D1795418

BEACON
BIBLE COMMENTARY

ISBN: 0-8341-0300-1

Library of Congress
Card Number 64-22906

Printed in the United States of America

BEACON
BIBLE COMMENTARY

In Ten Volumes

Volume I

GENESIS
George Herbert Livingston, B.D., Ph.D.

EXODUS
Leo G. Cox, M.A., B.D., Ph.D.

LEVITICUS
Dennis F. Kinlaw, M.A., B.D., Ph.D.

NUMBERS
Lauriston J. Du Bois, M.A., D.D.

DEUTERONOMY
Jack Ford, B.D., Ph.D.
A. R. G. Deasley, M.A.

BEACON HILL PRESS OF KANSAS CITY
Kansas City, Missouri

BEACON BIBLE COMMENTARY

In Ten Volumes

I. Genesis; Exodus; Leviticus; Numbers; Deuteronomy

II. Joshua; Judges; Ruth; I and II Samuel; I and II Kings; I and II Chronicles; Ezra; Nehemiah; Esther

III. Job; Psalms; Proverbs; Ecclesiastes; Song of Solomon

IV. Isaiah; Jeremiah; Lamentations; Ezekiel; Daniel

V. Hosea; Joel; Amos; Obadiah; Jonah; Micah; Nahum; Habakkuk; Zephaniah; Haggai; Zechariah; Malachi

VI. Matthew; Mark; Luke

VII. John; Acts

VIII. Romans; I and II Corinthians

IX. Galatians; Ephesians; Philippians; Colossians; I and II Thessalonians; I and II Timothy; Titus; Philemon

X. Hebrews; James; I and II Peter; I, II, and III John; Jude; Revelation

Preface

"All scripture is given by inspiration of God, and is profitable for doctrine, for reproof, for correction, for instruction in righteousness: that the man of God may be perfect, throughly furnished unto all good works" (II Tim. 3:16-17).

We believe in the plenary inspiration of the Bible. God speaks to men through His Word. He has spoken unto us by His Son. But without the inscripted Word how would we know the Word which was made flesh? He does speak to us by His Spirit, but the Spirit uses the written Word as the vehicle of His revelation, for He is the true Author of the Holy Scriptures. What the Spirit reveals is in agreement with the Word.

The Christian faith derives from the Bible. It is the Foundation for faith, for salvation, and sanctification. It is the Guide for Christian character and conduct. "Thy word is a lamp unto my feet, and a light unto my path" (Ps. 119:105).

The revelation of God and His will for men is adequate and complete in the Bible. The great task of the Church, therefore, is to communicate the knowledge of the Word, to enlighten the eyes of the understanding, and to awaken and to illuminate the conscience that men may learn to "live soberly, righteously, and godly, in this present world." This leads to the possession of that "inheritance [that is] incorruptible, and undefiled, and that fadeth not away, reserved in heaven."

When we consider the translation and interpretation of the Bible, we admit we are guided by men who are not inspired. Human limitation, as well as the plain fact that no scripture is of private or single interpretation, allows variation in the exegesis and exposition of the Bible.

Beacon Bible Commentary is offered in 10 volumes with becoming modesty. It does not supplant others. Neither does it purport to be exhaustive or final. The task is colossal. Assignments have been made to 40 of the ablest writers available. They are trained men with serious purpose, deep dedication, and supreme devotion. The sponsors and publishers, as well as the contributors, earnestly pray that this new offering among Bible commentaries will be helpful to preachers, teachers, and laymen in discovering the deeper meaning of God's Word and in unfolding its message to all who hear them.

—G. B. Williamson

Acknowledgments

Quotation from copyrighted material is gratefully acknowledged as follows:

Abingdon Press, *The Interpreter's Bible,* edited by George A. Buttrick, *et al.,* Volumes 1 and 2; and *The Interpreter's Dictionary of the Bible,* edited by George A. Buttrick, *et al.*

John Knox Press, *The Layman's Bible Commentary,* edited by Balmer H. Kelly, *et al.*

Moody Press, *The Wycliffe Bible Commentary,* edited by Charles F. Pfeiffer and Everett F. Harrison.

Fleming H. Revell Company, G. Campbell Morgan, *An Exposition of the Whole Bible;* Charles R. Erdman, *The Book of Leviticus.*

Soncino Press, J. H. Hertz, ed., *The Pentateuch and Haftorahs.*

Scripture quotations have been made from the following copyrighted sources:

The Amplified Old Testament. Copyrighted 1964, Zondervan Publishing House.

The Berkeley Version in Modern English. Copyright 1958, 1959, Zondervan Publishing House.

The Bible: A New Translation, James Moffatt. Copyright 1950, 1952, 1953, 1954 by James A. R. Moffatt. Used by permission of Harper and Row.

The Bible: An American Translation, J. M. Powis Smith, Edgar J. Goodspeed. Copyright 1923, 1927, 1948 by The University of Chicago Press.

Revised Standard Version of the Holy Bible. Copyright 1946 and 1952 by the Division of Christian Education of the National Council of Churches.

The Basic Bible: Containing the Old and New Testaments in Basic English. Copyright 1950 by E. P. Dutton and Co., Inc.

Quotations and References

Boldface type in the exposition indicates a quotation from the King James Version of the passage under discussion. Readings from other versions are put in quotation marks and the version is indicated.

In scripture references a letter (*a*, *b*, etc.) indicates a clause within a verse. When no book is named, the book under discussion is understood.

Bibliographical data on a work cited by a writer may be found by consulting the first reference to the work by that writer, or by turning to the bibliography.

The bibliographies are not intended to be exhaustive but are included to provide complete publication data for volumes cited in the text.

References to authors in the text, or inclusion of their books in the bibliography, does not constitute an endorsement of their views. All reading in the field of biblical interpretation should be discriminating and thoughtful.

How to Use "Beacon Bible Commentary"

The Bible is a Book to be read, to be understood, to be obeyed, and to be shared with others. *Beacon Bible Commentary* is planned to help at the points of understanding and sharing.

For the most part, the Bible is its own best interpreter. He who reads it with an open mind and receptive spirit will again and again become aware that through its pages God is speaking *to him.* A commentary serves as a valuable resource when the meaning of a passage is not clear even to the thoughtful reader. Also after one has seen his own meaning in a passage from the Bible, it is rewarding to discover what truth others have found in the same place. Sometimes, too, this will correct possible misconceptions the reader may have formed.

Beacon Bible Commentary has been written to be used with your Bible in hand. Most major commentaries print the text of the Bible at the top of the commentary page. The editors decided against this practice, believing that the average user comes to his commentary from his Bible and hence has in mind the passage in which he is interested. He also has his Bible at his elbow for any necessary reference to the text. To have printed the full text of the Bible in a work of this size would have occupied approximately one-third of the space available. The planners decided to give this space to additional resources for the reader. At the same time, writers have woven into their comments sufficient quotations from the passages under discussion that the reader maintains easy and constant thought contact with the words of the Bible. These quoted words are printed in boldface type for quick identification.

Illumination from Related Passages

The Bible is its own best interpreter when a given chapter or a longer section is read to find out what it says. This book is also its own best interpreter when the reader knows what the Bible says in other places about the subject under consideration. The writers and editors of *Beacon Bible Commentary* have constantly striven to give maximum help at this point. Related and carefully chosen cross-references have been included in order that the reader may thus find the Bible interpreted and illustrated by the Bible itself.

Paragraph Treatment

The truth of the Bible is best understood when we grasp the thought of the writer in its sequence and connections. The verse divisions with which we are familiar came into the Bible late (the sixteenth century for the New Testament and the seventeenth century for the Old). They were done hurriedly and sometimes missed the thought pattern of the inspired writers. The same is true of the chapter divisions. Most translations today arrange the words of the sacred writers under our more familiar paragraph structure.

It is under this paragraph arrangement that our commentary writers have approached their task. They have tried always to answer the question, What was the inspired writer saying in this passage? Verse numbers have been retained for easy identification but basic meanings have been outlined and interpreted in the larger and more complete thought forms.

Introduction to Bible Books

The Bible is an open Book to him who reads it thoughtfully. But it opens wider when we gain increased understanding of its human origins. Who wrote this book? Where was it written? When did the writer live? What were the circumstances that caused him to write? Answers to these questions always throw added light on the words of the Scripture.

These answers are given in the Introductions. There also you will find an outline of each book. The Introduction has been written to give an overview of the whole book; to provide you with a dependable road map before you start your trip—and to give you a place of reference when you are uncertain as to which way to turn. Don't ignore the flagman when he waves his warning sign, "See Introduction." At the close of the commentary on each book you will find a bibliography for further study.

Maps and Charts

The Bible was written about people who lived in lands that are foreign and strange to most English-speaking readers. Often better understanding of the Bible depends on better knowledge of Bible geography. When the flagman waves his other sign, "See map," you should turn to the map for a clearer understanding of the locations, distances, and related timing of the experiences of the men with whom God was dealing.

This knowledge of Bible geography will help you to be a better Bible preacher and teacher. Even in the more formal presentation of the sermon it helps the congregation to know that the flight into Egypt was "a journey on foot, some 200 miles to the southwest." In the less formal and small groups such as Sunday school classes and prayer meeting Bible study, a large classroom map enables the group to see the locations as well as to hear them mentioned. When you have seen these places on your commentary maps, you are better prepared to share the information with those whom you lead in Bible study.

Charts which list Bible facts in tabular form often make clear historical relationships in the same way that maps help with understanding geography. To see listed in order the kings of Judah or the Resurrection appearances of Jesus often gives clearer understanding of a particular item in the series. These charts are a part of the resources offered in this set.

Beacon Bible Commentary has been written for the newcomer to Bible study and also for those long familiar with the written Word. The writers and editors have probed each chapter, each verse, every clause, phrase, and word in the familiar King James Version. We have probed with the question, What do these words mean? If the answer is not self-evident we have charged ourselves to give the best explanation known to us. How well we have succeeded the reader must judge, but we invite you to explore the explanation of those words or passages that may puzzle you when you are reading God's written Word.

Exegesis and Exposition

Bible commentators often use these words to describe two ways of making clear the meaning of a passage in the Scriptures. *Exegesis* is a study of the original Greek or Hebrew words to understand what meanings those words had when they were used by men and women in Bible times. To know the meaning of the separate words, as well as their grammatical relationship to each other, is one way to understand more clearly what the inspired writer meant to say. You will often find this kind of enriching help in the commentary. But word studies alone do not always give true meaning.

Exposition is a commentator's effort to point out the meaning of a passage as it is affected by any one of several facts known to the writer but perhaps not familiar to the reader. These facts may be (1) the context (the surrounding verses or chapters), (2) the historical background, (3) the related teaching from other parts of the Bible, (4) the significance of these messages from God as they relate to universal facts of human life, (5) the relevance of these truths to unique contemporary human situations. The commentator thus seeks to explain the full meaning of a Bible passage in the light of his own best understanding of God, man, and the world in which we live.

Some commentaries separate the exegesis from this broader basis of explanation. In *Beacon Bible Commentary* writers have combined the exegesis and exposition. Accurate word studies are indispensable to a correct understanding of the Bible. But such careful studies are today so thoroughly reflected in a number of modern English translations that they are often not necessary except to enhance the understanding of the theological meaning of a passage. The writers and editors seek to reflect a true and accurate exegesis at every point, but specific exegetical discussions are introduced chiefly to throw added light on the meaning of a passage, rather than to engage in scholarly discussion.

The Bible is a practical Book. We believe that God inspired holy men of old to declare these truths in order that the readers might better understand and do the will of God. *Beacon Bible Commentary* has been undertaken only for the purpose of helping men to find more effectively God's will for them as revealed in the Scripture—to find that will and to act upon that knowledge.

Helps for Bible Preaching and Teaching

We have said that the Bible is a Book to be shared. Christian preachers and teachers since the first century have sought to convey the gospel message by reading and explaining selected passages of Scripture. *Beacon Bible Commentary* seeks to encourage this kind of expository preaching and teaching. The set contains more than 1,000 brief expository outlines that have been used by outstanding Bible teachers and preachers. Both writers and editors have assisted in contributing or selecting these homiletical suggestions. It is hoped that the outlines will suggest ways in which the reader will want to try to open the Word of God to his class or congregation. Some of these analyses of preachable passages have been contributed by our contemporaries. When the outlines have appeared in print, authors and references are given in order that the reader may go to the original source for further help.

In the Bible we find truth of the highest order. Here is given to us, by divine inspiration, the will of God for our lives. Here we have sure guidance in all things necessary to our relationships to God and under Him to our fellowman. Because these eternal truths come to us in human language and through human minds, they need to be put into fresh words as languages change and as thought patterns are modified. In *Beacon Bible Commentary* we have sought to help make the Bible a more effective Lamp to the paths of men who journey in the twentieth century.

A. F. Harper

Abbreviations and Explanations

The Books of the Bible

Gen.	Job	Jonah	I or II Cor.
Exod.	Ps.	Mic.	Gal.
Lev.	Prov.	Nah.	Eph.
Num.	Eccles.	Hab.	Phil.
Deut.	Song of Sol.	Zeph.	Col.
Josh.	Isa.	Hag.	I or II Thess.
Judg.	Jer.	Zech.	I or II Tim.
Ruth	Lam.	Mal.	Titus
I or II Sam.	Ezek.	Matt.	Philem.
I or II Kings	Dan.	Mark	Heb.
I or II Chron.	Hos.	Luke	Jas.
Ezra	Joel	John	I or II Pet.
Neh.	Amos	Acts	I, II, or III John
Esther	Obad.	Rom.	Jude
			Rev.

LXX	The Septuagint
Amp. OT	Amplified Old Testament
Amp. Bible	Amplified Bible
ASV	American Standard Revised Version
BB	The Basic Bible Containing the Old and New Testaments in Basic English
Berk.	The Berkeley Version
CWB	Commentary on the Whole Bible
ERV	English Revised Version
NBC	The New Bible Commentary
NBD	New Bible Dictionary
PC	Pulpit Commentary
RSV	Revised Standard Version
BBC	Beacon Bible Commentary
IB	Interpreter's Bible
ICC	The International Critical Commentary
IDB	The Interpreter's Dictionary of the Bible
NBD	The New Bible Dictionary
TDNT	Theological Dictionary of the New Testament

c.	chapter	OT	Old Testament
cc.	chapters	NT	New Testament
v.	verse	Heb.	Hebrew
vv.	verses	Gk.	Greek

Table of Contents

VOLUME I

THE PENTATEUCH 17

GENESIS

Introduction 23

Commentary 31

Bibliography 165

EXODUS

Introduction 171

Commentary 175

Bibliography 315

LEVITICUS

Introduction 319

Commentary 324

Bibliography 394

NUMBERS

Introduction 399

Commentary 405

Bibliography 501

DEUTERONOMY

Introduction 505

Commentary 510

Bibliography 622

MAPS AND CHARTS 625

The Pentateuch

The Bible opens with a group of five books of outstanding importance. We know them as "the Pentateuch," from a Greek term meaning "fivefold book." Genesis, Exodus, Leviticus, Numbers, and Deuteronomy have from the very earliest times been recognized as the core of the Old Testament canon.

The Pentateuch is the first of the three major divisions of the Hebrew Scriptures. There it is known as the *Torah,* or law—a term which includes also the idea of "teaching, instruction, or guidance."

The Bible itself describes the Torah (or portions of it) as "this book of the law" (Deut. 29:31; 30:10; 31:26; Josh. 1:8); "the book of this law" (Deut. 28:61); "the book of the law of Moses" (Josh. 8:21; 34:6; II Kings 14:6), which was equivalent simply to "the book of the law" (Josh. 8:34) or "the book of Moses" (II Chron. 25:4).

"The book of the law of the Lord" (II Chron. 17:9) was used in Jehoshaphat's time to teach the people. The scroll discovered in the Temple by Hilkiah the priest is described as "the book of the law" (II Kings 22:8, 11), "the book of the covenant" (II Kings 23:2, 21; II Chron. 34:30), "the book of the law of the Lord by the hand of Moses" (II Chron. 34:14), and "the book of Moses" (II Chron. 35:12).

Ezra 6:18 speaks of "the book of Moses." "The book of the law of Moses" and "the book of the law of God" are used in parallel passages in Neh. 8:1, 3, 8, 18; and 9:3. Neh. 13:1 identifies Deut. 23:3-5 as coming from "the book of Moses." "The law of Moses" is mentioned in I Kings 2:3 and Dan. 9:13.

The New Testament likewise alludes to "the book of Moses" (Mark 12:26) and "the law of Moses" (I Cor. 9:9), and attributes authoritative commands and statements to Moses (Matt. 19:7; 22:24; Mark 7:10; 10:3; Acts 3:22; Rom. 9:15; 10:19). There are also numerous New Testament references to "the law" as a court of final appeal.

Content and Form

The books of the Pentateuch contain a number of different kinds of material. There are history (Genesis), legislation (Exodus), ritual (Leviticus), government (Numbers), and rhetoric

(Deuteronomy)—with many combinations and much overlapping of literary types. The historical record spans a tremendous period of time—from creation to the death of Moses, at least longer than the rest of the Bible history all together.

That the five books of the law were originally prepared as separate books would appear from the fact that each is a literary unit, and each is just about the maximum length that could be accommodated on an ancient scroll. The books are obviously related, however, in continuity of historical sequence and by their necessary order. After Genesis, each book presupposes the one or ones that precede it.

Authorship

The problem of the authorship of the books of the Pentateuch is a complex one. Within their own text, these books are anonymous and contain nothing which would indicate the overall source of the whole. Ancient Jewish and Christian tradition credits them in their entirety to Moses. The books themselves attribute portions of Exodus and Numbers, and most of Deuteronomy, directly to the hand of Moses, and conservative scholarship finds no reason to question such statements (Exod. 24:4; 34:28; Num. 33:2; Deut. 1:1; 4:44; 5:1; 27:1; 29:1; 31:1, 9, 22, 30; 32:44; 33:1).

On the other hand, the text itself in the references just cited differentiates between what Moses wrote or spoke and what was written about him. There are also some non-Mosaic elements which a thoughtful reading makes apparent. Gen. 14:14 uses the name "Dan" for the place to which Abraham pursued the five kings who had raided Sodom. This name was not given until the time of the judges (Judg. 18:29), implying that this verse was written (or edited) after the time of Moses.

Gen. 36:31 speaks of the kings of Edom who reigned before "any king over the children of Israel," words which would imply a time of writing after the coronation of Saul (I Sam. 8:5 ff.).

The description of the work of Moses in Exodus, Leviticus, and Numbers is in the third person, quite unlike the first-person account recorded in Moses' speeches in Deuteronomy. There are two well-deserved tributes to the great lawgiver which must have been written by someone else: Exod. 11:3, "Moreover the man Moses was very great in the land of Egypt," and Num. 12:3, "Now the man Moses was very meek, above all the men which were upon the face of the earth."

Exod. 16:35, "And the children of Israel did eat manna forty years, until they came to a land inhabited; they did eat manna, until they came unto the borders of the land of Canaan," could have been written only after the death of Moses and the crossing of the Jordan (Josh. 5:10-12), since the eating of manna is spoken of in the past tense.

Num. 21:14-15 quotes from "the book of the wars of the Lord." This was apparently a book of poetry describing the acts of God in behalf of His people during the wilderness years. Nothing is known of it otherwise. It may have been one of the writings of Moses himself.

Num. 32:34-42 describes the cities built by the tribes of Reuben, Gad, and Manasseh in the territory they were granted east of the Jordan. They did not possess this territory until after the conquest of Canaan, in which they assisted (Josh. 22:1-9).

Deut. 2:10-12, 20-23 are parenthetical passages added later to explain the meaning of terms and conditions no longer current. Deut. 34:1-12, the account of the death of Moses, was apparently written after the appearance of the prophets (v. 10) during the time of Samuel.

Citations elsewhere in the Bible to what Moses wrote can all be traced to the one Book of Deuteronomy, with the possible exception of Ezra 6:18, which locates passages from Numbers in "the book of Moses"; and Mark 12:26, which cites "the book of Moses" for the Exodus account of the call of Moses at the burning bush. In these references, it is at least possible that "the book of Moses" may mean "the book about Moses" or "the book based on Moses' authority." I and II Samuel, for instance, are named after this great prophet although his death is recorded in I Sam. 25:1, many years before the events of II Samuel occurred.

Considerations such as these rather than the reconstructions of modern literary and historical criticism lead conservative scholars to the sound cautions expressed by Professor G. Ch. Aalders in his epoch-making work, *A Short Introduction to the Pentateuch.* What is important is the recognition of the authenticity and integrity of this most significant portion of God's Word.

The consensus of the biblical tradition would certainly establish the Mosaic authority of the Pentateuch. When this is clearly recognized, the question as to whose hand actually inscribed the books may safely be left where Origen left the problem of the authorship of the Book of Hebrews: "God only knows."

Interested students will find the conservative position strongly stated in Professor Aalders' book mentioned above (Chicago:

Inter-Varsity Christian Fellowship, n.d.); Oswald T. Allis, *The Five Books of Moses* (Philadelphia: The Presbyterian and Reformed Publishing Co., 1949); David A. Hubbard, "Pentateuch," *The New Bible Dictionary,* edited by J. D. Douglas (Grand Rapids: William B. Eerdmans Publishing Company, 1962), pp. 957-64; as well as Aalders' brief treatment in "The Historical Literature of the Old Testament," *The New Bible Commentary,* edited by Francis Davidson (Grand Rapids: William B. Eerdmans Publishing Company, 1956), pp. 31-34.

—W. T. Purkiser

The Book of

GENESIS

George Herbert Livingston

Introduction

A. Title

In the Hebrew OT, the first word of the text, *bereshit,* "in the beginning," serves as a title for the book. Taking the first phrase or word of a literary work to designate it was a common practice in the ancient Near East. The Greek translation, called the Septuagint (LXX), roughly approximated this opening phrase with the word *genesis,* which means "origin" or "source." The Greek word has continued into English versions, because it describes remarkably well the contents of the book. It is the book of the beginnings: the beginning of the universe, of man, of sin, of salvation, of the Hebrew nation, of the covenant relationship.

Martin Luther was the first to append the phrase, "The First Book of Moses," to the ancient title and it has been preserved in most English versions. Luther considered it appropriate since the Book of Genesis is the first of the books of the Pentateuch and traditionally Moses had been regarded as the author of all five books.

B. Authorship

A brief treatment of authorship cannot possibly do justice to the mass of literature nor to the complexity of the problems. Controversy has swirled about whether the Book of Genesis, as we know it in all extant manuscripts, was the product of Moses and his times or of unknown writers at a much later time. For the past two centuries scholars have been split between those who have accepted Mosaic authorship or authority and those who have seen the work of many unknown "authors" in the material we have in the Book of Genesis. (See discussion in "The Pentateuch," p. 18.)

The text of the book does not mention Moses' name, and as noted above, Luther (1483-1546) was the one who appended the notation about Moses to the title. Since even the latest event in Genesis is depicted as occurring long before the time of Moses, orthodox scholars have held that he moulded ancient material to its present form. This opinion has rested chiefly upon internal evidences in (*a*) the other four books of the Pentateuch to the effect that they came from Moses, or at least from his lifetime and from his direction; (*b*) the rest of the OT, which ties the content of the total Pentateuch to Moses; and (c) the NT, which refers to books of the Pentateuch (chiefly Deuteronomy) as being Mosaic.

C. Date and Composition

These items are closely tied to the discussion of authorship, so, in a sense, all three must be dealt with together.

Johann Eichhorn, a professor in the University of Jena in Germany, toward the end of the eighteenth century, is usually credited with the widely accepted rejection of the Mosaic authorship of the Pentateuch. He rested his case on two alleged sources in Genesis labeled *J* for Jehovah and *E* for Elohim, which he declared came into being after the time of Moses. Actually, this source analysis was pioneered by a French physician, Jean Astruc, several decades before Eichhorn. Through the first three-quarters of the nineteenth century German professors argued whether there were many sources, two sources, or just one source in the Book of Genesis. They dated these sources all the way from the time of Solomon to the time of Ezra. Using the occurrence of several divine names, differences of vocabulary, and alleged divergency of theological viewpoints as clues, the controversy raged between a fragmented history of composition and a basic unity in construction.

Julius Wellhausen[1] was the first to popularize successfully the idea of three main sources in Genesis: *J* and *E* and *P*. *J* was dated in the ninth century B.C.; *E* was dated in the eighth century B.C.; and *P* was dated in the fifth century B.C. This view became standard among his followers and highly popular in Protestant and Jewish circles throughout the Western world. The Roman Catholic church reacted negatively to the theory.

Hermann Gunkel[2] sought to enlarge upon the Wellhausen position by examining the literary forms of ancient storytelling as illustrated in Genesis. He concluded that before 1000 B.C. there was a long period of oral transmission of much of the content of the Book of Genesis before it became congealed into the so-called *J*, *E*, and *P* documents.

In more recent years, scholars who reject Mosaic authorship are more favorable to the idea of a long period of oral tradi-

[1]*Prolegomena to the History of Israel* (Edinburgh: Adam and Charles Black, 1885).

[2]*The Legends of Genesis* (New York: Schocken Books, 1964, though first published in 1901).

tion developing around tribal and cultic centers, rather than the existence of written sources as such. Otto Eissfeldt[3] has been the leading proponent of this approach. There has also been a tendency to regard the book as completed by exilic times and substantially Mosaic in character. W. F. Albright has championed this position.[4]

Conservative scholars have consistently found the theory described above to be unacceptable and have been heartened by the mass of contrary evidence which studies in the ancient Near East have provided. With new vigor they have insisted that more recently discovered evidence not only makes the composition of Genesis in Moses' time possible, but also highly probable. Various scripts, including the alphabetic type, were in use centuries before Moses' day, leaving behind an impressive amount of literature, much of it significant for studies in Genesis. Oral transmission of important memories, especially if enshrouded in sanctity, is now known to have a degree of accuracy which is no less than amazing.

More and more scholars are seeing that the contents of Genesis 1—11 must have come into Hebrew lore no later than the time of Abraham. The social, economic, and political orientation of the stories of the patriarchs is now conceded to be rooted solidly in the period of 2000 to 1500 B.C.[5] The one barrier has to do with theology. There has been a growing concession that monotheistic beliefs were prevalent among the Hebrews in Moses' time,[6] but only conservative scholars have dared to hold that monotheism was the faith of the patriarchs from the beginning.[7]

The issue resolves itself into a basic question: Was Genesis Mosaic, or was it a composite in composition and origin? This commentary holds to the conservative position that Genesis was Mosaic in its composition and date.

[3]*The Old Testament* (New York: Harper and Row, 1965).

[4]*The Archaeology of Palestine* (Baltimore: Penguin Books, 1963), pp. 224-26.

[5]G. E. Wright, *Biblical Archaeology* (Philadelphia: The Westminster Press, 1957), pp. 43-44.

[6]Y. Kaufmann, *The Religion of Israel* (London: George Allen & Unwin, Ltd., 1961), pp. 127-49.

[7]M. F. Unger, *Introductory Guide to the Old Testament* (Grand Rapids: Zondervan Publishing House, 1951); E. J. Young, *An Introduction to the Old Testament* (Grand Rapids: Wm. B. Eerdmans Publishing Co., 1956); G. L. Archer, *A Survey of Old Testament Introduction* (Chicago: Moody Press, 1964).

D. Structure

The Book of Genesis has an introduction (1:1—2:3) and 10 divisions, each of which, in the English, begins with the phrase, "These are the generations of." In Hebrew the word translated "generations" is *toledot,* which scholars have come to recognize as meaning "history," "story," or "account," rather than simply a genealogy. These divisions come at 2:4; 5:1; 6:9; 10:1; 11:10; 11:27; 25:12; 25:19; 36:1; 37:2. The book may also be divided into two main sections: the first from 1:1—11:26 and the second from 11:27 to the end. The first of these larger divisions deals basically with primeval origins, and the second with the establishment of God's covenant relationship with the ancestors of the Hebrew people. Or following G. C. Morgan,[8] the divisions can be viewed as threefold. The first division would be 1:1—2:25, concerned with generation; the second would be 3:1—11:32, dealing with degeneration; and the third would be 12:1—50:26, centering on regeneration.

After the introductory creation account, the book primarily focuses on key men and their descendents. These men are Adam, Noah, Abraham, Isaac, Jacob, and Joseph. Lesser figures related to these worthies are normally treated by simply listing their genealogies.

In Genesis there is an undulating movement of sequence from the universal to the specific. The story of the creation of the universe zeroes in on Adam and his wife, Eve; it then spreads out to trace sketchily the increase of his descendents through the lineages of Cain and of Seth. Having pithily described the corruption of these people in 6:1-4, the account announces the decision of the Almighty to punish them by means of a mighty flood but, at the same time, to save a remnant by providing protection for Noah and his family in an ark. Noah's descendents are also presented in their increase of numbers and their spread through migration, by way of a genealogical list. Abraham then comes to the forefront.

Geographically, the first 11 chapters are oriented to the Mesopotamian valley (see map 1). After Abraham's response to God's call to move out, the stories related to him are mostly centered in Canaan (see map 2), with only a few tied to Egypt or the former home in Haran. Aside from having a wife from Haran, Isaac is wholly limited to life in Canaan, but Jacob spent some 20 years in Haran, and the waning years of his life in

[8] *The Analyzed Bible* (New York: Fleming H. Revell Co., 1907), I, 9-27.

Egypt, though his youth and middle years were in Canaan. Aside from his youth, Joseph spent his mature years in Egypt, partly in prison and partly as a powerful official of the government.

E. Purpose and Message

The main purpose of the Book of Genesis is to show how God selected the people of Israel for a covenant relationship with himself by relating how He dealt with their progenitors. Though there are striking similarities between other ancient writings and the biblical stories of creation, of the fall of man, and of the Flood, the biblical interest in the origin of the universe is basically theological. Its concern is to declare that all things came from and are sustained by the one Creator-God. Polytheism and its overtones are studiously ignored.

In the Book of Genesis, interest in the origin of man and the origin of sin is primarily concerned with the nature of the relationship between man and God, both in its original fellowship and in its later negative, disobedient defiance of God's will. The original relationship is ever regarded as the ideal and goal of all future dealings of God with man. The mercies of God are extended to men in order that the positive relationship might be reestablished through the saving activity of God, which is set in a covenant framework. The glimpses of the future realization of God's redemptive purposes are oriented toward a grand fulfillment of not only individual, but national, international, and universal reconciliation of God and man. Hence, Messianic themes in the later OT and in the NT are found in Genesis.

Theologically, the content of Genesis is uncompromisingly monotheistic. Paganism is not openly disputed or rejected; it is largely ignored. Genesis depicts only limited instances of idolatrous practice and those are either indirectly (as in Genesis 22) or directly (as in Genesis 23) repudiated. The rationale and the religious thrust of paganism in Mesopotamia, in Canaan, and in Egypt are almost totally absent.

The limited number of religious motifs and literary phrases which can be found in both the ancient Mesopotamian literature and the material in Genesis are incidental to the main emphases of the stories of Genesis. They have been largely overrated in importance by some OT scholars.

The Book of Genesis challenges the validity of polytheism, dualism, deism, and pantheism, not by negative analysis of their weaknesses, but by positive affirmation of divine unity, sovereignty, and personal reality. In Genesis there is a presentation of the personal and dynamic qualities of the divine-human covenant relationship, chiefly in narrative form, and secondarily by means of genealogical summarizations.

Outline

I. Individual Crises and Collective Decay, 1:1—11:26
   A. The Creator in Action, 1:1—2:3
   B. The Creator in Relation to the Created, 2:4—3:24
   C. Murder and Its Aftermath, 4:1-24
   D. Expansion from a New Beginning, 4:25—6:8
   E. Universal Corruption and Its Aftermath, 6:9—11:26

II. Abraham, the Man Whom God Chose, 11:27—25:11
   A. Terah's Family Relationships, 11:27-32
   B. A Stranger in a New Land, 12:1—14:24
   C. God's Covenant with Abraham, 15:1—17:27
   D. Waiting for the True Son, 18:1—20:18
   E. Old Loyalties Tested, 21:1—22:19
   F. Bearing Responsibilities for Others, 22:20—25:11

III. Ishmael, the Man Whom God Set Aside, 25:12-18

IV. Isaac, the Man Whose Life God Spared, 25:19—28:9
   A. A Birthright for Bean Stew, 25:19-34
   B. Isaac's Dealings with His Neighbors, 26:1-33
   C. Isaac and His Family, 26:34—28:9

V. Jacob, the Man Whom God Remade, 28:10—35:29
   A. Confronted by God, 28:10-22
   B. Love Thwarted Does Not Die, 29:1-30
   C. A Painful Competition, 29:31—30:24
   D. Clever Shepherds, 30:25—31:55
   E. A Profound Spiritual Crisis, 32:1-32
   F. Brothers Reunited, 33:1-17
   G. Tragedy at Shechem, 33:18—34:31
   H. The Covenant Renewed at Bethel, 35:1-15
   I. A Journey Shadowed by Sorrow, 35:16-29

VI. Esau, the Man Who Took His Brother Back, 36:1-43
   A. Esau's Wives and Their Sons, 36:1-8
   B. Esau's Sons and Grandsons, 36:9-14
   C. The Prominence of Esau's Descendents, 36:15-19

D. The Sons of the Cave Dwellers, 36:20-30
E. Edom's Kings, 36:31-39
F. Areas Where the Edomites Lived, 36:40-43

VII. Joseph, the Man Whom God Preserved, 37:1—50:26
A. Sold as a Slave, 37:1-36
B. The Moral Laxity of Judah, 38:1-30
C. Joseph's Trials in Egypt, 39:1—40:23
D. Joseph's Dramatic Rise to Power, 41:1-57
E. Mysterious Problems in Egypt, 42:1—45:28
F. The New Home in Egypt, 46:1—47:31
G. Anticipations of the Future, 48:1—50:26

Section I Individual Crises and Collective Decay

Genesis 1:1—11:26

In a highly compressed series of stories and genealogies, this section of the book touches upon the origin of the universe, the origin of order on this earth, the origin of life, the origin of man, the origin of sin, of violence and disorder, and the origin of national and linguistic differences.

A. The Creator in Action, 1:1—2:3

For brevity and beauty of composition and of expression this vignette on creation has no equal. Dominating the scene is the Creator-God who speaks and order springs quickly into being, providing a well-stocked, beautiful dwelling place for the highest creation of all, man. Majesty and power mark every sentence.

1. *The Initial Act* (1:1-2)

In answer to the question, Who made all things? the Scripture boldly declares, **God created** (1). In answer to the question, Who is prior to and greater than all things? with equal boldness the Scripture announces, **In the beginning God.**[1] The heaven and the earth are not God nor gods; neither is God the same as nature. God is the Creator and nature is His handiwork.

Though made by God, the earth was not yet ready for man. It was still in disarray, **without form, and void** (2), and there was no light. However there was activity. **The Spirit of God** was continuously moving above **the waters.**

2. *The Day of Light and Darkness* (1:3-5)

Energy is a vital necessity for man's habitat, and light is energy. Hence God's first command was, **Let there be light** (3).

[1]For the grammatical construction of Gen. 1:1-3 see J. Skinner, *A Critical and Exegetical Commentary on Genesis* ("The International Critical Commentary"; ed. S. R. Driver, *et al.;* Edinburgh: T. & T. Clark, 1930), I, 12-19; J. P. Lange, "Genesis," *Commentary on the Holy Scriptures* (Grand Rapids: Zondervan Publishing House, reprint, n.d.), I, 161-65; E. J. Young, "The Interpretation of Genesis 1:2," *Westminster Theological Journal,* XXIII, May, 1961, 151 ff.

Emphasis on God's spoken word is so great that each creative day begins with a command or an expression of the divine will.[2] Then comes the execution of the command, and the climactic statement, **It was good,** or its equivalent (4, 10, 18, *et al.*).

3. *The Day of Divided Waters* (1:6-8)

The waters were separated, and above the earth was a **firmament** (6). The English word goes back to the Latin *firmamentum,* which in turn rests upon the Greek *stereoma,* both of which carry the idea of solidness.[3] However, the emphasis in the original Hebrew word *raqia* is not on the material itself but on the act of stretching out or the condition of being expanded. The word "expanse" (ASV, marg.) is more appropriate.

In several places in the OT the act of stretching out the heavens is prominent (see Job 9:8; 26:7; Ps. 104:2; Isa. 45:12; 51:13; Jer. 51:15; Zech. 12:1). Evidence that God is the Creator rests upon the act of stretching out rather than upon the character of that which was formed.[4] Throughout the OT interest

[2]For discussions concerning the length of the "day" of Genesis 1, see: Tayler Lewis, "Genesis" (Introduction), in Lange, *op. cit.,* pp. 131-43; H. E. Dosker, "Day," *The International Standard Bible Encyclopedia,* ed. James Orr, *et al.* (Grand Rapids: Wm. B. Eerdmans Publishing Co., reprint, 1949), II, 787-89. Dr. H. Orton Wiley states: "The Genesis account of creation is primarily a religious document. It cannot be considered a scientific statement, and yet it must not be regarded as contradictory to science. It is rather, a supreme illustration of the manner in which revealed truth indirectly sheds light upon scientific fields. The Hebrew word *yom* which is translated 'day' occurs no less than 1,480 times in the Old Testament, and is translated by something over fifty different words, including such terms as *time, life, today, age, forever, continually* and *perpetually.* With such a flexible use of the original term, it is impossible to either dogmatize or to demand unswerving restriction to one only of those meanings. It is frequently assumed that originally orthodox belief held to a solar day of twenty-four hours, and that the church altered her exegesis under the pressure of modern geological discoveries. This as Dr. Sheed points out is one of the 'errors of ignorance.' The best Hebrew exegesis has never regarded the days of Genesis as solar days, but as day-periods of indefinite duration. . . . Nor is this a metaphorical meaning of the word, but the original, which signifies 'to put period to' or to denote a self-completed time" (*Christian Theology* [Kansas City, Mo.: Beacon Hill Press, 1940], I, 454-55).

[3]S. R. Driver, *The Book of Genesis,* "Westminster Commentaries," ed. W. Lock (London: Methuen and Co., Ltd., 1911), I, 6-7.

[4]K. M. Yates, "Genesis," *The Wycliffe Bible Commentary,* ed. Charles Pfeiffer, *et al.* (Chicago: Moody Press, 1962), p. 3.

centers in God's relationships to nature and to man. God is the Creator, and from that declaration the OT moves on to show that nature is a creature and a tool. Likewise God judges, delivers, and cares for man.

4. *The Day of Land and Sea* (1:9-13)

God's third act was concerned with forming a future habitat for man, who is a land creature. Man's food, vegetation, grows on land. So at God's command land and sea separated, and shape, life, and beauty graced the earth. No description of how these separations took place is presented, nor is there a list of the dynamic, natural forces involved. Instead, the relationship of a mighty Creator to an obedient, pliable creature is kept clearly before the reader at all times.

Dramatically, God turned to the now visible earth and commanded it to assist Him. **Let the earth bring forth** (11) was not an admission that inorganic substances possessed inherent power to produce life.[5] Quite the contrary, life itself rests ultimately upon the creative word of God, and quickly springs forth in response to it.

Following a pattern of pairs, light—darkness, waters above—waters beneath, land—sea, there now occurs a series of triplets. **Grass, and herb yielding seed,** also **the tree yielding fruit** (12) are very generalized groupings and should not be regarded as botanical classifications in the modern sense.

The phrase **after his kind**[6] indicates limits to the powers of reproduction. But it does not provide a blueprint, outlining the boundary lines. What it does point to is the observable dependability of nature; clover produces clover, wheat produces wheat, etc. **It was**—and still is—**so.**

5. *The Day of the Two Rulers* (1:14-19)

The pagans worshiped the sun, moon, and stars as gods and goddesses of fearful power. In the account of this day of creation the **greater light** (16) and the **lesser light** are not even named. In a few deft sentences, these heavenly bodies are depicted as created and then appointed to perform servant duties in the

[5]E. F. Keven, "Genesis," *The New Bible Commentary*, ed. F. Davidson (Grand Rapids: Wm. B. Eerdmans Publishing Co., 1953), pp. 77-78.

[6]J. B. Payne, "The Concept of 'Kinds' in Scripture," *Journal of the American Scientific Affiliation*, X, No. 2 (June, 1958), 17-20.

skies.[7] Theirs is a delegated rulership and no more. **The stars also** receive no more than honorable mention. What a blow to paganism!

6. *The Day of Birds and Fish* (1:20-23)

Because light and darkness are common to both, the first day (3-5) and the fourth day (14-19) are related. Also the second (6-8) and the fifth (20-23) are related in that they deal with the expanse above and the waters below. On the fifth day God spoke a word to **the waters** (20) and they brought forth creatures, and birds filled the air. In v. 21 we see another triad: **great whales** ("great sea monsters," ASV, RSV), **every living creature that moveth . . . and every winged fowl.**

The text does not tell us how **the waters** may have aided the Creator, but to emphasize the close tie between God and these creatures the verb **created** is employed.[8] The striking differences between botanical and biological life are thus attributed to a divine act. **God** also **blessed them** (22). In the OT a divine blessing is a creative act, enabling the recipient to fulfill its destiny according to the will of God. In this case, God's will is that they reproduce **abundantly, after their kind** (21). This served to annul the former "void" (2).

7. *The Day of Animals and Man* (1:24-31)

Again giving the command, **Let the earth bring forth** (24), God filled the earth with creatures: **the beast of the earth** (wild animals, 25), **cattle . . . and . . . every creeping thing** (26).

But this day was to have a crowning creative act. The Godhead in counsel said, **Let us make man** (26).[9] This creature was to be different. God said that **man** was to be **in our image,** having some semblance to the reality but lacking its fullness. Man was to be **in our likeness,** having general similarity to God but not being an exact duplicate. He was not to be a little God, but definitely he was to be related to God and was to be the bearer

[7]John Calvin, *A Commentary on the First Book of Moses Called Genesis,* trans. by John King (Grand Rapids: Wm. B. Eerdmans Publishing Co., reprint, 1948) I, 86-87.

[8]H. C. Leupold, *Exposition of Genesis* (Grand Rapids: Baker Book House, 1950), I, 79-81.

[9]U. Cassuto, *A Commentary on the Book of Genesis,* trans. by Israel Abrahams (Jerusalem: The Magness Press, 1961), pp. 55-57.

of spiritual distinctives which mark him as uniquely higher than the animals.[10]

In 1:26-30 we find "Man Made in God's Image." (1) A spiritual being capable of immortality, 26*ab*; (2) A moral being bearing God's likeness, 27; (3) An intellectual being with capacity for reason and rulership, 26*c*, 28-30 (G. B. Williamson).

One mark of the **image** was God's grant to man of the status and power of a ruler. Man's right to **have dominion** (28) points to the fact that God equipped him to act as a ruler. Fitness to rule implies an adequate intellectual capacity to reason, to organize, to plan, and to evaluate. Fitness to rule implies an adequate emotional capacity to desire the highest welfare of the subjects, to appreciate and to honor that which is good and true and beautiful, to dislike and to repudiate that which is cruel, false, and ugly, to have a deep concern for the well-being of all nature, and to love the God who created him. Fitness to rule implies an adequate volitional capacity to choose to do at all times that which is right, to obey God's command positively and quickly, to surrender gladly all powers to God in joyous worship, and to participate in a wholesome fellowship with both nature and God.

God created man to be a person who possessed self-consciousness, self-determination, and inward holiness (Eccles. 7:29; Eph. 4:24; Col. 3:10). The image was distributed without distinction to the male and to the female, making them both equal before God.

As God had blessed (22) that which He had previously created (21), so again **God blessed** (28) this phase of His work, charging man with responsibility to reproduce and to subject the earth, and all within it, to his oversight. The English word **replenish** is misleading. It should be rendered "fill," as in 22, since both phrases are exactly alike in the Hebrew text.

The act of blessing mankind is broader in meaning than that of blessing animals (22). Man is capable of being aware of that blessing and can respond to it. "Blessing" in relation to a rational being is an act of conveying a sense of God's will to the one blessed. This is especially significant for man, for the command to procreate sets upon the act of reproduction the approval of

[10]P. Heinisch, *Theology of the Old Testament,* trans. by W. G. Heidt (Collegeville, Minn.: The Liturgical Press, 1955), p. 170.

God. Essentially, the relationship of man and woman in procreation is good, is within the will of God, and is basic to their well-being.

In the OT there are two aspects to the act of bestowing a blessing. On God's part, there is the act of a superior Being granting favor to those dependent upon Him. On man's part, there is the return of gratitude to the Bestower of gifts (Gen. 24:48; Deut. 8:10; *et al.*).

An important aspect of God's blessing was the grant of power and ability to **subdue** (28) and **have dominion** over the other created beings which inhabit the earth. But it was a delegated authority, a subordinate reign, for which man was accountable before God. It can be assumed that the responsibility to control animal life did not entail the right to abuse it, else it would not have been good.

God granted to man the right to use the fruits of plant life for food (29). This did not give him the privilege to exploit nature, leaving behind waste and desolation. Proper care of the fruits of plant life must of necessity entail cultivation (2:15) and the conservation of natural resources.

The fact that the animals, which were subject to man's control, must also feed upon plants, **every green herb** (30), further points up the responsibility resting upon man to control nature in such a way that nature would serve the needs of all living creatures and not just the needs of man (see 9:3 for permission to eat meat).

The death of animals is not touched upon, though there is no reason to assume the absence of animal death before the Fall. The stress is on life, harmony, order, and fitness of form and function for man's earthly abode.

In 1:1-5, 26-31 we see "Creation by Omnipotent Will," with the central idea in v. 1. (1) Adequate cause, 1-2; (2) Evident design, 2-5; (3) Godlike man, 26-30; (4) All-wise conception, 31 (G. B. Williamson).

8. *The Day of Holy Rest* (2:1-3)

The first three verses of this chapter properly belong to the content of c. 1, since it is the seventh day in the creation series. During the six days God had been creating and forming inorganic matter, plants, animals, and man. All of these occupy and are related to space in some way. Man had been given a specific command to subdue that which is in the spatial realm. God had surveyed the whole and had called it very good; He had brought to completion all that He had intended to create.

Some of the ancient rabbis were bothered because they thought they saw here an implication that God did some work on the Sabbath. Rabbi Rashi declared that what the world still lacked was rest, so God's last act was the creation of the Sabbath in which are quiet and repose.[11]

In the Ten Commandments, the relation of six days of God's labor with material things to one day of rest serves as the basis for man's observance of a day of rest (Exod. 20:8-11). This is a day established by God and is to occur regularly. Other important holy days may be established by man and fluctuate with the seasons, but this day is independent of the seasons or the problems of fixing a specific date. On this day God's command to man to conquer nature is laid aside and man recognizes a higher law, that he yield himself to God.

In Ps. 95:11 there is a hint that God withholds a "rest" (a sabbath) from those who disobey Him. The writer of the NT Book of Hebrews takes up this cue and declares that a Sabbath rest still remains for God's people, "Therefore give diligence to enter into that rest" (Heb. 4:11, ASV). The Sabbath would thus carry a suggestion of cessation from works of disobedience and an acceptance of God's rule over the inner being.

Contrary to the Babylonian's *sabbattu,* in which dangerous demons roamed freely, the Sabbath instituted here was **blessed** of God. It was to be a day of joy and gladness, of inner renewal, of praise to a merciful God. In pagan belief, certain natural forces, things, places, animals, or people were intrinsically holy, even divine; but nowhere in this creation story is holiness ascribed to anything which comes from nature. All that God had created was very good, but nothing was said to be holy. That which is first declared to be holy is the Sabbath portion of time. God set apart the Sabbath so that in it man might know most keenly his relationship to God.

In the seventh day of creation God made holy a day by giving it a special relationship to himself. So in the Ten Com-

[11]A. Cohen, *The Soncino Chumash* (Hindhead, Surrey, England: The Soncino Press, 1947), p. 8.

mandments man is to make the Sabbath holy repeatedly, recognizing that he has a special relationship to God.[12]

The fact that, basically, sanctity was associated with time and not with a fixed place made possible in the Exile the rise of the synagogue, which could be located anywhere. The twin institutions, the Sabbath and the synagogue, were thus able to withstand all the vicissitudes of dispersion; they remain powerful forces in Judaism to this day.

The same has been true of the Sabbath and the Christian Church throughout history. The basis of the Sabbath has been shifted from the event of the creation to the event of the Resurrection; hence the time has been shifted from Saturday to Sunday. Yet the same underlying principle persists; six days are given to man's mastery of nature, but the seventh is the Lord's Day.

B. The Creator in Relation to the Created, 2:4—3:24

The special significance of man as the highest creation of God is the central thrust of this story. The ideal relationship between God and man is depicted, which in turn is the basis for an ideal relationship between man and woman in marriage. In contrast, there is set forth the nature of sin, which brings chaos into these relationships.

The story has a clear sequence. There is a general setting (2:4-14), a command (2:15-17), an interjected creative act (2: 18-25), an act of violation (3:1-8), an interrogation (3:9-13), a judgment (3:14-21), and an expulsion (3:22-24). Because c. 3 contains the account of violation and judgment, its mood of doubt, fear, and anger is strikingly different from that of c. 2, which possesses an atmosphere of peace, harmony, and loveliness.

1. *The Man with the Inbreathed Life* (2:4-7)

The expression **generations** (4) has a broader meaning than does the term genealogy. The concept of origins is not essential to the word. It occurs 10 other times in Genesis (5:1; 6:9; 10:1; 11:10, 27; 25:12, 19; 36:1, 9; 37:2), once (37:2) with no genealogy given; but in most cases many significant events, as well as a genealogy, are presented.

[12] A. J. Heschel, *The Sabbath* (New York: Farrar, and Straus and Young, Inc., 1951), pp. 3-32.

Some would place the first part of v. 4 with the preceding material, but elsewhere in Genesis the expression, **These are the generations of,** serves as a heading for that which follows. It is retained as such here.

There is some parallel between vv. 4-5 of this chapter and 1:1-2. However, c. 2 gives little about any of the intermediate creative events which lead up to the creation of man. There is no clear indication that the story in c. 2 has any interest in the time sequence of the appearance of plants and animals. On the contrary, attention is drawn to the fact that without **rain** and the watchful care of **man** the earth was originally barren. Hence God provided moisture and **formed man,** so that plants which need cultivation might be fruitful.

More extended detail about the creation of man is given here than in 1:27. In 2:7, man is set forth as an earth creature. He is formed of dust. With intimate concern God breathed life into him, an act which highlights the fact that man's vitality and inner dynamic come directly from God. Any other object of man's affection and hope is a delusion. He is made for two worlds; therefore to be cut off from God is to wither like fruit on a severed vine.

The two expressions **the breath of life** (7, *nishmat chayyim*) and **living soul** (*nefesh chayyah*) have much in common. Both may be used of animals as well as man. **Breath** (*nishmat*) is more often associated with man, but is ascribed to animals in Gen. 7: 22. **Living soul** is translated "living creature," and is applied to all kinds of beasts in Gen. 1:20-21, 24, 30; 2:19; 9:12, 15-16.

Nefesh has a broader connotation than *nishmat.* Both may mean "breath," but *nefesh* also includes meanings like living being, soul, life, self, person, desire, appetite, emotion, and passion.[13] Man is unique. He is what he is because **God . . . breathed into his nostrils the breath of life.** God never did this for an animal.

2. *The Garden of Delight* (2:8-14)

The word **garden** (8) is a translation of the Hebrew *gan,* which designates an enclosed place. The LXX renders the Hebrew as "paradise," *paradeison,* a Persian term which means a park.

[13]F. Brown, S. R. Driver, C. A. Briggs, *A Hebrew and English Lexicon of the Old Testament* (Oxford: Clarendon Press, 1952), *ad loc.*

Eden is not translated, but transliterated into English. Basically, it means "pleasure" or "delight." It seems to indicate a region. Eden may come from the Assyrian word *edinu,* which means plain, prairie, or desert, and designates the land between the Tigris and the Euphrates rivers. If the phrase **a river went out** (10) is understood as oriented upstream, the garden could be placed in the lower Mesopotamian valley. If it is understood as oriented downstream, it would have to be placed in Armenia, where the heads of both the Tigris and the Euphrates originate near each other (see map 1). No definite conclusion is possible at the present time.

More important to the story is the presence of **the tree of life** (9) and **the tree of the knowledge of good and evil.** The first mentioned tree seemed to be the source of life from which man must be separated after his sin (3:22-24). A "tree of life" is mentioned in Prov. 3:18; 11:30; 13:12; 15:4, where it represents a source of happiness, wisdom, and hope in a figurative sense. The phrase is also found in the Book of Revelation as the supreme gift to the faithful (2:7) and as a symbol of eternal life (22:2, 14).

In regard to **the tree of knowledge of good and evil,** the two opposites **good and evil** represent the extremes of knowledge and thus serve as an idiom for completeness—in this case, omniscience and power. In Deut. 1:39 and Isa. 7:14-17, lack of knowing good and evil indicates immaturity, whereas in II Sam. 19:35 full maturity is by indirection associated with the ability to discern between good and evil. But Gen. 3:5 suggests that this power is a divine attribute, and Prov. 15:3 clearly makes the assertion that it is an equivalent to omniscience (see II Sam. 14: 17; I Kings 3:9).

The river **Pison** (11) has never been satisfactorily identified, though guesses have been offered, among them the Indus River of India. **Havilah** refers to a sandy country productive of fine **gold.** That land also yielded **bdellium** (12), seemingly a gum of great worth which was familiar to the Israelites (see Num. 11:7). Whether **onyx stone** is the correct translation of the Hebrew (*shoham*) is uncertain; the LXX suggests beryl.

The identification of **Gihon** (13) is unknown. The Nile River has long been a favorite conjecture because the LXX, the Vulgate, and the English identify the Hebrew word *kush* with **Ethiopia.** But because in Gen. 10:7-10 the descendents of Cush were Arabian and Mesopotamian tribes or cities, some have held that

Gihon is the Araxes River, which flows into the Cyrus River, then into the Caspian Sea. Cush would then be the Hebrew name for the Cassites who lived in that area.

The third river . . . Hiddekel (14) is the well-known Tigris River (see map 1), which in ancient Akkadian was called *idiqlat.* The Euphrates runs parallel to the Tigris, with which it joined to water the Mesopotamian valley. It is still an important river. The Assyrian name was *puratu,* but the old Persian was *ufratu,* which served as the basis for the Greek *euphrates.*[14]

3. *The Command Which Set the Limits* (2:15-17)

When God placed man in the **garden** (15), He gave him two tasks: **to dress it and to keep it.** In an agricultural context, **dress** means cultivation, which includes the act of pruning vines.

When **God commanded the man** (16), He made clear His own sovereign relationship to man and man's subordinate relationship to Him. God had this right because He is Creator and man is creature.

The strongest possible manner of expressing a prohibition in Hebrew is employed to place **the tree of the knowledge of good and evil** (17) out of bounds for man. Since direct speech is inherently personal, the command, **Thou shalt not eat,** is personal and the quality of the Hebrew negative makes it permanent. The importance of the command is augmented by the severity of the punishment. This is made very strong in the Hebrew syntax, the force being somewhat preserved in the English **surely.**

4. *The Woman God Built* (2:18-25)

There was one aspect of God's creation which was not totally satisfactory. The fact that man was still **alone** (18) was **not good.** Isolation is unwholesome. By implication, social relationship, i.e., fellowship, is good. Hence God determined to provide man **an help meet for him,** literally, a helper corresponding to him, one who was equal and adequate for him. In English, **meet** has the meaning of suitable, fit, proper, equal. *The Berkeley Version* reads, "a suitable helper, completing him." *The Confraternity Bible* has, "a helper like himself."

Since there are no tense forms in Hebrew, it does not necessarily follow that God formed the animals after He had formed man. It could just as easily mean that *after* man was placed in

[14]Driver, *op. cit.,* p. 40.

the garden, the animals that God had formed *previously* were **brought** to **Adam** (19). Time sequence is not the important item here.

One aspect of the image of God was demonstrated by Adam's power to discern the nature of each animal and give it a suitable **name,** for in the Hebrew, name and character coincided. When **Adam gave names** (20), he was himself able to discern that none of the animals were **an help meet for him.** He, as well as God, must know this in order to appreciate what God was about to do.

The **deep sleep** (21) is the kind in which the sensibilities cease their normal functioning. See Gen. 15:12; Job 4:13; 33:15, where the phrase is connected with visions; and I Sam. 26:12 and Jonah 1:5, where the condition is not related to visions. See also Isa. 29:10, in which the term suggests lack of spiritual sensitivity. **The rib** (22) can mean both the bone and the flesh attached to it. It is the part of the body nearest the heart, which to the Hebrew was the seat of the affections. Woman was not made of an inferior substance.

To stress the uniqueness of this act, a different verb (*yiben*), which means "built," is used, a point quite lost in the English word **made.** God **brought her unto the man** for his approval and appraisal. Thus part of the story follows the sequence of the creative days in c. 1—namely, the decision (18-20), the creative act (21-22), and the approval (23).

Immediately **Adam** (23) saw the appropriateness of this helper. She was an intimate part of himself, **bone of my bones, and flesh of my flesh,** thus suitable for him. But he also demonstrated his place of authority by naming her.

In effect, this was the institution of the marriage relationship. From the beginning God intended that marriage should be exclusive and intimate. Woman was not simply to cling to man as an appendage. To make man's responsibility clear, God ordained that a man **shall cleave unto his wife** (24) in the mutual commitment of a true union. Marriage is to remain unbroken throughout life, for it is said, **They shall be one flesh,** i.e., a complete identification with each other. And in this they **were not ashamed** (25).

5. *The Woman the Serpent Beguiled* (3:1-5)

The serpent (1) slipped into the peaceful garden like a sinister alien. Throughout ancient Semitic speech, reptiles were related to demonic influences and this verse depicts the creature as **more subtil than any beast of the field.** As the story progresses, the serpent is everywhere presented as the tool of some hidden spirit-power. In the NT, Jesus relates the serpent to the devil (John 8:44), as do Paul (Rom. 16:20; cf. II Cor. 11:3; I Tim. 2:14) and John (Rev. 12:9; 20:2). In all these instances the source of temptation is objectively distinct from either God or the human self. In no case is the serpent regarded as simply a "personification of temptation,"[15] or "representative of the power of *temptation.*"[16]

The serpent opened the conversation with an expression of surprise, **Yea, hath God said?** and then proceeded to misquote God's original command, thus making it absurd. The original prohibition was concerned with only one tree, but the serpent said **of every tree,** a phrase which in 2:16 is found in the permissive command but not in the negative command (2:17). Thus the serpent brought into question the goodness of God; He was too restrictive, withholding unnecessarily benefits of great worth.

That first question was seemingly innocent but it tricked **the woman** (2) into misquoting the command also. She made the prohibition much stronger than it really was. God had not said, **Neither shall ye touch it** (3). But He had made the threat of punishment much stronger than **lest ye die.** She had, unwittingly, made the command unreasonable and the punishment merely a possibility rather than an inescapable result. The woman had lost her golden opportunity to defeat the serpent's suggestion. Had she correctly quoted the command and stuck with it, he would have been unable to proceed further.

The serpent saw his advantage and moved to deny sharply the truth of God's statement of punishment by flatly declaring, **Ye shall not surely die** (4). He pressed his attack by kindling resentment against restraint and by stirring desire for ultimate power. Was not God using the finality of death as a device to keep mankind from discovering—**Your eyes shall be opened** (5)? Was He not preventing man from possessing a good which it was man's right to have? The serpent was accusing God of an improper motive, that of selfishly keeping man on a low level of

[15]A. Richardson, *Genesis I—XI* ("Torch Bible Commentaries"; London: SCM Press, Ltd., 1953), p. 71.

[16]Driver, *op. cit.*, p. 44.

being. Man's true destiny, the serpent hinted, was to **be as gods.** The main characteristic of being divine was the power of **knowing good and evil.**[17] This **knowing** was not abstract knowledge, but a practical ability to know all things, including intelligence to devise and establish ethical standards.

Cleverly the serpent had suggested that breaking God's command would actually provide, not death, but a full, rich life for man. No positive promises were given, only a suggestion of possibilities which were alluring and mysterious. Here was the core appeal of paganism, the belief that great achievements, profound thought, or carefully observed ritual would usher one into the divine realm. Here is also the basic sin of man, to reach for the state of being absolutely free and self-sufficient.

In 3:1-6 we find "The Serpent's Appeal." (1) To physical desire, 6*ab*; (2) To intellectual curiosity, 5; (3) To the disposition to self-assertion, 1, 3 (G. B. Williamson).

6. *The Act of Violation* (3:6-8)

The serpent's arguments appealed to three facets of the woman's nature, each a legitimate part of her creatureliness. Her physical hunger was excited, for **the tree was good for food** (6). Her aesthetic appetite was quickened, for **it was pleasant to the eyes.** And her capacity for wisdom and power was enticed, for it could **make one wise,** which included the ability to dominate others (cf. with Jesus' temptation, Matt. 4:1-11; Luke 4:1-13; and I John 2:16).

The woman had long since in reality been defeated and her contemplation soon issued into action. The commandment of God was broken and, amazingly, **her husband** followed her in disobedience. After both had eaten, their **eyes . . . were opened** (7), but not in the way that the serpent had suggested. Instead of moving to a higher level of being, they fell to a lower level. **They knew that they were naked.** Instead of becoming united with God by attaining equal essence with Him, they became estranged from each other through an awareness that their act had not produced what they had anticipated.[18] Their frustration was related to their new knowledge of nakedness. Disobedience had

[17]H. Renckens, *Israel's Concept of the Beginning* (New York: Herder and Herder, 1964), pp. 273-77.

[18]*Ibid.*, pp. 277-79.

begotten guilt and shame. In reaction to their sense of shame, the two gathered **fig leaves,** of which they **made themselves aprons** (marg., "things to gird"). They were simple, wrap-around loin-cloths.

The man and woman must have been familiar with the **voice of the Lord** (8) as related to a frequent fellowship with God. **The cool of the day** is an idiom for evening, for in the Near East a brisk breeze moves in upon the land at sundown. The pair were not prepared for meeting God this time. The phrase **the presence** is characteristically vivid in Hebrew. It is not a vague, indefinable influence, but a direct, well-defined, personal confrontation. The guilty pair **hid themselves,** but it was of no avail.

7. *The Summons to the Presence of God* (3:9-13)

The question, **Where art thou?** (9), was not uttered because God was ignorant, but because He wanted to elicit response and to bring the man and the woman out into the open by their own confession.

Adam's response, **I was afraid** (10), clarifies the motive for the hiding. Partaking of the fruit of the tree had not made him like God, as the serpent had suggested, but had rather compromised his own true essence of being a man before God.

God knows good and evil from the vantage point of divine, sovereign goodness. But man, being a man and dependent upon God, could know good and evil only from the vantage point of obedience to God's will or from the vantage point of disobedience, which is a rejection of God's expressed will. Man's reach for divine status could only cast him in the role of disobedience; hence his knowledge of good and evil was mixed with guilt and fear.

The first question was put directly to the man, **Hast thou eaten?** (11) Adam was without excuse, for he knew what the command had been. It was a simple, clear-cut prohibition. But Adam would not face his responsibility; he shifted blame from himself to his wife—**She gave me** (12)—and had not God given her to him? Surely she was trustworthy as a guide to action.

The woman (13), too, tried to evade responsibility by saying, **The serpent beguiled me.** She saw now, though, that the serpent had "played her for a fool."

In 3:6-11, G. B. Williamson points out "God and the Sinner." (1) Sin causes personal guilt, 7, 10-11; (2) Sin separates God and man, 8*b*; (3) God seeks sinful man, 8*a*, 9; (4) God pardons man's guilt, 21.

8. *The Sentences Pronounced* (3:14-19)

The sins which had been committed are reflected in the punishments which were meted out. **The serpent** (14) was **cursed. Above all** is not in the sense of "more than," thus suggesting that other animals were cursed too, but in the sense of "apart from" or "separated out from among." Moffatt translates, "A curse on you of all creatures!" The serpent had posed as supremely wise, but its manner of movement would ever be a symbol of its humiliation. The phrase **upon thy belly** does not mean that the serpent originally had legs and lost them at the moment the curse was put upon it, but rather that its customary mode of locomotion typified its punishment.

The clause, **Dust shalt thou eat,** is idiomatically equivalent to "You shall be humiliated" (cf. Ps. 72:9; Isa. 49:23; Mic. 7:17, where the phrase "lick the dust" clearly has this meaning).

The punishment would involve **enmity** (15), hostility between persons. The serpent's **seed,** which Jesus alludes to as wicked men (Matt. 13:38-39; John 8:44), and the woman's **seed,** both have a strongly personal sense.[19] The serpent was told, The Seed of the woman shall **bruise thy head.** Compare Paul's allusion to this in Rom. 16:20. The serpent could only **bruise his heel.** Actually, **bruise** is not strong enough for the Hebrew, which can mean grind, crush, destroy. A crushed head that leads to death is contrasted with a crushed heel that can be cured. Verse 15 has often been called the "proto-gospel," for it contains a promise of hope for the sinful pair. Evil is not destined to be all-victorious; God had in mind a Victor for the human race. There is a strong touch of the Messianic in this verse.

In 3:14-15 we see "The Bruised Heel." (1) The Saviour promised was the Seed of the woman—the God-man; (2) This Holy Seed would bruise the serpent's head—conquer sin; (3) The serpent would bruise the heel of the Saviour—on the Cross, He died (G. B. Williamson).

The woman's punishment was to be the opposite of the "delight" she sought in v. 6. She would know **sorrow** (16) in childbearing, which is quite different from the new kind of life

[19]The singular pronoun **it** (*hu*) can designate an individual.

she had tried to achieve through disobedience. Likewise, the future binding of her **desire** to her **husband** was a rebuke to her decision to seek independence. She would ever be dependent upon him.

In 3:1-15, Alexander Maclaren sees "How Sin Came In." (1) The inducement to evil, 1-5; (2) Yielding to the tempter, 6; (3) The fatal consequences, 7-15.

A curse was put upon the soil instead of upon the man directly. Adam had been commissioned to work with the soil (2:15), but no longer was it to be a pure joy. The man had easily submitted to the woman's appeal that he eat of the forbidden fruit. Now his labor on the soil would be mixed with **sorrow** (17). On every hand he would be faced with competitors, **thorns . . . and thistles** (18), which grow profusely without cultivation and yield no food for man. In Hos. 10:8 these plants appear as symbols of judgment and desolation in a place of worship. Compare also Judg. 8:7, 16; II Sam. 23:6; Ps. 118:12; Isa. 32:13; 33:12; Jer. 4:3; 12:13; Ezek. 28:24. In every case a bad connotation is attached to the nature of these plants (see also Matt. 13:7; Heb. 6:8).

Physical death was not to be immediate, but it was to be inevitable, for **unto dust shalt thou return** (19). The immediate kind of death which man was to suffer was spiritual, a separation from God.

In 3:14-19 we find portrayed "The Curse Caused by Sin." (1) Upon the serpent, 14; (2) Upon woman, 15-16; (3) Upon Adam, 17, 19; (4) Upon the earth, 17*b*-18 (G. B. Williamson).

9. *The Expulsion from the Garden* (3:20-24)

In the dark gloom of judgment there were to be rays of hope and mercy. The man was able to see the possibility of a future through his wife. He now named her **Eve** (20), meaning "life," for from her would come a posterity.

Mercifully, God then provided for them **coats of skins** (21). These may have come from sacrificed animals though the text does not specifically say so.

There is a touch of irony in the divine observation that these human beings had **become as one of us** (22). The preposition **of** (*min*) points to a sharp distinction between God and man rather than to identity. It is thus in contrast to **as one,** which denotes unity. The man and woman had sought to be as God, **to know good and evil,** as beings who are sovereign. But they could never achieve this status. They possessed only the breath (2:7) and the image (1:26-27) of God. Consequently their intrusion into a realm not their own was a denial of their creaturehood and a rebellion against the uniqueness of the Creator. Therefore man must be cut off from **the tree of life,** lest he become fixed in his rebellion.

The **Cherubims** (24) were angelic beings representing the power of God, often related to His throne. Two figures of cherubim were on the lid of the ark (Exod. 25:18-22; 37:7-9), and many were woven into the curtains of the Tabernacle (Exod. 26:1, 31; 36:8, 35) and carved upon the walls and doors of the Temple (I Kings 6:23-35; II Chron. 3:10-13). Ezekiel described them as being a composite of four faces: a lion, an ox, an eagle, and a man, and having the hands of men, feet of calves, and four wings (cf. the four creatures of Rev. 4:6-8). These creatures were charged with the task of keeping man from **the tree of life** as long as he was laden with the burden of sin.[20]

C. Murder and Its Aftermath, 4:1-24

A terrifying aspect of sin is that it cannot be isolated nor obliterated easily. It progressively performs its devasting work throughout society from generation to generation. The sin of Adam and Eve did not bring disaster into their lives alone; it continued on from son to son, from age to age. The story in c. 4 poignantly illustrates this fact and the genealogies amplify the repercussions of evil throughout the generations.

1. *The Murder of a Trusting Brother* (4:1-16)

In general structure, this story is much like the previous one. It has a setting (4:1-5), an act of violation (4:8), a judgment scene (4:9-15), and the execution of the sentence (4:16).

The story of the first two boys born to **Adam** and **Eve** (1) highlights the repercussions of sin within a family unit. The boys, **Cain** and **Abel** (2), possessed strikingly opposite temperaments. Cain liked to work with growing plants. Abel enjoyed being with living animals. Both had a religious frame of mind.

[20]E. H. Browne, "Genesis," *The Bible Commentary*, ed. F. C. Cook (New York: Charles Scribner's Sons, 1892), I, 49-52.

The sons of Adam brought sacrifices **unto the Lord** (3), the first recorded incident of sacrifice in the Bible.

That **Abel . . . brought of the firstlings of his flock and of the fat thereof** (4) does not necessarily make the point that animals are superior to plants for sacrificial purposes. Why **the Lord had respect unto Abel and to his offering** (5) becomes apparent as the story unfolds.

The first clue comes forth almost immediately. Cain could not take second place to anyone. The Lord's preference for Abel filled Cain with anger. Only Cain could be "number one."

The Lord was not absent from the hour of worship. He met Cain and gave him a warning. God did not condemn him directly, but by a play on words He let Cain know that he was in real danger. In Hebrew, the word **accepted** (7) is, literally, "lifted up," and stands in contrast to **fallen** (6). A downcast look is not the proper companion for a clear conscience or for a right action. The thrust of God's questions was to bring Cain to self-examination and to repentance.

If Cain had done **well** (7), surely God would have graciously received him. But what if Cain had not done well? Here was the real issue which Cain was ignoring, for he was projecting blame upon Abel. A threat to his spiritual life was not far away. Sin was just outside **the door,** ready to bring Cain to ruin.

There is need to look at two words in v. 7. The word for **sin** (*hatt'at*) can mean either **sin** or sin offering. The latter seems out of the question, because the presence outside **the door** does not appear to be helpful; rather it is sinister. The word **lieth** (*robesh*) is a verbal noun. The problem for the translator is, Does this word serve as a verb, **lieth,** or as a noun, giving the sense, "Sin is a croucher"?

E. A. Speiser points out that Akkadian, a parent of biblical Hebrew, has basically the same word, *rabishum* (note that the first three consonants are the same), which means "demon." The biblical story before us comes from the same geographical location; so if we regard *robesh* as borrowed from Akkadian, the solution is at hand.[21] Sin is depicted as a vicious demon, ready to pounce on Cain should Cain leave God's presence unrepentant. Graciously, however, God offered to Cain the power to overcome sin: **Thou shalt rule over him.**

[21]*Genesis* ("The Anchor Bible"; Garden City, New York: Doubleday & Co., 1964), pp. 32-33.

The last portion of 7 may be paraphrased: "You have let the fire of anger flame within; hence, when you leave my abode, sin will take you. It is best to rule over your anger, lest destruction overwhelm you."

But Cain left God's presence and anger changed to jealousy, which in turn became murderous hate coupled with sly planning. In the fields one day the evil deed was done—**Cain . . . slew** (8) Abel, deliberately and without provocation.

But Cain could not avoid **the Lord** (9). A judgment scene soon developed. **The voice of thy brother's blood crieth unto me** (10), is a vivid idiom meaning, "You may try to forget your act of violence, but I cannot. Whatever happens to one of My children is a matter of personal concern to Me." The privilege of cultivating plant life was taken from Cain and he was banished to the desert to be **a fugitive and a vagabond** (12).

The exposure of his sin changed Cain. Arrogant hate became craven fear mixed with self-pity. He would be open to the same fate which he had dealt his brother. He could not bear the thought. But God did not mock him. Again His mercy softened the punishment. He **set a mark upon Cain** (15). So Cain went out to face a totally new life, away from God. The designation **land of Nod** (16) means "land of wandering," and does not seem to be the name of a specific region other than its general direction to **the east of Eden.**

From 4:2-9, G. B. Williamson discusses "Cain and Abel." (1) The difference in men—even brothers, 2*b*, 5*b*-6, 8-9; (2) The significant difference in their offerings, 3-5*a*; cf. Heb. 11:4; (3) Here is a revelation of the goodness and severity of God, 7*a*.

2. *Cain's Creative but Godless Descendents* (4:17-24)

The significance of Cain had been exhausted, and his lineage of rebellious posterity is sketchily set forth in brief genealogical form.

Cain's wife was, by implication, a sister (cf. 5:4) who went with him into exile. Cain began to build a fortified dwelling, **a city** (17), and pridefully named it after his first son, **Enoch.** The search of Cain and his sons for security was symbolized by the erection of heavy walls, by the begetting of many sons through multiple wives, and in the power of craftsmanship, weaponry, and hatred. The first poem of the Scripture (23-24) serves as an illustration of the fierce bitterness which poisoned the spirits of these men. The meaning of 23 is, "I have slain a man [merely] for wounding me, and a young man [only] for striking and bruising me" (*Amp. Bible*). They reached heights of skill and achievement but they also wallowed in the depths of evil.

D. Expansion from a New Beginning, 4:25—6:8

In the Book of Genesis, the less important strands of thought or groups of individuals are given but brief attention and then dismissed. Interest is focused on doctrines or people which are central to God's redemptive dealings with man.

1. *Adam's Third Son* (4:25-26)

The boy who replaced the murdered Abel was well named. **Seth** (25) means "appointed" or "placed," which signified God's mercy. He gave to **Adam** and Eve a son who would preserve faith in the one true God. It was in his family that the fires of true worship were kept burning brightly. Here was basis for hope that godliness was possible among men.

2. *Abundance of Years but Scarcity of Faith* (5:1-32)

Verses 1-2 are a synopsis of 1:27-28, and in form strongly suggest that this genealogy is a unit in itself. The true goal of God's creative act was that man should be **in the likeness of God** (1). That **likeness** had been corrupted by the sin in the garden. **The likeness** had been distorted even in the cultural achievements of Cain's line of descendents. And Seth was not truly **in the likeness of God.** He possessed the corrupted state of sinful man, for he was in Adam's **likeness.** No number of years on earth could change that fact. The result of sin was physical death, and the only way one could bypass that fate was illustrated in Enoch's life. He had **walked with God: and he was not; for God took him** (24). The only escape from death was through intimate fellowship with God, coupled with a delivering act of the Almighty. Apart from that each man **died** (5, 8, 11, *et al.*).

A comparison of genealogies in both Testaments soon makes clear several of their characteristics. They are highly selective and do not necessarily list every generation. A study of "father" and "son," which can be done adequately only in the Hebrew, reveals that these terms often can be applied to any ancestor or any descendent. The role of genealogies in the Scripture is not always to provide a historical chronology; their function varies from place to place.

It is of interest to note a point of comparison between the line of Cain and the line of **Seth.** The seventh after Cain was Lamech, who was the epitome of angry hostility, though his three sons were creative geniuses. The seventh in Seth's line was pious **Enoch,** whom **God took** to himself. **Noah** (29), the tenth in Seth's line, and his three sons were to begin a new population after the Flood.

There is no easy way to account for the length of life attributed to the patriarchs listed in c. 5. The shortest is that of Lamech, 777 years. The longest is that of Methusaleh, 969. Conservative scholars have usually taken one of two possible interpretations. Some (notably John Davis in his widely used *Bible Dictionary* and more recently Bernard Ramm) have suggested that the names represent not only the individual man but his clan as well. A biblical parallel is found in Acts 7:16, where the name "Abraham" refers to his family or clan, since the transaction reported took place after the patriarch's death. Others point out that in the infancy of the race, before prolonged and persistent sinning had reduced human vitality and diseases had developed as we have them now, extreme age and long vigor may well have been possible.

3. *The Great Apostasy* (6:1-8)

The genealogies of Cain and of Seth are capped by a story which is powerful in its indictment. Yet extensive controversy has swirled about this passage.

One aspect of the problem has centered in the meaning of the phrase **the sons of God** (2). Because this phrase appears in Job 1:6; 2:1; 38:7; Dan. 3:25 as a designation for heavenly beings or angels, it has been argued that fallen angels came to earth and married women (cf. Ps. 29:1; 89:6, where "ye mighty" and "sons of the mighty" refer back to God).[22] Yet nowhere in the Scriptures are heavenly beings depicted as corrupting mankind. They are always beneficial in their relationships with man. Jesus clearly stated that those who would be resurrected "neither marry, nor are given in marriage, but are as the angels of God in heaven" (Matt. 22:30). Hence this view is contrary to the general tenor of the Bible.

[22]See Kevan, *op. cit.*, p. 83, and Yates, *op. cit.*, pp. 11-12.

The widespread presence of mythological stories among ancient pagans, going as far back as the Hurrians (1500-1400 B.C), depicting nature gods and goddesses engaged in illicit relations among themselves has led some to hold that this passage is a mythological tale. Nevertheless it is readily admitted that erotic mythology does not appear elsewhere in Scripture. It is then concluded by these scholars that the writer of Genesis altered a mythological tale and, with an embarrassed air, presented it as justification for God's judgment which was soon to come.[23]

Another popular view is that **the sons of God** were descendents of Seth. Of importance here is the word **God** (*ha'elohim*), which elsewhere in the OT means "the only true God" and thus distinguishes Him from pagan deities. This view seems to rule out the mythological theory.

It cannot be truly argued that the concept of a son relation between God and His worshippers is foreign to the OT. This matter does not simply rest upon a precise phrase; it rests on a concept.[24] In reference to the true God there is a statement in Deut. 32:5 which says, "Their spot is not the spot of his children" (Heb., *banaw*, "his sons"). Also in reference to God, the Psalmist (73:15) said, "Behold, I should offend against the generation of thy children" (Heb., *banayka*, "thy sons"). Surely in these contexts "his children" and "thy children" are equivalent to **sons of God.** And more clearly, Hosea (1:10) said of Israel, "There it shall be said unto them, Ye are the sons of the living God [*'el hay*]." In OT thought *he'elohim* and *'el hay* could hardly have been two separate Gods. Note also in Hos. 11:1 the phrase "my son," which refers back to the Lord.

In the NT the phrase "sons of God" occurs with reference to human beings in John 1:12; Rom. 8:14; Phil. 2:15; I John 3:1; and Rev. 21:7. These NT passages would not be drawn from paganism but would be solidly based on the OT concept noted above.

The conclusion that the worshipers of the Lord (Gen. 4:26) of the Seth lineage were also **the sons of God** bridges the gap between the genealogies and the Flood in a natural manner. These men did not pick their wives on the basis of faith but on the basis of impulse, with no regard for religious background. Corruption followed in the wake of this loose living and God reacted with divine wrath.

[23]See Speiser, *op. cit.*, pp. 45-46.

[24]Leupold, *op. cit.*, I, 250-54.

The Hebrew word for **strive** (3, *yadon*) is capable of several meanings. The KJV reading rests upon the meaning "judge, restrain." But the verb formation could point back to roots which mean "abide," "be humbled," or going to the Akkadian, "shield, protect." Either **strive** or "shield" fits the context well. Man was not to be pampered simply because he **also is flesh.** He was put on probation for **an hundred and twenty years.**

In 6:3 there is the arresting thought "Not Always." (1) The Spirit of God strives with man; (2) The Spirit will not always strive; (3) Man can find grace in the eyes of the Lord, 8 (G. B. Williamson).

The translation **giants** (4, *nefilim*) goes back to the LXX. The context of the other instance where it appears (Num. 13:33) suggests unusual stature, but actually physical size has nothing to do with the meaning of the word. Literally, *nefilim* means either "the fallen ones," or "those who fall upon [attack] others." In any case, they were vicious people. They preceded and coexisted with the commingling of **the sons of God** and **the daughters of men.** Nothing in the text supports the idea that they were the latter's offspring, who rivaled them as **men of renown,** i.e., men of notoriety.

The reaction of God to the affairs in human society heightened in intensity as sinful corruption became dominant on a universal scale. The degradation of man was inwardly complete, **only evil continually** (5).

The phrase, **It repented the Lord** (6), and phrases like it (see Exod. 32:14; I Sam. 15:11; Jer. 18:7-8; 26:3, 13, 19; Jonah 3:10), have troubled many Bible students. The ordinary concept of repentance is related to turning from immoral acts. Thus a change of direction, of character, and of purpose is inherent in the act.[25] However, twice OT passages definitely state that God does not lie and repent as man does (Num. 23:19; I Sam. 15:29). A study of the passages listed above shows that divine repentance does not spring from sorrow for evil deeds done. Rather, changes in man's relationship to God issue in changes in God's dealings with man. When man turns from God to sin, God changes the relationship of fellowship to a relationship of judgmental rebuke. When man turns from sin to God, He establishes a new relation-

[25] R. H. Elliott, *The Message of Genesis* (Nashville: Broadman Press, 1961), pp. 64-65.

ship of fellowship. This is divine repentance. In our text (6), God turns from fellowship to judgment.

The changes in relationship which God executes are never depicted in the OT as impersonal or passive. God is ever deeply involved. Since the change of relationship is personal, what better human terms could one use than profoundly emotional expressions? And so here, **it grieved him** (God) **at his heart.** When man sins, God judges; but He also suffers deeply.

So God did not glory in the coming act of judgment. Every word of the pronouncement is freighted with agony. **Whom I have created** (7) suggests "The products of My loving creativity must all be destroyed, except one." One man alone was a worshiper of God: **Noah found grace in the eyes of the Lord** (8).

From 6:5-8, G. B. Williamson discusses "The Flood." (1) Judgment for sin is inescapable, 5-7; (2) Righteousness is indestructible, 8; (3) God's faithfulness to men who trust and obey is unchangeable, 8.

E. Universal Corruption and Its Aftermath, 6:9—11:26

An individual comes to the front again as the principal object of God's concern. After delivering Noah and his family from the "day of doom," God set up a covenant relationship with them. But the vows were scarcely said before defilement entered to muddy the relationship, and matters did not improve as posterity increased and spread across the earth. It appears to be a dull repetition of an old story.

1. *The Exploits of Righteous Noah* (6:9—9:17)

Though this story is popularly known as "The Story of the Flood," there is little detail about the Flood itself. The main emphasis is upon God's relations with mankind, especially the one with whom He chooses to deal directly, and their responses to His claims upon them. Noah is the prominent character of the story and his obedience is of importance to God's act of salvation, not simply of judgment alone.

The sequence of the story is composed of a setting (6:9-12), a series of commands (6:13—7:5), the execution of judgment (7:6-24), an extension of mercy (8:1-22), and a covenant (9:1-17).

a. A just man in a corrupt world (6:9-12). Immediately **Noah** (9) is pinpointed as an unusual person, though the characteristics associated with him are not uncommon among God's men in both the Old Testament and the New. He was **just** (*tsadik*); i.e., he lived according to a standard, marking his life as one of obedience to God and concern for mankind. He was **perfect** (*tamim*); i.e., he was undivided in his loyalty, oriented toward a definite goal, and motivated by a controlling passion.[26] As Enoch (5:24), **Noah walked with God**; i.e., enjoyed a continual, intimate fellowship with God. Such a walk infused the previously mentioned traits with a warmth and depth of interpersonal relationship with God that transcends formal religion.

The moral condition of Noah's generation not only contrasts with Noah's own life but throws light upon the terms which describe him. The people's corruption stands out as opposite to Noah's righteousness. Noah displayed fidelity and conformity to God's will; the people did not. Noah's genuineness, his wholesomeness of life (*tamim*) was radically different from the **violence** (*chamas*, 11) which permeated society of his times. A comparison of vv. 11-12 with 5 would indicate that this **violence** was inward, heavily contaminated with immoral imagery and corrupt tendencies.

The statement, **God looked** (12), does not mean that He needed information, but that the situation on earth was very much His concern and demanded His serious consideration. Note similar meanings of this phrase in 30:1, 9; 50:15. In each case an evaluation of the situation issued in decision and then in action.

b. God's judgment on the race (6:13—7:5). The divine word, **The end of all flesh is come** (13), rang like a death knell through the consciousness of Noah. The fact of **the earth** being **filled with violence** could not continue unchecked. God had made a decision and He was ready to move into action. The lawlessness of the people had been unrestrained, so the punishment was to be drastic. Both mankind and its home, **the earth**, were to be destroyed. The earth was destroyed in the sense of ceasing to support life for the duration of the Flood.

The judgment was not to be devoid of an opportunity for salvation. Directions were specifically given to Noah. He was

[26]A. Richardson, ed., *A Theological Word Book of the Bible* (New York: The Macmillan Co., 1951), *ad loc.*

to take **gopher wood** (14) and build a large, boxlike structure. It is not known what **gopher wood** was really like but the **pitch** was an asphalt material fairly common to the Mesopotamian valley. If a cubit is regarded as about 18 inches in length, the ark would be about 450 feet long, 75 feet wide, and 45 feet high. Ventilation was to be provided through **a window** (16) or an opening for light, which may have been spaced all around the top edge. On matters of construction detail, the text says little. A **door** was to be on the side of the ark, but there is no indication how the door was related to the three floors of the ark.

A flood of waters (17) was to be the means of judgment, but a **covenant** (18) was to be established with Noah (see 9:9-17). This is the first time the word **covenant** appears in the OT. In later passages it is a favorite mode of describing the personal relationship between God and the people whom He chose to enter into a special relationship with Him. In this case Noah and his immediate family, including daughters-in-law, were to be the chosen few. Here the **covenant** relation was only a promise.

The Lord next informed Noah that he was to take pairs of birds and animals into the ark. The phrase **after their kind** (20), which is found also in Gen. 1:21, 24-25 in reference to animals, is unclear in regard to the classifications of animals intended. Only the general groupings are mentioned specifically: **fowls** (*of*), **cattle** (*behemah*), and **every creeping thing** (*remes*, 20). In present thinking, "kinds" of animals are species, of which there are about one million. It would be an error to assume that ancient people thought of kinds of animals in the same sense. Their concept may have been nearer to our terms "classes, orders, families, or genera," but there is no way now to determine this point. **Food** (21) was also taken into the ark.

Unusual though God's word was, Noah followed out instructions obediently. In Heb. 11:7 there is an observation that Noah was "moved with fear," as he obeyed God. Peter called him "a preacher of righteousness" (II Pet. 2:5).

From 6:9-22, Alexander Maclaren preached on "The Saint Among Sinners." (1) The solitary saint, 9-11; (2) The universal apostasy, 11-12; (3) The stern sentence, 13; (4) Noah's exact obedience, 22; (5) The vindication of faith, 7:21-23.

After the ark was completed, **the Lord** came to **Noah** (7:1) again. He was commended for his obedience, which was identified by the word **righteous.** What **Noah** had done met with God's approval.

In the listing of the animals to enter the ark, a distinction is made between **clean beasts** (2) and those **not clean.** Those which were **clean,** in a ritualistic sense, were privileged to come in **by sevens.** Whether seven pairs are meant or three pairs plus an extra single is not clear. Of the unclean only one pair each was allowed. No classification is made of unclean and clean **fowls** (3), but they too were to come **by sevens.** Noah had **seven days** (4) to load the ark before the judgment began. It was to come in the form of a flood that would **destroy** man and beast. He quickly obeyed the message from God in detail.

c. *The Flood* (7:6-24). It is noted that **Noah was six hundred years old** (6) at the time of this catastrophe. The entrance into the ark is depicted as a calm and orderly event, taking place just as God had commanded that it be done. According to schedule **the waters of the flood** (10) appeared.

The second chronological notation mentions even the month and the day when the Flood broke loose. The source of the waters was twofold: they burst forth from beneath, out of **the great deep** (11), and they poured out of **the windows of heaven.** Such brevity of description has caused a rash of conjecture concerning the meaning of these phrases.[27] The Bible is content to say only that this turbulence continued for **forty days and forty nights** (12). Before the Flood began, Noah and his family, with the animals, were within the ark in accordance with God's command. God then sealed them in so that they floated safely upon the rising waters, which **increased greatly** (18) until **the high hills . . . were covered** (19).

We are told that the waters rose **fifteen cubits upward** (20), a distance of about 22½ feet, but we are not told whether this measurement was from the top of the highest mountain to the surface of the water or from some other starting point.[28]

The water carried out its deadly purpose, destroying the creatures which are more at home on **the dry land** (22) than on or in water. The destruction is stressed twice (21, 23), for the

[27]B. Ramm, *The Christian View of Science and Scripture* (Grand Rapids: Wm. B. Eerdmans Publishing Co., 1955), pp. 229-49.

[28]J. C. Whitcomb, and H. M. Morris, *The Genesis Flood* (Grand Rapids: Baker Book House. 1961), pp. 1-2.

Chronology of the Flood

Genesis 7—8

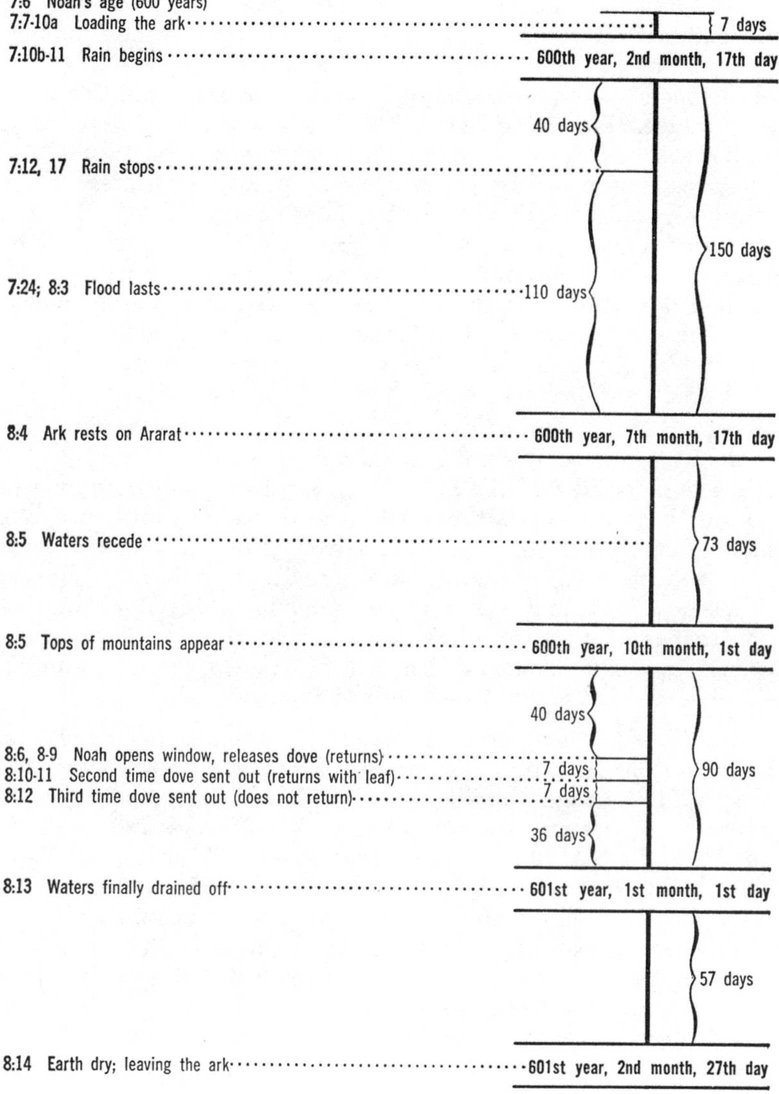

Total time from beginning of Flood, one year and 10 days

judgment was an awesome affair. Only those in the ark escaped from the fury of the storm, the aftermath of which continued for a total of **one hundred and fifty days** (24).[29]

d. But God remembered (8:1-19). The statement that **God remembered** (1) is like a ray of light in a gloomy scene. Violence and corruption bring a harvest of destruction, but the faithful obedience of a few evokes expressions of kindness from the heavenly Judge. The Flood was not to last forever, nor were those in the ark to stay in it as though it were a prison. Again God acted, causing a drying wind to sweep across the water, which steadily receded from the mountaintops. Soon **the ark** (4) was grounded upon **Ararat,** a mountain range in eastern Turkey. Slowly the lower **mountains** (5) came into view, but when **Noah opened the window of the ark** (6) and sent forth the **dove** (8), there was as yet no dry land on which it could alight, and so it **returned . . . into the ark** (9). A week later he sent out **the dove** (10) again and it came back with **an olive leaf** (11).

After another **seven days** (12), **the dove** was released a third time. This time it did not return, which prompted Noah to remove **the covering of the ark** (13). He did not allow anyone to go out, however, until the earth was thoroughly **dry,** 57 days later. Note in v. 13 that **the waters were dried up** (*harevu*), but that in the next verse **was the earth dried** (*yavesah*). The change of Hebrew verb indicates a more complete drying than the disappearance of water from **the face of the ground** (13). In response to God's command, **Noah** (18) opened the ark, and all that had been in it **went forth out of the ark** (19).

e. Sacrifice and promise (8:20-22). Coming from the ark, Noah first directed his thoughts and actions Godward. Upon **the altar** (20) were sacrificed some of the **clean** animals and birds, of which there was an excess number (7:2, 8-9), and God responded. Here the phrase **smelled a sweet savour** (21) does not indicate that God was greedily hungry, but that He was aware of Noah's act and approved.[30] God is depicted as making an inner resolve not to use a flood as a means of punishment again. The grounds for such punishment still remained, **for the imaginations of man's heart is evil from his youth** (21), but God's mercy would preclude a flood as a punishment. This does not mean that punishment would cease. As long as sin persisted among

[29]*Ibid.*, pp. 3-7.

[30]Browne, *op. cit.*, p. 73.

men, punishment would come, though by other means. As a sign of His decision God set up an orderliness of natural sequences which would encourage man to have hope for the future.

f. God's covenant with Noah (9:1-17). Reminiscent of Gen. 1:28-29, **God blessed Noah and his sons** (1) and a like command to populate the earth was laid upon them. They were to dominate all other creatures on the earth. In addition to having plants for food, they were now permitted to eat flesh, with one limitation. They were not permitted to partake of flesh in which **blood** (4) remained. **Blood** was the symbol of life, and in man particularly was not to be treated lightly. Man had been made **in the image of God** (6), and thus had a special status.

Having made clear man's unique role on earth, God proceeded to highlight further His special relationship with man by establishing a **covenant** (9) with Noah and his descendents. The emphasis of this **covenant** was to be on mercy rather than on punishment—mercy extended to all creatures. The fact that a **bow in the cloud** (13) was to be the peculiar sign of this covenant does not mean that rainbows had never appeared before. Its close association with rain seems to have been its prime value as a sign of God's covenant that a universal flood would not occur again. The point is so important that it is reiterated six times in verses 11-17.

The theological overtones of Noah's experiences related to the Flood are often only implicit but nevertheless they are clear. The root of the difficulty lay in man's rebellion against God, his evil imagination and propensity. Also, God does not tolerate sin beyond measure. There is a terminal point which issues in judgment for man, but not without pain to God (6:6). God took the first step in preparing for the judgment by providing for those who lived obediently before Him. The others came under judgment because they shut Him out of their lives. Noah's experiences depict God as complete Master of all natural forces, some of which He uses as tools for judgment or salvation. God's concern in the midst of judgment is pointed up in the statement that He remembered those in the ark. Dangerous though their situation was, they were never absent from His thoughts. When the danger was past, the Lord evidenced His concern by entering into a personal covenant relationship with man and creature, freely giving promises of future mercies. God's relationship with man was not in the nature of a complex of natural forces called gods and goddesses characterized by whim and caprice. He is the Creator-God who demands righteousness and punishes corruption. His dealings with man are profoundly personal.

2. *Spiritual Disintegration* (9:18—11:26)

In spite of the lessons of the Flood, men were not all true to God after it had passed.

a. Folly in Noah's family (9:18-29). Noah was a tiller of the ground, even as Cain had been. Caring for plants became his great love and among these plants was the grapevine. This is the first time production of wine is referred to in the Bible, and it is significant that it is connected with a situation of disgrace.

Noah may have been innocent, not knowing the effect that fermentation has on grape juice nor the effect that fermented wine has on the human brain. This did not prevent shame from entering the family circle. Losing his senses, Noah stripped off his clothes and lay naked. Nakedness was abhorred by early Semitic peoples, especially by the Hebrews, who associated it with sexual looseness (cf. Lev. 18:5-19; 20:17-21; I Sam. 20:30).

One of Noah's sons, **Ham** (22), entered the tent. Seeing his father, he did not help him but disrespectfully made light of Noah's condition to his brothers. The other two sons immediately **covered the nakedness of their father** (23), discreetly backing into the tent while they did so.

Regaining his senses, Noah took note of what had happened and spoke to his sons. He left Ham without a blessing and concentrated his reprimand upon Canaan, whose descendents historically became a people marked by sordid morals and a chief source of corruption for the Israelites. The Canaanite Baal worship descended to the lowest depths of moral degradation. Though the Canaanites gained some power, as Phoenicians, through sea traffic in the Mediterranean, they never rose to become a great nation. They were almost always dominated by other peoples.

The blessing placed upon **Shem** (26) has a strong religious emphasis, and this line of descendents from Noah indeed played a major role in bearing the message of redemption to the world. The most prominent of these nations was Israel, to whom the revelation of God preserved in Scripture was given. Particularly in the time of David and Solomon, Israel ruled over the

Canaanites, using them to assist in building the first Temple in Jerusalem.

The blessing given **Japheth** (27) involved a play on words, for the name means "enlarging." The line of Japheth rose to play a superior role as bearers of political power through the Persians, the Greeks, and the Romans. Evangelized by Paul and others, they were, of all peoples, the most receptive to Christianity and thus came to **dwell in the tents of Shem** (27). There was little else significant about Noah's latter days. As those before him, **he died** (29).

b. The spread of Noah's descendents (10:1-32). We have here the same procedure in giving genealogies as in c. 5, where the sons of Cain are merely listed, in order that attention might be centered on Seth. Thus the lines of Japheth and Ham are briefly told and then dismissed. Verse 5 states clearly that this list is based, not only on family divisions, but upon nationalistic and linguistic distinctions. Though the names may go back to individuals, the genealogies primarily relate to nations descended from Japheth. They occupied the northern regions, stretching through Turkey, the islands of the Mediterranean Sea, and into southern Europe. The languages of these people have been mostly Indo-European.

Gomer (2) has been identified with Cimmerians of Assyrian records. **Magog** probably is a term for all northerners (see Ezek. 38:2; 39:1, 6), but particularly those in eastern Turkey, where **Tubal** and **Meshech** apparently were located.

Madai was the ancient Median nation, which in the sixth century B.C. teamed up with the Persians to form the Persian Empire. **Javan** was the Ionian Greek nation, which was prominent in Homer's works. **Tiras** probably was the Greek Tyrsenoi, who lived on Aegean islands. Some think they may have been the Etruscans.

Ashkenaz (3) possibly was located in the Caucasian range near the Black and Caspian seas (cf. Jer. 51:27). There may be some tie with the Mesopotamian name *Ashguza*, who were the Scythians. **Riphath** apparently lived in Anatolia or Turkey. **Togarmah** appears to be the same as the Mesopotamian name *Tegarama*, located near Carchemish on the Euphrates River. **Elishah** (4) also appears on cuneiform lists as *Elashiya*, an ancient name for Cyprus. **Tarshish** may also have been Cyprus in older times, but the Greeks located the *Tartesos* on the southern

ern coast of Spain just west of Gibraltar. The **Kittim,** the same as the Greek *Kition,* were located on Cyprus. The **Dodanim** may have been the Dardanians of Anatolia or the inhabitants of Rhodes, an Aegean island. In the Septuagint (LXX), the Greek translation of the OT, this name is spelled with an initial *r.* In the Hebrew the characters *d* and *r* are almost alike and are easily confused.

Cush (6) is connected with two different geographic areas. This people early established Kish in the Mesopotamian valley and then become the Kassites. Some of them also seemed to have migrated to southern Arabia, for all those families listed in 10:7 were inhabitants of that land. There was then a movement into Abyssinia in eastern Africa (modern Ethiopia). The descendents of Cush who stayed in the Mesopotamian valley honored a hero named **Nimrod** (8), who built a **kingdom** (10) of prominent city states: **Babel, Erech, Accad, and Calneh.** The label **hunter** (9) seems to refer to Nimrod's tendency to victimize people and to exploit natural resources. The **hunter** stands in contrast to the common Semitic word "shepherd," which designates a ruler who has his people's welfare at heart. Nimrod's rule extended up the Tigris River, where the later Assyrian power center, composed of **Nineveh, and the city Rehoboth, and Calah** (11), **and Resen** (12), were built. It is of interest that the modern name for the ruins of **Calah** is Nimrud.

Mizraim (13) is the Hebrew name for Egypt, which has had its home in the Nile valley. To the west of Egypt is the land of the **Ludim,** the Libyans. The others listed in 13 have not yet been identified. The **Pathrusim** (14) are now known as the people of Pathros in upper Egypt. The **Casluhim** are listed as in the homeland of the **Philistim,** or Philistines, from whom Palestine gained its name. The **Caphtorim** were the people of Crete, which was also the original home of the Philistines.

The Canaanites became a Semitic-speaking people and were known to the Greeks as Phoenicians. Their main cities were **Sidon** (15) and Tyre, which still exist in modern Lebanon. The Canaanites were long politically dominated by the Egyptians. **Heth** would be the Hittites, who built a power center in central Anatolia (Turkey), but some established colonies in Palestine, the best known of which was at Hebron (Gen. 23:23-24). **Jebusite** (16) stands for the Hurrian inhabitants of Jerusalem before it was captured by King David (II Sam. 5:6-10). The **Amorite** clans held the highlands of Palestine and of Transjordan. **Hivite** (17) was also a name for Hurrian colonists in Palestine, but the **Girgasite** group are obscure in history.

The people listed in v. 14 all lived north of Sidon as far as the Orontes River and generally were under the political control of Egypt in early OT times. The description of **the Canaanites** (19) as occupying the Mediterranean coastal area as far south as **Gaza** and down the Jordan valley as far as the Dead Sea accords well with traces of their settlements lasting from about 1750 to about 1300 B.C. which archaeologists have uncovered in ancient Palestine.

The children of **Eber** (21), a name which was later narrowed to mean only the Hebrew people, here designates the Semitic-speaking people in and around the Arabian Desert. However **Elam** (22), which lies east of the Mesopotamian valley, was non-Semitic. The people of **Asshur** (Assyria) overcame the Sumerians, the people of Shinar, about 2200 B.C., and became a mighty empire.

Arphaxad seems to be northeast of the Assyrians. **Lud** became the Lydian nation. **Aram** became the influential Aramaic (Syrian) people, whose language and script came to be the international means of communication during the period of the Assyrian, Babylonian, and Persian empires. Damascus was the capital of Syria. **Uz** (23) lay east of the Jordan along the Arabian Desert. Job was of this group (Job 1:1). Nothing is known of **Hul, and Gether, and Mash.**

Most of those mentioned with **Joktan** (25) are unknown, but Arabian inscriptions tell of **Hazarmaveth** (26), of **Obal, and Abimael, and Sheba** (28), **and Ophir, and Havilah** (29). **Sheba** is famous because the queen of Sheba once traveled to Jerusalem to see King Solomon (I Kings 10:1-13). There was a great deal of intermarriage between all of these people, but basically there was a division between them according to language groups. So we tend to speak of them in terms of the Indo-European, the Semitic, and the Hamitic characteristics of their speech.[31]

c. *The confusion of tongues* (11:1-9). The setting of this short but intriguing story is simply that after the Flood the

[31]E. A. Speiser, "Ethnic Divisions of Man," *The Interpreter's Dictionary of the Bible,* ed. G. A. Buttrick (Nashville: Abingdon Press, 1962), Vol. *K-Q,* pp. 235-42.

descendents of Noah were bound together by a common language and soon began to migrate into new territories. Chronologically, the story is related to the very early phases of migration, for 10:25 speaks of a division of the people by the time of Peleg and 11:8 tells of a scattering of the clans. Seemingly the account was placed after the three genealogies of c. 10 so that their relationship to the prophecy of Noah (9:25-27) would not be disturbed.

Moving out of the Mount Ararat area, the people settled in **Shinar** (2), which is the Mesopotamian valley, the location of the very earliest remains of civilization known to us. The valley is watered by the Tigris and the Euphrates rivers and is very fertile.

The story tells us that the new inhabitants of **Shinar** made a decision in a council meeting quite apart from the will of God. The purpose of the proposed action is clear. They wanted fame: **Let us make us a name** (4). And they wanted security: **lest we be scattered abroad.** Both aims were to be secured by human achievement alone. There is no doubt about the people's ingenuity. Lacking stones, they manufactured substitutes from clay and then burned **them thoroughly** (3). They saw the utility of the crude **slime** (asphalt) common to the area and used it **for morter.** Persistently they labored until enough **brick** was available for the building project.

The main interest of these people was in a **tower** (4), though they were constructing **a city** too. The tower was to **reach unto heaven.** Nothing is said of a temple at the top of the **tower,** so it is not clear whether the **tower** was like the ziggurats of later Babylon. These were huge, artificial mounds made of brick, some rising to as much as 300 feet above the surrounding plain. Placed in the center of cities, they were topped by a temple to a pagan deity, and, in ancient inscriptions, are actually described as reaching to heaven.

Paganism seems to be involved indirectly in this story, for there was a skyward thrust to the building and the one true God was definitely left out of all planning and of all goals. But God was not inactive. He was observing what was going on and soon made known His evaluation of the situation. Man had not been created as a being independent of God. Being "in our image" (1:26) meant that man was endowed with great powers, but also that man was totally dependent on God for his life essence and for his reason for being.

There is irony in the Lord's soliloquy. The people were united, they had open communication with each other, yet they had subverted these blessings into rebellion against their Creator. God would not be ignored, and the folly of man's delusion that possessions and creative activity were ultimates would not go unchallenged.

God's judgment unveiled these delusions quickly. To demonstrate that human unity was superficial without God, He simply introduced confusion of sound into human language. Immediately there was chaos. The great project was abandoned and the united but godless society was shattered into confused segments. In Hebrew, a play on words in v. 9 is pungent. **Babel** (9) means "confusion," and diversity of language issues in a babble. The word play carries through even into English.[32]

d. The lineage of Shem (11:10-26). This genealogy is more selective than the one in 10:21-32. It seems to pick up where the genealogy in c. 5 leaves off, and has some of the same characteristics. Thus the ages of various men are given, and as Noah was tenth from Adam, so **Terah** (24) was tenth from **Shem** (10). Three sons are named with Noah and three sons are named with **Terah.** In contrast to the lineage of Shem in 10:21-32, this list traces the line through **Arphaxad** (11), ignoring the other sons of Shem. The genealogy then picks up the sons of **Peleg** (16), who do not have a place in the other list. By means of this genealogy, the story is brought quickly from Noah to **Abram** (26), the next major character of the redemption story.

[32]I. Asimov, *Words in Genesis* (Boston: Houghton Mifflin Co., 1962), pp. 103-4.

Section II Abraham, the Man Whom God Chose

Genesis 11:27—25:11

One of the most outstanding men of ancient times now becomes the focal point of interest. Abraham is honored by being exalted as a man of God in three important faiths in the world today: Judaism, Christianity, and Islam. During his earlier years his name was **Abram** (27), which means "Exalted Father."[1] The stories related to his life before God are straightforward, presenting the highlights of his spiritual adventures. But also the embarrassing hours are recorded when unbelief smote his soul and he became entangled in unpleasant situations with others.

A. Terah's Family Relationships, 11:27-32

Many names in this brief genealogy still persist in names of cities in the upper Mesopotamian valley. Probably the names of early settlers were given to new cities, even as now. In ancient Assyrian records, a place called "mound of Terah" can be found. The city of **Haran** (27) exists today on the banks of the Balikh River.

Ur of the Chaldees (28) was one of the wealthiest city-states yet excavated of the older cultures of the Mesopotamian valley. The moon god Nannar was worshiped there, and one of Ur's most famous kings was Ur-Nammu. Josh. 24:2 states that Terah's family worshiped idols. The city was destroyed about 2100 B.C. and soon afterwards there was a great migration toward the west. The families who moved west were called Amorites. Terah's family was among these migrants. Evidently they first planned to go to **Canaan** (31) but were detained—and **Terah died in Haran** (32).

B. A Stranger in a New Land, 12:1—14:24

Abram's response to the divine call to move to another country has caught the imagination of many searchers after the will

[1]C. A. Potts, *Dictionary of Bible Proper Names* (New York: Abingdon Press, 1922), p. 17.

of God. His journey in faith was not a fantastic fairy tale but has the hallmarks of a down-to-earth struggle in a hostile world. Abram suffered setbacks but he persevered in pursuit of what he believed was the will of God.

1. *Command and Response* (12:1-9)

The structure of this story is simple. There is a command mixed with promise (1-3), Abram's act of obedience (4-6), and the theophany or appearance of God to Abraham marked by promise, to which Abram responded by worshiping (7-9).

God's command was clear-cut but stringent. **Abram** (1) had to leave home and **kindred** and move out into a new land. When he arrived in that land, the Canaanites (6) were there, but God promised, **Unto thy seed will I give this land** (7). The other promise was concerning a posterity which would become **a great nation** (2). Abram's descendents were to be possessors of the new **land.** Abram was to know God's blessing and was to be known as a great man. He was to be a channel of **blessing** (2) to others. In fact he was to be related to them in such a way that their destiny would be determined by the way they treated him. God would be gracious to those who helped him and would punish those who cursed him. Abram's influence would be worldwide, a benediction and a blessing to many nations.

Instead of arguing with God, **Abram departed** (4), even though he **was seventy and five years old.** He did not go alone, for **Sarai his wife, and Lot** (5), and a sizable group of servants accompanied him. **The land of Canaan** is presently known as Palestine.

Abram's first major stop was at **Sichem** (6), also known as Shechem (see map 2; Gen. 33:18-19; Josh. 24:1) or Sychar (John 4:5). Today a nearby city is called Nablus. In ancient times the city was important because an east-west and a north-south trade route intersected here. Mount Ebal soared abruptly above the city to the north and Mount Gerizim reared its head to the south. The phrase **plain of Moreh** would be better translated as "oak of Moreh" (ASV).

Abram had come to the land promised; but others had arrived before him, for **the Canaanite was then in the land.** The promise of God was seemingly annulled by this fact. To encourage Abram, God renewed and strengthened the promise by declaring specifically, **Unto thy seed will I give this land** (7). In response, Abram constructed **an altar** and worshiped God.

Moving farther south, Abram located on a ridge between **Beth-el** (8; see map 2) and **Hai.** The latter name means "the ruins." Recent archaeological work has revealed that this site had already been abandoned for at least 500 years by the time Abram arrived. The ruins had originally been a fortress city, evidently built by the Egyptians in 2900 B.C. and destroyed about 2500 B.C. On this ridge Abram built another **altar** and worshiped. Soon he continued **toward the south** (9).

In this passage (12:1-9) we see "An Example of Faith." (1) The divine command and promise, 1-3; (2) The obedience of faith, 4-5; (3) The life in the land, 6-9 (Alexander Maclaren).

2. *Instead of a Blessing, a Troublemaker* (12:10—13:4)

God had promised that Abram would be "a blessing" (2) and that in him "all families of the earth [would] be blessed" (3). But when **Abram went down into Egypt** (10; see map 3) due to **a famine** in Canaan, he was far from being a blessing to the people of that country.

The severity of the **famine** sent **Abram** and his party to the well-watered delta of the Nile River in search of food for their cattle and for the families which served Abram. Apparently he had heard of the loose morals of the Egyptians, and moved by fear—**they will kill me** (12)—he asked his wife, **Sarai** (11), to lie about their relationship.[2]

The danger which Abram anticipated was real, for soon the **princes** (15) took note of Sarai and took her to **Pharaoh's house.** At the moment Abram prospered (16), for gifts of animals and slaves were showered upon him.

Matters did not go so well with the **Pharaoh** (17). **The Lord plagued** him and his house, because his lust threatened to annul the divine promise that Abram would have a posterity. Discovering that Abram had not given the full truth about his wife, the **Pharaoh called Abram** (18), severely reprimanded him, and expelled him from Egypt.

It was a humiliating experience for Abram, and in spite of his wealth, his return to Canaan was hardly a victory march. Slowly making his way back to **Beth-el** (3) the patriarch bowed

[2]Speiser, *Genesis, op. cit.*, pp. 91-94.

before the **altar, which he had made there at the first** (4), and worshiped. His trip to Egypt had been a blessing to no one. **The south** (1) would be the "country of Judah" (Amp. Bible).

3. *The Choice That Pointed Downward* (13:5-18)

Not only Abram was rich in **flocks, and herds, and tents** (5), but his nephew **Lot** also had extensive herds. Lacking in good year-round pasturage, the highlands of Palestine could not provide enough food and water. **Strife** (7) broke out between the **herdmen** in the fields, so that a conference between uncle and nephew was imperative. The presence and implied threat of the **Canaanite** and **Perizzite** in the land is noted. Such was the setting of one of the crucial decisions made in Abram's family circle.

Next comes the dialogue between **Abram** (8) and **Lot.** According to the customs of the day, the solution of the problem would have been fairly simple. The leader of the clan would work out a solution which would protect his own interests and give little regard to the interests of the contestant. But **Abram** preferred to step aside. He did insist that Lot **separate** himself (9) from Abram's family circle, but he gave to the younger man first choice of the area of Palestine in which to pasture his flocks.

From the place where they were encamped near Bethel, the Jordan valley lay visible before them to the east. Lot chose to go in that direction. Around Jericho, as now, fields were watered by abundant springs, and on the southeast side of the Dead Sea streams from the highlands fed rich fields. The area was so verdant that two symbols of fertility, **the garden of the Lord** (10) and **the land of Egypt,** seemed the only adequate means to describe it. This was in sharp contrast to the dry central mountain range of Palestine.

At the time Lot did not know of the fate which was to fall upon the land he had newly adopted. But the story is heightened with suspense by noting that destruction was due **Sodom and Gomorrah.** Especially is **Sodom** (13) mentioned as a morally unhealthy city, for its **men . . . were wicked and sinners before the Lord exceedingly.**[3]

In 13:5-13 we see "Lot's Choice." (1) Lot's choice revealed his character, 10-11; (2) Lot's choice led to Sodom, 12-13;

[3]H. E. Ryle, *The Book of Genesis* ("Cambridge Bible for Schools and Colleges"; Cambridge: University Press, 1921), p. 165.

(3) Lot's choice resulted in incalculable loss, 13; cf. 19:1-28 (G. B. Williamson).

After Lot had departed, **the Lord** appeared to **Abram** and renewed His previous promises, with additions (14). Commanding Abram to survey **the land** (15), the Lord told him that all of it was a gift to his descendents, who would be as numerous **as the dust of the earth** (16). But Abram was also to claim it as his own to travel in wherever he pleased. Immediately Abram moved south and settled in the rich pasturelands around **Hebron** (18), then known as **Mamre.** It was the third place where Abram **built . . . an altar** at which he worshiped **the Lord.** Lot's choice seemed to promise the most returns at the moment but it was related to a potentially explosive situation. Abram's generosity seemed to have been self-damaging, if judged in the light of the customs of that day. But decisions which are difficult must sometimes be made when a man seeks to do God's will. Nevertheless, by virtue of the Lord's promises and His help, Abram's future held rich returns.

4. *Crisis in the Valley* (14:1-24)

Unexpectedly, danger from the north became a reality in the form of a vicious attack by four kings. An identification of **Amraphel** (1) with Hammurabi, an important Babylonian monarch, had a strong appeal to some OT scholars several decades ago.[4] However, archaeological materials related to Hammurabi date him later than Abraham's time. Yet **Shinar** was an ancient name for Babylon. **Arioch** is remarkably like the ancient name *Ariukki,* to the north of Babylon in the land of the Hurrians. Nothing is known of a **Chedorlaomer,** but **Elam** was the name of the highlands east of the Tigris River. **Tidal** was one of the Hittite kings called *Tudkhula* or *Tudhaliya.*[5]

The five kings who joined in a defensive alliance in the **vale of Siddim** (3), an area south of the Dead Sea, were ill prepared to ward off the invaders. They surrendered and for **twelve years** (4) they were satellites of the foreigners. Then they rebelled and the results were disastrous. The invaders returned and ruthlessly slaughtered the inhabitants of the high plateau east of the

[4]R. D. Wilson, *A Scientific Investigation of the Old Testament* (Chicago: Moody Press, 1959), pp. 26, 64-66.

[5]Speiser, *Genesis, op. cit.,* pp. 106-8.

Dead Sea (see map 2). Some of these people were remembered as giants. For **Rephaims** (5) see Gen. 15:20 and Deut. 2:11; also 3:11, where the term is translated as "giants." The **Zuzims** were the same as the "Zamzummims" of Deut. 2:20. For **Emims** see Deut. 2:10-11. The term **Horites** (6) seems to have been used of the aboriginal inhabitants of Edom (Gen. 36:20; Deut. 2:12, 22). The latter were near the rich copper ore deposits of the southern part of the Arabah, and evidently this ore was what the kings were primarily interested in.

After the victories described in 5-6, the kings swung out into the desert to the south and west of the Dead Sea, looting the rich oasis of **Kadesh** (7, Kadesh-barnea; see map 3) and destroying the settlement at **Hazezon-tamar,** which is modern En-gedi. The major battle with the defending kings took place **in the vale of Siddim** (8) and ended in a complete rout and chaos. The victors carried off much booty and many slaves, among whom was **Lot . . . and his goods** (12).

A fugitive from the raid told **Abram** (13) of the fate of Lot. The ordinarily peace-loving patriarch gathered a band of **three hundred and eighteen** (14). By skill and sheer courage they managed to rescue Lot, many other captives, and much of the booty after an arduous pursuit of more than 100 miles northward to Dan (see maps 2 and 3).

On the return trip to Hebron, Abram and his party passed by ancient Jerusalem, through **the valley of Shaveh** (17), possibly the Kidron valley. There he was met by a party of distinguished and grateful leaders of the land. For the first time, Abram had proved to be a blessing to his neighbors (see 12:2-3).

Melchisedek (18), the dignified priest-king of **Salem** (Jerusalem), provided food and drink for the victors and pronounced a blessing on Abram (19). The name **most high God** (18) was a common designation of Divinity in the country of Palestine at that time. In response Abram **gave . . . tithes** (20) to Melchizedek. **The king of Sodom** (21) was less religiously inclined. He asked for his people back, yet was generous enough to offer Abram whatever booty remained from the fight. Abram had little respect for this man and replied that he had taken a vow not to keep any of the goods belonging to **the king of Sodom,** lest it be used against him later by that unsavory person. Abram also made it clear that his God carried the title **Lord** (22, "Jehovah," ASV) and was not just another Canaanite deity. The only thing Abram requested was that the soldiers have a reward for their services and that his allies, **Aner, Eshcol, and Mamre (24)**, receive a share from the booty.

The stalwart character of Melchizedek and his status as a respected priest-king became significant in later pronouncements about the longed-for Messiah. Psalms 110:4 relates the Messiah to "the order of Melchizedek" and the writer of the Epistle to the Hebrews quotes this portion of the Psalms to show that Christ is of this kind of priestly order rather than of the Aaronic order (Heb. 5:6, 10; 6:20; 7:1-21).

The writer of Hebrews places emphasis on the meaning of Melchizedek's name and status in order to note that both he and Christ were men of righteousness and peace (Heb. 7:1-2). The next correlation is a stress on personal strength and worth rather than on lineage. Thus their office did not pass to another automatically. Christ is a High Priest rather than merely a priest, and instead of giving a blessing only, Christ saves "to the uttermost" (Heb. 7:25-26).[6]

C. God's Covenant with Abraham, 15:1—17:27

Unlike the pagan religions of Abram's neighbors whose faith was polytheistic and nature-centered, the faith of Abram was monotheistic and covenant-centered. Neither Babylon, Syria, nor Egypt knew of a religion that was personal, with a dynamic relationship operative between God and man. But God established such a relationship with Abram and with his descendents by making a covenant with him.

1. *God's Covenant with Abram* (15:1-21)

In the society of the upper Mesopotamian valley, covenant making was common between men and between nations.[7] God used this form of personal relationship as the medium to convey His revelation to **Abram (1)** and his descendents. The communication came by way of a **vision** in which the Covenant Maker calmed the fear of Abram and identified himself as his **shield,**

[6]C. F. Keil and F. Delitzsch, "The Pentateuch," *Biblical Commentary on the Old Testament* (Grand Rapids: Wm. B. Eerdmans Publishing Co., 1949), I, 208-9.

[7]G. E. Mendenhall, *Law and Covenant in Israel and the Ancient Near East* (Pittsburgh: The Biblical Colloquim, 1955), pp. 24-50.

and . . . exceeding great reward. The term **shield** denotes protection; and **reward,** with its adjectives, conveys the idea of abundant graciousness. Both represent God as filled with concern for the anxieties which Abram had.

A dialogue ensues in which Abram makes known his deep distress. God had promised that Abram would have a child (12: 1-7; 13:14-17). But no child had come to bless his household. Why? Hurrian law, prevalent around Haran, from which Abram came, made provision for a childless couple to adopt a servant to care for them in their old age and to bury them. In turn the adopted heir received the wealth of the family. Evidently Abram had thus adopted **Eliezer of Damascus** (2), but he was not satisfied. This provision did not seem to correspond to the promise which God had made to him. **One born in my house** (3) is better "one belonging to my household" (Berk.).

In reply, **the Lord** (4) assured Abram that Eliezer was not to be the heir, but that God would still give Abram an heir of whom he would be the father. To reinforce the promise, God commanded Abram to **look now toward heaven, and tell** (count) **the stars** (5). The vast array of stars which sprinkled the sky would be comparable to the number of descendents which would count Abram as their father.

Abram's response was complete surrender to God's will and an acceptance of His promise as adequate to answer his questions. For the first time in Scriptures the word *believe* occurs (6). Basically, it means to be firmly established or rooted. In this context it means that Abram grounded himself in the integrity of God. In response, God accepted this act of faith as an act of **righteousness** which discounted the previous doubting.

This verse was very important to Paul, who used it to demonstrate in Romans 4 that believing God is the basis for obtaining salvation and that righteousness is a gift of God. Virtually the same argument is used in Galatians 3 (see commentary on these cc., BBC, Vols. VIII and IX).

In 15:1 there is suggested "The Faith of Abraham." (1) The record of faithfulness, **After these things,** cf. cc. 12—14; (2) The reward of faithfulness, 1-6 (G. B. Williamson).

The dialogue next concentrates on the relationship of the **land** (7) to Abram's seed. After a brief reference to His previous call to Abram, God repeated His promise that Palestine would be a home for the patriarch's children. Abram asked for some tangible evidence, since he did not own any of the land over which he roamed. It was in this context that the covenant was actually established.

Following ancient procedures of making covenants, God directed Abram to prepare three animals—**an heifer** (9), **a she goat,** and **a ram**—each **three years old,** and two birds—**a turtledove, and a young pigeon.** After sacrificing them, Abram split the carcasses of the animals and laid them on the ground, watching over them to protect them from the scavenger **birds** (10). Then, as **the sun was going down** (12), God appeared to Abram in the form of **an horror of great darkness** ("a terror and shuddering fear," Amp. Bible).

The message of the Revealer was filled with detail added to the previous promises. Of the **seed** (13), God said their possession of the land would not be immediate, but that Abram's descendents must first dwell in another **land.** There they would be servants for **four hundred years,** in which time they would know affliction. Yet God would **judge . . . that nation** (14) and would deliver Abram's people.

Abram would not possess the entire land himself, yet he would know a sense of **peace** (15) in his **old age** and death. Returning to the matter of the land, God indicated that **the Amorites** (16), who then inhabited it, must be given time to demonstrate their lack of responsibility and their abundance of iniquity. The wresting of the land from them would not occur until it could be on a firm moral basis.

At the moment that **the sun went down** (17), God manifested himself in a different manner. He symbolized His participation and His seal of the covenant by passing between the sacrificed animals as **a smoking furnace, and a burning lamp.** In Scripture fire often symbolizes God's presence.

The chapter has a summarizing remark, noting that the covenant promise included the boundaries of the Promised Land. They stretched **from the river of Egypt** (18), the Wadi el-'Arish, halfway between Philistia and Egypt, to **the river Euphrates.** Following that is a list of the 10 groups which dwelt in Canaan in Abram's times.

From 15:5-18, Alexander Maclaren preached on "God's Covenant with Abram." (1) God's promise, 5, 7; (2) A man's triumphant faith, 6; (3) Gospel truth, **He counted it to him for righteousness,** 6; (4) The covenant reaffirmed, 7, 13-18.

2. *The Substitute Wife* **(16:1-16)**

Time passed and **Sarai** (1) continued childless. God had not promised that the son would come from her (15:4) and the problem of an unfulfilled promise remained. To **Sarai** a custom from their homeland appeared to be the answer. This custom provided that a childless wife must provide her husband with a servant girl to serve in her stead. The offspring would be regarded as her own.[8] **Sarai** had an **Egyptian** servant named **Hagar,** whom she offered to **Abram** (2). Abram accepted the offer and in a short time Hagar was with child.

Intense emotions deep in the heart of each participant were entangled with the problem of interpreting a divine promise by means of legal provisions. **Hagar** (4) became arrogant toward her mistress, and **Sarai** became bitter and abusive (5). Going to her husband, she accused him of depriving her of basic rights as a wife and demanded that he act. *The Amplified Bible* renders 5*a*, "May [the responsibility for] my wrong *and* deprivation of rights be upon you!" It was contrary to their homeland custom for servant wives to show disrespect to the principal wife. **Abram** (6) declined to punish Hagar but permitted **Sarai** to act as she pleased.

The same custom which permitted a substitute wife refused to allow the expulsion of that wife after she became pregnant, whatever her attitude might be. But **Sarai** was resourceful. She **dealt hardly with her,** forcing the girl to run away.

Hagar was on her way to her homeland, Egypt, when **the angel of the Lord** (7) appeared to her at **a fountain** as she approached the wilderness of **Shur** (see map 2). In reply to his question, **Hagar** (8) confessed that she was fleeing from **Sarai.** Instead of showing sympathy, **the angel of the Lord** commanded the girl to **return to thy mistress** (9). In return for this submission to abuse, a promise of a numerous **seed** (10) was granted to Hagar. The child to be born was to be named **Ishmael** (11) as a reminder that God had heard her prayer of desperation. Yet the son would be unusual in character. He would not fit in well with the quiet family of Abram. Rather he would love the wild, free life of the desert. Few would be the men who would love his ways.

[8]C. F. Pfeiffer, *The Book of Genesis* ("Shield Bible Study Series"; Grand Rapids: Baker Book House, 1958), p. 51.

Hagar's response was one of gratitude and worship. God had taken note of her plight and she was thankful. Verse 13*ab* has been rendered, "So she called the name of the Lord who spoke to her, You are a God of seeing" (Amp. Bible). Instead of resenting the command, she faithfully turned her steps back to Sarai's tent. In honor of her great spiritual experience she named the well **Beer-lahai-roi** (14, "The well of him that liveth and seeth me"). She had solved no problems by running away. Now she faced her difficulty with Sarai with courage and with a new hope.

In due time the son was born and **Abram** (15), evidently aware of Hagar's experience at the well, named the child **Ishmael** (cf. 11). He had a son, but not the one whom God had promised.

3. *The Token of the Covenant* (17:1-27)

Thirteen years passed and again **the Lord appeared to Abram** (1). Typical of covenant-making occasions, the Divine One identified himself to **Abram.** He was **Almighty God** (*El Shaddai*). No other detail is given, but He had a command for Abram. It was brief but stringent: **Walk before me, and be thou perfect.** In an earlier time, Enoch had illustrated the first part of the commandment by living a life fully obedient and acceptable to God (5:24). Noah also had been designated as **perfect** (see 6:9), meaning that he was a man of one will, a man of integrity. Abram was to be like these men of God.

Reacting to the news that God desired to renew the **covenant** of promise (2) with him, **Abram fell on his face** (3), overwhelmed by the knowledge that **God** was talking to him. The patriarch's prostration was a common posture in his day to show reverence or extreme awe.

In 17:1-6 we see "God's Assurance to Abram." (1) God is all-sufficient, 1*a*, 4-6; (2) God is the all-wise Judge, 2-3; (3) God's eternal ideal for man is perfection, 1*b* (G. B. Williamson).

God's message to Abram came in four parts: 17:5-8, 9-14, 15-16, and 19-21—in two cases interspersed with conversation involving Abram.

God's first word reiterated the reality of the **covenant** relationship (4), but the promise of a seed was enlarged to **Thou shalt be a father of many nations.** The covenant was then reinforced by a change of Abram's name to **Abraham** (5). The promise was further expanded to include a posterity of **kings** (6). Another addition was the assurance that the relationship would be **everlasting** (7). It was also personal, so that Abraham's seed could claim the covenant-making **God** as their own **God.** This was possible because God himself had established the relationship, not because they had taken the initiative to seek Him. A new note was also introduced into the promise of the land: it was to be **an everlasting possession** (8).

"Waiting Faith Rewarded" is the theme of 17:1-9. (1) God's character and our duty, 1; (2) The sign of the covenant, 5; (3) The substance of the covenant, 2, 4, 7-8 (Alexander Maclaren).

The second word concentrated on the keeping of the **covenant** (9) and the **token of the covenant** (11). It was a series of commands. **Every man child among you shall be circumcised** (10), was the basic stipulation. The normal time of circumcision was to be when the child was **eight days old** (12). There were to be no class distinctions, for those in servitude were to rank equally with free men in the covenant. Servants could participate in **the everlasting covenant** (13), but of those who were not circumcised it was said, **That soul shall be cut off from his people** (14). As far as is known, the institution of the rite of circumcision among Abraham's people struck the first blow against the evil of slavery and for human equality before God.

The third word was concerned with the relationship of **Sarai** (15) to the birth of the promised son. This point had never been clarified in previous conversations between God and Abraham. She was to have a change of name. The more archaic form **Sarai** was to be changed to a new spelling, **Sarah** (15). As far as is known both spellings mean simply "princess." She was to have a divine blessing and would be the mother of **a son** (16), but more, **a mother of nations** and **kings.**

For the second time **Abraham fell upon his face** (17), but this time he **laughed.** His age and that of his wife would seem to preclude the fulfillment of such a promise. Surely it would be better to think in terms of the welfare of **Ishmael** (18). But **God** was insistent. **Sarah** was to be a mother, and the son's name was to be **Isaac** (19). Here is a play on words, for **Isaac** actually means "laughter." That which seemed laughable from the human viewpoint would truly be a reality.

As for **Ishmael** (20), God had plans to bless him as the ancestor of **twelve princes,** of a **great nation.** Nevertheless, the **covenant** was not to be with his lineage; it was to be **with Isaac** (21), whom **Sarah** would **bear** in due time.

Having received God's commands and promises, Abraham obeyed immediately. He had all the males in his **house** (23) circumcised the selfsame day. At that time **Abraham was ninety years old and nine** (24), and **Ishmael** (25) was **thirteen.** Circumcision became the sign of the Hebrew commitment to a religious faith which was to stand for centuries throughout OT times. It was a faith strikingly different from any of the surrounding people. Here was a faith based upon a revelation from God set in a framework of personal relationship with man, instead of a framework of natural forces.[9]

D. Waiting for the True Son, 18:1—20:18

These three chapters stand between the promise that Sarah would bear the true heir and the fulfillment of that promise. Chapters 18 and 19 return one to the content of cc. 13 and 14. The fortunes and misfortunes of Lot are common to both sets of chapters. Chapter 20 also harks back to a previous event, the deception of the Pharaoh of Egypt concerning the true kinship of Sarah to Abraham. As in the previous chapters, Abraham's character shines brightly in contrast to that of Lot, but not so well in contrast to the alien monarch.

1. *Not a Laughing Matter* (18:1-15)

Lest the reader be misled by the detail of the story, the first verse makes it clear that what is involved is a theophany, an appearance of **the Lord** (1), at Abraham's **tent** in **Mamre.** The word **plains** probably should be translated "oaks, or terebinths" (Amp. Bible). Abraham was resting in the shade during **the heat of the day,** i.e., the hour or two before and after noon.

Looking up, Abraham was surprised to see **three men** (2). He immediately responded with the hospitality which still survives among the common folk of Palestine today. Bowing before them, Abraham begged the strangers to stop at his tent, have the dust of the road washed from their **feet,** and relax under **the tree** (4). The patriarch assured them that food would be served

[9]J. P. Milton, *God's Covenant of Blessing* (Rock Island, Ill.: Augustana Press, 1961), pp. 88-91.

them and then they could travel on. **For therefore are ye come** (5) means, "That is why you have come to your servant" (Amp. Bible). The strangers responded graciously to the invitation, and **Abraham** (6) hurried to the flocks for a calf after asking **Sarah** to prepare **cakes upon the hearth,** a small clay oven. The **butter** (8) could have been made from the milk of cows, of goats, or of camels. The **milk** was probably sour. Such curdled milk is still highly regarded as a refreshing drink on a hot day in Palestine. According to custom, the women of the camp did not show themselves while visitors were present, nor did the host eat with his guests. His duty was to attend to their every need.

The inquiry about his **wife** (9) must have struck Abraham as quite lacking in good manners, for his reply carries an overtone of surprise. The movement shows a growing comprehension that one of the visitors was different from the others. It was **he** (10) who promised that Sarah's coming motherhood was to be a reality. Though Abraham had received this news before (17: 15-19), Sarah had not been informed. She now **laughed** (12) to herself, musing on the improbability of motherhood at her age. But she was shocked with fright when she heard the stranger, now designated as **Lord** (*Yahweh,* 13), question her husband about her secret unbelief. He queried, **Is any thing too hard for the Lord?** (14), and then reasserted, **Sarah shall have a son.** The woman was so taken off guard that she mumbled a denial, only to receive a rebuke in return. Thus did Sarah learn of her future role in God's purposes for His people, and she had stumbled at the threshold of the impossible, humanly viewed.

In this story (18:1-4, 9-14) we find evidence that (1) God permits impossible situations to develop, 10-12; (2) God can do the seemingly impossible, 13; (3) God is glorified in the proof of His power, 14 (G. B. Williamson).

2. *A Persistent Intercession* (18:16-33)

There was another aspect of the men's visit which was reserved for Abraham's ears. Having reaffirmed God's promise of a son coming by means of Sarah, and having demonstrated a divine ability to know a woman's secret thoughts, **the Lord** (17) had little difficulty convincing **Abraham** of the gravity of the next item of news. The brief soliloquy (17-19) reveals the confidence **the Lord** had in this man, based upon careful evaluation of his character. Abraham could be trusted to rule and to teach

his children in such a way that the divine will revealed to him would continue into future generations. Thus there would be continuity in **justice** (19, *tsedakah*), which is more often translated "righteousness." It connotes adherence to proper standards, whether moral or judicial. The preservation of **judgment** (*mishpat*), i.e., the maintenance of harmonious relations between people, would not be just a one-generation affair. Continuity in these values was what the Lord wanted and Abraham, with his descendents, gave promise of a fulfillment of His will. Thus He felt justified for unveiling a portion of His personal burden to Abraham.

The divine concern also involved **Sodom and Gomorrah** (20), for the cries of complaint which had come to **the Lord** indicated that **their sin** was **very grievous.** The Lord was now on His way to make a personal inspection of conditions. The strong anthropomorphism of this scene does not suggest ignorance on God's part. Rather, the point is centered on the Lord's intimate concern about social evils; they do not go unnoticed. Another emphasis is God's basic justice. He does not execute judgment on hearsay; He knows at first hand what the situation is. Furthermore, He is willing to give consideration to other means than destruction for correcting matters. He is willing to listen to and evaluate the prayers of those whom He trusts.

When Abraham heard the news about Sodom and Gomorrah, a deep burden gripped his soul, for he was fully aware of Lot's residence near these cities.

Abraham's sense of justice came quickly to expression. Surely the **righteous** (23, *tsaddik*), those who have been living acceptably before God, should not be punished with **the wicked.** Abraham began with high optimism. Suppose there were **fifty righteous within the city** (24), could God be just and destroy them? The divine response was that the Lord would deliver the city if **fifty** (26) could be found. But what if that number could not be found, would a shortage of five people (28) bring disaster?

Abraham well knew his own place before God, for in terms of power and authority he was **but dust and ashes** (27). Yet he persisted, lowering the figure from 45 to **forty** (29), to **thirty** (30), to **twenty** (31). Each time the Lord acceded to the patriarch's request. Finally he reached the number **ten** (32), which was almost the size of Lot's family. Receiving the assurance that judgment would be withheld should **ten** be found, Abraham ceased his intercession. The outcome must thereafter depend on the spiritual condition of his nephew's family.

In 18:20-33 our attention is directed to "The Just Judge." The focus is on v. 25. (1) The extension of God's mercy in answer to prayer, 23-26; (2) The execution of God's judgment upon the impenitent sinners, 20-21; cf. 19:23-24; (3) The exemption of the righteous, 26-32; cf. 19:12-22 (G. B. Williamson).

3. *There Were Not Even Ten* (19:1-29)

The story of this chapter has several distinguishable parts. The setting is in vv. 1-3. Then follow the crisis situation (4-11), the hour of decision (12-16), the act of deliverance (17-22), and the act of judgment (23-29).

Two of the men, now called **angels** (1), arrived in **Sodom** soon after leaving Abraham in Hebron, though the distance between the two places was an ordinary two days' journey. **Lot** was at **the gate** of the city, where men were accustomed to gather at the end of a day's work. Often legal affairs were transacted at the gate (Ruth 4:1-12). Lot extended greetings and offered lodging to the strangers. Yielding to his persistence, the angels were treated with generous hospitality.

Just before time for bed, Lot and his new friends became aware of a commotion outside his house. It was a multitude of **the men of Sodom** (4) of every age, fired with bestial lust. The famed sin of the city was being displayed in all its ugliness. The men wanted the strangers delivered to them so they could engage in homosexual acts with them, a sin which has become known as sodomy.

Lot was shocked and confused by the demand. In his confusion, Lot unwittingly unveiled another major sin of his day, a tragic devaluation of womanhood. Placing more value on the honor of his male visitors than on the welfare of his **two** young **daughters** (8), Lot offered them to the men to be abused as they saw fit. But the men took the offer as an insult and accused Lot of being an arrogant alien. *The Berkeley Version* translates 9*cd*, "This fellow came here as an immigrant and he keeps acting as a judge."

Seeing Lot's danger, the visitors rescued him from the mob and afflicted the men **with blindness** (11). The underlying Hebrew indicates that the blindness was caused by a dazzling flash of light.

The angels did not need to press the investigation further. The moral condition of Sodom was abundantly clear. Therefore they urged **Lot** (12) to warn every member of his household, including his sons-in-law, to prepare for flight out of the city. There was no question now of the imminence of judgment. Lot obeyed the command but met with rebuffs from **his sons in law** (14). Only four in the family remained, far from the minimum which Abraham had set for saving the city from destruction (18:32).

As the hour for departure arrived, Lot seemed too paralyzed for action. The **men** (16) had to take both **his hand** and that **of his wife,** as well as the **daughters,** in order to get them to move out of the city. Under the terms of Abraham's request, the men were not under obligation to do this. They showed concern for Lot and his family only because of **the Lord being merciful unto him.**

At the edge of the city more directions were given. The family was told, **Look not behind thee, neither stay thou in all the plain; escape to the mountain** (17). But **Lot** (18) still was not fully aware of the magnitude of the disaster that was to come. He was more afraid of the vague dangers of the mountains and pled for the privilege of hiding in a nearby village called **Zoar,** which meant **little one** (20). One of the angels granted him that concession but urged him to get to the village as fast as possible. Lot arrived in **Zoar** (22) in the nick of time, for the hour of destruction was at sunrise.

The fate of **Sodom** and **Gomorrah** (24) was awesome. The text does not mention an earthquake, but one could possibly have occurred, releasing from the earth explosive gases which, mixed with the deposits of sulphur in the area, created a fearsome scene. Not all even of the fleeing family escaped. Lot's **wife looked back** (26), disobeying the command of the angel, and she died, becoming **a pillar of salt.**

In the story of Lot's escape (19:15-26) Alexander Maclaren sees "The Swift Destroyer." (1) Lot's lingering and rescue, 15-16; (2) Escape for your life, 17-22; (3) Grim destruction, 23-25; (4) The fate of the loiterer, 26.

Another sad figure surveyed **the smoke of the country** (28) from the safe heights east of Mamre. He was aware of the cause of the smoke, but he did not as yet know that the angels had mercifully delivered his nephew Lot from the holocaust. He did not yet know that this deliverance had taken place because **God remembered Abraham** (29).

4. *Lot's Drunkenness* (19:30-38)

The final story of Lot's life is not a savory one. Like Noah (9:20-23), Lot became entangled with **wine** (32) after experiencing a remarkable escape from death. But in this instance the man's daughters were involved. **Lot** had retired into the mountains in spite of his earlier fears (19) and had set up a home in a remote cave.

One must judge the incident with compassion, for the series of disasters which had struck the three were by no means trivial. They did not know whether anyone in the valley had escaped beside themselves. The girls were in desperate straits. Where was a man to marry them, and where was there a son to preserve their father's name? That was a question of no small importance in their society.

The solution they devised was a shocking one, though they managed to rationalize it to their own satisfaction. But they knew better than to discuss it with their father. Their scheme was to reduce their father to insensibility with wine and then in turn have sexual relations with him. They succeeded and in due time gave birth to sons.

The story does not seem to be appended to the account of the destruction of Sodom and Gomorrah in order to condemn either Lot or the daughters. Rather its purpose seems merely to relate how the Moabites and the Ammonites came into being and why they were regarded as close relatives to the Hebrew people. On the other hand, there is no sense of moral approval.

5. *Failing to Be a Blessing* (20:1-18)

Abraham was gripped by a deep fear whenever he moved into close relationship with a political power which was stronger than his own. The reputation of his pagan neighbors probably gave him reason for fear. Here, as in the account of Abraham's journey to Egypt (12:14-20), the patriarch's distrust of the pagan rulers centers in their lust for a variety of women in their harems. Neither story denies that such lust existed. Rather, both stories casually depict both the Pharaoh and **Abimelech** (2) as taking **Sarah** into their entourage soon after they discovered that she was but a sister to **Abraham.** It was Abraham's fear for his own life that motivated him to fail to clarify the peculiar sister-wife relationship common to his homeland but not understood in Palestine or Egypt.

The result of Abraham's failure to tell the whole truth about Sarah's relationship to him was a situation filled with irony. God intervened in the matter but not to His own servant first. To **Abimelech** (3) **God** revealed himself in a **dream** and set the true facts of the case before him, pointing out his personal danger for committing this sin.

Abimelech protested ignorance and claimed that both he and his people were **righteous** (4) in the matter. He had trusted the truth of statements made by both Abraham and Sarah, so he claimed **integrity** (*tam,* basically the same word translated "perfect" in 17:1) and **innocency of . . . hands** (5). The former deals with inner motivation, the latter with actual deed.

In v. 6, **God** was willing to accept Abimelech's ignorance as witnessing to his **integrity of . . . heart,** but He also added that His own providential activity had prevented **Abimelech** from the actual deed of **sinning.** A command was then issued by God. Abimelech was to return Sarah to Abraham and seek his prophetic gift of intercession that Abimelech's life might be saved (7). The alternative was severe punishment.

Abimelech's immediate obedience is to his credit. He **called all his servants** (8) and, having told them of the dream, ordered Abraham to report for a personal conference. The pagan ruler bitterly upbraided the patriarch for what he had done and demanded an explanation. Abraham admitted that he had acted on the presumption that **the fear of God is not in this place** (11) and that they would kill him. He went on to explain the unusual marital customs of his homeland. A woman could both be a man's **sister** (12), in this case a stepsister, and a **wife.** He had left home obedient to God but fearful of the pagan world into which he was traveling, so he had agreed with his wife that everywhere they went she was to say, **He is my brother** (13).

Abimelech did not argue with Abraham, but returned his wife along with a gift of cattle and servants and told him to roam where he pleased. He then **reproved** (16) the woman, indicating that she should never be ashamed of claiming Abraham as her husband: **He is to thee a covering of the eyes** (16).[10]

The final verses take note of the fact that God had already partially punished Abimelech and his people by afflicting the women with barrenness. Abraham's function as a prophet here is that of intercession, a spokesman for Abimelech (17) before God. This was the way he was to be a blessing to these pagan neighbors. His influence for good could have been far greater. Nevertheless God mercifully responded to the prayer and removed the affliction.

E. Old Loyalties Tested, 21:1—22:19

The center of discussion shifts back to the fulfillment of the promise of a child, with Sarah as the mother. The arrival of Isaac created a series of crises in the household of Abraham involving Hagar and her son. Even the ultimate role of Isaac himself seemed imperilled in the complex of personal attachments which made up the patriarch's life. In 21:22-34 there is a story of covenant making with Abimelech, the first clear-cut, friendly relationship which Abraham had established with his pagan neighbors.

1. *A Painful Act of Separation* (21:1-21)

The story has several parts: the fulfillment of promise (1-8), the problem of jealousy (9-11), divine instruction (12-13), the separation (14-16), the divine promise (17-18), and the fulfillment of promise (19-21).

The word that **Sarah** (1) would have **a son** (2; cf. 17:15-17; 18:9-15) was fulfilled on schedule. In every respect it was understood as an unusual act of divine creative power, for both parents were beyond the age of childbearing. The child was born and was named Isaac according to the Lord's command (17: 19) in recognition that both parents had laughed at what was apparently impossible. Their first laughter had sprung from the incredulity of doubt, but **Sarah** (6) was caused **to laugh** now because of the joy of a realized impossibility. God had kept His

[10]Speiser, *Genesis, op. cit.,* p. 150. Others understand v. 16 to mean that Abimelech's gift cleared the reputation of Abraham and Sarah: "Before all men you are cleared and compensated" (Amp. Bible).

word. He had the power to bring forth life whenever He chose, regardless of natural circumstances.

No time data is given in regard to the weaning of Isaac, but this event was sometimes postponed until the child was three years old. The event was often celebrated by a feast, a custom which is still commonly observed in the Near East. The occasion brought to the surface an old tension which had existed since the conception of Ishmael (16:4-6). But this time it was Ishmael who was **mocking** (9) the baby Isaac. It was more than Sarah could take. She approached **Abraham** (10) in a stormy rage, demanding the expulsion of **this bondwoman and her son.**

Actually, the birth of Isaac had been a serious blow to Hagar and Ishmael. Being the only son of Abraham, Ishmael had been the heir apparent to all that his father owned and to the place of leadership over the clan. According to the law of Abraham's homeland this position of heir was negated by the birth of Isaac. Whether Hagar and Ishmael were aware of this fact is not known, but Sarah knew it and stressed the point to her husband.

The thing was very grievous in Abraham's sight (11) because the law of his homeland held that, if a son was born of the true wife, the substitute wife and her child were to continue under the care of the father of both children.[11] But **God** (12) was also concerned about the matter and gave special instructions that custom was not to rule in this case. Hagar must go out from the family in order that Isaac's position would be crystal-clear. God would, nevertheless, extend His care to Hagar and her **son** (13), making of them **a nation** for Abraham's sake.

Early in the morning (14) a supply of **bread, and a bottle of water** were given to **Hagar,** and she left with her boy for the desert. Soon **the water** (15) was exhausted and strength of body was spent. Leaving the boy **under one of the shrubs,** Hagar moved away a short distance, expecting **death** (16) to come soon. While weeping, she heard an **angel of God** (17) speak to her, calming her fears and promising a great future for the lad. She obediently returned to her boy, and looking around **saw a well** (19), from which she drew water to quench their thirst. The sequel was a future blessed of God materially and physically. The boy became a great **archer** (20), roaming **the wilderness of**

[11]C. F. Pfeiffer, *The Patriarchal Age* (Grand Rapids: Baker Book House, 1961), p. 110.

Paran (21), and soon married. God had demonstrated His mercies to the unfortunate, and Hagar had learned important lessons of faith. Abraham's loyalties to Sarah and her new son remained unchallenged because God had given him needed guidance in a time of crisis.

2. *The Bonding of Friendly Ties* (21:22-34)

Despite the unpleasant aspects of Abraham's first contact with Abimelech, this king of Gerar (20:2) had been impressed by the patriarch's manner of life among his people. Now he and his foremost soldier, **Phichol** (22), approached **Abraham** and requested a pact of friendship. Abimelech's opening words were complimentary. He recognized the fact that **God is with thee;** so he desired assurances that Abraham would **not deal falsely** (23) with him or his **son** in the future. The incident involving Sarah still stung his memory (20:1-18). He now used his own **kindness** to Abraham at that time as the basis for a plea that the patriarch would be kind to him. It was offering the golden rule in reverse (be kind to me, as I have been kind to you) as the grounds for lasting friendship.

Abraham proceeded to set up a covenant ceremony according to the customs of his forefathers. It is the first such covenant between equals recorded in the Scriptures. Abraham first laid out a grievance which had strained relationships between his own shepherds and Abimelech's men. A well which had watered the flocks had been **violently taken away** (25). **Abimelech** expressed surprise and claimed ignorance of the incident (26). Evidently he promised to correct the wrong, for **Abraham** presented a gift of cattle to the visitor.

The patriarch's next move puzzled Abimelech, for **seven ewe lambs** (28) were separated from the flock. Why? The answer was that they were to **be a witness** (30) that the **well** by which the men sat belonged to Abraham. Contrary to the pagan customs of his ancestors, Abraham did not call on a series of gods and goddesses to witness the agreement. Instead he substituted a gift which would serve as a seal of their **covenant** (32). Solemnly the two men swore an oath of commitment and the ceremony was completed. The well took its name from the occasion. Actually the name **Beer-sheba** (33, still the name of a city in Israel) can mean either "well of swearing" or "well of seven."

The word in Hebrew for *sware* and for *seven* (in this case the **seven ewe lambs**) is spelled the same.

Abraham (33) made the place one of the centers of his extensive grazing activity. He **planted a grove** and worshiped his **Lord, the everlasting God.** For the first time Abraham had gained the respect of a nearby pagan ruler and established a formal relationship which was mutually beneficial. It was the first stage in fulfilling the promise that he would be a blessing to the people among whom he moved (see 12:2-3).

3. *A Convincing Demonstration of Love for God* (22:1-19)

The structural elements of this story are the setting (1), the divine command (2), the act of obedience (3-10), and the ensuing blessing (11-19).

Portrayed here is one of the more profound experiences which is recorded in Genesis. It touches at the very foundations of the believer's assurance that the God who gives promises is faithful, even though He gives a command to destroy the evidence that His promises are being fulfilled. Would **Abraham** still cling to God though his dearest earthly treasure be blotted out?

For modern readers the KJV translation **tempt** (1) is confusing. It implies too much, raising the questions, Was God enticing this man to commit sin? and, Did God really want to humiliate and wound His most devoted worshiper? Actually, the Hebrew (*nissah*) means "to test" or "to put on trial," and most recent English translations preserve this meaning. In this instance God was testing Abraham's ultimate spiritual loyalties by touching the physical life of **Isaac, whom thou lovest** (2).

There were aspects of the command that were rationally inexplicable. A pagan community might justify human sacrifice on the grounds that the life of the sacrificed served to strengthen the community's gods in time of severe crisis. But no such crisis was facing Abraham or his clan. Killing Isaac could serve no clear purpose in the boy's life, in Abraham's life, or in the clan's corporate life. Even worse, it contradicted the promises of God.

The rationale of the act could not be easily understood by others, and the command did not reflect well on the moral nature of Abraham's God. The execution of the act could not possibly enhance the moral character of Abraham. Telling Sarah of what God had commanded could not conceivably contribute to her mental or emotional well-being, nor could telling the servants or Isaac of the true purpose of the trip inspire them to full cooperation.

Consequently, the reader is caught up in the extreme agony of the obedient father who, in silence, leaves the camp without telling the mother of the fate of her son. One senses the strain as the **wood for the burnt offering** (3) was cut and strapped to the beasts, as the father walked mile after interminable mile carrying a vessel in which coals of fire were being preserved. The father's stab of inner pain seems almost unbearable as he saw Mount **Moriah** (2) and could only say to his servants, **I and the lad will go yonder and worship** (5). And then the inevitable question, **Where is the lamb for a burnt offering?** (7) What a supreme effort of faith to reply, **God will provide himself a lamb** (8). There is infinite agony in the sentence, **So they went both of them together.** Did Isaac already suspect the outcome?

Every detail of preparing for the sacrifice was deliberate and meticulous. It was as though every stone of the **altar** (9) was mortared with the blood of the father, and every stick of the pyre soaked with his unwept tears. What must have been Abraham's agony as the cords were tied on wrists and ankles, and the boy's body was laid in place? What were the startled thoughts of the lad? And now the final act, the grasping of the sacrificial **knife** (10). When would God provide a lamb? The letter to the Hebrews says that Abraham was "accounting that God was able to raise him up, even from the dead" (11:19). But the text before us does not unveil this inner conviction. Rather, it leaves one in searing suspense as **the knife** moves from its resting place.

But a voice did cry out and **the knife** ceased moving. All Abraham's heart-rending suffering dissolved into wonder as he heard the word, **For now I know that thou fearest God** (12). He had **not withheld** Isaac, whom he dearly loved. So now God provided a sacrifice in substitution for the lad. **A ram caught in a thicket by his horns** (13) was nearby. Here was God's intended sacrifice.

Abraham's love for God had been threatened by a deep-rooted, fatherly love for Isaac. This son was both the evidence that God fulfilled His promises and the physical means by which a posterity could be assured. That Abraham really did love God above all else had to be tested in some such concrete situation so that there would be no confusion of loyalties. His reward for passing the test was a return of his son from the very edge of the grave. In this experience God renewed the promises concerning the multiplication of Abraham's **seed** (17), its power over its **enemies,** and its role as a channel of blessing to **all the nations of the earth** (18).

To Abraham, Mount Moriah was a new place. In honor of the revelation of God's grace in his hour of crisis he gave it a new name, **Jehovah-jireh** (14, "the Lord seeth" and will provide). One can be sure that the return home was far different from the journey to Moriah. Abraham had faced the devastating threat of death and had overcome its power by complete reliance on the integrity of God. On the other hand, God had clearly demonstrated that the sacrifice which He desires is one of the heart, of surrender to His command.[12]

In 22:1-14 we see "The Test of Faith." (1) The real test, 1-2; (2) The response of trust, 3-10; (3) The reward of obedience, 11-14 (A. F. Harper).

F. Bearing Responsibilities for Others, 22:20—25:11

Following a transitional genealogy, the stories in this group depict Abraham in relationship to his own family as the needs prompted by death and marriage demanded his attention.

1. *Nahor's Descendents* (22:20-24)

This family tree is of interest due to the appearance of **Rebekah** (23), who in c. 24 becomes a central figure as Isaac's wife. Also **Nahor** (20) had a wife and a **concubine** (24), as did Abraham. Both of these bore 12 sons, comparable to Ishmael's (25:13-16) and Jacob's 12 sons later on (35:23-26).

Two of Nahor's sons, **Huz** and **Buz** (21), have their counterparts in the "land of Uz" (Job 1:1) and "Elihu . . . the Buzite" (Job 32:6). Whether these sons were progenitors of tribes is not clear, though some speculation has centered on this possibility.[13]

2. *Sarah's Death and Burial* (23:1-20)

A record of the death and burial of a woman is unusual in the OT. But **Sarah** (1) was the mother of the long awaited son

[12]S. Kierkegaard, *Fear and Trembling* (London: Oxford University Press, 1939); a difficult exposition of this chapter but packed with insight.

[13]Driver, *op. cit.*, p. 223; Leupold, *op. cit.*, II, 638-39.

and she had gained a ripe old age of **one hundred and seven and twenty years.** She is prominent in the story because she was the first of Abraham's family to die. Respect and common decency demanded that the body be placed somewhere. But the real significance of this story is that, at long last, a portion of the Promised Land actually became a possession of the patriarch. **Came to mourn** (2) is better understood as by Moffatt, "going indoors."

In Abraham's day it was the custom to bury the dead in caves and Abraham knew that a cave near **Kirjath-arba,** later known as **Hebron** (see map 2), was adequate for his needs. He was anxious to have a clear title to the property, so that it would be known as his beyond any possible dispute.

The proper way to negotiate such a purchase was to bargain for the property in the presence of an assembly of leaders in the community. In this case they were **the sons of Heth** (3), who could have been colonists from the land of the Hittites or long-time residents in the locality. Abraham was at a disadvantage and he knew it. He publicly admitted that he was but **a stranger and a sojourner** (4), i.e., something comparable to a resident alien. So he made a strong plea to **the children of Heth** (5) that he be allowed to buy land for a burial place.

Abraham quickly gained the approval of the influential family **of Heth,** who called him **a mighty prince** (6; marg., "a prince of God"). The next step was to gain their services as intermediaries between him and **Ephron the son of Zohar** (8), who owned the cave of **Machpelah** (9). Abraham assured everyone that he was willing to pay for the property **as much money as it is worth.**

Ephron (10) now spoke. He offered to make a gift of **the field** (11) along with **the cave** to Abraham. This was really a roundabout way of beginning the bargaining. But Abraham did not want a gift. He wanted a legally attested title to the property, and only an outright purchase could accomplish this purpose. In typical Near Eastern fashion, **Ephron** (13) casually mentioned an exorbitant price of **four hundred shekels of silver** (15). Probably to the surprise of everyone Abraham did not haggle for a lower price. He brought out his supply of currency and promptly weighed out the **four hundred shekels of silver** (16). The phrase **current money with the merchant** means that the silver was valued at the rate then agreed upon by the merchants of the locality. There is no way to know the value of the silver in present-day terms, but compared with the 17 shekels of silver which Jeremiah paid for land at Anathoth (Jer. 32:9), the price seems excessive.

The content of v. 17 impresses one as the wording of a deed to a piece of land. The location and the various aspects of the property, including **the field** (17), **the cave,** and **the trees,** were attested in the presence of everyone in the assembly. At long last a portion of the land, small though it was, belonged to **Abraham** (19) and his descendents. In the cave **Sarah** was promptly **buried.**[14]

3. *In Quest for the Right Girl* (24:1-67)

As the patriarch of the clan, Abraham had the responsibility to provide a bride for Isaac. The story which relates how this quest was fulfilled is one of the best written and most attractive narratives concerning Abraham. The setting comprises vv. 1-9. Next comes the search and its fulfillment (10-27), then the negotiation scene (28-61), and finally the marriage (62-67).

According to the customs of his time, and still true in the less westernized families of the Near East, the old father had an important duty to perform for his son.[15] Abraham had never been impressed with the moral character of the people about him in Canaan, so his thoughts turned back to the homeland, where his relatives still lived. He wanted a girl with a religious background similar to that of Isaac.

The text does not make clear whether the **eldest servant** (2) was the Eliezer mentioned in 15:2 but some commentators feel that this was the case.[16] The importance which Abraham attached to the project of finding a wife can be measured by the fact that a solemn vow was demanded of the **servant.** The form described was customary in the East. At Abraham's request, the man placed his hand under his master's **thigh** and received his instructions.[17] Isaac's wife must not be **of the Canaanites** (3) but

[14]G. Cornfeld, *Adam to Daniel* (New York: The Macmillan Co., 1961), pp. 73-77.

[15]R. de Vaux, *Ancient Israel: Its Life and Institutions* (New York: McGraw-Hill Book Co., Inc., 1961), pp. 29-32.

[16]T. Whitelaw, "Genesis," *The Pulpit Commentary,* ed. H. D. M. Spence, *et al.* (Grand Rapids: Wm. B. Eerdmans Publishing Co., 1961), I, 296.

[17]M. H. Pope, "Oaths," *The Interpreter's Dictionary of the Bible* (Nashville: Abingdon Press, 1962), pp. 575-77.

from **his kindred** (4). If a girl refused to come to Canaan, Isaac must not be taken back north, because God had given a promise that Abraham's **seed** (7) would claim **this land.** However, Abraham was sure that God would provide **a wife** by sending **his angel before** his servant. Abraham was depending on God to carry out His promises. Therefore if the girl refused to come the servant was released from the **oath** (8).

The details of preparing for the trip, and of the trip itself, are passed over with no more mention than that **ten camels** (10) made up the caravan. By this time there was a **city of Nahor,** perhaps in honor of Abraham's grandfather (11:22-26). The old servant picked a spot at **a well of water** (11) where the women were most likely to congregate.

The religious faith of Abraham had had profound influence on his servant, who was also a deeply pious man. Stationed at the well just before the time for the **women . . . to draw water,** he lifted up his voice in prayer. His prime desire was that the choice of the wife for Isaac should not be his own decision but that it might be God's choice. Knowing his own handicaps in discerning the will of God, he asked that the **Lord God** (12) make known His will by a series of events. These events were also to serve a secondary purpose, i.e., to reveal the character of the girl herself. She must be a young woman who possessed a concern for the stranger, one who was willing to do the extra task which denoted generosity. On God's part the series of events would demonstrate fidelity to covenant promises. The word is translated **kindness** (12, *chesed*) but carries a broader meaning of loyalty to promises made, and of mercy in times of crisis. Eliezer's prayer was one of deep trust and of high expectancy.

The servant was at the right place at the right time and had submitted his needs to God. **Before he had done speaking** (15) the answer to his prayer began to unfold before his eyes. **Rebekah,** Abraham's niece, appeared at the well. She met all physical and legal requirements, but this was not enough; so the servant asked the key question. Without hesitation he was given a **drink** (18), and then, spontaneously, she began **to draw water** (20) for **his camels.** Struck dumb with wonder, Eliezer saw his request fulfilled to the letter.

Recovering, the old man brought forth a heavy **golden earring** (22) and **two bracelets . . . of gold.** Breathlessly he asked about the maiden's family. The news that she belonged to Abraham's lineage unleashed great joy, so that without embarrassment he **bowed down his head** (26) and uttered a prayer of praise. His master's God had made good on His promises, thus showing **mercy** (27, *chesed;* translated **kindness** in 24:12, 14) and **truth** (*emet*). God's actions in the lives of His followers correlated with His promises to them. But there was another reason for this remarkable outcome. The servant had been **in the way,** promptly obedient and completely open to being **led** by **the Lord.** Thus the concern of Abraham for his son, the complete obedience of the servant, and the wholehearted generosity of the girl combined with the guidance of the Lord to bring about a wonder-filled execution of divine promise.

The news about the stranger stirred Rebekah's family into action. **Laban** (29), a brother, found the man by **the well** (30), brought him to the house, and gave **the camels** food (32). Before Abraham's servant sat down **to eat** (33) he insisted that he must tell why he had come.

He told an impressive story about the wealth of Abraham and all that would be passed on to Isaac. He repeated the content of the oath to which his master had caused him to swear; and then reviewed the details of the incident by the well, including his prayer, and the series of actions which coincided with his request of God. Finally, the matter was placed squarely before the family: Would they let Rebekah return with him to be Isaac's wife? The main difference between the final words of the servant to the family and the words of his prayer by **the well** (27) is that the words **kindly** (*chesed*) and **truly** (*emet*) are shifted from God to the family (49). Up to this point God had been faithful to His promises. Would the family now participate in the full realization of the promise given in regard to Isaac? Much depended on their response, for if they should refuse, the fulfillment of the promise could be frustrated.

The response was positive. **Laban and Bethuel** (50) recognized the dealings of the Lord and set aside their own human authority. This was a decision of such importance that Abraham's servant again **worshipped the Lord** (52). He then gave each member of the family rich gifts.

In the morning (54) the servant had surprising news for the family. He wished to begin his journey back to Canaan immediately. His task was completed and he wanted to deliver the girl to Isaac as soon as possible. The family protested that they should have a few days more with their loved one, but they were willing to let Rebekah decide for herself. What if she refused the servant's request? But she did not. Instead there was a quick response, **I will go** (58). Thus a series of crucial personal decisions, which if negative could have hindered the will of God, were made in obedience to the divine purpose, bringing the venture to a happy ending.

With the blessing of her family (60) ringing in her ears, Rebekah headed south with the camel caravan. At the end of the journey the courageous girl caught her first glimpse of the man she had chosen wholly by faith, and she was not disappointed. Modestly, **she took a veil, and covered herself** (65). A marriage without a previous courtship, but with much guidance of the Lord, was consummated with love.

4. *Distributing Gifts* (25:1-6)

Abraham took yet another wife and this union proved to be fruitful. **Keturah** (1) bore six sons (cf. I Chron. 1:32-33) and from these came seven grandchildren and three great-grandchildren. This completes the genealogical evidence offered in Genesis that God's promise that Abraham would be the father of many nations (17:4) had been fulfilled.

Abraham (5) still had responsibilities to Isaac and to these other descendents. The superior rights of Isaac as the true son must be preserved, but the claims of the other children must be recognized as well. The patriarch's solution was to divide his wealth. **All that he had** (i.e., the major portion) went to Isaac, and lesser portions designated as **gifts** (6) to the other children. The latter were sent **eastward** out of Canaan, so that there would not be disputes in the future about claims to the Promised Land.

5. *Abraham's Death and Burial* (25:7-11)

The span of Abraham's life was 175 years. Quietly, with a sense of fulfillment, the patriarch **was gathered to his people** (8). This phrase means more than dying. It includes the practice of placing the body in a grave with the remains of the ancestors (cf. 25:17; 35:29; 49:29, 33; Num. 20:24; 27:13).[18] From the phrase itself it is not clear that life after death is a part of its ordinary meaning. However, a comparison of Gen. 15:15 with

[18]de Vaux, *op. cit.*, pp. 56-61.

Heb. 11:13-16, and with Christ's words in Matt. 22:31-33, leaves no doubt that life after death was inherent in the expression. The phrase does not include the concept that the dead leader in death moved from a human status to a divine status—an idea common to pagan notions of the time.

Carefully Abraham's body was laid beside the remains of **Sarah his wife** (10), and the two **sons Isaac and Ishmael** (9) returned to their daily tasks. **Isaac** (11) made his home near **the well Lahai-roi,** where God had previously appeared to Hagar, Ishmael's mother (see 16:14; 24:62). God's blessings were focused on Isaac.

Several traits set Abraham off as a most unusual man for his day. He obeyed God's clear instructions (12:4; 15:10; 17:23; 21:14; 22:3), though when the instructions were not wholly clear, he sometimes wavered (16:4; 17:17). He is never depicted as worshiping other than one God (12:7-8; 13:4, 18; 15:10-11; 17:3; 19:27; 20:17; 21:33). He possessed respect for, and sometimes fear of, men of authority in the lands which he visited (12:12-13; 14:17-18; 20:1-13). He was generous of spirit and free from greed (13:8-9; 14:23; 17:18; 18:3-8; 21:14). He knew how to forgive and to intercede for others (18:22-23; 20:17; 21:25-31). He was capable of unswerving love for God (22:16), and knew how to carry responsibility for others (23:1-2, 19; 24:1-9, 67; 25:5-6). Above all, he knew how to believe God when visible evidences were lacking (15:6).

In regard to the covenant, one learns from Abraham's life that God initiates the covenant (12:1; 13:17), protects the covenant partner (12:17; 18:1), binds himself by giving promises (12:1-3, 7; 13:14-17), and places man under obligation (17:1, 9; 18:19).

The categories of faith and obedience in Abraham's life set the thrust of the remainder of the Old and New Testaments.

Section III Ishmael, the Man Whom God Set Aside

Genesis 25:12-18

One of the characteristics of style in the Book of Genesis is the dismissal, by means of a genealogy or genealogies, of persons closely related to those whom God chose. Compare the similar dismissals of Cain (4:17-24), Japheth (10:2-5), Ham (10:6-20), the descendents of Shem other than Terah's family (11:10-26), and later the dismissal of Esau (36:1-43).

The time had come to remove Ishmael's family from the record of the mainstream of God's dealing with the covenant people. The genealogy is a demonstration, in part, that God's promises to **Hagar** (12) had been fulfilled (see 16:12; 21:18).

The 12 sons of Ishmael were not only **princes** (16) but their followers filled many tent encampments and were scattered over a wide territory. **Castles** in KJV is a poor translation, which is better rendered "villages." They were nomads and traversed the land from the edge of **Egypt** (18) eastward across central Arabia to the southern borders of **Assyria** along the Tigris River (see map 1).

Section IV Isaac, the Man Whose Life God Spared

Genesis 25:19—28:9

The life of Isaac is overshadowed in the Book of Genesis by the daring faith of his father, Abraham, and the dramatic qualities of the life of his son Jacob. Yet Isaac's early life was not lacking in the unusual. He was a miraculous gift of God to his aged parents, fulfilling a promise of long standing. In the most crucial moment of his youth he submissively yielded himself to his father, though he realized his father was about to kill him. Doubtless the deliverance of his life from death on Mount Moriah left an abiding effect upon his religious outlook. An incident which could have begotten fear of his father gave birth to a firm faith in his wisdom. Isaac responded with trust to Abraham's efforts to obtain a wife for him and received the bride with a gratitude which quickly ripened into love. The remainder of his life is mainly recorded in two chapters. He was a solid bridge between generations.

A. A Birthright for Bean Stew, 25:19-34

The genealogy which opens this section is extremely brief, listing only the father, the son, and his wife, whose family tree includes only her father and brother. **Padan-aram** (20), Rebekah's homeland, is the stretch of highlands between the upper Euphrates and Tigris rivers (see map 1).

Like Sarah, **Rebekah** (20) was **barren** (21); and like **Abraham** (19), **Isaac** was deeply distressed by this misfortune and prayed that **the Lord** would grant them children. A comparison of vv. 20 and 26 shows that 20 years passed before their first children were born. During her pregnancy **Rebekah** became distressed by the excessive activity within her. The RSV renders the last part of 22, "If it is thus, why do I live?" In desperation she sought help from **the Lord.** It was then that she learned for the first time that she was carrying twins, that they were different in character and would be the fathers of two different people. She was also told that the descendents of the younger of the two (which v. 26 indicates was determined by the sequence of their birth) would produce the stronger nation. This news the mother never forgot.

At birth the difference between the babies produced reactions of apparent wonder in the parents and moved them to name them accordingly. The first boy was covered with **red** hair (25, *admoni se ar*). These Hebrew words have obvious ties with *Edom* and *Seir,* names commonly associated with the future homeland of this boy's descendents. Likewise the name **Esau** means "hairy." The name of the second boy was prompted by the unusual fact that he was grasping his brother's **heel (26)** as he was being born. The name **Jacob** (26) means "heel catcher."

The difference between the boys was intensified as they grew to manhood. Being a robust fellow, hunting was Esau's first love. He enjoyed the art of shooting wild animals. Jacob found pleasure in caring for domestic animals. Perhaps this is the reason he is called **a plain man** (27). The Hebrew word is *tam,* which is translated by "perfect" in Gen. 6:9.

The contrasting character of the boys brought out contrasting likes and dislikes in their parents, which tended to drive an emotional wedge between them. The genteel **Isaac** (28) developed a strong preference for the rugged **Esau;** the vivacious **Rebekah** focused her attention on the less aggressive **Jacob.**

Without doubt the mother had confided to Jacob the content of God's message to her before the birth of the boys (23). Both must have been aware that the customs of their ancestors favored the firstborn as the legal heir to the father's tribal position. Jacob also knew that birthrights could be transferred to a younger brother by agreement.[1]

Craftily, Jacob chose his opportunity and caught Esau in his weakest moment, when he was physically exhausted and hungry after a strenuous hunt. **Jacob** (29) was a good cook and had prepared a tasty stew (**sod pottage** is old English for a "cooked stew"). This he used as leverage to bargain with **Esau,** who was too hungry to care. Almost flippantly Esau sold his birthright for the stew. **Jacob** (34) had taken advantage of **Esau,** but **Esau** had completely misjudged the value of **his birthright** (cf. Heb. 12: 15-16).

[1]C. H. Gordon, *Introduction to Old Testament Times* (Ventnor Pub., Inc., 1953), pp. 112-13.

In 25:29-34 we see "Esau's Barter." (1) Esau traded eternal values for temporal satisfaction, 31-32; (2) Esau's barter was irrevocable, 33; (3) Jacob's sharp bargain was not clear gain; cf. 27:36, 41 (G. B. Williamson).

B. Isaac's Dealings with His Neighbors, 26:1-33

Similar to Abraham's relationships with his pagan neighbors, Isaac's contacts with the people of Canaan was a checkered pattern of distrust, forbearance, and reconciliation. Even God's blessings of prosperity on the patriarch seemed to hinder Isaac's efforts to establish some kind of peace with them.

1. *The Covenant Promises Given to Isaac* (26:1-5)

A famine (1) had forced Isaac out of the semiarid land south and west of Canaan to seek pasturage along the coastal plain east of the Mediterranean Sea (see map 2). This was in the territory of **Abimelech king of the Philistines,** near to the borders of Egypt. But the richer delta area of Egypt was evidently luring Isaac in that direction. It was then that **the Lord appeared unto him** (2).

God told Isaac to stay away from Egypt. He then renewed the promises granted to Abraham, and applied them to Isaac. Canaan was to be Isaac's home and there he would know the presence of God. The prospect of **seed . . . as the stars of heaven** (4) was reemphasized and the assurance was stressed again that **the nations of the earth** would reap blessings from his descendents. God's promise was being passed on to Isaac **because that Abraham obeyed** (5).

This incident probably occurred before the birth of Esau and Jacob. The story of Isaac calling Rebekah his sister which follows in 6-11 would seem improbable if active boys were romping about Isaac's tents. The words about the seed doubtlessly undergirded Isaac's entreaty for a son (25:21).

2. *Deceit Did It Again* (26:6-16)

Fear made it difficult for the patriarchs to establish an effective relationship with their pagan neighbors. The moral values of these people were such that an alien family could feel justified in harboring fear. The pagan kings were understood to have connubial rights to any woman who pleased them. Like Abraham

(12:10-13; 20:2, 11-13), Isaac took refuge from imagined personal harm in the peculiar sister-wife marriage custom of his ancestors. In this arrangement even a cousin or a non-relative would be adopted into the family as a sister of the bridegroom and thus legally be both a sister and a wife.

Isaac let the Philistines know about the **sister** (7) angle but not the **wife** aspect of his relationship to **Rebekah.** The pagans, however, made no move to indicate a desire for Rebekah. **Abimelech** (8) chanced to see **Isaac** in what would have been a compromising situation with a sister and he suspected the truth. He called Isaac in, verified his suspicions, and then rebuked him. Abimelech declared that Isaac could have misled a Philistine into sinning against Rebekah. Isaac's deceit, prompted by fear, lowered the pagan's opinion of him, negating an opportunity for the patriarch to be a blessing.

Isaac continued in the territory, making good use of **the wells** (15) dug **in the days of Abraham.** The remarkable yield of grain appears to have been the result of irrigation which was made possible by the water drawn from **the wells.** This feat has been duplicated widely in Israel today. The patriarch's increasing wealth, because of God's blessing on him, engendered envy in the hearts of **the Philistines,** who filled up all the wells and expelled Isaac (16).

3. *Demonstrating Patience Under Pressure* (26:17-25)

Reopening more of Abraham's **wells** (18) in another neighborhood, Isaac tried to prepare new fields for grain. Instead of learning important new methods of agriculture from Isaac, **the Philistines** foolishly continued to fill the wells and drive the patriarch to a new place. **Esek** (20) means "quarrel"; **Sitnah** (21) is "feud"; **Rehoboth** (22) means "room." Rather than fight, Isaac moved on, dug new wells, saw them filled again and again, then moved completely out of the region, settling at **Beer-sheba** (23).

In 26:17-22 we find "Room—Rehoboth"; see v. 22. (1) Room for men who seek peace to live in peace, 21-22; (2) God's resources are sufficient for all to have enough, 22; (3) Patience is rewarded in peace and prosperity, 22 (G. B. Williamson).

For the second time, God met Isaac and reaffirmed the covenant promises first revealed to **Abraham** (24) concerning an abundant posterity. The Lord took pains to allay his fears and to assure him of continued divine presence. Isaac responded in grateful worship at a freshly built **altar** (25).

In vv. 24-25 we see "Some Elements in Human Happiness." From the human side, (1) Worship, **he builded an altar there,** 25; (2) Family life, **pitched his tent there,** 25; and (3) Financial security, **Isaac's servants digged a well,** 25. These were matched on the divine side by (4) God's guidance, **Go not down . . . dwell in the land,** 2; (5) His presence: **I am with thee,** 24; and (6) His blessing: **and will bless thee,** 24; also 26:12, 29.

4. *Patience Begets Peace* (26:26-33)

Presently **Abimelech** (26), with a friend **Ahuzzath,** and **Phichol** (probably a military title) visited **Isaac** (27) at Beersheba. Isaac was suspicious and accused them of hating him. To his surprise the visitors testified to being impressed by Isaac's forbearance and told him they had become convinced that **the Lord was with** him (28). They requested that old grievances be set aside by recognizing only the better aspects of their relationships. The request was somewhat of a modified golden rule, "Deal with us on the basis of the **good** [29] things we have done to you." They wanted a covenant to govern the future relationships between them.

Isaac responded without hesitation by providing **a feast** (30). The next morning they concluded the pact of friendship by giving solemn promises to each other in the form of oaths. It was a dramatic example that, if two parties of a conflict mutually forgive and forget, **peace** (31) can be a reality.

The climax was the happy discovery of water in a newly dug **well** (32), which gave cause for Isaac to reemphasize the name which Abraham gave to the spot, **Beer-sheba** (33; see 21:30-31). The first part of the name means "well." The last part means "seven" or "oath."

C. Isaac and His Family, 26:34—28:9

When one reads cc. 26—27, a striking contrast looms. In spite of fumbling because of fear of the morals of his new neighbors, Isaac was quick to admit his fear and his lie. Basically he was a man of peace and did everything in his power to avoid trouble. He was quick to make a covenant to clear up old tensions. On the other side he was not so successful with his own family. Their unethical shrewdness drove him into a most embarrassing situation. His indulgent desires and insensitivity to God's promises to his wife gendered strife and misunderstanding rather than peace.

1. *Esau's Poor Choices* (26:34-35)

Esau's lack of value judgment when he sold his birthright to Jacob (25:29-34) was matched by his unconcern for his parents' wishes in regard to his wives. He followed the call of his physical appetites exclusively when he chose two pagan girls for his mates. He ignored the custom of being guided by the parents' judgment, and he disregarded the fact that the moral standards of the culture from whence these girls came were far lower than those of his ancestors. **Grief of mind** (35) is the phrase used to describe the deep hurt of **Isaac and . . . Rebekah.**

2. *A Blessing by Stealth* (27:1-29)

Isaac had become **old** (1) and blind, and probably also quite sick. At least he believed he was about to die, though actually he lived for another 40 years (35:28). He decided that the time had come to pass on the patriarchal blessing to his successor. According to the customs of his ancestors this belonged to **Esau his eldest son.**

Calling Esau to him, the old man requested that the son obtain wild game and prepare the meat for a ceremonial feast preparatory to giving the blessing.[2] Such action ignored God's message to Rebekah that "the elder shall serve the younger" (25:23), which Isaac surely knew about. It also ignored the sale of the birthright to Jacob, which Isaac probably knew about (25:29-34). But **Rebekah** (5) had not forgotten, nor had **Jacob** (6).

The reactions of Rebekah and Jacob to Isaac's plan do not reflect well on their characters. In fact all four participants in this story are consistently presented in a bad light. The parental partiality for one son over the other by both father and mother (25:28) had led to a breakdown of understanding between them. Isaac ignored Rebekah and she was unable to talk to him about his mistake.

In desperation Rebekah turned to **Jacob,** enlisting his support in a plan of deceit. He was to get **two good kids of the goats** (9), so she could prepare the kind of **meat** that Isaac loved. Jacob was to take it to Isaac and receive the blessing before Esau re-

[2]*Ibid.*, pp. 114-15.

turned. The old man's inordinate desire for a certain **savoury meat** was the open door to this scheme.

Jacob (11) did not protest the plan but he did see a serious weakness in it. His body did not have the abundant hair that Esau's did, and Isaac might insist on touching Jacob to make identification certain. The **blessing** (12) might become **a curse.** Flippantly the mother retorted, **Upon me be thy curse** (13), and commanded the boy to do as told. By the time Jacob returned, **Rebekah** (15) had decided how to solve the problem. The **skins of the kids** (16) would be put on Jacob's **hands** and around his **neck.**

The scheming pair overlooked one item, the difference between the voices of the two sons. The old father caught the difference immediately and reacted suspiciously when Jacob identified himself as **Esau thy firstborn** (19). The aged **Isaac** (20) almost tripped him over the quickness of delivering the meal; Jacob could only mutter, **Because the Lord thy God brought it to me.** The tense moment came when Isaac insisted on feeling Jacob's body (21). Partially satisfied, Isaac called for the meat and ate. But clearly the sound of that voice troubled him. Under the ruse of asking for a kiss, the father **smelled . . . his raiment** (27). But Rebekah had anticipated that (15). Finally convinced, Isaac proceeded to give the blessing.

The patriarchal blessing was a form of last will and testament. Oral blessings were considered as binding on all parties as a written contract.[3] Isaac desired that prosperity for his son spring out of the richness of the soil, but he also bequeathed to him lordship over other **nations** (29) as well as over his own family. The recipient of the blessing was to be protected by divine justice; whoever had contact with him was to receive punishment for cursing him and blessing for being gracious to him. When the blessing was over, Jacob slipped away.

3. *The Shock of Discovery* (27:30-40)

Close by, **Esau** (30) was busy preparing meat he had brought in from the hunt. Unaware of Jacob's act, he took the **savoury meat** (31) to **Isaac his father** (32), fully expecting to receive the blessing. The father was amazed to hear his voice and knew immediately what had happened. He had been tricked. The old

[3]Speiser, *Genesis*, *op. cit.*, pp. 212-13.

man was shaken till he **trembled very exceedingly** (33). The blessing he had given was of the "once for all" type and could not be revoked. The measure of Esau's reaction is seen in his **great and exceeding bitter cry** (34) and his plaintive plea that his **father** would still **bless** him. Heb. 12:17 notes that Esau's serious mistake was his sale of the birthright (25:29-34) and that now his efforts to repair that error were too late, for he had never really repented of his earlier foolishness. Esau placed the entire blame on **Jacob** (36), but his brother's guilt could not justify his own.

Isaac could think only of the completeness of his act of blessing Jacob and it was only after Esau's persistent pleading that he consented to grant Esau a lesser blessing.

Esau was also to have prosperity but he would have to live **by thy sword** (40) and accept the role of a servant to Jacob and his descendents for a time, after which he had the right to **break his yoke from off thy neck.** The expression **when thou shalt have dominion** is better, "When you grow restive" (Moffatt). This blessing wasn't much, but it did have a ray of hope for Esau.

4. *A Brother's Hate, a Fearsome Thing* (27:41-46)

Esau's disappointment and bitterness congealed into a resolve to **slay my brother Jacob** (41). Like Cain, he allowed his reaction to the advantage gained by the younger brother to be governed by negative emotions. **Esau** (42) had not kept his thoughts to himself and soon word got to **Rebekah** and then to **Jacob,** causing fear and giving birth to new schemes. Ever resourceful, Rebekah counseled Jacob to leave home for safety's sake. She envisioned such a trip to last but a short time, for Esau's **fury** (44) would surely be short-lived. She had no intention to lose Jacob after her tricky scheming had completely alienated Esau from her.

Rebekah's immediate problem was how to justify Jacob's trip to Haran. Esau must not be led to suppose that evasive action was being taken in order to thwart his intent to kill Jacob, or he might act even before his father's death. Rebekah's first move was to complain about Esau's wives, **the daughters of Heth** (46), and then to point out her feeling that if Jacob married local girls, **what good shall my life do me?** The stratagem was shrewdly conceived and highly effective.

5. *Commissioned to Find a Wife* (28:1-9)

Rebekah's criticism of the wives of Esau convinced **Isaac (1)** that there must not be more pagan daughters-in-law. He was unaware that, at the same time, Rebekah was successfully covering up a scheme to get **Jacob** away from Esau's presence.

The old father **called Jacob, and blessed him, and charged him** to return to their ancestral homeland and find there **a wife** (2). This time, by choice rather than by ignorance, **Isaac** granted to Jacob a new blessing to be given by **God Almighty** (3), promising an abundant posterity. The covenant promises of **seed** and **land** given to **Abraham** (4) were repeated in essence. Jacob was now openly and beyond dispute the bearer of the covenant into the new generation. His departure from the family circle was justified in the sight of all.

When Esau saw (6) that Jacob's new status was tied to his willingness to take a wife from among his relatives in **Padan-aram** (5), new thoughts ran through his mind. Perhaps he could regain the esteem of his parents if he took a **wife** from among close relatives. But he was not interested in those located in faraway lands; he assumed that the daughters of Ishmael would be good enough. He did not realize that Jacob would have been sent to Ishmael if this had been so. The silence in v. 9 which follows the account of Esau's act speaks most eloquently.

The role of Rebekah in Isaac's life began on a high level but deteriorated to the depths of disappointment and fear. When Rebekah first appears on the pages of Scripture she shines as the model of purity (24:16), of hospitality (24:18), of willingness to work without thought of reward (24:19-20), of capacity to make decisions in accord with the evident will of God (24:58). She had courage to tread untried paths in giving herself to an unknown bridegroom (24:67), and ability to provide comfort to a lonely man (24:67). She demonstrated willingness to seek God's help and to accept His word (25:22-23).

As her sons began to grow, Rebekah began to change. She reacted to Isaac's preference for Esau by centering her affection upon Jacob (25:28). In the crisis hour when she heard Isaac's plans to bless Esau, she fell to pieces morally. All of her resourcefulness, her ability to make quick decisions and to plan a course of action, became warped by fear—fear that her favorite would not be recognized properly. She yielded to the devices of deceit (27:6-17) and to clever stratagems well camouflaged by professed concern for a proper mate for Jacob (27:46) but actually motivated by selfish interests: "Why should I be deprived?" (27:45) She planned to call Jacob home again (27:45), but her view of the departing favored son proved to be her last glimpse of him. Her closing days must have been empty and cheerless.

Isaac's life was spared, and his death at the ripe age of 180 years is recorded in Gen. 35:28-29. But with Jacob's departure to Padan-aram, Isaac also passed from the scene of God's active dealings with the bearers of the partriarchal covenant.

Though different in temperament from either Abraham, his father, or Jacob, his son, Isaac was a man whom God could use in His own way. Born as the son of promise, Isaac could have been an arrogant type. But each time he appears in the stories of Abraham's walk with God he is portrayed as submissive (22:6, 9), possessing a boyish trust in his father and in God (22:7-8). He did not interfere with Abraham's efforts to obtain a wife for him. In the episode he is depicted as meditative (24:63), capable of tender love for both his late mother and his new bride (24:67). He knew how to pray (25:21; 26:25).

Section V Jacob, the Man Whom God Remade

Genesis 28:10—35:29

Out into a strange world, Jacob walked alone. Behind him was an aging father, who failed to see that his favoritism for Esau could have led him into thwarting the will of God as it had been revealed to Rebekah (25:23). Behind him also was a bitter and angry brother, who, having no sense of true values, thought only that he had been robbed by clever Jacob. Behind him was a distraught mother, who, knowing something of God's will for Jacob, complicated the divine purpose through ill-planned subterfuge.

But Jacob was not alone for long; God met him, and a girl met him. A marital arrangement not to his liking and a father-in-law not too trustworthy pained his heart. Nevertheless God led out into a new, transforming experience, into a reconciliation with his brother, into patterns of light and shadow which slowly matured and mellowed his life before God.

A. Confronted by God, 28:10-22

God's major visitations with Jacob were dramatic, shattering. The incident at Bethel was no exception; he scarcely expected the events of that night, nor was he ever to forget the significance of what happened to him. Before that moment, apparently, Jacob never gave much thought to God's will for him. After that experience, his life was dominated by a serious concern for the divine will.

1. *A Hard Headrest* (28:10-11)

The trip to **Haran** (10; see map 1) was well over 300 miles and the distance to the **certain place** (11) was about 70 miles from **Beer-sheba.** Since night had already come and he was tired, Jacob constructed a crude bed on the ground, gathering a few **stones** (11) for **pillows** (*mera ashotaw;* lit., a headrest). The story gives no hint that Jacob either expected or sought for an unusual spiritual experience.

2. *The Surprise Visit* (28:12-15)

The dream came without human inducement and its content was determined by **the Lord** (13), who dominated it. The **ladder** (12) was a visual connecting link between the earthly and the heavenly. The **angels of God** were the messengers, the line of communication between man and God. There was no image of God in the dream, only the awareness of a sovereign relationship of God standing **above** (13) everything. The element of surprise is emphasized by a threefold **behold** (12-13) in the description of the dream.

Common to visitations of God to man in a covenant context is an opening statement which identifies the One who first speaks. In this case, the Speaker made it clear that He was the same One who had visited Jacob's grandfather, Abraham, and his father, Isaac. Polytheism was not involved here. In each instance the same God was the Communicator of the covenant.

The content of the promises of God remained the same. The **land** (13), even that on which he was lying, was a gift of God. It was not for him alone, but for his **seed** (14), which would multiply like the **dust of earth,** beyond computation, and like the points of the compass moving out toward all parts of the world. This would involve contact with other nations, and, as with Abraham (12:3), it was God's will that those contacts be **blessed,** i.e., contribute to their welfare and spiritual enlightenment.

Several of the promises had a more personal import. Like Isaac (26:24), Jacob was to know the intimate presence of the Lord, but a new pattern was also set. Jacob was to go out and he was to return—a sequel which was to be repeated many times in the history of his descendents. The stability of God's presence was tied to His faithfulness to actualize His purposes in the affairs of men.

3. *Jacob's Response* (28:16-22)

The dream and the message jarred Jacob wide-awake, thoroughly overwhelmed by a meeting with God for which he was quite unprepared. Fear seized his heart. To him the place was **dreadful** (17), i.e., awe-inspiring. He clearly apprehended the supernatural, but at the same time he did not lose his senses. He was well aware that a most unusual event had happened which involved God. His terms for it were **house of God** (*Beth-el*) and **gate of heaven.**

Jacob responded with three significant actions. The first was ritualistic in nature. To memorialize the event, the **stone** (18) was upended and anointed with **oil.** This was not because he was a primitive man who believed in spirit stones, but because he was convinced of the integrity of his encounter with God and wished to witness to that faith. The second act was to rename the spot in order to bring the name into line with the new experience. To Jacob, **Luz** (19) was meaningless, but **Beth-el** would never lose its import. The third act was a commitment sealed with **a vow** (20). Because the first word Jacob uttered was a conditional **If God will be with me,** some have pictured him as engaged in a hard bargaining session with the Almighty quite in line with his deals with Esau.[1] But the context depicts Jacob as a subdued man. He was ready to meet the undeserved promises with a voluntary declaration of loyalty to God. In acceptance of God's self-disclosure as genuine, and in recognition of His sovereignty, Jacob was ready to give back a **tenth** (22) to God.[2]

In 28:10-22 we find "Unexpected Encounter with God." (1) The story background, 27:1—28:9; (2) An unexpected revelation, 10-11; (3) Discovering the connection between earth and heaven, 12-15; (4) Right response to God's revelation, 16-22 (A. F. Harper).

B. Love Thwarted Does Not Die, 29:1-30

Little of the rest of the journey from Canaan is recorded, except that **Jacob . . . came into the land of the people of the east** (1). This probably designated, primarily, the region around Damascus, but may have included Haran also (see map 1).

Jacob burst upon the quiet community of Haran with dash and vigor. He knew why he had come, and the first girl he met was exactly the one he wanted. She was willing but her father

[1]H. M. Buck, *People of the Lord* (New York: The Macmillan Co., 1966), p. 342.

[2]W. H. Griffith-Thomas, *Genesis* (Grand Rapids: Wm. B. Eerdmans Publishing Co., 1946), pp. 264-65.

was not. Laban's dealings with Jacob were to prove most disconcerting, especially on Jacob's wedding day.

1. *The Flocks in the Field* (29:1-8)

The fact that Jacob came on shepherds who knew his relatives is to be taken as a fulfillment of God's promise to be with him. Being a shepherd himself, Jacob noticed things that were different from his own procedures in caring for a flock. It was noon and **three flocks** were already gathered at **a well** (2)—probably a cistern—but were not being watered. Covering the **well** was **a great stone.** An explanation of the delay in watering the sheep is given in vv. 3 and 8, but Jacob did not learn of it until he had inquired about the identity of the shepherds and their knowledge of Laban.

The shepherds were not lazy. They were waiting for Laban's daughter to arrive with her flock, so all could cooperate in removing **the stone** and covering the well again. As in the story in c. 24, this narrative points up the personal security of women in Haran's society, even in the open fields.

2. *Boy Meets Girl* (29:9-14)

The sight of his cousin **Rachel** (10) changed **Jacob** into a paragon of strength. The great stone, which demanded the combined power of a group of shepherds, now moved readily under the mighty tuggings of the stranger from Canaan. Jar after jar of water was hauled to the surface for the girl's sheep. **Rachel** must have been pleasantly surprised when she was **kissed** (11) by the emotional **Jacob,** who identified himself as her cousin. The term **brother** (12) here has the sense of kinsman; Jacob was actually the nephew of Laban.

Like Rebekah (24:28), Rachel ran home with the news of the stranger's arrival. The response of the household was immediate and hospitable. Laban, in true Eastern fashion, **embraced** and **kissed** his relative. At the meal with the family, Jacob thrilled them with the story of his trip. During the month which followed, there was no hint that Laban had other than thoughts of pure affection for Jacob. One item stands out clearly: Jacob's arrival lacked the expressions of deep religious piety evident in Abraham's servant when he arrived in the same home years before (24:32-49).

3. *The Double Marriage* (29:15-30)

During the month's stay, evidently **Jacob** (15) had been working with Laban's flocks, so **Laban** suggested that an agreement on wages be worked out. Without doubt he had noticed Jacob's interest in **Rachel** (16) and saw an opportunity to take advantage of him. This daughter was not his eldest, a point which gave the father an important legal advantage. **Leah** means "wild cow." She was **tender eyed** (17), which does not necessarily mean that she had a visual defect. It could as well mean that she had attractive eyes—one physical trait in her favor. On the other hand, **Rachel** (which means "ewe") was a beauty and **Jacob loved** (18) her.

Jacob had been thinking about the matter too and had an immediate proposition. He would work **seven years for Rachel.** He was unaware of the complications behind his offer, but Laban knew and bided his time.[3]

The agreed date for the wedding came and Jacob was eager for his loved one to be his very own. **Laban** made ready the customary bridal **feast** (22). However, that night he presented, not Rachel, but **Leah** (23), to Jacob as wife. The bridal veil and the darkness hid this switch from the young man's knowledge.

The next **morning** (25) Jacob's surprise and chagrin knew no bounds. Angrily he berated **Laban** for his duplicity, but Laban was unimpressed. To give a younger daughter in marriage while the oldest daughter was still unmarried was illegal (26), but there was a remedy. If Jacob would work for another **seven . . . years** (27), Laban would give Rachel to him the very next week after Leah's week of bridal festivities had been completed.

For Laban the whole transaction appeared to be a very good deal. He had successfully married off his unattractive eldest daughter and had a promise of seven more years of free labor from Jacob. He made no effort to justify his failure to inform Jacob of local marriage laws when the request for Rachel was first made. Now in accordance with local custom, he provided his daughters with a personal maid each.

C. A Painful Competition, 29:31—30:24

The record of strife which developed in Jacob's family is not a pleasant story, and it gives concrete basis for a later prohibition

[3]Gordon, *op. cit.*, pp. 115-16.

against the marriage of sisters to one man at the same time (Lev. 18:18). Just as important, this section provides information on the origin of the names of the 12 tribes of Israel by describing the circumstances of the birth of each of Jacob's sons. Each name reflects something of the inner motives, emotions, and piety of the two sisters.

1. *The Unloved Was Blest* (29:31-35)

The Hebrew word for **hated** (31, *senuah*) does not always carry the strong negative connotations of the English. The context of this instance favors a weaker meaning (cf. v. 30). Jacob showered affection on Rachel but he did not despise or reject Leah. The fact that she gave birth to children by him demonstrates that their relationship lacked no more than the warmth of true love.

No explanation is given for the favoritism which **the Lord** (31) showed to Leah except as her faith in divine mercy is expressed in v. 32. As for Rachel, she was the third wife in succession in this family who temporarily suffered from barrenness —Sarah, Rebekah, and now Rachel.

The names of Jacob's sons were mostly based on sounds of words or phrases rather than on a direct literal meaning. The name of the first son, **Reuben** (32), was an exclamation, meaning, "Look, a son!" The verb *look* is carried over into Leah's testimony. Her hope for true love from her husband, however, was not realized. Her second son's name, **Simeon** (33), is based on the verb *shama,* which means "hath heard." It is embedded in another testimony to God's mercy even though she was unloved by her husband.

The third son's name, **Levi** (34, "attachment"), is tied to the phrase **will . . . be joined** (*yillaweh*). It gives a glimpse into the depths of Leah's yearning for the human affection which Jacob steadfastly denied to her. She had yet another son, **Judah** (35, "praise"), which suggests a swing of her emotions from an inner ache to outgoing thanksgiving to **the Lord.**

2. *The Loved One Desperate* (30:1-8)

Beautiful and beloved though she was, **Rachel** (1) soon found that strong feelings of envy stirred in her heart against Leah. The values of her day placed a high premium on children and she had none. Unreasonably she demanded that Jacob give her children, to which he angrily replied, **Am I in God's stead?** (2) But Rachel remembered, as did Sarah before her (16:2), that local law allowed a childless wife to gain posterity through a substitute wife. Impulsively she gave Jacob her **maid Bilhah** (4), who was soon with child—a child Bilhah could not claim as her own, for legally it belonged to Rachel. When she named the boy **Dan** (6), meaning "judge" or "vindication," she was not thinking of God as condemning her, but rather as judging her worthy of mercy.

The name which Rachel gave Bilhah's second son, **Naphtali** (8), means "wrestling" and is based on **great wrestlings have I wrestled.** Because the first part of the phrase is literally "wrestlings of God" (*naphtaley elohim*), some have held that Rachel was indulging in magic. But there is no reason to believe that she was doing other than praying earnestly to God, though her emotions were tinged with envy.

3. *The Counter Play* (30:9-13)

Leah also had a maid, whom she promptly gave to Jacob as another substitute wife, and who in turn gave birth to two sons. Though the name **Gad** (11) can mean **troop,** its most common meaning is "good fortune," which fits much better this context and is accepted in most recent translations. The next boy's name, **Asher** (13, "blessed"), was also an exclamation of deep satisfaction that Leah and her maid were outproducing Rachel.

4. *Not Magic but God Grants Life* (30:14-24)

Being but a child, **Reuben** (14) innocently brought some **mandrakes** from the **wheat** fields to **his mother.** The yellow berries of this plant were highly prized as having magical ability to induce fertility. When Rachel saw them she yielded to the temptation to obtain them as a cure of her barrenness.[4] To do so, she made a sordid bargain with her sister. Paganism's emphasis on magical superstitions was luring the women into unsavory practices. Jacob neither objected nor resisted.

In spite of the overtones of distorted moral values, God granted fruitfulness to Leah, and Rachel discovered that magic could not touch her problem. Leah at least recognized the activity of God, though she misunderstood the reason for God's mercy. Her

[4]Skinner, *op. cit.*, pp. 388-89, fn.

misunderstanding was imbedded in the name of her fifth child, **Issachar** (18), which means "hire." The name was based on the agreement made between Leah and Rachel. **The sixth son** (19), **Zebulun** (20, "dwelling"), reflects Leah's lingering yearning for affection from her husband, which even six sons did not gain for her. This name is the only one of the 12 sons which has a Mesopotamian parallel. The Akkadian word *zubullu* means "bridegroom gift" and thus gives a tie to the phrase **good dowry** (20).

Only one **daughter** (21) is accounted to Jacob. Her name was **Dinah,** meaning "judgment," but no personal testimony was attached to the name. This girl was to figure in a tragic scene at a later time (Genesis 34).

To **Rachel** (22) the mandrakes proved worthless. When she finally bore a child she understood it to be a special act of divine mercy. **God remembered** is a term usually associated with answered prayer. The name she gave the boy was **Joseph** (24, meaning "addition"). By faith she looked forward to another child as a gift from God. For her, pagan superstition had lost its appeal.

D. Clever Shepherds, 30:25—31:55

After the marriage of Jacob to the two sisters, the story centered on their struggle with each other in the realm of childbearing. Now the struggle was between Jacob and Laban until they parted in an uneasy peace.

1. *An Agreement Reached in Bad Faith* (30:25-43)

When **Jacob** (25) had fulfilled his second seven-year period of service, he approached **Laban** concerning the future. Jacob began by making a request that he be allowed to take **his wives** (26) and family and return to his own **country.** But Laban prevailed upon him to stay, for he had profited from his work. Jacob had apparently planned a second proposition, should this be Laban's attitude.

On the surface, Jacob's wage demands seemed curiously stupid to Laban. In that country, normally, the goats are solid black or dark brown, and the normal color of the sheep is solid white, though variations do occur. Jacob wanted to cull out the off-colored goats and the dark-colored sheep and build his herd from them. He would keep only those odd-colored goats and sheep which appeared among the offspring of the base flock. This division would be an easy way to avoid misunderstanding as to who owned which animals. In the RSV, Jacob says, "So my honesty will answer for me later, when you come to look into my wages with you" (33).

Laban agreed but had misgivings, so he quickly and secretly culled out of his flocks the colors which Jacob wanted and sent them far away (vv. 35-36). This act was a violation of the spirit of the agreement, but Jacob could do nothing about it at the moment. However, he had his own devices. Outwardly his procedure appears to have been a superstitious kind of magic, but he confessed later to his wives that God had instructed him in selective breeding (31:10-12). **Pilled white strakes** (37) is better "peeled white streaks" (Moffatt). Actually he was limiting his male breeding stock to the rams with the peculiar coloring, and sorting out the offspring into separate flocks, thus radically increasing the number of the off-colored kids and lambs from season to season. Further, he kept only the very best animals for the selective breeding, and left inferior animals for Laban's flocks. This was the real reason why his own flocks did so well (31:9).

2. *A Family Council* (31:1-16)

Jacob's success with the flocks had given occasion for **Laban's sons** (1) to make malicious remarks about Jacob's honesty. They refused to recognize his skill as a breeder or God's providence in Jacob's life. Worst of all, Laban believed his sons, overlooked his own dishonesty, and became hostile toward Jacob. Evidently Jacob became fearful for his life and sought guidance from God. The Lord gave him permission to **return** (3) and stressed again His promise, **I will be with thee.**

Not trusting the people at the main camp, Jacob requested that **Rachel and Leah** (4) come out to his **field** location for a family council.

Noting the change in Laban's attitude, Jacob stressed God's presence in his affairs, his personal diligence as a shepherd, and Laban's dishonesty. Jacob gave **God** (9) full credit for whatever prosperity had come to him, for guidance in breeding the flock, and for the new proposal to flee to Canaan.

On this matter **Rachel and Leah** (14) were of one mind. They agreed that their father had been unjust. They remembered with keen resentment that Laban had debased them by selling them like property, and had used **money** (15) which belonged to them and their children. They willingly gave their consent to go to Canaan.

3. *The Flight and the Chase* (31:17-24)

Jacob shrewdly took advantage of the fact that **Laban** had gone out to distant flocks to **shear his sheep** (19). Unknown to anyone else, Rachel took with her **the images** which were equivalent to deeds to Laban's property.[5] Without leaving word of their intentions, Jacob and his wives drove their flocks south across the Euphrates **river,** down past Damascus to the highlands east of the Sea of Galilee called **mount Gilead** (21; see maps 1 and 2). When Laban heard of the flight, he gathered some **brethren** (23), i.e., relatives, and **pursued** Jacob until he caught him. But before **Laban** (24) found Jacob, **God** met him **in a dream,** warning him to treat **Jacob** neither **good or bad.** God was demonstrating that He has many ways to help His own.

4. *The Investigation* (31:25-42)

The dramatic meeting of Laban and Jacob is artfully told. Varied emotions are skillfully and subtly revealed and suspense is maintained to the end, with twists of irony seasoning the whole.

Laban first made an angry assault on Jacob, accusing him of being a thief who trafficked in human lives. He accused his son-in-law of gross discourtesy in fleeing. With a touch of self-pity, Laban depicted himself as a most generous man who had been deprived of displaying affection to his daughters and the hospitality of giving a farewell feast. Self-righteously, Laban declared he had the power to punish severely but was desisting because God had intervened.

Laban next belittled Jacob as a homesick boy who just had to go back to his **father's house** (30). But he also accused him as a vicious scoundrel who had **stolen** Laban's **gods.**

Jacob did not defend himself. He simply admitted that fear had motivated him, a fear that was based on a deep distrust of Laban's integrity and of his irresponsible use of **force** (31). But Laban's last charge stung Jacob, and impulsively he gave his father-in-law permission to search the camp, adding that anyone caught with the **gods** (32) must die. **Jacob** was unaware that his

[5]J. Paterson, "The Hurrians," *Studia Semitica et Orientalia,* II (1945), 113-14.

beloved wife, **Rachel,** was the guilty party. But **Rachel** was resourceful and claimed disability as the reason for not moving for her father. **The camel's furniture** (34) would be "the camel's saddle" (RSV). She was sitting on **the images** (35).

Chagrined that his accusation seemed unfounded, Laban's anger faded. Now Jacob became enraged and began to upbraid his father-in-law, demanding an explanation for his actions. Laban had accused him of theft but had produced no evidence. In turn, Jacob accused Laban of longtime dishonesty and ill treatment toward him. In contrast to Jacob's diligent and unstinted service, Laban had been exploitive. Only the provident mercies of the **God** of Jacob's fathers had brought him through, and what was more, God had **rebuked** (42) Laban in the recent dream.

5. *The Covenant of Peace* (31:43-55)

Laban (43) was in an awkward spot, yet he weakly protested that the women and their **children** and **the cattle** all belonged to him. If Jacob had been a slave, this would have been true in that day, but Jacob claimed to be a true son-in-law. Some scholars have concluded that he may have been actually an adopted son, in which case there would be no question about property ownership.[6]

The father-in-law was willing now to forget legal niceties in favor of **a covenant** (44). The external details of the covenant making were all according to practices current in that day—the upright **stone** (45), the raised pile of **stones** (46) on which a meal was eaten, and the vows or oaths taken there. Each named the place in his own native language, Laban in Aramaic, and Jacob in Hebrew. Both the Aramaic, **Jegar-sahadutha** (47), and the Hebrew, **Galeed,** mean "The heap of witness."

The place was also called **Mizpah** (49), meaning "watchtower." The statement in 49 has become a benediction among Christians. Yet in this immediate context the word carries a warning. The Lord was to see to it that Jacob would not move north of that boundary marker nor Laban south of it to harm each other (cf. 52). Being the stronger party, Laban did lay down several limitations for Jacob in the future. He was to treat Laban's daughters decently and refrain from taking any more

[6]J. M. Holt, *The Patriarchs of Israel* (Nashville: Vanderbilt University Press, 1964), pp. 98-102.

wives. The sense of the last part of 50 is, "Although no man is with us, remember, God is witness between you and me" (RSV). In conclusion, each took an oath, Laban in the name of **the God of Abraham, and the God of Nahor** (53). Jacob took his vow in the name of the "Fear [God] of his father Isaac" (RSV). After the vows they ate a communal meal of the meat of a sacrificed animal. **In the morning** Laban was a different man, bidding farewell with affectionate kisses (55) and a divine blessing.

Laban had been an unpredictable man. On the one hand he had shown hospitality to Abraham's servant (24:31) and then to Jacob. Outwardly he gave the appearance of kindliness until the final argument with Jacob. On the other hand, he cleverly took advantage of Jacob's ignorance of local law and did his best to exploit his daughters and Jacob to his own advantage. Ironically, he finally lost his daughters, his best shepherd, his grandchildren, and much of his flocks. After the covenant at Galeed, he was never to see them again. He gave the appearance of being pious but in fact placed no value on righteous living.

E. A Profound Spiritual Crisis, 32:1-32

Affairs with Laban had been settled, but now a greater threat lay to the south. The impending meeting with Esau shook Jacob to the depths of his soul and set the stage for one of the significant spiritual struggles and victories in the Book of Genesis. Peniel, where that event took place, has become synonymous with a spiritual crisis experience which radically transforms the soul.

1. *Stirrings of New Spiritual Awareness* (32:1-2)

Ever since Laban had become hostile to him, Jacob had been more sensitive to God's dealings and had experienced times of help and guidance. Now a visitation of **the angels of God** (1) awakened him anew and in a measure prepared him for the crisis which was to come. **Mahanaim** (2) means "two camps." It refers to Jacob's own camp and the invisible, surrounding camp of **angels of God** which protected Jacob and his family.

From 32:1-2, Alexander Maclaren preached on "Mahanaim: the Two Camps." (1) Angels of God meet us on the dusty road of common life, 1; (2) God's angels meet us punctually at the hour of need, 2; (3) The angels of God come in the form that we need, **God's host,** 2.

2. *Fear Goaded by Guilt* (32:3-8)

Jacob well knew that he must now deal with Esau, whom he had so grievously sinned against in time past, and who, as far as he knew, still intended to do him harm. But Jacob was willing to seek peace by making the first move to establish a new relationship. To that end he **sent messengers** (3) southward toward **the country of Edom** (see map 2) with the story of Jacob's success and a request that he might **find grace** (5). This phrase is equivalent to asking forgiveness for past wrongs. The **messengers returned** (6) with the news that **Esau** was headed north with **four hundred men,** apparently with evil intentions toward Jacob. Evidently, **the messengers** of Jacob had not talked to **Esau.**

Fear gripped Jacob's heart and he quickly took countermeasures. With disregard for the lives of some of his followers, he set them out ahead to take the brunt of the expected attack. This might enable others to escape.

3. *A Plea for Divine Help* (32:9-12)

Jacob's second move was to pray to God for deliverance. He possessed no pagan concept of many gods. He addressed his prayer to the **God of my father Abraham, and God of my father Isaac** (9). He identified this God with **the Lord** who had given him commands and promises. It was the same God who met His servants at any time and at any place He chose. He was the God who had the right and the power to say, "Go," and, **Return;** He had the integrity and the power to fulfill His promise to be with Jacob and to **deal well with** him.

There was no self-righteous arrogance in Jacob's prayer. He readily admitted his unworthiness to receive divine **mercies** (10), i.e., deeds of kindness. **Truth** would be messages of command, promise, and instruction. Jacob's rise from poverty to riches was wholly due to God's help. However, because of normal human fear the caravan was now split into **two bands** due to the anticipated assault by Esau.

The aim of the prayer was to gain divine deliverance, for Jacob was gripped by fear. His own death and the slaughter of his wives and children seemed imminent. He closed his prayer by again pleading the validity of the divine promises and God's faithfulness to fulfill them through preventive protection.

4. *Gifts of Reconciliation* (32:13-23)

After the prayer, Jacob added a new dimension to the purpose of his divided camp. The first groups were not simply to take the impact of an attack but were to serve as emissaries of peace, bearing gifts for Esau. Instead of two groups there were now three, each with presents and a message that Jacob was coming. Jacob's hope was to **appease** Esau's wrath (20), so that when he arrived on the scene Esau would **accept** him kindly.

The word **appease** (*kipper*) literally means "cover" but came to signify the offerer's sorrow for having committed a wrong action and his desire to ask forgiveness so that a proper and workable relationship could be established. This is the first instance where the word is used in the Bible with this meaning. When this symbolic message was conveyed to the one who had been sinned against, it was expected that anger would be changed to mercy, with a response of openness which would make reconciliation a reality.

Jacob and his family were camped at the time by the **Jabbok** (22), a river which cuts down through a deep valley from the eastern highlands to the Jordan River about halfway between the Sea of Galilee and the Dead Sea (see map 2).

5. *Crisis in the Night* (32:24-32)

Jacob had sent all others to the south bank of the river and spent the night **alone** (24). At least it started that way. In the darkness **a man,** who is identified as God in v. 30, **wrestled** with his soul. During the struggle Jacob suffered a dislocated hip, but he prolonged the combat by insisting that he would not cease **except thou bless me** (26). Jacob needed help desperately, but before he gained it he had to confess the sin which was symbolized by his name, "heel-catcher," or "deceitful one."

In response, God changed his name to **Israel** (28), "one who strives, or prevails with God." The change of name, as with Abraham and with Sarah, indicated a change in status as well as a changed inner being. Jacob was not quite sure who was struggling with him until the end of the match. He then arose and testified to his new understanding by calling the place **Peniel** (30), or **Penuel** (31), meaning "face-to-face with God." His own new physical disability was to be a constant witness to him that the battle had indeed been real. His descendents were also to memorialize the event by abstaining from eating the **thigh** (32), or sciatic muscle, of animals which they used for food.

In 32:22-30 we see how "Jacob Becomes Israel." (1) Jacob the supplanter, 27; (2) Jacob the wrestler, 24-26; (3) Jacob the prevailer, 28 (G. B. Williamson).

Jacob's nocturnal struggle bore the basic characteristics of the significant spiritual experiences of men and women in both the Old and the New Testaments. Charles Wesley understood the Peniel episode to be a type of Christian experience, basing upon it his well-known hymn "Come, O Thou Traveler Unknown."

The fact that sin against others is also an act which affects God's relationship with man is central to this event. Jacob must not only face Esau; he must face God first of all. Actually, God faced him in the caldron of his guilt to bring him to a full recognition of the sinfulness of his being, and the need for a radical change.

Jacob was faced with a difficult problem. If he failed to meet his alienation from Esau realistically, or tried to solve it in a devious, inadequate manner, he ran the risk of further inflaming Esau's anger. Likewise, if he did not confess his sin to God, he would incur divine displeasure.

At first Jacob tended to resort to devious devices. He feared Esau's power and he loved his own life and his wealth. He was therefore willing to sacrifice some of his retinue to Esau in order to escape with his life and a few possessions. He next thought of sending gifts and mediators before him to Esau. In prayer he admitted his unworthiness but did not admit his sin. He wanted a blessing but loathed to repudiate his own deceitful nature.

But Jacob won the victory because he stayed on solid spiritual ground throughout his struggle. He asserted God's lordship over his life and claimed the promises God gave to him at Bethel and in Haran. He rested his future on their validity and God's faithfulness to fulfill them. He stated his needs, pled for help, and with determination held on for a blessing even at the price of confessing the sin of his inner perversion. He then publicly witnessed to God's help by giving a name to the place.[7] Jacob established a basic gospel dictum: faith is acceptance of undeserved mercy from God.

[7]A. Clarke, "Genesis," *The Holy Bible with Commentary and Critical Notes* (New York: Carlton and Porter, n.d.), I, 200-202.

In 32:9-12, 24-30 we see where "God Confronts a Man the Second Time." (1) A man whose resources were not enough, 9-12; (2) A man alone with God, 24; (3) A man who would not be denied, 26; (4) The confession that brings the blessing, 27-30 (A. F. Harper).

F. Brothers Reunited, 33:1-17

There are earlier stories in the Book of Genesis which describe fatal conflicts between brothers (4:1-8) and deep differences between brothers (9:22-23; 21:9-14). This is the first recorded instance of a reconciliation between brothers who had been separated by strife. The story is skillfully told.

1. *A Meeting Filled with Emotion* (33:1-4)

Jacob was still unsure of his brother's intentions and even made another rearrangement of his family. This time he put the two secondary wives, Bilhah and Zilpah, with **their children** (2) out in front, then **Leah and her children,** and finally **Rachel and Joseph.** This order indicates something of the relative value he placed on the various members of his family. But this time, instead of remaining behind as he first intended (32:20), he limped ahead of them all, and bowed himself to the ground **seven times** (3).

To the surprise of everyone, **Esau** (4) was not hostile, but deeply moved with joy as he **embraced** his brother **and kissed him.** Together **they wept.**

2. *Getting Acquainted Again* (33:5-11)

Esau knew Jacob but not the others, so Jacob introduced his family group by group, and each group in turn courteously **bowed themselves** (6). The older brother had been puzzled by the three bands of servants with presents which had already met him. Jacob explained that the presents were given in order that he might **find grace** (8) with his estranged brother. But Esau had long since forgotten his grudge against Jacob, and indicated that he did not need the presents. However he took them when Jacob insisted. They had not been needed to mollify Esau's anger, for God had long since prepared his heart to forgive Jacob. But Jacob's heart had only been prepared that very morning, so now the presents represented gratitude and affection instead of appeasement.

3. *Preparing to Part* (33:12-17)

Esau wanted Jacob to return home with him to the rugged, mountain fastness of **Seir** (14), located southeast of the Dead Sea (see map 2). But Jacob pleaded that his flocks and family burdened him too much to keep pace with Esau and his men. He requested and was granted permission to move south at his own speed. The separation was amicable and in marked contrast to the way the brothers had parted 20 years previously.

G. Tragedy at Shechem, 33:18—34:31

This painful story begins a series which center on the qualifications of various sons of Jacob as worthy bearers of the covenant promises and responsibilities. The community at Shechem followed different standards in regard to women than those honored by Jacob and his family. When Dinah was harmed by the clash of these standards, the savage nature of several of Jacob's sons boiled to the surface.

1. *Settling in a New Community* (33:18-20)

After some time near **Succoth** (17) on the east bank of the Jordan, Jacob's family moved into the highlands to the west and seemed to like what they found there. Abraham had also lived briefly at **Shechem** (18; cf. 12:6, where Sichem equals Shechem). But Jacob decided to take permanent advantage of the rich pastures east of the city. He purchased land and set up a place of worship which he called **El-elohe-Is-ra-el** (20), that is, "God, the God of Israel."

2. *The Shameful Deed* (34:1-5)

As indicated by the stories of Rebekah (24:15-28) and of Rachel (29:6-12), the people of Haran allowed their girls considerable freedom of movement away from the house or the camp, because the moral standards of the area secured their safety. Jacob's family seemingly expected the same consideration for their women from the Shechem community. They were in for a jolting surprise.

Dinah (1) had gone alone to see some friends and was molested in the field by the young **son** (2) of the local **prince. Shechem the son of Hamor the Hivite** probably belonged to a Hurrian group which had migrated into the area sometime before. It must have already been a decade since Jacob had said his second farewell to Esau, for **Dinah** was the seventh child of Leah and she was now a teen-ager.

Shechem assaulted **Dinah** and then tried to persuade—**spake kindly** (3) is not strong enough—her to accept his advances on a permanent basis. He was successful, for he took her to his home and demanded that his father get the girl for him as a **wife** (4). The youth had no sense of wrongdoing but was quite arrogant in the way he spoke to his father. When **Jacob** (5) heard the news, he did not make a move until **his sons** returned from the fields with their flocks; they acted as a family unit in making their decisions.

3. *The Negotiations* (34:6-19)

The crisis required a conference between the two families involved. **Hamor** (6) and **Shechem** represented one side, and **Jacob** and his angry **sons** (7) represented the other. On the surface the meeting was polite, but a seething resentment boiled in the hearts of Jacob's sons, for to them this **thing** (Dinah's defilement) **ought not to be done.**

Hamor's argument was simply that Shechem wanted Dinah. But he extended an inducement. Jacob's family would be granted full citizen rights of intermarriage, free movement, participation in **trade** (10), and property ownership. **Shechem** impulsively interjected the possibility of a sizable dowry (11), for he desperately wanted Dinah for a wife.

It was **the sons of Jacob** (13) who replied with an innocent-sounding proposition, which nevertheless had lethal overtones. They insisted that their own peculiar custom of circumcision be accepted by the entire male population of the city; otherwise they would leave the area. Not suspecting a ruse, the father and son agreed to the plan.

4. *Open Trust and Hidden Guile* (34:20-31)

Hamor and Shechem (20) carried the proposition back to the **city,** where the men were accustomed to gather for community discussions and decisions in **the gate of their city.** The arguments of the father and son convinced their fellow citizens of the advantages of intermarriage with Jacob's family and it was agreed that submitting to circumcision was not a high price. **All that went out of the gate of his city** (24) is an idiom for men capable of bearing arms. They were all **circumcised,** an operation which incapacitated them for several days.

Simeon and Levi (25) knew that the circumcised males would not be able to fight, so at the opportune moment they moved into town, **slew all the males,** including **Hamor and Shechem** (26), and rescued their sister. The other **sons of Jacob** (27) then followed up with a general looting of the city and the flocks. They took the survivors captive.

Jacob was deeply shocked, and rebuked the two who had carried out the crime. He knew what the reaction in the surrounding countryside would be, and that his own clan could be wiped out. But the boys were unrepentant, retorting with the question: **Should he deal with our sister as with an harlot?** (31) The answer, of course, is "No!" But in their passion, the sons of Jacob were blinded to other alternatives to violence. Jacob realized that the event had clearly disqualified these two older sons as worthy to bear covenant responsibilities in the future. He did not forget, but he reserved his greater punishment until later (cf. 49:5-7).

H. The Covenant Renewed at Bethel, 35:1-15

In the previous incident, Jacob had been largely in the background, yet seriously hurt by all that transpired. In this story he has a dominant role again, leading his family into significant experiences which culminated at Bethel, where he had first met God.

1. *A Divine Command* (35:1)

In the depths of his acute spiritual suffering, due to the crime against Dinah and the crimes of his sons against Shechem, **Jacob** (1) was met by **God.** The word was clear-cut and simple. Jacob was to **go up to Beth-el** and worship the God whose only outward expression was to be **an altar.** The visit to **Beth-el** was to be significant because it was there that **God** had first appeared to Jacob.

2. *Rejection of Idolatry* (35:2-5)

Apart from the brief reference to images which Rachel had stolen (31:19, 30-35), this is the first description of idol possession within the patriarchal family. Evidently Jacob had been aware of their presence but had not taken drastic action until now. In this context the command, **Be clean** (2), means to be rid of idols and the practices associated with them. The other command, **Change your garments,** seems to have had a symbolic meaning, denoting a change of religious loyalties and practice. In exchange for worship of nature gods and superstitions, Jacob promised a time of worship of the true **God** (3), who had answered his prayers and had made real His presence through many years. God was distinct from nature, yet ever powerful in His personal relationship with those who yielded to Him. The power of His presence was sensed by all in the family, as indicated by their obedience. The **earrings** (4) were also an expression of heathen belief, a kind of good-luck charm. Moffatt calls them "their amulets of ear-rings." The clan had been in mortal danger, but God saw to it that in place of violence against Jacob's family **terror** (5) would be felt by the inhabitants of the area.

3. *The Second Divine Appearance at Bethel* (35:6-15)

It must have been a solemn occasion for Jacob as he came back to **Beth-el** (6) and built the **altar** (7) preparatory to worship. Vivid memories of the event which took place so many years before must have flashed through his mind. A note of sorrow was added to the other emotions when **Deborah Rebekah's nurse died** and **was buried** (8). Scripture leaves no record of Rebekah's death or of when her nurse had joined Jacob's family circle, but she was evidently with them long enough to gain their affection. They called the grave site **Allon-bachuth,** which means "oak of weeping."

The first element of God's appearance to Jacob was a blessing which included a reiteration of the new fact of Jacob's life, the change of his name to **Israel** (10). Since this was related to two important divine visitations, it would take on added meaning for the patriarch and for his descendents.

The other element was a repetition of the covenant first made with Abraham. After God identified himself, He gave a command (11) much like the one He had given to Adam and Eve (1:28). This command was related to the promises long since given to Abraham (17:5-6), that his posterity would include **a nation and company of nations . . . and kings** (11). The promise was repeated that **the land** (12) was to be his and his children's as a gift. The theophany (divine appearance) was an act of God's commitment to past promises, and a validation of present spiritual realities.

Jacob's response was much like his first encounter with God at the same place. He **set up a pillar . . . of stone** (14) and

poured oil on it. This was a public witness that Jacob's God was in truth the God who reveals himself to man. The proclamation of the place's new name, **Beth-el** (15, house of God) was likewise a witness to Jacob's faith.

I. A Journey Shadowed by Sorrow, 35:16-29

God's presence did not eliminate sorrow or pain from Jacob's life, but it did prepare him and sustain him during the time of sorrow. His disposition now was one of gentleness and compassion, showing a remarkable capacity to bear heartache.

1. *Loss of Beloved Rachel* (35:16-20)

Jacob's favorite wife, **Rachel** (16), delivered a second son, but at the cost of her life. With her last breath, Rachel named the child **Ben-oni** (18, son of my sorrow), but Jacob broke precedent and overruled Rachel's choice. Instead, he called the boy **Benjamin,** literally, "son of the right hand." Since, for the Semitic people, the right hand was a place of honor and strength, some commentators have assumed that this new name signified "Son of Good Fortune."[8] In view of the circumstances, another explanation seems more probable. When an inhabitant of Palestine designated directions, he customarily stood facing the east; hence the right hand would be south. Rachel's second son was the only child in Jacob's family born south of Haran; therefore it is possible that the name meant "son of the south" or "southerner."[9]

Tradition has long held that Jacob's retinue was camped on a hilltop about two miles south of present-day Jerusalem. The place still carries the name *Ramat Rahel,* i.e., "Hilltop of Rachel." Presently there is a small building along the road to **Bethlehem** (19), a few miles south of *Ramat Rahel,* which is known as the "Tomb of Rachel." Whether this is the actual location of the **pillar** (20) which Jacob reared in honor of Rachel is not known.

2. *Lust Overcame Reuben* (35:21-22*a*)

The tower of Edar (21) has come down in history only as a place where a gross sin was committed. Otherwise its location is unknown. The incident that happened there compounded Jacob's sorrow. His eldest son, **Reuben** (22), violated the standards of

[8]Leupold, *op. cit.,* II, 924. [9]Speiser, *Genesis, op. cit.,* p. 274.

morality by committing incest with **Bilhah,** one of Jacob's secondary wives. The act was not only a flagrant sin against the sanctity of marriage; it was also a contemptuous challenge of his father's tribal authority. Jacob did not punish Reuben immediately but he did not forget (see 49:3-4). As far as Jacob was concerned, the act ruled **Reuben** out as a covenant leader.

3. *A Roster of Jacob's Sons* (35:22*b*-26)

The sons of Jacob (22) are listed according to their mothers, not according to their ages. Also the sons of the wives, **Leah** (23) and **Rachel** (24), are placed before the sons of the handmaids, **Bilhah** (25) and **Zilpah** (26). This summary is a bridge which ushers in the stories that depict the fortunes of his sons.

The phrase **which were born to him in Padan-aram** (26) is modified by the story of Benjamin's birth (35:16-18). It was not deemed necessary to repeat that which was obvious.

4. *Isaac's Death* (35:27-29)

Finally, Jacob returned to his aged father, whom he had wronged through deceit many years before. Isaac's earlier sickness (27:1-2) had not been fatal. Rebekah had long since passed away. Old wounds had healed and the homecoming was in peace. So also Isaac's death was in peace, for the two brothers, **Esau and Jacob** (29), joined in the burial of their father in the cave of Machpelah.

This series of three experiences (19-29) pointed up a real problem for Jacob. There were no more sons, and the oldest members of the 12 were showing distressing signs of moral turpitude. The past generation was now gone and Jacob was the only bearer of the covenant responsibilities alive. Was the covenant to die with him? If not, who was worthy to take his place?

Section VI *Esau, the Man Who Took His Brother Back*

Genesis 36:1-43

This chapter is a compilation of six ancient lists which are related to Esau and his posterity. They are placed here in order to give him an exit from the story of God's dealings with the lineage of Abraham. From this point on the Scriptures depict the Edomites as in some way opposed to the Israelites. Never are the Edomites pictured as being genuinely religious, though archaeological research has shown that they did possess pagan idols.

The first list (36:1-8) deals with Esau's wives and their children and is oriented toward Canaan. The second one also includes the grandchildren but is tied to the land of Edom (Seir, see map 2), an area southeast of the Dead Sea, rising to over 3,000 feet above sea level in some spots. The third list designates the sons of Esau as heads of clans. The fourth gives the family tree of the Horites, "cave dwellers," who occupied the land prior to the coming of Esau's family. The fifth genealogy records a group of Edomite kings who preceded the appearance of kings in Israel. The sixth list enumerates descendents of Esau according to geographical areas which became, more or less, their respective homes in ancient times. A list very similar to these six appears in I Chron. 1:35-54.

A. Esau's Wives and Their Sons, 36:1-8

In 26:34 and 28:9 the wives of Esau are listed as Judith, Bashemath, and Mahalath. Since in the ancient Near East girls often changed names at the time of marriage, it would seem that Bashemath (26:34) was the same as **Adah** (36:2), and that Mahalath (28:9) was the same as **Bashemath** of 36:3. The Judith of 26:34 appears to have been a different girl from **Aholibamah** (36:2). Evidently "Judith the daughter of Beeri the Hittite" (26:34) either was childless or died at an early age, and **Aholibamah** was taken as a replacement. It is to be observed that the name of her father, **Anah,** and grandfather, **Zibeon,** appear in the list of Seirites (36:20). The Samaritan, Greek, and Syriac texts have "daughter of Anah, son of Zibeon," which is likely the correct reading. The term **Hivite** should probably be understood as a synonym for "Horite" (36:20), which happens frequently in Scripture, or as a textual variant, since the Hebrew characters for *w* and *r* are only slightly different in shape.

The departure of Esau for **mount Seir** (8) seems to have been a peaceful separation from Jacob. The phrase **the land . . . could not bear them** (7) suggests that there was insufficient pasturage for their extensive holdings of livestock.

B. Esau's Sons and Grandsons, 36:9-14

The Edomites were now in **mount Seir** (9) and this genealogy carries the lineage into another generation. **Eliphaz** (12) had a secondary wife, whose son was Amalek. His descendents were to become implacable foes of the people of Israel.

C. The Prominence of Esau's Descendents, 36:15-19

Notable in this record is the presence of the Hebrew term *alluf,* which KJV translates as **dukes** (15), following the Latin Vulgate, *dux.* The root meaning of the term is "ox," but a close cousin, *elef,* means "thousand." This has led some to suppose that what is meant here is "leader of a thousand."[1] Some translators prefer "chief." It has been proposed that a better translation is "clans" on the basis of the recurring phrase, **in the land of Edom** (16).

D. The Sons of the Cave Dwellers, 36:20-30

This list related to the people **who inhabited the land** (20) before Esau's arrival seems to indicate that Esau's descendents and the Seirites, who already dwelt in the land, soon intermarried and blended into one people.

These people were descendents of the **Horite.** The term means "cave dweller," which seems to have been the mode of living for early inhabitants of Seir. **Horite** is also a name which the Hebrews used for a non-Semitic nation known to us as Hurrians which dominated the Upper Tigris valley, but had colonists in Palestine (see comments on Genesis 34). It is doubtful

[1]Skinner, *op. cit.,* pp. 432-34.

that any physical relationship existed between the Hurrians and these people.[2]

E. Edom's Kings, 36:31-39

The focus of interest here returns to the Edomites with the spotlight on the power which Esau's descendents gained.

The office of king was not determined by heredity but was granted to men who had proved themselves as leaders of men. For centuries this was a characteristic of the Edomites. At that early date **Edom** (31) did not have an established city.

Some have argued that the phrase **before there reigned any king over the children of Israel** shows that Moses did not write the Pentateuch. The assumption would be that the phrase indicates a date during Israel's kingdom period or later for the composition of the Pentateuch. But it has not been proved conclusively by archaeological research that Edom did not have kings at Moses' time. It should also be observed that, even if this phrase came from a later period, it can be understood as a marginal note which crept into the text with no bearing on Mosaic authorship *per se.*

F. Areas Where the Edomites Lived, 36:40-43

If, in this list, the name **Elah** (41) is understood as a shorter form of Elath, then all the names recorded here would be designations of geographical areas to the southeast and to the south of the Dead Sea.

The term **dukes** (40, *alluf*) appears here again and the same problem arises as in 36:15-19. Is the best translation of the word "chiefs" or "clans"? Or is it here a name for the territory governed by these people? The issue is not easily solved and at present there is no answer to this question.

[2]See C. A. Simpson "Genesis" (Exegesis), *The Interpreter's Bible,* ed. G. A. Buttrick (New York: Abingdon-Cokesbury Press, 1952), I, 746, which has a contrary view to Speiser, *Genesis, op. cit.,* pp. 282-83.

Section VII Joseph, the Man Whom God Preserved

Genesis 37:1—50:26

The narrative of Joseph's trials and triumphs is one of the best loved stories of the OT. With c. 37, the focus of the Book of Genesis shifts from Jacob to his favorite son. Joseph at first appears as a typical spoiled child. He lacked an easy rapport with his brothers, who regarded him as an insufferable informer to their father. And his dreams, which Joseph told with relish, were effective in creating strong hostile feelings toward him. As a result, a series of tragedies overwhelmed Joseph, finally sending him to a dismal prison. But Joseph was a young man of strong faith, and God had not forgotten him. A sudden turn of events brought him to power in one of the great nations of the ancient Near East.

From his new position of power, Joseph was able to help his family when they came to Egypt for grain. He was also able to chastise his brothers and then to forgive them. As a result, a grief-burdened Jacob found new hope and a new joy in life; also his family found a new home in the land of Goshen in Egypt.

A. Sold as a Slave, 37:1-36

Deceit had played an unsavory role in Jacob's youthful dealings with Isaac and with Esau, also in Laban's relationships with him. Now it was to reenter the family circle through the tension which had built up between Jacob's older sons and Joseph. The suffering it left in its wake was to follow Jacob for many years, due to the cruel sale of Joseph to foreigners by his brothers.

1. *Joseph's Favored Position* (37:1-4)

Jacob's father, Isaac, had the weakness of preferring one of his sons above another (25:28). Now **Jacob** (1) himself was doing the same, perhaps because Joseph reminded him of Rachel. The result was a rift between **Joseph** (2), who was now **seventeen years old,** and his half brothers. Part of their resentment seems justified, for Joseph was given to tattling, especially on the less favored **sons of Bilhah** and **Zilpah.** Added to this was Jacob's provision of a special attire for Joseph which set him off from the others.

How to translate the Hebrew *ketonet passim,* which KJV has as **coat of many colours** (3), has long been a problem. There is no question about *ketonet;* it means "coat, tunic, or undergarment." The other word, *passim,* has the meaning of "extremity," or "wrist," and perhaps "ankles." Hence some translators have used the phrase "coat of sleeves." In II Sam. 13:18 the same Hebrew phrase occurs as descriptive of the special garments worn by Tamar and other daughters of the king.

There is a parallel expression in Akkadian, *kitu* (*kutinnu*) *pisannu.* It designates a robe, decorated with gold ornaments, which was placed on images of goddesses. This has led some recent scholars to suggest the translation, "ornamented tunic."[1] In any case, the garment set Joseph off from the others. The half brothers recognized it as a mark of distinction, and **hated him** (4) for it.

2. *Dreams That Aggravated* (37:5-11)

Perhaps it was innocent naiveté, or it might have been an artless arrogance—nevertheless **Joseph** (5) loved to tell his half brothers of unusual dreams which he experienced. It served only to increase their hatred of him.

On the surface, the first **dream** (5-8) which Joseph told was harmless. The dream was a harvesting scene, but the **sheaves** (7) set up by his half brothers **made obeisance** to Joseph's **sheaf.** His listeners immediately caught the implication and indignantly asked, **Shalt thou indeed reign over us?** (8) To them the answer could only be an emphatic No. Little did they realize that it would indeed come true.

The other **dream** (9) had to do with objects in the sky. **The sun and the moon and the eleven stars made obeisance to** Joseph. Hearing an account of the dream, Jacob **rebuked** (10) the boy, for he understood that the sun symbolized him, the moon represented Rachel, and the eleven stars his other sons. But the father was sobered by the story and **observed the saying** (11), i.e., kept it in his memory.

[1]Speiser, *Genesis, op. cit.,* pp. 289-90.

3. *The Errand Boy* (37:12-22)

In the highlands of central Palestine, flocks range over a great expanse of territory to find forage. Jacob's sons had been out for some time, pasturing near **Shechem** (13) and he desired information concerning their welfare. He doubtless remembered dangers due to revenge for his sons' attack on the people of the land (cf. 34:24-30). Jacob therefore sent **Joseph** (13) on the trip to **Shechem** (14), which would be about 60 miles from **Hebron** (see map 2). From a friendly man at **Shechem,** Joseph discovered that the flocks had moved on to **Dothan** (17), about 20 miles farther to the northwest.

When Joseph appeared on the horizon, the brothers quickly **conspired against him** (18). They had murderous intent but plotted that no one should discover their involvement. Their alibi would be that **some evil beast hath devoured him** (20). They hoped thus to nullify the predictive force of Joseph's **dreams.** But one of the brothers disagreed. **Reuben** (21) would not listen to plans to shed blood, and talked them into imprisoning the boy in a **pit** (22), or cistern, nearby. He intended to secretly release Joseph, so he could return to **his father.**

4. *The Nefarious Sale* (37:23-28)

Joseph must have been surprised and shocked to be treated so brutally by his half brothers. In moments he was **stript** of his clothing (23) and lowered into an **empty** cistern (24).

While the brothers were eating, a company of **Ishmeelites** (25) approached. They were transporting goods **from Gilead,** which is the highlands east of the Jordan River (see map 2). The shipment included **spicery** (tragacanth gum, which exudes from a low bush); **balm,** which is harvested by cutting incisions in the bark of the mastic tree; and **myrrh,** another gum which exudes from the leaves of the cistus rose.[2] The Egyptians bought these for their embalming industry and for medicine.

Judah (26), who had no stomach for his brothers' plans, persuaded them to sell Joseph to the **merchantmen** (28). The fact that the name **Midianites** appears here and in v. 36, whereas **Ishmeelites** occurs in 25 and in the last part of 28, has been confusing to many readers. Some scholars have assumed that two

[2]W. Walker, *All the Plants of the Bible* (New York: Harper & Bros., 1957).

stories of the incident have been interwoven here. However, these are simply two names for the same men—descendents of Abraham and of nomadic and trader habits. Midianites are identified as Ishmaelites again in Judg. 8:22-24.

When the caravan arrived at the brothers' camp, they (the brothers, not the Midianites) raised the boy from **the pit** and sold him for **twenty pieces of silver** (28). These were not coins but pieces of metal weighed in balances. Compare this price with the values expressed in Lev. 27:3-7. The normal price of a slave in Moses' time was 30 pieces of silver (Exod. 21:32; Zech. 11:12; cf. Matt. 26:15). The caravan took **Joseph into Egypt.**

5. *The Lie and the Agony* (37:29-36)

While the brothers were eating, **Reuben** (29) evidently had been caring for the flock as a ruse so that he could secretly release **Joseph.** But when he finally got to the **pit,** he was shocked to find Joseph gone. He was so overwhelmed with grief that **he rent** (tore) **his clothes.** He expressed his grief to the others (30) but they ignored him. To cover their deed, they **killed a kid of the goats,** and **dipped the coat** (31) which belonged to Joseph **in the blood.** This they brought to their father, knowing he would assume that **Joseph** had been killed by **an evil beast** (33).

Jacob's reaction was immediate and painful. Following the custom of his day, as had Reuben (29), **Jacob rent his clothes, and put sackcloth upon his loins** (34). His expressions of prolonged sorrow alarmed the family and they tried **to comfort him** (35). Ironically, they could have allayed some of his sorrow by telling him the truth of the matter, but even Reuben did not divulge the secret. Meanwhile Joseph had been **sold** (36) to an Egyptian **officer** called **Potiphar.**

B. The Moral Laxity of Judah, 38:1-30

This story seems like an intrusion into the story of Joseph. Perhaps it was inserted here to clarify why Judah, who figured significantly in the story later, was disqualified to be the fourth-generation leader in the covenant with God. It strikingly reveals the acute moral temptations which living among the Canaanites brought into the lives of Jacob's sons.

The events of the story cover a period of time parallel to Joseph's trials and triumphs in Egypt, and offer a partial explanation for the final move to Egypt. If the integrity of the covenant people was to be preserved, they must, for a time, be removed from the corruption of Canaan's religious and social life.

1. *A Marriage Lacking Covenant Convictions* (38:1-5)

In his dealings with his **Canaanite** (2) neighbors, **Judah** one day saw a Canaanite girl who attracted him. He married **Shuah** and in due time she gave birth to three sons, **Er** (3), **Onan** (4), and **Shelah** (5). These all grew up heavily influenced by the lax moral standards of their Canaanite mother and her relatives.

2. *A Levirate Marriage Gone Awry* (38:6-11)

When **Er** was old enough to be married, normally in the mid-teens, Judah obtained a Canaanite girl called **Tamar** (6) as **a wife** for him. But **Er** was a **wicked** (7) fellow and met an early death before a child was born to the couple. The text indicates that the boy's death was an act of divine judgment.

The custom of levirate marriage was widely practiced among people of the ancient Near East because great importance was placed on preserving the name of the eldest son by means of a son.[3] If the oldest son died prematurely without a son, it was the responsibility of the next oldest son to take the widow as his own wife. However, the children born to this union would legally belong to the dead brother rather than to the actual father.

In this instance the next oldest son, **Onan** (8), refused to carry through with his responsibility. He showed disdain for Er and contempt for Tamar in a shameful manner. His punishment was death, ordained by **the Lord** (10). The third boy was too young for marriage yet, so **Judah** (11) told **Tamar** to wait in her **father's house.** But Judah could not resist the suggestion that she may have been at fault for his other sons' deaths.

3. *Judah's Evasion of Responsibility* (38:12-23)

After proper mourning for his deceased wife, Judah was busy shearing sheep with his friend and possibly his father-in-law, **Hirah** (cf. vv. 1-2). **Tamar** (13), tired of waiting for **Shelah** (14), who was now fully grown, decided to force Judah to act.

She was much more concerned about the legal aspects of her situation than with morals. The common law held that she

[3]E. W. Heaton, *Everyday Life in Old Testament Times* (New York: Charles Scribner's Sons, 1956), pp. 77-78; de Vaux, *op. cit.*, pp. 37-38.

had the right to have children by a brother, or at least a relative, of her dead husband. In fact, she had an obligation to provide a son for him. Since Judah seemed to be deliberately keeping **Shelah** from her, she decided to involve Judah himself. She had no legal recourse to courts, so she depended on clever deception.

Making careful note of Judah's movements, she saw that he was going alone to Enaim or Enam (Josh. 15:34). **An open place** (14) is more correctly a translation of the town's name, **Enaim.** At exactly the right moment she changed clothes for a **veil,** the garment of a common **harlot** (15, *zonah*). She stationed herself by the roadway to lure **Judah,** who reacted just as she thought he would. Tamar was not so interested in pay—the **kid from the flock** (17)—as she was in obtaining something from Judah that would positively identify him later. She insisted on and got his **signet** (18), which was a seal, probably cylindrical in shape with a hole through the center lengthwise and a distinctive device carved on it. The **bracelets,** or better, "strings," were passed through the seal to suspend it about the neck. She also got a **staff** which the leader of a clan or tribe carried as a symbol of authority. No one could mistake the ownership of these items.

After the affair was completed, Tamar returned home immediately and put on **the garments of her widowhood** (19), and Judah returned to his flocks. Judah was sensitive, perhaps with an underlying sense of guilt, about personally taking the **kid** (20) to the supposed harlot, so he sent it by a **friend.** The **Adullamite** friend did not inquire about the location of a common prostitute (*zonah*) but for a Canaanite temple prostitute (*qedeshah*), who had a higher status in Canaanite social circles. Everyone professed ignorance of such a person in the vicinity. So the Adullamite reported back to **Judah,** who immediately realized that he could **be shamed** (23, blackmailed) by the person who possessed the articles which identified him. Judah seemed frustrated and nonplussed. In self-justification he said to his friend, "You see, I sent this kid, and you could not find her" (RSV).

4. *The Trap Sprung* (38:24-26)

Three months after this incident (24) the rumor came to Judah that **Tamar** was **with child.** Clearly she had been unfaithful to her obligations to Judah's remaining son. This infuriated Judah and he demanded that she be publicly **burnt** alive (cf. Lev. 21:9 and Deut. 22:20-24).

When Tamar was brought out for execution, she requested only one privilege, the identification of the man who owned certain objects in her possession. As soon as **Judah** (26) saw them, he realized what Tamar had done and how his own moral looseness had made him vulnerable to her devices. He admitted that he was the man responsible for her condition.

Judah's remark, **She has been more righteous than I** (26), provides an interesting sidelight on the meaning of the Hebrew term *tsedeqah.* Basically it has the legal connotation of "being in the right" or "having a just cause." To us Tamar was morally shameless, but in a technical sense, within the levirate marriage law, she was in the right. She had obtained a child by the man who was responsible for seeing to it that a relative of her husband be given to her as a substitute husband. Judah was publicly shown to be derelict in his duty of giving Shelah to Tamar, and to have been the man responsible for making pregnant the woman he had angrily condemned to death. Obviously, neither could come up to the highest concepts of righteousness in the Bible, but Judah was more in the wrong than Tamar.

5. *Tamar's Twins* (38:27-30)

The account of the birth of the children describes an unusual incident which gave rise to the names of Judah's twin sons. The hand of one twin appeared and was marked with **a scarlet thread** (28), but the hand drew back and the other child was born first. The name, **Pharez** (29), means "to make a breach," or "to forge through," so it designated his aggressive character. The meaning of the other name is uncertain. It was through **Pharez** that the line of descent ran to Boaz, to David, and to Jesus Christ (I Chron. 2:3-15; Matt. 1:3-16; Luke 3:23-33).

C. Joseph's Trials in Egypt, 39:1—40:23

Joseph's reactions to stress and misfortune were remarkably different from those expressed by his brothers when they were faced with difficult situations. They had reacted with strong negative feelings involving jealousy, lust, and hatred which issued in murder (34:25), in incest (35:22), in plots to kill, then to sell into slavery (37:20-28), in callous deception of their father (37:31-33), and in irresponsible immorality (38:15-26).

In contrast, Joseph was a young man of remarkable moral strength who did not give way to bitterness, self-pity, or despair.

Instead, he overcame his difficulties with a courageous sense of responsibility and of high moral values. In every situation he demonstrated confidence in God, kindly wisdom in his dealings with others, and honesty in regard to every trust bestowed upon him.

1. *Imprisoned on a False Charge* (39:1-20)

Joseph's new Egyptian master, **Potiphar** (1), soon noticed the unusual qualities of his new slave's character and entrusted more and more of his household tasks to him. The testimony of the text is that **the Lord was with Joseph** (2) and that even the pagan master observed this fact. As a result, the Word says that **Joseph found grace in his sight** (4). This expression means that Potiphar reacted with benevolence and kindliness toward Joseph and elevated him to a more personal relationship of service in the affairs of the household. With the raise in status there was an enlargement of responsibility, which Joseph met with skill, so that through Joseph **the Lord blessed the Egyptian's house** (5), i.e., the affairs of the master prospered.

The phrase **well favoured** (6) speaks of Joseph's fine appearance and sets the stage for the incident that follows. It illustrates well the dangers of high office in a pagan home. The **master's wife** (7) was a pampered and impulsive person with nothing to do. She lacked moral standards, and when her husband was away found other men altogether too attractive. Joseph soon became a mark of her attentions and at the first opportunity was propositioned by her.

In contrast to Judah (38:16), Joseph resisted the invitation. He gave a reasoned explanation of how his position with its burden of accountability would make such an act a violation of trust. **Wotteth not** (8) means "knows not." Above all that, it would be a **great wickedness, and sin against God** (9). The woman didn't see it that way, so continued to tease and invite him. Finally, at an advantageous moment she became insistent, grabbing **his garment** (12) to pull him toward her. Joseph got free and ran from the house, but in doing so he left **his garment** behind, which she used effectively against him. When **she called unto the men of her house** (14), she accused the **Hebrew** (taking full advantage of race prejudice) of improper advances and claimed that she had resisted by crying out **with a loud voice.** She repeated this charge to her husband later, and as a result

Joseph was put in prison. The fact that Joseph was not immediately killed suggests that the **master** (20), though angry, was not wholly convinced of his wife's innocence in the matter.[4]

2. *An Interpreter of Dreams* (39:21—40:23)

Joseph's control of his own attitudes was important. But the writer of this story understood that his good rapport with **the keeper of the prison** (21) was due to the Lord's **mercy** (*chesed*). This word is intimately tied up with the covenant relationship and it thus becomes clear that Joseph had been selected by God as Jacob's successor in the covenant framework. Soon Joseph was in charge of many details of prison life. This was also due to the fact that **the Lord was with him,** and **made it to prosper** (23). More than attitude control and efficient work was involved. In Joseph's life there was an all-important plus, God's active concern and **mercy.**

Being a servant in the court of **the king of Egypt** (1) was risky business. Soon two of the king's servants arrived **in ward** (3, in **prison**), due to some unnamed indiscretions. They were put in Joseph's care.

One night each of the new prisoners had **a dream** (5) which puzzled and depressed him. **According to the interpretation of his dream** is better "each dream with its own meaning" (RSV). They told Joseph, who in turn offered to assist, saying, **Do not interpretations belong to God?** (8) Whereupon each related his **dream.**

The chief butler (9) said that his **dream** was of a **vine,** which had **three branches** (10) that produced **ripe grapes.** The butler took the **Pharaoh's cup** (11), squeezed the juice of **the grapes** into it, and put it into the **Pharaoh's hand.** Joseph's interpretation was that **the three branches are three days** (12), and that within that time the butler would be restored to his old job. **Lift up thine head** (13) is better "release you" (Moffatt) or "summon you" (Smith-Goodspeed).

Joseph took advantage of the moment to make a personal appeal that, when reinstated, the **butler** would **shew kindness** (14) by mentioning to the **Pharaoh** the injustices which had put Joseph in prison in Egypt. He hoped that this would lead to his release.

[4]Keil and Delitzsch, *op. cit.,* pp. 345-46.

The chief baker (16) next told his dream, in which he was carrying **three white baskets** (16, *salley hori*). **White** is a good translation of this term if it is understood to refer to white bread, but the same phrase can mean "wicker baskets." Again the number three designated **three days** (18). But this man would not be restored. He would also be summoned by the Pharaoh, but as RSV puts it, "Pharaoh will lift up your head—from you!" The **birds** (17) pecking at the baked goods gave this ill omen, for they would consume his **flesh** (19) while his body was hanged **on a tree.** The term **lifted up the head** (20) is employed the third time to denote release from prison. The fate of each man was as Joseph had predicted. However, to Joseph's dismay, the man whose life was spared **forgat him** (23).

D. Joseph's Dramatic Rise to Power, 41:1-57

Joseph's case seemed hopeless until **two full years** later (1) the **Pharaoh** had a dream which defied the interpretative prowess of Egypt's best diviners. The impasse caused the butler to remember Joseph, who, when brought to the Pharaoh, accurately revealed the dream's secret. He was rewarded not by simply being released from prison but by being elevated to a position of power which was next to the Pharaoh himself.

1. *The Cryptic Dream* (41:1-8)

The Pharaoh's dream was deceptively simple. Standing by **the river** (1) which, in Egypt, could be only the Nile River, the **Pharaoh** saw **seven well favoured kine** (2), or cows, come out of the water and feed in a nearby **meadow. Seven other** (3) cows came from the water also, but were **leanfleshed.** What was unusual was that these lean cows ate up the fat cows.

The Pharaoh wakened, but falling asleep again he **dreamed** (5) that **seven ears of corn** (5) appeared, coming forth from **one stalk.** The word **corn** is the British term for grain, such as wheat or barley, not the American corn. **Rank** (5) here has the sense of being vigorous and healthy. In contrast to their good condition, **seven** (6) other heads of grain, **thin** and **blasted with the east wind,** grew up and consumed the healthy grain.

Disturbed by the dreams, the Pharaoh **called for all the magicians** and **wise men** (8, diviners). Relating the dreams to them, the **Pharaoh** sought for an explanation, but none could provide one. Such dreams were understood to possess secret messages concerning future events and it was important that they be decoded.

2. *The Secret Made Known* (41:9-36)

It was at this juncture that **the chief butler** (9) called to mind the occasion in the prison when he and the **baker** (10) had dreamed and Joseph had correctly interpreted their dreams for them. **According to the interpretation of his dream** (11) is better "a dream with its own meaning" (RSV). The butler told Pharaoh the story. Joseph was sent for, and after hastily preparing for an audience with the **Pharaoh** (14), he was ushered into his presence. When told that he had a reputation as an interpreter of dreams, Joseph protested that he did not possess the power in himself but in **God** (16). The pagan diviners boasted of innate powers, though oftentimes in conjunction with some god or goddess. Joseph, like all believers in the one true God, regarded predictions of the future to be a divine gift. Accurate predictions could be dispensed only as God chose to grant them to His servants.[5] **God shall give Pharaoh an answer of peace** (16), is translated by Moffatt, "It is God's answer that will answer to Pharaoh."

Pharaoh (17) related the content of the dreams with a few touches of personal reaction. He had been particularly impressed with the scrawny **kine** (19) which ate up the **fat** (20) ones with no resulting change in their physical appearance. None of his **magicians** (24) had been able to decipher the dreams.

Joseph (25) had no difficulty giving an interpretation. But in doing so he pointedly noted that the one true **God** (*ha elohim*, the Heb. term has the emphatic definite article which denotes distinctiveness) was going to act in Egypt. This was an amazing testimony in the presence of the monarch who was regarded by his people as the sun god in physical form, yet who was in this case helpless. This true God had **shewed Pharaoh what he was about to do.**

The two dreams were really a unit with a message related to future crop conditions in Egypt. **The seven good kine** (26) and **the seven good ears** symbolized **seven years** of abundant harvests. Their opposite kind represented **seven years of famine,** which would follow **the seven years of great plenty** (29).

[5]Y. Kaufmann, *op. cit.*, pp. 40-52, 78-101.

Rain is not a significant factor in Egypt's climate, being almost completely absent in Upper Egypt. The prophecy, therefore, could only mean that the floods of the Nile River, which occur in the summer months and fertilize the valley, would be functioning normally for seven years. But for the following seven years they would be inadequate for Egypt's crops to mature properly. For ages, Egypt's food supply has been dependent on the Nile floods, which have not always been sufficient for agricultural needs.[6]

Joseph noted that, since both dreams meant the same thing, the situation was urgent, for **the thing is established by God** (32) and would happen soon. Joseph then proceeded to give the Pharaoh some practical advice which was not strictly a part of the interpretation. He suggested that **a man discreet and wise** (33) be given responsibility of gathering and storing all excess grain during the **seven plenteous years** (34) in order that there would be food during **the seven years of famine** (36).

3. *The Surprise Appointment* (41:37-45)

In a council meeting, **Pharaoh** and **his servants** (37) decided that Joseph's interpretation and advice were excellent. **Pharaoh** (38) characterized him as **a man in whom the Spirit of God is,** and reported to **Joseph** (39) that they had agreed he should be the man to supervise the grain storage plan. His rank would be next to Pharaoh himself in power and authority.

To symbolize Joseph's new office, **Pharaoh** gave him **his ring** (42) which bore the seal of authority, clothed him in **fine linen, and put a gold chain about his neck.** A **chariot** (43) was assigned to him and he was paraded publicly with the proclamation that he was to be honored by the populace. The next act was to change his **name** (45) to **Zaphnath-paaneah,** which means "abundance of life," or "the god speaks and he lives." Finally, Joseph was married to a girl from a high-ranking family of the priestly city of **On** (45). This city was called Heliopolis by the Greeks; it is still a suburb of modern Cairo. The girl's name was **Asenath,** meaning "one belonging to the goddess Neith."[7] Joseph was thrust into intimate contact with Egypt's paganism, but he was not overcome by it.

[6]L. Casson, *et al., Ancient Egypt* (New York: Time, Inc., 1965), pp. 28-49.

[7]Leupold, *op. cit.*, pp. 1034-36; Speiser, *Genesis, op. cit.*, p. 314.

4. *The Crop Conservation Project* (41:46-57)

Joseph had been taken to Egypt when he was only 17 (37:2). He had been in Egypt for 13 years, and was still a young man of **thirty years** (46), when he became the second most powerful ruler in Egypt. He knew exactly what to do. During the years of abundant harvest, he gathered all grain beyond the people's immediate needs and stored it in a number of Egypt's **cities** (48). **Brought forth by handfuls** (47) is better "brought forth abundantly" (RSV). During this time **two sons** (50) were born. The first was named **Manasseh** (51, "forgetting") as a testimony that God had erased from Joseph's soul thoughts of sadness about his years of **toil, and all my father's house.** The second son was named **Ephraim** (52, "double fruitfulness") as a witness to God's provisions of mercy **in the land of my affliction.**

"The Song of an Exile" is given in 41:50-52. (1) Forgetfulness of toil, 51; (2) Fruitfulness in times of hardship, 52 (W. T. Purkiser).

When **the seven years of dearth** (54) came, **Egypt** was prepared with a large supply of food stored for the emergency. But the drouth reached beyond Egypt to Palestine and other neighboring countries. Within Egypt itself, people were soon hungry and pled for food, which Joseph provided according to a plan already worked out. The people were permitted to purchase the stored grain and so had enough to eat. People from other countries heard of Egypt's supply and came in order **to buy corn** (57, grain).

E. Mysterious Problems in Egypt, 42:1—45:28

The drouth drove Jacob's family to buy grain outside of Canaan and the only place that had an excess supply was Egypt. But when Jacob's sons came to Egypt they ran into unexpected difficulties. For some reason the vizier, or premier, made seemingly unjust charges against them and issued demands which defied ready explanation. But the vizier knew with whom he was dealing and was determined to extract the utmost advantage from the fact that Jacob's sons did not know him.

The affair ended in an unexpected and dramatic way. It was an ending which convinced Joseph of his brothers' change of heart; it surprised them by revealing that the brother they had sold was the man of authority who stood before them; and it overjoyed a burdened and grief-stricken father who heard with wonder that the boy he thought dead was alive.

1. *Suspicion and Accusation* (42:1-28)

In view of the drouth Jacob remonstrated with his sons, "Why stand looking at each other?" (1, Moffatt) So **ten** sons were dispatched **to buy corn** (grain) **in Egypt** (3). The youngest was kept at home, for Jacob was loath to let **Benjamin** (4) go, **lest peradventure mischief befall him.** The father's reluctance reveals both his painful memory of Joseph's disappearance and a lingering, gnawing fear that the others deeply disliked Rachel's sons.

To obtain grain they had to secure permission from the man in charge of the program, especially since they were foreigners. Instantly Joseph **knew** (7) who they were and decided to make himself as **strange** to them as possible, putting them through an unfriendly interrogation. He accused them of being **spies** (9), but they protested that they were **true men** (11). **The nakedness of the land** (9) is better "how defenceless the land is" (Moffatt). They regarded themselves as honest, a claim which must have caused Joseph to laugh silently to himself. As Joseph persisted in his accusations, they provided an accurate account of the situation in their family. The fact that Benjamin was not with them gave Joseph an opportunity to apply pressure. He did not mete out revenge, yet he used his authority to test them severely and to cause them to reveal their true selves. **That is it** (14) means, "It is as I said to you, you are spies" (RSV).

The accusation that they were spies was intended to bring out their purpose for coming to Egypt; their imprisonment was to impress them with the extent of his power over them. Joseph's demand that they send someone to fetch Benjamin was designed to uncover their real attitude toward his full brother, the other son of Rachel. **By the life of Pharaoh** (15) is a kind of oath, "as sure as the Pharaoh lives" (Moffatt).

After **three days** (17) he changed his tactics somewhat, for he had devised new ways to carry out his test. Calling them to his presence, he said that they could go home. But one must remain as a hostage, until their **youngest brother** (20) was brought to Egypt. This development revealed a collective conscience that was both tender and frightened. The memory of what they had done to Joseph had become more acute with the years. Doubtless **Reuben** (22) had worked on that conscience many times, and he now reminded them that justice was catching up with them.

Joseph had been conversing with them through **an interpreter** (23), so they had no way of knowing that he understood their conversation in their native tongue. But he heard their words and was moved so deeply he had to leave, for his emotion could not be contained. Privately, he **wept** (24), probably with relief and some joy that hardness and hate had given way to soul distress over their past sin. The selection of **Simeon** as the hostage may be an indication that he had been the ringleader of the plot against Joseph.

Without the brothers knowing it, Joseph gave orders that the **money** (25) paid for the grain be placed in each man's **sack.** At the first stop on the way home, the **money** was discovered when one **sack** was opened to get grain for the animals (27). The explanation for this turn of affairs was beyond them, but they fearfully suspected that **God** (28) had something to do with it.

The brothers had a strange tale to relate to **their father** (29). On hearing of the Egyptian's demand for Benjamin, his retention of Simeon, and the mysterious refund of money, Jacob became almost hysterical in his grief and fear. He accused his sons of responsibility for all his misfortunes, his loss of **Joseph** (36), of **Simeon,** and now of the threatened loss of **Benjamin.**

Reuben (37) sought to allay Jacob's fears by offering to give his **two sons** as hostages who could be put to death if he did not bring Benjamin back safely from Egypt. But Jacob could not be convinced. He had a deep distrust of his older sons and a fearful concern for the only remaining son of his beloved Rachel. To lose Benjamin would bring Jacob in **sorrow to the grave** (38).

2. *The Fear-filled Return to Egypt* (43:1-34)

The continuation of **the famine** (1) forced Jacob's family to go to **Egypt** (2) the second time for grain. **Judah** (3) insisted that they dared not go without Benjamin. **Israel** (6, Jacob) could but weakly protest that they should not have told Pharaoh's officer about Benjamin. But **Judah** (8), like his brother Reuben (42:37), offered to **be surety** (9), i.e., guaranteed, that Benjamin would return safely.

Facing bravely what seemed the inevitable, **Israel** (11) instructed his sons to take a **present** to **the man,** consisting of some of the delicacies of Canaan. They were to take back **double money** (12) for the first purchase, just in case the refund was really **an oversight.** The old father concluded with a note of resigned trust in the **mercy** of **God Almighty** (14) that his sons would be returned—but he was now ready to accept their loss, if it came to that.

When Joseph saw Benjamin (16), he was satisfied that his brothers were greatly changed in their attitudes and ordered his servants to prepare a banquet for them. The brothers were mystified about the trip to the officer's **house** (18) and immediately suspected that harm would come to them. They feared that they would be accused of stealing the money that was in their sacks and then be enslaved. As a precaution they sought to explain **to the steward of Joseph's house** (19) that they had been puzzled about the money and now had it to return to Joseph. They further assured him that they had other funds to pay for more food. **Money in full weight** (21) is interpreted "our money in full" (Smith-Goodspeed).

The steward's reply must have surprised and further mystified them. He spoke to them kindly and admitted that he had been responsible for the money in their sacks—"I received your money" (23, RSV). They did not know it but they had just given proof that they were not the greedy men who had sold their brother for 20 pieces of silver. They were indeed acting like honest men.

Simeon (23) was brought from the prison and joined the others. All were properly taken care of, including their animals. Anxiously they waited with present in hand for Joseph's arrival for the **noon** meal (25). They presented the gift, bowing humbly at his feet. Questioning them about their father, **Joseph saw his brother Benjamin** (29) again. It was too much. Choked with emotion, he left his brothers, and in the quiet of his room he **wept** (30). Finally he gained control of his emotions, **washed his face** (31), and returned to the dining room.

In typical Eastern style, they ate in separate groups according to rank and ethnic distinctions. **The Egyptians** (32) were particularly careful to keep themselves separate from the others, being strongly prejudiced against **the Hebrews.**[8] As the meal continued, so did the pattern of inexplicable incidents. They

[8]S. Davis, *Race-Relations in Ancient Egypt* (London: Methuen and Co., 1953), pp. 74-88.

found themselves seated in order from the eldest to the **youngest** (33). Also Joseph not only shared some of his food with them but made **Benjamin's mess,** i.e., portion of food, **five times** more than theirs (34). Otherwise the occasion was a **merry** one (34).

3. *The Mysterious Refund* (44:1-13)

Joseph was not yet finished with his brothers. They had already demonstrated to his satisfaction that they were telling the truth about his family in Canaan. They had been honest in regard to the money replaced in their bags. Jacob had entrusted Benjamin to their care and he had arrived safely, but the length of time between their trips must have suggested to him that Jacob had been very unwilling to let Benjamin come. Joseph intended now to test the extent of their trustworthiness in regard to his brother. He wanted to see whether they would abandon Benjamin, as they had abandoned him.

To gain this information he instructed **the steward** (1) to replace the **money** in the **sacks** for the second time. But in Benjamin's sack he was to hide Joseph's personal **silver cup** (2). After the caravan had left, he sent **his steward** (4) to accuse them of stealing the cup. **He divineth** (5) means to foretell future events or to discover hidden knowledge.

Like Jacob with Laban (31:32), the brothers vehemently denied the charge of stealing and boldly asserted that whoever should do such a thing ought to **die** (9), and they themselves would be willing to become **bondmen,** i.e., slaves. To their amazement and chagrin, the cup was found in **Benjamin's sack** (12).

4. *The Accusation and the Plea* (44:14-34)

The brothers were completely crushed by the new developments and **fell before** Joseph **on the ground** (14). **Wot ye not** (15) would be, Do you not know? In deep agony, utterly unable to defend themselves, they said, **God hath found out the iniquity of thy servants** (16). Joseph then appeared to relent somewhat, for he offered to let them go free. Benjamin, though, would have to remain as a slave. On the surface it looked like a merciful gesture, for it gave them an opportunity to leave without any charges or any punishment leveled against them.

But **Judah** (18) could not leave without his brother Benjamin. Approaching the Egyptian officer, he poured from his soul a plea which stands as a literary masterpiece.

Judah first reviewed the case up to that moment. He recalled that the Egyptian official had inquired of their family, had discovered that the youngest was very dear to their father, and then had demanded that he be brought to Egypt. Although this would cause great pain to him, they had told their **father** (24) of the demand. Judah skillfully played on the pathos of the father, who had lost his most dearly loved son and was loath to let the other son of his beloved wife go, fearing his loss also. He stressed Jacob's words, **If . . . mischief befall him, ye shall bring down my gray hairs with sorrow to the grave** (29). The words were designed to make the greatest possible emotional appeal to the man before him. Next, Judah emphasized his own pledge to his **father** (32) to bring the boy back or **bear the blame . . . for ever.** To prove the earnestness of that pledge, Judah offered to become a slave himself in order that Benjamin might go home. His last thrust was personal, for to go home to see his father die of grief would be too painful. He would rather live as a slave.

To Joseph, the change he saw in Judah must have been amazing. This was the man who had urged his brothers to sell Joseph as a slave, and now he was willing to become a slave himself, and thus to defend Benjamin with his life. Judah, who had aided in deceiving Jacob about Joseph's death, was now standing bravely loyal to Jacob at great personal cost. He had not dared to take a stand openly against his brothers when the plot was being hatched, but now he was boldly standing before a man of great power. Previously greed and passion had guided his life, but now he was willing to pay a supreme sacrifice for the sake of another.

5. *The Startling Disclosure* (45:1-15)

Judah's plea gained its purpose; it deeply affected the man before him who held so much power over their lives. Stirred with emotion, **Joseph** (1) ordered all others out of the room and then began to weep loudly, to the amazement of everyone. His doubting heart was satisfied; his brothers were no longer the heartless men who had sold him into slavery.

Dramatically he announced, **I am Joseph** (3), and asked again about his **father.** The brothers were speechless, unable to believe what they had just heard. If this was Joseph, surely he would punish them. But Joseph reassured them, requesting that they not berate themselves for what they had done to him, **for God did send me before you to preserve life** (5).

Now it could be seen by Joseph that God had overruled the evil intent of his brothers. God had made it possible for him as a high official in Egypt to open the way for his family to move out of drouth-stricken Canaan to the land where he had stored food for the famine. His brothers had thought to get rid of him by selling him as a slave. But God had used him to save them from starvation. **Neither . . . earing nor harvest** (6) would be "neither plowing nor harvest" (RSV). **Made me a father to Pharaoh** (8) is better "has made me Pharaoh's prime minister, head of all his palace" (Moffatt). By transforming evil intent into good and by providing strength during distress, God showed that His ultimate purpose is redemptive and that His relationships with men are informed with love.

Joseph gave in detail his plans to have the entire family move to **the land of Goshen** (10; see map 3). Verse 12 is rendered clearly by Smith-Goodspeed, "You can see for yourselves and my brother Benjamin for himself that it is I who speak to you." Then throwing aside lordly dignity, he embraced his brother **Benjamin** (14) and they **wept** together. This he did with each of **his brethren** (15), following which they **talked with him.**

The road to full reconciliation had been painful for both Joseph and his brothers. The brothers had to face up to their guilt, confess their sins (42:21-22), and recognize that God was punishing them (42:28). They had to plead for mercy (44:27-32) and demonstrate that they actually were changed men (44:33-34). For Joseph, the ordeal was also painful. He had to assure himself of their new sincerity by putting them through embarrassing situations, some of which would bring pain to his father. He had to maintain his disguise as an Egyptian, though he yearned to make himself known. When the hour of unveiling came, his rank and his power made it difficult for his brothers to believe that he was Joseph and that he really was forgiving them.

6. *Orders to Move* (45:16-24)

The fame (16, news) that the men who came from Canaan were in fact the brothers of the vizier of Egypt stirred the royal court. When it reached the ears of Pharaoh, he responded with an order that Joseph's family should take back food and **wagons** (19) in order to transport the entire clan to **Egypt.** The expression **regard not your stuff** (20) means, "Never mind your goods" (Smith-Goodspeed). Joseph took charge of equipping his brothers for the move. To each he gave gifts, but he showered **Benjamin** (22) with an overabundance, and sent a great amount for **his father** (23). **See that ye fall not out by the way** (24), means, "Do not quarrel on the road" (Moffatt).

7. *The Son Who Was Dead Is Alive* (45:25-28)

The return home was different this time. There were no mysteries and no disconcerting demands, only unbelievable news. Word that **Joseph** (26) actually was **alive** was almost a greater shock than the news that he had been killed by a beast. Only the detailed story of what happened in Egypt and **the wagons** (27) which had been sent loaded with food and gifts convinced Jacob. Then his **spirit . . . revived** (27). Jacob's burning desire for Joseph was to **see him before I die** (28).

Already the aftermath of forgiveness and reconciliation could be traced. An abundance of food was available without price. Jacob's life had been spared due to Benjamin's return and the news that Joseph was alive. Family unity had been restored, and freedom from guilt and fear was realized.

F. The New Home in Egypt, 46:1—47:31

In spite of the news that Joseph was in Egypt, it was not easy for Jacob to leave Canaan, for it was the Promised Land. But with divine permission, Jacob made the move with his sizable retinue, received a joyous welcome from Joseph, and saw his family settled in a well-watered and productive portion of the delta of the Nile. It was a blissful conclusion to a life full of mistakes, adventures, tension, adversity, sorrow, and joy, and above all, it had been a life full of the mercies of God.

1. *Jacob Received Permission to Move* (46:1-7)

Evidently Jacob and his family had kept their headquarters at Hebron (37:14; see map 2). On hearing the astounding news that Joseph was alive and was a high official in Egypt, **Israel** (1, Jacob) set out at once for Egypt. As he traveled toward **Beersheba,** Jacob probably remembered that his grandfather Abraham had gone through an unpleasant experience in Egypt (12:10 ff.), and that God had told Isaac not to go to Egypt (26:2). He must also have recalled that God had told Abraham that his descendents would one day reside there (15:13-16).

With mingled thoughts, therefore, Jacob worshiped, offering **sacrifices unto the God of his father Isaac.** Though not recorded, a prayer for guidance and protection doubtless was offered at this time. God's answer did not come until the nightfall, but the word was positive: **Go down into Egypt** (3). The message also contained promises. Jacob's family would become **a great nation;** God would **bring** Jacob **up again** (4), being with him always; and **Joseph** would **put his hand upon thine eyes,** i.e., be present at his death.

Jacob arose from that place with all doubts settled. This was not a new God but the only true God, who had appeared to his father. In the Hebrew, the definite article *ha* distinguishes this speaking God from all false gods. Everything and everyone connected with Jacob moved toward Egypt and soon arrived at its borders.

A momentous turn of events had occurred in the life of the patriarch and his family, and God's stamp of approval was upon it. God's purpose seemed to be to preserve the patriarch's family as a unit, by separating it from the spiritual rot of Canaanite immorality and idolatry. Already, several of the older sons had been tainted by that rot. The Egyptians would be sufficiently different, so that intermarriage and idolatry would not have so strong an appeal as in Canaan. Yet Jacob's descendents would be closely associated with the positive achievements of culture. They would be living beside the main international trade routes of the day.

2. *A Register of Jacob's Sons* (46:8-27)

In this list, the family of Jacob is separated according to the mothers; the number of children, grandchildren, and great-grandchildren is totaled. Since Judah's sons **Er and Onan died in the land of Canaan** (12), it can be assumed that Dinah and Jacob or some unnamed second daughter or daughter-in-law are included in the total of **thirty and three** (15).

A granddaughter of **Jacob** and **Leah** (15) is mentioned in connection with **Asher** (17), son of **Zilpah** (18), giving a grand total of **sixteen souls** in this branch of the family. Besides the two sons of **Joseph** (20), 10 sons are assigned to **Benjamin** (21), though he was still young. Perhaps multiple births were a characteristic of his family. The Greek translation gives three sons, six grandsons, and one great-grandson to Benjamin, an improbable situation for one so young.

The two sons of **Bilhah** are listed as having five sons between them. The total of all those recorded here is 70 people, but the actual count of 66 omits Jacob, Joseph, and his two sons. The wives of none of the men are counted, and only one daughter and one granddaughter are clearly included in the total.

The reference in Acts 7:14 to Jacob's move to Egypt mentions 75 people; it follows the Greek translation, which includes five more descendents of Joseph through his sons.

3. *The Dramatic Father-Son Meeting* (46:28-34)

Jacob sent **Judah** (28), the new leader of the brethren, on ahead to work out details of the settlement in Egypt and to arrange for the best possible occasion for the reunion of father and son.

Being a high official, Joseph had access to Egypt's best means of transportation, a **chariot** (29), and he was not long in reaching his **father.** They embraced each other and **wept . . . a good while.** When the embrace was completed, the aged **Israel** (30, Jacob) was ready to **die,** as though the entire goal of his life had just been achieved. His son who was lost had been found.

Joseph turned his attention to the great need immediately before them, to gain formal approval of **Goshen** (34) as the part of Egypt in which Jacob's family would reside. Because he had intimate knowledge of royal procedures in Egypt, Joseph gave detailed instructions concerning how to approach **Pharaoh** (33). The situation was delicate because **the Egyptians** (34) rated shepherds as of low social status, and it must be made clear that their visit would be temporary. The Egyptian records show that this was not the first time people from Canaan had come to Egypt in famine years. Probably no other group had had as high representation before Pharaoh as did Jacob's family.

4. *Permit for Temporary Residency* (47:1-6)

In modern terms, it might be said that Joseph gave Jacob's family visas for entrance. But a permit for temporary residence of some years must come from **Pharaoh** himself (1). Knowing Egyptian procedures, Joseph himself made proper approaches to Pharaoh. The **five** brothers selected (2) made the plea that Joseph had coached them to make. However, they stressed the fact that dire necessity had motivated them to move to **Egypt** (4).

The Pharaoh was impressed and, happily, permission was granted to live **in the land of Goshen.** Pharaoh also made an unexpected request. Jacob's family was offered employment privileges in the Egyptian economy—"If you know of capable men among them, put them in charge of my own livestock" (6, Berk.)

5. *The Man of God Meets Pharaoh* (47:7-12)

The next step was to introduce **Jacob** to the **Pharaoh** (7), an incident filled with interesting contrasts. The **Pharaoh** was regarded as a divine being, the son of the sun and ruler over a polytheistic nation.[9] **Jacob** had personally met the one true God several times and was in a covenant relationship with Him. The **Pharaoh** had the power to receive or to reject Jacob now, but Jacob had a promise from the true God that He would bring the Israelites back to Canaan again, and no Pharaoh could prevent it. The Pharaoh was supposed to have power over all aspects of Egypt's life. But it was Joseph, Jacob's son, who actually ran the country during its time of crisis. In time the line of Pharaoh was to be destroyed, but Jacob's descendents and their religious faith are still powerful today.

Pharaoh noticed that Jacob was an old man, whose age was much beyond the life-span of the average Egyptian. When asked, **How old art thou?** (8) Jacob gave his age but did not boast. Men of long life have their memories of tragedy. Also, even **an hundred and thirty years** (9) were **few** compared to those of Jacob's ancestors. Here was another contrast between the short-lived man-god and the longevity of a man of God.

On entering and on leaving Pharaoh's presence, Jacob **blessed** him (7, 10). Heb. 7:7 declares that "without all contradiction the less is blessed of the better."

Under Joseph's watchful eye Jacob's family fared well. All things needful were provided for them. **The land of Rameses** (11) was a title for Goshen common at the time when the Pentateuch was written.

6. *Joseph's Welfare Program* (47:13-26)

The drouth, which in **Egypt** (13) would be the failure of the Nile River to flood the land at its regular time in the summer, continued to leave the people without a harvest. Joseph's grain-storage plan proved to be invaluable. But the dole was not handed out gratis. Food must be purchased with whatever property was available. Coins or printed currency were not known in

[9]P. Hamlyn, *Egyptian Mythology* (London: Paul Hamlyn, Ltd., 1965).

Joseph's time, so the **money** (14) brought in by the people was probably precious metals and jewels. When these were gone, **cattle** (16) were turned in to the government, then privately owned land, and finally the people became serfs in exchange **for bread** (19).

In theory, all land, cattle, and people belonged to the Pharaoh, and in certain periods of Egypt's history this was the actual situation. But there had been periods of royal weakness when private property and enterprise held sway. The famine was a means by which the ancient absolutism was reestablished. There was only one exception. **The land of the priests** (22) could not be touched by the ruling class.

To temper the hardships of **the people** (23), Joseph granted **seed** to them with the understanding that one-fifth of the increase was to be turned over to the government. This is much less than the 50 percent or more that sharecroppers often pay, and it is a lower tax than many citizens in civilized countries pay today.

7. *Joseph's Vow to His Father* (47:27-31)

For **seventeen years** (28) the patriarch lived in **Egypt,** seeing his family prosper **in the country of Goshen** (27). Feeling the end drawing near, he **called . . . Joseph** (29) to his side. **Israel** must be certain that his remains would be placed in the cave of Machpelah. Using terms common to the covenant language, such as **grace** and **deal kindly and truly,** he requested that Joseph solemnly vow to bury him in Canaan in accordance with God's promises recorded in 28:13-15 and in 35:11-12. When Joseph took his vow, he followed custom (see 24:2) by placing his **hand under** Jacob's **thigh.** It was a high moment of faith for Jacob and, as soon as Joseph committed himself, the dying patriarch worshiped. The KJV states that **Israel bowed himself upon the bed's head** (31). Heb. 11:21, following the Greek Septuagint, reads "leaning upon the top of his staff." In the Hebrew language the difference is *mittah,* "bed," and *matteh,* "staff." Only consonants were written in Hebrew manuscripts, so the difference arises from two separate traditions of pronunciation.

G. Anticipations of the Future, 48:1—50:26

The final chapters of Genesis are rooted in both the crises of death in the present, or immediate future, and the long-range future of the descendents of Jacob. Always it is stressed that the land of Egypt is not the permanent home of these people. They must have their eyes on Canaan. To emphasize this point, Jacob was buried in the family burial cave and Joseph was embalmed for future burial in Canaan.

1. *Jacob's Adoption of Joseph's Sons* (48:1-22)

A turn for the worse in Jacob's health brought **Joseph** (1) and his **two sons** to the aged man's bedside. With difficulty Jacob sat up to receive them. It was an important meeting, about which father and son evidently had talked previously.

Jacob's memories harked back to that eventful moment at **Luz** (3, Bethel; see 28:10-22). At that time **God Almighty** had appeared to him, becoming personally real and conveying the covenant promises to him. Now Jacob intended to pass these covenant promises, along with attendant obligations, to his descendents. He had already come to know the will of God concerning which son would be singled out for this privilege, but had told no one.

Jacob's first step was to adopt Joseph's two sons as his own. In fact he placed them on a par with **Reuben and Simeon** (5), his two oldest sons.[10] Jacob had never forgotten his loss of Rachel, so he intended to honor her by elevating these grandchildren to the status of sons and eventually as tribes in Israel. However, Joseph's name would be perpetuated through other sons apt to be born (6). **Ephrath** (7) is an older name for **Bethlehem,** which is inserted by the writer to make the location clear.

Jacob's **dim** eyes (10) now noticed two other figures in the room. Ascertaining that they were Ephraim and Manasseh, he performed the ritualistic gestures of adoption which were customary among his people. Legitimate sons were received by the father by placing them **between his knees** (12); so also were these adopted sons recognized.

The next step was the formal act of pronouncing the blessing which was to Jacob's people irrevocable. Not knowing his father's intentions, Joseph arranged his sons according to custom, i.e., the oldest son opposite the tribal father's **right hand** (13). Jacob anticipated this move, so crossing his hands, he pronounced the covenant blessing on the youngest, **Ephraim** (14). From that moment Ephraim was to be the covenant representative before God. Dissatisfied with his father's actions, Joseph tried to change

[10]de Vaux, *op. cit.*, pp. 51-52.

the position of Jacob's hands, only to be told that what had been done was intentional. **Wittingly** (14) would be "knowingly." For the third time, the younger son in the line of the patriarchs had taken the place of an older son (see 17:19-20; 27:27-29).

In the blessing, Jacob testified of **the Angel which redeemed me from all evil** (16). This is the first time the word "redeem" (*go'el*) appears in the Scriptures. It is rooted in the obligation of a kinsman to buy back the mortgaged property of an unfortunate relative, or to buy the relative back from slavery (Lev. 25:25-55).

Jacob had come to see his own dishonesty with Esau, and his troubles with Laban as an **evil** which threatened to entrap him. But God had helped him to settle things with Laban, and to effect a reconciliation with Esau. God had also brought him out of the evil ways of his own older sons, and had given Joseph back to him. These were the acts of God which had brought hope and joy to his heart. He looked upon these events as redemptive, for he owed everything to what God had done for him. He who had worked so effectually in the past would surely **bless the lads** and work redemption for these grandchildren.

In addition to the special blessing upon **Ephraim** (17), blessing was also given to Manasseh (cf. 27:39-40). The form of this blessing, **God make thee as Ephraim and as Manasseh** (20), is still used among Jewish people. Moreover, Jacob gave Joseph the promise that he too would return to Canaan someday (21), for it was God's will. Furthermore, Joseph was to have a **portion** (22) of that land for his own. It was located by Shechem. No other record remains of the battle with **the Amorite** which is connected with Jacob's ownership of this parcel of land. However, Josh. 24:32 states that Joseph's embalmed body was buried on a plot of ground which was purchased from "the sons of Hamor" (see also John 4:5-6).

2. *Jacob's Blessings on His Sons* (49:1-28)

Except for the first verse, this portion of Scripture is poetic in form, rich in parallelism of thought, wordplay, and metaphor. It was a solemn hour, for the patriarch was dispensing his final will and testament before dying.

There is a strong tinge of irony in Jacob's address to **Reuben** (3). As the **firstborn,** his was a place of high privilege and responsibility. He should have been a leader of **might, strength,**

dignity, and **power.** But Reuben had turned his back on the highest and had stooped to the very lowest level. He had sought to demonstrate his leadership by defiling his **father's bed** (4) in a gross act of incest (cf. 35:22). Jacob had not forgotten and now Reuben was to pay a high price for his folly.

"The Tragedy of Spiritual Instability" is illustrated in Jacob's words about Reuben: (1) A man of great possibilities, 3; (2) Reuben's lost excellence, **shalt not excel,** 4; (3) The fatal flaw, **unstable as water,** 4 (W. T. Purkiser).

Simeon and Levi (5) are grouped together, for they had led the bloody massacre of Shechem (34:25-29). Jacob's shock, when he heard of this incident, is vividly depicted in this condemnation of their rash act. Moffatt renders it: "Their plans, my soul, never share; heart of mine, join not their council!" Neither was to have a tribal territory in Canaan, but would be scattered among the others (see Josh. 19:1-9 and 21:1-42).

Judah (8) had proved himself to be a better man in maturity than in youth and, prior to moving to Egypt, had demonstrated his leadership ability. The name means "praise" and so he was to be the **praise** of Jacob's family as their military and political leader. His courage would be like that of **a lion** (9); but above all, royalty would issue from Judah's tribe (I Sam. 16:1-13; II Sam. 2:1-4; 5:1-5).

A great deal of controversy has swirled about the word **Shiloh** (10), which can be understood as meaning "rest" or "rest giver." This is the name of the town where the ark rested until Samuel's time (I Sam. 4:1-22). But since that site was never important in Judah's history, there seems to be no tie to this prophecy in v. 10. An early Aramaic translation reads "until Messiah comes," and this interpretation has held a strong place in Jewish and Christian understanding of the text. The Greek, the Samaritan, and the Targum of Onkelos give a reading pointing to a Hebrew compound word meaning, literally, "which is his" (cf. Ezek. 21:27). This also was understood to have Messianic import, but it has been challenged.[11]

Evangelical Christians have been quite united in seeing Christ as the fulfillment of this prediction which came from Jacob's lips. So understood, this prophecy meant that beyond the tribes of Israel the people of the world would become obedient

[11]Skinner, *op. cit.*, pp. 521-24.

to the One who was to come.[12] Smith's translation has caught the mood of royalty in this description of Judah's leadership:

"He tethers his ass to the vine,
And his ass's colt to the choicest vine;
He washes his garments in wine,
And his robes in the blood of grapes;
His eyes are darker than wine,
And his teeth whiter than milk" (Smith-Goodspeed).

The main characteristic of **Zebulun** (13) was association with **sea** commerce. These people would be energetic traders.

Issachar (14) was to be related to the laborer's task and he would do his work faithfully if not imaginatively. He was to be the epitome of "Mr. Taxpayer."

The name **Dan** (16) means "judge." But what a poor one he was to be! Instead of justice, treachery was to mark his decisions, which would afflict the plaintiff like the poison of the **adder** (17). As Jacob uttered this pronouncement, he could not help but cry with pain, **I have waited for thy salvation, O Lord** (18).

The words about the next three sons were short. **Gad** (19) was to be oppressed, but would **overcome** finally. **Asher** (20) would be prosperous, having a surplus of food. **Naphtali** (21) would know freedom and would be blessed with the ability to utter **goodly words.**

In contrast to these three, Jacob overflowed with predictions of a **fruitful** future for **Joseph** (22). Persecuted though he had been, this son was sustained by **the mighty God of Jacob** (24). This was the God who had been Jacob's own **shepherd**, Protector, and **stone of Israel** throughout his life. **The Almighty** (25) would be liberal with His **blessings,** five of which are enumerated. Joseph was unlike any of **his brethren** (26). Moffatt renders parts of 24-25 meaningfully:

"Jacob's Mighty One upholds him,
Israel's Strength sustains him—
ay, your father's God who aids you,
God Almighty who will bless you . . ."

In 49:22-26, G. B. Williamson points out "Joseph, a Fruitful Bough." (1) Joseph's tribulations, 23; cf. 37:17-36; (2) Joseph's temptation, 24; cf. 39:7-20; 40:14, 23; (3) Joseph's triumph, 25-26; cf. 4:39-46.

[12]Huffman, *op. cit.*, pp. 42-44.

Benjamin (27) is described as wolflike, "devouring prey in the morning and dividing spoil at evening" (Smith-Goodspeed). Violence would attend his acquisition of wealth.

3. *Jacob's Death* (49:29-33)

Having completed his blessings, Jacob made known the wish he had earlier revealed to Joseph (47:29-31). He was to be buried **in the cave . . . of Machpelah** (29-30), which had been purchased by **Abraham** (23:1-20). It was the grave of his ancestors and of **Leah** (31), his wife. Jacob wanted to be sure that in life and in death his sons were to have their eyes on Canaan as their true home.

The last detail had been cared for and there was no need to tarry. **Jacob . . . was gathered unto his people** (33), as were Abraham and Isaac before him.

4. *The Burial of Jacob* (50:1-14)

Joseph (1) was overwhelmed with emotion. Casting dignity of high office aside, he **wept upon** the lifeless form of his father. But he also knew his duty. In death, Jacob was to have the best. For **forty days** (3) the body was in the process of being **embalmed,** and 30 more days were spent in mourning, something which had not happened to Abraham or to Isaac.

Joseph next went to **the house of Pharaoh** (4), i.e., the proper officials of the court, to explain the vow to which Jacob had committed him and to seek permission to perform the vow. A promise was made that Joseph would **come again** (5). The request was passed on to **Pharaoh** (6), who granted permission to leave the country and, more significantly, assigned a group of official representatives to attend the funeral.

The sizable company of Israelites and Egyptians made their way to the cave of Machpelah. At **the threshingfloor of Atad** (10), presumably close by the burial cave, **seven days** of mourning for Jacob were observed.

The native **Canaanites** (11) were overwhelmed by the presence of so many officials from Egypt and their mourning over Jacob, whom they knew well. Their reaction was to rename the threshing floor **Abel-mizraim,** which means "the mourning of the Egyptians." Interment in **the cave of the field of Machpelah** (13) was formally carried out and the funeral retinue returned to Egypt.

5. *The Fearful Brothers* (50:15-21)

Jacob's death brought to the surface fears which had been submerged in his sons' minds for several years. Would Joseph unleash reprisals against them as soon as Jacob died? They could not believe that he had ever fully forgiven them. Together they determined to make clear that they were indeed sincere in their contrition for past deeds, though that contrition had never been voiced (cf. 45:4-15).

Discreetly, the brothers sent a message to Joseph before they sought for an interview. For the first time in the biblical record a plea for forgiveness is openly stated, though Jacob's words to Esau, "to find grace in thy sight" (33:8, 10), approach this. The contents of the note touched Joseph's heart, and another deeply moving scene of reconciliation took place. The prostrate forms of the brothers remind one of Joseph's dream against which they had bitterly reacted (37:5-8). Though Joseph possessed supreme human power to achieve vengeance, his soul was swayed by a greater influence, the readiness to forgive. The one true God had overruled human hate and had **meant it unto good . . . to save much people alive** (20). The kindness of Joseph cast out the nagging fears, and the brothers parted truly united in mutual respect and love.

6. *Joseph's Last Request* (50:22-26)

The time had come for the fourth of the great patriarchs to die. Death held no terror for either Abraham (25:7-11), Isaac (35:27-29), or Jacob (49:28-33). The same was true of Joseph. As with Jacob, so Joseph must make certain his remains would eventually be laid to rest in the Promised Land.

Gathering his **brethren** (24), Joseph reiterated his father's faith that Canaan was the true home of the Israelites. He gained from them an oath, **Ye shall carry up my bones from hence** (25). That cared for, Joseph died peacefully, **being an hundred and ten years old** (26). He was **embalmed,** placed **in a coffin,** and, for the time being, his mummy remained with his brethren **in Egypt.**

From 50:22-26, Alexander Maclaren expounds the theme of "Joseph's Faith." (1) Faith is always the same though knowledge varies; (2) Faith has its noblest office in detaching us from the present; (3) Faith makes men energetic in the duties of the present.

Bibliography

I. COMMENTARIES

BROWNE, E. H. "Genesis." *The Bible Commentary.* Edited by F. C. COOK, Vol. I. New York: Charles Scribner's Sons, 1892.

CALVIN, JOHN. *A Commentary on the First Book of Moses Called Genesis.* Translated by J. KING. Grand Rapids: Wm. B. Eerdmans Publishing Co., reprint, 1948. Vols. I-II.

CASSUTO, U. *A Commentary on the Book of Genesis.* Translated by I. ABRAHAMS, Vol. I. Jerusalem: The Magness Press, 1961.

CLARKE, A. "Genesis." *The Holy Bible with Commentary and Critical Notes,* Vol. I. New York: Carlton & Porter, n.d.

COHEN, A. *The Soncino Chumash.* Hindhead, Surrey, England: The Soncino Press, 1947.

DRIVER, S. R. *The Book of Genesis.* "The Westminster Commentaries." Edited by W. LOCK, Vol. I. London: Methuen and Co., Ltd., 1911.

GRIFFITH-THOMAS, W. H. *Genesis.* Grand Rapids: Wm. B. Eerdmans Publishing Co., 1946.

KEIL, C. F., and DELITZSCH, F. "The Pentateuch." *Biblical Commentary on the Old Testament.* Translated by JAMES MARTIN, Vol. I. Grand Rapids: Wm. B. Eerdmans Publishing Co., 1949.

KEVAN, E. F. "Genesis." *The New Bible Commentary.* Edited by F. DAVIDSON. Grand Rapids: Wm. B. Eerdmans Publishing Co., 1953.

LANGE, J. P. "Genesis." *Commentary on the Holy Scriptures.* Translated by PHILIP SCHAFF, Vol. I. Grand Rapids: Zondervan Publishing House, reprint, n.d.

LEUPOLD, H. C. *Exposition on Genesis.* Grand Rapids: Baker Book House, 1950. Vols. I-II.

LEWIS, T. "Genesis" (Introduction). *Commentary on the Holy Scriptures.* Translated by PHILIP SCHAFF, Vol. I. Grand Rapids: Zondervan Publishing House, reprint, n.d.

PFEIFFER, C. F. *The Book of Genesis.* "Shield Bible Study Series." Grand Rapids: Baker Book House, 1958.

RICHARDSON, A. *Genesis I—XI.* "Torch Bible Commentaries." Edited by JOHN MARSH, *et al.* London: SCM Press, Ltd., 1953.

RYLE, H. E. *The Book of Genesis.* "Cambridge Bible for Schools and Colleges." Edited by A. F. KIRKPATRICK. Cambridge: University Press, 1921.

SIMPSON, C. A. "Genesis" (Exegesis). *The Interpreter's Bible.* Edited by G. A. BUTTRICK, Vol. I. New York: Abingdon-Cokesbury Press, 1952.

SKINNER, J. *A Critical and Exegetical Commentary on Genesis.* "The International Critical Commentary." Edited by S. R. DRIVER, *et al.*, Vol. I. Edinburgh: T. & T. Clark, 1930.

SPEISER, E. A. *Genesis.* "The Anchor Bible." Edited by W. F. ALBRIGHT, *et al.*, Vol. I. Garden City, New York: Doubleday & Co., 1964.

WHITELAW, T. "Genesis." *The Pulpit Commentary.* Edited by H. D. M. SPENCE, *et al.*, Vol. I. Grand Rapids: Wm. B. Eerdmans Publishing Co., 1961.

YATES, K. M. "Genesis." *The Wycliffe Bible Commentary.* Edited by CHARLES PFEIFFER, *et al.* Chicago: Moody Press, 1962.

II. OTHER BOOKS

ALBRIGHT, W. F. *The Archaeology of Palestine.* Baltimore: Penguin Books, 1963.

ARCHER, G. L. *A Survey of Old Testament Introduction.* Chicago: Moody Press, 1964.

ASIMOV, I. *Words in Genesis.* Boston: Houghton Mifflin Co., 1962.

BROWN, F., DRIVER, S. R., and BRIGGS, C. A. *A Hebrew and English Lexicon of the Old Testament.* Oxford: Clarendon Press, 1952.

BUCK, H. M. *People of the Lord.* New York: Macmillan Co., 1966.

CASSON, L., *et al. Ancient Egypt.* New York: Time, Inc., 1965.

CORNFELD, G. *Adam to Daniel.* New York: The Macmillan Co., 1961.

DAVIS, S. *Race-Relations in Ancient Egypt.* London: Methuen & Co., 1953.

EISSFELDT, O. *The Old Testament.* New York: Harper and Row, 1965.

ELLIOTT, R. H. *The Message of Genesis.* Nashville: Broadman Press, 1961.

GORDON, C. H. *Introduction to Old Testament Times.* Ventnor, N.J.: Ventnor Publishers, Inc., 1953.

GUNKEL, H. *The Legends of Genesis.* New York: Schocken Books, 1964.

HAMLYN, P. *Egyptian Mythology.* London: Paul Hamlyn, Ltd., 1965.

HEATON, E. W. *Everyday Life in Old Testament Times.* New York: Charles Scribner's Sons, 1956.

HEINISCH, P. *Theology of the Old Testament.* Collegeville, Minn.: The Liturgical Press, 1955.

HESCHEL, A. J. *The Sabbath.* New York: Farrar, and Straus and Young, Inc., 1951.

HOLT, J. M. *The Patriarchs of Israel.* Nashville: Vanderbilt University Press, 1964.

HUFFMAN, J. A. *The Messianic Hope in Both Testaments.* Butler, Ind.: The Higley Press, 1945.

KAUFMANN, Y. *The Religion of Israel.* London: George Allen & Unwin, Ltd., 1961.

KIERKEGAARD, S. *Fear and Trembling.* London: Oxford University Press, 1939.

MENDENHALL, G. E. *Law and Covenant in Israel and the Ancient Near East.* Pittsburgh: The Biblical Colloquium, 1955.

MILTON, J. P. *God's Covenant of Blessing.* Rock Island, Ill.: Augustana Press, 1961.

MORGAN, G. C. *The Analyzed Bible.* New York: Fleming H. Revell Co., 1907.

PFEIFFER, C. F. *The Patriarchal Age.* Grand Rapids: Baker Book House, 1961.

POTTS, C. A. *Dictionary of Bible Proper Names.* New York: Abingdon Press, 1922.

RAMM, B. *The Christian View of Science and Scripture.* Grand Rapids: Wm. B. Eerdmans Publishing Co., 1955.

RENCHENS, H. *Israel's Concept of the Beginning.* New York: Herder and Herder, 1964.

RICHARDSON, A. *A Theological Word Book of the Bible.* New York: The Macmillan Co., 1951.

UNGER, M. F. *Introductory Guide to the Old Testament.* Grand Rapids: Zondervan Publishing House, 1951.

VAUX, R. DE, *Ancient Israel: Its Life and Institutions.* New York: McGraw-Hill Book Co., 1961.

WALKER, W. *All the Plants of the Bible.* New York: Harper and Bros., 1957.

WELLHAUSEN, J. *Prolegomena to the History of Israel.* Edinburgh: Adam and Charles Black, 1885.

WHITCOMB, J. C., and MORRIS, H. M. *The Genesis Flood.* Grand Rapids: Baker Book House, 1961.

WILEY, H. ORTON. *Christian Theology,* Vol. I. Kansas City, Mo.: Beacon Hill Press of Kansas City, 1940.

WILSON, R. D. *A Scientific Investigation of the Old Testament.* Chicago: Moody Press, 1959.

WRIGHT, G. E. *Biblical Archaeology.* Philadelphia: The Westminster Press, 1957.

III. ARTICLES

DOSKER, H. E. "Day." *The International Standard Bible Encyclopedia.* Edited by JAMES ORR, *et al.* Grand Rapids: Wm. B. Eerdmans Publishing Co., reprint, 1949. Vol. II, pp. 787-89.

PATERSON, J. "The Hurrians." *Studia Semitica et Orientalia,* II, 113-14.

PAYNE, J. B. "The Concept of 'Kings' in Scripture." *Journal of the American Scientific Affiliation,* X, No. 2 (June, 1958), 17-20.

POPE, M. H. "Oaths." *Interpreter's Dictionary of the Bible.* Edited by G. A. BUTTRICK, *et al.* New York: Abingdon Press, 1962. Vol. *K-Q,* pp. 575-77.

SPEISER, E. A. "Ethnic Divisions of Man." IDB, Vol. *E-J,* pp. 234-42.

YOUNG, E. J. "The Interpretation of Genesis 1:2." *Westminster Theological Journal,* XXIII (May, 1961), 151 ff.

The Book of
EXODUS

Leo G. Cox

Introduction

Exodus takes its name from the Septuagint (LXX), a Greek translation of the OT in use at the time of Christ. The Hebrew title was merely the first words of the text, "Now these are the names of" (Exod. 1:1).[1] The word Exodus gives the theme of the first half of the book, since it denotes a large number of people leaving a land. However the latter half of this book describes the establishment of the institutions, the laws, and the worship of Israel.

A. Author and Date

It is fairly clear that the author was an eyewitness to the events. The vivid descriptions of the plagues upon Egypt, of the thunderings at Mount Sinai, and of the manna in the wilderness require a witness who was there. The minute details concerning the wells and palm trees at Elim, the two tables of stone, the worship of the golden calf, and many others testify of a personal eyewitness.[2] Since there is little or no evidence of later additions to the book, it may be safely assumed that the writer of Exodus composed his material during or shortly after the experiences recorded in the book.

If it is granted that a contemporary Israelite wrote the accounts in Exodus, it is easily assumed that Moses was the writer. The author could have been no ordinary Israelite; he was highly gifted, educated, and a cultured man. Who was better prepared among all these people of slavery than Moses? Jesus affirmed that the law was written by Moses (Mark 1:44; John 7:19-22); His disciples also attested this fact (John 1:45; Acts 26:22). There is internal evidence in the book itself that Moses wrote certain parts (17:14; 24:4). Connell writes: "Nothing within the book conflicts with this claim that Moses was the author. The frequent mention of Moses' name in the third person has its parallels in the books of Isaiah and Jeremiah, whilst the

[1]J. Coert Rylaarsdam (Introduction and Exegesis), and J. Edgar Park (Exposition), "The Book of Exodus," *The Interpreter's Bible*, ed. George A. Buttrick, *et al.* (New York: Abingdon-Cokesbury Press, 1952), I, 833.

[2]George Rawlinson, "Exodus," *Commentary on the Whole Bible*, ed. Charles J. Ellicott (Grand Rapids: Zondervan Publishing House, n.d.) I, 188-89.

record of his call in chapter iii carries the same marks of authenticity as do the accounts of theirs."[3]

Higher criticism has attacked the claim that Moses wrote the Pentateuch and has held that these books are a compilation of documents written at much later times. This radical position that denied Mosaic authorship to the Book of the Law is not as widely held today as earlier. "Though many liberal scholars still question the Mosaic authorship of the Pentateuch, archaeological discoveries have given scholars of every theological background a higher respect for the historicity of the events it describes."[4] There is no sound reason in the light of present-day research to abandon the traditional view that Moses wrote Exodus during the wilderness wandering.

The actual date of the exodus from Egypt and the giving of the law has been a problem to scholars for centuries and has not yet been resolved. Dates have been suggested as early as 1580 B.C. and as late as 1230 B.C. Archaeological evidence "seems to point to a date some time in the thirteenth century," though this is in apparent conflict with the date in I Kings 6:1. The issue "is not a matter of doctrine, but simply a matter of historical enlightenment."[5]

B. Contents

The material found in Exodus follows naturally the Book of Genesis. The word "now" (Exod. 1:1) connects this account with what goes before. In fact the material in Exodus would be rather meaningless without the accounts in Genesis. However, after a brief reference to what came before, the author launches into a description of the changed situation. God's people, once the favored guests of Pharaoh, have become a nation of slaves. Jehovah undertakes to deliver this people from her oppressors, and make her into a nation under God with institutions and laws given by divine revelation. Exodus is a picture of the mighty-working God, redeeming and creating a people for himself.

The theme of Exodus is clearly redemption by the mighty acts of God. The leader of Israel is the Almighty operating on

[3]"Exodus," *The New Bible Commentary,* ed. R. Davidson (Grand Rapids: Wm. B. Eerdmans Publishing Co., 1954), p. 106.

[4]Philip C. Johnson, "Exodus," *The Wycliffe Bible Commentary,* ed. Charles F. Pfeiffer and Everett F. Harrison (Chicago: Moody Press, 1962), p. 51.

[5]*Ibid.*

and through His servant Moses. The task of deliverance seemed impossible, but God accomplished it with a mighty hand. The establishing of these difficult people in a new homeland as a godly nation appeared hopeless, but the book closes with a triumph of God's grace. The focus is on God's character as the One who reveals himself as mighty and just, yet tender and forgiving. Israel would look back on these events through these pages of history, and see, perhaps even more clearly than did the Israel of the Exodus, the God who had revealed himself to His people.

The purpose in writing the book is evident. This account of God's acts in delivering His people from Egypt and giving to them their laws and institutions would be a constant reminder of God's special concern for Israel and a uniting factor in their worship. Israel could never have become and continued to be the people whose God is the Lord without the awareness of these divine events in their history. The recounting of the events created faith in the later generations of Israel. These same events are spiritualized into the great redemption wrought by Jesus Christ on the Cross. Christians look back to these divine manifestations as symbolic of God's work for them in Christ (see John 1:29; Heb. 8:5; 10:1).

Outline

I. Oppression in Egypt, 1:1—11:10

A. Introduction, 1:1-22
B. Preparation of the Deliverer, 2:1—4:31
C. Prelude to Deliverance, 5:1—7:13
D. The Plagues in Egypt, 7:14—11:10

II. Deliverance and Victories, 12:1—18:27

A. The Passover, 12:1-36
B. The Exodus, 12:37—15:21
C. The Journey to Sinai, 15:22—18:27

III. The Covenant at Mt. Sinai, 19:1—24:18

A. The Covenant Proposed by God, 19:1-25
B. The Ten Commandments, 20:1-17
C. The People's Fear, 20:18-20
D. The Laws of the Covenant, 20:21—23:33
E. Ratification of the Covenant, 24:1-18

IV. The Worship of God Established, 25:1—40:38

A. God's Plan for the Tabernacle, 25:1—31:18
B. The Covenant Broken and Restored, 32:1—34:35
C. Building the Tabernacle, 35:1—38:31
D. Making the Garments, 39:1-31
E. The Completed Materials Presented to Moses, 39:32-43
F. Erection of the Tabernacle, 40:1-33
G. The Divine Dedication, 40:34-38

Section I *Oppression in Egypt*

Exodus 1:1—11:10

A. Introduction, 1:1-22

1. *Israel's Growth in Egypt* (1:1-7)

The writer of Exodus ties this book directly to the preceding one with the word **now** (1). He is not relating a new and different story but an additional chapter in the life of God's people. All of God's revelations are tied together with the later ones fulfilling the earlier.

a. From a small beginning (1:1-5). **These are the names of the children of Israel, which came into Egypt** (1). God knows His children whether small or large in number. His repetition of their names many times (see 6:14-26; Gen. 35:23-26; 46:8-26) emphasizes His interest in them and His desire for posterity's familiarity with them.

Each one of the sons of Jacob came to Egypt with **his household.** No one was left behind. The 11 persons here named (2-4) along with **Joseph** (5), who was **in Egypt already,** made up Jacob's family of 12 sons. All but one were born to him while he was in the vicinity of Haran (see map 1) with his father-in-law, Laban. Benjamin, the youngest, was born on the journey back to Canaan (Gen. 35:23-26). Jacob brought all his family to Egypt to be with Joseph. The total number of **souls,** or persons, was **seventy** and all were direct descendants of Jacob. Likely there were others in the households who were not **of the loins** (descendants) **of Jacob.** Abraham's clan comprised 318 adult males (Gen. 14:14), and on the same basis the various families with their servants which came into Egypt might have numbered into the thousands.[1] Even so, there was a tremendous growth of Israel in Egypt although reckoned on the basis of a beginning this large.

[1]George Rawlinson, "Exodus" (Exposition and Homiletics), *The Pulpit Commentary,* eds. H. D. M. Spence and Joseph S. Exell, I (Grand Rapids: Wm. B. Eerdmans Publishing Co., 1950), 1.

b. Leaders will die (1:6). Fathers and leaders must die; this is the way of life on earth. **Joseph died, and all his brethren** (6). Those upon whom one depends most will ultimately depart. In fact growth is dependent on death. "Except a corn of wheat fall into the ground and die, it abideth alone" (John 12:24). One generation passes away and a new one takes over. Thus it is with God's people as well as with the rest of the world.

c. Fulfillment of God's promise (1:7). **And the children of Israel were fruitful, and increased abundantly.** Even though God's chosen men die, He watches over their children. He made a promise to Abraham of the increase of his seed (Gen. 12:2; 15:5; 17:1-8) and here in Egypt that promise was being fulfilled. By the time Israel left Egypt the total became about 600,000 men in addition to the women and children (12:37). This was not necessarily an unusual growth in this length of time.[2] Yet considering the hostile environment it showed God's special providence.

What God had promised to mankind at creation (Gen. 1:28) was now being fulfilled in His chosen family. The words **increased abundantly** come from Hebrew that means "to teem or swarm" as in marine or insect life (see Gen. 1:20; 7:21).[3] Not only great in number, Israel became **exceeding mighty.** Obviously health and vigor are indicated. Moses recognized this gracious providence when he wrote, "A Syrian ready to perish was my father, and he went down into Egypt, and sojourned there with a few, and became there a nation, great, mighty, and populous" (Deut. 26:5).

The **land** that **was filled with them** refers to Goshen, where Jacob and his sons were first placed (Gen. 47:1, 4-6, 27). No doubt in time they outgrew this place and began to mingle with the Egyptians in other sections. Their increasing numbers soon attracted the king's attention.

2. *Israel Enslaved in Egypt* (1:8-14)

a. Favors forgotten (1:8). The brief words, **a new king . . . knew not Joseph,** convey considerable history. Joseph's part in the preservation of Egypt was appreciated by his contemporaries. Now a new dynasty, as these words likely mean, took over in Egypt. The Hyksos dynasty ruled Egypt from about 1720 until

[2]*Ibid.*, p. 9.

[3]J. Coert Rylaarsdam, *op. cit.*, I, 853.

1570 B.C. These kings were foreigners and were expelled by this **new king.** It would appear that the new dynasty, the eighteenth, hated all persons associated with the earlier kings, especially the Hebrews.[4] The new king not only did not know Joseph, but apparently cared little for Egypt's past.

Forgetting Joseph meant also forgetting God. By disregarding God's people Pharaoh set his mind and heart against Jehovah. Often a refusal to remember the past results in present rebellion. It is an evil day for any man who sets his face against God.

b. Oppression excused (1:9-10). Evil men seek for reasons to justify their ways before other men and in their own eyes. This new king first exaggerated the problem by saying that **the people . . . are more and mightier than we** (9). He was frightened by the numerical increase of the Israelites and by the strength they possessed. God's favor for His people made the king jealous.

The ruler feared the possibility of Israel joining with Egypt's **enemies** in a war (10). There is no evidence that Israel had warlike intentions, but it is amazing what evil a carnal heart can read into the intentions of other men.

In the king's mind, the ultimate disaster would be that the people might **get them up out of the land.** Possibly Israel's hope of later settlement in Palestine was known. If Pharaoh feared their presence in Egypt, why did he not send them out, rather than try to destroy them (16, 22)? Possibly he feared their becoming a neighboring strong nation.

c. Cruelty devised (1:11, 13-14). Worldly wisdom often devises cruel methods. The king wanted to break down the power of Israel by weakening their will as a group and causing them to become like the Egyptians. Apparently, according to later evaluations (Josh. 24:14; Ezek. 20:7-9), some of the Israelites did just this. Under normal circumstances such methods would have fulfilled the king's design.

The **taskmasters** (11) were general supervisors whose cruel methods were well-known. Likely some foremen were Israelites (5:14). "There is . . . room to think that they not only worked them unmercifully, but also obliged them to pay an exorbitant

[4]Johnson, *op. cit.*, p. 53.

tribute at the same time."[5] **Treasure cities** were "store-cities" where provisions and arms were stockpiled.

The tasks for the Israelites became very **bitter with hard bondage** (14). **Service in the field** may refer either to irrigation projects or to the care of the royal herds,[6] or possibly to carrying brick to the places of construction.[7] The bondage was as cruel as man could make it short of death.

d. Intentions thwarted (1:12). When God intervenes for His people, men's evil designs cannot succeed: **The more they afflicted them, the more they multiplied and grew.** This is a reversal of natural law, but such a divine intervention has frustrated persecutors of God's people many times. By giving special favor to His own, God counteracted tyrannical power. Deliverance from the bondage did not come, but vigor and strength remained in the people.

These unusual results baffled the taskmasters. They could not understand what was happening, so **they were grieved**—"The Egyptians were in dread of the people" (RSV). "There was something eerie and unnerving about this."[8] It only increased their fear and cruelty.

3. *Israel's Existence Threatened* (1:15-22)

The writer of Exodus is laying the background for the birth and miraculous preservation of Moses. The wicked king of Egypt and his counselors were baffled and must resort to more severe methods to break Israel.

Their actions illustrate the "Increasing Boldness of Evil." (1) General oppression of the good, 8-14; (2) Secret murder of the innocent, 15-21; (3) Total and open destruction of life, 22.

a. The secret scheme foiled (1:15-21). Since Israel multiplied even in bitter bondage, the king decided to strike at the secret of strength, the male child. To avoid publicity he sought the cooperation of the **Hebrew midwives** (15) in destroying the male children at birth. These midwives may have been Egyptians, but were assigned to the Hebrew women.[9] The two named likely

[5]Adam Clarke, *A Commentary and Critical Notes* (New York: Abingdon-Cokesbury, n.d.), I, 293.

[6]*Ibid.*

[7]*Ibid.*, p. 294.

[8]Rylaarsdam, *op. cit.*, I, 855.

[9]Rawlinson, P.C., I, 17.

were heads of an organized order of midwives, since two could hardly serve for all Israel.[10] The king's design was to destroy the males and amalgamate the females into the Egyptian population. This plan would end Israel as a nation. The **stools** (16) were birthstools designed to be used in childbirth and were common in Egypt, Mesopotamia, and among the Hebrews.

The king's intention was thwarted again. These **midwives feared God** (17) and did not carry out his command. Apparently Israelitish influence upon their neighbors had been effective. The reason given by the midwives to the king for their failure was true—**the Hebrew women . . . are lively** (19); they gave birth before help arrived. God thus aided the Hebrew mothers for their protection and provided the midwives with an excuse satisfactory to the king. "Faith in God enables men to give a reason for not doing wrong."[11] God honored these midwives with **houses** (21, "families," RSV). It is possible they married Israelites and became members of God's chosen people.[12]

b. The open threat (1:22). When men fight against God, they ultimately come to desperation. Egypt's king was at his wit's end. He had tried twice to reduce Israel's strength, but to no avail. Drastic measures appeared necessary. He must come out in the open and demand the destruction of the Hebrews.

This time it was not just the taskmasters or the midwives whose help was required. **Pharaoh charged all his people** to drown the male children. Although the word "Hebrew" is not stated in 22, it is assumed. Apparently by this time Israel was more widely scattered among the people of Egypt than when they were concentrated in Goshen. They were, therefore, more vulnerable. Without God's providence this decree would have ended Israel.

Chapter I pictures how "God Guards His People": (1) When small in number, 5-7; (2) When under oppression, 8-14; (3) When threatened with extinction, 15-22.

[10]John Peter Lange, *Exodus* ("Commentary on the Holy Scriptures"; Grand Rapids: Zondervan Publishing House, n.d.), p. 3.

[11]Joseph S. Exell, *Homiletical Commentary on the Book of Exodus* (The Preacher's Complete Homiletical Commentary on the Old Testament"; New York: Funk and Wagnalls Co., 1892), p. 10.

[12]Matthew Henry, *Commentary on the Whole Bible* (New York: Fleming H. Revell Co., 1706), *ad loc.*, fn.

B. Preparation of the Deliverer, 2:1—4:31

1. *Birth, Preservation, and Discipline of Moses* (2:1-25)

The Egyptian oppressor from every earthly point of view had made an edict that spelled the extinction of Israel. With every male child to be drowned in the river, how could a nation survive? Since all the people were commissioned to assist in this evil design, there seemed to be no human means of resistance. It appeared that the end had come.

a. God's secret providence (2:1-10). God had a man and woman of the **house of Levi** (1) whom He could entrust with His secret. Moses was not their first child, for Miriam, a sister, was old enough to watch over her brother (4; Num. 26:59). Furthermore, Moses' brother, Aaron, was three years his elder (6:20; Num. 26:59). It would appear that the king's edict went into effect after Aaron's birth, and that Moses was the first of these parents' children whose life was in danger because of the royal proclamation.

The faith of the parents (Heb. 11:23) is clearly portrayed in that the mother saw he was **a goodly child** and **she hid him three months** (2). Then she placed him in **an ark** and **laid it in the flags by the river's brink** (3). Faith always results in action, even when action is risky. Living by her faith, the mother also showed cleverness. She placed the babe in the water where the princess of Egypt normally came. She also arranged for her daughter to be at a strategic point where the right question could be asked at the right moment (4, 7). **To wit** (4) means to know or to observe. It was also an act of faith for a Hebrew woman to commit her child into the hands of the Egyptian princess. This mother, like Hannah and Mary at later times, was convinced that her child was chosen of God and she was willing to trust him to God's providence.

God's grace is revealed in the **compassion** shown by Pharaoh's daughter (6). Even when wicked men do their worst, God still by His gracious power can place goodwill and tender love in the hearts of people near a tyrant. Little did that wicked king know how God was working His plan secretly and surely even while it appeared that the worldly ruler was succeeding. Also some of Pharaoh's money was used to pay the Hebrew mother to **nurse** her own **child** (9). This is another example where man's wrath is made to praise God.

It can be supposed that **Moses** (10) was trained as a young Egyptian prince and received the best education possible for a youth of that day. His name, **Moses,** was a constant reminder of his origin, for the Hebrew meaning is "drawn out" and the Egyptian meaning is "saved from the water" (Berk., fn.). It appears certain that his mother's early words produced a fruit that lived on in the lad's heart. In him were developed a sense of right and a hatred for injustice which came to the surface in his later actions.

b. Moses' premature actions (2:11-15). The injustices that were being heaped upon the Israelites gave to Moses a sense of mission. When old enough to act on his own, he examined in person the burdens of his brethren. When **he spied an Egyptian smiting an Hebrew** (11), his longing to help his people rose to the surface. He felt he was right in punishing the wicked doer, yet he also knew such an act would be dangerous. **He slew the Egyptian** (12) only when he thought no one would know. He had no authority from Egypt to correct these evils, and God had not yet commissioned him. Acting on his own, he got into trouble.

When Moses attempted to settle a difference between two Hebrews the following day, he learned that his killing of **the Egyptian** was **known** (14). He also learned that injustice was present even among his brethren. Moreover, a people who would not support a man who wanted to help them were not yet ready for a deliverer. Also a self-appointed **prince** and **judge** would not do. Moses must await God's time, and receive further instructions from a Higher Authority. The king soon learned what Moses had done, but before Pharaoh could act, Moses **fled** to the **land of Midian** (15; see map 3), where 40 years later (Acts 7:30) he would receive his commission.

c. Moses in Midian (2:16-25). The Midianites were a people descended from Keturah and Abraham (Gen. 25:1-4). It appears that they dwelt in the vicinity of Mount Sinai, on the Sinaitic peninsula east of Egypt beyond the Red Sea. This mountain was also called Horeb (3:1).[13] **The priest of Midian** (16) is called **Reuel** (18), meaning "friend of God."[14] Elsewhere he is known as Jethro (3:1; 4:12, *et al.*). He had seven daughters who cared for their father's sheep, but who had difficulty with the shepherds who mistreated the girls. Moses, always ready to help

[13]Johnson, *op. cit.*, p. 54 [14]*Ibid.*

the abused, came to their rescue. How he managed a group of shepherds by himself is not said, but he succeeded in holding them off until the girls had **watered their flock** (17). As a result of this kindness **Moses** found a home and a wife (21). Here he became a father of his first son **in a strange land** (22). The name **Gershom** "suggests not merely 'stranger,' but exile, banishment" (Berk., fn.).

During the time of Moses' sojourn in Midian, his oppressed people in Egypt began to feel more deeply the crushing weight of their burdens (23). Apparently the leaders of Egypt had resorted to cruel **bondage** to keep the Hebrews in subjection, rather than by continuing the policy of killing the male children.

However, God still watched over His own. He **heard their groaning** and **remembered his covenant** (24). God postponed the deliverance of Israel until both Moses and Israel were ready. Moses needed the disciplines of the wilderness, and Israel's desire for freedom needed to grow. The continued bondage in Egypt united the people of Israel in their desire for liberty, and in their faith that only God could free them. God hears the cries of His people but waits until "the fulness of time" to bring the victory. **Had respect unto them** (25) means "God concerned Himself about them" (Berk.).

2. *Call and Commission of Moses* (3:1—4:17)

a. The burning bush (3:1-6). According to Stephen (Acts 7:23), Moses was 40 years old when he slew the Egyptian, and after 40 more years he met the Lord at the burning bush (Acts 7:30). After these years in the wilderness, God saw that His people and Moses were ready for the miracle of deliverance. Moses' father-in-law is here called **Jethro** (1), although it is possible that Jethro was the son of Reuel and therefore Moses' brother-in-law.[15] Still a shepherd, Moses was in the vicinity of **Horeb,** the **mountain of God** (1), also called Sinai (see map 3). It is likely that **Horeb** was the name applied to the range of mountains, while Sinai was a smaller group, or a single peak.[16]

The angel of the Lord (2) at the burning **bush** is often reckoned by Bible scholars to be the preincarnate Christ,[17] although He is never referred to as such in the New Testament. In the

[15]Rawlinson, CWB, I, 198.

[16]Johnson, *op. cit.*, p. 54.

[17]Clarke, *op. cit.*, I, 303.

Bible a flame of fire often symbolizes the presence of God (Heb. 12:29). Moses' curiosity was attracted and God spoke to him. Then he **hid his face: for he was afraid to look upon God** (6). He could not stand lightly in God's presence, and he learned that the Divine Presence sanctifies even the ground where He appears (5).

In vv. 1-6 we see the "Servant of God." (1) The employment in which he was engaged, 1; (2) The sight which he witnessed, 2; (3) The resolution he made, 3; (4) The prohibition he received, 5; (5) The announcement he heard, 6.[18]

b. The divine plan (3:7-10). God involved himself in the plight of His people. He said, **I have surely seen, I have heard,** and **I know** (7). He may have waited many years, but He was attentive all the while. These words give assurance of God's attentive listening to cries of sorrow, and His knowledge of the human plight.

God is always acting in the world, "for in him we live, and move, and have our being" (Acts 17:28). However, He moves into history at special times to make himself known and to accomplish His will. He told Moses that He had **come down to deliver** (8) His people from Egypt. He had a place prepared for them in a land **good** and **large** and **flowing with milk and honey.** This does not mean that Canaan was more fertile than Egypt, but it was a good land, fruitful, and large enough for Israel. It was a land identified by the names of peoples whose iniquities were full, and they must relinquish the land to the chosen of God (Gen. 15:16-21).[19]

Though God could have delivered Israel by a word directly, He chose His servant through whom He would work. Moses was told, **I will send thee unto Pharaoh** (10). This man, once a self-appointed deliverer, was to go to the proud king and lead Israel out of Egypt under God's direction.

"God's Involvement with His People" is seen in five statements: (1) **I have surely seen,** 7; (2) **I have heard,** 7; (3) **I know,** 7; (4) **I am come down,** 8; (5) **I will send thee,** 10.

c. The divine instructions (3:11-22). At first Moses objected to God's plan to use him. He saw (*a*) his own inability—**Who am I?**—and (*b*) the impossibility of the task—**bring forth the children of Israel out of Egypt** (11). The self-confident prince

[18]Exell, *op. cit.*, p. 32. [19]Johnson, *op. cit.*, p. 54. Cf. BBC, II, 35-36.

of 40 years before now feared the assignment. He was wiser as regards man's ability to bring about a deliverance, but he must yet learn the power of God. How often one hesitates when he looks at himself—and he should; but there need be no fear when one looks to God!

Certainly I will be with thee (12) suggests that God's choice of a messenger is not on the basis of man's ability, but on his submission to God's will. God assured Moses that he and the people should **serve God upon this mountain** after Israel was delivered from **Egypt.** The expression **this shall be a token** is better, "This shall be the sign for you" (RSV).

Moses realized that, as a spokesman for God, he must persuade his people. They would ask, Who is this God who is sending you? **What is his name?** (13) Egyptian gods had names, and the people would want to know the name of their God.

Here at Horeb, God said, **I AM THAT I AM** (14). The original is a form of the word *Yahweh* (Jehovah). The tense is indefinite, so can mean equally past, present, or future.[20] God "revealed himself to Moses not as the Creator—God of power—Elohim, but as the personal God of Salvation, and all that 'I am' contains shall be manifested through the ages to come."[21] This name also revealed His eternity—He was the **God of your fathers** and this was to be His **name for ever:** His **memorial unto all generations** (15). This divine Being later was said to be He "which is, and which was, and which is to come, the Almighty" (Rev. 1:8). It is evident from Gen. 4:26 (where *Yahweh* is translated "the LORD," as usual in the KJV, RSV, and many other English versions) that Moses received here an explanation of a name long known (cf. also 6:3, and comments there).

Moses was commissioned to **gather the elders of Israel together** (16), inform them who God was and that He had heard their cries. He was to make known God's promise of their deliverance from Egypt and their inheritance of **the land** of Canaan (17; cf. BBC, II, 35-36). God told Moses that the people would **hearken** (18) to him. They would be willing to carry their petitions to the king.

Asking for a **three days' journey** in order to **sacrifice to the Lord** (18) was a test of Pharaoh's willingness to cooperate with God. "There was reticence [withholding information] here, no

[20]Connell, *op. cit.,* p. 109. Cf. BBC, II, 110, fn. 1.

[21]Johnson, *op. cit.,* p. 55.

doubt, but no falseness."[22] God gave Pharaoh every opportunity to cooperate with Him. Yet He knew that the king would not yield, not even with **a mighty hand** upon him (19). God knows even what He does not make so by decree.

God promised to do great **wonders** in Egypt, so that ultimately Israel would be permitted to leave (20). When they left, **every woman** was to **borrow** ("ask," RSV) from **the Egyptians** (22), who would show **favour** to these people (21) by giving of their treasures. Since they had been enslaved so long, Israel had a right to this remuneration. **Spoil the Egyptians** (22) means "despoil" (RSV) or "strip" them (Berk.).

In vv. 14-22 there is a revelation of "The Eternal God": (1) He reveals His name, 14-16; (2) He unveils His plan, 17-18; (3) He assures of His power, 19-22.

d. The divine signs (4:1-9). Moses was very human, and his faith was yet weak. He said of the Hebrews, **They will not believe me** (1). God therefore patiently led him on to further assurance. Using the common shepherd's staff, God gave Moses evidence of His supernatural power (2-3) by turning the **rod** into **a serpent.**

The second sign to Moses was the **hand** that became **leprous** (6-7). If the people would not believe the first and second signs, they would believe the third; this was to be the turning of **river** water into **blood** when some of it was poured out on the **dry land** (9).

In addition to their miraculous nature, these signs taught important lessons. The **rod,** symbol of the shepherd, or common worker, when surrendered to God, becomes a wonder and power. Leprosy, symbol of sin and defilement in Egypt, can be instantly cured by the power of God. The **blood,** sign of war and judgment, assured retribution upon the wickedness of the Egyptians.[23]

e. The divine method (4:10-17). Moses had every reason, after these signs were given, to accept God's assignment and believe His word. But his unwillingness was still present, and a further excuse was offered—**I am slow of speech, and of a slow tongue** (10). Moses had not yet felt any change even though he had talked with God; he still felt **slow of speech.** But God assured him of victory for himself (11-12), even as He had prom-

[22]Rawlinson, PC, I, 58.

[23]*Ibid.*, pp. 87-88.

ised to overcome the problem of the people's unbelief. However Moses was not convinced; frankly he did not want to go to Egypt. The meaning of v. 13 is, "Oh, my Lord, send, I pray, some other person" (RSV).

Because of this **the anger of the Lord was kindled against Moses** (14). Nevertheless, the only punishment given to Moses was the sharing of leadership with his brother. Aaron would be the **spokesman** (16) and Moses would be the prophet. Moses apparently was willing for this arrangement, and his objections ceased. God had an answer for all of this man's misgivings. Yet the arrangement was really a second-best. Aaron often proved to be as much a hindrance as a help (e.g., 32:1-25; Num. 12:1-2).

The secret of Moses' success was to **take this rod in thine hand** (17). In this chapter, taking "The Rod of God" meant (1) The full surrender of oneself to God, 2-4; (2) The means by which people would recognize God's presence, 5; (3) The avenue through which God's power would be demonstrated, 17.

3. *Moses' Return to Egypt* (4:18-31)

a. The account (4:18-20). **Moses,** submissive now to God's plan, first obtained permission from **Jethro** to leave for **Egypt** (18). He did not give all of his reasons for going, but the reason he gave was sufficient to gain approval. His **brethren** were his kinsmen, the Israelites. Jethro said, **Go in peace.** He gave Moses freedom, and thus put no obstacle in the way of God's plan.

God gave Moses further assurance by declaring that those who had **sought** his **life** were **dead** (19). Moses began his journey with **his wife and** two **sons** (20; cf. 18:3-4), though apparently after the circumcision episode (24-26), he sent them back to Jethro (18:2) and proceeded on alone with Aaron (29). Obviously the statement that **he returned to the land of Egypt** (20) is a general statement not fulfilled until v. 29. It may be rendered "set out to return."[24]

b. The message repeated (4:21-23). God again instructed Moses to perform the **wonders before Pharaoh** when he arrived in **Egypt.** But God also warned him that He would **harden** Pharaoh's **heart** and the king would **not let the people go** (21; see comments on 7:13 concerning the hardening of Pharaoh's heart). God's victory over this tyrant was not to be a quick one,

[24]Rawlinson, CWB, I, 204.

but the final victory would be the Lord's (cf. 3:20). God gave every opportunity to Pharaoh. Early he was to be warned that, since Israel was as God's **firstborn** (22), refusal to obey would mean death to the king's **firstborn** (23). Increasingly it was to be made clear to Pharaoh that he was oppressing God's people and refusal was rebellion against the Almighty God.

c. *Discipline for Moses* (4:24-26). These three verses are difficult to interpret. Though Moses was obeying God in returning to Egypt, there had been one point of failure. God had instituted the rite of circumcision for all sons of Israel. It seems that Moses had himself been circumcised and had performed the rite on his first son. The reaction of **Zipporah** (25-26) indicates her strong disapproval of the act and suggests that Moses had allowed the omission of circumcision for his second son in order to please his wife. However God demanded obedience, and brought Zipporah to terms by what appears to have been some serious affliction for her husband (24). Obedience brought healing to Moses (26), but the incident apparently resulted in Zipporah's return to her own home (18:2).

d. *The report to Aaron* (4:27-28). **The Lord** instructed **Aaron** to **go into the wilderness to meet Moses** (27). God did His preparatory work in both brothers. It appears that they met at Sinai after Zipporah had returned home. Moses reported to Aaron all that God had said to him, and also told him about **the signs** (28). The account is brief, but Aaron obviously accepted without question God's revelation to Moses.

e. *The report to the people* (4:29-31). The two brothers returned to Egypt and called a conference of **the elders** (leading men) of the Israelites (29). While Moses had told Aaron God's words at their first meeting (28), it was Aaron who **spake all the words** and **did the signs** before **the people** (30). As God had promised (3:18), **the people believed** the words and signs (31). It was a joyful occasion when these oppressed Hebrews learned that God had heard their cries and was ready to act; **they bowed their heads and worshipped.**

C. Prelude to Deliverance, 5:1—7:13

1. *First Visit to Pharaoh* (5:1-23)

The time had arrived when the real test must be made. Moses and Aaron were equipped and instructed. The people were informed and appeared ready to follow God. It was time to confront the tyrant.

a. The refusal of the king (5:1-5). God's word, **Let my people go** (1), was given to the man in whose power Israel was held. No doubt it came as a surprise to **Pharaoh** because he thought of Israel as his people. The Hebrews had been in Egypt over four centuries. How could anyone else claim their loyalty and require a sacrificial feast from these slaves?

Furthermore, **Pharaoh** recognized no authority over himself. He asked, **Who is the Lord, that I should obey his voice?** (2) There were many gods in Egypt, and this king knew about them. But for him gods were to be manipulated, not obeyed. His ultimatum was, **I know not the Lord, neither will I let Israel go.**

Moses and Aaron continued to entreat. They told the king, **The God of the Hebrews hath met with us** (3). They asked for permission to take a **three days' journey** in order to **sacrifice** to their **God.** In the only kind of language Pharaoh could understand, they warned of judgment from the Lord: **lest he fall upon us with pestilence, or with the sword.** Yet the king refused.

Pharaoh accused them of being idlers, seeking to evade responsibility in an appeal to religion. He saw it as laziness and challenged, "Why do you take the people away from their work?" (4, RSV) Despots find it hard ever to believe their subjects have a righteous cause.

b. Increased labor (5:6-14). The king in anger immediately commanded the Egyptian **taskmasters** and Israelite **officers** (6)[25] to increase the work of the slaves. Rather than supplying the straw from the fields already cut and ready for use, the taskmasters required the people to **gather** the stubble **for themselves** (7). The **straw** was mixed with clay to make stronger sun-dried brick. The stubble was the lower part of the grain stalk. Though there was extra work to gather the straw, the **tale** (number) of brick to be made was to remain the same (8). This tyrant, blind to all reason, was determined to break the will of the people. But little did he realize that he could not break God. He could be cruel to God's people, but the words he had heard were not **vain words** (9).

This order of Pharaoh was carried out by **the taskmasters** (10-11). The slaves **scattered** over **all the land of Egypt to**

[25]Johnson, *op. cit.*, p. 56.

gather stubble (12). The **taskmasters** (13), fearful of their own positions, pushed the Hebrew officers hard. When the quota of brick was not fulfilled, the officers **were beaten** (14). It appeared that Moses' and Aaron's attempts had backfired.

c. *The three appeals* (5:15-23). The Israelite **officers** (15) thought that some mistake had been made. Surely Pharaoh would not demand impossible tasks of these slaves. So they went direct to the king to appeal their case: **Wherefore dealest thou thus with thy servants?** They thought that the fault was in the king's **own people** (16). But these Hebrew officers learned the truth. It was the king himself who had made this demand. He claimed that the people were **idle** ("lazy," Amp. OT) because they wanted to **sacrifice to the Lord** (17). He cruelly renewed the demand for their labors (18).

The second appeal was made by the officers to **Moses and Aaron** (20). They saw that the door was closed with Pharaoh and that they were in a bad situation. **In evil case** (19) is better "in grave trouble" (Berk.). They placed the blame upon **Moses and Aaron** (20), claiming that they had made the Israelites (not **our savour,** but simply "us," RSV) **to be abhorred** by both **Pharaoh** and **his servants** and had placed **a sword in their hand** (21); i.e., jeopardized the lives of the Hebrews.

Young faith may often be weak. These men had believed Moses at first, but this severe trial made them doubt. Surely Moses was wrong! How could God be in an action where matters got worse? They had yet to learn that often it gets darkest just before day, that all things must be counted as loss (Phil. 3:8) before God becomes all, and that God delivers when one gets to the end of himself.

The third appeal was made by Moses to **the Lord** (22). Rather than trying to answer the officers, he went directly to God. Often it is futile to do otherwise, especially when one's own mind is baffled. It was plainly evident that matters were worse. There were no outward signs that God had even started a deliverance. Moses asked, **Why is it that thou hast sent me?** (22)

The Lord is pleased when one comes with his "whys" and "wherefores." While faith is growing it will have its setbacks. God often brings a person low before He shows His strong arm. Many saints have cried out, "How long, O Lord?" (Rev. 6:10) but God watches every move of His suffering children.

2. *The Renewed Promise and Command* (6:1-13)

God had not let Moses down. A delayed deliverance was not a forsaken promise. God was working out His purpose. Verse 1 is translated by Smith, "Now you shall see what I will do to Pharaoh; compelled by a mighty power he will not only let them go, but will drive them out of his land" (Smith-Goodspeed). **Further evil had come to Israel** (5:19), but God's promise was still secure.

The value of the promise was in the God back of it. **I am the Lord** (2). Their forefathers knew of **God Almighty** (3), the God of might and "overpowering strength." "Here the primary idea of Jehovah is, on the contrary, that of absolute, eternal, unconditional, independent existence."[26] Both names were probably of great antiquity and widely known (Gen. 4:26; 12:8; 17:1; 28:3), but God had manifested himself primarily by the name of *El Shaddai,* **God Almighty.** Now, for this great deliverance, God himself made known the full meaning of *Yahweh,* "the Lord." This is not a new and different account of the call of Moses, as many liberal scholars contend,[27] but a renewal of promises to Moses with added emphasis for a discouraged people.[28]

The new revelation in this name pictured God as One who bound himself by a **covenant** (4) with His people. This **covenant** began with the patriarchs and included the promise of **Canaan,** where they had wandered as **strangers** and pilgrims for many years (Gen. 15:18). The **covenant** was now **remembered** when God **heard the groaning of the children of Israel** because of their **bondage** (5). He had not forgotten; He had only waited until His children were ready to enter into their part of the covenant.

Moses was commanded again to reassure the people. They were to be told that they would be delivered from Egyptian **bondage,** that God would **redeem** them **with a stretched out arm** ("special and vigorous action," Amp. OT), **and with great judgments** (6) upon the oppressors. Israel was to be God's special **people** and He would give them **the land** of promise for their **heritage** (7-8). These reassuring words were backed by the declaration, **I am the Lord.**

Though the promise was strongly given, the leaders of **Israel**

[26]Rawlinson, CWB, I, 208. [27]IB, I, 888, Exegesis.

[28]Lange, *Exodus,* p. 17.

. . . hearkened not unto Moses for anguish of spirit, and for cruel bondage (9). Although they had earlier believed (4:31), the increased cruelty had brought them so low that mere words of promise were not enough. Sometimes God must work before the promise can be believed. Afterwards men will remember the words of promise.

When **Moses** (10) could not convince Israel, he doubted that he could convince **Pharaoh** (11), to whom God now directed him. If Israel would not hear him, why would Pharaoh listen? **Uncircumcised lips** (12), according to the Hebrew idiom, would be an imperfection which interferes with efficiency.[29] An uncircumcised ear was an ear that would not hearken (Jer. 6:10), and an uncircumcised heart was one that did not understand. So here Moses' lips were not able to speak clearly. But in spite of man's weakness, God had spoken. His **charge** to **Israel** and **Pharaoh** had been made, and the matter would be done (13).

"Problems for Faith," found in 5:22—6:13, are: (1) God's delays in action, 22-23; (2) Crushed and broken spirits, 9; (3) Unresponsive people, 12; (4) Infirmities of the flesh, 9.

"Assurances for Faith" in vv. 1-8 include: (1) God's power, 1; (2) God's name, 3; (3) God's response, 5; (4) God's relationship, 7; (5) God's promise, 8.

3. *The Genealogy of Aaron and Moses* (6:14-27)

The author of Exodus had here reached the end of a preliminary account of the deliverance from Egypt. The drama of the actual victory was about to begin. It was his desire, as well as God's, to keep the account clearly tied to history, and especially to the history of God's people. It was the task of Moses and Aaron to lead this people out of the land of Egypt (13). These were the two men about whom he was writing (26-27) and their names were found in the official genealogy. Hence the writer includes that portion of the genealogy here.

The list began with **Reuben** (14) and **Simeon** (15), the two older brothers of Levi. These first two and their descendants were mentioned, probably to show where Levi came in the list and also to suggest that God's choices often bypass the firstborn.[30] The names given were the heads of families, or "clans," and no

[29]Rawlinson, CWB, I, 209.

[30]Connell, *op. cit.*, p. 111.

names beyond those of the first generation of sons were given for these two elder brothers.

The primary concern here was the account of the family of Levi, from which Moses and Aaron came. The giving of the ages of **Levi** (16), **Kohath** (18), and **Amram** (20) was not for chronological reasons, but to show God's good providence to this family even before the tribe was selected for priestly work.[31] The genealogy of the tribe of Levi is given in detail here for the first time (cf. Gen. 46:9-11; Num. 3:18-33).

The **Amram** of 18 cannot be the same as the one in 20 because several generations occur between them. This method of recording genealogy was not unusual for the Hebrews.[32] Though the author gave the descendants of relatives of Moses and Aaron (19, 21, 22, 24), his primary concern was these two leaders. **Korah** (24), cousin to Moses, was mentioned even though later he perished; he is included because his children survived (see Num. 16:1; 26:11).

Jochebed (20, the mother of Moses) was an aunt of **Amram,** and probably about the same age. Such marriages were not unusual before the giving of the law (Lev. 18:12).[33] Moses' descendants are not mentioned here, but Aaron's son **Eleazar** (23) and grandson **Phinehas** (25) are listed. The name of Aaron's wife, **Elisheba** (23), is better known in its Greek form "Elizabeth."

The author made certain that his readers knew who Moses and Aaron were. No one was to mistake their identity. **These are that Aaron and Moses** (26) who heard from God and **spake to Pharaoh** (27). **Their armies** (26) does not necessarily mean equipped armies of men; it refers to the orderly arrangement by tribes and families when Israel was marshalled for exit.

4. *Second Visit to Pharaoh* (6:28—7:13)

a. The word to Pharaoh (6:28—7:7). Verses 28-29 repeat God's command to these two leaders about going to Pharaoh. Moses was still reluctant because of his speech impediment (30; cf. v. 12, comment), and God's plan to use Aaron was again emphasized. Yet Moses' place was of vital importance. He was to seem like a **god to Pharaoh** (1). Often the Lord sets His people

[31]Rawlinson, CWB, I, 210. [32]*Ibid.*, p. 204.

[33]Connell, *op. cit.*, p. 112.

as a god to their children and to their neighbors, in positions of authority and responsibility which they would not seek. How important in these roles that we speak **all** His word (2)!

Even though it was clear that **Pharaoh** would be hardened and **not hearken** (4), they were to speak anyhow (see comment on the hardening of Pharaoh's heart, 7:13). Along with the hardening of the king would come multiplied **signs** and **wonders** (3) and **great judgments** (4). For **mine armies** see comment on 6:26. God was about to punish Egypt, and to show mercy to His people. He was ready to do both in such a way that **the Egyptians shall know that I am the Lord** (5). God's actions were not now to be secret; they were to display His power and glory. He had been working behind the scenes with Moses and Aaron, and earlier with their parents, in secret. He had opened the hearts of the elders when the first report was given to them. But the God who had patiently waited for so many years was now ready to break forth into the open where all must see. With assurance in that word **Moses and Aaron** (6) acted. Their exact ages are given as a date for these tremendous events (7).

b. First miracle before Pharaoh (7:8-12). **When Pharaoh** should ask for confirmation in the form of **a miracle,** Moses and Aaron were to be ready with the **rod** of God which Moses had now entrusted to **Aaron** (9). The purpose of the miracle was to prove their claims of supernatural guidance. When the rod was **cast down . . . before Pharaoh . . .** it **became a serpent** (10). Pharaoh then called in his **wise men** and **sorcerers** (11), and these **magicians** ("wizards and jugglers," Amp. OT) also made their rods into serpents **with their enchantments.** "Magic was very widely practised in Egypt, and consisted mainly in the composition and employment of charms, which were believed to exert a powerful effect, both over man and over the brute creation."[34] Whether the actions of these **magicians** was entirely a result of human manipulation or whether there was present supernatural power from evil spirits is not clear.[35] In either case the action tended to discredit the miracle of Aaron's rod. This was offset by **Aaron's rod** swallowing the others (12). Whatever power God allows His enemies to possess, His strength is still greater. Yet it appears that God permits enough deception to be

[34]Rawlinson, CWB, I, 211.

[35]Cf. the suggestion in Connell, *op. cit.*, p. 112.

present along with His miracles that the hard hearts who choose to do so may harden still further (13; cf. 22).

c. *Pharaoh's heart hardened* (7:13). There is a problem concerning the hardening of Pharaoh's heart. Verse 13 should be translated, "Pharaoh's heart was hardened" (RSV), but in v. 3 it is clearly said by God, "I will harden Pharaoh's heart." It is also said that Pharaoh hardened his own heart (8:15). Possibly in this we have three stages. First, the person knowingly hardens his own heart (8:15, 32; 9:34). Pharaoh set his mind to resist and oppose God's will and thus made his own heart more stubborn. Second, as a result, the heart is hardened by the action of psychological laws ("heart was hardened," 7:14, 22; 9:7, 36). Third, when God saw that Pharaoh was determined to resist, He directly hardened the hard heart (7:3; 9:12; 10:1, 20, 27; 14:4, 8). This was done by divine judgment upon the individual (9:11-12) and by the extension of life, physical courage, and human power to continue his resistance to God.[36]

Certainly it must never be said that God causes a man to be wicked. Pharaoh was responsible for his own evil choice and for the turning of his heart from God. However, when people set their wills against God, then God gives them up to their base desires (Rom. 1:24); when "they did not like to retain God in their knowledge, God gave them over to a reprobate mind" (Rom. 1:28). God shows mercy to those who yield to Him and hardens those who resist Him (Rom. 9:18). It appears that God's judgment may place some who turn away from the light where they cannot return to Him (Heb. 10:26-30). God extended the life and ability of Pharaoh in his resistance in order to give a greater display of His power and glory.[37] God hardens only those who begin first to harden their own hearts. He can do this hardening both by extraordinary intervention or by the ordinary responses to the experiences of life.[38]

D. The Plagues in Egypt, 7:14—11:10

1. *The Water Turned into Blood* (7:14-25)

a. *Announced to Moses* (7:14-19). God was now ready to challenge the resistance of Pharaoh. Moses was commanded to

[36]Exell, *op. cit.*, p. 139.
[37]Connell, *op. cit.*, p. 110.
[38]Johnson, *op. cit.*, p. 58.

go to the king when he went to **the water** (15). This going to the Nile **in the morning** was likely for worship.[39] **Against he come** means "to meet him" (Berk.). While resisting the Lord, Pharaoh still trusted his own gods. This first plague was a direct challenge to an Egyptian object of worship. For this sign Moses was again to use his **rod.**

Moses was to warn the king of what he was going to do, and why (16-18). Pharaoh could clearly see that these things were done at the word of God's servants. He was to be told that **the Lord God of the Hebrews** had **sent** Moses (16) and that this judgment was to make him know that *Yahweh* was God—**I am the Lord** (17).[40]

b. Performed before Pharaoh (7:20-25). **Moses** passed God's word along to **Aaron,** who now **smote the waters that were in the river** (20). The command included the waters in the **streams, ponds, pools,** and **vessels** (19). Likely the water, turned to blood, came into the subsidiary places as a result of the plague on the Nile, the main source of water supply.[41] The change in the water was such that it killed **the fish** and the people **could not drink** it (21). The Egyptans were forced to dig shallow wells **for water to drink** (24).

Again the **magicians** (22) were able to counterfeit the miracle. Where they found the water on which to work their **enchantments** is not said. They may have gotten a small supply from the new wells. Their deception was sufficient to cause Pharaoh's heart to harden more. He refused to **hearken** to Moses and Aaron, **as the Lord had said.** God was able to foretell this hardening because He knew that Pharaoh would harden his heart, and also knew that the first plague would not change him. God knows even those things which He does not determine. Where before Pharaoh had caused Israel to suffer, now he and his people were beginning to feel the weight of God's hand. He knew this to be true, but did not **set his heart to it,** i.e., had "no concern even for this" (23, Smith-Goodspeed).

The plague continued **seven days** (25), which could have been shortened had Pharaoh yielded. But he probably had some water from the wells for his own use, so gave no thought to the plight of his people.[42]

[39] Lange, *Exodus*, p. 20.

[40] Connell, *op. cit.*, p. 112.

[41] *Ibid.*

[42] Rawlinson, CWB, I, 213-14.

Verses 14-25 reveal the "Faithful Servant of God." (1) He listens to God's instructions, 15-19; (2) He does precisely what God says, 20; (3) He witnesses the mighty power of God, 21-25.

2. *The Plague of Frogs* (8:1-15)

a. Moses and Aaron instructed (8:1-5). Moses was asked again **to go unto Pharaoh** and demand, **Let my people go** (1). Repetition may become monotonous, but in this case it was necessary in order to keep the issue clear. God was asking but one thing of Pharaoh, and this one thing Moses was to repeat until it became a never-forgotten demand: **Let my people go.**

Pharaoh had endured the plague of blood for seven days. Continued refusal would now result in **frogs** (2). The issue was clear, for God said, **If thou refuse . . . I will smite.** Here was merciful warning for the king, who could have avoided this plague. But hard hearts challenge even the warnings of God.

These **frogs** were to **come up** from **the river** Nile (3) and other bodies of water (5). The original word indicates that the frogs came from the mire of the marshes from which water had receded.[43] These loathsome creatures, though not dangerous in themselves, could make life miserable. The plague would affect the bedroom and the **bed,** where Egyptians were especially clean. The **ovens** (open pits in the ground) and **kneadingtroughs** (bowls) would be filled with frogs and thus make baking almost impossible. The plague would affect both the king and his **servants** (officers) as well as the common **people** (4).

b. The reaction of Pharaoh (8:6-15). Since the river Nile was reckoned as sacred by the Egyptians, to them this plague, like the others, was a contest of gods. Also frogs themselves were objects of worship,[44] and as such were not to be killed. One can imagine the distress to the pious Egyptian when he could hardly walk, or open his door, without crushing the creatures.

Again the Egyptian **magicians** were able to counterfeit the act of Aaron (7). Possibly at best they could only add a few more **frogs** to the multitudes God had already brought (6). These magicians apparently could not take away the frogs.

For the first time Pharaoh's obstinacy was weakened; he called on Moses and Aaron for help. In the case of the water becoming blood, he could be supplied from the wells, even though

[43]Lange, *Exodus*, p. 211. [44]Rawlinson, CWB, I, 214.

his people suffered, but there was no relief from these frogs. He could not sleep or eat, so he asked for mercy. He seemed convinced that God had sent the frogs and that He could remove them. Whether sincere or not, he promised to **let the people go** (8).

Moses was willing to listen to Pharaoh and grant the request. The words, **Glory over me** (9), are difficult to translate from the original; they must have been an Egyptian idiom not used in Hebrew. It seems to have meant, "I submit to thy will," or, "I am content to do thy bidding." Likely it was an expression of courtesy from an inferior to a superior.[45] Moffatt and *The Berkeley Version* both suggest the idea, "You may have the honour of saying when."

Rather than asking for immediate relief, the king said, **To morrow** (10). There was an underlying hope that by then the frogs would go by some natural means. But Moses was unafraid. He allowed the king's request to stand in order that Pharaoh might **know that there is none like unto the Lord our God,** who could both bring judgment and show mercy. By this time Moses had become much more confident of God's purpose and power.

When Moses went out from Pharaoh, he **cried unto the Lord** (12) to take away the frogs. Although he knew God would do it, yet the intercession was necessary. It pleases the Lord for man to pray earnestly even for that which He has already promised. God answered this prayer by killing the frogs (13) rather than by driving them back to the river, as the promise suggested (11). Thus the Lord left with the people a reminder of His judgment upon them (14).

It is interesting to note that, when God spoke, Moses and Aaron responded (5-6). When Pharaoh made request of Moses, he responded (8-9). When Moses cried unto God, the Lord did as Moses said (12-13). The only break in this circuit was the lack of sincerity on Pharaoh's part.

That Pharaoh's penitence was shallow is seen in that **he hardened his heart** when the judgment was lifted (15; cf. 7:13, comment). The word **respite** means literally "open space." "As soon as he 'got air' he hardened his heart."[46] Like many others, this man broke under the affliction, but did not yield his will to God. When the pressure was off, he was the same obstinate person as before, or worse.

[45]*Ibid.*, p. 215.

[46]Johnson, *op. cit.*, p. 58.

One can see in vv. **1-15** "The Judgment and Mercy of God." (1) Trials are given to lead one to repentance, 1-6; (2) Under trials the repentance of men may be temporary, 8, 15; (3) The mercy of God is shown to the proudest sinner, 12-13; (4) The servant of God should be helpful to penitent souls, 9-11.[47]

3. *The Plague of Lice* (8:16-19)

This time, without warning or offering an opportunity for surrender, God told Moses to have Aaron **smite the dust** that it might **become lice** (16). The lice could have been "gnats" (RSV, Berk.) or "mosquitoes" (Moffatt, Smith-Goodspeed). These insects came upon **man** and **beast** (17). They attacked the skin, the nose, ears, and eyes, and thus caused great irritation, and even death.[48] With so many of them—**all the dust of the land**—there was no place to find relief.

For the first time the **magicians** were unable to counterfeit with their magic (18). For one thing, in this case they had no advance notice of what was expected. Then, the point had come where the work of God became clearly His own. God permits wicked men to go so far, but there is a boundary where they are stopped. The confession, **This is the finger of God** (19), was not necessarily admitting Jehovah's superiority so much as it was acknowledging the end of human magic. There was no way this time that they could produce a deceiving duplication. Their **enchantments** would not work.

However, Pharaoh's earlier lie and disobedience (8, 15) had left his heart so hard that even such a confession did not daunt him; **he hearkened not unto them**—neither Moses nor his own servants.

4. *The Swarms of Flies* (8:20-32)

a. The warning and plague (8:20-24). Again Moses was asked to confront Pharaoh **in the morning** on his way **to the water,** probably for a religious ceremony (20; cf. 7:15). He was to repeat the demand, **Let my people go,** and to warn Pharaoh that if he refused there would be a plague of **flies** (21). From the Hebrew it is not clear what these insects were (note that **flies** is italicized in KJV), whether **flies,** "gnats" (Moffatt), beetles, or a mixture of insects.[49] *The Berkeley Version* calls them "gadflies."

[47]Exell, *op. cit.*, p. 164. [48]Rawlinson, CWB, I, 215.

[49]Johnson, *op. cit.*, p. 59.

Whatever their form, they were **grievous,** and **the land was corrupted,** i.e., destroyed by them (24).

These insects were also sacred to the Egyptians, and it was wrong to kill them. They could come into houses, ruin decorative furniture, and make life unbearable for the people. There was no human power to overcome them.

A new thing happened with this plague. While before, the Israelites in **Goshen** apparently suffered with the Egyptians, now God separated His people from the others (22). He saved His own people from the judgment. This act clearly set forth that the Lord of these plagues was the God of the Hebrews. God's people may suffer some of His judgments sent upon wicked men by reason of a common humanity, but a point is reached when they are spared the worst.

b. Pharaoh's reaction and compromise (8:25-32). Pharaoh's reaction to the new plague was immediate. He suggested a compromise: **Go ye, sacrifice to your God in the land** (25). But Moses was ready with an answer. It would not do for Israelites to sacrifice in Egypt because the sacrifice of animals sacred to them would be an **abomination** to **the Egyptians** (26) and they would likely **stone** the Israelites. Moses stood by his request for a **three days' journey into the wilderness** (27). When God has commanded, there is no room for bargaining with wicked men.

Pharaoh apparently recognized that Moses was right. He was therefore willing for Israel to go at least a short distance into the desert (28). Moses took Pharaoh at his word (apparently understanding the **not . . . very far away** as three days' journey) and promised to **intreat the Lord** (29). However, he warned, **Let not Pharaoh deal deceitfully any more.** God **removed the . . . flies** at Moses' word and **there remained not one** (31). The complete reprieve from this plague only made the king more stubborn, **neither would he let the people go** (32). In the face of so great light Pharaoh made his own heart harder (cf. comment on 7:13). He was setting his will more and more against God and His people.

Verses 20-32 show "The Rebellious Heart." (1) Suffers in judgment, 20-24; (2) Suggests a compromise, 25-26; (3) Deceitfully makes a concession, 28; (4) Receives tokens of God's mercy, 29-31; (5) Willfully refuses God's plan, 32.

5. *Death of the Cattle* (9:1-7)

God in patience continued to demand from **Pharaoh** (1) the release of His people. He warned that, if the king continued to **hold them** (2), still another plague would come. God could instantly have destroyed Pharaoh and taken His people, but He chose to appeal to the will of this wicked tyrant. The **cattle** of Egypt became the target for this fifth plague (3). **Horses** are here mentioned for the first time in the Bible. The nature of this **grievous murrain** is not known, but it was fatal to the cattle (6).

The miraculous aspects of this plague were its occurrence upon the **cattle . . . in the field** (3), removed from close contact with infected animals; the exemption of **the cattle of Israel** (4); and the exact timing of the event (5).

The statement that **all the cattle of Egypt died** (6) must not be understood in an absolute sense. In Hebrew the term **all** frequently designates a great number, rather than completeness.[50] There were still cattle that suffered in the seventh plague (20-21). Also this disease was to affect the cattle **in the field** (3). Furthermore, the cattle that died were Egypt's, as contrasted with Israel's (4), and this could be the meaning in v. 6.

Pharaoh's heart was hardened again when he discovered that Israel's cattle were exempt (7; cf. 7:13, comment). He allowed jealousy and anger to produce further willfulness against God. It is possible that he reckoned on requisition of Israel's cattle to replace those he had lost.

6. *The Boils and Sores* (9:8-12)

In the sixth plague, as in the third, there was no repetition of the demand upon Pharaoh and no warning given to him. Moses stood before the king, took **ashes** from **the furnace** (the kiln where brick was made), and threw them in the air. The **ashes** "became boils breaking out in sores on man and beast" (10, RSV). The miracle was in the ashes becoming **small dust** (9) and spreading over all of Egypt, producing the boils. It is assumed that Israel escaped this plague as well.

The magicians (11) are mentioned again, but this time they were afflicted with the boils and were unable to contest God's power or even to remain in Moses' presence. We hear of these magicians no more in this record.

[50] *Ibid.*

Here for the first time it is said that God **hardened the heart of Pharaoh** (12), which act was forecast in 7:3. The judgment of God had begun on this wicked man, making his heart still harder. When men persist in disobedience, the time comes when God sends "strong delusion, that they should believe a lie" (II Thess. 2:11). On the hardening of Pharaoh's heart see comments on 7:13.

7. *The Hail and Fire* (9:13-35)

a. The appeal to Pharaoh (9:13-17). This plague was prefaced by the often repeated demand and warning (13-14). By now Pharaoh should have been expecting his unwelcome visitors **early in the morning.** Apparently he was helpless to rid himself of these men who were omens of evil.

Though the plagues did not follow each other with increased intensity, there was an overall increase of danger to life. Moses was to say to Pharaoh, **I will at this time send all my plagues upon thine heart,** as well as on **thy servants** and **people** (14). The contest was to get closer to the wicked king and the impact was to be of greater intensity. God's purpose was clear, **that thou mayest know that there is none like me in all the earth** (14).

There were several new features in this plague: "(1) It is ushered in with an unusually long and exceeding awful message (verses 13-19). . . . (2) It is the first plague that attacks human life; and this it does upon a large scale: all those exposed to it perish (verse 19). (3) It is more destructive than any previous plague to property. . . . (verse 31). (4) It is accompanied with terrible demonstrations . . . (verse 23). (5) It is made to test the degree of faith to which the Egyptians have attained . . . (verse 20)."[51] Hail and thunder, or even rain, were rare in Egypt, and such phenomena as accompanied this storm were unknown to the Egyptians.

The words, **Now I will stretch out my hand** (15), are best translated, "Now I could have put forth my hand" (RSV). The original conveys, not future, but a past possibility. God was telling Pharaoh that He could have made a quick end to him and his people. He had not done so because He wanted to show His **power** and get glory for His **name** (16). God had extended the life of Pharaoh and allowed him to continue resistance so that

[51]Rawlinson, CWB, I, 219.

He could reveal His greater powers on His people's behalf. Through these mighty acts His name would be **declared throughout all the earth.** Probably no event in history is any more widely known than that of Israel's deliverance from Egypt. Verse 17 is a challenge in the form of a question to Pharaoh, "Are you still setting yourself up against My people not to let them go?" (Berk.) A king exalting himself against divine power became a means of greater glory for God.

b. The warning and promise (9:18-21). The warning (18) gave the Egyptians, who by now were aware of the conflict between Pharaoh and Moses, an opportunity to protect themselves and their livestock. They were to bring home their men and animals for protection (19). Some of the Egyptians **feared the word of the Lord** (20) and acted hastily for self-preservation. Others, however, **regarded not the word of the Lord** (21) and did nothing. These facts remind us of New Testament times. When Jesus spoke, some believed His word, and others did not.

c. The intensity of the plague (9:22-26). The phenomena of **hail, and fire** must have been terrifying (23-25). The stones were so large that they killed **man and beast** and broke the trees (25). There had been **none like it** ever before in **Egypt** (24). The crops of barley and flax were sufficiently developed to be destroyed, while the wheat and rye (*holius sorghum,* not rye in the usual sense)[52] were yet undeveloped, so unharmed (31-32). God's protecting hand was upon the Israelites, who escaped the storm **in the land of Goshen** (26).

d. Pharaoh's reaction (9:27-35). This time Pharaoh was really frightened. He confessed, **I have sinned,** and, **The Lord is righteous** (27). He asked for mercy and promised, **I will let you go** (28). Moses granted the request of Pharaoh, so that he would know **that the earth is the Lord's** (29). However, Moses knew by now that this king and his people would **not yet fear the Lord God** (30). It is easy for men whose hearts are hard to harden themselves still more when the pressure is off (34; cf. 7:13, comment). Many men confess sin, make vows, and appear penitent under judgment, only to reveal their true selves when the evil passes. The depth of one's change becomes known when the outward circumstances change. In v. 31, **The flax was bolled** means, "The flax was in bud" (Moffatt).

[52]*Ibid.,* p. 221.

Verses 27-30 picture "False Repentance." (1) It possesses the feature of confession, 27; (2) It acknowledges God's righteousness, 27; (3) It recognizes personal inability and seeks help of God, 28; (4) It promises amendment, 28; (5) It lacks the fear of God, 30.[53]

8. *The Plague of Locusts* (10:1-20)

a. Reasons for hardening Pharaoh (10:1-2). God gave to Moses two reasons for His hardening of Pharaoh's heart and the hearts of his servants. First, He wanted to **shew these my signs before him** (1). Had Pharaoh yielded sooner, the last and greater wonders would not have been wrought. In such an instance some of the Egyptians would not have been convinced. God prolonged the agony until all would see His glory.

Second, God wanted the future generations of His own people, Israel, to know and recount again and again this marvelous deliverance (2). The increased intensity of the **signs** and their multiplication made deep impression upon the Israelites and convinced them beyond any reasonable doubt that God was **the Lord.** The words **what things I have wrought** are more correct as "how I have made sport" (RSV). There was divine irony in the fact that Pharaoh's obstinacy led to greater manifestations of God's glory and power.[54] These repeated assurances to Moses prepared him for the obduracy of Pharaoh, since he was often told that God had a hand in it (cf. 7:43, comment).

b. Announcement to Pharaoh (10:3-6). Moses went to Pharaoh and gave his new message clearly and hurriedly. The prolonging of these agonies was because of Pharaoh's pride, **How long wilt thou refuse to humble thyself before me?** (3) This time **locusts** (4) would be brought into the land. **They shall cover the face of the earth** (5) and **shall eat** all that remained from the other plagues. These locusts would enter **houses** and constitute a greater menace than ever occurred before (6).[55] After this announcement, Moses and Aaron **went out** quickly.

c. An attempt at compromise (10:7-11). **Pharaoh's servants** (7), those officers of court nearest to him, now began to plead. First, the magicians had been impressed by God's power (8:19). Second, some of the people believed sufficiently to remove their livestock and servants from the field when the plague was threat-

[53]Rawlinson, PC, I, 220-21.

[54]Johnson, *op. cit.*, p. 60.

[55]See Joel 1:1-4.

ened (9:20). Now some high officers believed that what Moses said would come true. They pled with Pharaoh no longer to allow this Moses to **be a snare** unto them. The only salvation for Egypt was to relent and let this people go. The word **men** here refers to all the people. The **servants** knew, apparently better than Pharaoh, that Egypt was nearly destroyed.

On this occasion **Moses and Aaron were brought** (8) before the king. For the first time Pharaoh relented before the plague began. He gave permission for them to go, but tried another compromise. He would allow the men to go if they would leave their families and their flocks. He wanted to destroy the whole proposition by objecting to the details. Moses made clear that all were going—the **old,** the **young,** the **sons** and **daughters,** the **flocks** and **herds** (9). It is always well to know for certain one's plans when dealing with an opponent of truth. Verse 10 is best translated as a kind of oath, "Let the Lord be with you, if ever I let you go with your little ones! See, you have some evil purpose in mind" (Amp. OT). The king looked on granting their full request as he would look upon blasphemy: "As little as I will let you go with your children, so little will ye go on your journey, so little shall Jehovah be with you."[56] It angered Pharaoh to feel this pressure and to see the firmness of Moses. He might compromise, but never give in fully.

Pharaoh now admitted what he knew all along. These people wanted their freedom. He accused them of an **evil** intent (10). He would assure their return to Egypt by keeping the **little ones.** The **men** (adult males, cf. 7) might **go now** (11); Pharaoh implied that was all they wanted anyhow. He was exasperated and immediately drove Moses and Aaron out of his **presence.**

d. The extent of the locusts (10:12-15). Without further warning God sent the **locusts** (12). The miracle aspect is seen in that the insects came when Moses **stretched forth his rod** (13). The wind blew 24 hours, bringing the locusts from a great distance. It was unusual for them to go **up over all the land of Egypt** (14). The infestation was greater than ever before or since.

When the record says that **they covered the face of the whole earth** (15), it means the earth in Egypt, except, we assume, the land of Goshen, where Israel dwelt. Had Israel suffered in this plague, after exemption from the others, it would

[56]Lange, *Exodus*, p. 30.

have been worse for them than for the Egyptians, since they would have had more to lose. We understand that God's division between Israel and Egypt continued for all the plagues beginning with the flies (8:22). Whether covering **the face of the whole earth** meant the thickness of the locusts on the ground or the thick clouds of them in the air is not clear. Likely the former is meant.[57] For a description of locust invasions read the accounts in Clarke and Rawlinson.[58]

e. Pharaoh's relenting (10:16-20). Under pressure of this judgment, Pharaoh called again for Moses to bring relief. Often men who act willfully are more moved by momentary emotions than by reason. This time Pharaoh admitted that he had **sinned against the Lord** and against Moses (16). He asked for forgiveness for his sin and wanted relief from **this death,** the plague (17). On the surface it all seemed sincere.

When Moses **intreated the Lord** (18), God sent a **strong west wind** (likely northwest from the Mediterranean), which blew the locusts into the **Red sea.** Not a one remained in the land. No one with a reasonable mind could doubt the fact of God's hand in this plague and its removal. But neither the emotions of fear and concern nor the rational powers of his mind could change the heart of Pharaoh. His heart was so set against God that he would not yield. God now had made him a slave of his own stubbornness and was driving him to the bitter end (cf. 7:13, comment). Since Pharaoh was determined to resist God, he was going to be made an example of how evil a wicked heart can be and of how powerful Almighty God can be.

9. *The Darkness* (10:21-29)

Of this ninth plague no warning was given. At God's command, **Moses stretched forth his hand toward heaven,** and **thick darkness** came into the **land of Egypt** for **three days** (22), a darkness that could **be felt** (21).

Most scholars agree that this darkness was probably brought about by the *hamsin,* a sandstorm so dreaded in the East.[59] The miracle was that it came at God's word (21) and did not occur where God's people dwelt (23). The darkness was so great that men could not see **one another.** It is not necessary to suppose

[57]Rawlinson, PC, I, 224-25.

[58]Clarke, *op. cit.,* I, 340-41; Rawlinson, CWB, I. 222-24.

[59]Johnson, *op. cit.,* p. 60.

that there was no artificial light or that men could not move about in their houses.[60] However, all business activity ceased and the people stayed in their own homes.

Pharaoh was now ready with another compromise. He said to Moses after calling him, **Go ye, serve the Lord; only let your flocks and your herds be stayed** (24). How like Satan! He relents when forced, but seeks for some small concession. Many people succumb to his suggestions and accept the compromise. But not Moses! He declared, **There shall not an hoof be left behind** (26). Moses knew God's command even though he did not yet know all the reasons. He expected further instructions as events unfolded.

Christians will never attain full victory so long as they give a place to the devil. Some insist that a little sin will not hurt, or that some evil must still reside in the heart. But God's Word is plain, "Put off . . . the old man" (Eph. 4:22); "Put off all these" (Col. 3:8); "Neither give place to the devil" (Eph. 4:27). No compromise with Satan ever results in full victory or freedom for God's child.

The Lord was not finished with Pharaoh. It must yet be shown what God will do to him who resists to the full. Rather than allowing Pharaoh to send Israel on her way, God gave fur ther hardening to his heart (27; cf. comment on 7:13). Anger broke in fury upon Moses, as Pharaoh ordered God's servant away from him forever with the threat of death if he came again (28). Moses heard the voice of truth in Pharaoh for once, and replied, **Thou hast spoken well, I will see thy face again no more** (29). God was about finished with Pharaoh. There was little more this tyrant could do, caught as he was in the bonds of his own haughty heart.

In cc. 8—10 one can see the "Dangers of Compromise." (1) Abiding close to the world—**sacrifice . . . in the land,** 8:25, 28; (2) Neglecting family religion—let the **men** go, 10:8-11; (3) Reserving the material things—let **flocks** and **herds** remain, 10:24; (4) Overcoming by full commitment—**not an hoof be left behind,** 10:26.

10. *Announcement of the Last Plague* (11:1-10)

a. God speaks to Moses (11:1-3). These verses appear to be parenthetical, because vv. 4-8 continue the account of Moses' last

[60]Rawlinson, CWB, I, 225.

visit before Pharaoh. Some scholars hold that the translation should be, **The Lord** had **said unto Moses** (1).[61] The thought is that God had formerly told this to Moses (see 3:21-22), who inserted the words at this juncture. Others doubt the validity of this translation and hold that God gave these words to Moses while he was standing before Pharaoh.[62] In either case the message was clear. There was to be one more plague, which would cause Pharaoh to **thrust** Israel out of Egypt.

When this moment arrived, the children of Israel, both men and women, were to **borrow** (ask) of the Egyptians **jewels of silver, and . . . gold** (2). The idea is not borrowing with thought of later return, but actually asking and taking from the Egyptians treasures of value. As a conquering army they were to "spoil the Egyptians" (3:22).

The provisions with which Israel would be thrust out of the country were augmented by their being in **favour in the sight of the Egyptians** (3). Verse 3 gives a behind-the-scenes glimpse of Egypt while the public contest between Pharaoh and Moses was occurring. On the public front it appeared that Moses was failing, with Pharaoh refusing his requests and accusing him of evil design and insubordination. But the common people were being impressed by the God of Israel and were beginning to honor His servant and people.

By the time of the ninth plague the people of Egypt had begun to regard the Israelites as God's people and to wish them well. The reason for this favor lay largely with the leader, Moses, who was by now "very greatly esteemed in the land of Egypt" (3, Smith-Goodspeed). His contest with Pharaoh and the resulting victories had lifted Moses high in their eyes and placed him equal with Pharaoh, who was revered as a god on earth.[63]

b. Moses speaks to Pharaoh (11:4-8). In v. 4 the conversation with Pharaoh continues from 10:29. The king could probably have avoided this final catastrophe had he acted wisely and sanely, but his heart was too hard.

The **midnight** (4) of disaster indicated the time of day, but not which day. In this judgment God acted directly without further action on Moses' part. The **firstborn** always referred to

[61]Clarke, *op. cit.*, I, 345; Johnson, *op. cit.*, p. 60; Rawlinson, CWB, I, 226.
[62]Exell, *op. cit.*, p. 220.
[63]Rawlinson, CWB, I, 226.

males, and they were the pride and joy of the Egyptians. The elder son "was the hope, stay, and support of the household, his father's companion, his mother's joy, the object of his brother's and sister's reverence." He was the "hereditary crown prince" and was successor to his father. "No greater affliction can be conceived, short of the general destruction of the people, than the sudden death in every family of him round whom the highest interests and fondest hopes clustered."[64] These **firstborn** sons, from the king's palace to the lowest maidservant's hovel, would die on that night (5). **The maidservant that is behind the mill** may be "the slave girl behind the hand mill" (Berk.).

This disaster would create a **great cry** (6) resounding throughout **all . . . Egypt.** Those who have travelled in the East know what a shrill cry is uttered by mourners.[65] This would be the greatest cry ever heard before or after. In this judgment God would protect His own people (7). Not even a **dog** would bark among the Israelites—no one would die there. It was God who put a difference between His people and the Egyptians.

The urgency of the **servants** of Pharaoh was forecast by Moses. They would **bow to** Moses and insist that he and the people leave (8). At that time, Moses promised, **I will go out.** Moses now had his last word with Pharaoh; he would see him no more. This wicked king had sealed his doom and was ready for God's final judgment. Moses left **in a great anger,** but not because of frustration. Rather, he felt the righteous indignation of God that was due this man who thought he was strong enough to defy God and who by his obstinacy had wrought havoc among his people. There was nothing left for Pharaoh but God's final punishment. He had sinned away his day of grace.

c. *General summary* (11:9-10). These last two verses of c. 11 give a general summary of the encounters with Pharaoh. The king's refusals resulted in God's mighty works. These things were foretold (9) and they were accomplished (10). In spite of the hardhearted tyrant, God Almighty would yet accomplish His purpose, and that with a mighty hand.

"God's People" in c. 11 are: (1) Honored and respected by their enemies, 2-3; (2) Protected by God from the ravages of judgment, 4-7; (3) Delivered from bondage by God's mighty hand, 1, 8-10.

[64]*Ibid.* [65]*Ibid.*, p. 227.

Section II *Deliverance and Victories*

Exodus 12:1—18:27

A. The Passover, 12:1-36

The deliverance of Israel from Egypt was a tremendous event that would be remembered for all time by Israel. The term *passover* can be understood in several senses. The actual event was the passing over in safety of Israel's sons when God destroyed the Egyptian firstborn (27). The feast at the time of the event was **the Lord's passover** (11). This feast was to be commemorated in a **memorial** celebrated annually by Israel (14). The word passover is used to describe all three of these occasions.

1. *Moses Instructed on the First Passover Feast* (12:1-13)

God instituted a new year for Israel. The custom had been to begin the year in the autumn with the month Tisri. But now Abib (13:4) was to be **the first month of the** religious **year,** six months earlier than the beginning of the civil year.[1] Abib became known as Nisan after the Exile.[2]

Moses was to instruct the Israelites to take **a lamb** for each household (3) on **the tenth day of this month.** Verse 3 is clarified thus, "Each man shall secure a lamb for his paternal family, one lamb for each home" (Berk.). If the lamb was too much for one family, neighbors were to join together according to the number who could eat one lamb (4). The choosing of the lamb four days before the feast (cf. v. 6) was probably for observation of the animal. They were to make certain it was **without blemish** (5) and under a year old. Innocency was implied in the younger animal. This **lamb** (*seh*) could have been either a sheep or young goat, although in practice only sheep seem to have been used.[3]

On **the fourteenth day** the lamb was to be killed **in the evening** (6, lit., "between the evenings"). This could mean between sunset and dark, or between the decline of the sun and sunset. Lange believed it to be the early evening, since this gave more

[1]Rawlinson, *ibid.,* p. 227.
[2]Johnson, *op. cit.,* p. 61.
[3]Rawlinson, CWB, I, 228.

time for the paschal activities.[4] Moffatt translates, "Every member of the community of Israel shall kill it between sunset and dark." The **blood** of the lamb was to be placed on the "doorposts" (RSV) and **on the upper door post** (7), or lintel. This may have meant a latticed window above the door.[5] **The flesh** was to be eaten that **night,** having been roasted **with fire** (8). The **bitter herbs** are not named but traditionally included endive, watercress, cucumber, horseradish, lettuce, and parsley. The whole lamb was to be roasted, including the **head, legs,** and **purtenance** (9) or entrails. "The Jewish commentators say that the intestines were taken out, washed, and cleansed, after which they were replaced, and the lamb roasted in a sort of oven."[6] **Nothing** was to **remain until the morning;** what was not eaten must be burned (10).

The details of vv. 5-10 may be understood as a type of "Christ, the Lamb of God." (1) Was unblemished and spotless, 5; (2) Died in the late afternoon, 6; (3) Applies His blood to the hearts of believers, 7; (4) Becomes the Substitute for the bearing of God's wrath, 8-9; (5) Is to be wholly received by the believer, 10. He is to be received without the leaven of sin and in the godly sorrow of repentance, 8.

While eating, the Israelites were to be ready for travel, with the long robes gathered together, and fastened about the **loins** with a girdle (11).[7] Their **shoes** were to be on, and their staffs in hand, while they ate **in haste**—an action at least in part symbolic of the Christian's readiness for Christ's coming. During the night God would **smite** the Egyptians and **execute judgment** upon **all the gods of Egypt** (12). Death to all the firstborn beasts of Egypt would be seen by the Egyptians as a judgment upon their gods.[8]

The blood shall be to you for a token ("a sign for you," RSV) which God would see and would not smite those in the houses where the blood had been sprinkled (13).

2. *The Feasts of Commemoration* (12:14-20)

This day, the fourteenth of Abib, was set aside by God as a perpetual **ordinance** for Israel (14). Here was to be an annual

[4]*Op. cit.*, p. 36.
[5]Rawlinson, PC, I, 259.
[6]*Ibid.*, p. 260.
[7]Rawlinson, CWB, I, 229.
[8]*Ibid.*

reminder of the great deliverance from Egypt. It was to be kept **for ever.** Only in Christ could this **ordinance** truly be fulfilled eternally. The Christians celebrate the Lord's Supper, the memorial for the slain Lamb of God. This shall continue until it is observed anew in God's kingdom (Matt. 26:29).

The Feast of Passover was to be followed immediately by the feast of **unleavened bread** (15). It is not necessary to reckon that verses 15-20 were added after a later institution of this feast.[9] The close connection with the Passover made this feast an essential part of the first event. The Israelites had no leavened bread at the Passover, and because of their hasty departure had no time to prepare it. Also leaven, a symbol of Egypt, was left behind.[10]

The Feast of Unleavened Bread was to last **seven days,** beginning on the day following the Passover. The first and last day of the feast were each to be a **holy convocation** (sacred gathering), in which **no . . . work** was done (16). These two days were not Sabbaths in the strict sense, but were days of worship. The feast was a memorial of the Exodus, the actual journeying out of Egypt. **Armies** (17) is better "hosts" (RSV).

The important lesson of this feast was the complete separation from **leaven.** There was to be no leaven in the bread, not even any in the **houses** (18-19). Any person who ate leaven (persistently and knowingly) would **be cut off from the congregation of Israel,** that is, no longer allowed the privileges and rights of an Israelite.[11] This command applied to both the Israelite by birth—**born in the land**—and the **stranger** who joined with them by choice. The unleavened bread was to Israel the sign that they had entered a new life with God, free from the evils of Egypt. Leaven is a type of corruption being caused by fermentation.[12] It symbolizes the old life of sin, and the evil nature in man. Paul wrote, "Purge out therefore the old leaven . . . therefore let us keep the feast, not with . . . the leaven of malice and wickedness; but with the unleavened bread of sincerity and truth" (I Cor. 5:7-8). In both the Old and New Testament the teaching of complete cleansing from all sin is clear.

3. *Instructions to the Elders* (12:21-28)

Moses was now ready to pass along what God had told him. How necessary it is that the man of God first know what his

[9]Johnson, *op. cit.*, p. 61.

[10]Lange, *op. cit.*, p. 88.

[11]Clarke, *op. cit.*, I, 353.

[12]*Ibid.*, p. 351.

message is to be! **The blood** was to be placed on the **lintel and the two side posts** with **hyssop** (22). This plant was especially "suitable for sprinkling of blood" and "from its frequent use for this purpose it came to be a symbol of spiritual purification" (cf. Ps. 51:7).[13] The Israelites were commanded not to leave the house where the blood was sprinkled **until the morning** (22).

Moses assured the **elders** that the Lord would **pass over** Israel when He came to smite the Egyptians with **the destroyer** (23). Safety was assured the firstborn **when he seeth the blood.** It required the blood applied as well as the blood provided—a fact not without meaning for our day in reference to the atonement of Christ (I Pet. 1:18-19). **This service** (25, the activity of the night) was to be renewed annually as a memorial, or object lesson, to their children (24-27). When the people heard of God's plans, they **bowed the head and worshipped** (27). God's promise of special favor to them brought humility and holy emotions. Having met God in worship, they **went away, and did as the Lord had commanded** (28).

4. *Death in Egypt* (12:29-36)

As God had foretold, **all the firstborn** in **Egypt** were smitten at the **midnight** hour (29). Rather than "the maidservant" (11: 5), who was mentioned as the lowest in the prophecy, it was now **the captive that was in the dungeon.** Apparently there was little difference between them socially.

Pharaoh should have known this plague would occur, for Moses had told him (11:4-5), but his own hard heart blinded him even to the things about which there should have been no doubt. However, when the event occurred, there was no evasion of truth—the firstborn were dead. The **great cry** had come; every house held a dead son (30). While it was yet night, Pharaoh **called for Moses and Aaron** and commanded—not just permitted—them to leave Egypt, taking everything with them (31-32). This order was one of desperation, rather than willing consent. His words, **Bless me also,** simply expressed a desire for averting further calamity. Here was extreme humiliation "without heart contrition."[14] Since Moses had said that he would see Pharaoh no more (10:29), it may be assumed here that Pharaoh's message was given to Moses through his servants.

[13]Connell, *op. cit.*, p. 115. [14]*Ibid.*

Not only Pharaoh and his servants, but all **the Egyptians were urgent upon** Israel to get out—"The Egyptians urged the people to hurry" (Berk.). They feared that soon **all** would be **dead men** (33). Moffatt's translation of v. 34 indicates the haste with which the people of Israel left: "So the people snatched up their dough, unleavened as it was, and wrapped their kneading-bowls inside their mantles, carrying them on their shoulders." They had already asked (RSV) **jewels** from the Egyptians in such amounts that the Egyptians were impoverished (35-36). It would appear that many helped Israel get ready to go even before the Passover. They were now insistent that they go quickly. So it was that Israel fled from Egyptian slavery after an awesome night of victory. The KJV reading, **borrowed** (35), is a term that implies obligation to return and has created unnecessary ethical problems. The Hebrew *sha'el* may equally well be translated "asked" or "demanded." Only by extension does it mean "borrowed." Virtually all more recent versions use "asked." The Hebrews were due a considerable amount in wages for unpaid and involuntary labor.

God's victory for Israel brought "The Great Salvation" observed in verses 26-36. (1) Its prerequisite—**Israel . . . did as the Lord had commanded,** 26-28; (2) Its protection—God **passed over the houses of the children of Israel,** 27, 29-30; (3) Its provision—**The Lord gave the people favour,** 31-36.

B. The Exodus, 12:37—15:21

1. *The Departure from Egypt* (12:37-42)

a. The number in the march (12:37-39). The day following the night of death to the Egyptians, **Israel journeyed . . . to Succoth** (37). The certain location of this place is unknown, though it was apparently a short day's journey **from Rameses** east toward the Red Sea (see map 3). Getting this large a group to a central point must have been a big task; apparently some planning had been done as the time of victory drew near.

There has been much controversy as to the actual number that departed from Egypt. Liberal scholars, unwilling to assume miraculous providence, refuse to accept so large a number as **six hundred thousand** men implies.[15] They object to the possibility

[15]Rylaarsdam, *op. cit.* (Exegesis), I, 925.

of Israel's increasing to such a large number in the time allowed and under the adverse conditions described. They also reject the possibility of survival of so many people in the desert. There is the possibility that the Hebrew word for **thousand** (*elep*) "could be translated 'clan' or 'family,' as it is elsewhere (e.g., Judg. 6:15)."[16] In this case the total number of 600 clans would be much less.

However, taking into consideration God's special blessing, one can accept that Israel had grown to a number estimated at nearly 3 million persons.[17] Also, under God's special power the provisions in the wilderness would have been adequate.

The **mixed multitude** (38) that departed with Israel were likely Egyptians who had become attached to Israel and its religion; possibly also, other foreign slaves seeking freedom in this manner, or those who had married Hebrews. These people later became a snare for Israel (Num. 11:4). Interestingly, Israel possessed **flocks, and herds.** These were already theirs before the plagues and had been protected from destruction (9:4). How the Israelites were able to possess so much livestock in Egypt is not said. It may be assumed again that God's blessings were on Israel during the bondage. Chadwick suggests that an earlier revolt may have gained certain privileges for these slaves in Egypt.[18] In any case, God had supplied them with **very much cattle.**

The sudden departure from Egypt left Israel partly unready, for they had not **prepared for themselves any victual** (food, 39). They ate only **unleavened cakes.** This they were to do for seven days during the memorial feast (15).

b. *The date of departure* (12:40-42). The time of **sojourning of the children of Israel** was **four hundred and thirty years** (40). The author did not say whether all this sojourn was in Egypt, or included also the time in Palestine. Paul (Gal. 3:17) implied that the law was given 430 years after Abraham. Yet Stephen (Acts 7:6) said that Israel was in bondage in a strange land for 400 years. The round figure of 400 agrees with the number in Gen. 15:13, which passage also implies that these years were spent in affliction. It is safe to assume that the writer here meant

[16]Johnson, *op. cit.*, p. 62. [17]Rawlinson, CWB, I, 232-33.

[18]"The Book of Exodus," *The Expositor's Bible*, ed. W. Robertson Nicoll (Grand Rapids: Wm. B. Eerdmans Publishing Co., 1947), I, 170.

the years in the land of Egypt.[19] In fact, the time was dated on God's clock with an exactness that proved the Word divine (41).

What a night to be remembered! "That was a night when the Lord kept watch" (Berk.)—He kept a close eye on His children (42). It was to be celebrated as a "night of watching" by all generations of Israelites in the future. To Israel it was like a day of new birth, which to a Christian is remembered as, "Happy day, happy day, when Jesus washed my sins away!"

2. *The Law of the Passover* (12:43—13:2)

Further instructions were here given to Moses concerning the celebration of the Passover feast: (*a*) **no stranger** (foreigner) was to eat of it (43); (*b*) strangers and servants, when **circumcised,** became as Israelites, and might eat (44, 48); (*c*) the lamb was to be eaten **in one house** and no part of it was to be removed (46); (*d*) no **bone** of it was to be broken (46); (*e*) the same law applied to both the **homeborn** (native) and the **stranger** (49).

The last three points above emphasize unity in fellowship. In the congregation of Israel there was to be no division—the lamb was one and the people were one. So in Christ all are one; divisions have no place in His body (I Corinthians 1—3).

The response of the Israelites was immediate (50). Recent victory made their hearts obedient. When God works, victory is complete. **Armies** (51) is better "hosts" (RSV). But God's blessings upon a people carry responsibilities. Since the Lord had spared the **firstborn . . . both of man and of beast,** these were now to be consecrated to Him (2). God laid a claim upon these men to give Him what was His. To **sanctify** as used here, and often throughout the OT, has the meaning of consecrating or setting apart for special divine ownership, as compared with the NT meaning, which includes moral purity (Eph. 5:25-27; Heb. 9: 13-14). **Sanctify** in this broader OT sense is used of both persons and things.

3. *The Speech of Moses* (13:3-16)

a. The day of remembrance (13:3-10). **Moses** was now to relate to the **people** the instructions that God had given to him. Verses 3-7 repeat much of what was given in 12:14-20 (see com-

[19]*Ibid.*

ments there). In v. 5, Moses named five of the seven nations whose land Israel would inherit. The other two were the Perizzites and Gergashites, who probably were less important (cf. BBC, II, 35-36).

The importance of remembering **this day** (3) must be passed on to the children (8). The **sign unto thee upon thine hand** and the **memorial between thine eyes** (9) were not to be physical writings, or "phylacteries" (cf. Deut. 6:4-8).[20] Rather, the feast and the words of mouth coming from the heart were to be the continual reminders.[21] Physical objects may help remind one of God's gracious acts to a degree, but **the Lord's law . . . in thy mouth** (9)—the full heart of praise and testimony, passed on to the children—is the most effective means of transmission. God knows that it is easy for men to forget Him, so He commanded: **Thou shalt therefore keep this ordinance in his season** ("at its appointed time," RSV) **from year to year** (10).

b. Consecration of the firstborn (13:11-16). Another constant reminder was to be the giving of the firstborn to God (2, 12) and the answers to the sons' questions (14) about the ceremonies. All the firstborn males of cattle were to be God's (12) and given in **sacrifice** (15). **All that openeth the matrix** (15) refers to "all the males that first open the womb" (RSV). The **all** here must be taken as referring to the clean animals.[22] The unclean animals, such as the **ass** (13), were to be redeemed by the substitution of a **lamb,** or kid. If not redeemed, the unclean animal was to be killed. The **ass** was mentioned here because it was the sole beast of burden taken from Egypt.

A special arrangement was made for the male child. Since he could not be sacrificed as an offering, he was to be redeemed (15). The obligation for service to God was later transferred to the Levites, and the price of substitution for the firstborn male was set at five shekels or about five dollars in our currency (Num. 3:47).[23] This payment served as an acknowledgment of God's claim upon the firstborn.

The reason for this requirement is clear. God brought Israel out of Egypt by destroying the Egyptian **firstborn** (15). Therefore every son, especially the firstborn, was to be told the story repeatedly. This act of redemption, as well as the one of sacrifice,

[20]Rawlinson, CWB, I, 235.

[21]Johnson, *op. cit.*, p. 63.

[22]Rawlinson, PC, I, 300.

[23]Pfeiffer, *op. cit.*, p. 63.

was to be a reminder—**a token upon thine hand, and for frontlets between thine eyes** (16; see comment on v. 9).

4. *The Pillar of Cloud and of Fire* (13:17-22)

The direct, northern route from Egypt to Palestine (see maps 2 and 3) was about 200 miles and could have been covered in about two weeks. However, when God led Israel out of Egypt, He took them on a longer route to avoid encounter with the warlike **Philistines** (17). The people of Israel were untrained for battle and their faith in God was weak. They might **repent when they** saw **war,** and **return to Egypt.** The Lord knew the limited strength of this people and protected them from undue temptation (see I Cor. 10:13). Often God's way may not appear the most simple and direct. Thus He led Israel by **the way of the wilderness of the Red sea** (18; see comments on the Red Sea in 14:2).

The word **harnessed** (18), though a military word in the original, must have referred to the organized manner of march. Moffatt says, "The Israelites left Egypt in orderly array." This organization may have been planned during the time of contention with Pharaoh.[24]

Fulfilling the request of **Joseph** when he was dying (Gen. 50:25), **Moses took the bones** (19) of this patriarch with him. Surely Moses knew much about this earlier leader and was strengthened in faith by the strong hope that had been in Joseph. Israel faithfully buried Joseph's bones in Canaan in due time (Josh. 24:32).

The next stop of Israel after **Succoth** was **Etham, on the edge of the wilderness** (20; see map 3). The location of these places is uncertain, largely because the place of crossing the Red Sea is uncertain.[25] But wherever the location, God was the Leader. He appeared before Israel in the form of **a pillar of a cloud** (21, likely of smoke) **by day,** and **of fire** by **night.** The pillar remained long with Israel as a guide in their journeys. It symbolized the Holy Spirit, a Fire (Matt. 3:11), who guides the Christian in his walk.

"God's Guiding Light" is seen in 17-22. (1) It leads God's

[24]Rawlinson, CWB, I, 236.

[25]See discussion of possible theories in Emil Kraeling, *Bible Atlas* (New York: Rand McNally and Company, 1956), pp. 101-6.

children away from the paths of greatest danger, 17; (2) Sometimes in circuitous paths to unwelcome places, 18*a*; (3) In an orderly and obedient fashion, 18*b*; (4) With strong evidence that He is with them, 21-22.

5. *Crossing the Red Sea* (14:1-31)

a. A perilous place (14:1-4). Since it is not clear where the exact crossing occurred, it is best to assume that the children of Israel were moving from Goshen (see map 3) to the border of Egypt where they could cross over into the wilderness. Then God asked them to **turn** (2; "turn back," RSV) and **encamp by the sea.** Whether they turned north to the Lake Manzaleh,[26] or south to the Bitter Lakes,[27] is not clear. What is clear is that there was a body of water before them as an obstacle to their crossing.

Pharaoh began to reevaluate his release of the slaves. He may have heard of their apparently aimless journeying, and assumed that they were **entangled in the land** (3) and **the wilderness** had **shut them in.** To him, their God, who was powerful in Egypt, was helpless in the wilderness. He thought they were hopelessly lost. Certainly Israel would have been finished were it not for Almighty God. He sometimes leads us into tight places so that He can deliver us and show that He is **the Lord** (4).

b. Pursuit by Pharaoh (14:5-9). Smarting under his recent defeat and the frustration caused by losing so many of his laborers (5), **Pharaoh** and **his servants** (advisers) changed their minds. Thinking that Israel was virtually cornered in the wilderness, the king **made ready his chariot** (6) and **took his people** ("army," RSV) **with him.** Also he had **six hundred chosen** ("picked," RSV) **chariots** (7) and as many others as could be quickly assembled (so the term **all the chariots** should be understood).[28] With this array of human might, Pharaoh hurried after the Israelites. His hard heart was made harder because to him these slaves had left **with an high hand** (8; "defiantly," RSV). Contrast this with the great fear (10) they were soon to feel. He pressed in upon them where they were encamped **by the sea** (9; see map 3). **Pi-hahiroth** means "sedge-place, on the Egyptian side of the Red Sea" (Berk., fn.).

[26]Johnson, *op. cit.*, p. 64. [27]Rawlinson, CWB, I, 237.

[28]*Ibid.*, p. 238.

c. The people's fear (14:10-12). The sight of Pharaoh's army melted the hearts of the people and they **cried out unto the Lord** (10). It was a hopeless cry, for they saw nothing but death ahead, and chided **Moses** for bringing them out of Egypt **to die in the wilderness** (11). For them bondage was better than death, and Moses should have left them **alone** in Egypt (12). In terms of a modern slogan, they felt that they would be "better Red than dead."

These Israelites, like so many new converts, even though freed from the bondage of slavery, still possessed "an evil heart of unbelief." They were full of fear and doubt, having soon forgotten the mighty acts of God in their behalf. They had gone along with the leaders, but now, with apparent catastrophe at hand, their lack of full commitment was revealed.

d. God's purpose (14:13-18). How often faith weakens just when God is ready to do His greatest work! But God had His man of faith. How much Moses was trembling underneath is not said, nor is it apparent that he yet knew just what God would do. But his past encounters assured him that God was leading. There was nothing his people could do except to quiet their fears, to **stand still, and see the salvation of the Lord** (13). God had told Moses (4) that another victory would come, and he believed God's word. He was able to declare, **The Lord shall fight for you, and ye shall hold your peace** (14). "You have only to be still" (RSV).

Actually, there was no need for further crying unto God. The time for march had come. Clearly it was a march of faith, for only treacherous water was before them; yet God's command was, **Go forward** (15). One ultimately comes to the place in his spiritual walk when fearful praying stops and the step of faith must be taken.

All the time Israel was fearing that God had let them down, He was working out His purpose. The barrier of water before them would **divide** as Moses' **hand** was stretched out with his **rod** (16). Pharaoh's hard heart would cause him to presume upon God by following Israel, but God's plan was to destroy this Egyptian army and thus gain glory and **honour** to himself (17). It would be too late for **Pharaoh** and **his horsemen** (18), but the rest of the **Egyptians** would **know** who is **the Lord.**

In v. 15 we see God's challenge to His people, "Go forward." (1) Their history pushed them forward, 1:13-14; (2) The present prodded them forward, 14:9-10; (3) The future pulled them forward, 3:8; 14:13-14 (G. B. Williamson).

e. The protecting pillar (14:19-20). The **angel of God** (19), called the "angel of the Lord" in 3:2, had been going before Israel, but now moved to the rear of the camp. The invisible movement of God was seen in the visible movement of **the pillar of the cloud,** which now moved from **before** them and **stood behind them.** This pillar came between the two camps, keeping the Egyptians from coming near Israel **all the night** (20). The KJV gives the correct idea, though not the exact translation. The pillar brought **darkness** to the Egyptians, while Israel had **light** in their camp.[29]

The process of "Overcoming Fear" can be seen in 10-20: (1) Startled by looking at Satan's power, 10; (2) Expressed in distress at God's providences, 11-12; (3) Relieved when God's word is clearly given, 13-18; (4) Fully quieted when God's presence is manifest, 19-20.

f. The path through the sea (14:21-25). That night, when **Moses stretched out his hand over the sea . . . the waters were divided** (21). A **strong east wind** is mentioned, serving to make **the sea dry land,** perhaps by drying up the bed from which the waters rolled back. One should be cautioned against forcing poetic language (15:8; Ps. 78:13) into narrow literalism and requiring belief that the waters defied gravity, or congealed as a solid.[30] The word **wall** (22) referred to the barrier of water that lay on both sides of Israel as they marched across.[31]

The distance across the sea and the width of the passage are not given in the record. The area was enough for nearly 3 million people to pass over in one night, and enough for all of Pharaoh's host to be in **the midst** of it (23). Either **the Egyptians** looked upon the opening in the sea as a natural event or else they in their hardness presumed upon God's mercy when they marched into the opening. Whether Pharaoh went in with his hosts it does not say, but **all** his **horses, chariots,** and **horsemen** (23) went in (the "army," v. 9, is not listed as going in).

In the morning watch (24), between 2 and 6 a.m.,[32] God

[29]Connell, *op. cit.*, p. 116. [30]Rawlinson, CWB, I, 239-40.

[31]Clarke, *op. cit.*, I, 371; Connell, *op. cit.*, p. 116.

[32]Johnson, *op. cit.*, p. 64.

troubled the **Egyptians.** Likely the dark pillar began to flash, maybe with lightning. Fear came to the Egyptians, and they were having trouble with the **chariot wheels** (25), "clogging" or "binding" (RSV) so that they drove **heavily.** Apparently the dry bed of the sea was breaking through with the weight of the horses and chariots. They said, **Let us flee . . . for the Lord fighteth for them against the Egyptians.** Once more these wicked men acknowledged the power of God. The confusion of the Egyptians gave time for Israel to complete the crossing and for all the pursuing Egyptians to get into the sea bed.

g. Perishing of the Egyptians (14:26-31). God now reversed His action and the waters returned to their former place (26). Whether there was a reversal of the wind is not stated (see 15:10). The return of the waters was such that they overwhelmed **the Egyptians** as they tried to flee and they were destroyed (27-28). The same waters that served as **a wall** for the people of God (29) became the means of destruction for the Egyptians.

This latest contest of God with Pharaoh, resulting in final and complete victory for the Lord, greatly impressed the Israelites. The situation had looked hopeless the night before. Now **Israel saw the Egyptians dead upon the sea shore** (30). The turbulent waters, or tide, had washed the bodies ashore. The Lord had **saved** Israel; all the needed evidence was before their eyes.

When **Israel saw that great work** (31), the **people feared the Lord, and believed.** This mighty act removed the fear that had torment (10) and implanted a true fear of God—a fear that led to a living faith. From this manifestation "the Israelites were to discern not only the merciful Deliverer but also the holy Judge of the ungodly, that they might grow in the fear of God as well as in the faith which they had already shown."[33] The word for **believed** (31) means "believed in" (RSV); this kind of faith takes a firm hold on a person. They could now rest their case on God and **his servant Moses** because their faith became more personalized.

In 10-31, we see "God's Mighty Deliverance." (1) In behalf of a fearful people, 10-15; (2) With power over natural obstacles, 16, 19-24; (3) From the rebellious enemies of God, 17-18, 25-28; (4) In the creation of a believing people, 29-31.

[33]*Ibid.*

6. *The Songs of Deliverance* (15:1-21)

a. The song of Moses (15:1-19). What is more natural than singing songs of praise when God has wrought a great deliverance? After a time of deep oppression and a dark night of despair, to realize suddenly that victory has come brings billows of joy to the heart. Into the record went this song of Moses, which will become the title of the song of the redeemed on that last day (Rev. 15:3).

Critics claim that this song, or parts of it, was composed at a much later time than Moses and inserted here by later editors.[34] They base their opinions primarily on ideas found in 13 and 17, of the **holy habitation** and the place for God to dwell, **the Sanctuary.** Their argument presupposes that Moses could not have known about these concepts in the future of Israel. But one who accepts the fact of divine inspiration for men like Moses has little or no problem here. The use of a prophetic past or present (as in 13) is not at all uncommon in the OT (e.g., Isa. 9:6). The poem's simplicity as well as its graphic power of description "points to the time of Moses for the composition."[35]

(1) *God is the Hero* (15:1-3). God is great, for He threw the **horse and his rider . . . into the sea** (1). **The Lord,** a **strength** and **song,** is also the singer's **salvation** (2), as well as his **father's** (forefather's) **God.** To **prepare him an habitation** is better rendered "praise him" (ASV). His victory over the Egyptians proved that God was **a man of war** (3), an anthropomorphism describing simply His power in battle. This kind of speaking of God in human terms is frequently found in the OT. His name is *Yahweh,* translated **the Lord,** even though Pharaoh would not acknowledge Him.

(2) *The Lord, supreme over all* (15:4-12). The Lord's **right hand** (6), another anthropomorphism, shattered the enemy by sinking them in the sea, and they **sank into the bottom** as **a stone** (5). As Israel watched, the armed captains sank quickly in the returning flood. God, who is excellent in majesty, overthrew His adversaries and in **wrath** He **consumed them as stubble** (7). The wind that moved the waters is described as a **blast** from God's **nostrils** (8). Poetic language often uses human analogies to describe an activity of God without intending strict literalism. When God moved, **the waters** were as **an heap, and**

[34]IB, I, 941.

[35]Rawlinson, CWB, I, 241.

the depths were congealed in the heart of the sea. This may refer to the water as walls on each side of Israel,[36] or to the closing of the sources from which the water could come.[37]

The defiant attitude of the enemy is shown in v. 9. His proud assurance and **lust** (intentions or will) were clear. But when God **didst blow** with His **wind,** they were drowned (10). A new fact is here suggested; a wind was also used to return the waters of the sea. God is greater than all **the gods** (11); none can attain unto His glory, **holiness,** and power. This is the first explicit mention of the holiness of God in the OT (cf. 3:5). He stretched out His **hand** and the **earth swallowed them** (12). Here the sea is thought of as part of **the earth.**

(3) *The Lord is King of Israel* (15:13-19). God **led forth** and **redeemed** (13) His people; He has **guided** (is guiding) **them.**[38] **Thy holy habitation** is surely the Promised Land. As the writer anticipated the movement into **Palestina** (*Palestine* comes from the enemy's name, Philistia), he could see the concern and fear upon **the inhabitants** because of God's power (14). **Edom, Moab,** and **Canaan** (15) will feel the dreadful fear. **Dukes** are princes. **Fear and dread,** caused by **the greatness** of God's **arm** (16), will immobilize the enemies until Israel crosses over the border. Ultimate establishment in Canaan was assured. Settlement in the land and establishment of **the Sanctuary** yet to come are spoken of as certainly as if they were an already accomplished fact (17). The Lord reigns **for ever** (18) while Pharaoh's host was destroyed and Israel was spared (19). The song writer was full of rejoicing for this tremendous event.

b. The Song of Miriam (15:20-21). **Miriam . . . the sister of Aaron** (20) apparently had equal rank with Aaron, though not with Moses. She was a **prophetess,** the first mentioned in the Bible. The **timbrel** was a tambourine. "Solemn dances as an expression of worship, although appropriate to the times of Moses and the psalmists, are liable to abuse and have never found a generally accepted place in the worship of the Christian Church."[39]

It is thought that when **Miriam answered them** (21; cf. v. 1), she and the women sang the words of this refrain in response following each of the parts of the song of Moses. They played the

[36]Connell, *op. cit.*, p. 116.

[37]IB, I, 943-44.

[38]Rawlinson, CWB, I, 243.

[39]Connell, *op. cit.*, p. 117.

instruments and moved gracefully among the singers in a "stately and solemn dance."[40]

C. The Journey to Sinai, 15:22—18:27

1. *At Marah and Elim* (15:22-27)

Israel **went three days** into **the wilderness of Shur** (east of the Red Sea) and **found no water** (22). The faith of the people needed further testing. A great victory like the Red Sea crossing gave a wonderful view of God's omnipotence; it did not train their faith for everyday problems. The daily need of food and drink tries some people's faith more than the bigger obstacles. But God was training His people in all of life, so He brought them to the **bitter** waters of **Marah** (23; see map 3). Imagine the keen disappointment of a thirsty people finding water, only to learn that it was undrinkable.

The extreme bitterness of springs is well attested by travelers in this area of the **wilderness of Shur** (or Etham, Num. 33:8), which is "treeless, waterless, and, except in the early spring, destitute of herbage."[41]

The people murmured against Moses (24). Leadership is costly because the blame for adversity falls on leaders. These people knew Moses was God's man; thus their sin was also against God. Great experiences with God do not necessarily cure the evil heart of complaining. Only when self is crucified and Christ fully enthroned does murmuring cease (Eph. 4:31-32).

Moses **cried unto the Lord** (25), the only thing he could do. No doubt God would have provided sweet water in response to Israel's patient faith if they had held steady. The Lord may sometimes satisfy a person's whims to the detriment of his faith. Here the **waters were made sweet** when Moses threw **a tree** into them, but Israel's faith remained weak. This miracle cannot be explained by any known natural means.

God used this occasion to teach Israel a lesson, by establishing **a statute and an ordinance** (25). If the people would listen to God and fully obey His word, they would be healed of all the **diseases . . . brought upon the Egyptians** (26). As God healed the bitter waters of Marah, so He would heal Israel by supplying physical needs and, more important, healing the people of their

[40]Rawlinson, CWB, I, 245. [41]*Ibid.*

own corrupted nature. God wanted to take the spirit of complaint out of them and to grant them a strong faith.

Not all experiences of life are bitter. Israel's next encampment was at **Elim,** an oasis with **twelve wells** (springs) **of water** (one for each tribe), **and 70 palm trees** (27). Had Israel endured the bitterness of Marah's waters, they should soon have feasted at Elim. The thin patience of many believers dulls the keen edge of joyful victory when it comes. **Elim** was a beautiful place to camp, but it was not their destination.

2. *The Manna and the Quail* (16:1-36)

a. Israel murmurs again (16:1-3). Israel should have entered into God's "statute" and believed His "ordinance" (15:25) but they did not. Their failure to do so resulted in more complaining. They had left one wilderness (Shur) and entered another **(Sin)** on the way to **Sinai** and had been traveling for one **month** (1). Apparently food supplies were lessening and there was no outward evidence of any new supply. God permitted the problem to arise as a test for Israel's faith. But they **murmured against Moses and Aaron** (2) and wished to have **died** in **Egypt** with full stomachs rather than to be killed with **hunger** in the **wilderness** (3). Apparently they had eaten well in Egypt, and matters appeared worse for them now. Of course food is necessary for physical life, but God had not forgotten them. He would have supplied in a more satisfying manner had Israel held steady in patient faith.

b. Promise of bread and meat (16:4-12). No doubt God had in mind all the while just how He would feed Israel in the wilderness. When they murmured, the Lord made known His plan of supplying **bread from heaven** (4) for them at **a certain rate**—"a day's ration each day" (Smith-Goodspeed). However, even in the giving of the bread there would be a test **whether they will walk** in His **law** or not. In conformity with the Sabbath law, the people would find the amount on **the sixth day** sufficient for two days (5).

God wanted these people to know that the One who brought them out of Egypt was still with them. **At even . . . ye shall know** (6) and **in the morning . . . ye shall see** (7). **The glory** of v. 7 referred to the realization of God's hand in the coming of bread, while **the glory** of v. 10 was a special manifestation of God in the cloud.

Moses chided the people for murmuring against him and Aaron because they were as nothing—God was the One who was leading (7). When God gave them **flesh** and **bread** to eat, they would know that He had heard their **murmurings . . . against** Him (8). In a sense, supplying food in this manner was a rebuke. God did not supply the food simply because they complained; He wanted them to know He was the Lord and it was not His servants but himself against whom they murmured.

Israel was to be humbled before God. Aaron assembled them, saying, **Come near before the Lord: for he hath heard your murmurings** (9). When they drew near and **looked toward the wilderness,** suddenly **the glory of the Lord appeared in the cloud** (10). "The unmistakable evidence of God's presence in the fiery pillar authenticated the words of Moses and prepared the people for the more veiled glory of the miracle to come."[42] It gave these weak followers of God an opportunity to see the evil of their own hearts as they contemplated the faithfulness of God to them. His miracle of **flesh** and **bread** would come; then they would **know** that the **Lord** was their **God** (12). He was patient with these weak believers whose faith needed growth; later, after they had time for maturing (Num. 14:11-12), they were punished because of continued unbelief.

c. *God sent quail and bread* (16:13-21). The **quails** which **came up, and covered the camp** (13) normally migrated "across the Red Sea in large numbers at this time of year, and, exhausted by their long flight . . . could easily be caught near the ground."[43]

The following morning there was a **dew** about the camp (13). **When the dew . . . was gone,** there was found a "fine, flakelike thing, fine as hoarfrost on the ground" (14, RSV). When the people **saw it,** they asked, "What is it?" (15, RSV) Moses answered, **This is the bread which the Lord hath given you to eat.** "The name manna may have arisen from the question [What is it?], or the similarity in sound may have related the two words."[44]

Some have tried to identify the scriptural manna with natural substances found in this region. Though similar in some respects, these natural substances do not fit the biblical account. They are not large in quantity, nor could they be a principal

[42]Pfeiffer, *op. cit.,* p. 66. [43]Connell, *op. cit.,* p 117.

[44]Pfeiffer, *op. cit.,* p. 66.

food. Also, they appear only during a short season of the year. The manna of the Bible (1) was to be Israel's chief nourishment for 40 years; (2) it was supplied in large quantities; (3) it was given throughout the whole year; (4) it came only six out of the seven days of the week; and (5) it bred worms if kept two days except on the Sabbath.[45] Clearly this manna was a miracle of God and is a type of the Christ who came down from heaven (John 6:32-40).

The instructions about gathering the manna were clear. Each family was to collect enough for one day, **an omer for every man** (16), about three pints, and **according to the number of . . . persons** in the family. Apparently by a miracle of expanding or diminishing according to the need present,[46] those who took **much had nothing over** and those who took **little had no lack** (18).

Moses made clear that none of the manna should be left until **morning** (19). However, some folk who still needed to learn about explicit obedience kept a supply of manna until morning, but it **bred worms, and stank** (20). Since the manna kept over for the Sabbath did not spoil (24), the disobedience of the offenders was made apparent and was punished by the spoiling.

God's lesson for Israel in this episode, as for Christians, is that believers must depend on Him day by day. The life of Christ in a Christian is retained moment by moment by abiding in God. Daily and careful obedience results in orderly provision; carelessness brings disturbance and judgment. Israel learned to gather in the **morning** before the **sun** melted the manna (21); spiritual food gathered early stands the heat of the day.

d. Sabbath observance (16:22-31). When **the sixth day** arrived, and some began to gather double amounts of manna, **the rulers of the congregation** (22) seemed not to understand. Moses again made the rule clear; there would be no manna on the **sabbath** (25). On the sixth day they were to **bake** and **seethe** (used as bread or porridge) what they needed and lay it up for the morrow (23). They learned that the manna held over for the seventh day **did not** spoil (24).

These verses indicate a knowledge of the Sabbath prior to the giving of the Ten Commandments (20:8-11). God set up a day of rest at the creation of the world (Gen. 2:2-3); it was

[45]Rawlinson, CWB, I, 247-48.

[46]Connell, *op. cit.*, p. 118.

likely known to Abraham, since it was observed in a certain sense by the Babylonians. However, neither the early Hebrews nor the Egyptians knew of a seven-day week.[47] Since there is no mention of the Sabbath after creation until this event, one can assume this to be a renewal of Sabbath observance. During the Egyptian oppression, observance would have been impossible; so for these people the words of Moses were new.[48]

Even though Moses made clear that there would be no bread on **the sabbath** day (26), **some of the people** went out **to gather** just the same (27). There are always those who will not believe God's word, so they **refuse** to **keep** His **commandments** and **laws** (28). The order became more explicit; **no man** was to **go out of his place on the seventh day** (29). No one was to go outside the camp; the people were to rest **on the seventh day** (30). See further comment on the Sabbath in 20:8-11.

The **manna** was **like coriander seed** (31), "a small, grayish-white seed, with a pleasant spicy flavor, used widely as a spice for cooking."[49] It tasted like **wafers** made of wheat flour, oil, and **honey.** God's gift of food was pleasant to the taste.

e. The memorial manna (16:32-36). **A pot** containing **an omer full of manna** (33) was laid **before the Lord** in God's house **before the Testimony** (34). Here it was to be **kept for** future **generations** (32). The writer to the Hebrews mentioned the "golden pot" of "manna" in "the Holiest of all" (Heb. 9:3-4). Whether the command of God was given at this time, or later when the ark of the covenant was constructed, is not said. It can be assumed that Moses added this section (32-36) to the Book of Exodus near the end of his life.[50] **The Testimony** (34) refers to the Ten Commandments which were also deposited in the ark of the covenant.

For the record, Moses affirmed that Israel ate **manna . . . until they came unto the borders of . . . Canaan.** This does not mean that they had no other food along the way, but always there was manna provided. Joshua reported the cessation of this miracle after arriving in the land of promise (Josh. 5:10-12). The **omer** and **ephah** (36) were measurements used in Egypt, and this note was needed since only the **ephah** continued as a measure

[47]Rawlinson, CWB, I, 247.
[48]*Ibid.*, p. 249.
[49]Pfeiffer, *op. cit.*, p. 66.
[50]Rawlinson, CWB, I, 250.

with Israel.[51] An **ephah** was approximately one bushel. The **omer** would be about one and a half quarts.

In c. 16, God's food for Israel points to the Living Bread of the New Testament, "Christ, Our Manna." (1) Is given to a hungry and disturbed people, 1-3; (2) Becomes the manifestation of God's glory, 4-12; (3) Satisfies fully those who gather, 13-18; (4) Effective through a day-by-day obedience, 19-30; (5) Is an experience memorialized forever, 31-34.

3. *The Rock at Rephidim* (17:1-7)

Israel now journeyed on **from the wilderness of Sin** "by stages" (1, RSV) to **Rephidim** (see map 3), likely the Wadi Refayid, a valley not far from **Horeb** (6). This name may identify the mountain range which included Sinai.[52] The word **Rephidim** means "rests" or "resting-places."[53] The people needed water and were expecting some at this place, but none was to be found. God was not making the way easy in every respect.

The people again chided **Moses** and demanded **water** (2). His acquaintance with this region may have made them think he ought to know where there was water. But Moses had not chosen to bring Israel to this place. He was only God's representative. This chiding of him was to **tempt** ("test" or "try") God. Had not God proved himself adequate for all occasions? Could He not be trusted to provide water? Moses was finding these people a trial to his patience.

Without divine help, there was good reason for alarm. Unless **water** could be found, they would die, as well as their **children** and their **cattle** (3). One cannot blame them for their concern, but where was their faith? Had they not seen enough of God's power to assure them that He would not let them down? Some of the people at least were yet unconvinced and could soon stir up enough trouble to affect the whole crowd. They were fast becoming dangerous.

Moses cried unto the Lord (4). There was nothing else he could wisely do; the people **were almost ready to stone** him.

[51]*Ibid.*

[52]Pfeiffer, *op. cit.*, p. 66. Most Bible geographers, however, consider Horeb and Sinai to be different names for the same peak, the present Gebel Musa.

[53]Rawlinson, CWB, I, 250.

Moses and, hopefully, others were willing to await God's time, knowing that God would not forsake them. The Lord might wait awhile and thus perform a greater wonder, as He did with Lazarus when Jesus tarried until His friend was dead (John 11:20-23). But what could Moses do with this riotous people? They would not wait for God any longer.

In mercy, God instructed him what to do. He was to **go on** ahead with some **elders** (appointed leaders) **of Israel** and with the **rod** of God in his **hand** (5). What a comfort that **rod** must have been to Moses! With it he had accomplished some mighty wonders.

God promised to stand before Moses upon **the rock in Horeb** (6), probably in the same mountain range as Sinai (see footnote 52 above for an alternative explanation). When human effort failed, God was there to carry on with His power. Moses was to **smite the rock** from which water would come. His act brought forth water sufficient to meet the needs of this large host of people and their cattle. God knew where the water was and was able to cause springs in the desert. The **elders** were witnesses to this great miracle.

Moses named the place **Massah** and **Meribah,** "proof" and "contention" (RSV, marg.), because the people found fault and forced God to prove himself (7). What more beautiful names might be given one's experiences if only he could, without fault-finding and unbelief, patiently await God's time and let Him work!

Christ is the Water that quenches the spiritual thirst of man (John 7:37). He is the "spiritual Rock" from which the "spiritual drink" comes (I Cor. 10:4). That "Rock" was smitten before the grace could flow forth, reaching all mankind (see Gal. 3:1).

In 1-7 we see "God, Our Rock." (1) A stumbling block to the unbelieving, 1-4; (2) Must be smitten before grace could flow, 5-6; (3) Satisfies the thirst of those who drink, 6*b*; (4) Symbolizes the Cross, an emblem of shame, 7.

4. *Defeat of the Amalekites* (17:8-16)

a. The battle (17:8-13). In the midst of the miracle at the rock, the Amalekites struck at the children of Israel (8), attacking the "feeble" in the rear while they were faint and weary (Deut. 25:18). Since the attack took place **in Rephidim** (cf. 1), it probably first involved those who had not yet caught up with the camp. **Amalek** was a descendant of Esau (Gen. 36:12, 16), though not a part of Edom as a nation.[54] The Amalekites' disregard of God and their attack on His people brought them under the judgment of God.

Joshua (9), mentioned here for the first time, was first known as Oshea (Num. 13:16), but Moses called him "Jehoshua" (contracted to **Joshua**), meaning "Jehovah is Salvation."[55] This helper of Moses (24:13, "his minister") was asked to form an army with which to **fight** the enemy. This army may have been armed with the equipment from the dead Egyptians (14:30-31), and Joshua led the host out to face the enemy (10).

Apparently the battle was in the valley, because Moses went to **the top of the hill with the rod of God** (9), taking with him **Aaron, and Hur** (10). **Hur,** who assisted Aaron when Moses went up into the mountain (24:14), was the grandfather of Bezaleel (31:2), the skilled workman for the Tabernacle. Jewish tradition according to Josephus identified him as the husband of Miriam.[56]

When Moses held up his hand (11), with the rod extended (9), **Israel prevailed,** but **Amalek prevailed** when the arm became weary. **Aaron and Hur stayed up his hands** (12) by placing a **stone** under Moses for a seat, and supporting his arms until the close of the day. Thus Joshua, under God, "mowed down Amalek" (RSV) and his hosts with **the sword** (13).

The rod of God here clearly suggests the importance of prayer and faith. Victory in the battle with Satan comes when prayer is effective. The unseen forces of Satan are routed when God's people pray in faith. Support of others in prayer aids in this victory. Leaders responsible in the work of God would fail without the prayer support of the people.

"Prayer" (1) Is needed when the enemy attacks, 8; (2) Becomes powerful on the hill of God, 9-10; (3) Needs the support of others, 11-12; (4) Prevails in effective victory, 13.

In 8-16 we see that "Prayer Brings Victory." (1) God's work prospers by prayer, 8-11; (2) There is need for united prayer, 12-13; (3) Altars testify to future generations that God answers prayer (G. B. Williamson).

[54]Pfeiffer, *op. cit.*, p. 66.

[55]Connell, *op. cit.*, p. 118.

[56]IB, I, 960.

b. The memorial (17:14-16). The battle with the Amalekites was not ended, but there would come a final victory. The phrase **in a book** (14, "the book," Amp. OT) indicates that the books of Moses were already in process of composition.[57] The successor to Moses must also know God's plan, so God commanded Moses to "read it aloud to Joshua" (14, Moffatt). **Amalek** would ultimately be annihilated.

Moses built an altar (15), **and called** it **Jehovah-nissi** ("the Lord is my banner," RSV). This was to be a sign that the Amalekites, who had put "a hand upon the banner of the Lord" (16, RSV), would be under God's judgment until destroyed. God's people had been attacked by an enemy of God; therefore continual warfare was threatened against them. King Saul was later punished because he failed to carry out God's command to destroy the Amalekites (I Samuel 15). It was in the days of Hezekiah that these people were finally annihilated (I Chron. 4:41-43). We may see in this God's foreknowledge of the continued impenitence of those fierce and warlike people. The strife of nations results in the judgment of the One who makes even the wrath of man to praise Him (Ps. 76:10). Over and over in the Scriptures, sin—whether personal or national—proves to be self-destructive.

5. *The Visit of Jethro* (18:1-27)

a. The coming of Jethro (18:1-5). **Jethro, the priest of Midian, Moses' father in law** (1; see comments, 2:18) heard by indirect means what God had done for Israel. **Zipporah, Moses' wife** (2), had returned to her parents' home after the beginning of the journey to Egypt (4:18-26) and remained there until Israel approached Horeb. The **two sons** (3) were born to Moses while he was living with his father-in-law in Midian (2:22; 4:25) and had remained there with their mother. The first son, **Gershom,** was so named because Moses was **an alien in a strange land.** The second son was called **Eliezer** (4), because Moses had been **delivered . . . from the sword of Pharaoh** (2:15). Their ages at this time are unknown; they may have been quite young, or possibly nearly 40, since Moses had been in Midian 40 years (see Acts 7:23, 30).

Apparently **Jethro . . . came** just as Israel was nearing the

[57]Rawlinson, CWB, I, 252.

vicinity of Sinai, called **the mount of God** (5; cf. 3:1; 17:6; and 19:1), shortly after the defeat of the Amalekites, but before the arrival at Sinai.

b. Moses reports to Jethro (18:6-8). Verse 6, rather than being a direct word to Moses by Jethro, likely was a message sent to Moses or a report by some third party of Jethro's coming (RSV). After getting the word, **Moses went out to meet** Jethro (7). In accordance with oriental custom, Moses **did obeisance** ("bowed in homage," Amp. OT), **and kissed** his **father in law.** The relationship between these men was always of a high order. They sought each other's good in everything.

Moses reported to Jethro **all that** God **had done** for Israel and how the Lord had given victory over **Pharaoh** and **the Egyptians** (8). He was careful to give God all the glory and took none to himself. He also told of the hardships that had come to them along **the way** and how God had **delivered them.**

c. Jethro's praise (18:9-12). For a man to rejoice as **Jethro** did at this report indicates his open heart before **the Lord** (9). Often nations are spoken of as enemies of God, and the Midianites were such later on (Numbers 35). God did not count Egyptians, Amalekites, or others His enemies simply because they were not Israelites; a nation was wicked because the people of that nation were wicked. But God often has His children living among people who are wicked. When a righteous person such as Jethro was found, he was honored by God (cf. Melchizedek, Gen. 14:18-20; Abimelech, Gen. 20:6; and Job, Job 1:1, 8).

How much Jethro knew about Israel's God before this event is not known. His ancestors were descendants of Abraham. He was a "priest" (cf. v. 1) and as such was a religious man. Moses had lived with him 40 years, but this was before the burning-bush experience. At least Jethro's heart was open. When he heard of the Lord's doings, he was able to say, **Blessed be the Lord** (10, *Yahweh*), and thus identified the God of Israel's victory. It is true that he spoke of **the Lord** as **greater than all gods** (11), rather than as the only God. However, this language is similar to that of Solomon at the dedication of the Temple (II Chron. 2:5) and of the Psalmist in his praise (Ps. 135:5). Jethro's idea of other gods was the opposition they gave the Lord (11). Therefore they were evil spirits. The last part of 11 has been rendered, "He delivered the people from under the hand of the Egyptians, when they dealt arrogantly with them" (RSV). The words, **Now I know,** imply a new knowledge for Jethro and may mean that at this time he became a convert to *Yahweh.*[58]

Jethro's religious devotion moved him to offer a **burnt offering and sacrifices for God** (12). **Aaron** and **the elders of Israel** joined in the occasion and had fellowship with Jethro. They joined in the worship of the same God, even though of different nations and cultures. Jethro did not become an Israelite, but he became one with Israel in their love for *Yahweh.*

d. Jethro's counsel (18:13-23). The next day Jethro observed Moses as he judged **the people** (13). Apparently Moses took the full load as judge for these 2 million or more people without sharing responsibility with others. Jethro questioned Moses' wisdom in serving **alone** (14) and keeping the people waiting all day for decisions.

Moses gave his reasons (15-16) for doing the job this way: (1) he sought God's mind to settle the disputes that had arisen, and (2) he used the occasion to teach the people **the statutes of God, and his laws.** Since he was the one who heard God's word, he felt it necessary to act directly in connection with every problem.

But Jethro was not satisfied with these reasons. What Moses was doing was **not good** (17). Even a man of his strength must remember that he was human and would **wear away** (18) on this kind of schedule. Jethro said, **Thou art not able to perform it thyself alone.** Moses should have known this, but he, like many others, needed a friend to tell him so. This method not only was hard on himself, but it also caused difficulties for the people who were forced to wait in line.

One cannot but admire the courtesy and boldness of Jethro. Who would have courage to correct a man who, under God, had brought plagues upon Egypt, opened the sea, brought water and bread into a desert, and led over 2 million people? Moses, who had listened to God directly, now must **hearken** to one who had a message from God for him. Jethro did not deny Moses' place as God's mouthpiece; he was still to be **for the people to Godward** (19); that is, their representative before God (RSV). It would also still be Moses' task to **teach** the **ordinances and laws**

[58]Pfeiffer, *op. cit.,* p. 67.

(20) and direct the people in **the way** they should go and in what they should **do.**

However, to carry out wisely God's purposes, Moses should choose **able men, such as fear God, men of truth, hating covetousness, and place** them over the people as **rulers of thousands, hundreds, fifties,** and **tens** (21). These numbers may have referred to families rather than persons.[59] The men were to serve as higher and lower courts, each leader of a smaller group responsible to the one above him. Persons not satisfied with a decision of the lower judge likely could appeal to a higher. This would mean that multitudes of decisions could be made without their coming to Moses (22).

One wonders that Moses had not used this or a similar plan. He already had elders and rulers who had represented the people on several occasions. The ideas were known in Egypt and apparently Jethro was acquainted with this kind of organization.[60] The qualifications for these judges were sound; they were to "be concerned only for God's approval, not man's, candid in their verdicts, and impervious to bribes" (21).[61]

Jethro was careful to recognize the authority of the man to whom he was speaking. He wanted it to be Moses' own decision—**If thou shalt do this thing** (23). He also knew that Moses acted on divine authority—**If . . . God command thee so.** If Moses could see the wisdom of this, and God would direct him in it, then he would **be able to endure** and the **people** would be at **peace.**

e. The new plan instituted (18:24-27). **Moses** saw the wisdom of the plan suggested by Jethro and **did all that he had said** (24). It can be assumed that Moses sought and obtained God's permission for this method. He chose the necessary men and **made them heads over the people** (25). These men were **rulers** and **they judged the people** (26). They brought **the hard causes** to **Moses,** but cared for the small matters **themselves.**

In Deut. 1:9-18, Moses recounted the appointment of these judges, called there "captains" and "officers." They were appointed at the time Israel was ready to leave Sinai after the law was given. There, it appears, the people had some voice in the selection of the officers (Deut. 1:13). This may mean that, though Jethro gave the counsel before Sinai and the giving of the

[59]*Ibid.*

[60]Rawlinson, CWB, I, 255.

[61]Connell, *op. cit.*, p. 119.

law, the organization was not fully effected until Israel was ready for movement again.[62]

The ministry of Jethro was finished. **Moses let** him **depart** to **his own land** (27). Zipporah and her sons apparently stayed with Moses.

The "Qualifications for Leaders" can be found in 13-23: (1) Humility in counsel, 13-17; (2) Recognition of human weakness, 18; (3) Concern for God's best, 19-20, 23; (4) Integrity of character, 21-22; (5) Willingness to obey, 24-26.

[62]Rawlinson, CWB, I, 255.

Section III *The Covenant at Mt. Sinai*

Exodus 19:1—24:18

Israel had finally arrived at the place where God designed to make them into a religious community that would be peculiarly His. The months "at Sinai accomplished two things: (1) Israel was given the law of God and instructed in God's way; and (2) the multitude that had escaped from Egypt was unified into the beginnings of a nation."[1] This period is of great importance for understanding God's will as it was revealed in the heart of the law.

The critical theories of the nineteenth century, which denied the existence of the Tabernacle and made most of these laws merely a reflection of the customs of later centuries, have been largely abandoned in recent years. Most scholars now admit that the core of these laws was given at Sinai by Moses. Those who hold that the law is the revelation of God accept it in its present form as substantially that which Moses received. Even when critics deny this, they cannot agree which of the laws are later ones.[2]

A. The Covenant Proposed by God, 19:1-25

1. *Introduced by God at Sinai* (19:1-8)

In the third month after leaving Egypt **the children of Israel** reached the **wilderness of Sinai** (1; see map 3). Jewish tradition holds that this day was Pentecost and that the Feast of Pentecost celebrated the giving of the law. However, the Hebrew expression, **the same day,** is not specific enough to indicate an exact day.[3]

When **Israel camped before the mount** (2) **of Sinai,** they were in the wide area in front of the mountain. It has been identified as modern Jebel Musa[4] by most scholars. The area

[1]Johnson, *op. cit.*, p. 61.

[2]*Ibid.*

[3]*Ibid.*

[4]Connell, *op. cit.*, p. 119.

before the mountain is large enough to accommodate a large number of people and was well supplied with water.[5]

Moses **went up unto God** (3), who manifested His presence on the mountain, as indicated by the fact that the cloud (cf. 13: 21) covered it. On Moses' way up, **the Lord called unto him** and commanded him to give a message to Israel. They **have seen,** God said, **what I did unto the Egyptians** (4), and how mercy was shown to Israel. What God had done was fully open to their view. He had borne them **on eagles' wings.** These **eagles**—the "griffin-vulture, a large majestic bird abundant in Palestine,"[6]—carried their young on their wings until able to fly. God had brought Israel out of Egypt with a high hand.

And God had **brought** them to himself. They had been in slavery in Egypt, where they had belonged to Pharaoh. Through divine power they had been snatched from the usurper and brought back to the bosom of God. They were now His in a new way.

God was ready to bring His people into a **covenant** (5) relationship with himself. Such a **covenant** had the significance of a bond or agreement. In social practice there were two kinds. One was the agreement between equals, where obligations and privileges were shared, and where each in effect lost his own right to act independently. The other was a covenant between parties not equal, as between a king and his people. In this the stronger party made a promise or gift "conditioned upon certain demands or obligations to be met by the weaker party." The freedom of the stronger party was not destroyed by such a covenant. For Israel at Sinai the covenant was "the promise of God, backed by the gift of deliverance already given," that Israel would be His "special possession and instrument." The fulfillment of the promise depended on Israel's faith and obedience.[7]

Israel was to be God's **peculiar treasure** (5) **above all** other **people,** but only if Israel fulfilled the conditions of the covenant. "While claiming a peculiar right in Israel, God does not mean to separate Himself from the other nations, to cease to care for them, or give them up to their own devices."[8] Actually, Israel was to be a blessing to all other nations.

[5]Rawlinson, CWB, I, 256.

[6]Johnson, *op. cit.*, p. 68.

[7]Rylaarsdam, *op. cit.*, I, 841.

[8]Rawlinson, CWB, I, 256.

As God's people, Israel was to be unto God a **kingdom of priests, and an holy nation** (6). In a certain sense every individual was a priest having direct access to God. The universal priesthood of all believers is taught here (see I Pet. 2:5). The holiness of God is the "originating cause of the creation of a holy people. . . . Jehovah keeps Himself pure in His personality, He protects His glory by His purity, His universality by His particularity—thus is He the Holy One. And so He creates for Himself a holy people that in a peculiar sense exists for . . . [Him], and keeps Himself aloof from notions and forms of worship that conflict with true views of His personality."[9] To bring man back from the evil ways of sin to the life of holiness was God's purpose in redemption.

Moses . . . called . . . the elders of the people (7, leaders of tribes and families) and "set before them" (RSV) the **words** which God had spoken. Apparently the people were deeply moved and responded: **All that the Lord hath spoken we will do** (8). It is easy for people to make vows to God when moved by deep religious feeling. Often they may not realize all that is involved in the promise, but the vows can be sincere and will be a later reminder to them of their responsibility. If left to make decisions without this godly awe, men will go the way of unbelief.

Religious emotion is not coercion. These people were free to accept or reject God's proposals. He does not force men to enter into covenant with Him, but He does create the atmosphere that makes a favorable choice possible. Without God's working first, man could never act in favorable response.

2. *The People Sanctified* (19:9-15)

The people were now to be made ready for the greatest experience in human life—the hearing of God's voice. God told Moses three things—**I come unto thee in a thick cloud**; the people will **hear when I speak**; and they will **believe thee for ever** (9). Some Israelites had refused to recognize Moses as God's spokesman; often when in trouble most of Israel were doubtful about him. In spite of all that Moses had said and done, irreligious people could still claim that it was only his voice and that he could work magic. But now these people would "see" God in the

[9]Lange, *op. cit.*, p. 70.

thick cloud and **hear** God's voice directly. Thus Moses' words would be verified.

In many ways it is impossible for people really to believe that the words a man speaks are the words of God until they personally hear God speak directly to them. The Israelites apparently heard a sound, other than Moses' voice, which they recognized as God speaking to them (20:1; see Deut. 4:11-12). For most Christians the voice of God is heard through the voice of His Spirit in the heart (Rom. 8:16). When His voice is heard, then the word of God through man, audible or written, becomes a means of faith. The promise concerning the people who **believe** in Moses **for ever** remains true, since Christians and Jews alike hold Moses to be God's mouthpiece.

In order for Israel to be prepared to listen directly to God, Moses was to **sanctify them to day and to morrow** (10). This outward sanctification, a symbol of the inward purity which only God can give (cf. comment on 13:2), was to take two full days. The external cleansing included (1) washing of the person, (2) washing of the clothes, and (3) abstinence from sexual intercourse.[10] Even after this sanctification the people were to be separated from the mountain by **bounds** (12), or fences, so that no man or beast would touch the mountain. If one did, he was to be put to death. If a person or beast broke through the fence, "No hand shall touch him" (13, RSV), for in so doing it would indirectly touch the mountain. Such an offender must be killed by stones or arrows.

All of these regulations were to teach the people the necessity of holiness, the awesomeness of God, and the absolute obedience God required. Carelessness was not condoned; even an innocent animal must die if its owner failed to keep it from the mountain. **The people** could have God come near in their **sight** (11), but they must not presume to be familiar with Him. The way was not yet open to come boldly into His presence (Heb. 4:16).

Though forbidden in v. 12 to come to the mountain, there was permission for some to come **when the trumpet soundeth long** (13). It would appear that the **they** of 13 refers to a special group of people—Moses, the priests, and the 70 elders (24:1-2)—who were later permitted to ascend.[11] Yet even they must not

[10]Rawlinson, PC, I, 1. [11]*Ibid.*, p. 117.

come until **the trumpet** blew. The verse may refer to the gathering together of the people when God was ready to speak,[12] though the Hebrew seems to mean more than this. The sense in 16-17 favors the view that the trumpet called Israel from the camp to the foot of the mountain. For **Moses . . . sanctified the people** (14; cf. comment on 13:2).

3. *God on Mt. Sinai* (19:16-25)

With all their preparations and warnings the people **trembled** (16) when God made His presence known. The moment had arrived for them to meet God, so "they took their stand at the foot of the mountain" (17, RSV). The whole experience was designed to create a true fear of God in the people and prepare them to respect God's law.

In addition to the **thunders and lightnings** (16) and the loud **trumpet,** the mountain was aflame; **smoke . . . ascended** from the fire as from **a furnace, and the whole mount quaked greatly** (18). **Altogether on a smoke** is better "was wrapped in smoke" (RSV). Even Moses was made to tremble with fear at the sight (Heb. 12:21). Yet for all this fear, at the longer and louder sounding of the trumpet, **Moses spake, and God answered him by a voice** (19). The same voice that he had heard at the burning bush now spoke from the mount in a clear and awesome sound that all could hear.

The Lord called Moses to ascend the **mount** (20), an act forbidden to the others, **and Moses went up.** Quickly, however, God sent Moses back to renew the warning to the people against trespassing on the holy mountain (21). Especially was the message directed to the **priests, which come near to the Lord** (22). For **sanctify themselves,** cf. comment on 10 and 13:2. These persons were not the Levites, who had not yet been appointed; they probably were firstborn who performed priestly functions (see 24:5).[13] They might have presumed that they had as much right to ascend the mount as Moses had. God knew their intentions and so ordered Moses to return and thus avoid a catastrophe. For the Lord to **break forth upon them** would be in plague, or fire, or direct death, as in the case of Uzzah (II Sam. 6:7-8).

Moses, in his ignorance of the people's possible intentions, reminded God that all precautions had been taken and none

[12]Henry, *op. cit.*, fn.

[13]Connell, *op. cit.*, p. 120.

could unwittingly **come up to mount Sinai** (23). But God knew better; Moses must again tell the people that only he and **Aaron** could **come up** (24). Here God is making clear that He can choose whom He will, and others must abide by His will. Also it is important to discern God's voice, and follow it, even when one thinks there is no danger. God knows men's hearts when others do not. For **sanctify it** (23), cf. comment on 13:2. **Moses** obeyed (25) and thus averted a tragedy.

In c. 19 is revealed "The Holiness of God," which: (1) Requires holiness in those who approach Him, 5-6, 10-11; (2) Sets Him apart from all His creatures, 12-13; (3) Manifests His presence in awesome grandeur, 16-20; (4) Communicates to erring men, 7-9, 21-25.

B. The Ten Commandments, 20:1-17

God spake (1) out of the burning mountain to the people. In Deuteronomy it is clearly stated that these commandments to the assembly were given by God "in the mount out of the midst of the fire, of the cloud, and of the thick darkness, with a great voice" (Deut. 5:22). How God spoke in audible voice is not said, but Israel understood that the voice they heard was that of God. This was "an audible and terrible voice, the voice of Jehovah, sounding like a trumpet over the multitude (Ex. 19:16; 20:18)."[14] This way of describing the event does not assume that God has vocal cords like a man, but it does declare that God created an audible sound that enunciated His words to man in intelligible form. After the people had heard, it was enough; they preferred that **Moses** do the speaking (19).

It is important to know that it was the **Lord thy God** who was speaking (2). In this modern day, when there is talk of a "new morality" and when some theologians announce that "God is dead," one needs to know where his authority is. These words were given by God to His people as the guiding rules for all mankind. It will not do to claim that they are relevant only to the day in which they were given. "God would have the Israelites clearly understand, that He Himself gave them the commandments."[15]

Furthermore the people heard **all these words** (1). In the Bible the Ten Commandments are called in the original "ten

[14]Johnson, *op. cit.*, p. 68.

[15]Rawlinson, PC, I, 130.

words" (34:28; Deut. 4:13; 10:4; hence the title Decalogue, lit., 10 words). They were not borrowed from Egypt, or other nations, as some suspect. "The noble utterances of Sinai are wholly unlike anything to be found in the entire range of Egyptian literature."[16]

God gave these words, not as a means of salvation, for these people were already saved from Egypt, but as rules for guidance. Since obedience was a condition of continuing the covenant (19:5), these words became the basis for perseverance as God's people. Paul made clear that the observance of the law is not the means of one's personal salvation, but rather, justification is by faith in Christ (Gal. 2:16). The law leads to Christ, but does not save (Gal. 3:24). "If it is not true that we can keep it and so earn heaven, it is equally false that we may break it without penalty or remorse."[17] Actually then this moral law was given as a proving ground for the faith of God's people. Those who love Him will observe His law.

The dividing of the law into moral, ceremonial, and civil is helpful in one way, but misleading in another. Certainly the moral law of the Decalogue is basic and expresses a responsibility for all men. However, the other laws given to Israel were just as binding for them. God's laws were an exhibition of His righteousness by means of symbols and they provided a discipline through which Israel might be conformed to God's holiness.[18] Social and ceremonial laws may change, but the fundamental relationships between God and man, and among men, as found in the Decalogue, are eternal.

The division of the Ten Commandments has been variously understood. The Lutheran and Roman Catholic churches follow Augustine in counting vv. 2-6 the first commandment and dividing v. 17 on coveteousness into two. Modern Judaism reckons v. 2 as a command to believe in God and as the first word; it combines vv. 3-6 into the second. The earlier division, however, made verse 3 the first commandment and verses 4-6 the second. This position was "supported unanimously by the early church, and is held today by the Eastern Orthodox and most Protestant churches."[19]

The first four commandments make up the first table of the

[16]*Ibid.*

[17]Chadwick, *op. cit.*, I, 191.

[18]Johnson, *op. cit.*, p. 68.

[19]*Ibid.*, p. 69.

Decalogue and reveal man's proper relationship to God. They are fulfilled in the first great command, "Thou shalt love the Lord thy God with all thy heart, and with all thy soul, and with all thy mind" (Matt. 22:37). The last six deal with human relations and are fulfilled in loving one's neighbor as himself.

1. *The First Commandment—No Other Gods* (20:3)

Verse 2 introduces the first commandment with **God** identifying himself as the One bringing Israel out of Egyptian **bondage.** Since He did this for them and proved His supremacy, they were to make Him their God. There was no place for any competitor. All other gods were false.

Before me (3) means "side by side with me" or "in addition to me."[20] God did not expect that Israel would give Him up; He knew that their danger lay in the direction of giving equal allegiance to other gods. This command underlines the monotheism of Judaism and Christianity.

"The first commandment prohibits every species of *mental* idolatry, and all inordinate attachment to *earthy* and *sensible* things."[21] There is no true happiness apart from God, for He is the Fountain of all joy. Those who seek joy elsewhere break the first commandment, and end up in misery and tragedy.

2. *Second Commandment—No Graven Images* (20:4-6)

"As the first commandment asserts the unity of God, and is a protest against polytheism, so the second asserts his spirituality, and is a protest against idolatry and materialism."[22] Though some forms of idolatry may be nonmaterial—e.g., covetousness (Col. 3:5) or sensuality (Phil. 3:19)—yet the second command primarily condemns the making of images (4) as objects of worship. This kind of idolatry has always existed among the more simpleminded pagan peoples of the world. That this temptation was a snare to Israel is apparent in her history.

These pagan images were made in the form of things seen in the sky, on the earth, and in the waters. No such images were to be made objects of worship: **Thou shalt not bow down thyself to them** (5). Verses 4 and 5 must be taken together. There is no condemnation for making images so long as they are not

[20]Rawlinson, CWB, I, 260.

[21]Clarke, *op. cit.*, I, 402.

[22]Rawlinson, PC, I, 131.

made objects of veneration. Sculptured work was used in the Tabernacle (25:31-34) and in the first Temple (I Kings 6:18, 29). Idolatry consists in making an image an object of worship and ascribing to it the powers of the god it represents. If pictures or images of people are looked upon as possessing divine powers and are adored, they become idols.

God's reason for this prohibition was given. He is **a jealous God,** in the sense that He will not permit the respect and reverence due Him to be bestowed upon another. God does not, as did the Greek gods, begrudge success or happiness to others. It is for His people's sake that they are to hallow and reverence His name.[23]

Disobedience will be punished (5) and obedience rewarded (6). Many have questioned the judgment upon the children of offending parents, but these judgments are temporal (see Ezek. 18:14-17) and apply to the consequences such as disease that naturally follow evildoing. The fear of harming a child should exercise a wholesome check upon parents' conduct. The disadvantages given a child because of parental disobedience may lead parents to repentance. At worst, penalty is **unto the third and fourth generation,** while **mercy** will be shown to a thousand generations when love and obedience are present.

3. *Third Commandment—God's Name in Vain* (20:7)

To take God's **name . . . in vain** is "to call upon unreality, i.e., that which is not an expression of divine character, by means of the divine name."[24] Such unholy usage of God's name occurred in perjury, in the practice of magic, and in the invocation of the dead. The prohibition is against false swearing, and would also include flippant oaths and the profanity so common in our day. "This commandment does not preclude the use of God's name in true and solemn oaths."[25]

God hates dishonesty, and for someone to use His name to cover up an evil heart, or to make himself appear better than he is, is a serious sin. People who try to cover up evil lives while professing the name of Christ break this third commandment. Such persons are guilty before God (7) and can receive no mercy until repentant. Righteous men revere God's name as holy and sacred.

[23]Connell, *op. cit.*, p. 120.

[24]IB, I, 983.

[25]Connell, *op. cit.*, p. 120.

4. *Fourth Commandment—the Sabbath Is Holy* (20:8-11)

The use of the word **remember** (8) implies that it is easy to neglect God's holy day. It was to be held in continual remembrance and kept holy, i.e., "withdrawn from common employment and dedicated to God" (Amp. OT). All common labor was to be done on the **six days** (9), while **the seventh day is the sabbath of the Lord thy God** (10). It was a day set apart, to be given wholly to God.

No one was to work on this **seventh day.** A master was not to make his servants work. Even the work animals were to rest. Specific prohibitions were given, such as the command against gathering manna (16:26), lighting a fire (35:3), gathering sticks (Num. 15:35). Though the negative is emphasized, the law allowed for necessary work, such as the work of priests and Levites in the Temple, caring for the sick, and the rescue of a beast (cf. Matt. 12:5, 11).

The reason given for observing the Sabbath is that God made the earth **in six days** and He **rested the seventh day: wherefore the Lord blessed the sabbath day, and hallowed it** (11). Though the Scriptures do not list the things a person is to do on the Sabbath, the day is clearly implied to be one of rest and worship. Secular and materialistic pursuits are to be replaced with spiritual activities. Christ condemned the legalism that made the day a harsh and heartless form, yet He did not do away with the sacredness of the day. It was given for man's good (Mark 2:23-28).

The observance of the Lord's Day (Sunday) as the Christian Sabbath preserves the moral principle laid down in this command. The change from the Jewish Sabbath to the Christian Sabbath was gradually made with no necessary loss of God's purpose in this holy day.[26] It may be noted that vv. 9-10 do not specify Saturday nor "the seventh day of the week" as the day of Sabbath rest. The letter of the commandment is fulfilled by observing the next day after six days of labor, as the Christian indeed does.

5. *Fifth Commandment—Honoring Parents* (20:12)

Honour thy father and thy mother, is the first command in relation to men and governs the earliest relationship a person has

[26]John D. Davis, *The Westminster Dictionary of the Bible* (Philadelphia: The Westminster Press, 1944), p. 362.

with others, that of children to parents. This commandment is so basic that it is fairly universal. Most societies recognize the importance of obedient children. The best exegesis of this verse is the exhortation of Paul in Eph. 6:1-3, where he points out the responsibilities of parents and children.

With this commandment came a promise. Long life was assured to those who honor their parents. This promise was probably intended for both the nation in her continuance in Palestine and for the individual who obeys. The promise is still true: the nation whose children are obedient continues under God's blessing, and individuals obedient to parents have promise of longer life. There will be exceptions to this rule, but its general application has been shown.[27]

6. *Sixth Commandment—Thou Shalt Not Kill* (20:13)

Life is man's most prized possession and it is wrong to deprive one of his life without just cause. It is clear from Israel's history that this command is not absolute. Later provision was made for excusable (21:13), accidental (Num. 35:23), and justifiable homicide (22:2). Also Israel was authorized to destroy her enemies. No reasonable exegesis can condemn capital punishment or war simply on the basis of this command. Jesus made its meaning clear when He quoted it, "Thou shalt do no murder" (Matt. 19:18).

There can be no justification for the instigation of riots, unnecessary rebellions, or other conditions that may lead to bloodshed. Responsibility is apparent for proper care in travel, construction projects, and sports where danger is present. Individual and community effort is needed in the preservation of human life. Yet this command does not call for nor justify the prolonging of a life by modern drugs when hope for normal life has passed.

7. *Seventh Commandment—No Adultery* (20:14)

Sexual purity is the underlying principle of this command. Adultery was usually defined as unlawful sex relations of a married person. It was thus sinning against the family. But this commandment is applicable to all kinds of sexual immorality. The modern idea that exceptions can be made to this rule cannot be justified. Jesus made clear that adultery is found in the heart and

[27]Rawlinson, CWB, I, 262.

occurs before any outward act (Matt. 5:28). This command condemns all sexual intercourse occurring outside the marriage bond. It also implies a prohibition of acts that precede and lead to the sexual act.

8. *Eighth Commandment—Thou Shalt Not Steal* (20:15)

The right of personal property is allowed by this command. It is wrong to take from another what is rightfully his. It is also stealing when one takes what rightfully belongs to a business firm or an institution. There can be no justification for "appropriation" even when one feels it is his due. This commandment is broken if one intentionally reports falsely on a tax form and thus withholds taxes due his government, even though he disapproves of the government.

It is also stealing to take advantage of others in the selling of property or products, or in the conducting of any business deal. To pay lower wages than deserved is wrong. The love of money is the basic sin condemned by this command. Only with a pure heart can obedience be perfect.

9. *Ninth Commandment—No Dishonesty* (20:16)

While stealing robs a man of property, the bearing of a false witness may rob a person of his good reputation. Whether in court or elsewhere, one's word should always be true. A report should never be repeated until its truth is verified. The passing on of gossip is immoral; before one speaks he should make certain that what he says is correct. There may be times when even a true report should not be passed on to others—one is not commanded to bear witness to all he knows as true. But when one speaks, what he says should, to the best of his knowledge, always be true.

10. *Tenth Commandment—No Coveting* (20:17)

This final command underlies the four preceding ones since it strikes at the purposes of the heart. Killing, adultery, stealing, and lying result from wrong desires that inflame a person's being. It is unique that the Hebrew law included this challenge to thought and intent. "Ancient moralists did not usually recognize this," and they did not condemn evil desires.[28] But it is in the heart where all rebellion begins, and this commandment reveals the inward aspect of all the commandments of God.

[28]*Ibid.*, p. 263.

Paul recognized this inward aspect of the law when he was awakened to his sinful condition (Rom. 7:7). Many people are innocent of wrongdoing on the basis of outward acts, but are nevertheless condemned when they consider their inward thoughts. These covetous desires may be for property belonging to a neighbor (17) or for his **wife.** Such evil desires need to be purged by the Spirit of God; only then can one live in perfect obedience to God's holy law.

C. The People's Fear, 20:18-20

What an experience for these Israelites to stand near a burning mountain and to hear the voice of Almighty God! When the people saw these things, they backed away and **stood afar off** (18). Fear overcame them. They asked Moses to be an intermediary for them, and said, **Let not God speak with us, lest we die** (19). In these circumstances they discovered that they were not as ready to question Moses' place as the prophet of God as they had been earlier disposed to do (17:1-4).

Moses gave Israel the reassuring word that they need not fear unduly, for **God is come to prove you** (20)—that is, "to test whether you will respect His commandments."[29] They were not to be afraid of the **lightnings,** but there was to be a **fear** lest they sin against God. Children of God need not fear divine providences, but a godly fear that leads to reverence and obedience is essential.

D. The Laws of the Covenant, 20:21—23:33

1. *The Law of the Altar* (20:21-26)

While the people stood in fear at a distance from the burning mountain, **Moses drew near unto the thick darkness where God was** (21). The same phenomena that repelled the people drew Moses. The real difference was in the heart. Moses' faith drew him to God.

God now gave to His servant what is called the book of the covenant (20:22—23:33). Rather than speaking directly to the people, He used Moses as a mediator, as they had requested (19). God wanted the people to know that He who spoke through Moses was the same One who **talked with you from heaven** (22)

[29]Connell, *op. cit.*, p. 121.

when He gave them the Decalogue. Whether God speaks directly or through His minister, what is conveyed is His word.

Israel was not to make representations of gods out of **silver** and **gold. Ye shall not make with me** (23) means "to rival me" (Berk.). Jehovah alone was their God, so there was to be no fashioning of images of any kind. False gods were not to share with Him His glory nor to share the worship of the people. These restrictions further implement the second commandment.

The approach to God was to be at an **altar of earth** (24) made by the people. The elevation symbolized the lifting up of man toward the God of heaven. The simplicity of the altar directed man's attention from himself and material things to the Exalted One. Obviously the **burnt** and **peace offerings** were commonly known to Israel at this time even though their use in Egypt may have been restricted.

"In every place where I cause my name to be remembered" (24, RSV) indicates God's purpose to meet Israel and bless them. **Places where I record my name** (24) probably referred to places where He made himself known to them as they journeyed. In later times, when a more permanent memorial was desired, Israel's altars were to be made of unhewn **stone;** using tools on the stones would pollute them (25). The use of the stone in its natural form restricted Israel from using artistic embellishments at this time, probably because of the danger of idolatry. In the later, permanent structures, more elaborate altars were allowed (27:1-8; 30:1-5). God taught His people by beginning with the simple and leading on to the more complex as their spiritual growth would justify.

The restriction in 26 was given before the instructions concerning priestly garments (28:42). The loose robes of the priestly heads of tribes were not suitable for mounting steps in the presence of people, so there were to be no steps on the altar. God always wants matters decent and in order.

2. *Laws Concerning Slaves* (21:1-11)

It must be remembered that **these . . . judgments** (1, detailed laws) were given to Israel for the social situation in which they lived. God applied His moral principles to their present needs. The law did not require slavery, but since it was present, these rules would guide in maintaining right relations. The ethical principles themselves were to apply in whatever social structure prevailed. The Israelites had to judge what were right actions under their system, therefore the necessity of these rules.

a. Concerning the male slave (21:2-6). Poverty was the reason a man would sell himself to another who could buy him. The time of service would be limited to **six years; and in the seventh he shall go out free** (2). These rules applied only to Hebrew slaves (Lev. 25:44-46). The regulations were to protect individual rights. In the sabbatical year the slave was to go free with **his wife** if she had come into slavery with him (3).

However, if he married one of the slaves of his master, he could not take her when he went, nor the **children** (4). If his **love** for his family or **master** (5) was such that he wanted to remain a slave, he could. When he made clear a desire to remain, **his master** was to take him to **the judges** for confirmation (6). A continuing proof of his free intention was given by boring **his ear through with an aul.** By this token he would become a slave **for ever.** The ear was the organ of hearing and thus symbolized willing obedience. In this manner a man's freedom of choice was maintained, even in slavery.

b. Concerning the female slave (21:7-11). Actually the daughter sold into slavery was protected more than the man. If she remained single, she could go free as any male slave at the end of six years (Deut. 15:12, 17), though this may have been a later provision. The situation here appears to be that a father would **sell his daughter** (7) to become a wife, either to **her master** (8) or to **his son** (9). If the master was not pleased with her, she was to **be redeemed** (8), i.e., bought back, but he could not sell her to a foreigner. If she became the wife of his son, he was to treat her as a daughter (9). Even if a second wife were taken by the husband, her **food, raiment,** and marital rights continued in the household (10). If there were failure in **these three** conditions, she was to be set **free** (11) without charge.

Probably the purpose of this practice was for a father to better the situation for his daughter. She could become a part of the household of a better family. These rules prevented a master from taking advantage of the poor family by mistreatment of the girl. The regulations were given, not for upholding the institution of slavery, but for protecting the rights of individuals already in the system.

3. *Laws Concerning Capital Crimes* (21:12-17)

The sixth commandment made clear that killing was wrong. These rules clarified the law and stated the penalty, which was capital punishment, usually by stoning. Those who oppose capital punishment merely by quoting the sixth commandment do not rightly interpret scripture. The same Lawgiver who commanded not to kill instructed that the murderer **be put to death** (12).

God distinguished between willful, premeditated murder and killing that was unintentional on the part of the slayer. If a man did not **lie . . . in wait** (13) for another but in God's providence slew him (there are no accidents with God), then the slayer could flee to a place of refuge (Num. 35:22-28). Here the man was safe until the matter could be tried and the truth determined by a proper court. If the man were guilty of purposeful murder, he was to be taken from the **altar** and executed (14). It is possible that altars were commonly considered as places of refuge. Many in the ancient world had scruples against removing a criminal from an altar for punishment, but Mosaic law regarded this unqualified scruple as a superstition and refused to sanction it.[30]

Striking a parent was reckoned a capital crime (15). Apparently the blow was considered as serious a wrong as if it resulted in death. Certainly it was assumed to be purposeful. Children were to honor their parents, who were God's representatives to them. Parents were reckoned as equal, and the penalty was the same for striking either. It would appear also that the child held responsible in this way would be old enough to be accountable for his act.

Stealing, or kidnapping, **a man** and holding him as a slave or selling him into slavery was reckoned a capital crime (16). To do this was as bad as murder since it took away a person's liberty, which was treasured as life. The common practice of enslaving people by force was here condemned in the Mosaic law.

Cursing a parent (17) was an appeal by oath to God to join against His own representative on earth and was a crime punishable by death.

4. *Laws Relating to Non-capital Offenses* (21:18-32)

a. Quarreling men (21:18-19). Mosaic law recognized the depravity of men—they quarrel and strike (18). When one struck

[30]Rawlinson, CWB, I, 267.

with a **stone or fist** (apparently with no intent to kill) and the victim did not die, but was able to **rise** and **walk** with a **staff** (19), the penalty was payment for **loss . . . of time** and for medical care. The man's responsibility to his victim did not end until he was **thoroughly healed.**

b. Death of a slave (21:20-21). In pagan society few, if any, rights were allowed to the slave. But God recognized the worth of such persons; He placed both the male and the female on a high level by requiring punishment for the master who killed a slave (20). Whether this penalty was death is not clear.[31] However, if the slave survived **a day or two** (21), there was no penalty. This was probably because survival proved that the master did not desire to kill the slave but was beating him for correction. If the slave died later, the economic loss of the slave was the master's penalty.

c. A woman with child (21:22-23). Often when **men strive,** a wife tries to intervene and gets hurt. If the woman was pregnant, and lost her child, the man who hurt her must pay a fine to her **husband** as required by the **judges.** Since the death of the child was accidental, the death penalty was not imposed. However, if further harm resulted (23), such as the death of the woman, the death penalty was applicable, unless the slayer could prove his act was unintentional (cf. 13-14).

d. Retaliation law (21:24-25). Rawlinson believes that the "law of retaliation was much older than Moses, and accepted by him as tolerable rather than devised as rightful."[32] Similar laws were prominent in ancient society and are found in the Code of Hammurabi.[33] The requirement that an offender should suffer an equivalent injury was difficult to administer, and was later commuted to a money fine except for murder.[34] Jesus did not say that this law was unjust, but He asked that love and forgiveness prevail (Matt. 5:38-48). In actual practice, the "lex talionis," as this is called, resulted in a code of justice more merciful than that prevailing in many pagan codes, where the most extreme punishment was meted out for comparatively minor offenses. Here the punishment was limited to the extent of the crime.

e. Harm to slaves (21:26-27). A modification of the law of retaliation is given immediately. If a master should destroy an

[31]*Ibid.*, pp. 267-68.

[32]*Ibid.*, p. 268.

[33]IB, I, 1000.

[34]Connell, *op. cit.*, p. 122.

eye, or even a **tooth,** of his own slave, he must set him **free,** whether male or female. The eye was reckoned a man's most valuable asset, and a tooth the least. Such a restriction on masters would serve as a restraint in their punishment of slaves, since even the accidental knocking out of a tooth could deprive him of his servant. This law reflects a recognition of a human worth found nowhere else among nations of that period.

f. Hurt by an animal (21:28-32). **If an ox** should **gore** a person to death, the animal was to be **stoned** and its **flesh** could **not be eaten** (28). **Shall be quit** means "shall be without blame." The owner of the ox was held responsible further for the tragedy if he knew the animal to be dangerous and had done nothing to prevent the killing—it would be criminal negligence. In this case he was guilty of a crime equivalent to murder and must **be put to death** along with the animal (29).

However, provision was made for a ransom in such cases. Apparently the family of the slain person could ask a **sum of money** (30) which the owner of the ox could pay, and thus save his life. Such a **ransom** was also allowed if the slain person were **a son** or **daughter** (31). Likely if a family asked too high a ransom, the judges were called in for a settlement (cf. 22).

In the case of slaves killed by an **ox,** the **master** was paid the amount set by law as the price of a slave—**thirty shekels of silver** (32). **The ox** was **stoned,** as in the death of a free man, and thus the human dignity of the slave was recognized.

5. *Laws Relating to Property Rights* (21:33—22:17)

The above laws on capital and non-capital crimes implement the sixth commandment, "Thou shalt not kill." In contrast, the following legislation concerning property is related to the eighth commandment, "Thou shalt not steal." The right of private property was recognized by these rules, and proper reimbursement was required when these rights were trespassed.

a. An open pit (21:33-34). Pits in the ground were common in the East, used for the storage both of water and of grain. These were dangerous when left uncovered. The person responsible for the open **pit** must pay for any damage to an animal which fell into it (33). When he had reimbursed the owner for the value of the animal, he could claim the dead beast. Apparently there was the right of open range for the livestock.

b. Ox versus ox (21:35-36). Out on open range the animals grazed together and one ox might kill another. When this happened, the owners of the two oxen would share the value of the **live ox** and **divide** the **dead** animal (35). However, if it was **known that the ox** doing the damage was dangerous, his owner must pay the full price of the dead ox to its owner, and might then take the animal for **his own** (36). In disputed cases, there would normally be witnesses before a panel of judges. It is apparent that proof of serious negligence was reckoned as important in these decisions.

c. Stealing (22:1-4). Cattle and sheep were the most common animals, so these are used as examples of theft. The reason for restoring **five oxen for an ox, and four sheep for a sheep** (1) is not clear. Possibly the loss of oxen was more serious, since they were work animals and not, as sheep, raised chiefly for wool and meat.

Breaking up (2) was digging through a clay wall into another's property by a thief. If the intruder was caught in the act and slain, there was no guilt to the one killing him. This was justifiable homicide. However, if time had elapsed, as the words **If the sun be risen upon him** (3) can be taken to mean, then to slay the thief was not justifiable and such a slayer would be guilty.[35] It is possible that the meaning conveyed is that killing the thief in the night brought no guilt, while in the day it did. In any case, if the thief lived, he had to make **full restitution,** or if unable to pay, was to **be sold** as a slave (3).

If the thief had not killed or sold the animal he stole, he could make restitution by restoring **double** (4) rather than four- or five-fold (1). In this case he would restore the stolen animal, and one other.

d. Trespassing (22:5). Though it appears that animals were free to roam together in certain places (21:33-36), there were also private fields or vineyards where trespassing was prohibited. The Hebrews allowed for private land as well as personal property. If a man purposefully grazed his lifestock in his neighbor's **vineyard** or **field,** he must pay back with the best in **his own field** and **vineyard.**

e. Fire (22:6). In the fields dead brush was piled and burned at certain seasons of the year. If by carelessness the fire

[35]Lange, *op. cit.*, p. 91.

spread and burned the stacked or **standing** grain in the fields, the one who **kindled the fire** was required to pay in full. Such rules taught carefulness and encouraged respect for the rights of others.

f. Trust goods (22:7-13). In primitive societies where banking was unknown, goods were often left in the hands of others for safekeeping. In such cases there was need for protective laws. If money or goods so entrusted had been stolen by a thief who was apprehended, the culprit must **pay double** (7). **If the thief** was **not found,** the trustee must appear before the **judges** for a determination of the case (8). The word here translated **judges** may be rendered "God," although the context would indicate that judges were meant, acting as representatives or agents of God (see Amp. OT).

Verse 9 explains what happened when two parties each claimed the same object. The controversy, which could also arise in the circumstances described in v. 8 if the owner charged the trustee of his goods with dishonesty, was to be settled before God by **the judges.** The phrase **another challengeth to be his** means "which anyone says is his" (BB). Whatever decision was made, the condemned person must **pay double** to the other.

Not only were goods and money put in trust with neighbors, but also livestock (10). If while in trust an animal died or was hurt or disappeared, an "oath before the Lord" (11, Amp. OT) between the parties was required to prove the innocence of the trustee. When this was accepted by the owner, no restitution was required.

However, if the animal had been **stolen** while in trust, **restitution** must be made (12). This rule differed from the one about money or goods in v. 7. It was probably reckoned that shepherds, if responsible, could prevent theft of an animal, while money was more easily taken. If an animal was slain by another beast, the trustee was free from guilt if he could bring the slain animal as evidence (13). An alert shepherd might not be able to prevent the attack of a wild beast, but he could recover a part of the carcass as proof. In this case no restitution was necessary.

g. Borrowing (22:14-15). A person was responsible for that which he borrowed. If an animal that was borrowed was hurt or died, and **the owner** was not present, the borrower must make full restitution (14). However, **if the owner** was **present** when the animal was hurt or died, no restitution was necessary (15).

Being present made him responsible even when another was using the animal.

If it be an hired thing, then the matter was different. "Damage to a thing hired was not to be made good by the hirer, since the risk of it might be considered to have formed a part of the calculation upon which the amount of the hire was fixed."[36] The words **It came for his hire** may be rendered, "The damage is included in its hire" (Amp. OT).

h. Seducing a virgin (22:16-17). The seduction of a virgin was regarded as a form of stealing. A father expected his daughter's marriage to bring him a dowry. **If a man** enticed her (with her consent) and had sexual intercourse, he was required **to endow her to be his wife** (16). Should the father refuse to allow her to be the seducer's wife, as a penalty the culprit must **pay money according to the dowry of virgins** (17). What this amount was is not said. It may be assumed to be larger than the dowry for a wife.[37] Apparently this act was not considered an offense against the commandment on adultery, but against the commandment on stealing.

6. *Other Crimes Punishable by Death* (22:18-20)

A witch (18) was a woman who practiced sorcery, a form of reliance upon evil spirits.[38] This rule was not an acknowledgment of any reality of genuine intercourse with evil spirits, but condemned the challenge that sorcery presented to belief in the true God. Also this practice often led to injury to the bodies and lives of others. The **witch** dispensed mixed herbs and thus became a mixer of poisons.[39] When such a person persisted in these unholy and dangerous practices, she was not to be permitted to live.

Sexual intercourse with beasts (19) was often practiced in pagan religions. Such wickedness could not be condoned in Israel, so the offender was not permitted to live.

Any acknowledgment of false gods (20) was utterly condemned in the Mosaic code (Deut. 13:1-16). God would have no rival; all semblance of false worship was to be abandoned. Persons attempting to instigate or perpetuate relics of pagan religion in Israel were to be **utterly destroyed.**

[36]Rawlinson, CWB, I, 271.

[37]*Ibid.*

[38]Connell, *op. cit.*, p. 122.

[39]Lange, *op. cit.*, p. 93.

7. *Sundry Duties* (22:21-31)

a. Against oppression (22:21-24). A **stranger** (21, foreigner) was not to be vexed or oppressed by God's people. Israel was to remember that she had been a stranger **in the land of Egypt.** Mistreatment of foreigners is ever obnoxious to the Heavenly Father.

God had special sympathy for the **widow** and orphan (22). His ear was tuned to their **cry** in oppression (23). The offender against these unfortunate persons would suffer under God's **wrath** (24). This wicked man would be killed and his wife and **children** left desolate. The history of Israel's punishment at the hands of the Babylonians reflects the fulfillment of this threat. Interestingly, these offenses of Israel were punished more directly by God through enemy nations than by officers of Israel. Likely such offenses as these were committed more often by the very men in Israel who were authorized to administer justice.

b. Lending (22:25-27). God had regard for the poor and prohibited the rich person from taking advantage of them. When a poor man had to borrow (probably taking an advance on his wage in order to obtain food), there was to be no **usury** (25, interest) charged. The idea of interest on commercial loans was not considered here, as this practice was a later development. Even if the creditor took a garment as a **pledge,** it was to be returned by nightfall (26). This garment was the outer, flowing cloak not needed during the day, but especially needed by nomadic people for sleeping during the cool nights (27). To retain such a pledge, and cause suffering to a poor man unable to pay, brings God's disfavor. He is **gracious** (compassionate) and expects His people to have a similar spirit.

c. Obligations to God (22:28-31). The word **gods** (28) in this context should be rendered either "the judges" or "God."[40] Israelites were to hold foreign gods in contempt (Isa. 41:29; 44:9-20). No one was to **revile** God, or the judges duly selected, nor was he to **curse the ruler** of the **people.** The **ruler** was the chief person in each tribe and was reckoned as God's representative.

Apparently **delay** (29) in giving to God His share of the **ripe fruits** was a common fault. The command here required the

[40]Rawlinson, PC, I, 192. "Again the name Elohim is used, which usually stands for God, but balanced, Hebrew fashion, with 'rulers' in the next clause, it must denote judges as it did previously [in 22:7]" (Berk., fn.).

immediate bringing to God for sacrifice that which He claimed for himself. **Liquors** is better translated the "outflow of your presses" (RSV).

The firstborn as belonging to the Lord are mentioned in 13:12. They were to be redeemed by the payment of a stipulated sum. However, males of the firstborn **oxen** and **sheep** were to be brought for sacrifice. The only delay allowed for these was the first **seven days** with the mother (30). This was an act of mercy to the animal's mother, which needed the newly born for her comfort and health for this length of time. The animal was to be brought **on the eighth day.**

God commanded His people, **Ye shall be holy men** (31). Essentially this meant to become holy in heart and spirit. But this inward holiness was foreshadowed by compliance with God's outward signs of purity. These holy men were not to eat animals **torn of beasts in the field.** Such animals were made ceremonially unclean by the unclean beasts which tore them to pieces, and also by the blood left in the flesh. Men holy at heart want to be like God. They therefore find it easy to follow the clearly defined laws of God.

Verses 18-31 show "The Nature of God." (1) Severe in punishing evil, 18-20; (2) Compassionate towards the needy, 21-27; (3) Deserving of respect and obedience, 28-30; (4) Expecting holiness in His people, 31.

8. *Ethical Instructions* (23:1-9)

a. Bear no false report (23:1-3). One should neither **raise a false report** (1) nor "repeat" it (Amp. OT). God's man must never become an **unrighteous witness,** in court or anywhere else. A man has joined **with the wicked** when he breaks the ninth commandment.

Even if **a multitude** (2) are on the wrong side, God's man must stand alone for the right. One can often expect the crowd to do wrong, because many go the broad road (Matt. 7:13-14). The meaning of 2*b* is, "You must not . . . bear witness in court so as to side with an unjust majority" (Moffatt).

Nor should one be partial to **a poor man in his cause** (3). Though the law especially protected the poor, enthusiasm for the cause of the poor must not pervert justice. A judge or jury must judge according to principle, not according to popular appeal. In a day when there is a popular movement toward civil rights, criminal rights, and relief of poverty, the rights of other citizens must also be protected.

b. Help your enemy (23:4-5). "It was not generally recognized in antiquity that men's enemies had any claims upon them."[41] But the New Testament emphasis on love is anticipated in this exhortation to aid a personal enemy (4). If his animal strays, **bring it back to him.** If one met his enemy with an animal fallen under its **burden,** he was to **help** lift the load (5). A clearer rendering of the last part of the verse is, "You shall refrain from leaving the man to cope with it alone, you shall help him to release the animal" (Amp. OT). Working together in helping an enemy get his donkey back on its feet could soften the ill feelings between the men.

c. Do not pervert justice (23:6-8). These instructions appear to have the judges in mind. The **poor** (6) must be given righteous **judgment** even though the temptation to do otherwise was common. Whenever a **false** charge has been brought, the judge must not give a sentence that would **slay** the **innocent and righteous** (7). God will not **justify** a **wicked** judge under any circumstance. Nor must a judge ever accept a **gift** (8, bribe). The need for this rule is always present. Israel later fell far into the pernicious evil of taking bribes (I Sam. 8:3; Isa. 1:23; 5:23).

d. Remember the stranger (23:9). The admonition of 22:21 is repeated, though the idea here was concerned especially with action in legal matters. Israel knew in her heart how foreigners felt, so had good reason to be kind and righteous toward them.

9. *Sabbath Observance* (23:10-13)

a. The sabbatical year (23:10-11). A year of rest for the land in every seven was unknown to any other nation. For an agricultural people it may have appeared too drastic. According to one interpretation of II Chron. 36:21, it was neglected 70 times, or about half the time, between the Exodus and the Captivity. The law was given to test the obedience of the Israelites, to give **the poor** an advantage, since they could partake of any fruit in **the seventh year** (11), and to give time for special communion with God.[42]

b. The sabbath day (23:12-13). No new word is given here beyond the statement in the fourth commandment. The purpose

[41] Rawlinson, CWB, I, 273. [42] *Ibid.*, p. 274.

of **rest** and refreshment to the animals, slaves, and aliens is repeated. This seventh day was God's day, and **no mention of the name of other gods** was to be **heard** (13). These Sabbaths were a constant reminder to the Jews of their obligations to the God of Israel.

10. *The Great Festivals* (23:14-19)

a. The three feasts (23:14-17). **Three times in the year** all the males were to appear before God at a special feast (14, 17). The first one was **the feast of unleavened bread** (15) which was connected with the Passover (cf. 12:14; Lev. 23:5). After the Passover the feast was continued seven days (see comments on 12:15-20). This feast especially commemorated the flight from Egypt and was celebrated by bringing gifts to God. Verse 15 says, "None shall appear in My presence empty-handed" (Berk.).

The feast of harvest (16) was Pentecost (Lev. 23:15-22; Num. 28:26-31; Deut. 16:9-12), at which were exhibited the **firstfruits** of the field where grain had been sown.

The **feast of ingathering** was also called "the feast of tabernacles" (Lev. 23:34-43; Num. 29:12-40; Deut. 16:13-14). This was held in the autumn after all crops had been gathered. It was like a harvest-home celebration, and lasted for a week. It was a time of thanksgiving. Rawlinson writes: "Viewed religiously, the festivals were national thanksgivings for mercies received, both natural and miraculous—the first for the commencement of harvest and the deliverance out of Egypt; the second for the completion of the grain-harvest and the passage of the Red Sea; the third for the final gathering in of the fruits and the many mercies of the wilderness."[43]

b. Offerings at the feasts (23:18-19). The offering of **blood** (18) was primarily at the Passover and was not to be offered with **leavened bread.** Nothing of the lamb, even **the fat,** was to **remain until the morning;** whatever was left was to be burned (12:10). At these feasts **the firstfruits** (19) were to be brought to God's house, symbolizing the consecration of the whole.

The instruction **not** to **seethe a kid in his mother's milk** seems strange, but it may indicate the wrong of letting what was ordained for life (**milk**) become the means of death. Some think that a kid so prepared was a delicacy too fancy for these feasts.[44]

[43]*Ibid.*, p. 275.

[44]Lange, *op. cit.*, p. 97.

But the prohibition was more likely given because of a Canaanite practice in which eating meat so cooked was supposed to promote fertility. Its connection with this pagan ceremony therefore made it unsuitable for God's people.[45] God wanted Israel to copy no practice that could easily lead to idolatry.

11. *God's Promise of Victory* (23:20-33)

a. Victory through His Angel (23:20-22). This **Angel** was God's messenger, the uncreated Spirit in whom God revealed himself. "He is called in 33:15, 16 the face of Jehovah, because the essential nature of Jehovah was manifested in him."[46] The pillar of cloud and fire was an outward symbol of the **Angel.** He was sent before Israel to guard them and **to bring** them **into the place** that God had **prepared** for them (20). This **Angel** must be obeyed, because **transgressions** against **his voice** will not be pardoned (21). He has the authority of God **in him.** Obedience will mean victory, because God will fight for Israel and her **enemies** will be defeated (22).

b. Victory over enemies (23:23-24, 27-33). The enemies that Israel would encounter in Canaan were again named (23; cf. BBC, Vol. II, pp. 35-36). The promise was given that God's **Angel** would **go before** His people, and that He would **cut . . . off** Israel's enemies ("blot them out," RSV) as nations. The special warning was often repeated that Israel must **not bow down to** nor **serve** the **gods** of these nations (24). God's people must not follow these heathen practices in their worship. In fact, Israel was required to **utterly overthrow** these false religions and **break down their images.** Conquerors usually liked to preserve objects of worship from vanquished nations as relics, but these would be only **a snare** (33) to God's people. It was failure at this very point that brought ultimate judgment upon Israel.

God's promise of complete victory for His people over the nations in Palestine was repeated (27). God's **fear** would be upon the Canaanites; He would drive them out as if **hornets** were after them (28). Some take the **hornets** to be literal, but the expression was most likely used figuratively in describing the pursuit of the enemy by Israel's armies. God did not promise instantaneous deliverance; the inhabitants of the land would be vanquished gradually as Israel was enabled to increase and **inherit the land** (30). Too sudden destruction would leave

[45]Johnson, *op. cit.*, p. 73.

[46]*Ibid.*

the land **desolate** and prey to wild beasts (29). Spiritually, God's deliverance from an evil heart is instantaneous, but there are many enemies to be overcome by the sanctified Christian in his daily walk. As we grow, we are enabled to overcome more of such enemies and inherit more of God's land of promise.

Israel's boundaries were to extend from the **Red sea** (31) on the south to **the sea of the Philistines** (Mediterranean) on the west. On the east was **the desert** and on the north **the river** Euphrates (see map 2). Only under Solomon did Israel reach these bounds (I Kings 4:21, 24; II Chron. 9:26). Failure to maintain possession of all this land was because of disobedience.

There was to be **no covenant** (agreement) with the nations of Palestine **nor with their gods** (32). These pagan peoples were not to **dwell in** the **land** as nations for fear of leading Israel into sin; **their gods** would surely be **a snare** to Israel (33). God wanted these peoples with their pagan worship to be destroyed as nations. Lange writes: "It appears that the destruction announced by Jehovah on the Canaanites was intended primarily for them in their collective and public capacity, not for the individuals. The individuals, in so far as they submit, Jehovah will allow, as individuals, to live."[47]

c. *Temporal blessings* (23:25-26). If they obeyed God, the people of Israel were assured, not only of the destruction of their enemies, but also of their **bread** and **water** (25). God also promised to **take . . . away** their **sickness.** Abundant increase of animals and people was assured, along with long life (26). Obedience to God and righteous living assure temporal blessings as a usual result, although for Christians there will be tribulation in this world (John 16:33). Complete fulfillment of this promise will be in the age to come.

Verses 20-33 picture "The Victorious Child of God." (1) Obedient to God's voice, 20-22; (2) Confident in His promises, 23-28; (3) Patient with His plan, 29-31; (4) Alert to His warnings, 32-33.

E. Ratification of the Covenant, 24:1-18

1. *The Covenant Sealed by Blood* (24:1-8)

Moses had been in the mountain (19:3) receiving the **book of the covenant** (7), which was now to be sealed. Having come

[47] *Op. cit.*, p. 98.

down to the people (19:25), he was told to return to God's presence in the mount with **Aaron** and his two sons and with **seventy of the elders of Israel** (1). These elders were the heads of the tribes and families of Israel who had been leaders in Egypt; through them Moses had communicated to the people (3:16; 4:29; 12:21; 17:5-6). They were to come up for **worship** but to remain afar off from God. Only **Moses** could **come near the Lord** (2); the others were to be farther away. **The people** were not allowed on the mountain at all (see 19:12-13). In the OT there was not the same open access to God that we have in Christ (cf. Heb. 10:19-22).

Before the group ascended the mount, Moses **came and told the people all the words** (3) the Lord had given him. These **words** and **judgments** were what was recorded as the Book of the Covenant (20:22—23:33). After **the people** heard, they **answered with one voice, and said, All the words which the Lord hath said will we do.** In the awe and inspiration of the moment, perhaps without realizing the great difficulty they would experience in their obedience, they made their vow to God.

After writing **all the words of the Lord** (4), Moses **early in the morning** built an **altar** with **twelve pillars** "at the foot of the mountain" (RSV). The altar represented God, and the **twelve pillars** stood for the **twelve tribes.** Here was being enacted an agreement between these people and the Lord.

Burnt offerings (5) were both expiatory and marks of self-dedication, while the **peace offerings** indicated man's thankfulness for God's mercies. These were offered by especially selected **young men** in behalf of Israel. The offerings showed thankfulness for being included in the covenant and marked Israel's determination to be consecrated wholly to God's service.[48]

Half of the blood (6) from the sacrificed victims was placed in **basons** to be used later; the other **half** Moses **sprinkled on the altar.** This blood on the altar denoted the consecration of the sacrifice which represented the people to God. The blood also represented God's part in the covenant.

In the presence of the sacrifice and the altar Moses **read** to the people what he had written in **the book of the covenant** (7). He had earlier reported this message to them orally (3) but they needed to know clearly the covenant into which they were enter-

[48]Rawlinson, CWB, I, 278.

ing with God. Again the people promised to **be obedient.** Moses took the other half of the **blood** reserved in **basons** (6) **and sprinkled it on the people** (8); he called it **the blood of the covenant.** This was the first covenant made with Israel and it was sealed with the blood of animal sacrifices. The new or second covenant as described in the NT replaced the old and was sealed with the blood of Christ (Heb. 8:6—9:28). If the old covenant required the obedience of the people to the will of God, certainly no less is expected of him who enters into the new covenant (Heb. 12: 18-29).

2. *The Meeting with God* (24:9-11)

The group that had been requested to ascend the mountain (v. 1) **went up** (9) after sealing the covenant with the blood. The priests, **Aaron, Nadab, and Abihu,** were the spiritual representatives of the people, while the **seventy . . . elders** were the political leaders. They were called **nobles** (11), indicating that they were of noble birth and highly respected by the people they represented.

It appears that in this experience of meeting with God, all partook of a sacrificial meal, for they **did eat and drink** (11). "A sacrifice involved a sacrificial meal, and Moses, following the command of v. 1, took the elders up to the mount, there to eat the flesh of the sacrifice and so commune with God to whom it was offered."[49]

During this meal the participants had a special experience with God. It is said that **they saw God** (10-11). This vision of the Lord must be understood as a manifestation of God, a theophany, when the eye is able to see clearly a representation of the divine Person. "We must not go beyond the limits drawn in ch. 33:20-23 in our conception of what constituted the sight of God; at the same time we must regard it as a vision of God in some form of manifestation which rendered the divine nature discernible to the human eye."[50] In this appearance, God was revealed in His loveliness as a Guest at a meal rather than in fearsome thunderings and earthquakes, as at other times. **Under his feet** (10) was **a sapphire stone** pavement as clear as **heaven.** The **nobles** (11) were not frightened; rather they were able to **eat and drink** with joy in the divine presence without fear of

[49]Connell, *op. cit.*, p. 124.

[50]Johnson, *op. cit.*, p. 74.

death. Moffatt translates 11*a*, "The Eternal did not strike down these headmen of Israel [as they might have expected]. This gentle, lovely, attractive side of God's character was shown to them, instead of the awful and alarming one; and they were taught to look forward to a final state of bliss, in which God's covenanted servants would dwell in His presence continually."[51]

This gracious experience also pointed forward to the day when under the new covenant God's children would enjoy their highest privilege, the realizing of the presence of Christ in the holy sacrament of the Lord's Supper.

"A Covenant with God" is portrayed in 3-11. (1) The terms clearly stated, 3*a*, 4, 7*a*; (2) The vows confidently made, 3*b*, 7*b*; (3) The blood freely sprinkled, 5-6, 8; (4) The Divine gloriously manifested, 9-11.

3. *Moses Returns to the Mount* (24:12-18)

The Decalogue and the Book of the Covenant had been given to Israel. But now, after its ratification by the nation, God had further instructions for His special people. In order to sustain their religious life they needed a form of worship defined, and regulations covering externals such as holy persons, places, rites, and ceremonies. The laws contained in the Decalogue and the Book of the Covenant were important, but the ritual and ceremonial laws which form the main subject of the rest of the Book of Exodus were also needed by Israel.

a. The call (24:12-14). Moses was commanded to ascend **the mount** in order to receive the **tables of stone, and a law, and commandments** (12), which God had written. The Ten Commandments were **written** on the tables (cf. 31:18 and Deut. 5:22). In contrast, the **law, and commandments,** recorded elsewhere, probably included the instructions for the sanctuary and the priesthood and the ritual laws found in Leviticus and Deuteronomy.[52] The purpose for recording these was so that Moses could transmit them to the people.

Moses took **Joshua** with him (13). It is not said whether Joshua entered the cloud (18), but the statement in v. 2 implies that only Moses came near to God. Before he left, Moses asked **the elders** to remain with the people and to bring any matters to

[51]Rawlinson, CWB, I, 278.

[52]Johnson, *op. cit.*, p. 74.

Aaron and Hur (14) in his absence. Apparently he would be away for some time.

b. The approach to God (24:15-18). When Moses ascended, **a cloud covered the mount** (15)—identified as **the glory of the Lord** in 16. This cloud of glory remained on the mount **six days** with no voice heard. These were days of preparation for Moses before going directly into God's presence. Joshua was probably with him during these days. Israel was able to see the cloud and it appeared to them as a **devouring fire on the top of the mount** (17), but they knew Moses was to meet God in **the cloud.**

On the **seventh day** God **called** Moses and he **went into . . . the cloud.** He remained in the mount **forty days and forty nights** (18) without food (Deut. 9:9). Joshua must have remained at some distance (32:17). The people remained in the valley, and soon revealed their lack of faith by a terrible sin (32:1-6) while Moses was in the mount.

Section IV *The Worship of God Established*

Exodus 25:1—40:38

While Moses was on the mountain for those 40 days, God gave him the plans of worship for His people. The instructions were given to Moses and later the objects used in worship were made by the people themselves. The failure of Israel while Moses was out of their sight is recorded between the revelation of the plans to Moses and the making and erection of the sanctuary. This final section of the Book of Exodus reveals the patience of God in dealing with His rebellious people, and also the minute detail in which He revealed requirements for their worship of Him.

A. God's Plan for the Tabernacle, 25:1—31:18

1. *The Offering for the Tabernacle* (25:1-9; cf. 35:4-19)

Before the Lord could have a dwelling place, the gifts of the people must be brought. Each must give **willingly with his heart** (2). The offering for God's house was not a tax but rather freewill giving.

The precious metals which Israel possessed at this time came from ancestral wealth and from the rich gifts received from the Egyptians at the time of the Exodus. Further wealth had come from the plunder of the Amalekites. Their supply of **gold** (3) was plentiful; **silver** and **brass** (likely bronze) were also to be brought.

The **blue, purple,** and **scarlet** (4) referred to linen yarn. **Fine linen** was a soft, white thread spun from flax. **Goats' hair** was commonly used for making tents and still is today in the Near East.[1]

North Africa was famous for its **skins dyed red** (5); Israel likely carried these from Egypt. **Badgers** were not native to north Africa, so the original word probably refers to some sea crea-

[1]Rawlinson, CWB, I, 280.

ture.[2] The **shittim wood** came from the acacia tree, found widely on the Sinaitic peninsula.[3]

The **oil for the light** (6) is later described in more detail (27:20). The **spices** were needed for the **anointing oil** and for **incense.** It is not clear just what the **onyx** was (7).

Israel was to make God a **sanctuary** in which He could **dwell** (8). Though He cannot be contained in a dwelling, it pleased Him to manifest himself through a building. It was to be made according to the **pattern of the tabernacle** given on the mount (9; cf. Heb. 8:5).

The **sanctuary,** or holy place, referred more generally to the whole structure including the court, while **tabernacle,** or "tent of meeting" (27:21, RSV), applied to the tent only. Other names used are "tabernacle of the Lord" (Num. 16:9) and "tabernacle of testimony" (38:21). Later the name "temple" was applied to the **sanctuary** after it was more permanently located (I Sam. 1:9; 3:3).

2. *The Tabernacle Furniture* (25:10-40; cf. 37:1-29).

a. The ark of the testimony (25:10-22). The **ark** (see Chart *A*) was considered the most sacred object in the Tabernacle. It was called the **ark of the testimony** (22), the "ark of the Lord" (I Sam. 4:6), the "ark of God" (I Sam. 3:3), and the "ark of the covenant" (Deut. 10:8).[4]

The **ark** was a box or chest made of acacia **wood** (10), about 3 feet 9 inches long and 2 feet 3 inches wide and deep. **A cubit** is about 18 inches. The ark was overlaid **with pure gold** (11) on both the inside and outside; probably gold plates were used. The **crown of gold** was apparently a "molding of gold, forming a rim."[5]

Rings of gold (12) were located at the four **corners.** Through these rings poles, also overlaid **with gold** (13), were placed for the purpose of carrying **the ark** (14). The poles, or **staves,** were

[2] *Ibid.* RSV and Berk. call them "goatskins."

[3] Johnson, *op. cit.*, p. 75.

[4] "Sacred chests were in use among other peoples of antiquity. They were employed by the Greeks and Egyptians, and served as receptacles for the idol or for symbols of the deities, or for other sacred objects" (Davis, *op. cit.*, p. 41).

[5] *Ibid.*

never to be removed from **the ark** (15), thus avoiding the necessity of ever touching the ark itself; also always reminding the people of the mobility of God.

In the **ark** was to be placed the **testimony** which God would give Moses (16), probably the two tables of stone (31:18) containing the Decalogue (cf. 16:34).

The **mercy seat of pure gold** (17) was a slab serving as a lid to the ark (see Chart *A*) and made with exactly the same dimensions. It was called the **mercy seat** because it was the place of atonement where mercy was symbolized. The **cherubims** (18), first mentioned as guardians of Eden (Gen. 3:24), were a high order of angels usually associated with the very presence of God. *Cherubim* rather than **cherubims** is the Hebrew plural of **cherub** (19). The more predominant idea is a human form with wings, such as the Egyptian "ma, or truth, so often seen inside Egyptian arks" and sheltering some emblem of deity.[6]

There was to be **one cherub** on each **end,** with **their wings** lifted **high** over **the mercy seat** while **their faces** looked down upon the ark (20). In this manner they guarded God's revelation to man while in humility they turned their faces away from God's glory.

There, **from above the mercy seat,** God promised to **commune with** Moses, and reveal to him all His will (22).

There are beautiful lessons that the **ark** and the **mercy seat** teach in spiritual things. The **pure gold** was precious, as is God's holy presence. The **gold** inside the ark where it could not be seen pictured the purity that God desires in the hearts of men. Placed in the gold-covered ark the commandments became precious and beautiful, symbolizing the law written upon the hearts of men.

The mercy seat was placed over the ark because God's "mercy transcends justice." Rawlinson writes:

> The teaching of the ark in this respect was, primarily, that of David in the eighty-fifth psalm: "Mercy and truth have kissed each other." Mercy without justice is a weak sentimentality, subversive of moral order. Justice without mercy is a moral severity—theoretically without a flaw, but revolting to man's instinctive feelings. The synthesis of the two is required. The law, enshrined in the holiest place of the sanctuary, vindicated the awful purity and per-

[6]Rawlinson, CWB, I, 282.

fection of God. The mercy seat, extended above the law, assigned to mercy its superior directive position. The Cherubim figures showed the gaze of angels riveted in astonishment and admiration on God's mode of uniting mercy with justice, by means of vicarious suffering, which he can accept as atonement. Finally, the Divine presence, promised as a permanent thing, gave God's sanction to the expiatory scheme, whereby alone man can be reconciled to him, and the claims both of justice and of mercy [can be] satisfied.[7]

b. Table of showbread (25:23-30). This was a plain **table** made of **shittim wood** (23, acacia wood), as was the ark, and overlaid **with pure gold** (24). It was 3 feet long, 18 inches wide, and 2 feet 3 inches high. There was **a crown of gold,** or border, around the top edge for decoration; it also probably served to prevent the bread from sliding off the table (see Chart *A*).

The **border of an hand breadth** (25) was a band about three inches wide probably placed between the legs just below the crown of gold. This band could serve as a support for the legs. A **crown** of gold on the band was a **border** or rim of gold for decorative purposes.

The **rings of gold** (26) for the poles were similar to those on the ark. Verse 27 seems to indicate that they were placed at the band near the middle of the legs. **The staves** (28), or poles, were like the ones for the ark and were to be used in carrying the table.

The dishes (29, "plates," Amp. OT) were for carrying the bread. The **spoons** were "cups for the frankincense that was to be placed on the bread, identifying it as a sacrifice (Lev. 24:7)."[8] The **covers** ("flagons," Amp. OT) and **bowls** were for holding and pouring out the wine of the drink offering. These were all of **pure gold.**

The **shewbread** (pronounced showbread, 30) was to be placed on the **table** before God continually. It was the "bread of the Presence" (RSV). This was not food intended for God but a symbol of the spiritual bread by which Israel was to be nourished. As such, it reminded the Israelites of their dependence upon God for their daily needs.[9] There were 12 loaves, representing all the tribes. The bread was to be changed every Sabbath (Lev. 24:5, 8). The **shewbread** also signified the continual communion

[7]PC, I, 250-51.

[8]Johnson, *op. cit.*, p. 75.

[9]*Ibid.*, p. 76.

of God's people with Him. The bread pointed forward to the Christ, who is the Living Bread (John 6:35).

c. *The lampstand* (25:31-40). Some biblical critics have doubted the origin of the Tabernacle during Moses' time and consider that much of the material found in these descriptions was written at a much later date.[10] They have asserted that the lampstand as described here was not known until hundreds of years later. But recent discoveries by W. F. Albright confirm the existence of lampstands such as the one described here as early as 1200-1400 B.C. (Amp. OT., fn.).

The **candlestick** (31) was more properly a lampstand made of **pure gold** (see Chart *A*). **A talent** of gold (39), weighing about 94 pounds, was used in its construction. The **shaft** and **branches** are more correctly "base" and "shaft" (RSV), the shaft being the upright center stem, called the **candlestick** in 34. The **bowls, knops,** and **flowers** were "its cups, its pomegranates, and its blossoms."[11] These were for decorations on the stem and branches.

Out from the main stem or shaft went three **branches** on each side—the **six branches** (32) with the center stem making seven holders for the lamps, like a candelabrum. There were **three bowls** (cups shaped like almond blossoms) on each branch, each with its pomegranate and **flower** (33), while on the main stem there were four such cups (34). It is supposed that each branch had a cup decoration at each end and one at center, while the center stem had one at each point where the branches joined it (35) and at the top. The repetitions in v. 35 simply say, "Make a calyx [the green base of a flower's blossom] under each pair of branches" (Berk.). These cups were made right in the material of the branches and stem (36).[12]

The **lamps** (37) were placed at the top of the **six branches** and the one stem. It is not said what these were like, but it can be supposed that they were shaped like bowls, or saucers, possibly with one end pinched at the rim. These lamps were lighted during the night to give light in the room. Oil was placed in the saucer, and a wick extended from the pinched part.[13]

[10]Rylaarsdam, *op. cit.*, I, 1020-26. [11]Rawlinson, CWB, I, 284.

[12]For a diagram of this lampstand see Chart *A*; also Lange, *op. cit.*, p. 116.

[13]Johnson, *op. cit.*, p. 76.

The tongs (38) were for trimming the lamps in the mornings. The excessive ash was trimmed from the wick and placed in the **snuffdishes,** where the **tongs** were also laid.

Verse 40 is a final warning to Moses to make all these things according to the **pattern** shown **in the mount.** It appears that God gave him a vision of the Tabernacle and its furniture, and then gave to him further detailed instructions.

Light is often used in the Bible as a symbol of God; Jesus is the Light of the World. These lamps in the Tabernacle gave forth their light from the oil, a type of the Holy Spirit. Israel was to be a light in the world, as are Christians. John referred to the "seven lamps of fire burning before the throne, which are the seven Spirits of God" (Rev. 4:5), a clear allusion to the Holy Spirit.

3. *The Tabernacle* (26:1-37; cf. 36:8-38)

a. The coverings (26:1-14). The framework of the Tabernacle proper was 15 feet by 45 feet (see Chart *A*). The **curtains** (1, coverings) were to go over the wooden structure (18-30) and serve as the top. These **curtains** for covering were made of the colored **fine . . . linen** with forms of **cherubims** woven into the cloth. There were to be **ten curtains,** each one 28 by 4 **cubits** (42 by 6 feet). These were **coupled together** (sewed) in groups of **five** (3), making two large coverings 42 by 30 feet each.

On the 42-foot side of each of these coverings, 50 **loops of blue** (4) were to be made. **The selvedge** is the border or edge of a piece of fabric. The loops were to match (5) so that these two large curtains could be joined together with **fifty taches** (clasps) **of gold** (6), thus making one large curtain 42 by 60 feet. The purpose of having the two parts was so they could be separated for moving. This covering was to be placed over the holy structure. Just how this was done is not said. Probably there were poles at each end with a ridgepole lengthwise down the middle. The curtain was large enough to cover the full 45 feet of the structure with 15 feet extending either over the front as a porch, or at the rear, or partly at both ends. It could also extend over the sides several feet, depending on the height of the ridgepole, and be fastened to the ground with ropes and pegs.

Over this first covering was to be placed a second **covering** made of **goats' hair** (7). This was made in a similar manner, except that the curtains were two feet longer (8), and there were

11 of them (9). Joined together, these made the second covering three feet wider and six feet longer, or 45 feet by 66 feet. The two sections, one made up of five curtains and the other of six, were joined by **brass** (11, bronze) clasps rather than gold. Placed over the inner covering, this one extended one and one-half feet farther down on each side (13), like a valance. The extra length was folded over partially as a decoration at the front of the Tabernacle (9) and the remaining length could hang down at the rear (12).

Two more coverings over the first two were necessary (14), one of **rams' skins** and the other of **badgers' skins** (see comment on 25:5). These were more weatherproof and kept out the rain and heat. Their size is not given, but certainly they were large enough to cover the area directly over the Tabernacle proper.

b. The wooden structure (26:15-30). The **boards for the tabernacle** (15), made of **shittim** (acacia) **wood,** were 15 feet long and 27 inches wide (16). The thickness is not given. Since the acacia wood in this area was small, these boards were probably made up with several pieces joined together. These boards were stood up on end side by side around the building, forming the two sides and the rear wall. The **two tenons** were pegs (lit. "hands") on the bottom end of each board for securing it to **sockets** in the bases of **silver** (19).

There were to be **twenty boards** on each side of the Tabernacle (18, 20) with two sockets of silver, fairly heavy in weight (see 38:27), for the foundation of each board (19, 21). The two **tenons** on each board fastened securely to these two sockets, making the board stand firm. **On the south side southward** (18) literally means "on the south side to the right." An Oriental faced east when giving directions. Since the Tabernacle faced east, the south would be on the right, the north on the left, and the west would be the rear.[14]

On the west side were to be **six boards** (22) with **two** additional **boards** to make up the two **corners** (23). Just how these corner posts were arranged is not clear (24), but apparently they were set in such a manner that the width of the building was 10 cubits (six boards would be only nine) or 15 feet. These **eight boards** (25) on this end had the same number of sockets

[14]Rawlinson, PC, I, 263.

and tenons as the ones at the side. This made 48 boards in all and 96 sockets for their bases.

Bars of acacia **wood** (26) were made to hold the boards together, **five** for each side and five for the end. The last clause of 27 is better rendered "for the boards of the rear end of the tabernacle, for the back wall to the west" (Amp. OT). One **bar,** the **middle** one, placed midway on the upright **boards** (28), was full length for sides and end. Apparently the other four on each wall were shorter. All these **boards** and **bars** were overlaid with **gold** (29), while the **rings** on the boards through which the bars were placed were also **of gold.**

Again Moses was reminded to erect this building according to the pattern shown **in the mount** (30). The general picture to this point is clear. There was a boarded wall 15 feet high with 45-foot sides, a 15-foot rear wall, and an open front. Over this structure was stretched a four-layer curtain, probably on a ridgepole, completely covering the structure.

c. *The veil and screen* (26:31-37). A **veil** (31), similar in construction to the first covering (1), was to be made to separate the Tabernacle into two rooms (33). There were to be **four pillars . . . overlaid with gold** (32), and placed on **sockets of silver** similar to the boards of the walls, on which to hang the veil. There being an even number of pillars suggests that they were equal in length and therefore not reaching all the way to the tent roof—assuming the roof was pitched.

The veil was placed **under the taches** (33) or clasps (6, 11) joining the coverings. Unless this statement is very general, it would mean that the veil dividing the two rooms was placed about the middle of the Tabernacle. It is supposed that the **holy place** was 30 feet long and the **most holy** place was 15 feet, although the Scriptures nowhere state this.[15] It is possible that the 15-foot extension on the covering (see comments on 6) was at the rear; this would make the joining of the covering directly over the traditional place of the veil. Interestingly, the theory of a flat roof described by Davis also allows for this kind of division.[16]

In the **most holy** place, which was **within the veil** (33), was

[15]Lange, *op. cit.*, p. 117 (see footnote where there is a discussion by the translator).

[16]*Op. cit.*, p. 588.

to be placed the **ark of the testimony,** with the **mercy seat** placed **upon the ark** (34). **Without the veil** (outside or beyond it), in the holy place, were to be placed **the table** of showbread and **the candlestick** (35). **The table** went **on the north side,** or left when one faced the front, and the lampstand stood on the **south** side. The altar of incense (30:1-6) also was placed in the holy place near the veil (see Chart *A*).

Another **hanging,** called a "screen" (RSV), was to be made for the opening at the front of the Tabernacle (36). It was less elaborate since it lacked the cherubim, probably because it was farther from the ark and was used commonly by the priests. This screen was supported by **five pillars** (37), which were overlaid with **gold** and had gold **hooks,** although the **sockets** were made of bronze, since the use of this entrance was more common. Since there were **five pillars,** it is supposed that they were unequal in length, with the center one serving as support for the ridgepole which held the coverings.[17]

There are spiritual lessons that may be drawn from c. 26. The beautifully colored covering that underlay the other coverings could be seen from the inside only. From the outside the goats' hair, ram and seal skins made for a very common appearance, but from within the beauty could be viewed. From the outside, God's way often looks drab and uninviting, but to the Christian the inside view is glorious.

Many of the articles—the table, the ark, the boards, the altar of incense—were made of common acacia wood, but overlaid with gold. This wood typifies humanity, common, rough, and faulty, but clothed with the presence of God. People who have no worth on their own are made rich with the gold of His glory.

There were degrees in the approach to God. Outside was the world, separated from the holy place by a curtain. Spiritually this curtain is entered by repentance and faith. Once inside, the daily joy of living bread and light are given the worshiper, as well as constant thanksgiving typified by the altar of incense. Even for these worshipers, a veil separated them from the most intimate presence of God. On the Cross the veil was rent in two (Matt. 27:51), making access to God possible by faith. Yet Christians must have "boldness to enter into the holiest by the blood of Jesus" (Heb. 10:19). Some Christians by faith enjoy the rich-

[17]Rawlinson, PC, I, 264.

er experience of spiritual fullness, while others stand outside the veil.

4. *The Great Altar* (27:1-8; cf. 38:1-7)

A bronze altar was an important part of Israel's worship. Set outside the sanctuary proper, it came first as one approached the holy place. It was a constant reminder of the need for atonement and repentance. On it the sacrificial animal was offered to God as an expiation for guilt.

This **altar** (1) was to be made of **shittim wood** (acacia) overlaid with bronze (2). The shape was square, seven and one-half feet on each side, and four and one-half feet high. It was a **hollow** box (8) open at both ends, and equipped with poles placed through **rings** for the purpose of carrying it (6-7) in a fashion similar to the furniture of the Tabernacle.

Since Israel was to have altars only of earth or unhewn stones (20:24-25), it has been thought that this boxlike altar was filled with earth whenever Israel stopped.[18] The sacrificial animals were placed on top of the earth which filled the bronze-wood frame.

Horns (2) were placed at **the four corners** of the altar and were a part of the frame. These probably were shaped like an animal horn. They were significant as symbols of power and protection (I Kings 1:50). Also the blood of the sacrificial animal was smeared on the horns (Lev. 4:7). These horns, extending toward heaven, "spoke of the God to whom the altar was reared, and indicated his ability to help, protect, and succour his worshippers."[19] They might also indicate the victory of man over sin through the expiation symbolized by the altar.

The implements used in connection with the altar were made of bronze. There were the **pans to receive** the **ashes** (3), **shovels** for removing the ashes, **basons** to receive the blood, **fleshhooks** for arranging the pieces of flesh, and **firepans,** likely used for carrying coals of fire to the altar of incense. It is not clear what the **network** (4-5) was for, or where it was placed, since the identification of **the compass** (5) is impossible. It could have been a grating near the top of the altar to catch pieces of the animals that might fall off, or it may have been at the bottom to keep the feet of the priests from touching the altar.[20]

[18]Rawlinson, CWB, I, 288.
[19]Rawlinson, PC, I, 271.
[20]Rawlinson, CWB, I, 289.

5. *The Court* (27:9-19; cf. 38:9-28)

Interestingly, the altar was described before the **court** (9) which surrounded **the tabernacle,** as was the furniture of the Tabernacle before the structure itself (25:10—26:30). This court was to serve as an enclosure for the Israelites who came to worship before the Tabernacle. It separated them from the world on the outside and gave sanctity in the approach to God's presence. See Chart *B*.

The court was a rectangle 150 feet long and 75 feet wide. Each side, the **south** and **north** (9-11), was to have **twenty pillars** with **sockets** made of **brass** (bronze), and the **west** end needed **ten** pillars (12). For **the south side southward** (9) see comment on 26:18. These **pillars** were probably held to the ground on **their sockets** by means of ropes fastened to the ground with tent **pins** (19). Between the pillars were **fillets of silver** (11). Most likely bars between pillars on which the curtain was hung with **hooks** made of **silver** (17). A curtain of **fine twined linen,** probably white,[21] 7½ feet high (18), was hung around the sides and rear, and in the front where there were **three** pillars on each side of **the gate** (14).

On the east, or front, there was a **gate** (16) in the center 30 feet wide. It was made of a curtain **of blue, and purple, and scarlet** as well as **fine twined linen,** supported by the **four** center **pillars** on this end. **Filleted with silver** (17) is better "connected by silver bands" (Berk.). Whenever the Tabernacle was set up, the front always faced east. The curtain for the gate was similar to the one that hung at the front of the Tabernacle (26:36-37).

The Tabernacle and the court teach successive steps in one's approach to God. The more precious materials were in the most holy place; the holy place was less ornate, while the materials in the court were the most simple. The closer one gets to God, the more glory and grace there are. Only the high priest could enter the most sacred shrine. Other priests ministered in the outer room. The lay Israelite could come only as far as the court, and then only when ceremonially clean. The unclean had to remain outside the court. In Christ, the veil was rent in two and all may now come to the holiest. Yet there are those who still remain outside, at a distance from God, because of a lack of faith and dedication.

[21]Johnson, *op. cit.*, p. 78.

6. *The Oil for the Lamp* (27:20-21)

Instruction concerning the oil for the lamps in the holy place was now given to Moses. The **pure oil olive** (20) was to be **beaten** rather than ground as in a mill. The purest oil, best for burning, was obtained in this manner from olives picked just before ripening. This procedure required more care than the customary process and such oil is widely considered a type of the Holy Spirit. The oil was **to cause the lamp to burn always.** This did not mean both day and night, since there was the lighting of the lamps in the evening (30:8; I Sam. 3:3). It was to burn every night **always.**

Verse 21 assumes the priesthood of Aaron's family and ascribes to them the task of keeping oil in the lamps and the **evening to morning** activity. **Without the veil** would be in the holy place beyond the curtain enclosing the holy of holies. **Shall order it** means "shall do it." Keeping the lamps burning was to be **on the behalf of the children of Israel.** God's ministers are to keep the light of God shining brightly.

In vv. 20-21, "The Shining Light" results from the (1) Work of the people—preparation, 20*a*; (2) Work of the ministers—perpetuation, 21; (3) Work of the Holy Spirit—illumination, 20*b*.

7. *The Garments for the Priests* (28:1-43; cf. 39:1-31)

a. Introduction (28:1-5). God chose Moses' brother, Aaron, and his descendants to serve as priests. Until this time Moses was the only mediator, but Aaron's rather than Moses' family was now chosen to **minister** before God for Israel (1). These priests were to have special **garments** which were reckoned **holy** (2). As typical of the inner purity of God's people, outward objects were set apart for holy purposes. These garments also were **for glory and for beauty.** For the priest to minister in drab clothing in the beautifully colored Tabernacle would be inconsistent and lacking in glory. God, the Author of all that is good and beautiful, desires beauty for His people and beauty in their worship of Him.

God granted His **spirit of wisdom** (3) to **wise hearted** men in order to enable them to **make** these **garments.** God, who created beauty, gives to man his appreciation for beauty and his ability to create it. Some productions called art may be perverted, but true art is of God.

The articles for the high priest are named in v. 4 as a group and described separately in the following verses. The materials were the same as for the curtains of the Tabernacle (5) except that **gold** was added.

b. Ephod (28:6-14). This garment was a waistcoat with a front and back held together with straps over each shoulder and a belt or **girdle** at the waist (6-8).[22] **Curious girdle** (8) is better "the skilfully woven band" (RSV). It was richly colored (6) and the shoulder straps were inset with **onyx stones** with **the names of the children of Israel** engraved upon them (9), **six** to each **stone** (10). **According to their birth** would be in the order of their births. Obviously some of the Israelites had learned engraving while in Egypt as slaves. The names were set into the stones **in ouches of gold** (11), i.e., settings of gold filigree.[23]

These names were borne on the priest's **shoulders** as he ministered **before the Lord** (12), symbolic of the responsibility of ministers in bringing their people to God. Also those names were before God when the priest was in His presence. Here was assurance that God watches over His people and remembers them.

The **ouches of gold** (13) appear also to have been fasteners for the **chains of pure gold** (14) holding them to the ephod. They may have been used to fasten the breastplate to the ephod (see 22-26).[24]

c. The breastplate (28:15-30). Fastened securely to the ephod was a **breastplate of judgment** (15), made of the same material as the ephod. **Judgment** here means "oracle" or "judicial"; this was a means "by which God's will was sought and usually found" (Berk., fn.). **Cunning work** would be "skilled work" (RSV). The material was folded to form a pouch about **a span** (nine inches) square (16). In it were set **four rows** of three precious **stones** each (17). The real nature of the stones is not known, though efforts have been made to identify them.[25] The **enclosings** (20) would be the settings of the stones. **The names** of the **twelve** tribes **of Israel** were to be engraved on these **stones** (21). This **breastplate** was fastened at the top to the shoulder straps of **the ephod** with **chains . . . of pure gold** linked

[22]Rawlinson, PC, I, 279.

[23]Johnson, *op. cit.*, p. 78.

[24]Rawlinson, PC, I, 286.

[25]Johnson, *op. cit.*, pp. 78-79.

into gold **rings** (22-26; see also 13-14). At the bottom of the breastplate **two other rings** were fastened to the **girdle of the ephod** (27) with **a lace of blue** (28).

Thus the high priest not only bore **the names of the children of Israel** upon his shoulders, the place of strength, but also **upon his heart** (29), in order that he might with wisdom and compassion be their mediator before God.[26] **The Urim and the Thummim** (30) were likely stones placed upon the breastplate representing **judgment** concerning the will of God. The high priest was the judge of his people and may have arrived at his decision by means of these stones.[27] At least they symbolized his power and wisdom in making decisions.

In c. 28 can be seen "God's Representative for Man" as (1) Intercessor for his people, 12; (2) Compassionate in behalf of his people, 29; (3) Wise judge of his people, 30.

d. Robe of the ephod (28:31-35). This garment was woven in one solid piece with an opening for the head (32). The Hebrew word translated **the hole of an harbergeon** is of uncertain meaning. The concept seems to be a hemmed edge reinforced—to prevent tearing. The robe was probably sleeveless. The color was **blue** (31), and it was worn under the ephod and breastplate.[28] The contrast between it and the breastplate would make the latter prominent. On **the hem** of this garment, which would reach at least to the knees, were to be placed **pomegranates** made of colorful material and **bells of gold** (33), one following the other (34).

There is disagreement as to the meaning of the decorations on the hem of the robe. Pomegranates symbolize fruitfulness or possibly nourishment for the soul. The bells ring out praise to God and symbolize the joy in service. The **sound** of the bells could be heard by the Israelites in the court while the priest ministered before God in **the holy place.** Thus the worshipers could participate with the high priest in prayer and praise as they listened, even though they could not see. The threat **that he die not** (35) was made to warn the priest of failing the people if he did not have the bells ringing while he served.[29] The ministry of God's servants today should be such that the people can partici-

[26]*Ibid.*, p. 78.

[27]Connell, *op. cit.*, p. 127.

[28]Rawlinson, PC, I, 289.

[29]*Ibid.*

pate in worship with him and not be mere spectators. Worship becomes only form when the congregation are only observers.

e. Turban and shirt (28:36-39). On the head of the high priest was to be **the mitre** (37), better understood as a turban, similar to a crown. It was to be made **of fine linen** (39). On the front of the turban was to be the **plate of pure gold** (36), upon which was engraved **HOLINESS TO THE LORD.** As the high priest appeared before the people, the striking objects in his attire first to meet the eye would be the jeweled breastplate with the names of Israel, and the gold plate on his forehead proclaiming holiness to God.

Israel's God was always to be portrayed as holy and righteous. Pagan religions created gods like men, unholy and impure. But God to Israel was revealed as absolutely pure and holy. The purpose of this revelation was not to make the Israelites continuously ashamed of themselves, but to inspire them to become like God. "Ye shall therefore be holy, for I am holy" (Lev. 11:45), was a command ever before God's people. The lack of holiness in His people was pointed out whenever this plate of gold was seen. However, the priest went in before God bearing **the iniquity of the holy things** (38), that is, making atonement for the guilt created by man's sin. Thus, boldness before "the throne of grace" is seen in this ministry by an erring priest for an erring people as he stood confidently before a holy God expecting acceptance by Him (Heb. 4:16). As the priest stood before the mercy seat making atonement for his people, he and the people through him not only received God's forgiveness; but as they beheld His holiness, they were "changed into the same image from glory to glory, even as by the Spirit of the Lord" (II Cor. 3:18).

To minister before God with **HOLINESS TO THE LORD** written on the forehead while iniquity is shielded in the heart is hypocrisy. To proclaim the necessity of continued sinfulness on the part of the worshipper who had yielded himself to the Holy One degrades God's power to purge. Surely a holy God who desires a holy people can "purify unto himself" people like unto himself (Titus 2:14). The work of the minister is to lead his people into "holiness, without which no man shall see the Lord" (Heb. 12:14).[30]

[30]*Ibid.*, pp. 291-92.

The undergarment of the priest was a **coat of fine linen** (39), more correctly a shirt or tunic,[31] and a **girdle.** The shirt had sleeves and most likely extended nearly to the ankles. It would show only at the sleeves and below the robe. "It was bound about the body with a richly colored sash or girdle embroidered like the tapestries of the sanctuary."[32] This **girdle** and most of the shirt would not be seen by the people. But even so, the inner garments must also be sound, since God sees, just as the motives of the believer must be pure, since God knows even our inmost thoughts.

f. Garments for the sons (28:40-43). Compared to the garments of the high priest those of the ordinary priests were simple, although fine linen was a rich and highly prized cloth in those days. These lesser priests wore a coat (40) or shirt fastened about the waist with a girdle, or sash. The **bonnets** or "caps" (RSV) were likely bands of linen or skullcaps. This garment, though simple, was white, symbolic of the purity of the saints. For **sanctify them** (41), cf. comment on 13:2. The other garment, **linen breeches** (42), was the trousers or drawers worn by both the ordinary priests and the high priest.

Verse 41 anticipates the investiture found in the next chapter (see comments on 39:7-9). Moses was to have the garments made and then to consecrate his brother's family for the priesthood.

These garments were to be worn by the priests whenever they ministered in the sanctuary. The **holy place** (43) must have included the court where the great altar was. The priests were reckoned guilty if they neglected proper clothing in their ministrations, and were subject to the death penalty. This **statute** was to be **for ever.**

8. *Consecration of the Priests* (29:1-46)

After describing the priestly attire, God told Moses how to ordain the priests for their holy duties. These priests were to offer sacrifices for their own sins, to be clothed with their garments, to be anointed with the holy oil, and to eat of the sacrificial offerings.

a. Introduction (29:1-9). As a preparation for the installation of the priesthood, a **young bullock, and two rams without**

[31]Rawlinson, CWB, I, 296. [32]Johnson, *op. cit.*, p. 79.

blemish (1), with **unleavened bread** and **cakes** and **wafers** in a **basket** (2:3), were to be prepared. **Tempered with oil** would be "mixed with oil," and **anointed** would be "sprinkled with oil" (Berk.). These were to be brought with **Aaron and his sons** (4) to the **door of the tabernacle.** Here the priests were to be washed **with water.** Such outward washing is a symbol of inward cleansing and corresponds to Christian baptism. The laver (30:17-21) was used by the priests for this purpose (cf. Chart *B*).

The investiture of Aaron is very briefly given here (5-6). A more complete account is recorded in Lev. 8:7-9, where the process included nine acts: placing upon Aaron (1) the linen shirt, (2) the under-girdle, (3) the robe of the ephod, (4) the ephod, (5) the girdle of the ephod, (6) the breastplate, (7) the Urim and Thummim, (8) the turban, and (9) the plate on the turban. Here the account of the investment leaves out steps two and seven, and the order of five and six is reversed. Also the golden plate on the turban is here called **the holy crown,** indicating the royal character of the high priest.

The anointing oil (7) described in 30:22-33 was to be poured upon Aaron's **head,** an act symbolic of the baptism with the Holy Spirit. The shirts, **girdles,** and caps (8-9), in three actions, were to be placed upon Aaron's **sons.** Such acts of investiture and anointing inducted these men and their successors into the priestly office for life in a **perpetual statute.** Only in Christ can the fulfillment of the eternity of this office be seen (Heb. 5:6).

b. The offerings (29:10-18). The sin offering and the burnt offering were first to be made for the priests. Since they were men and sinners, they had to offer for their own sins as well as the people's (Heb. 5:3). The **bullock** (10), after being brought to the altar, was to be killed when **Aaron and his sons** laid **their hands upon the head,** an act signifying that their sins were being laid upon the animal. Its immediate death showed the penalty for sin, but also pointed to the atonement in the sacrifice of Jesus on the Cross. Placing **the blood** (12) on **the horns of the altar** and at its base emphasized the necessity of the giving of life for salvation. Parts of the animal's body, including **the fat,** were burned **upon the altar** and the rest was removed outside **the camp** for burning (13-14), typifying Christ, who "suffered without the gate" (Heb. 13:11-12). **The caul** was the "lobe" or "appendage" of the liver. No part of this offering was eaten by the priests, nor were sin offerings generally eaten (Lev. 4:11-12; cf. Lev. 10:17-20).

The **burnt offering** (18) was one of the rams brought to the consecration ceremonies (1). It was slain in a fashion similar to the sin offering and its blood was sprinkled about the altar. Verse 17 is clarified by the RSV, "Then you shall cut the ram into pieces, and wash its entrails and its legs, and put them with its pieces and its head." The whole ram was then burned on the altar as a **sweet savour** (18) unto the Lord. In the **burnt offering,** the idea of self-sacrifice rather than expiation was intended. Such a self-sacrifice is pleasant to God, as compared to the sin offering, which was never considered sweet-smelling.[33] This offering represented the surrender of the persons to God for service in a spirit of adoration.

c. *The sacrifice of installation* (29:19-37). The second **ram** (19), called a **ram of consecration** (22), was killed in the same manner as the other animals (19). Some of the blood was placed first upon **the right ear, the thumb** of the **right hand,** and upon **the great toe** of the **right foot** of each of the priests (20). After the blood was placed on the altar, some of it was taken, along with oil, and sprinkled **upon Aaron** and **his sons** and their **garments** (21).

Blood **upon the tip of the right ear** dedicated the hearing to God; **upon the thumb** the blood symbolically consecrated service rendered by the hands; blood **upon the great toe** set apart to God the whole walk in life. The mixing of the blood and oil is best viewed as "symbolising the intimate union which exists between justification and sanctification—the atoning blood, and the sanctifying grace of the Holy Spirit."[34] Both the persons of the priests and their garments were **hallowed** (21), that is, made holy by being set apart for holy service.

Parts of this **ram of consecration,** along with portions of the **bread,** cakes, and wafers within the basket (22-23; see v. 2), were to be laid by Moses upon the **hands** of the priests. By a horizontal motion toward the altar, the priests were to **wave** the **offering,** thus symbolizing its being given to God (24). Then Moses was to **burn** God's portion **upon the altar** (25) as a pleasing morsel to God. He retained **the breast** for himself (26), the

[33]Chadwick, *op. cit.*, I, 224.

[34]Johnson, *op. cit.*, p. 296.

part that would normally go to the priest who officiated in the **wave offering.**[35]

Ordinarily the **breast** and the **shoulder** of the **peace** offering —as this kind of offering may be called (28)—were to be portions for the priest (27). The **breast** was waved in a horizontal movement and the **shoulder** was **heaved** up in a vertical movement as acts symbolic of giving them to God. For **sanctify,** cf. comment on 13:2.

The holy garments (29) of the high priest were to be passed on to his son for his consecration to this priestly function (29). This period of installation for the new priest was to be **seven days** (30).

After a diversion in 27-30 describing the permanent aspects of this ritual, the record returns to the consecration. Those portions of meat not burned on the altar or given to Moses were to be boiled (31) and eaten by **Aaron and his sons** (32) along with the remaining contents of the **basket** of **bread** (cf. 23). This sacrificial meal occurred also in the making of peace offerings, when the offerers ate a portion of the sacrifice. This eating sanctified and consecrated them, a type of the bread and flesh of Christ, which give life and holiness to the believer. In this particular case only the priests could eat, and any part of the sacrifice remaining until **morning** must be burned (33-34). This sacrificial meal was a mark of fellowship with God and of the priests with each other. For **sanctify them** (33), cf. comment on 13:2.

The continuation of the consecration ceremonies was to be **seven days** (35), God's perfect number. It appears that the sin offering was repeated **every day** (36). The same offering that cleansed and consecrated the priests also dedicated the altar. This altar was also anointed (Lev. 8:11, 15) and reckoned to be **most holy** (37; cf. comment on 13:2). Anything that touched the altar must be **holy** or the altar would be desecrated.

d. The conclusion (29:38-46). Leading on from the consecration of the priests, the writer pointed out the requirement for the daily sacrifices on **the altar** (38). **Two** young **lambs,** symbolizing early surrender to God, were offered daily, one **in the morning** and **the other** in the evening (39). With both of these sacrifices were to be meat and drink offerings of bread and **wine** (40), largely for the convenience of the priests.[36] **A tenth deal**

[35]IB, I, 1050.

[36]Rawlinson, PC, I, 300.

was about seven pints, and **an hin** was about a gallon and a half. These were **for a sweet savour** to God (41), pleasant to Him, in contrast to the idea that the wickedness of evil men is a smoke in His nostrils.

As the people made their offerings to God, He would **meet** with them (42) while He spoke to the priest, their representative. The true sanctifying power is God's **glory** (43), not the material objects which He has sanctified. Israel's obedience to God in these ceremonies assured them of His sanctifying power (cf. comment on 13:2). God would sanctify both the **tabernacle** and the **altar** for their special uses, and the house of **Aaron** for its peculiar task (44). Because of this sanctification Israel would be God's children and He would **dwell among** them (45). Thus they would **know that I am the Lord their God** (46).

How gloriously are these truths fulfilled in the Christian believer! He has brought his sins to the foot of the Cross and by faith has received the forgiveness of God. In humble obedience he offers up daily sacrifices of praise and prayer which are acceptable to God. With the law written on his heart, he experiences the holiness of God by obedience to the truth through the Spirit (I Pet. 1:22), and God's Spirit dwells with him continually.

In c. 29 may be seen the following "Believer's Privileges:" (1) Atonement in Christ seen in the sin offering, 10-14; (2) Surrender to Christ found in the burnt offering, 15-18; (3) Consecration and sanctification revealed in the sacrifice of dedication, 19-37; (4) Daily devotion observed in the continual sacrifices, 38-42; (5) Fullness of the Spirit promised in the indwelling Deity, 43-46.

9. *Matters Concerning the Sanctuary* (30:1-38)

a. The altar of incense (30:1-10). The reason for the discussion of the matters in this chapter at this juncture in the account is not clear. Either Moses was here describing what had been left out of the earlier writing or else God directed him to place it in this order. Certainly the instructions for the Tabernacle were incomplete without these added directions.

The **altar to burn incense upon** (1) was similar in form to the brazen altar, except that it was smaller (see Chart *A*). It was to be one and one-half feet square and three feet high (2). The **shittim wood** (acacia) was to be covered with **pure gold** (3), and all its parts, which included a **crown of gold,** most likely a rim similar to that on the table of showbread, were also gold-covered. It was to be carried as the other furniture with **staves** through **rings** of gold (4-5).

This golden altar was to be set **before the mercy seat** near the **ark** but in front of **the veil** (6). Of necessity it must be in the holy place, since the most holy place was entered only once a year and the **incense** was to be burned daily (7). Its location close to the most holy place accounts for the apparent listing of it as an article within the veil in Heb. 9:4.[37] It was at this altar that God would especially meet with the person offering the incense day by day.

The burning of the incense, the composition of which is described in 34-38, was to take place in the **morning** (7) when the lamps were lighted, and again at evening (8). The idea of **perpetual incense** refers to its continuity daily, rather than the maintaining of a fire day and night.[38] This golden altar was not to be used except for the burning of proper incense (9); **strange incense** would be an offering other than the designated kind (see 34-38). Neither was this altar for **meat** or **burnt** offerings, or for **drink** offerings; these were offered only on the brazen altar.

However, **once in a year,** on the Day of Atonement, the high priest was to place **blood** on the **horns** of the golden altar in order to **make atonement** for the altar (10). Even the altar of incense would need atonement because of man's deliberate sins or unconscious errors.

The spiritual meaning of this altar is clear. The incense represented the prayers of the saints (Rev. 8:3). Atonement at the brazen altar reconciled the worshiper to God, while the sweet-smelling incense completed the transaction with communion. "In this respect, the incense-offering was not only a spiritualizing and transfiguring of the burnt-offering, but a completion of that offering also."[39] For the Christian this offering of prayer is continual, both in the sense of the constant attitude of prayer and also in habitual periods of meditation and intercession.

b. The ransom money (30:11-16). In all probability Moses was contemplating an accurate census for the Israelites. The earlier number given was perhaps only an estimate. God now

[37]Johnson, *op. cit.*, p. 80. [38]Rawlinson, PC, I, 304.

[39]Johnson, *op. cit.*, p. 81.

instructed him to require of **every man a ransom for his soul** (12). The word **ransom** means expiation and conveys the same idea as **atonement** in 15. Earlier (25:2) God told Moses to ask Israel for a freewill offering. Here a sort of poll tax was required. Failure at this point could mean a plague upon the offenders.

The amount required of each male was not large, a **half shekel** (13), about 33 cents in our currency. It was not a tax levied on the ability to pay, but based on the truth of all men's equality before God. **The poor** could feel himself equal with the rich in God's eyes; **the rich** could not buy God's favor, since he could give only the **half . . . shekel** (15). Only the mature males, **twenty years old and above** (14), were required to pay this ransom.

Why is it called **atonement money** (16)? Did not the sin offering make the necessary atonement? This payment was an acknowledgment of unworthiness before God and of the inability to atone for one's own sins. It was a recognition that only God could really pay the price of redemption; the **half shekel** was only a token or sign of the acceptance of God's covenant with Israel.

This first tax was to be for the **service of the tabernacle of the congregation** and was used for making the silver sockets for the Tabernacle (38:25-28). These sockets would be a constant reminder of Israel's obligation to God and of His atonement for them. This tax may have become an annual obligation (II Chron. 24:9). Most likely it was the one for which Peter found payment in the fish's mouth (Matt. 17:24-27).[40]

Verses 11-16 picture "Man's Redemption." (1) Required of all, 12-14; (2) The same for each person, 15; (3) Kept continually in mind, 16.

c. *The bronze laver* (30:17-21). A **laver** made **of brass** (18, bronze) was to be placed **between the tabernacle** and the brazen **altar** (see Chart *B*). The specifications are not given, though it is supposed that it was in the shape of a vase with a stem and base, all of solid metal. It was to hold the water for the ceremonial washings (19-20). It is possible there were "taps and cocks" fitted to it.[41] This laver was used by the priests for washing before they ministered in **the tabernacle** or at **the altar.**

[40]Chadwick, *op. cit.*, I, 226.

[41]Rawlinson, PC, I, 308.

Water is a means of purifying the flesh and is a type of the Holy Spirit, who cleanses the soul. The laver would be a constant reminder of the holiness required by God and that cleanliness is next to godliness.

d. The holy anointing oil (30:22-33). Moses was told to make a special anointing oil. The ingredients were to be **pure myrrh, sweet cinnamon, sweet calamus, cassia,** and **oil olive** (23-24). The **shekels** (23) here refer directly to weight rather than to money value as in v. 15. The four spices (twice as much of myrrh and cassia as of the other two) were to be mixed with **an hin** of **olive oil** (about six quarts). The **apothecary** (25) would be a druggist or perfumer. These spices, having both a healing quality and fragrance, made a perfumed substance suitably typical of the Holy Spirit, who sanctifies and anoints God's people.

This compound was to be used first for the anointing of **the tabernacle** and its furniture (26-29). These sacred articles were to be sanctified (29), i.e., set apart for holy uses. The **foot** of the **laver** (28) would be its "base" (RSV). Having been made holy, the Tabernacle furniture was to be touched by nothing except the **holy** (cf. comment on 13:2).

After the consecration of the Tabernacle, Moses was to **anoint** the priests for their special function (30; cf. 29:21). This act would consecrate them to their sacred office, symbolizing the anointing by the Holy Spirit upon God's servants.

Furthermore Israel was to be told that this oil was to be lasting (31); it was never to be used **upon man's flesh** (32), i.e., for common purposes; and it must never be duplicated. A curse was pronounced upon the one who made a compound **like it,** or wrongly applied the holy oil (33).

How like the Holy Spirit is this mixture of spices and oil! He brings fragrance and healing to the anointed soul; He makes holy all who receive Him; He cannot be counterfeited, and whoever tries to substitute for Him is under God's judgment; He is not given to the world, but to those who are redeemed by the blood of Christ; and He is ever the same.

e. The holy incense (30:34-38). The incense to be burned on the altar of incense was to be especially fragrant. The spices used, when mixed properly, were **a perfume** (35) put together so as to produce a solid; the portions then could be broken off for burning on the altar.[42] **A confection after the art of the apothecary** would be "an incense blended as by the perfumer" (RSV). It was offered on the altar where God came to **meet** with the priest (36) and thus it was to be reckoned **most holy.** There was to be no duplication of **the perfume** (37) because it was **holy for the Lord.** Anyone duplicating it would **be cut off** from Israel (38).

The odor of this burning incense was to remind the priests and the people of their devotion to God and of His acceptance of them.

"The Surrendered Life" is (1) Formed as God desires, 34-35; (2) Broken in order to burn, 36*a*; (3) Blessed with God's presence, 36*b*.

10. *Appointment of Bezaleel and Aholiab* (31:1-11)

To carry out the many details required in making the Tabernacle and all its furniture and furnishings, Moses would need skilled workmen. God did not intend to produce this place of worship by a miraculous act of His power but through men endowed for such work; here was a task His children could and should do. God does not perform for His creatures what they through Him can do for themselves.

It is well to recognize that God calls men in various ways. He had already **called by name Bezaleel** (2), as He had earlier called Moses. This call was now revealed to Moses, who would later inform **Bezaleel** and Israel of that choice (35:30—36:3). God called Moses directly but these men, as far as we know, were called through Moses with no direct word to them from God. Though God chose by name Bezaleel and **Aholiab** (6), obviously it was left to Moses to name many others for the work. It is inspiring to be **called by name** directly or indirectly by God, but it is also important to be appointed by those whom God authorizes to choose workmen.

God's Holy Spirit selects and anoints certain persons for the spiritual work of His kingdom, such as preaching or teaching. God also chooses, endows, and directs His servants in accomplishing material things. Bezaleel and his assistant, Aholiab, were called to create beauty in the material forms of the Tabernacle. For this task there was the filling **with the spirit of God,**

[42]Johnson, *op. cit.*, p. 81.

in wisdom, and in understanding, and in knowledge, and in all manner of workmanship (3). Men were here called **of God** to do artistic things with gold, silver, bronze, wood, cloth, and stones (4-5). The detailed instructions given to Moses were to be carried out (7-11) **according to all that I have commanded** (11). These men were to use their skill and direct others—**all that are wise hearted** (6)—in the performance of this part of God's work.

Wisdom denotes "compass of mind and strength of capacity"; it is the "power of judging" what is best to be done. **Understanding** is the capacity to comprehend the different parts of a work and its complete form. **Knowledge** denotes acquaintance with material through practice and experience.[43] Skill for making beautiful and useful things is a gift of God. Here are seen both a natural endowment trained and perfected and a gift of grace through the Holy Spirit. The gifts of the Spirit are largely these natural endowments dedicated to God and inspired by the Spirit. These gifts are found in voice and brain, but also in hands and eyes.

It is true that natural and God-given abilities may be perverted. Many have rejected the artistic because of perversion in this kind of skill. However, in all gifts, the true and Godlike must be distinguished from the false and humanistic. God loves beauty, and has created many beautiful things for man's enjoyment; He has endowed His creatures with powers to create beauty, and His handiwork may be seen here.

To be sure, Christians must not live for this world in the sense that they become attached to things of time and forget the eternal. However, in expressions of art, whether it be in church architecture or in the home, in painting, music, or mechanics, recognition of the eternal prevents secularization and thus adds value to both time and eternity. The man who works on machines may become a slave to his machine, but he need not if he sees in his work a creation of God's Spirit through his powers. It is possible that modern man may destroy himself with his scientific genius, because, unfortunately, the controls of the products of science often fall into the hands of evil men. But Christian men should seek to use scientific skills for God's glory.

It is possible to dedicate one's skills to God, whether these are used directly in church work, in the improvement of so-

[43]Clarke, *op. cit.*, I, 461.

ciety, or in the earning of means with which to support the cause of Christ.

11. *Observance of the Sabbath* (31:12-17)

In this passage there is a return to the emphatic demands upon Israel regarding the holy Sabbath. It is not fully clear why the subject is again treated at this juncture in the record unless there was fear that Israel with new instructions about the Tabernacle might forget the earlier statements concerning the holy days. There are two new aspects of the Sabbath given in these verses.

God told Moses that the Sabbath was **a sign between me and the children of Israel** (17; cf. 13). The earlier sign given to Israel was circumcision; God now added the **sign** of the Sabbath as a distinguishing mark for His people. This Sabbath-sign distinguished Israel from other nations more than circumcision, because "no other nation ever adopted it. It continued to Roman times the mark and badge of a Jew."[44] It thus became a "sacramental bond" between Israel and God. **Throughout your generations** (13; cf. 16) means "through all ages" (Moffatt).

It is declared here that pollution of the Sabbath was punishable with **death** (14-15). This may appear drastic to moderns, but Israel's covenant with God was unique. The Sabbath was both a part of that covenant and its sign. Anyone breaking the Sabbath committed an offense of the gravest character and, as far as he was concerned, destroyed the entire covenant between God and Israel. A person so annulling the covenant was **cut off from among his people** (14), that is, separated or excommunicated from them. He had forfeited his right to live as a child of God.

"It is to be noted that this outward observance, along with other outer signs, such as circumcision, the dietary laws, *et al.*, are specifically translated in the NT into inward, spiritual evidences of discipleship (cf. Rom. 2:28, 29; Gal. 4:9, 10; Col. 2:16, 17."[45] The observance of the Christian Sabbath, Sunday, is of a spiritual nature and is a law written on the heart. It is a day for rest and refreshment, as the Sabbath was for Israel (17).

12. *The Tables of Testimony* (31:18)

As a conclusion to his whole experience on the mount during the 40 days, Moses was given by God **two tables of testimony,**

[44]Rawlinson, PC, I, 318.

[45]Johnson, *op. cit.*, p. 82.

made of **stone,** and **written with the finger of God.** These were the tables referred to when God asked Moses to come to the mount (24:12); they were to be placed in the ark (25:16); they were the stone tables that Moses broke in anger (32:19). God later renewed them (34:4), and Moses placed them in the ark (40:20). These are the tables that were to give significance to the whole Tabernacle.

On these tables the Decalogue was inscribed by **the finger of God.** By this we are not to understand "a literal hand, but some unseen divine power" (cf. Luke 11:20).[46] The method God used to produce these tables we do not know.

B. The Covenant Broken and Restored, 32:1—34:35

Chapters 32—34 record the apostasy of Israel while Moses was on the mountain; also the resulting punishment and subsequent restoration. The account naturally follows at this juncture in the record and could be understood only in this context. To view it as a later insertion creates more problems than it solves.

1. *Israel's Idolatry* (32:1-6)

The people became restless when their visible leader remained on the mountain for the 40 days (1; cf. 24:18). **We wot not** means "we do not know." Their unhappiness about it caused them to come as a group with a special request **to Aaron,** in whose hands they had been left. **Up,** they said, **make us gods, which shall go before us.** The word **gods** is usually translated God. The request did not necessarily mean that these people were rejecting Jehovah; it would appear that they wanted a visible form among them to represent God. Moses, who had been as God to them, had disappeared and their patience in awaiting his return was exhausted.

Aaron's reaction to their request may have been an attempt to avert the disaster. In asking that they **break off the golden earrings** (2) and **bring them** to him, he may have hoped that they would refuse.[47] For women and children to give up their ornaments is not easy and their opposition could have stalled the men's request for a god.

If Aaron expected opposition to his request, he was quickly

[46]Connell, *op. cit.*, p. 129. [47]Rawlinson, CWB, I, 309.

disappointed, because **all the people brake off the golden earrings** (3) and gave them to him. The carnal heart will sacrifice much to satisfy its evil desires.

Since Aaron had started going along with this wicked request, he could not now stop. **He received** the gifts of gold and **fashioned** a god for the people (4). At a time when he could have proved himself an able leader, Aaron miserably failed.

Most ancient images were made of wood and plated with gold.[48] This idol was made in the form of a **calf,** or young bull, a common form among the Egyptians, representing fertility and strength. Or, as Rawlinson suggests, Aaron may have reverted back to the "gods on the other side of the flood" (Josh. 24:14), found in Babylon, thinking that these would be a safer representation of the God of Israel.[49] When the calf was finished, **they** (the people) **said, These be thy gods, O Israel, which brought thee up out of the land of Egypt** (4). How quickly may the carnal heart be turned away from the true worship of God!

When Aaron saw (5) how far the people were going, it appears that he tried to control them by erecting **an altar** before the image and proclaiming a **feast to the Lord.** He may have hoped to retain a semblance of the worship of God by keeping the name *Yahweh* in the festival. His act reminds one of attempts to retain a form of godliness without its power (II Tim. 3:5) and of the syncretism found in much of nominal Christianity.

Whatever Aaron intended, he failed completely in retaining any worship acceptable to God. The people gave way to an emotional outburst that led to idolatry and apostasy. **They rose up early** (6) **to eat and to drink, and . . . to play.** Though eating and drinking in worship were part of God's plan, in this case there was no spiritual worship—only a satisfaction of carnal lusts. "They gave full rein to their passions in the 'play,' the orgiastic dance which followed and which almost invariably accompanied idolatrous rites. See also verse 25 and cf. I Cor. x. 6, 7."[50]

"Steps in Backsliding" can be seen as (1) Impatience with God's providence, 1*a*; (2) Desire for visible signs in worship, 1*b*-4; (3) Compromise with true forms of worship, 5; (4) Surrender to carnal passions, 6.

[48]Johnson, *op. cit.*, p. 82. [49]PC, I, 322.

[50]Connell, *op. cit.*, p. 129.

2. *Moses Informed of Israel's Sin* (32: 7-14)

a. God's evaluation and threat (32: 7-10). Moses would have returned to the camp completely ignorant of Israel's idolatry had not God warned him of it. It was an act of mercy to reveal this tragedy to Moses before he left the mount. God also used this occasion to test the faith and courage of His servant.

Moses was told, **Get thee down; for thy people, which thou broughtest** from **Egypt,** have sinned (7). God's language seemed to disown this people and to reckon Moses as their leader and deliverer. Sin always separates from God, though He never gives us up easily or quickly. In Moses' position the easiest thing he could have done was to disclaim any further responsibility for this people, but experiences across the past months had done something for this man. He was not Israel's leader by his own choice and he had been helpless many times before a rebellious following. Only through God had he come to this point, and the God who had led thus far must not fail now.

God's evaluation of this wicked crowd is clearly given: they had **corrupted themselves** (7); they **turned aside quickly** and substituted a **calf** for himself (8); they were **a stiffnecked people** (9); He was very angry with them (10). **Stiffnecked** is a word applied to a rebellious horse or ox which refuses to be controlled by a rein. Israel had refused to follow the covenant she had made with God.

Here was probably the greatest test Moses had sustained. **Let me alone,** God said, **that I may consume them: and I will make of thee a great nation** (10). That God could have done this very thing in justice must not be denied; that He would have carried out this threat had Moses not interceded seems apparent. However, God knew His servant and knew that he would stand this test and that he would become a mediator. Moses saw the reality of God's wrath, rejected the opportunity for selfish glory, and pled for his people and for God's glory.

b. The prevailing prayer (32: 11-14). Moses turned the words of God around by insisting that these were His people that He had **brought forth out of the land of Egypt** (11). He was willing to accept his own personal part in the deliverance from Egypt, but Moses knew it was God who had really exercised the **great power** and the **mighty hand.** To destroy this people now would only disgrace God in the eyes of **the Egyptians**

(12) by implying that He had acted with an evil intent. All the past glory that had been attained in the eyes of the Egyptians would be lost if God consumed His people in anger.

With a boldness that could come only from a strong faith, Moses pled, **Turn from thy fierce wrath, and repent of this evil against thy people.** He asked God to **remember** His promises to the patriarchs to whom He had sworn by His own name to give the **land** of promise **for ever** (13). In this defense before God are three arguments against the Lord destroying His people: (1) it would annul past victories; (2) it would give the Egyptians occasion to glory; (3) it would break the promise to Abraham. All of these are pleas based upon the glory of God—certainly a true example in intercessory prayer.

God was pleased with Moses' intercession; He was now able to set aside His threat. The word **repented** (14) is used here as an anthropomorphic expression describing God's change of action toward His people since there would come a change in them. God's eternal purpose never changes, but He condescends to work with men in their changing modes of action, and this work is described in the language of human action. Repentance also conveys the idea of pain in the heart of God in the event of the destruction of His people.[51] When holy anger is present with holy love, the tempering of the wrath with the suffering of love brings the offer of mercy. This would be God's kind of repentance especially revealed in the atonement in Christ. This same quality may be felt by godly parents when they find a pained love overcoming anger and showing mercy to a child who rebels against them and commits willful sin.

In vv. 7-14 is a picture of "The True Intercessor." (1) Recognizes the threat of God's anger, 7-11*a*; (2) Pleads for the glory of God, 11*b*-13; (3) Gains response from the heart of God, 14.

3. *Moses Confronts the Sinful Israelites* (32:15-24)

a. The tables of testimony broken (32:15-19). There is an emphasis on **the tables** (15) of stone at this point that gives significance to the action of Moses in breaking them. Containing the Ten Commandments, they represented the heart of the law; having been written on stone, **on both . . . sides,** pictured permanency and completeness; being **the work of God, and the writ-**

[51]Johnson, *op. cit.*, pp. 82-83.

ing of God (16) gave to them authority and perfection. They were the essence of the covenant between Israel and God and were to be placed in the most sacred shrine. They were supernaturally wrought and given to Moses to present to Israel.

Joshua (17) must have been left at a point on the mount where he had awaited Moses' return. He did not know about Israel's sin, but he heard **the noise** from the camp and interpreted it to mean a sound **of war.** Moses replied that it was neither a sound of **mastery** (victory) or of **being overcome** (defeat). It was simply a sound of **them that sing** (18), perhaps a cry that was undefined.[52] At this point Moses did not share with Joshua his knowledge of events in the camp.

When Moses came near **the camp** and saw directly the sin of his people—**the calf** and their **dancing**—his **anger waxed hot** (19) and he broke the tables "at the foot of the mountain" (RSV). When the report of this evil was indirect, Moses in compassion pled for abatement of God's wrath (11). When he saw for himself the evil of the people, he experienced the same anger that God had expressed (10). One need not suppose here that Moses' anger was uncontrolled passion. To a person whose heart is pure, there always comes an awareness of the terrible dishonor that sin brings to God. Holy people experience deep emotions of holy anger against wickedness.

But holy wrath is to be tempered with loving compassion. Moses held in his hands the very law that condemned to death these rebellious people. If the threat of the law were now allowed, Israel must die. The people had broken that law. As Moses stood before the people and observed their lewdness, he lifted the law above his head, and probably in their view, dashed the tables to the ground. He had brought to them something of which they were unworthy. They were completely unfit to receive this gift of God.[53] Either the tables must be broken or the people must be destroyed. Moses broke the tables.

There is no indication here or elsewhere in Scripture that Moses was censured for this act. What he did here in a moment must have made a lasting impression. His act declared both the wrath of God and His mercy. Israel's covenant was broken; the evidence lay at Moses' feet, as well as in the acts of the people. If God continued with Israel, it must be through mercy and a renewed covenant.

[52]Connell, *op. cit.*, p. 129.

[53]Rawlinson, PC, I, 334-35.

b. The image and Aaron (32:20-24). Moses made quick work of the image; he **burnt it in the fire, and ground it to powder,** then scattered the ashes and dust **upon the** drinking **water,** and forced the people to **drink of it** (20). The wooden core of the idol would burn and the gold plate was reduced to powder.[54] Thus the people were made to suffer for their sin.

Aaron was next asked to give an account of his actions (21). He placed the blame on **the people,** saying, **They are set on mischief** (22, "wickedness," Berk.). **We wot not** (23) is better "we do not know." The people were determined to have things their way and Aaron went along with them. He reported that he took their gold, placed it in the fire, and **there came out this calf** (24). It would seem that Aaron was trying to make it appear that a miracle had occurred.[55]

How easy it is for religious leaders to act as did Aaron! Before they act they sound out public opinion. They think it unwise to be too firm. It is necessary, they think, to allow for carnal weaknesses, and to go along with present-day tendencies. One cannot succeed, they believe, unless he keeps with the crowd; to them it is better to compromise than to lose influence with the people. So they allow an infiltration of the world with the hope that some semblance of the divine can be retained. What will their answer be in that day?

4. *Punishment of the Idolaters* (32:25-29)

Even though God intended mercy to this people because of Moses' intercession (14), this grace could be extended only to the penitent. Some of the people were still rebellious. **Naked** (25) may best be translated "broken loose" (RSV). They were dishonoring God in the eyes of Israel's enemies—most likely some of the Amalekites were still around. So the call went forth, **Who is on the Lord's side? (26)** In response, many of the **sons of Levi** (the Heb. word for **all** does not necessarily mean everyone) came to Moses. This was the tribe later designated as the priestly family; their devotion to God was evident in this act.

These Levites were told to take their swords and go through **the camp, and slay,** if necessary, even brothers and companions (27). It appears that some of the Levites also had to be killed. It may be assumed that these strokes fell upon the rebellious

[54] *Ibid.*, p. 339. [55] *Ibid.*

who refused to submit to Moses and the Lord.[56] **Three thousand men** (28) died before order was restored.

This act of obedience on the part of the Levites consecrated them to God. The RSV translates v. 29, "Today you have ordained yourselves for the service of the Lord." The **blessing** bestowed upon them was their being chosen as the tribe devoted to God's service (Num. 3:6-13).[57] God here used those chosen for a priestly task to carry out His judgments. His ministers must be firm in justice as well as rich in mercy. Aaron had failed at this point.

5. *Moses' Intercession for Israel's Sin* (32:30-35)

Moses' earlier intercession for Israel (11-14) was a plea for God to spare His people from immediate destruction because of His hot anger against them. He had succeeded in that plea; Israel as a nation had been spared, and the idolatry had been destroyed. The rebellious had been slain or subdued, but the tables containing the law had been broken; the covenant no longer existed. Moses must now find a way back to a covenant relationship with God.

With a penitent Israel awaiting God's verdict, **Moses** reminded the people of their **great sin** (30). Then he promised to **go up unto the Lord** to see if **an atonement** for their sin could be made. In God's presence Moses confessed Israel's **sin** in making **gods of gold** (31). He wanted the people to be restored to God's favor by divine forgiveness—**If thou wilt forgive their sin—** (32). Words such as "it is well" need to be supplied at the dash ahead of the semicolon.[58] However, if God would **not** forgive them, Moses asked that he be blotted **out of thy book which thou hast written. To blot out** means "to cut off from fellowship with the living God, or from the kingdom of those who live before God, and to deliver over to death."[59] Moses' love for his people was so great that he did not care to live unless God forgave them. Atonement for sin was a greater thing than Moses knew. Only God could provide it, and the basis for universal forgiveness could be found only in God's gift of His Son. But the love prompting such atonement was found in Moses' heart, as Paul also later experienced in himself (Rom. 9:2-3).

[56]Connell, *op. cit.*, p. 130.

[57]Rawlinson, PC, I, 340.

[58]Connell, *op. cit.*, p. 130.

[59]Johnson, *op. cit.*, p. 83.

God's answer to Moses was that the individual who sins is the one whose name is blotted out of the **book** (33). Moses could not atone for Israel, but their forgiveness is assumed in God's approval of Moses' continued leadership of **the people** to the Promised Land (34). The same promise of His **Angel** going before them (23:20, 23) was given Moses, with the difference indicated in 33:2-3 that God himself would not go. The penalty for the broken law would not be completely removed, though modified sufficiently for Israel to proceed.

In vv. 31-34 is seen "The True Intercessor." (1) Confesses the sins of his people, 31; (2) Seeks forgiveness for his people, 31*a*; (3) Offers himself in behalf of his people, 32*b*, (4) Receives an answer from God for his people (33-34).

Though Israel was forgiven and permitted to continue as God's people, certain penalties would remain. The presence of God with them would be mediated through His **Angel,** though a day of final reckoning would ultimately come. When **the Lord plagued the people** (35), some of them suffered immediately for their sins, most likely through afflictions among them. Though God forgives people for their sins through Christ and restores them to His favor, certain consequences follow as reminders of the broken law. Also it must be noted that impenitent hearts cannot be forgiven; even though penalties may not fall immediately, a day of reckoning will come.

"Intercession" is the theme of 30-34. (1) Intercession needed, 30; (2) Intercession illustrated, 31-33; (3) Intercession rewarded, 34 (G. B. Williamson).

6. *Israel's Repentance and Reconciliation* (33:1-23)

a. God's offer of modified justice (33:1-3). Moses was told by God to lead the people to the land promised to **Abraham, to Isaac, and to Jacob** (1). A way had been found by which the promise of God could be fulfilled. His **angel** (2) would **drive out** their enemies, and the land would be fruitful **with milk and honey** (3). Material blessings were assured to the people.

However, an important aspect of the earlier promise was omitted. Though God promised to send **an angel,** He himself would not go. This people were **stiffnecked** and would be in danger of God's wrath if He were leading them. The Angel spoken of in 23:20, 23 must have been the Son of God, who as God himself was directly leading His people. Here the **angel** was a being who would adequately represent God, but God in His most immediate personal presence would be absent.[60] However it is possible that the last part of v. 3 was a warning. The repentance it produced brought a renewal of God's promised presence later (vv. 14-17).

b. Israel's mourning (33:4-6). To the people, these were **evil tidings** (4). This threat awakened in them the realization of their loss. They could remember the pillar of cloud (13:21), God's counsel when needed (15:25), His aid in battle (17:8-13), and His close presence (13:22). People of the world may seem to get by very well without God, but men who have experienced His presence know that they cannot get along without Him. This realization has brought many wanderers back to God.

When one is awakened to his sin and the emptiness it brings, he is willing to repent in sackcloth and ashes. God asked Israel to lay aside their **ornaments** (5) as a sign of penitence, but their willingness to do so came with their godly sorrow even before they were asked (4). These **ornaments** "may have consisted of armlets, bracelets, and, even perhaps, anklets, all of which were worn by men in Egypt at this period."[61] These were removed as a test of their obedience "from Mount Horeb onward" (6, RSV) and were later used for the construction of the Tabernacle (35:22).

c. God's meeting with Moses (33:7-11). **And Moses took the tabernacle, and pitched it without the camp, afar off from the camp, and called it the Tabernacle of the congregation** (7). The KJV makes no distinction in translating two Hebrew words, both meaning **tabernacle** or tent. The tabernacle of v. 7 was not the same as the one described in cc. 26—31. This was probably Moses' own tent (Amp. OT) where he had met with God and counseled the people.[62] After their sin of idolatry Moses removed this tent outside the camp because God could no longer dwell among His people (3). Its presence outside the camp reminded Israel of their sin. They must go outside to seek the Lord.

When Moses went out unto the tabernacle (8), **the people** stood at their own tent doors and watched Moses enter his tent. As he **entered,** the **cloudy pillar descended, and stood at the**

[60]Connell, *op. cit.*, p. 130. [61]Rawlinson, PC, I, 348.
[62]IB, I, 1071-72.

door of this tent while God **talked with** him (9). Since they were penitent, **the people** stood and **worshipped** (10) while God talked **face to face** with Moses, **as a man speaketh unto his friend** (11). When Moses returned to **the camp, Joshua** remained in this tent, a possible preview of the favor to be shown to Joshua later as Moses' successor.

Three great lessons may be learned from this account. (1) God is grieved by sin in His people, and His presence is withdrawn from them because of it. There is an emptiness experienced whenever a believer disobeys God and thus grieves the Holy Spirit. A quick and easy restoration to God's favor is not taught here or in the NT (cf. I Cor. 5:1-5; II Cor. 7:6-13). (2) God, however, may still be approached by the penitent if he goes to Him (Heb. 13:13). There the Presence may be seen and His word heard. (3) For the one whose heart is pure there is face-to-face communion with God. Moses' encounter with God assures every believer of the rich joy when there is nothing between the soul and the Saviour.

The Church today needs to recover this sense of awe and respect for God's holy presence. Too often God is seen as one who condones sin, overlooks failure, and makes the path to divine favor an easy one. Repentance is seen as a simple "I'm sorry." However, God is deeply grieved by sin; Calvary proved this. Free sinning today with the hope of easy forgiveness tomorrow disregards God's holy nature and assumes cheap mercy. True penitence is costly but it is the only way to faith and God's redeeming presence. Israel here saw that it was costing both them and God something to complete a restoration.

d. The promise of God's presence (33:12-17). These verses picture a third time that Moses interceded for his people. The first time (32:11-14) he obtained the abatement of God's wrath on the people. The second time (32:30-35) he obtained forgiveness for them and a modified promise to lead them to Canaan. Here Moses received assurance of Israel's full restoration to God's favor and of the restored presence of God with them.

Moses knew that God had renewed the command for him to **bring up this people** (12) to Canaan; he also knew that God had favored him with personal **grace.** However he was puzzled as to how or with **whom** the journey would be made. He pled for a revelation of **thy way** (13), so that he could **know** God even more clearly and distinctly and **find** added **grace** in His

sight. Moses was not spiritually selfish; he was not asking God's blessing just for personal enjoyment. Thus he added, **Consider that this nation is thy people;** he felt inadequate to lead the people without the assurance that God would go with him.

In fact Moses did not want to lead this people unless God were with them—**If thy presence go not with me, carry us not up hence** (15). This presence of God in His fullness would reveal a full restoration to **grace** for both Moses and the **people** (16), and be the true mark of their uniqueness from other nations. The only excuse for the existence of Israel as a nation was being wholly the Lord's. When the Church loses the fullness of God's Spirit, she ceases to be distinct as an instrument of God.

Moses' pleas prevailed. God said, **My presence shall go with thee, and I will give thee rest** (14). What a glorious assurance! Moses' uneasy spirit had pled with God to spare the people. He had broken the tables of stone, destroyed the idol, and directed the execution of offenders; yet he could not rest until he was assured that God's grace was fully restored to His people. God's servants cannot be at peace until they know that He has answered their prayers. When He answers, and His presence is assured, there is a great calm.

God condescends to answer the call of man. He said to Moses, **I will do this thing also that thou hast spoken** (17). There are some things God can do because man prays that otherwise He will not do. The personal integrity of the intercessor is vital; God said, **Thou hast found grace in my sight, and I know thee by name.** The one who pleads with God must first be certain of his own right relation with God. "The effectual fervent prayer of a righteous man availeth much" (Jas. 5:16).

"The Divine Presence" is seen in vv. 1-17. It (1) Is subject to provocation, 1-6; (2) Honors separation, 7-11; (3) Responds to intercession, 12-13, 15-16; (4) Grants restoration, 14, 17.

e. *Moses asks to see God's glory* (33:18-23). Most men are satisfied with their experience of God's presence much sooner than was Moses. Here was a man to whom God had given more than to any other, and yet he wanted still more. The closer one gets to heaven, the more of heaven he wants; the more one experiences God, the more of God he wants to experience. Moses implored, **Shew me thy glory** (18). "God's glory is manifested to mortal minds by the evidences of His goodness, yet this revelation to Moses was to be, in some way incomprehensible by us who have not seen it, a direct vision of His goodness undimmed by the limitations of its usual manifestations through earthly forms."[63] What Moses desired, therefore, was a sight of the glory or essential being of God, without any figure, and without a veil."[64] This was a bold request.

God promised Moses a partial granting of his petition. **All** of His **goodness** (19) would be made to **pass before** Moses. God's anger was now past and the threats were set aside. He was ready to reveal His great mercy and compassion toward those who, though unworthy, were to experience His grace. The proclamation of **the name of the Lord** was a proclamation of mercy, grace, love, and faithfulness (cf. 34:6).

However, Moses was told that he could not see God's **face** and **live** (20). Only in the next world can one possess in full the beatific vision. Moses must be satisfied, while mortal, with something less than he desired. One is not now permitted to reach across and lay hold on all that awaits the future. But in that day we shall see "face to face" (I Cor. 13:12).

God here promised the theophany (a visible manifestation of himself) to Moses which he would later experience (cf. 34:5-7). God promised to place him **upon a rock** (21) and His glory would pass by. When it did, God would **cover** Moses **with** His **hand** (22) while He passed by, but would remove His hand so that Moses could see His **back** (23). In this way Moses could see the "afterglow which He leaves behind Him, but which may still suggest faintly what the full brilliancy of His presence must be."[65] For this experience language would be inadequate, even as for Paul when he was caught up into the "third heaven" (II Cor. 12:4). God's children with pure hearts do experience visions of God that are enigmas to the worldly mind, and incomprehensible to the carnal heart. But for the holy person these bring heaven to earth while the longing still remains for the glories of heaven.

7. *The Return to the Mount* (34:1-9)

a. The second tables of stone (34:1-4). With the people of Israel now restored to divine favor, God accepted them as having renewed their part of the covenant.[66] However, it remained

[63]Connell, *op. cit.*, pp. 130-31.
[64]Johnson, *op. cit.*, p. 84.
[65]*Ibid.*
[66]Rawlinson, PC, I, 359.

for God to renew His part by again writing the law on other tablets of stone. The broken law must be restored. Moses must again ascend into the mount, receive the law, and return to the people. When a people sin against God, it is necessary that the first works be done again (Rev. 2:5). Time must be taken to restore the backsliders. It is unfortunate that transgression should come to the church and disturb its peace and witness. But when it comes, restoration is necessary before further progress can be made.

Moses was asked to **hew thee two tables of stone,** upon which God promised to **write . . . the words that were in the first tables** (1). Moses must make the stones, but God would do the writing. On the first occasion God had both made the stones and done the writing (32:16), but now Moses was required to do a part. This was not a punishment to Moses for breaking the stones; but it suggests that the way back to God, after transgression, may require more for the penitent backslider than for the unconverted sinner.

This time Moses was to ascend the mountain alone (3); all others were to remain in the camp. Though brief, the instructions to Israel were the same as earlier (19:12-13). Moses was careful to follow God's explicit instructions. He made the **tables of stone** (4) and **went up** the mount **early in the morning** as he was **commanded.**

b. The vision of God (34:5-9). God now fulfilled His promise to reveal himself. **The Lord descended in the cloud** (5). Modern men may decry biblical language of a God "up there," "coming down" or "going up in a cloud"; but these anthropomorphic phrases retain a concept of God that is safer and more meaningful than reducing Him to an abstraction such as the "ground of being" or an "inevitable inference." Though it is clear in this appearance to Moses that the reality of God was somewhat evasive, yet the experience was dramatic and real. **The name of the Lord** was **proclaimed** in a new way (5); this name was *Yahweh, Yahweh elohim.* **The name of the Lord** was a clue to His nature. He revealed himself as **merciful and gracious, longsuffering, and abundant in goodness and truth** (6). God had just shown that He had **mercy for thousands** in Israel, **forgiving iniquity and trangression and sin** (7).

Iniquity conveys the idea of "sins committed from an evil disposition"; **transgression** is "rebellion against God." The original word for **sin** means to miss the mark; and is "the most general word for sin in the Old Testament."[67] God's **mercy** is broad, reaching to every evil in the human race. Interestingly, mercy is here proclaimed first and is followed by a warning against the presumption that God would condone iniquity (cf. 20:5-6). God cannot and will not forgive the impenitent who persist in their sin. Though He is great in mercy, the wicked will be destroyed, even if those wicked have once tasted of God's grace (cf. Heb. 6:4-6).

For the man who had asked for a direct vision of God, this experience of viewing only God's back (33:23) brought humility: **Moses made haste, and bowed his head . . . and worshipped** (8). Not in vain repetition but with strong and urgent desire, Moses prayed, **Lord . . . go among us . . . pardon our iniquity . . . and take us for thine inheritance** (9).

The theme of 1-8 is "The Tablets of Stone." (1) The commandments are permanent, 1; (2) The commandments are benevolent, 5-7; (3) The commandments are transcendent, 8 (G. B. Williamson).

8. *The Covenant Renewed* (34:10-28)

a. The promise of God (34:10-11). God now formally renewed the broken covenant with Moses. He promised to lead Israel by doing **marvels** (10) that would be greater in their eyes than anything yet done. He called it **a terrible thing that I will do with thee.** *The Berkeley Version* translates it, "What I am about to do with you inspires awe." He would **drive out** the enemies from the land of promise (11). The **marvels** were fulfilled later in such events as the fall of Jericho's walls (Josh. 6:20) and the killing of enemies with hailstones (Josh. 10:11). Though Moses did not live to see these victories, God's promise was fulfilled for His people.

b. Warning against idolatry (34:12-16). The evil of forming alliances with peoples of the Promised Land was now a real possibility. Israel must **take heed** (12) and make no **covenant with the inhabitants,** because this would be **a snare** to them. In order to protect themselves Israel must **destroy their altars, break their images, and cut down their groves** (13). They must not

[67]Connell, *op. cit.*, p. 131.

be allowed to exist. The **images** ("pillars," RSV) and the **groves** ("Asherim," RSV) were cult objects erected for the worship of male and female gods in the Canaanite mythology. They were connected with Baal worship, and "introduced by the Phoenician Jezebel into Israel (I Kgs. 18:19)."[68] "Grossly immoral rites were practised in connection with the pillars and groves, and these were a source of temptation to the Israelites continuously until the exile."[69]

Concerning the statement that God is **jealous** (14), see note on 20:5. Any **covenant with the inhabitants of the land** (15) might lead to joining with them in idol-feasts and intermarriages that could result in apostasy and idolatry (16). Marrying a person attached to a false religion is the quickest way to disobedience. **Sons go a whoring** after the **gods** of their wives. Idolatry, whether pagan or modern, is a form of spiritual adultery. One is unfaithful to his vows to God when his heart seeks after the gods of this world.

In our society it is almost impossible to save our children from exposure to these temptations. Thrown together in public school and neighborhood activities, children are subjected to these allurements every day. Our only hope is the instilling of courage and faith that will resist the pull of worldly "idols" and ungodly marriages. When wrong alliances and other failures come to one's own family, there is recourse to God's redeeming grace and the power of intercessory prayer through the Holy Spirit.

c. *Various injunctions* (34:17-26). Most of these injunctions are repetitions of earlier commands. Israel's recent sin made the repeated command to **make . . . no molten gods** (17) imperative. The instructions in vv. 18-20 are discussed in 12:14-20; 13:3-13; and 23:15. The command about the Sabbath (21; see comments on 23:12) adds the injunction to observe the holy day **in earing time and in harvest.** Temptation to plow on God's day when rain threatened or to reap when harvest was ready must be resisted. It was easy then, as it is now, to excuse work when pressure was on.[70]

For discussion of the contents of vv. 22-23 see comments on 23:16-17. In v. 24, Israel was promised enlargements of **borders**

[68]Johnson, *op. cit.*, p. 84. [69]Connell, *op. cit.*, p. 131.
[70]Rawlinson, PC, I, 370.

through obedience, and freedom from molestation of their **land** by others when they attended the annual feasts. Comments on the instructions given in 25-26 are found in 23:18-19.

d. Finalizing the covenant (34:27-28). Moses was told, **Write thou these words** (27)—the words that God had just given him (10-26). **After the tenor of** means "on the basis of these words" (Smith-Goodspeed). These agreements renewed the covenant of the Lord with His people. Clarke thought the transaction also included a copy of the tables of stone for Israel, since the originals would be placed in the ark.[71] In any case it was God who wrote **the ten commandments** on the two **tables** (28; the **he** here must be understood as God; see v. 1), and Moses wrote the remainder of the covenant. Moses was in the mount **forty days and forty nights,** as earlier, and fasted on both occasions (cf. 24: 18 and Deut. 9:9). God gave him special strength for these fasts.

9. *Moses' Shining Face* (34:29-35)

An unusual fact was discovered when **Moses came down from** the **mount. Moses wist not** (i.e., did not know it) but the people saw **that the skin of his face shone** (29), "because he had been talking with God" (RSV). His countenance glowed with a heavenly radiance as a result of his face-to-face encounter. **When Aaron** and others **saw** him, **they were afraid to come nigh him** (30); but Moses reassured them, so **Aaron** and **the rulers** came near to listen (31). **Afterward** (32) **all . . . of Israel came** and heard Moses' complete report. While Moses spoke, his face shone before the people; then after he had finished, he placed **a veil on his face.** The KJV implies that Moses veiled his face while speaking, but the Hebrew suggests that the veil was put on after speaking (cf. Berk., RSV, *et al.*). It appears that Moses took off the veil when he **went in before the Lord** (34), then **came out, and spake** his message with unveiled face, and afterwards covered himself (for the reason, cf. II Cor. 3:13, BBC, Vol. 8, pp. 527-28).

This visual evidence convinced Israel that Moses' message was of God. Some have thought that the radiance was man's likeness to God lost in the Fall (Gen. 1:27) and that it will be ours in the resurrection.[72] The glory on Moses' face was similar to Christ's radiance at the Transfiguration (Luke 9:29-31), shared

[71] *Op. cit.,* I, 473-74.

[72] Rawlinson, PC, I, 320.

then also by Moses and Elijah. It may be that Stephen had a radiance of this kind as he stood before the Sanhedrin (Acts 6: 15). Paul refers to this glory in II Cor. 3:7-18 as belonging to men in Christ who behold the realities of God "with unveiled face." This inner radiance of the believer will burst forth in the day of Christ's second coming and the resurrection (cf. I John 3:1-2).

Verses 29-35 describe "The Shining Face." (1) Received in an encounter with God, 29; (2) Discovered by those ready to listen, 30-32, 35*a*; (3) Veiled to those who are dull of hearing 33, 35*b*; (4) Renewed in returning to God's presence, 34.

C. Building the Tabernacle, 35:1—38:31

In the remaining chapters of Exodus, much of the material is a repetition of the instructions given earlier to Moses in the mount (see 25:10—31:11). The reader is referred to the comments in these earlier passages for the description of the Tabernacle and its furniture. The comments in this section are limited to new material and to variations that occur.

1. *Willing Offerings* (35:1—36:7)

Moses called the people **together** in order to instruct them about the needs for the Tabernacle (1). He first reminded them of the importance of the **sabbath** day (1-3). It is possible that religious zeal, even in building a house of God, might endanger the observance of this command.

Moses next exhorted those with **a willing heart** to bring **an offering** of the basic materials for the manufacture of the articles needed for the Tabernacle (4-9). He then insisted that **every wise hearted** (10; "able," RSV) man **make all that the Lord hath commanded** (10; cf. 10-19).

The people of Israel responded with dispatch. Their hearts were opened to the Lord and they returned with their gifts (20-29). Their hearts were **stirred** and their spirits **made willing** (21). They gave according to ability, since "every one who could make an offering" (24, RSV) **brought it** to the workmen. Also **the women** did what they could (25-26) in using their hands. More expensive gifts were supplied by **the rulers** (27). No one was expected to give or do where there was inability, and all who gave or performed did so out of willing hearts.

Moses made clear that **Bezaleel** (30) and **Aholiab** (34) were chosen for particular tasks because of their special skills (30-35). Not every person is able to do all the tasks in God's work. But it is important that each learn to do willingly those things that he can do. In fact one is obligated to develop the skills in which he is adept. God fills such men with His **spirit** and **wisdom** and **understanding** (31) in the work He has chosen for them to do. These chosen workers were also enabled to **teach** others who could help them in their service to God (34).

To these special craftsmen were committed the materials being brought by the people (36:1-3). When it was found that more than was needed was being brought (5), **Moses gave commandment** (6) that the people cease bringing further offerings. When the Lord opens men's hearts to give, there is never any want in His work. "God loveth a cheerful giver" (II Cor. 9:7).

In this section "The Gifts for God" (1) Originate in a willing heart, 35:21-22, 26; (2) Are supplied according to ability, 35: 10, 24-25, 35; 36:1-2, 4; (3) Result in abundance, 36:5-7.

2. *The Execution of the Work* (36:8—38:20)

This section records the implicit obedience of the workmen to the explicit instructions God had given Moses in the mount (see comments on 25:10—27:19). The exactness of this execution of the work is even clearer than the KJV indicates.[73] This repetition of detail gives evidence of Israel's careful adherence to God's instructions. Everything He said was important, and no detail must be overlooked. The record stands as witness to Israel's perfect obedience in these matters.

New information is given about **lookingglasses** brought by the women who **assembled at the door of the tabernacle** (38:8). These mirrors were made of bronze and polished highly. They were plentiful in Egypt and were made and used by the women there.[74] The Israelite women also had such mirrors and brought them as offerings for the bronze of the altar (2) and **laver** (8). Their sacrifice for the altar of God of that which had been created for personal use is here commended. This is a "triumph of female piety over female vanity."[75]

[73]Rawlinson, CWB, I, 325.

[74]Connell, *op. cit.*, p. 132.

[75]Rawlinson, PC, I, 389.

3. *Value of the Metals* (38:21-31)

The value of these offerings as here given is difficult to interpret in modern terms. Johnson writes:

> The gold amounted to 29 talents, 730 shekels, or about 40,940 ounces troy weight. The silver mentioned was only the atonement money (30:13, 14), which amounted to 100 talents, 1,775 shekels, or about 140,828 ounces troy. No account is made of the voluntary gifts of silver. Attempts to value the precious metals used in terms of modern currency do not mean much, as we have no way of knowing the comparable value in that day . . . The bronze used weighed about three tons.[76]

The amount was large and revealed the dedication of God's people. It is also significant that the building rested upon **silver . . . sockets** made from the **half a shekel** given in equal amounts by **every man** in Israel (38:26-27).

D. Making the Garments, 39:1-31

Here is the account of the workmen making the garments according to the instructions given Moses in the mount (28:1-43). There is only a slight change in the order at a few points. The careful and skilled work of the artisans is noted and the exactness of their adherence to God's instructions is emphasized. The words, **as the Lord commanded Moses,** are repeated six times in these verses (1, 5, 7, 21, 26, 31). The people wanted to follow God's words explicitly.

E. The Completed Materials Presented to Moses, 39:32-43

The entire work of making the Tabernacle and its furniture was accomplished in about six months.[77] When all was done, the finished pieces were **brought** to **Moses** (33) for his inspection. He was the one who had seen the pattern and was the only one who was qualified to pass final judgment. Had any part been faulty, it would have been rejected, but this was not necessary. The workmen had labored diligently, and Moses assured them that the work had been done **as the Lord had commanded** (43). They received the reward for any good workman—the assurance of a task well done. Moses then pronounced a blessing upon those who had so faithfully and skillfully wrought.

[76]*Op. cit.,* p. 85.

[77]Rawlinson, CWB, I, 331.

Connell writes: "We may wonder why all the minute details of the tabernacle and its accessories were repeated so fully in these chapters. At least two reasons for this are as follows: the inspired record shows how careful were these men to follow faithfully every detail of the pattern which God had commanded them; and how God delights in and keeps exact account of obedience of His own people."[78]

F. Erection of the Tabernacle, 40:1-33

Instructions were given to erect the Tabernacle **on the first day of the first month** (2), exactly two years after leaving Egypt. Verses 2-8 describe the placement of the furniture. When all were in position, Moses was to **anoint the tabernacle** and all its furnishings with **the anointing oil** (9-11). The oil, a type of the Holy Spirit, was to make these things sacred. Material objects set apart to God are made holy by the touch of God (cf. comment on 13:2).

In vv. 12-15 detailed instructions were given for the consecration of **Aaron and his sons** (12). From Lev. 8:1-13 it is apparent that the ceremony of anointing the Tabernacle and the priests awaited a later date.[79] The use of the word **everlasting** (15) can refer only to the continuing office of the priests in the same family for many generations; Christ's is the only truly perpetual priesthood (Heb. 7:17, 23-25, 28).

When the assigned date arrived—**in the first month in the second year, on the first day of the month** (17)—the task of erecting the Tabernacle was completed as ordered (16-33). Each part was put in place, beginning with **the tabernacle** itself (18-19), and then placing **the ark** in the holy of holies (20-21), and hanging **the veil.** The holy place was next furnished with its objects (22-27) and **the hanging** (curtain) **at the door** placed at the front (28). Finally **the altar, laver,** and **court** were set up (29-33). One can imagine the thrill and awe that came to all the people as they saw the results of their gifts and labors taking shape before them (see Charts *A* and *B*).

For the first time, as this memorable day came to a close, **the bread** was placed on the table (23), **the lamps** on the candlestick were **lighted** (25), and **sweet incense** was burned before

[78]*Op. cit.*, p. 132. [79]*Ibid.*

the Lord on the golden altar (27). **Moses and Aaron and his sons washed** at the laver as they began their ministry (31).

G. The Divine Dedication, 40:34-38

The people had done their best in their freewill offerings of goods and services; the skilled workmen had fashioned the materials into lovely pieces of art; Moses had accepted the finished products and had placed them according to instructions in proper order for the house of God.

Evening came to the camp of Israel with the new sanctuary in its midst. The people were pleased and so was Moses. Suddenly the **cloud** (34) which had been their guide moved over and rested upon the coverings of **the tent** and **the glory of the Lord** (a glowing fire) **filled** the holy place. The glory was so bright that **Moses,** who apparently tried to enter the sanctuary, **was not able** to do so (35). Even this man, who had talked with God face-to-face and who had glowed with a heavenly light, found the place too glorious to enter for the moment.

In vv. 36-38 the writer anticipated God's plan for the future. **The cloud** and **fire** rested **upon the tabernacle** as permanent features. Whenever **the cloud** moved, **the tabernacle** was to move; whenever **the cloud,** or fire, stood still, the house of God was to rest (36-37). **Throughout all their journeys** (38) this pattern was followed. Apparently the intensity of **the glory** (35) was later confined to the most holy place, since the priests were to minister in the holy place.

Israel could now rejoice in the assurance that God's favor had returned to them. The way back to God after their sin had been long and arduous, and it seemed for a time they would be left on their own, but now they knew that their God was with them in mercy. On this glorious note of perfect forgiveness and divine acceptance the Book of Exodus, an account of God's redemptive plan, comes to a close.

In these closing verses we see "God's Perfect Salvation." (1) Wrought by the implicit obedience of the seeker, 33; (2) Instantaneous entrance of the divine glory, 34-35; (3) Continual presence of the Holy Spirit (36-38).

Bibliography

COMMENTARIES

Chadwick, G. A. "The Book of Exodus." *The Expositor's Bible.* Edited by W. Robertson Nicoll, Vol. I. Grand Rapids: Wm. B. Eerdmans Publishing Co., 1947.

Clarke, Adam. *A Commentary and Critical Notes,* Vol. I. New York: Abingdon-Cokesbury, n.d.

Connell, J. Clement. "Exodus." *The New Bible Commentary.* Edited by R. Davidson. Grand Rapids: Wm. B. Eerdmans Publishing Co., 1954.

Driver, S. R. *The Book of Exodus.* "Cambridge Bible for Schools and Colleges." Edited by A. F. Kirkpatrick. Cambridge: University Press, 1918.

Dummelow, J. R. (ed.). *A Commentary on the Holy Bible.* New York: The Macmillan Co., 1946.

Exell, Joseph S. *Homiletical Commentary on the Book of Exodus.* "The Preacher's Complete Homiletical Commentary on the Old Testament." New York: Funk and Wagnalls, 1892.

Henry, Matthew. *Commentary on the Whole Bible,* Vol. I. New York: Fleming H. Revell Company, 1706.

Jamieson, Robert; Faussett, A. R.; and Brown, David. *A Commentary: Critical and Explanatory,* Vol. I. Hartford: S. S. Scranton & Co., 1877.

Johnson, Philip C. "Exodus." *The Wycliffe Bible Commentary.* Edited by Charles F. Pfeiffer and Everett F. Harrison. Chicago: Moody Press, 1962.

Lange, John Peter. *Exodus.* "Commentary on the Holy Scriptures." Grand Rapids: Zondervan Publishing House, n.d.

Lee, James W. "Genesis—Joshua." *The Self-Interpreting Bible,* Vol. I. St. Louis: The Bible Educational Society, 1911.

Lindsell, Harold. "Introductions, Annotations, Topical Headings, Marginal References, and Index." *Harper's Study Bible—The Holy Bible.* New York: Harper and Row, Publishers, 1952.

McIntosh, C. H. *Notes on the Book of Exodus.* New York: Fleming H. Revell Company, n.d.

McLaughlin, J. F. "Exodus." *The Abingdon Bible Commentary.* Edited by F. C. Eiselen, Edwin Lewis, and David G. Downey. New York: The Abingdon Press, 1929.

Parker, Joseph. "The Book of Exodus." *The People's Bible,* Vol. II. New York: Funk and Wagnalls Co., n.d.

Rawlinson, George. "Exodus." *Commentary on the Whole Bible.* Edited by Charles J. Ellicott, Vol. I. Grand Rapids: Zondervan Publishing House, n.d.

———. "Exodus" (Exposition and Homiletics). *The Pulpit Commentary.* Edited by H. D. M. Spence and Joseph S. Exell, Vol. I. Grand Rapids: Wm. B. Eerdmans Publishing Co., 1950.

Rylaarsdam, J. Coert (Introduction and Exegesis), and Park, J. Edgar (Exposition). "The Book of Exodus." *The Interpreter's Bible.* Edited by George A. Buttrick, *et al.,* Vol. I. New York: Abingdon-Cokesbury Press, 1952.

Unger, Merrill F. "Exodus." *The Biblical Expositor.* Edited by Carl F. H. Henry, Vol. I. Philadelphia: A. J. Holman Co., 1960.

OTHER BOOKS

Butler, J. Glentworth. *The Bible Work: The Old Testament.* Volumes I-II. New York: Funk and Wagnalls, Publishers, 1889.

Cook, F. C. *Exodus.* New York: Scribner, Armstrong and Co., 1874.

Davis, John D. *The Westminster Dictionary of the Bible.* Philadelphia: The Westminster Press, 1944.

Driver, S. R. *An Introduction to the Literature of the Old Testament.* New York: Charles Scribner's Sons, 1923.

Edersheim, Alfred. *The Exodus and the Wanderings in the Wilderness.* New York: Fleming H. Revell Co., 1876.

Free, Joseph P. *Archaeology and Bible History.* Wheaton: Scripture Press, 1956.

Kraeling, Emil. *Bible Atlas.* New York: Rand McNally and Company, 1956.

Kurtz, J. H. *Sacrificial Worship of the Old Testament.* Edinburgh: T. & T. Clark, 1863.

Maclaren, Alexander. *Expositions of Holy Scripture,* Vol. I. Grand Rapids: Wm. B. Eerdmans Publishing Co., 1932.

Morgan, G. Campbell. *An Exposition of the Whole Bible.* New York: Fleming H. Revell Company, 1959.

———. *Living Messages of the Books of the Bible.* New York: Fleming H. Revell Company, 1912.

———. *The Analyzed Bible.* New York: Fleming H. Revell Co., 1907.

Pfeiffer, Robert H. *The Books of the Old Testament.* New York: Harper and Brothers, Publishers, 1957.

Raven, John Howard. *Old Testament Introduction.* New York: Fleming H. Revell Company, 1910.

Taylor, William M. *Moses the Law-giver.* New York: Harper and Brothers, Publishers, 1879.

Thompson, J. A. *The Bible and Archaeology.* Grand Rapids: Wm. B. Eerdmans Publishing Co., 1962.

The Book of

LEVITICUS

Dennis F. Kinlaw

Introduction

A. Name

The name of Leviticus comes to us from the Septuagint (LXX) through the Vulgate. During the early centuries of the Christian era the Bible of the Christians was the Greek Bible. Jerome translated it into Latin in the fourth century (completed A.D. 405). This translation, called the Vulgate, became the Bible of the Western church until the Reformation. *Leveitikon* was the name of the third book of the Pentateuch in the Septuagint. In the Latin this became *Leviticus.* The name, of course, was given to the book because it is concerned with the Levitical system of worship in the Old Testament.

B. Authorship

The witness of the book itself is not to human authorship but to divine. Twenty of the 27 chapters begin with the formula, "And the Lord spake unto Moses, saying." Moses is usually commanded to convey a message either to Israel (1:1—3:17; 4:1—5:19, *et al.*) or to Aaron and his sons (6:9, 25; 8:1-2, *et al.*). Occasionally the text says that God spoke to Moses and to Aaron (11:1; 13:1; 14:33; 15:1). At least once God speaks to Aaron alone (10:8). The great majority of the material, though, is presented as coming directly from God to Moses. The traditional view in the Church was that Moses gave this book to Israel and thus to us.

The rise of modern critical scholarship saw this view rejected. The adoption of the documentary hypothesis (*J, E, D, P*) led to the view that Leviticus was part of the priestly code which was many centuries in compilation and received its final form only in the postexilic period. It was insisted that much of the material, like the so-called "Holiness Code," cc. 17—26, was older than the postexilic period, and some of the legal material might also be quite old. It was a firm conviction of most critical scholars, however, that *P* was the latest of the Pentateuchal strands.

Recent studies have shaken an apparent unanimity among scholars at this point. The work of men like J. Pedersen, Ivan Engnell, Yehezkel Kaufmann, and others has left some uncertainty.[1] Studies of law in the ancient Near East make this fact evident: there is little in Leviticus for which a parallel can be found in the ancient world that does not also find its parallel in the literature of the second millennium B.C. From the content of Leviticus that is common to ancient Israel's world there is no reason to suppose that Leviticus does not come from the Mosaic period.

Recent studies by men such as W. F. Albright have shown that it is reasonable to assume that the unique monotheistic character of Israel's religion goes back to the time of Moses.[2] Today scholars have an increased knowledge of the legal tradition of the world of the second millennium B.C. in the Fertile Crescent. In the light of this new knowledge it now seems possible that the legal character of Israel's religion as seen in Leviticus fits into the Mosaic period and might just as well be of Mosaic origin.

C. Pentateuchal Dating

The period allocated by the Pentateuch for the giving of this law and for the events embedded within Leviticus is precise. It was given between the erection of the Tabernacle in the first month of the second year after the departure of Israel from Egypt (Exod. 40:17) and the first day of the second month of that same year (Num. 1:1).

D. Message

In seeking the message of Leviticus it is important to see the progression of the Pentateuch. Genesis tells us of the calling of the patriarch Abraham and the election of his family to a covenant role in human history. Exodus tells of the mighty deliverance of Abraham's descendants, the Israelites, from bondage in Egypt and of the establishment of God's covenant with this people at Sinai. Exodus also indicates the legal character of this covenant and the witness to the covenant in the Tabernacle and the worship to be conducted there. Leviticus is a kind of manual given to the priests and to the people of Israel that they might know how to perform the worship demanded by this covenant in a manner effective for them and acceptable to the God of Israel. Leviticus is thus a manual of worship. Included, also, are varied

[1]Gleason Archer, *A Survey of Old Testament Introduction* (Chicago: Moody Press, 1964), pp. 83-131.

[2]*From Stone Age to Christianity* (Baltimore: Johns Hopkins Press, 1940).

instructions on how to live so that such worship would be acceptable to the Lord, the God of the covenant.

The content of the book reveals the basic principles of the religion of the Old Testament. The following affirmations are implicitly assumed throughout.

1. No fellowship with God is possible except upon the basis of atonement for sin. Thus the opening chapters of Leviticus describe the various offerings that are necessary if atonement and fellowship are to be realized.

2. Man is not able to atone for his own sins. A mediatorial system is necessary. Thus the role of the priests, the sons of Aaron, is played up throughout. The entire system presupposes a mediator.

3. Atonement must be according to divine plan. Note how much of Leviticus is direct speech from God. Note also the tragic end of Nadab and Abihu when they worshiped according to their own pattern rather than after the pattern given by Moses from God.

4. Only the good, the clean, and the whole (perfect) is acceptable as sacrifice to God. Man cannot approach God with empty hands. Strict stipulations are given by God as to what is acceptable to Him.

5. People who walk with God must be holy, because He is holy. This accounts for the heavy emphasis upon the difference between the clean and the unclean, the pure and the abominable, the holy and the unholy. Leviticus is thus a handbook on "the holy." The holiness demanded is not merely ceremonial. It is also ethical and social, as in c. 19, which is largely a recapitulation of the Decalogue. The concern of the book is inner, moral righteousness. It is from Leviticus that we get the command, "Thou shalt love thy neighbour as thyself" (19:18). The meaning of this requirement is spelled out, and that spelling out is in terms of personal and social righteousness.

6. Fellowship with God involves the commitment of the total life. The book makes it very clear that no area of one's personal existence is beyond the right of the God of Israel to control. There are instructions about eating, sexual habits, possession of property, offerings to God, the time demands of true worship, and one's relations with his neighbor and the stranger. The Holy One of Israel demanded that all of the life of those who would walk with Him be brought under His sovereign control and His sanctifying influence.

From the above it is not difficult for one who knows the New Testament to see the roots of Christian piety laid down here. The expression may not be as developed as that found in the New Testament, but the principles are remarkably the same. And even Leviticus feels the need for a better way. This need is spelled out in the requirements for the mediators of the Levitical system, the Aaronic priests. The mediatorial efforts necessary for themselves are indicative that this system is not the ultimate. It was only a type that pointed to a "better way," a way made plain in Christ and His new covenant which is foreshadowed here.

Outline

I. A Manual for Worship, 1:1—7:38
   A. Instructions for the Israelites, 1:1—6:7
   B. Instructions for the Priests, 6:8—7:38

II. Consecration of the Priests, 8:1—10:20
   A. Moses Consecrates Aaron and His Sons, 8:1-36
   B. Aaron Assumes the Priestly Office, 9:1-24
   C. A Case of Sacrilege, 10:1-20

III. Laws Concerning Uncleanness, 11:1—15:33
   A. Uncleanness from Animals, 11:1-47
   B. Uncleanness from Childbirth, 12:1-8
   C. Uncleanness from Leprosy, 13:1—14:57
   D. Uncleanness from Issues, 15:1-33

IV. The Day of Atonement, 16:1-34
   A. Aaron's Preparation, 16:1-19
   B. The Scapegoat, 16:20-34
   C. Some Conclusions

V. Holiness in Daily Living, 17:1—20:27
   A. Killing Domestic Animals, 17:1-16
   B. Social Regulations, 18:1—20:27

VI. Holiness of the Priest, 21:1—22:33

VII. Holy Days and Festivals, 23:1-44
   A. The Sabbath, 23:1-3
   B. The Passover, 23:4-8
   C. The Offerings of Firstfruits, 23:9-14
   D. The Feast of Weeks, 23:15-22
   E. The Holy Days of the Seventh Month, 23:23-44

VIII. Holy Oil, Holy Bread, and the Holy Name, 24:1-23
   A. The Holy Oil, 24:1-4
   B. The Holy Bread, 24:5-9
   C. The Holy Name, 24:10-23

IX. Holy Years, 25:1-55
   A. The Sabbatical Year, 25:1-7
   B. The Jubilee, 25:8-55

X. Final Words of Promise and Warning, 26:1-46
   A. Idolatry, Sabbaths, and the Sanctuary, 26:1-2
   B. Promise, 26:3-13
   C. Warning, 26:14-46

XI. An Appendix: On Vows and Tithes, 27:1-34

Section I A Manual for Worship

Leviticus 1:1—7:38

The relationship of Leviticus to Exodus is indicated in the opening sentence of the book. In Exodus, God is speaking from the mountain. Here He speaks from the Tabernacle. Exodus closes with the account of the dedication of the Tabernacle, and the coming of the glory of God to fill it. Now God begins to speak to His people from the place where He has chosen to dwell among them. The word which He speaks has to do with how this people, now redeemed by the mighty hand of God, shall worship and serve their God. Leviticus is the handbook for worship of the ancient Hebrews. It begins with a manual for sacrifice.

A. Instructions for the Israelites, 1:1—6:7

Immediately the reader is made aware of the divine origin and the consequent authority of the message that is being given. **And the Lord called unto Moses, and spake unto him out of the tabernacle of the congregation** (1). Moses is not permitted to go into the Tabernacle (Exod. 40:35), so God within speaks to Moses without. S. R. Hirsch suggests that the intention here is to establish the fact that the word of God came to Moses rather than simply arising within him as a product of his own religious consciousness.[1] The word spoken is of supernatural origin.

The expression **tabernacle of the congregation** is better translated "tent of meeting" (RSV). The word for **tabernacle** is the common Hebrew word for "tent" (*'ohel*). The term translated **congregation** is from a Hebrew root (*y'd*) which means "to appoint." Thus the best reading would be "tent of appointment." Worship is not an option with the people of God. It is an obligation. God made an appointment with man at an appointed place (the Tabernacle). The appointment was intended for fellowship according to appointed procedures (cc. 1—22) and at appointed times (cc. 23—25). It is not the Hebrews who here decide how

[1]*The Pentateuch Translated and Explained.* Rendered into English by Isaac Levy. Vol. III, 2nd ed. (London: Isaac Levy, 1962), p. 3.

and when they will worship. Those decisions are initially made by God for the redeemed ones.

1. *Law of the Burnt Offering* (1:1-17)

a. God's command (1:1-2). This manual for worship begins with the offering of sacrifices: **If any man of you bring an offering unto the Lord** (2). The words **bring** and **offering** are both from the same basic root, which means "to come near, to approach." Thus the question to which Leviticus addresses itself is how a Hebrew can live in "nearness" to God. And that involves offerings, or sacrifices. **Offering** (*qorban*) is the closest thing to a general term in the OT for "sacrifice." It is the term used for all kinds of offerings that are presented to God. The root idea, though, is neither "sacrifice" nor "offering" as we understand these words. It means "a thing brought near." It is used in the OT exclusively with reference to man's relation to God and indicates the purpose of this section of Leviticus; it was intended to instruct the Hebrews on how to draw near to God.

That worship involves sacrifice, or offerings, is a commonplace. Such sacrifice was by no means confined to Israel. It was an essential part of the religion of the world in which the Israelites lived.

Scholars have long sought to find a controlling idea behind religious sacrifices. Some have suggested that it is communion and is symbolized in a common meal. Others have emphasized propitiation, substitution, or joyous gratitude. It seems clear that sacrifice is a multi-faceted thing just as man's relationship to God is many-sided. It involves communion, but communion with God involves propitiation, gratitude, and petition. Thus our attention is turned back to the idea of nearness to God. All that is involved in drawing near to God is implicated in sacrifice. This explains the five varieties of offerings that are discussed in the following chapters: burnt, meal, peace, sin, and guilt (trespass) offerings. Each speaks of a different facet of nearness to God.

Leviticus assumes that when a man comes to God he will not come empty-handed. There is something about the relationship that makes it right and proper that a man should bring an offering. Since NT times it is easy to forget this. But one must always remember that, although the Christian believer may come boldly to God, he does not come with empty hands. Under the old covenant one came with his own gifts. Now the believer comes with God's own Gift, His Son, as the basis for his approach and his intimacy with the Divine.

The OT gifts were of different kinds. They could be animals from the herd or flock, birds, or cereal. They were accompanied by such things as salt, honey, frankincense, or wine. The purpose of all is given in v. 3, **He shall offer it of his own voluntary will . . . before the Lord.** The Hebrew is better translated: "He shall offer it for his acceptance before the Lord." Thus the entire system described here is provided in order that man might draw near with acceptance. This necessitates sacrifice.

It was obvious to the Early Church that the foundations were laid here for the NT teaching of the necessity of the sacrifice of Christ for true fellowship between man and God. The Jewish understanding of John the Baptist's identification of Jesus as the Lamb of God, who would take away the sin of the world, is determined heavily by this Book of Leviticus.

The animals for sacrifice came either from **the herd** or **the flock.** They were domesticated animals. Wild animals were not acceptable. Jewish tradition suggests that this was because they cost the offerer nothing.

b. *An offering of cattle* (1:3-9). The Hebrew term translated **burnt offering** (*'olah*) means literally "that which goes up." Since the *'olah* was burned upon the altar completely (except for the hide, which went to the priest), it came to be called the burnt offering. Sometimes it is qualified by the adjective "whole." In other sacrifices parts were eaten by the priests or even by the offerer himself. Here the offering all ascends to God for a sweet savor. Hirsch suggests that this indicates "the necessity for, and the aspiration to, 'striving to rise higher.' "[2] Micklem says that it "signifies total self-oblation to God in praise and love."[3] This self-giving and praise must not be separated from expiation, though, for v. 4 says it is **to make atonement for him.**

The whole of the offering is for God. It must meet His specifications. God is the One who determines what is given and how. It is to be **a male without blemish** (3). One wonders if thoughts

[2] *Ibid.*, p. 10.

[3] "Leviticus" (Exegesis and Exposition), *The Interpreter's Bible*, ed. George A. Buttrick, *et al.*, II (New York: Abingdon-Cokesbury Press, 1951), 15.

of this offering were not in Paul's mind when he urged the Romans to present their bodies a living sacrifice, wholly acceptable to God (Rom. 12:1-2). Only the best is good enough for God, and that has to be given without reservation if man is to be accepted by Him.

The identification of the offerer and the offering is indicated in the expression, **He shall put his hand upon the head of the burnt offering.** This is prescribed for all animal sacrifices. Compare the peace offering (3:2), the sin offering (4:4), the ram of consecration (8:22), the Day of Atonement ritual (16:21), and even the presentation of the Levites as a wave offering (Num. 8:10). The practice is not specifically mentioned in connection with the guilt offering, but since 7:7 says that there was one ritual for the sin offering and the guilt offering, it may well be that this was part of that ritual too. Jewish tradition indicates that the hand was to be laid on with some pressure and that it was accompanied by the confession of sin. Targum Jonathan says: "He shall lay his right hand with firmness." Other Jewish sources indicate that both hands were usually used. In other rituals this may have had different significance but here it seems to indicate a separation by the offerer of his gift to God and a full identification with it. Keil writes: "To render the self-sacrifice perfect, it was necessary that the offerer should spiritually die, and that through the mediator of his salvation he should put his soul into a living fellowship with the Lord by sinking it as it were into the death of the sacrifice that had died for him, and should also bring his bodily members within the operations of the gracious Spirit of God, that thus he might be renewed and sanctified both body and soul, and enter into union with God."[4]

This identification was in order that the offering might **make atonement for him** (4). The Hebrew word means "to cover over." Some have interpreted it as meaning "to cover the face of the one wronged." In the Bible it means to cover the sin so that God, who cannot look with equanimity upon sin (Hab. 1:13), does not see it. The purpose again is in terms of nearness to God; it indicates "acceptance," or "at-one-ment." This nearness, of course, is not spatial but spiritual and personal. Such

[4]C. F. Keil and F. Delitzsch, *Biblical Commentary on the Old Testament*, II (Grand Rapids: Wm. B. Eerdmans Publishing Co., 1949), 291.

nearness cannot come without sacrifice. The animal was killed and **the priests** (5), identified as the **sons** of Aaron, drained the blood and **sprinkled** it **round about upon the altar** so that it touched all sides. The animal was then **cut . . . into . . . pieces** (6) and placed **upon the altar** to be burned.

Any true understanding of this requirement must involve a discussion of the role of the blood in its relation to life and to death. Snaith insists that the primary reason for disposing of the blood in this manner is because "it is taboo, too sacred and too dangerous for the ordinary man to handle."[5] Blood was forbidden to the Israelite, as 17:11 shows, perhaps because the blood represented life. Some thus hold that it here represents life released from the body and now presented to God.[6] In this view the emphasis is not upon death but upon life. It seems unfair to the biblical evidence, however, to ignore the fact that the mass of references to blood in the OT involve death. When speaking of this sacrificial system and its relation to the sacrifice of Christ, it is necessary to emphasize that the basis of our fellowship with God includes Christ's death. Thus Paul says that "we were reconciled to God by the death of his Son." This does not deny the release of life. So Paul adds, "Much more, being reconciled, we shall be saved by his life" (Rom. 5:10).

The duties of the priests, **the sons of Aaron** (7), are clearly defined. It must be remembered that this arrangement represented a new departure in the life of the people of God. In the patriarchal period each family head acted as priest. Now, in the Mosaic covenant, a new order was being established that would prepare the way for understanding the ministry of Christ, the great High Priest, as seen in the letter to the Hebrews.

This **sacrifice** is to be **an offering made by fire . . . a sweet savour unto the Lord** (9). Noth says concerning the sweet savor that this phrase "seems to stem from the cultic speech and thought-forms belonging to the land of the two rivers." He notes that the flood narrative in the Gilgamesh Epic tells how " 'the gods smelt the sweet savour' of the sacrifice offered after the

[5]"Leviticus," *Peake's Commentary on the Bible*, ed. M. Black (New York: Thomas Nelson and Sons, Ltd., 1962), p. 242.

[6]L. L. Morris, "Blood," *The New Bible Dictionary*, ed. J. D. Douglas, *et al.* (Grand Rapids: Wm. B. Eerdmans Publishing Co., 1962), p. 160.

flood."[7] Micklem comments that to suppose that this passage implies "that the God of Israel literally enjoyed the smell would be as foolish as to imagine that incense is used in Christian churches because God is supposed to like the odor of it."[8] What is clear is that man's religious activity is to be pleasing to God, and that when it is performed according to His Word, it pleases Him.

The cutting of the animal into pieces and the arrangement of them upon the altar so that the fire passed between them may be compared with Gen. 15:9-10, 17-18, where the covenant of God with Abraham is sealed by the passage of the divine fire between the pieces of the offering.

c. An offering of sheep, goats, or fowl (1:10-17). Verses 10-13 explain the offering from the flock of a ram or a male goat. The ritual instructions are brief, not repeating the obvious. The information is added that the killing of the animal shall be on the north **side of the altar** (11). This may be due to the fact that **the ashes** were on **the east** side (16), vessels for washing on the west (Exod. 30:18), and the ramp on the south.

The concern of ancient Hebrew law for the poor is revealed in the provision of 14-17 that small birds might be used for the burnt offering (cf. 5:7). From this we see more clearly the status of Mary, the mother of Jesus, as revealed in Luke 2:24. Apparently the act of giving and the attitude behind the gift are of more importance than the value of the gift. Due to the size of the **fowls** (14) thus offered, the ritual was naturally different. There was no laying on of hands, and the blood was **wrung out** (15), not sprinkled. The first part of 17 has been explained, "Let it be broken open at the wings, but not cut in two" (BB). All of the bird that might be useful to man was thus to be offered to God.

2. *Law of the Meal Offering* (2:1-16)

a. Basic provisions (2:1-3). The way that time changes the meaning of words is illustrated for us in **meat offering** (1). This was the one offering that did not consist of meat. Rather it was a meal or cereal offering made from finely ground grain. The Hebrew word (*minchah*) denotes a gift or offering generally. It

[7]*Leviticus* ("The Old Testament Library"; Philadelphia: The Westminster Press, 1965), p. 24.

[8]*Op. cit.,* p. 17.

is used in Gen. 4:3 of Cain's offering, but in Gen. 33:10 it is used of Jacob's gift to his brother. In Judg. 3:15-18 it is used of tribute. When the word is used in connection with sacrifice, it carries either a broad meaning of something given to God or the narrower meaning found here of a grain or cereal offering. Such an offering was the result of human labor and the earth's fruitfulness. It represented the consecration to God of the fruit of one's labor.

The offering seems to have been voluntary, as implied by the phrase **and when any will offer a meat offering.** The **meat offering** is commonly presented in the OT as accompanying the animal sacrifices (Num. 15:1-6). The ritual here is suitable both for this dual offering and for the presentation of a meal offering by itself.

The meal offering could be uncooked (1-3) or cooked (4-16). If uncooked, it was accompanied by **oil** and **frankincense** (2). The oil was a vital part of the daily food of the ancient Hebrew. As such it signifies in the OT gladness, nourishment, and prosperity. The Hebrew word (*shemen*) means "fatness, richness." Note the use of the word in Deut. 32:13; Job 29:6; Isa. 61:3; Micklem suggests that it symbolized "a quickening and sanctifying power."[9] In the light of its connection with the anointing of the priests, and its use with the golden candlestick, Allis thinks that it symbolized "the gracious presence of the Holy Spirit in illumination and sanctification."[10] Certainly the seasoning presence of the Holy Spirit in the work and worship of the believer is what makes him acceptable with God.

Frankincense was a whitish-yellow, aromatic resin which was bitter to the taste but very pleasant-smelling. It was used in the holy anointing oil (Exod. 30:34), as incense (Jer. 6:20), burned as perfume (Song of Sol. 3:6), offered with the shewbread (Lev. 24:7), and presented as a priceless gift to Christ (Matt. 2:11). Erdman says that it symbolized prayer and praise.[11] Certainly there is biblical support for the notion that prayer and

[9] *Ibid.*, p. 18.

[10] "Leviticus," *The New Bible Commentary*, ed. F. Davidson, *et al.* (Grand Rapids: Wm. B. Eerdmans Publishing Co., 1953), p. 138.

[11] *The Book of Leviticus* (New York: Fleming H. Revell Company, 1951), p. 27.

praise are eminently acceptable to God when men present their gifts to Him.

He shall take thereout his handful (2) is clarified thus: He "shall take out a handful of the fine flour and oil . . . and the priest shall burn it on the altar" (Berk.).

The portion of the meal offering which was burned was called a **memorial.** This term (*'azkarah*) occurs only seven times in the OT, six in relation to the meal offering and once in connection with the frankincense which was burned with the presentation of the shewbread. Study of the usage of the verb "to remember" (*zakar*) in recent years has pointed out significant theological overtones.[12] When God remembers, a new situation develops in which help is available for the righteous, and judgment confronts the unrighteous. The converse of this implies that, when man remembers the faithfulness of God, new faith and obedience result. This becomes obvious when one recalls the role of "remembrance" in the institution and celebration of the Lord's Supper (Luke 22:19; I Cor. 11:24-25). At the heart of worship is a remembering by man and God of both covenant commitment and covenant promise.

The identification of this offering as **a thing most holy** (3) means that it could be eaten only by the male descendants of Aaron, the priests. Gifts to the Lord were either **most holy** (*qodesh qodashim*), reserved for the priests alone; holy (*qodesh*), to be used for the maintenance of the families of the priests; or simply **offerings** (*qorbanim*), which were for the maintenance of the Tabernacle or later the Temple. The reference in Mark 7:11 to "corban" is to a gift willed to Temple maintenance upon the death of the owner, which was thus not available for family needs.

b. The baked cereal offering (2:4-11). The cooked meal offerings could be prepared in three ways: (i) baked **in the oven** (4), (ii) cooked on a flat **pan** (5), or (iii) prepared in **the fryingpan** (7).

Neither **leaven** nor **honey** (11) were to be used. These could be offered as firstfruits but not as offerings to be burned upon the altar. The Hebrew seemed to feel that fermentation implied disintegration and corruption; it thus implied unclean-

[12]O. Michel, *Theological Dictionary of the New Testament,* ed. Gerhard Kittel, IV (Grand Rapids: Wm. B. Eerdmans Publishing Co., 1967), 675-83.

ness. In the rabbinical writers leaven is often used as a symbol of evil. Pagan writings show a similar attitude. Plutarch said: "Leaven is born of corruption, and corrupts that with which it is mixed . . . (A)ll fermentation is a kind of putrefaction."[13] Jesus in the Gospels (Matt. 16:6; Luke 12:1) uses leaven figuratively of the false teachings of the Pharisees and the Sadducees. Paul speaks of "the unleavened bread of sincerity and truth" (I Cor. 5:7-8). The proscription of leaven in the Passover feast is another matter. There the unleavened bread was a reminder of Israel's bondage and was called "bread of affliction" (Deut. 16:3). Honey seems to have been widely used in sacrifices among Israel's neighbors.[14] Perhaps this is why honey and milk, both important elements of the diet, were not offered in sacrifice.

As leaven was forbidden in the meal offerings, salt was required (13). Salt carried great value in the ancient world, and it was necessary for life. It symbolized permanence in that it gave resistance to corruption. It also indicated fellowship and fidelity in that covenants were sealed with a common meal in which salt was an important element. To share a man's salt was to establish a bond between host and guest. Note how God calls His covenant with Aaron and his sons (Num. 18:19) and His covenant with David and his descendants (II Chron. 13:5) covenants of salt. Hirsch suggests that, just as salt preserves meat from the influences of decay about it, so the covenant should protect the contracting parties from external influences detrimental to the bond established.[15]

c. *Meal of firstfruits* (2:12-16). This meal was composed of the tender, young grain in the ear, roasted and ground (14). It was presented to God as a proclamation that all increase comes from God. Just as the firstborn son and the firstborn of the flock and the herd belonged to God, the firstfruits of the field were given to Him. All was God's, but His acceptance of the firstfruits as representative of the whole meant that man was free to use the remainder in gratitude.

In 2:8-16 we see the spiritual meaning of "The Meat Offering." (1) The meat (meal) offering involves worship and ser-

[13]A. T. Chapman and A. W. Streane, *The Book of Leviticus* ("The Cambridge Bible for Schools and Colleges"; Cambridge: The University Press, 1914), p. 8.

[14]Hirsch, *op. cit.*, p. 67.

[15]*Ibid.*, p. 70.

vice, 8-10; (2) All fruits of man's labor belong to God, 12, 14; (3) The instructions for the meal offering are noteworthy: oil—the Holy Spirit; frankincense—prayer; no leaven—purity; no honey—nothing to ferment or decay; salt—preservation; fire—God's acceptance; sweet savor—God's pleasure, 9, 11, 13, 15 (G. B. Williamson).

3. *Law of the Peace Offering* (3:1-17)

To understand fully the peace offering, the reader should look also at 7:11-34. There it is seen that this offering is essentially a common meal in which priest and worshiper share and in which the choicest parts are given to God. **His oblation** (1) is an "offering" (RSV) or "present" (Berk.). In contrast to the burnt offering, only a portion is burned. The fat which is not intermingled with the flesh of the animal and which can be peeled away from intestines and kidneys is to be offered with the **kidneys** and **the caul** (lobe or appendage) of **the liver** (4-5). If it is a Palestinian sheep with its unusually fatty tail, the fat of the tail is to be offered too. All of this was placed upon the burnt offering of the day and consumed.

The giving of the fat to God corresponds to the disposal of the blood. The fat was looked upon as the "saved up riches of the animal," "a store against any future want."[16] Thus it is used metaphorically in the OT for the richest and the best. Such rightfully belongs to God. Having given this to God, the remainder of the animal was for priest and people to enjoy.

The **peace offering** seems to imply that the offerer is in fellowship with God. Otherwise he would not be permitted to eat of the flesh of the animal. Keil says that the object was "invariably salvation," either thanksgiving for salvation already received or supplication for salvation desired. Here salvation must be taken in the fullest sense. The Hebrew root of the word for **peace** (*shalom*) means "to be whole, sound, complete." As Keil continues, the word here denotes "the entire round of blessings and powers, by which the salvation or integrity of man in his relation to God is established and secured."[17] A study of the references to this sacrifice in the historical books supports this claim in that it reveals that the peace offering accompanied the burnt offering in times of great joy (II Sam. 6:17, *et al.*) and

[16] *Ibid.*, p. 80.

[17] *Op. cit.*, p. 299.

also in times of greatest need (Judg. 20:26, *et al.*). In Lev. 7:11, 16 we see that the peace offering could be a praise offering, a vow offering, or a freewill offering—an expression of one's sense of dependence upon and need for God in most varied circumstances.

The sacrifice could come from **the herd** (1, cattle), **the flock** (6, a sheep), or it could be **a goat** (12). Since the animal offered did not go to the altar, its sex and its age are not prescribed. It must nevertheless be **without** blemish (1, 6). The offerer must **lay his hand upon the head** (2, 8, 13), kill the animal, and present the parts to be offered to the priest who burned them upon the altar. The portion presented was **the food of the offering made by fire unto the Lord** (11), **for a sweet savour** (16). It is not necessary to see in this any reference to feeding God, as was found among Israel's neighbors. The God of Israel was not thus dependent upon His worshipers. He longed for fellowship with them, and wanted them to think of this peace offering as a fellowship meal. Note the use of the word "sup" even in a NT passage like Rev. 3:20. And consider the role of the Lord's Supper in the Christian Church.

The seriousness with which the ancient Hebrew was to take this legislation is indicated by the expression **a perpetual statute for your generations throughout all your dwellings** (17). This expression occurs 17 times in Leviticus.

4. *The Law of the Sin Offering* (4:1—5:13)

Our attention now is turned from the sweet savor offerings to the sin offering and the trespass offering. The importance of this shift is indicated by the introductory words, **And the Lord spake unto Moses, saying** (4:1). This formula becomes more common later in Leviticus, but this is the first occurrence since 1:1. In the remainder of the book it appears 28 times. Andrew Bonar, impressed by the frequency of this and similar formulas, remarked that there is no book that "contains more of the very words of God than Leviticus."[18]

This attribution of the institution and the regulation of these sacrifices to God must be more than just a claim that Israel's sacrifices were different from those of their neighbors. Is this not

[18]*A Commentary on the Book of Leviticus* (New York: Robert Carter and Brothers, 1863), p. vii.

the Old Testament's way of making clear to its readers that salvation is not merely the result of human religious sensitivity or reason? Salvation is based on sacrifice, and sacrifice that atones is instituted by God. The emphasis in the Hebrew sacrificial system is on something that is done for man. It is true that the man who sacrifices is involved in that he brings the offering, lays his identifying hand upon it, and kills it. The atoning work, however, is something that is done for him. The priest acts as mediator in a system instituted by God. The role of Christ is prophetically written into these rituals.

a. Rules for the offerings (4:1-35). The sin offering and the trespass offering represent a new type of sacrifice, that of expiation. Nothing was said in cc.1—3 about the occasions when the burnt offering, the meal offering, and the peace offering were to be presented. The sweet-savor offerings were voluntary. But here the sin offering and the trespass offering are described and the occasions on which they are to be offered are stipulated. These are obligatory for all who are within the covenant who become guilty of **things which ought not to be done** (2). The ritual for different classes is given: (*a*) the anointed **priest** (3-12), (*b*) the **congregation** (13-21), (*c*) a **ruler** (22-26), and (*d*) any of **the common people** (27-35). The animal used in the sacrifice varied with the importance of the person or persons who had sinned. The sacrifice for a **priest** (3) or for **the whole congregation** (14) was a bull. That for a **ruler** (22) was **a kid of the goats, a male without blemish** (23), while that for **the common people** (27) was either a she-goat (28) or a ewe **lamb** (32).

The seriousness of the guilt apparently varied with the position of the one sinning. The priest's sin was more serious than that of a ruler or a common man. As a representative of the people before God, his sin brought guilt upon all of the people. He seems thus to have defiled the very holy place itself. The blood from the sin offering for him was placed **upon the horns of the altar of sweet incense** (7) in the holy place, while that from the sin offering of ruler or commoner was placed **upon the horns of the altar of burnt offering** (25, 30) in the court of the Tabernacle. The blood from the offering for the whole people was handled as was blood from the sacrifice for the priests (cf. 7 and 18). Perhaps this was due to the fact that Israel was supposed to be a "kingdom of priests" (Exod. 19:6). The difference in the sin offering for the priest and for the people is seen likewise in that the flesh of the animals sacrificed for them was burned without the camp (cf. 12 and 21). The flesh of the sacrifices for rulers or commoners seems to have been eaten by the priests.

Other than the above difference, the ritual for the various classes was the same. The offerer brought his sacrifice, laid his hand upon its head, killed the animal, and gave it to the priest. The officiating priest there sprinkled **the blood** before the Lord, smeared some of it upon the horns of the altar, and then poured out the rest at the base of the altar of burnt offering; he burned the **fat,** the **kidneys,** and the **caul** (lobe or appendage) of **the liver** upon the altar of burnt offering. The influence of this ritual upon the NT understanding of Jesus' death is seen in the use of this terminology and these concepts in the Epistle to the Hebrews (Heb. 9:10-23; 10:19-22).

The name of the sin offering (*chattath*) is a noun based on the verb "to miss [a mark], to fall short." This is appropriate in that the offering is intended to cover sins **through ignorance** (22, *bishgagah*). Often these are referred to as sins committed "unwittingly." The opposite of such sins are those committed "with a high hand" (Num. 15:30, "presumptuously"; cf. Exod. 14:8); these were sins for which there were no sacrifices. The difference does not seem to be in the realm of knowledge as much as in the attitude of the heart. The sin "with a high hand" is committed with an attitude of haughty defiance of God, while that committed "through ignorance" arises from human weakness. Thus Keil can say: "But sinning *'in error'* is not merely sinning through ignorance (vss. 13, 22, 27, 5:18), hurry, want of consideration, or carelessness (5:1, 4, 15) but also sinning unintentionally (Num. 25:11, 15, 22, 23)."[19]

Here the NT believer can sense something of the inadequacy of the Levitical sacrificial system. There was no provision for the more heinous sins such as blasphemy, adultery, and murder. In the story of the exposure by Nathan of David's sin against Bath-sheba and Uriah there is no reference to sacrifice. The inability of this system to provide for the "presumptuous sin" points up the need for a better way—the way found in Christ.

b. Trespasses requiring a sin offering (5:1-13). Three cases are now enumerated that demand a sin offering. The first has to do with a man who has seen or come to know something that has

[19] *Op. cit.*, p. 303.

bearing upon a case but who has refused to disclose what he knows when called upon by the magistrate. The translation **hear the voice of swearing** (1) is confusing. The Hebrew word for **voice** is translated by Hirsch as "demand."[20] There are a number of occasions where "voice" could be translated "entreaty, request, demand" (cf. Gen. 3:17; 4:23). The RSV thus renders the expression "a public adjuration to testify." Moffatt translates the verse, "If anyone sins by remaining silent when he is adjured to give evidence as a witness of something he has seen or known." To adjure is to put on oath, on penalty of a curse.

It must not be assumed that a Hebrew, if he had concealed truth or misrepresented facts to the detriment of another, was freed from guilt by offering a sin offering. Verse 5 shows that he had to confess his sin, and 6:5 indicates that he had to make proper restitution. For examples of men keeping silence until put under oath, see Josh. 7:19; Judg. 17:2; Matt. 26:63; John 9:24. The fact that restitution is implied for this offense may be indicated by the statement, **He shall bear his iniquity** (1); in subsequent cases the text says only that the party involved is **guilty** (2-4).

The second case has to do with uncleanness contracted through touching an **unclean beast** (2, a wild beast), **unclean cattle** (domesticated animals from herd or flock), **unclean creeping things** (lit. "swarming things"), or **the uncleanness of man** (3). Leviticus 12—15 gives an extended discussion of cases of uncleanness. See the treatment there. Here the person seems to have defiled himself unknowingly and thus to have neglected the prescribed purificatory rites (11:24-31). Upon finding out about his uncleanness, the Hebrew was responsible for performing the needed sacrifice.

The third case involves a rash promise. If a man vows foolishly to do something that is **evil** (4), he would be wrong to keep the vow. He is guilty, though, of having made such a vow. If he promises to do something **good** and is unable to do it, he is guilty for this failure. In both cases the guilty one must **confess** (5) and present his sin offering. In 6, this is called a **trespass offering.** The actual discussion of trespass offerings does not begin until 5:14. The use of the term here is undoubtedly due to the fact that trespass means "guilt." There is, of course, a close relationship between the sin offering and the trespass offering.

[20]*Op. cit.*, p. 20.

The basic compassion inherent in the law is reflected in 7-13. In NT times the law was looked upon as a burdensome thing. Jesus accuses the scribes and Pharisees of making the law unbearable for men (Matt. 23:2-4). This Leviticus passage reveals concern for the poor. If a man could not **bring a lamb,** he could bring **two turtledoves, or two young pigeons** (7). If even this was too much, he could bring **the tenth part of an ephah** (seven pints) **of fine flour** (11). Note the similarity between this passage and 1:14-17.

Two birds were demanded and one of these was for **a burnt offering** (10). Allis points out that in the sin offering only the fat was burned upon the altar.[21] Since in the case of a bird it would be impossible to remove the fat, the flesh of one bird was consumed upon the altar as representing the Lord's portion of the sin offering (called a burnt offering because it was completely consumed upon the altar), while the other was given to the priest as representing his portion of the sin offering.

The offering of meal as a sin offering differed from the regular meal offering in that no oil or frankincense accompanied it. The memorial **handful** was burned upon **the altar** with **the offerings made by fire** (12). Thus it was mingled with the offerings on the altar and attained the value of a blood sacrifice and is no exception to the principle that "without shedding of blood is no remission" (Heb. 9:22).

5. *The Law of the Guilt Offering* (5:14—6:7)

The word that is translated **trespass** (15) comes from a root which means "to act unfaithfully, or treacherously." The context for this offense is the covenant. It must be kept in mind that these laws are not provided for men generally. They are given for the people of Israel, men who have committed themselves to a covenant with the Lord and have thus assumed certain responsibilities. The Lord is to be their God and they are to be His people. Undoubtedly this is why there is no provision for deliberate, willful violations of the covenant—sinning "with a high hand." Such sin would put the violator outside of the very covenant which these laws define. Note the wording: **If a soul commit a trespass, and sin through ignorance.**

Two cases are cited demanding the trespass (guilt) offering. One is an unintentional withholding of **the holy things of the**

[21] *Op. cit.,* pp. 139-40.

Lord. This refers to tithes, offerings, firstfruits, and the like. These belonged to God and were to be given to the priests. The offerer was to bring an offering, **a ram without blemish out of the flocks,** comparable in value to the loss which the priests had suffered. The meaning of the original is not entirely clear in the reference to **thy estimation by shekels of silver.** It appears to mean that a money value was to be placed upon the offering in order to calculate the amount of **the fifth part** (16, one-fifth of the value) which was to be paid in restitution as a fine. **The shekel of the sanctuary** (15) is identified in Exod. 30:13 as being based on the Phoenician measurement rather than the Babylonian shekel, which was of less value. The moral basis of the Levitical legislation is obvious here. Micklem says:

> Leviticus is concerned with the ritual of the *sin offering,* but that there is no superstitious idea that the offering of itself avails to take away sin is clear from the demand of penitence. There is no suggestion that apart from penitence there is atonement. If we raise the theological objection that God requires nothing but repentance for forgiveness, we overlook the demand for restitution so far as this may be possible. The true penitent says not only "I am sorry" but also "What can I do about it?"[22]

The second case of a guilt offering involves acts which are forbidden in the covenant law which demand restitution but which are unknown to the offender (17-19). Since no one knows what the loss has been, or even whether there has been a loss, the offerer brings the trespass offering without the added compensation. Note the desire to guard against the slightest offense. When seen in the light of the covenant and its gracious redemption, such a sacrifice is seen as the natural desire of the tender conscience to express positively its gratitude and its dependence. Note the attitude of Job in Job 1:5. The ideal is blamelessness.

The close of this section (6:1-7) deals with injuries done to a neighbor in matters of property. These concern deceit with respect to a deposit left for security by a **neighbour,** robbery, unjust gain by oppression (2), or appropriation of something **found** that belongs to another (3). These are the closest to conscious and willful acts of sin found in this section (5:14—6:7). They are matters that would not usually be known without disclosure by the offender. If discovered, such actions were punishable. See Exod. 22:7-13 for the legal procedures involved. The context

[22]*Op. cit.,* p. 29.

shows the inseparable relationship here between religion and ethics in Israel. To sin against another within the covenant was to sin against the God of the covenant. Thus one's relationship to his neighbors intimately affected his relationship to the Lord. The Lord is the Guarantor of the neighbor's property. To sin against a neighbor is to sin against God.

The word **fellowship** (2) seems to indicate a transfer of material goods in which something has been placed in another's hand. The LXX translates it *koinonia.* It would probably have to do with a business partnership. For **with thy estimation** (6), cf. comment on 5:15.

In cases of property damage, restitution was not enough. As a **trespass** demanded a guilt offering, a **fifth part** (5) of the value of the property involved must be added to the capital and restored to the owner. Then and then only was a guilt offering effective to atone for the trespass.

B. Instructions for the Priests, 6:8—7:38

1. *The Law of the Burnt Offering* (6:8-13)

The opening section of Leviticus (1:1—6:7) is addressed to the people of Israel (1:2) and is God's word to them about the sacrifices that He demanded. Now God addresses himself to the priests, **Aaron and his sons** (9), who are to perform these rituals. These instructions are helpful in understanding more about the Levitical sacrificial system and its significance.

First, we are informed that the fire was to be kept burning continually upon the altar (9-13). Exod. 29:38-39 informs us that a burnt offering was offered both morning and evening. It was the fat of the evening sacrifice that was used to keep the altar fire burning through the night. A perpetual flame burning before the deity is not unique to biblical religion. It is an expression of the human intuition that perpetual praise and worship should ascend from man to God. If this is felt by those who know little of divine grace, how much more appropriate that the heart of the Christian believer should be filled with unceasing prayer and perpetual praise! Micklem says concerning the fire:

> It points Christians to the eternal priesthood of the Lord Jesus Christ, the great High Priest, "who ever liveth to make intercession" for us (Heb. 7:25), who is "a priest for ever after the order of Melchizedek" (Heb. 5:6). He offers his eternal obedience to the

Father, an acceptable sacrifice, on behalf of all; he is the priest, and his obedience is the lamb, his obedience and his perfect love to God: these he offers on behalf of all men, for "he is not ashamed to call them brethren" (Heb. 2:11).[23]

The priest is given instructions concerning his dress for removal of **the ashes** every morning (11). The regular priestly garments were not to be worn for that task. It is surprising to many to see how much space is devoted in the Bible to clothing. This is especially true concerning dress for the priests. The idea is conveyed that it does matter how one appears before God. This is developed extensively in the NT and in Christian hymnody. Jesus spoke of the necessity of "the wedding garment" (Matt. 22: 11-14). In the Revelation we are counseled to buy "white raiment" (3:18) and to keep "garments" (16:15). We are also told of the bride of the Lamb, who is "arrayed in fine linen, clean and white: for the fine linen is the righteousness of saints" (19: 8). The concern in Leviticus, however, is the clothing of the mediator who stands between God in His holiness and worshiping man.

2. *The Law of the Meal Offering* (6:14-23)

The priest was to take a **handful** (15) of the meal offering with its **oil** and **frankincense** and offer this as a **memorial.** The **remainder** (16) of the meal offering was to be eaten without **leaven** (17) in the court of the tent by the chief priest and his sons. The expression, **It is most holy** (17), is used of the three offerings which were for the use of Aaron and his sons: the meal offering, the sin offering, and the trespass offering. It is also used of anything "devoted," that which could not "be sold or redeemed" (27:28).

This is further explained with the conclusion: **Every one that toucheth them shall be holy** (18). The exact meaning of this statement is not clear. Some feel that this is simply saying that everyone who touches holy things should be holy himself (Isa. 52:11). Others believe that it must mean also that those who touch the altar become holy and can never be returned to secular life. Jesus' reference to the power of the altar to sanctify a gift (Matt. 23:19) would indicate that both of these points of view are ultimately true. Num. 16:38 says concerning the censers

[23] *Ibid.*, p. 34.

of Dathan and Abiram: "For they offered them before the Lord, therefore they are hallowed." It is no light thing for men to present themselves to God. He takes a man seriously and subsequently claims for His own that which has been given to Him. Such consecration is amply illustrated in the OT.

The special meal **offering of Aaron and his sons** (20; i.e., the high priest) is described in 19-23. It is appropriate in that this entire section consists of instructions for the priests. This offering was to be made by the high priest **in the day when he is anointed** as high priest. The term **perpetual** indicates that subsequently the offering was to be made every morning and evening throughout his high priesthood. This offering was presented by the high priest for himself and for all priests. Thus it was to be **wholly burnt** (22). The priests shared in the most holy things offered by others. They could not partake of those offered by and for themselves (23).

3. *The Law of the Sin Offering* (6:24-30)

The sin offering also was **most holy** (25) and was to be **eaten** by the priests **in the court of the tabernacle of the congregation** (26). No unholy person was to **touch** it. All that it touched became holy and was to be devoted to God. Any garment **sprinkled** with the blood of the sin offering was to be washed **in the holy place** (27). The **vessel** (28) in which the meat was prepared for the priests was to be broken if pottery, or **scoured, and rinsed** if brass. Whatever touched it must be clean and removed from common use. Verse 30 is clarified thus, "However, no sin offering of which the blood is taken into the meeting tent for atonement in the sanctuary, shall be eaten; it shall be burned with fire." A footnote explains: "Its blood will be sprinkled on the mercy seat within the Holy of Holies; therefore the flesh, also, is too sacred for human food" (Berk.).

Moses indicates the sanctity of the sin offering in 10:17 by saying that it was given to the priests to eat to bear the iniquity of the congregation, to make atonement for them before the Lord. All of this ritual is presented to help emphasize the importance of distinguishing between the holy and the unholy. Inability or refusal to thus differentiate is always disastrous (see c. 10).

Many writers are quick to relate the concept of the "holy" found here to that present in pagan religious circles. Micklem's comparison is helpful.

Commentators are apt to speak of this "holiness" as a mere taboo, but the term is misleading. A taboo object (the term is taken from the primitive religions of Polynesia) is dangerous in its own right as the mysterious dwelling place of mana or supernatural power. That is not identical with the idea that an object is sacrosanct because it has been brought into relation with the living God. We can well believe that there was much superstition in Israel; but this conception of holiness is not superstition. To take a relatively inadequate instance from the contemporary situation, a modern man does not regard the gravestones "sacred to the memory" of his ancestors as containing any supernatural powers; but he treats them with reverence, and not as common stones, because of the use to which they have been dedicated. Such, but more vivid as we may suppose, was the sense of the holiness of things connected with the sacrifice in Israel.[24]

4. *The Law of the Guilt Offering* (7:1-10)

This section should be compared with the longer account in 5:1—6:7. The similarity of the **sin offering** and the **trespass** (guilt) **offering** is here emphasized (7). The priestly role in the trespass offering is made clearer, and the priestly shares of the **burnt offering** and **meat** (meal) **offering** are announced (8-10).

5. *The Law of the Peace Offering* (7:11-38)

Peace offerings were of three varieties: thank offerings (12), votive offerings (16), and freewill offerings (29). The first seems to have been offered for benefits received from God. Ps. 107:22 speaks of such a sacrifice after deliverance from peril. The peace offering is the only offering of which the worshiper is permitted to partake. The **thanksgiving** offering is to be **eaten the same day that it is offered** (15). Allis suggests that this was to encourage a spirit of sharing, "the inviting of friends or neighbors, especially the poor and needy, to share in this joyful occasion (Deut. 12:12)."[25] The perpetual goodness of God to His children should be a continual incentive to joyous sharing. Is there something to be learned from the fact that it is called a **sacrifice of thanksgiving** (12)? Is there, or should there ever be, any true thanksgiving that costs the thankful one nothing? **One out of the whole oblation** (14) means "one cake from each offering" (RSV).

[24]*Ibid.*, pp. 35-36.

[25]*Op. cit.*, p. 141

The sacrifice of his . . . vow (16, votive offering) is promised to God in hopes for His help (Ps. 66:13-14; 116:1-19). The voluntary or freewill offering seems to have been offered out of the consciousness of God's tender mercies and covenant faithfulness, with a resultant sense of obligation. It was with freewill offerings that the Tabernacle was originally built (Exod. 35:5, 21). *The Berkeley Version* suggests more clearly the voluntary character of this offering: "Whoever wants to present his peace offering . . . must bring a portion . . . as a donation" (29).

The character of the peace offering as an act of communion was not obvious in 3:1-17. Here it is made clear. The offering, whether from the herd, a lamb, or a goat, if it was for thanksgiving, was to be accompanied by various **unleavened cakes** and **leavened bread.** These were not meal offerings in that no incense was placed on them, and no portion was burned upon the altar. They accompanied the offering and contributed to showing the character of this offering as an occasion for communion between God, priest, and people. The use of the **leavened bread** (13) reveals the essential difference between this offering and the burnt offering, which was consumed entirely upon the altar, and the other offerings which were identified as most holy.

There are careful instructions about when the offerings could be eaten (15-17), who could eat them (20-21), what could be eaten (24-26), and which portions belonged to whom (31-35). These instructions and the serious penalty for disobedience—bearing one's own **iniquity** (18) or being **cut off from his people** (20)—reveal the seriousness of ritual propriety in Israel. This does not mean that the holiness demanded here was simply ceremonial. The differentiation between moral and ceremonial holiness is not a part of the Levitical legislation. The ceremonial performance was looked upon as a reflection of one's attitude toward the Lord, whose holiness was eminently moral.

The manual of instructions for the priests (6:8—7:38) concludes with a summary paragraph (37-38) reminding Israel that this legislation derived its importance and its authority from **the Lord,** who had redeemed them from Egypt and who had revealed himself to them at **mount Sinai** (38).

Section II *Consecration of the Priests*

Leviticus 8:1—10:20

The opening chapters (1—7) of Leviticus deal with the sacrifice demanded by the Lord in His worship. This section (8—10) gives instructions concerning the agents of mediation, the priests. The entire Levitical system assumes this mediatorial role of the sons of Aaron. In this it foreshadows the NT picture of true worship based upon the mediatorial role of Christ. The importance of correctness in performance of these matters is made evident by the continual emphasis that all is done according to the command of the Lord to Moses (cf. 8:4-5, 9, 13, 17, 21, 29, 34, 36, *et al.*).

Chapter 8 tells of the consecration of the priests, and c. 9 pictures the inauguration of the worship at the Tabernacle. Chapter 10 gives the story of Nadab and Abihu, and underscores the danger of failing to observe the worship of the Lord according to His own demands. The Lord is to be sanctified in those who come near Him, and this is to be done according to His good pleasure.

A. Moses Consecrates Aaron and His Sons, 8:1-36

The stipulations concerning the rites, sacrifices, and ceremonies in the installation of the priests commanded in Exodus 28—29 and 40 were now to be performed by Moses. It should be noted that Aaron and his sons were not selected by Israel. They were chosen by God (cf. Heb. 5:4-5). Nor did they consecrate themselves. Moses, as God's representative, performed this for them. Here is seen the limited character of the Levitical priesthood. The priests were not to control Israel but to minister before the Lord for Israel. The separation of the offices of prophet, priest, and king is affirmed here and was to be maintained until the Messiah should come, who could fill all three roles simultaneously.

1. *The Preparation* (8:1-9)

The gravity of the events recorded here is indicated in every detail. The consecration was to be done publicly in the presence of **all the congregation together** at **the door of the tabernacle of the congregation** (3). Aaron and his sons were never again to be looked upon as ordinary Israelites. They were **washed** (6), for uncleanness in the holy precincts could bring death (Exod. 30: 19-21). They were clothed with special garments. Carelessness or disobedience in dress when serving in the divine presence could be fatal (Exod. 28:35, 43).

A word should be spoken about the **ephod** and the **Urim** and **Thummim** (7-8). The description of the ephod is given in Exod. 39:22-26. It was an upper garment that extended from the shoulders downward to the hips and was tied about the waist. It was of gold, blue, purple, scarlet, and fine twined linen. An object of great value and beauty, it had attached to it a breastplate of similar material into which were worked precious stones. In the breastplate **the Urim and the Thummim** were found.

The Urim and the Thummim were the means by which the priest could declare the will of God (Num. 27:21; Deut. 33:8, 10). Perhaps as plausible an explanation as any as to the character of these is the suggestion that they were two flat pieces; on one side of each was written **Urim** (from *'arar,* "to curse") and on the other side of each was written **Thummim** (from the root *tamam,* "to be perfect"). Thus affirmative, negative, or indecisive answers could be secured. This type of oracular device was extremely common in the ancient world. Perhaps it is most significant that the references to this practice are very limited, cease with Saul, and do not reoccur until the postexilic period, when prophecy had ceased in Israel (Ezra 2:63; Neh. 7:65).

2. *The Anointings* (8:10-13)

The priests and Tabernacle furnishings were anointed with oil. In the OT, the prophet (I Kings 19:16), the king (I Sam. 9:16; 10:1), and the priest were thus anointed. The Hebrew word for "anoint" (*mashach*) is the root from which our word Messiah ("the anointed one") comes. The Messiah was to be anointed not just with oil but with the Holy Spirit (Isa. 11:2; 42:1; Luke 3:22). The anointing here symbolizes the separation of the priests unto God and the enduement with the divine power (*charisma*) necessary for the exercise of their holy ministry. Micklem says: "The priests under the old covenant were anointed with oil, symbolizing the Spirit, and with blood, symbolizing the atoning sacrifice, which were to come. The priests under the new covenant are symbolically anointed with oil and with blood, but not literally, for now the reality has come."[1]

Even the Tabernacle and all that was in it were anointed, indicating their separation unto the Lord and their ceremonial acceptance. Those who handled the vessels (Isa. 52:11) and the Tabernacle were to be holy. The distinction between persons and things was not as great in Israel as among modern men. Both could be holy and unholy.

3. *Three Sacrifices* (8:14-29)

The priests and the Tabernacle were to be atoned for also (15, 34). A **sin offering** (14), a **burnt offering** (18), and **consecration** (22, also ordination) offerings were made for Aaron and his sons. They, like the people whom they were to represent, needed atonement. The blood of **the ram of consecration** (22) was placed upon the tip of the **right ear,** the right **thumb,** and the right large **toe** (23). The priest was to *hear* the word of God, *fill* his hands with the ministry of holy things, and *walk* in holy places. It would seem that to the ancient Israelite no man should or could perform such ministry without the sprinkling of sacrificial blood and complete separation to holy things.

The character of this separation is indicated by the Hebrew word for consecration (*millu'im*), which is from the root *male'*, "to fill." Where our text reads, "Shall he consecrate you" (33), the Hebrew text literally says, "He will fill your hands." In 27, Moses took the **wave offering** (cf. 25-26) and filled the hands of Aaron and his sons, who in turn waved them before the Lord. The "filled hands" seem to symbolize the fact that the life of the priest was to be filled with nothing except holy things. He was not to own property nor support himself. He was to live from the Tabernacle service (31-32), and his life was to be devoted exclusively to the service of God for Israel. Is this not a pictorial way of saying that the priest, like Christ at 12 years of age (Luke 2:49), was to "be about" his "Father's business"?

[1]*Op. cit.*, p. 45.

4. *Consecration of the Priests* (8:30-36)

The separation from the rest of Israel and from normal pursuits to the Tabernacle and to the Lord was sealed by **seven days** (33) in which the priests were forbidden to leave the environs of the Tabernacle. Failure to observe this enforced separation would have brought death. Thus is given the great OT picture of consecration to the service of the Lord.

B. Aaron Assumes the Priestly Office, 9:1-24

This chapter is an OT pattern for worship. It records the first public sacrifices of Israel under the Levitical priesthood. In c. 8, sacrifices were offered in the ordination of Aaron and his sons, but the people only observed; they did not participate. Now the priests began their mediatorial ministry. This was a high day for Israel. **The Lord** himself appeared to crown this occasion (4, 23-24).

To prepare for God's appearance Aaron offered a **sin offering** and a **burnt offering** for both **himself** (7-8) and his sons. Aaron's sin offering was a **calf** (2, 8), and his burnt offering a **ram** (2). This is the only instance (with 3) in the sacrificial legislation where a calf is demanded. Rashi says concerning the calf: "This animal was selected as a sin offering to announce to him that the Holy One, blessed be He, granted him atonement by means of this calf for the incident of the golden calf which he had made."[2]

Traditional Jewish thought has always seen significance in every detail here. Snaith points out that **the ram** was a reminder of Abraham's obedience in binding Isaac (Gen. 22:9).[3] He also cites the significance attached to these offerings by the Jerusalem Targum where **the goat** (15) is seen as a reminder of the goat that Joseph's brethren killed (Gen. 37:31); **the calf** (8), of the golden calf (Exod. 32:4); and the **lamb** (3), of Isaac bound like a lamb for sacrifice (Gen. 22:7). The very eagerness to see significance in every detail indicates how important for ancient

[2]*Pentateuch with Targum Onkelos, Haphtaroth and Rashi's Commentary,* trans. M. Rosenbaum and A. M. Silbermann, *Leviticus* (New York: Hebrew Publishing Company, n.d.), p. 35.

[3]*Leviticus and Numbers* ("The Century Bible"; Camden, N.J.: Thomas Nelson and Sons, Ltd., 1967), p. 71.

Israel these events were. **According to the manner** (16) means "in the regular way" (Moffatt) or "according to directions" (Berk.).

The presentation by Aaron of the sin offering and the burnt offering for himself and for his sons reveals the Old Testament's self-understanding of the limitations in its own sacrificial system. No man, not even the high priest, Aaron, was prepared to serve God or to worship God until atonement had been made for him. The writer of the Hebrews (7:27) takes this as proof of the superiority of the new covenant and of Christ, the true High Priest.

The offerings of Aaron for the people formed a pattern for Israel's worship of the Lord. He here offered the **sin offering,** the **burnt offering** (3), the **peace offerings,** and the **meat** (meal) **offering** (4). The omission of the trespass offering confirms the fact that this offering was primarily for occasions where damage had been done and reparation was being made.

The order of the sacrifices reveals the Levitical understanding of the proper approach to God in worship. Keil says:

> The sin-offering always went first, because it served to remove the estrangement of man from the holy God arising from sin, by means of the expiation of the sinner, and to clear away the hindrances to his approach to God. Then followed the burnt-offering, as an expression of the complete surrender of the person expiated to the Lord; and lastly the peace offering, on the one hand as the utterance of thanksgiving for mercy received, and prayer for its further continuance, and on the other hand, as a seal of covenant fellowship with the Lord in the sacrificial meal.[4]

The appropriate conclusion for such worship is the presence of the living God manifest in His **glory** to **the people** (23). The word **glory** is a peculiarly biblical term. The root idea in the Hebrew (*kabed*) is "to be heavy, weighty." The noun form is used in the ancient world of the outward appearance of splendor accompanying a great personage. Brockington says that in the Scripture it refers to "that which men can apprehend, originally by sight, of the presence of God on earth."[5] Note the use of the term in Ezekiel 1. The word speaks of the experience of Israel

[4]*Op. cit.,* pp. 345-46.

[5]"Presence," *A Theological Word Book of the Bible,* ed. Alan Richardson (New York: The Macmillan Company, 1951), pp. 172-76.

at Sinai, of Solomon and the people when the Shekinah filled the house of God, of Isaiah in the Temple, of the shepherds outside Bethlehem, and of the disciples on the Mount of Transfiguration.

The name of the OT sanctuary, **the tabernacle of the congregation** (5), in the Hebrew is called "the tent of appointment." It is where God keeps His appointment with sinful man to meet Him when man has met the divine conditions. God does not fail to keep this appointment. The divine **fire** came and climaxed this day of worship and **consumed** the **burnt offering** upon the altar (24). God communed with His covenant people, Israel.

With the end of this chapter the role of Moses as mediator begins to change. Here it is he who leads Aaron into the Tabernacle. The subordination of the Aaronic priesthood is clearly demonstrated. At this point, however, Moses transmitted all priestly functions to Aaron and his sons.

Aaron and Moses returned from within **the tabernacle** and lifted their hands in blessing over **the people** (23) as **the glory of the Lord appeared unto all the people.** The blessing may have been that found in Num. 6:24-26. In His presence, the people **shouted, and fell on their faces** (24).

C. A Case of Sacrilege, 10:1-20

1. *Nadab and Abihu* (10:1-7)

In c. 9 the proper way to approach the Lord and the gracious consequences of that proper approach are pictured. In c. 10 the scene changes to one of tragedy. Israel sees the inevitable consequences of presumptuous drawing near to the Lord. The joy and awe at the appearance of God's glory in c. 9 are now replaced by the terror that comes when God moves in judgment against sin.

The nature of the sin of **Nadab and Abihu** (1) is not recorded. The commentators have suggested that the incense was not made according to Moses' instructions (Exod. 30:34-38), that fire other than that from the altar was used (Lev. 16:12), that the offering was at the wrong time (Exod. 30:7-8), that the wrong censers (their own) were used, that Nadab and Abihu assumed a role to be retained exclusively for the high priest, or that they were under the influence of alcohol (cf. 8-11). It is impossible to speak with certainty here. The main thing is that the two priests performed priestly functions in a manner contrary to that commanded by the Lord. Moses makes it clear that the Lord must **be sanctified** (3) in them that draw near to Him, in order that He may be **glorified** before **all the people.** This is an illustration that obedience was far more important in the OT than sacrifice (I Sam. 15:22).

The people **of Israel** were permitted to mourn this great tragedy (6), but Aaron and his two remaining sons were forbidden to show the normal marks of grief by uncovering their **heads** and loosing their hair or by tearing their **clothes.** They must not give the appearance before Israel of questioning or lamenting the judgment of God. Moses reminded them that **the anointing oil** (7) was upon them. The service of God cannot defer to personal matters. **The burning** (6) would be "the flame which the Lord has kindled" (Berk.; cf. v. 2).

2. *Strong Drink Forbidden* (10:8-11)

The seriousness of the role of a priest is indicated in the proscription of wine for the priest before his service in the Tabernacle. The priest was to distinguish for Israel **between holy and unholy, and between unclean and clean** (10). This Nadab and Abihu had failed to do and apparently with presumption. The seriousness of such failure is impressed here upon Israel. There is a proper way to approach God (c. 9). That approach brings blessing. Man dares not come to God on his own terms and in his own way if he expects to find acceptance. Attempts to do this bring destruction. Cf. the story of Ananias and Sapphira (Acts 5:1-11).

The proscription of alcohol for the priests when in divine service is applicable to the Christian today. The Christian is in perpetual need of the ability to think clearly in terms of the holy and the unholy. It is now statistically certain that a high percentage of automobile accidents involving fatalities are the result of impairment of human judgment due to alcohol. If the whole story of the damage done both spiritually and physically by this evil could be told, it would make us see the divine wisdom in such a command.

3. *Instructions to the Priests* (10:12-20)

Moses now spoke to **Aaron** about the portions of the **offering** that were to belong to the priests for their own consumption (12). The meal offering, the **breast** (called the **wave** offering), and the **shoulder** (which was called the **heave** offering, 14) were to be eaten by the priests and their families. The sin offering of the people (not that offered by the priests for themselves) was to be eaten by the priest in **the holy place** (12-13). It was given to the priest by God that he might **bear the iniquity of the congregation** (17).

Aaron, due to the sad events of **this day** (19), had felt unworthy to eat the offering and had burned it upon the altar. Moses rebuked him for his failure (16-18) but **was content** (20) when Aaron explained his motive. As c. 9 tells of a gloriously instructive day, c. 10 records a tragic one.

Section III *Laws Concerning Uncleanness*

Leviticus 11:1—15:33

Israel was to be a holy people. This was because they were in covenant with the Lord, the Holy One. That covenant demanded that their total life be brought into conformity with God's demands. Those demands as far as worship was concerned were spelled out in Leviticus 1—7. The establishment of the priesthood and the beginning of their ministry is given in the second section (8—10). The priests were to teach the difference between the holy and the unholy, the clean and the unclean (10:10). Now, in the third section of the book, what this covenant meant in terms of daily living is revealed (cc. 11—15). That revelation is in terms of what is clean and what is not. Matters of diet, contact with carcasses of animals, the uncleanness of persons, garments, furniture, and houses is dealt with. The purpose of all of this is clearly stated: that Israel should not defile itself (11:44).

A. Uncleanness from Animals, 11:1-47

The key words in this section are **clean, unclean, abomination, defile, sanctify,** and **holy.** A quick glance through c. 11 to count the occurrences of these words will underscore the purpose of this section; it was given in order to make a difference between the clean and the unclean. In cc. 11—15 the word "unclean" alone occurs some 100 times.

The differentiation made in these chapters seems strange to the modern man who reads and knows little of the ancient world. Perhaps the most important thing is not the specifications of what is clean and unclean but the underlying motivation that demanded the drawing of such a line. The truth here is that God is concerned with the total life of His people, that nothing is beyond His concern. However, according to the NT understanding of God's requirements it is obvious that many items mentioned have no moral or ethical significance.

Gen. 7:2 makes it clear that this custom of differentiating the clean and the unclean is much older than Moses. The study of other ancient peoples reveals a similar system. The old proverb, "The same thing done by two different people is not the same thing," may be applicable here. Eichrodt points out that these restrictions, so unusual to us, may have had far more religious, and thus ultimately more moral, significance than one first thinks. He suggests that through these laws everything which had to do with alien gods or their worship was condemned as unclean. Animals such as the pig figured in Canaanite sacrificial rites. Also mice, serpents, and hares—which were regarded as possessing special magical power—could thus be precluded.[1]

The processes of the sexual life and the practices connected with the dead were looked upon as having magical and spiritual significance. The identification of Canaanite gods and goddesses with generation and birth and of the Egyptian gods with the cult of the dead may help explain legal demands in things relating to these functions. The drinking of blood as a part of the worship of certain animals or as a means of inducing ecstatic prophecy or as a part of orgiastic rites in idolatrous contexts may bear upon the laws relating to blood. Diseases that forced the separation of men from their social group and thus cut off the Israelite from the community of the Lord were looked upon as defiling. This led Eichrodt to say that such ritual purity could easily be a symbol, an outward expression, of spiritual wholeness or moral perfection.[2] Certainly it can be said that the modern Church has not demonstrated sufficient ability to discriminate between the holy and the unholy and to commit itself with single mind to the former.

B. Uncleanness from Childbirth, 12:1-8

This chapter has traditionally been a difficult one for the commentators. The problem is to explain why childbirth should be associated with uncleanness. Fruitfulness was obedience to divine command according to Gen. 1:28. Children were looked upon as good gifts from God (Gen. 33:5) and were to be prized highly (Psalms 127—128). The woman who was fruitful was con-

[1]*Theology of the Old Testament*, trans. J. A. Baker ("The Old Testament Library"; Philadelphia: The Westminster Press, 1961), pp. 134-35. A recent medical explanation of many of these requirements is given by S. I. McMillen, M.D., *None of These Diseases* (Westwood, N.J.: Fleming H. Revell Co., 1963).

[2]*Op. cit.*, p. 137.

sidered blessed, while the woman who had no children was looked upon as under a curse.

Some scholars have seen here a latent dualism which felt that human flesh was associated with evil. Others have thought that uncleanness in childbirth was the result of the fall of man and is a witness to the fact that man is born to sin and lostness unless he finds God.

The key to an understanding here may lie in the association of childbirth with the mystery of sex, of life and with the emissions accompanying parturition. This discussion is in the same section of Leviticus as c. 15, which deals with the uncleanness attendant upon various emissions. Perhaps this treatment has a close association, particularly with 15:19-27. It must be remembered that there was infinitely more mystery in life for ancient man than for the modern mind. Micklem has paraphrased vv. 2-4: "When a woman has borne a son, proper feeling requires that she remain in seclusion for a week; then the child is to be circumcised; even then she is to stay at home for a month, and her first journey abroad is to be to church."[3] In a society like ours where much of the danger of childbirth has been removed by modern medicine and the mystery removed by biological knowledge, who is to say that some customs are not needed to restore the element of gracious mystery and sacredness to such events?

The close identification of some Canaanite deities with generation and birth may have contributed to the intensification of the Levitical legislation regarding uncleanness in connection with birth processes. The association of birth with magical and demonic powers among Israel's neighbors could likewise have been a factor. It should be said, though, that impurity in the Levitical texts is never a demonic power in itself. As Kaufmann has pointed out, impurity is nothing more than a condition and in contrast to pagan conceptions is not in itself a source of danger since it has no divine or demonic roots.[4] Thus, a passage as strange to modern ears as this one was from an ancient Near Eastern point of view quite understandable. The danger was that of bringing the impure into contact with holiness. Destructive power lay in the source of holiness. Thus some act was appropriate to restore

[3]*Op. cit.*, p. 60.

[4]*The Religion of Israel*, trans. Moshe Greenberg (Chicago: The University of Chicago Press, 1960), pp. 103 f.

the unclean one to redemptive fellowship with the covenant community and the covenant God. In this case it permitted the mother to return to participation in covenant fellowship and worship.

If the child was a male, he was to be circumcised the eighth day. Jesus' mother followed carefully this pattern (Luke 2:21). It was the sign of participation in the covenant that was given to Abraham. Critical scholars have said that circumcision became the symbol of initiation into Israel only during and after the Exile.[5] Genesis 17; Exod. 4:25; and this passage would indicate otherwise. To appreciate the significance of circumcision in the old covenant one should note the comparison with baptism under the new covenant as described by Paul in Col. 2:10-15.

C. Uncleanness from Leprosy, 13:1—14:57

The matter under discussion here is called in the Hebrew *tsara'at*. The LXX translated this term *lepra*. The result is that a collection of things here is subsumed under the English word derived from the LXX term, our word **leprosy.** This includes plagues that appear in the skin of human flesh, in garments that men wear, or in houses in which they live. The concern of the section has to do with the question of cleanness and uncleanness and thus limits the information to this aspect.

The term commonly used here is **plague** (13:2; lit., "stroke"). The uncleanness is serious enough that the person contaminated must be excluded from the camp (13:45-46). If it is in a garment, either the whole garment or the infected part must be burned (13:52, 57). If it is in a house, the stones contaminated must be taken out of the house to an unclean place outside the city (14:40). If the contamination is not arrested, the house must be broken down and the stones, timbers, and mortar carried away (14:45).

No mention is made of treatment of the diseased person. Some have drawn from this the deduction that the disease was incurable. The concern of this chapter, though, is primarily to identify the disease and make provision for dealing with the uncleanness involved. The reference to **cleansing** (14:2) seems clearly to indicate that it was curable. Waterson feels that **leprosy**

[5]Helmer Ringgren, *Israelite Religion*, trans. David E. Green (Philadelphia: Fortress Press, 1966), p. 203.

here may involve a variety of infectious conditions including true leprosy.[6]

1. *The Diagnosis* (13:1-59)

It was the duty of the priest to determine the presence of leprosy and instruct concerning the handling of uncleanness attending it. In this section information is given so that the priest can identify leprosy in the human body (1-46), in a garment (47-59), and in a house (14:33-48). It would seem that the leprosy in the garment was some kind of mildew or fungus. The leprosy in the house was probably a form of dry rot in the timbers or a contaminating lichen in the stone.

a. Leprosy in the body (13:1-44). Six different cases are dealt with here: **a scab** (2-8), **a spot** after **a boil** (18-23), after a **burning** (24-28), a plague in **the hair** or **beard** (29-37), **spots** in **the skin** (38-39), a sore in a man's **bald head** (42-44).

If the priest is able to diagnose the case immediately as **leprosy,** the person shall immediately be pronounced **unclean** (3). If the priest is uncertain, he shall **shut** the man **up** for **seven days** (4). If the plague has not **spread** after seven days, he shall be shut up for **seven days more** (5). If the disease has not **spread** then, **the priest shall pronounce him clean.** The man **shall wash his clothes, and be clean** (6). **If the scab spreads . . . the priest shall pronounce him** leprous (7-8). If he has **quick raw flesh . . . the priest shall pronounce him** leprous (10-11). **If the raw flesh turn . . . white,** or if the man becomes **white** all over, he shall be pronounced clean (16-17). In the case of **the burning,** if it has not **spread** after seven days, he shall be considered **clean** (28). A **scall** (30-37) refers to a spot or scabby disease of the scalp. Natural baldness was not a sign of uncleanness (40-41).

b. The isolation of leprosy (13:45-46). The person with leprosy was to separate himself from society. **His clothes** were to be torn, his hair let go loose (cf. "Let the hair of his head hang loose," RSV), and **his upper lip** was to be covered (45). These were signs of mourning (10:6). Banished from the fellowship of his people, he was to warn all who approached of his uncleanness. He was not only socially "dead" but the bearer of a con-

[6]Cf. "Leprosy," *Dictionary of Christ and the Gospels,* by E. W. Masterman. For a discussion of the diseases of the Bible see the article by A. P. Waterson in *The New Bible Dictionary,* pp. 313 ff.

tagion that would bring the same "death" to those who were yet socially "alive." No ritual is given here for cleansing the leper, but provision is made to pronounce him clean if he is free of the disease. The fact that Jesus let a leper touch Him is an indication of His own estimate of himself. He transcended the laws of ceremonial uncleanness that He urged others to observe. Also the cleansing of lepers is indicative of the radical ministry of Jesus' healings (Matt. 11:5).

c. *Leprosy in garments* (13:47-59). This was probably a fungus which appeared in clothes. These could be **linen, woollen,** or leather (47-48). If the garment had **greenish or reddish** spots in it (49), the priest was to remove the garment from use for seven days (50). **If the plague** had **spread** (51), it was leprous. The garment must be burned. **Fretting leprosy** (52) is "malignant leprosy" (RSV), and therefore contagious. If **the plague** had **not spread,** the garment was to be washed and put aside for **seven days more.** If it had **not changed . . . colour** then, the infected areas were to be burned. If the plague had changed color, the spots were to be torn from the garment. If the plague had spread, the garment was burned (53-57). If when the garment had been washed the plague disappeared, the garment was washed again and pronounced **clean** (58).

2. *The Law of Cleansing* (14:1-57)

This section is divided into two portions. The first deals with the regular law of cleansing for the leper himself. The second concerns the poor man who is unable to meet the usual requirements for cleansing. A third section prescribes the ritual for the cleansing of a house, following instructions for diagnosing "leprosy" in houses.

a. *The regular ritual for cleansing* (14:1-20). The procedure here given in detail reminds one of the consecration of the priest (cc. 7—9) and the ritual for the Day of Atonement (c. 16). Just as there had been a day when the leper was pronounced unclean, now there is a ritual and time for the restoration of the leper to the community. This ritual was not looked upon as a means of cleansing but of attesting cleanness.

The person who had the disease was **brought** to **the priest,** who met him outside **the camp** (2-3). The leper could not enter the camp until pronounced clean. If the priest found the disease healed, the unclean person was to take **two birds,** some **cedar wood, scarlet, and hyssop** (4). **One of the birds** was to **be killed** over **an earthen vessel** of **running** (fresh) **water** (5). **The living bird** (6), the **cedar wood,** the **scarlet, and the hyssop** were to be dipped **in the blood of the bird that was killed over the running water.** With these the priest was to **sprinkle** the unclean man **seven times** (7). Then the priest was to pronounce the man **clean** and release **the living bird . . . into the open field.** The man formerly unclean was to **wash his clothes,** shave **his hair,** bathe himself, and remain outside **his tent for seven days** (8). **On the seventh day** (9) he was to **shave** again **all** of **his hair . . . wash his clothes,** carefully bathe his body, and be restored to his family and society.

On **the eighth day** (10) sacrifices were to be made for the one formerly unclean. These included the full gamut of Levitical sacrifices: a guilt offering, a sin offering, a burnt offering, and a meal offering. **Three tenth deals** (10) is "six quarts" (Berk.); **one log** is "one pint" (Berk.). **Some of the blood** (14) from the guilt offering was to be taken by **the priest** and placed **upon the tip of the right ear,** the **thumb of** the **right hand,** and the large **toe of** the **right foot** of the one being pronounced clean. Note the similarity of ritual for restoring the leper to that used for the consecration of the priest (8:23-24). Then the priest was to take **oil** and **sprinkle** it before the Lord **seven times** (16), place some of the **oil** upon the **ear,** the **thumb,** and the **toe** as he had done with blood (17), and **pour** the remainder of the oil over **the head** of the one now being pronounced clean (18).

The purpose of such an involved ceremony was to restore a man to his place among the covenant people of God. Having been debarred from the community and its worship, he was now being introduced again into that kingdom of priests that Israel was supposed to be. The seriousness of separation from the community is seen in the detail with which this ritual of restoration is given.

It has been common to compare leprosy to sin and to see in this passage a parable. Leprosy is insidious (being scarcely noticed at first), progressive, pervasive, benumbing, loathsome, and isolating.[7] The way back into the fellowship demanded atone-

[7]Erdman, *op. cit.*, p. 68.

ment and consecration. Man was not made for such separation, and it is the Church's business to open the way back for the person who has been excluded.

b. The ritual for the poor (14:21-32). Adjustments here as elsewhere were to be made for the **poor** (21). **Two turtledoves** or **young pigeons** (22) replaced the **burnt offering** and the **sin offering;** a **tenth** of an ephah of **flour** (21; "three quarts," Berk.; cf. comment on v. 10) served for the meal offering. The **trespass offering** (24) was not reduced. Evidently this was the condition for restoration to fellowship for even the poorest. Some conditions must be met by all.

c. Leprosy in houses (14:33-57). It is significant that this guidance is given in prospect of the future settlement in Canaan. The passage bears witness to the promise given to Abraham (Gen. 12:7; 13:17; *et al.*). **The plague** (34) is probably a growth of fungus or lichen. Its source is from God (34*b*). The origin of leprosy is not in some baleful spirit. The OT takes little account of secondary causes and attributes none of these things to any demonic rival of the Lord.

If a man thinks there may be leprosy **in the house** (35), he must call **the priest.** If there is a question, all items must be removed immediately from **the house** (36), lest they become **unclean** and have to be destroyed. **Hollow strakes** (37, streaks), **greenish or reddish** in color, are the telltale marks. If they are present, the house must be **shut up** for **seven days** (38). If the plague spreads, the stones shall be removed to **an unclean place without the city** (40). **The house** is to be **scraped** (41) and the scrapings carried away. The house was then to be rebuilt. If **the plague** returned (43), the building was to be pronounced **unclean** (44), destroyed, and removed (45). Anyone entering the house **shall be unclean** (46) until evening. For **fretting leprosy** (44) see comment on 13:51.

The ritual for cleansing demanded **two birds,** some **cedar wood, scarlet, and hyssop** (49). The **cedar,** the **hyssop,** the **scarlet,** and a **living bird** were to be dipped **in the blood** of the other bird and in **running water** (51). With these **the house** was to be sprinkled seven times. **The living bird** was then released and let fly away into the **open** country. In this manner **atonement** was made **for the house** (53). The chapter concludes with a brief summary (54-57).

D. Uncleanness from Issues, 15:1-33

This chapter deals with issues from the genital organs and the attendant uncleanness. The word **flesh** (2) is used euphemistically for the primary sex organs. Four categories are dealt with: abnormal emissions (pathological) from men (2-15); normal sexual discharges from men (16-18); normal menstrual flow in women (19-24); and abnormal blood issues in women (25-30).

1. *Abnormal Emissions in Men* (15:1-15)

All discharges from the primary sex organs brought ceremonial **uncleanness** (3). Bodily emissions resulted in such uncleanness even after the active discharge ceased. This involved not only the person with the **issue** but also anyone who touched him or touched anything with which he had had intimate contact. The hygienic value of such legislation is obvious. It is difficult, though, to believe that such legislation had only hygienic intent. However, the sick seemed to have no place in the Tabernacle or in the worshipping community. Again we have an illustration of the fact that it was very difficult to successfully divide between the physical and the spiritual, between the religious and the purely secular in the OT world. Hygienic uncleanness made a man unacceptable for close communion with either God or man. Such externals were felt to have internal significance.

Purification here involves washing (10) for anyone or anything contaminated by the uncleanness, except for earthen vessels, which were to **be broken** (12). The person with the issue was to count **seven days** (13) from the cessation of the issue and then to wash himself and **his clothes.** Thus cleansed, he was to offer a sin offering and a burnt offering of **two turtledoves, or two young pigeons** (14) for **atonement** (15). It is clear that the reconciliation here is not moral but a social restoration to the religious community.

2. *Normal Sexual Emissions* (15:16-18)

The uncleanness from these emissions is similar to that in the preceding case except that no sacrifice is required for cleansing. Time (waiting until the evening) and washing of body and clothing remove the uncleanness. It must not be suggested that uncleanness here means something that God has forbidden. The only defilement forbidden to a lay Israelite was intercourse with a menstruous woman. The point here is to keep the legitimate but "unclean" separated from the "holy." To defile the holy was the danger to be avoided (note the reference to defiling the Tabernacle in 31).

3. *Normal Menstrual Issues* (15:19-24)

The uncleanness here is similar to that in the immediately preceding section. Time (here it is **seven days** instead of until evening), bathing, and laundering one's clothing removes the uncleanness. No sacrifices are necessary, since this is a normal part of a woman's life. **Her flowers** (24) means "her menstruation" (Berk.).

4. *Abnormal Menstrual Issues* (15:25-33)

This problem is dealt with in the same way basically as that in the opening paragraph of the chapter. **Seven days** (28) after the cessation of the issue the woman is to wash herself and her clothes (the text implies this though it does not state it). **On the eighth day** (29) she is to make her offerings. Two **turtles** (29) is better "two turtle doves."

A comparison of this chapter with comparable literature from Israel's pagan neighbors reveals the height to which Israel's faith rose in contrast to theirs. The concepts of cleanness and uncleanness are common to both Israel and her neighbors. The use of washings and sacrifices for purification were also common. In non-biblical literature this uncleanness is connected with demons and evil powers. Purificatory rites thus became a matter of conflict with evil forces. Incantations and magical spells became necessary. Not a trace of such conflict is implied in the Bible. The aura of fearfulness of the spirits producing uncleanness is lacking. Only the Lord is to be feared. And humble obedience to His laws always brings a man or woman back to where approach to God and a resumption of his place within the religious community is possible.

This chapter makes the story of Christ's healing of the woman with the issue of blood (Mark 5:25-34) the more remarkable. That she should touch Him tells of her faith that she could not defile Him. That He felt no need of washings reveals that, although He was born under the law (Gal. 4:4), He transcended the claims of the law. He was not bound by it. How the Pharisees must have marvelled and been angered that He felt no sense of defilement from her touch! A greater than Moses had come!

Section IV *The Day of Atonement*

Leviticus 16:1-34

This chapter is the high point of the Book of Leviticus. Here atonement for Israel is provided. Elsewhere atonement for individual persons or things had been made possible. Here it is atonement for the priests, the holy place itself, the tent of meeting, the altar, and all Israel. It was atonement for all uncleannesses, iniquities, transgressions, and sins. Here is the point at which the Lord and His people, through their high priest, come into the closest relationship possible under the old covenant.

The seriousness of this occasion is immediately intimated by reference to the death of **the two sons of Aaron, when they offered before the Lord, and died** (1). The ritual of this chapter was to make possible the approach of the high priest into the presence of the Lord without tragedy. Moses is told to remind **Aaron** that even the high priest could not approach God directly and at will. The religious organization of Israel was like that of a pyramid. From 12 tribes only one, the tribe of Levi, was selected that could serve in the priestly position. From that family, only one man could go into the presence of God in the holy of holies, the inner shrine of the Tabernacle. This man, the high priest, could do that only on one day in the year, the Day of Atonement. On that day he could go before God only under the most carefully prescribed circumstances. The Lord is holy and is not to be approached without the utmost care that holiness be not offended. How could the otherness of God—His holiness—and the sinfulness of man be more dramatically demonstrated than in the ritual of this day with its historic and national context?

Fortunately the commentator is not left to his own imagination and insight as to the interpretation of the figures and symbols given here. In the Epistle to the Hebrews, especially in c. 9, an interpretation of the atoning, mediatorial work of Christ is given in the language of this chapter. The New Testament writer felt that the Day of Atonement was a day that prefigured the redemptive work of our great High Priest, Jesus. The values of the Levitical system and its inadequacies are peculiarly and poignantly felt in a study of this chapter from Hebrews.

A. Aaron's Preparation, 16:1-19

Moses was commanded to remind Aaron that he could come into God's presence only according to God's command and in the prescribed way. The penalty for carelessness here was death (2, 13). God would meet Aaron on this day at the **mercy seat** (2). If he were not properly prepared, he would die. Aaron was told that the must **be attired** correctly (4), and must present a **sin offering** for **himself** and for **his house** (3, 6, 11). He must offer **incense** that would form a **cloud** to **cover the mercy seat** (13).[1] In addition he must sprinkle with blood **the mercy seat** (14) and the area **before the mercy seat** in atonement for himself and for his family. Aaron was likewise to **make . . . atonement for the holy place** (16) by sprinkling the blood of **the sin offering** of **the people** (15). In similar fashion **atonement** must be made for **the altar** (18) and **the tabernacle** (20). When man approaches God, even his religious acts need atonement for acceptance with God. *The Berkeley Version* translates v. 16, "Thus he shall make the atonement for the holy place because of the uncleanness of the Israelites, all their sinful transgressions. He shall do the same for the Dwelling, which stays with them in the midst of their impurities."

B. The Scapegoat, 16:20-34

Two goats figured prominently in the ritual of this day (5, 7-10, 15, 20-22). These were to serve for a sin offering to the Lord. Aaron was commanded to "cast lots" (8) over the two goats to select one "for the Lord" and the other to be a "scapegoat." The one selected for the Lord was to be slain as a sin offering and its blood used in the atonement for the holy place, the altar, and the sanctuary. The second goat was kept alive. Aaron was commanded to **lay both his hands upon the head of the live goat, and confess over him all the iniquities . . . transgressions,** and **sins** of Israel, **putting them upon the head of the goat** (21). **The goat** was then to be led into **the wilderness** (22), bearing away **the iniquities** of Israel. **Reconciling** (20) means

[1]"The incense altar, standing outside the veil, belonged to the Holy of Holies [see Chart *A*], but could not stand inside it because incense was offered on it daily. On the Atonement Day the high priest took the burning incense in his censer behind the veil into the Holy of Holies" (Berk., fn., *ad loc.*).

"atoning" (RSV). A **fit man** (21) is better "a man at hand" (Berk.) or "in readiness" (RSV).

The term "scapegoat" (8) was first used by Tyndale and has since been a part of both religious and common speech. It is really not an adequate translation for the Hebrew term (*'ez'azel*), and has evoked voluminous notes in the commentaries. In the apochryphal Book of Enoch 8:1; 9:6, *Azazel* is a demon who teaches men to make weapons of war, ornaments, and cosmetics. Ultimately *Azazel* came to be identified in Jewish thought with the devil. Noth says that people usually have seen in this term a reference to a "desert demon" who is to be satisfied with a he-goat sent to appease him.[2] If this explanation is accepted, the purpose of the ritual would be to ward off the demon and the dangers that he presented. Here is an example of the fact that if two interpretations are possible, and one tends to drag the OT to the level of Israel's pagan neighbors, that interpretation seems to be preferred by some critical scholars.

It is not necessary to associate this scapegoat ritual with the worship of satyrs or demons of the rocky wilderness places. Actually the Hebrew word *Azazel* is made up of two elements: *'ez,* which means "goat"; and *'azel,* which could easily be from the good Semitic root "to go away." Thus, as Snaith admits, the meaning could be simply, "The goat has gone away."[3]

The passage illustrates the use of a figure for forgiveness that is common in the OT, that of sin being borne away by another than the sinner. The word which is used for **bear** (22) is used frequently in the OT in the sense of "forgive" (Ps. 32:1; Isa. 53:4, 12; *et al.*). Thus the OT understands sin as something which has to be borne away, and forgiveness means to have another bear one's sins for him. This passage is consistent with many others in the OT. The groundwork is being laid in this and other passages for a correct understanding of the atoning work of Christ. Undoubtedly this is part of the background for a true understanding of the words of John the Baptist about Jesus, "Behold the Lamb of God, which taketh away the sin of the world" (John 1:29).

After the goat was thus sent away, Aaron was to change his **garments** (23), **wash his flesh** (24), and make a **burnt offering** for himself and for **the people.** The man who led the goat away

[2]*Op. cit.*, p. 125.

[3]*Op. cit.*, p. 113.

was also to **wash his clothes, and bathe** before returning to **the camp** (26). The one who carried the portions of **the sin offering** (27) outside **the camp** for burning was likewise to **wash his clothes, and bathe** (28) before entering **the camp** again.

The solemnity of this ritual was underscored by the fact that it was considered **a sabbath of rest** (31) and a day of fasting. (This is the meaning of the expression, **Ye shall afflict your souls** (29, 31). This fast is referred to in Acts 27:9 and was the most stringent of all fasts in Israel. The ceremony of this day was to be **a statute for ever** (31) for Israel.

C. Some Conclusions

It is not difficult to draw some clear inferences from this chapter about the OT understanding of sin and its forgiveness. One is the equality of need among all men under the old covenant. Here Aaron must make atonement for himself first, then for the very Tabernacle, the altar, and the holy place, as well as for Israel. All were in equal need of atonement. Nothing in Israel was ready of itself for fellowship with or use by God. The cover of atonement was needed by all.

Further, it is obvious that no man can adequately atone for his own sins. He needs the help of another. Here it was a goat that carried away the transgressions. Israel was being taught that it needed Another to bear its sins. This is made equally plain in Isaiah 53.

Finally, the inadequacy of the Levitical system is implied. The commands for this Day of Atonement were a perpetual statute for Israel. The day must be repeated annually. Final provision for forgiveness of sin is not envisioned in this system. It cries out for a better covenant, a great Priest, and a more excellent Sin Bearer. Leviticus is not enough. It needs the Epistle to the Hebrews to find its fulfillment. But it is certain that no one will truly understand or appreciate the glory of that NT letter who has not also understood the drama presented here.

Section V *Holiness in Daily Living*

Leviticus 17:1—20:27

A. Killing Domestic Animals, 17:1-16

Most critical scholars see in this section the beginning of what has come to be called the Holiness Code (cc. 17—26). It is looked upon as a separate document that was incorporated into the so-called "priestly material" said to make up the earlier part of Leviticus. Some, however, have felt that c. 17 stands in closest relationship with what has gone before and is a logical consequent. Allis has said:

> Since the day of atonement exhibits in a superlative degree the significance of sacrifice in the life of the covenant people, and points out the unique sacredness of the blood in that on this one day the sacrificial blood is brought into the holiest place and sprinkled on the ark of the covenant itself, to obtain the remission of all the sins of all the people, it is appropriate that in this next chapter the two aspects of sacrifice which specially concern all the people should be particularly emphasized.[1]

It is legitimate to ask here whether ancient documents should be forced to fit modern canons of logical consistency. The content of this and the subsequent chapters is material that was important to the priest for his service in the sanctuary and for his instruction of the people.

1. *Slaughter of Animals as Sacrifice* (17:1-9)

In the ancient world all slaughter of animals was considered sacrifice. In Hebrew the common word for sacrifice (*zabach*) originally meant "to slaughter." Some feel that in the ancient Near East the use of domestic animals for food was rare and that all slaughter was connected with sacrifice. This may well have been so. It must be remembered that the ancient world did not differentiate the sacred and the secular to the extent that Western man has come to do. Life itself was mysterious. Thus the slaughter of any animals may have had religious overtones. In this case the Hebrew is commanded to bring an **ox**, a **lamb**, or a **goat** (3) to **the tabernacle** (4) before killing it. Here they would be slaughtered as **peace offerings** (5) before **the Lord. The priest**

[1]*Op. cit.*, pp. 150-51.

officiating took an allotted portion of the animal (6) and returned the remainder to the one offering it. Thus the food was received by the offerer but not before he had ritually acknowledged that his daily bread came from God.

The passage also makes it clear that this practice was directed at a pagan custom common in the world of that day, namely, offering the slaughtered animal to the demons of the countryside. The Hebrew word translated **devils** (7) means "the hairy ones," or "the goats." The ASV translates it "he-goats" and the RSV "satyrs." The non-biblical world of antiquity was thought to be filled with spirits. Often the worship of these was accompanied by the grossest of conduct. Here to sacrifice to these **devils** was to go **a whoring.** The full seriousness of this practice is not known, but the passage is undoubtedly directed at preventing an association that would be detrimental to the religious faith of Israel.

2. *Significance of Blood and Its Proscription* (17:10-16)

The requirements of the preceding section may have had as their intended end the prevention of eating blood. This was not a new thing with the Levitical legislation (cf. Gen. 9:4). Blood was the most religiously significant thing in the life of the Israelites. God said, **I have given it to you upon the altar to make an atonement for your souls: for it is the blood that maketh an atonement for the soul** (11). As the seat of physical life and the most important element in expiation of sin, it was peculiarly the Lord's. To eat blood, then, was to invite excommunication from Israel—to be **cut . . . off from among his people** (10). This rule applied both to **the children of Israel** and **any stranger that sojourneth among you** (12). Even **the blood** of the animal killed in the hunt was to be carefully poured upon the ground and covered **with dust** (13), probably as an indication of the respect in which all blood was to be held. An animal that **died of itself** or was **torn with beasts** (15) was not to be eaten, since there was danger that the blood would have been left in it. Such animals could not be used for food in Israel.

B. Social Regulations, 18:1—20:27

The legislation in this section covers a wide variety of matters. It reveals the extent to which the law was designed to regulate all of human life. For those who stood in covenant relation with the Lord there was no part of life that could be exempted from His dominion. Characteristic of this section is the recurrence of the expression, **I am the Lord,** and the variation, **I am the Lord your God.** These expressions appear 20 times in cc. 18—19. Israel was to be different from other nations (18:3) because the Lord is different. That difference is His holiness. The concluding verses of this section (20:24-26) identify the God of Israel as **the Lord your God, which have separated you from other people** (24). In 20:26 the purpose of the separation is given—**That ye should be mine.** This section reveals something of what it means to be holy in social and religious relations.

This legislation reveals one of the things that makes it without parallel in the ancient world. As Eichrodt says, there is an expressed determination to relate "the whole of life to the one all-ruling will of God." And the appeal to the nature of God as the real sanction removes the law "from the sphere of human arbitrariness and relativism and bases it firmly on the metaphysical."[2] The appeal is not simply ethical; it is religious. An age when the appeal to men to do right has been based largely on utilitarian and humanitarian reasons and an age that has seen those appeals steadily losing their power might turn to these ancient pages for instruction. The basis for determining right and wrong is the Word of God. It has yet to be proven that society can survive where its ethic is without religious sanction.

1. *Unlawful Sex Relationships* (18:1-30)

a. Where does one get his standards? (18:1-5.) This chapter is directed to **the children of Israel** (2). The people are reminded that the **Lord** is their **God** and that they are to be different from the other nations of the earth. They must not take their standards from **Egypt** (3), whence they have come, nor from **Canaan,** where they are going. They are to take their standards from the Lord, who gives them these **statutes** and **judgments** (5). They are told that if they accept the Lord's way they will **live.** Here is seen the striking difference between the believer in God and the nonbeliever. The worldling takes his standards from his context; the believer, from his God.

b. Standards with respect to sex (18:6-23). This section deals with those family relationships where sexual intimacy is

[2]*Op. cit.*, p. 75.

forbidden. Commentators have tried to determine whether these commands have to do with marriage or not. It is obvious that some of the relationships discussed here were not envisioned as within the legitimate marriage bonds. However, it would not be improper to think that this section provided a basis for possible marriage ties. In fact, modern marriage laws are largely based on the limitations found here.

The section begins with the closest relationships, **father** and **mother** (7), moves to the more remote, e.g., a **brother's wife** (16). To **uncover their nakedness** (6) means "to have sexual relations" (Amp. OT). There are two Hebrew words used for "flesh." One means "the inner flesh, full of blood, next the bones," while the other means "the flesh next the skin."[3] The former is the one used throughout this chapter. In v. 6 both are used, "flesh of his flesh" being the literal translation of **near of kin.** So the prohibition here is that of incest. Levitical legislation is rigid in its attempts to protect the sanctity of the marriage bond from the problems resulting from promiscuity. God is concerned about the purity of the intimate relationships that are designed to be practiced within that bond. This standard was sharply at odds with the practice of Israel's neighbors.

Verse 16 has often been cited as being in opposition to levirate marriage (cf. comments on Gen. 38:8). In actuality v. 16 seems to be speaking against sexual familiarity with a brother's wife while he is yet alive.

The meaning of v. 18 is, "While your wife is still living do not take her sister for a rival" (Berk.).

The reference to **Molech** in v. 21 has been understood as referring to a pagan rite of throwing children into a raging fire in sacrifice. There is actually no reference to fire in the Hebrew text here; note that **the fire** is in italics, indicating that it is a translator's addition. Because of the context which is dealing with sexual irregularities, Snaith suggests that what is forbidden is the giving of children to the temple shrines for training as male or female prostitutes.[4] The references in the OT are not clear enough and our knowledge of Israel's neighbors is not extensive

[3]Francis Brown, S. R. Driver, and Charles A. Briggs, *A Hebrew and English Lexicon of the Old Testament* (Oxford: The Clarendon Press, 1952), p. 984b.

[4]*Op. cit.*, p. 125.

enough to know exactly what is involved here other than an illicit use of children, and that probably in sexual matters. Since homosexuality and bestiality were known within the Canaanite religious circles, vv. 21-23 could possibly go together. Practices such as these are what this legislation and Gen. 15:16 envision as the reasons for God's permitting the Canaanites to be dispossessed (cf. vv. 24-25).

c. *A warning for the covenant people* (18:24-30). This chapter closes with a warning to Israel. If Gen. 15:16; 50:24-25 are to be taken seriously, part of Israel's faith was the confidence that God was going to give the land of Canaan to Israel and dispossess the Canaanite. Now God warns the nation that this promise is not automatic nor unconditional. If Israel stoops to the iniquity of the people whom they are to drive out, then Israel too will be **spued out** (28) from **the land.** God is holy and His promises are morally conditioned. The solemn word, **I am the Lord your God** (30), is the sober guarantee of that truth.

2. *Holiness and Some Varied Laws* (19:1-37)

This chapter is obviously intended to be a unit in itself. This is evident from its introductory formula (1; cf. 18:1; 20:1). Its subject is indicated in the command, **Ye shall be holy** (2). What the Levitical legislation understood by holiness in daily living is indicated throughout this chapter. To the modern reader it appears to be a collection of different admonitions covering a score or more of subjects. There seems to be little organization to the list. However, its disconnected nature should not keep us from seeing it as a whole. It is a remarkable collection of sundry concerns that could be compared to Romans 12—13. Perhaps a study of these two passages would indicate the similarities and the differences in the understanding of holy living in daily life from the old covenant point of view and from the new. Some of the most exalted lines in the OT are found here.

Here in 19:1-4 we discover "Holiness, the Key Word of Leviticus." (1) God is the Source of all holiness, 1-2; (2) God is the Standard of holiness, 2; (3) Holiness is separation from evil and separation unto God, 3-4 (G. B. Williamson).

There is a sense in which this chapter is a miniature of the Levitical law. Note what is contained here: respect for parents, and respect for the **sabbaths** (3); abstinence from idolatry (4);

correct sacrifice of **peace offerings** (5-8); concern **for the poor and** the **stranger** by not gleaning thoroughly the fields (9-10); prohibition of stealing, dealing **falsely,** lying (11); swearing **falsely** and profaning God's name (12); prohibition of taking advantage of **the deaf** and **the blind** (14); prohibition of unfair **judgment** (15); talebearing (16); the hating of one's **neighbour** (17); taking vengeance (18); mixing breeds, seeds, or fabrics (19); eating the fruit of a newly bearing tree (23-25); eating **blood** (26); practicing the occult (26*b*, 31); cutting the hair wrongly or cutting the **flesh for the dead** (27-28); prostituting one's **daughter** (29); crooked business transactions (35-36); a demand of respect for the elderly (32); **love** for the **neighbour** and the **stranger** like the love that one has for oneself (18, 33-34). Simply to note the list indicates the humanitarian character of the Levitical law.

To **respect the person** (15) means to "be partial" to **the poor** (RSV). To **honour the person of the mighty** means to "show a preference" for them (Amp. OT). To **stand against the blood** of a **neighbour** (16) was to endanger his life by a false testimony (Amp. OT). The meaning of 17*b* is, "You shall reason with your neighbor, lest you bear sin because of him" (RSV).

The standard demanded here approaches that of the NT when it forbids vengeance, and demands love for neighbor and stranger like that which one has for himself. The mention of **the stranger** (34) makes it immaterial whether **neighbour** means "neighbour Israelite," as Snaith says, or "neighbour anybody."[5] This entire chapter is an extremely practical passage and was undoubtedly used to teach the ancient Hebrew what it really meant to live a holy life.

Most of the chapter needs little comment. Much of it is mandatory in character, stated either in a negative imperative or in straightforward, positive command in the second person. No difference is made between the ceremonial and the ethical requirements. The Lord is the sanction behind both. The concern here is for justice and social righteousness but also for proper religion.

Some items are strange to the modern reader. The prohibition of mixing **seed** and fabric materials (19) illustrates *the principle of separation*. It was called *habdalah* by the Jews, and was to characterize all of life. What God separated, they were to keep

[5]*Op. cit.*, p. 136.

separate. Hybrids seem to have been forbidden. It may be that elements are involved of which the significance has long been lost to us. Deut. 22:9-11 repeats and extends what is found here. The prohibition against eating the fruit of the new **trees** (23) is, as Snaith points out, a sound agricultural principle that would ultimately enable the trees to bear better crops.[6] The firstfruits were to belong to **the Lord** (24). Perhaps the fruit produced in those first three years was not felt to be an acceptable offering for the Lord. The expression **as uncircumcised** (23) is the Hebrew way of saying it is "forbidden to you" (Amp. OT).

The limitations of the old covenant are illustrated in vv. 20-22 in the case of the **bondmaid.** Here we see illustrated one of the great dangers of slavery. The girl involved would be wholly at the disposal of her master. The word **betrothed** (20) seems to be misleading. She evidently had been spoken for but no payment had been made. If the woman had been betrothed, the penalty would have been death for both (cf. Deut. 22:23-24). The woman here was as much at her master's disposal as was Hagar (Gen. 16:1), or Bilhah and Zilpah (Gen. 30:4, 9). The word used is *shiphchah,* not *'amah.* It means a female slave belonging to her mistress. The Levitical legislation apparently did not look upon this act as necessarily a violation of the seventh commandment. **She shall be scourged** (20) is better, "A court inquiry shall be conducted" (Berk.). **In meteyard** (35) would be "in measures of length" (RSV).

This chapter is an excellent example of the fact that the Levitical legislation attempted to bring the totality of a man's life and its relations under the sovereign control of the Lord. The chapter begins with the command to be holy because **the Lord** is Israel's **God** (2). It closes with the command to observe these statutes and ordinances because He is the one who **brought** them **out of the land of Egypt** (36). The claims of the Levitical law are thus really based upon the fact of grace.

3. *Molech, the Occult, Parents, and Aberrations* (20:1-27)

This chapter picks up much of what is contained in c. 18. Here, however, it spells out the penalties in an effort to reveal the extreme seriousness of these sins. It concludes with an exhortation to holiness longer than that at the end of c. 18.

[6]*Ibid.*, p. 133.

a. More about Molech (20:1-5). Not all that is involved in giving children **unto Molech** (3) is known to us (cf. comments on 18:21). Here we are told that the penalty was **death** by stoning. God would also set His **face against that man, and . . . cut him off from among his people** (3). God declared that to give one's **seed** to Molech was **to defile my sanctuary, and to profane my holy name.** It was spiritual adultery.

The determinative passage for most scholars in explaining this practice is II Kings 23:10, where the son or daughter is caused to pass through the fire to Molech. There is evidence in Punic discoveries that the Carthaginians burned children as sacrifices by placing them in the arms of a bronze statue of Kronos, from whence they rolled into the fire to be burned. These references in Leviticus have been interpreted accordingly.[7] It must be remembered, though, that the chronological gap between the Punic material and these references is very wide. As mentioned at 18:21, Snaith suggests that it means the giving of sons and daughters for temple prostitution.

b. Concerning the occult (20:6-8, 27). The biblical prohibition of magic is important for an understanding of how revolutionary monotheism was in its world. Pagan religions often forbade black magic, that is, the magic which brought injury to men. But the Bible makes no differentiation. It will make no concession to any claim that there is supernatural help for man outside of the Lord. To try through the occult to get help was a denial of the sovereignty of the Lord and was thus equivalent to idolatry. Sorcery, witchcraft, and magic are not as serious a problem in our society as in the ancient world. Nevertheless, the Christian should be as careful to keep himself deliberately dependent upon the Lord alone as Israel was commanded to do. Use of the occult (6) or the practice of it (27) here meant death. **Sanctify yourselves** (7) here means to "set yourselves apart" for the purpose of obeying God.

c. Respect for parents (20:9). Equally serious was the sin of cursing one's parents. In Exod. 21:17 the penalty for this sin was death. The clause, **His blood shall be upon him,** meant that the laws of blood revenge did not apply (cf. Ezek. 18:13).

[7]Roland de Vaux, *Ancient Israel: Its Life and Institutions* (New York: McGraw-Hill Book Company, Inc., 1961), pp. 444-45.

d. Sexual aberrations (20:10-21). This paragraph on illegal sexual conduct is like that found in 18:6-20, 22-23, except that here penalties are prescribed. Sex relations were forbidden **with another man's wife** (10), with one's **father's wife** (11, not the son's own mother), his own **daughter in law** (12), a person of the same sex (13), with an animal (15), with a **mother** and her daughter (14), with a **sister** or a half sister (17), with a menstruous women (18), with an aunt (19), an **uncle's** wife (20) or a **brother's wife** (21). All these sins were forbidden on pain of death, of being cut off from one's people, or of being divinely afflicted with childlessness. The reference to dying **childless** may mean the sentence of death for the participants, which would preclude the possibilities of progeny. **Confusion** (12) here means "incest" (RSV).

e. Warning and exhortation (20:22-26). This paragraph is much like 18:24-30. Israel is told that the land will **spue it out** if it does not separate itself from the ways of the Canaanites. The Israelites must be a **holy** people to live in a holy land and walk with a **holy** God.

Section VI *Holiness of the Priest*

Leviticus 21:1—22:33

The key to this section is in 21:6, 8. The priests were to be holy to the Lord because they presented **the offerings (6)** to God. They must protect themselves from the defilement that came from contact with **the dead** (1-2; except in cases involving the closest of kin, like **mother, father, son, daughter, brother,** or unmarried **sister**). The references to cutting the hair, the **beard,** or the **flesh** (5) had to do with mourning for the dead. In 19:27-28 such mourning procedures are forbidden to all Israel.

The **wife** (7) of the priest must also be acceptable. At marriage she must be a virgin. The text stipulates that she cannot be an harlot. This undoubtedly reflects the fact that temple prostitution was common among Israel's neighbors. The **daughter of any priest** (9) was likewise to keep herself pure. Harlotry by a priest's daughter was punishable by death. Not only the priest but also his immediate family were to be holy.

The stipulations for **the high priest** (10) were even more stringent. He was **not** to **uncover his head, nor rend his clothes**—the tokens of mourning that were permitted to the priest. He had to marry **a virgin** (14) from the daughters of Israel—otherwise **his seed** (15) would be profaned. He was the symbol of the highest purity. There was to be nothing in him that would defile **the sanctuary** (12). The expression, **Neither shall he go out of the sanctuary,** probably refers to his leaving for purposes of mourning, not to any permanent residence within the Tabernacle.

The priest was to have no physical **blemish** (17). In this he was to be like the animals that were offered for the major sacrifices. He was to be physically sound and sexually whole (20*d*). A blemish would preclude a son of Aaron from service in the holy place, but it did not deprive him of the other rights that belonged to a priest (22). It simply meant that no man could approach **the veil** or **the altar** (23) who was not physically whole.

The priest was not to touch the **holy things** (22:2) when he was **unclean** (6) for any reason (22:1-9). A list of the ways in which a man could become unclean is included here. The **unclean** priest (and every priest would be unclean at times) must wait until the evening (6) and bathe before he could eat of the holy things (cf. c. 13 and 15:1-12). To be careless in such matters was to bring **sin** (9) upon the priest and to cause his death. **Sanctify them** here means, "I am the Lord who sets them apart" (Berk.) for a special ministry.

All of the true members of the priest's family could share in the **holy thing.** But a **stranger,** a **sojourner,** a **hired servant** (10), or a **daughter** who was now a part of her husband's family (12) could not participate. Any legal member—a **priest's daughter** who was a **widow** or **divorced** (13), or a slave (11)—could partake. If one ate by mistake of the holy things, a return of an equal amount plus a **fifth** was necessary as reparation (14). Verses 15-16 are a summary statement, "The priests shall not profane the holy things the Israelites offer to the Lord" (15, Amp. OT).

The final paragraph in this section (22:17-33) emphasizes that no offering that contained **a blemish** (20) was acceptable to God except in the case of the **freewill offering** (23). The offering was to be perfect. The priests were not to accept defective sacrifices either from the Israelites themselves or from **a stranger's hand** (25), i.e., from foreigners. A newly born animal was not acceptable until the **eighth day** (27). A mother and its offspring could not be killed the same **day** (28). Obedience in these matters reflected the separation of Israel unto **the Lord** (31) and enabled Him to **hallow** them unto himself (32).

Section VII Holy Days and Festivals

Leviticus 23:1-44

In this chapter are given the appointed meetings of Israel with its God. The term which is translated **feasts** (1) is the Hebrew word for "appointed time" (*mo'ed*). Thus the list given here is of the **holy convocations** (2). Included are the three great annual feasts (*chaggim*). The emphasis in the word **feasts** (*mo'ed*) is on the setness of the time and the meeting, while that of **convocations** is upon its festive, or joyous, character. Israel's worship was to be a thing of joy to them. Compare our "holiday" and "holy day." There is true freedom when duty is a delight. This was God's plan for Israel.

A. The Sabbath, 23:3

The sabbath was a special sign of the covenant of God with Israel (Exod. 20:8-11; 31:12-17), though it was not unknown prior to the giving of the Decalogue. In Genesis the Sabbath is pictured as based upon the divine pattern set down in the creation (Gen. 2:1-3). God underscored this for Israel in the giving of the manna (Exod. 16:5, 22-26). It seems to have been distinctly an Israelite observance, not shared with her Canaanite neighbors.[1] It was the Lord's Day, and the basic reason for observing it was that it belonged to Him. The giving of the one day to God was a great acknowledgment that all time was His, just as the giving of the tithe acknowledged His sovereign ownership of all things. To desecrate the Sabbath was looked upon as extremely serious. Violation could bring the death penalty (Num. 15:32-36). This was the basic holy day for Israel as is evidenced by its position in this chapter.

The proper observance was cessation from all work. The **rest** here indicated is more complete than that for the other sacred times. Note the difference between **no work** (3) and "no servile ['laborious,' RSV] work" (7, 8, 21, 25, 35, 36). Perhaps

[1]H. H. Rowley, *Worship in Ancient Israel* (Philadelphia: Fortress Press, 1967), p. 91.

Israel's attitude toward the Sabbath as the basic religious institution has something to say to our age in which the Lord's Day has become almost indistinguishable from the others.

B. The Passover, 23:4-8

Here attention is turned to the true **feasts** (4) of Israel. The first is the feast of **passover** or **unleavened bread** (5-6), the most important of the annual festivals. In current critical thought there is strong insistence that this festival, as well as the Feast of Weeks, and the Feast of Tabernacles were originally agricultural feasts which Israel borrowed from its pagan neighbors and slowly transformed into the biblical festivals presented here. It can only be said that there is no reflection of such origins in the text as it has come to us.

It is true that Israel's neighbors had their agricultural and pastoral festivals which were in some sense analogous. Even in Israel there was a strong consciousness of the natural cycle, and these three feasts commemorate three stages in the agricultural year: the cutting of the first sheaf of grain. the end of the barley and wheat harvest, and the gathering of the grapes. Israel was aware that her Lord was the Giver of nature's bounty (cf. c. 26). Thus it was right that she should acknowledge in her festivals her dependence upon Him for daily bread.

The unique thing in Israel was the historical reference given to her festivals. Thus the Feast of Unleavened Bread may have been a celebration of the season of the year, but it had a higher significance. It was also the Passover, the commemoration of Israel's redemption from Egypt. The uniqueness of Israel in her world is seen in her religious faith. The festival was not geared just to the natural cycle but primarily to a sovereign God who works generally in nature but specifically in election-love in redemptive acts in the life of His own. The feasts recalled to Israel the Exodus and its theological implications. In this the OT is consistent with the New. The faith of the Christian Church is based upon the historical events of the incarnation, passion, resurrection, and ascension of Christ and the coming of the Holy Spirit at Pentecost.

The evangelical believer likewise finds the empirical basis of his faith in experiences in *his own history* of new birth, the Spirit's witness and baptism, and perhaps divine call. This faith can be pegged to a calendar as clearly as Wesley's when he said that "about a quarter before nine" in a chapel on Aldersgate Street on May 24, 1738, he experienced the redeeming grace of God.

Israel had known such a redemption and remembered both it and God's providential provision in these annual festivals. The Passover, which is mentioned here, was the old covenant's counterpart to the supper of the Lord instituted under the new covenant. Both pointed to a lamb slain and a people redeemed.

C. The Offerings of Firstfruits, 23:9-14

Four laws are given in Leviticus that were to be obeyed when Israel came into the land of Canaan. This is the third (for the other three cf. 14:34; 19:23; 25:2). This commandment has to do with the beginning of the harvest. Since all of the produce of the earth comes from the Lord, who made and sustains it, the giving of **the firstfruits** (10) acknowledges His ownership. The presentation of this **offering** (14) meant the sanctification of the rest of that harvest, for not until the Israelites had presented this offering were they permitted to partake of their produce. It is another of the innumerable reminders in Scripture that our daily bread is given by God. For the symbolical use of this ceremony in the NT see Rom. 8:23; 11:16; 16:5; I Cor. 15:20, 23; and 16:15. **Two tenth deals** (13) would be "a fifth of a bushel," and **the fourth part of an hin** would be "three pints" (Berk.).

D. The Feast of Weeks, 23:15-22

This is the Feast of Harvest. As the presentation of the firstfruits indicated the beginning of the harvest, this feast commemorated its end. It is the most "naturalistic" of the feasts of Israel. This is evident in the use of **leaven** (17) in the loaves offered and in the fact that its historical association does not come from the OT but was added later. The festival was a joyous acknowledgment of the gracious faithfulness of **the Lord** (20) in giving another harvest, and gladly acknowledged His good hand in the normal daily life. It is fulfilled in the NT festival of Pentecost. Is it not fitting to recall that, in Luke 11:11-13, Jesus speaks of an earthly father's willingness to give bread, meat, and eggs to his children, and an even greater willingness in our Divine Father to give to us His Holy Spirit? It is certain that in the gift of the divine fullness our every daily need finds its satisfaction.

This festival came at the conclusion of the harvest. Since God had given of His bounty to His children, it was especially appropriate that they should remember **the poor** and **the stranger** (22).

E. The Holy Days of the Seventh Month, 23:23-44

The sacredness of the number seven is a common theme throughout the Pentateuch. Perhaps the unusual number of high days in this month is due to the fact that it was the seventh month. As the seventh day was holy, so was the seventh month.

1. *The Feast of Trumpets* (23:24-25)

The first day of **the seventh month** (24) was to be an especially holy day in Israel, a **sabbath,** a **holy convocation.** No **servile** ("laborious," RSV) **work** was to be done (25).

Israel had more than one way of reckoning time. This was the seventh month of the ecclesiastical year, but it was also the first month of the civil calendar. Thus it was a new year's festival as well. Payne says that the **blowing of trumpets** (24) was an anthropomorphic way of reminding God of the needs of His people.[2] It also announced the beginning of the month that was to include the great Day of Atonement and the joyous Feast of Tabernacles.

2. *The Day of Atonement* (23:26-32)

In c. 16 this holy day was described from the standpoint of Aaron and the priests. Here it is presented in terms of the people and their responsibilities (cf. comments on 16:29-34). Note the seriousness with which this day was to be approached. It was a day in which they were to **do no work** (28)—a day of complete **rest** (32). It was also a day when **ye shall afflict your souls** (27; "humble yourselves," Berk.; cf. also 29 and 32). The approaching Feast of Tabernacles was the most joyous season of the year. It was to be preceded by true repentance and faith in the Feast of Atonement. Failure to keep it with full reverence could mean excommunication or death (29-30).

[2]*The Theology of the Older Testament* (Grand Rapids: Zondervan Publishing House, 1962), p. 406.

3. *The Feast of Tabernacles* (23:33-44)

For other scriptures that illuminate this festival see Num. 29:12-38; Deut. 16:13-15; 31:10-13; Ezra 3:4; and Neh. 8:18. This feast was like that of the Passover and Unleavened Bread in that it lasted for eight days. The first and last days were to be the days of **holy convocation** (35-36) with **no servile work** to be done on either day. **Solemn assembly** (36) is called a "day of restraint" (marg.). *The Berkeley Version* renders the sentence, "It is a festive gathering; you shall do no hard work." Numbers 29 tells us that the daily burnt offerings were 13 young bulls for the first day and one less each succeeding day. The Israelites were also to offer 14 lambs and two rams each day with appropriate grain and drink offerings, a male goat for a sin offering, and the regular burnt offering with its grain and drink accompaniments. The eighth day the offerings were to be a bull, a ram, seven lambs, cereal and drink offerings, and the regular burnt offering with its accompaniments.

The feast commemorated the ending of the agricultural year, when the produce **of the land** (39) had been gathered; it was intended to express gratitude to God for His provision. A **palm** frond (40) was bound together with a **thick** (myrtle) branch on one side and a willow branch on the other. It was called a *lulab.* This was carried, and waved at appropriate intervals, along with fruit in the religious celebration. Tradition says that Psalms 118 was part of the ritual recited during the feast.

The chief characteristic of this feast was the custom of making **booths** (42) from leafy branches and living in them during the feast. Thus the people remembered the provision of God for **Israel** (43) during the long years of wandering in the wilderness. As the Passover was a reminder of the Exodus, this feast recalled the wilderness experience. The gifts of God through nature's bounty and through divine grace were both recalled here. Little wonder that it was looked upon as an occasion of intense joy (40). With this occasion the sacred calendar of Israel was completed.

Section VIII *Holy Oil, Holy Bread, and the Holy Name*

Leviticus 24:1-23

A. The Holy Oil, 24:1-4

The illumination of the Tabernacle was provided by a great golden **candlestick** (4, lampstand) with seven lamps (see Chart *A*). Its construction is described in Exod. 25:31-40, while the preparation of the oil and its supply are detailed in Exod. 27:20-21. It was to burn perpetually **in the tabernacle** (3) before the Lord. The **candlestick** was placed on the south side of the holy place (see Chart *A*), a room which had no other source of light. It was to be supplied with the finest of olive **oil** (2). The symbolical significance of this lamp may be indicated in the promise that Israel was to be a light among the nations of the world. The vision of Zechariah 4 would support this, as would the vision of John in Rev. 1:12-20. Note also the role of the Christian believers in Phil. 2:15. This role is to be a perpetual one and is possible only through the enabling of the Holy Spirit, symbolized in the **pure oil.** The expression, **He shall order the lamps** (4), means, "He shall keep the lamps in order upon the lampstand" (RSV).

B. The Holy Bread, 24:5-9

In this section we find the instruction concerning the shewbread. In Exod. 25:23-30 the table for it is described (see also Chart *A*). Here the priests are told the use of **the pure table** (6). **Twelve cakes** (5, loaves of bread) were to be prepared and kept **before the Lord** (6) at all times. Pieces of **frankincense** (7) were to be placed **on the bread.** According to Jewish tradition, the frankincense was burned on the altar of burnt sacrifice with the offerings of oil and wine when the old bread was replaced by new each week. The old bread then was to be used as food for the priests (9). The loaves could have symbolized the fact that man's daily bread is a gift from God. They might also suggest that the labor of man's hands is to be given back to God, who gives to man that with which he works.

C. The Holy Name, 24:10-23

A story is inserted about a man who **blasphemed the name of the Lord** (11) and the penalty that resulted. The Decalogue gave no specific penalty for profanation of the divine name. Hence Moses sought from **the Lord** (12) a decision as to what to do with the guilty one. **In ward** (12) would be "in custody" (Amp. OT). A similar story about a violation of the law of the Sabbath is inserted in the same fashion in Num. 15:32-36. In this case of blasphemy the one involved was only half Israelite, his father being **an Egyptian** (10). He could thus represent that "mixed multitude" mentioned in Exod. 12:38. The answer that is given shows that there is no difference between the Israelite and the non-Israelite in such matters—**Whosoever curseth his God shall bear his sin** (15).

Here is an illustration of the fact that there were no sacrifices provided for violation of the Decalogue as such. The sacrifices were only for those within the covenant, and violation of the Decalogue was a repudiation of the covenant. It is difficult for modern men to understand such severity for what is called a mere verbal sin. But the ancient world looked upon verbal sins as having genuine reality. And what, we may ask, demonstrates one's attitude toward the sacred and the holy God more than the way in which a man uses holy words? Erdman writes:

> Nothing is more perilous or more injurious to a community or a nation than irreverence toward things which are sacred. Profanity and blasphemy are sins which involve exceptional guilt. Reverence toward God is the foundation not only of religion but of morality. There is a message for the present day even in this tragic episode which emphasizes the need for reverencing the Holy Name.[1]

This story of blasphemy is used to introduce a series (17-22) of examples of *lex talionis*—the principle of **eye for eye** and **tooth for tooth** (20). All have been mentioned earlier in the Pentateuch but are repeated here to show that this principle extends to both Israelite and non-Israelite (22).

[1] *Op. cit.*, p. 127.

It is often contended that Jesus repudiated this principle in the Sermon on the Mount, and it is true insofar as personal revenge is concerned. Allis is right, though, when he asserts that this incident is intended to be a law of public justice, not private revenge, and that compensation for injuries probably took the form of fines.[2] This position is supported by the facts (*a*) that only murder (Num. 35:31 f.) is excluded from crimes for which ransom is permissible, and (*b*) that Mosaic law opposed mutilation. It must be remembered that the principle of "an eye for an eye" is rather basic to all civilized law. In fact one cannot play a game except on the basis that what is right for one is right for the other and that every violation of this principle must receive its due penalty.

Interpersonal dealings are another matter. But even in this area, love that turns the other cheek says little to the offending party unless he and the offended both know the difference between justice and injustice.

[2]*Op. cit.*, p. 158.

Section IX Holy Years

Leviticus 25:1-55

In c. 23 the Sabbath as a day of rest was dealt with in connection with the sacred feasts. Now the same principle is extended to cover the seventh year (25:1-7) and the fiftieth year, the year which crowns seven cycles of seven years (25:8-55).

A. The Sabbatical Year, 25:1-7

The principle of the **sabbath** (2), an institution that seems to have been unique to Israel (see c. 23), is now extended to the years. The suspension of work on the seventh day is a hallowing of time. Here such rest is commanded for every seventh year. Time, as all other resources, belongs to God. The observance of the **seventh year** (4) illustrates God's claim upon Israel's time and His demand that Israel trust in Him for provision of its needs. Reference to this observance occurs in Exod. 23:10-11, where the context indicates a humanitarian concern. References also are found in Deut. 31:10; II Kings 19:29; Neh. 10:31; and in the Aprocrypha in I Macc. 6:49, 53. Josephus says that it was observed in the days of Alexander the Great (*Antiquities*, XI, viii, 6) and in the time of the Herods (XIX, xvi, 2). Tacitus also refers to it in his *History* (5:4).

Verses 6-7 seem to modify the limitation of v. 5. The probable meaning is that, while no formal cultivation, harvesting, and storing of crops shall be done during the sabbatical year, what grows of itself can be used for food at the time.

B. The Jubilee, 25:8-55

The actual observance of the Year of Jubilee in Israel has been seriously challenged. It has been suggested that this represents "priestly theorising and never an actual policy."[1] Snaith has pointed out, though, that in II Kings 19:29 (and Isa. 37:30)

[1]Snaith, *op. cit.*, p. 162.

different Hebrew words appear for "that which grows of itself in the first year" (*saphiach*) and "that which grows of itself in the second year" (*sachish*).[2]

This year was to begin **on the tenth day of the seventh month, in the day of atonement** (9), with the sounding of **the trumpet.** It was to be a year of release and **liberty throughout all the land** (10). The land and the people were given a sabbath (rest), and all property that had been alienated from the original owner was to be returned. An illustration of the principle involved here is found in the story of Naboth, who could not sell his vineyard to King Ahab because it belonged, as a family inheritance, to his descendents as well as to himself (I Kings 21:3).

This practice meant that land was valued **according to the number of years** away from **the jubile** (15) that the transfer of property was considered. Thus the purchase price was determined according to **the number of years of the fruits,** i.e., the number of crops rather than the land value itself. This was a dramatic underscoring of the OT teaching that the property belonged to the Lord—**the land is mine** (23). He had given it in trust to certain Israelite families, and it **shall not be sold** permanently to another. God was the permanent Owner.

Property within **a walled city** (29) was an exception to this law. It could be redeemed by the seller **within a . . . year;** otherwise it was sold in perpetuity (30). This limitation on redemption was not true of houses within Levitical cities, which could be redeemed by a Levite **at any time** (32), since such cities were their only **possession** in **Israel** (33; cf. Num. 35:1-5). If the property within the city was not redeemed by a Levite, it would return to him **in the year of jubile.** The **field of the suburbs** (34, pasturelands attached to the Levitical cities) could not be sold at all.

The Year of Jubilee was also to be a year of release for slaves (35-55). Introducing this section is a word expressing concern for the **poor** (35) in Israel. If a man could not maintain himself, it was expected that a Hebrew would see that he was maintained. Under the old covenant a man was not to accept **usury** (36, interest) for money loaned to the poor. Maintenance of the needy was a manifestation of a true fear of the Lord. God demanded this of Israel, since He had purchased them from **the**

[2]*Loc. cit.*

land of Egypt (38) and maintained them until He could establish them in the land which He *gave* them.

A Hebrew who became so **poor** (39) that he would sell himself to another Hebrew could not be treated as a slave, but as a **hired servant** or as a **sojourner** (40) until the Year of Jubilee. God said, **Thou shalt not rule over him with rigour** (43), i.e., with harshness (cf. 46, 53). Non-Hebrews could be owned as **bondmen** (slaves, 44) and could be bequeathed as family property (46). Not so with a Hebrew. Moreover, if a Hebrew were bought by **a sojourner or stranger** (47) in Israel, that Hebrew could be **redeemed** (48) by a kinsman at a value consistent with the time remaining until **the year of jubile** (50), when he would go free without payment. The reason given for this law (55) is the same as that applying to property. The Hebrews had been redeemed by God and were His property alone. It was not right for another to possess them. Their labors could be hired but they could be *possessed* only by God, who had redeemed them. Is there not here a word for us about the dignity of every child of God and of our mutual responsibility one for another?

Section X *Final Words of Promise and Warning*

Leviticus 26:1-46

Throughout the Pentateuch it is customary for sections of law to be closed with an exhortation to obedience (Exod. 23:20-33; Deut. 28:1-68). So this chapter gives a final word of promise and warning. First, there is a reminder of the prohibition of idolatry (1). This reminder is connected to a statement on the importance of reverencing the **sabbaths** and the **sanctuary** (2). Next is given a promise of multiplied blessing if Israel is obedient (3-13). Finally, there is an extended promise of chastening and judgment for disobedience, but the chastening and judgment will be moderated by the Lord's mercy and His remembrance of the covenant and His commitment to it (14-46).

A. Idolatry, Sabbaths, and the Sanctuary, 26:1-2

It would seem that this chapter should be the closing chapter of the book. It represents the heart of the covenant commitment of Israel and reminds her of the first table of the Decalogue. Four different terms are used here for idolatrous objects. The first, **idols** (*'elilim*), means false gods; it comes from a root which seems to mean "to be weak, worthless, a thing of nought." The next, **graven image** (*pesel*), means something hewn from wood or stone. **Standing image** (*massebah*) refers to a stone pillar. **Image of stone** (*maskit*) was understood by Rashi to mean a carved stone on which men prostrated themselves or at which one looked.[1] The non-iconic nature of the worship of the God of Israel was in absolute contrast to the religion of all of Israel's neighbors and the Scripture never lets us forget it. In this passage the Sabbaths and the reverencing of the sanctuary are made of equal importance with the adherence to the one true God.

B. Promise, 26:3-13

The gracious benefits of obedience to the Lord are now pointed out. The unity of all of life is reflected in this passage

[1]Snaith, *op. cit.*, p. 169.

of promise. The sympathetic relationship between man and nature found in the prophets is portrayed here. If man is right with his Maker, all of life will respond helpfully. Physical plenty (4-5), national victory (6-8), **peace,** and family fruitfulness (9) will follow. Best of all, God says, **I . . . will be your God, and ye shall be my people** (12). This passage recalls the paradise from which man was expelled (Genesis 2—3) and envisions that of which the prophets were yet to speak (Ezek. 48:35; Amos 9: 11-15). The personal character of this promise is reflected in the common use of the first person here as God speaks to His covenant people. His good intent toward them in this promise is guaranteed by His past deliverance of them when they were **bondmen** (13).

Smith clarifies the meaning of 5 thus: "Threshing shall last for you until the time of vintage, and the time of vintage shall last until sowing time, so that you shall eat all that you want of your food" (Smith-Goodspeed). **Eat old store, and bring forth the old** (10) is better, "You shall eat what had long been stored, then clear it out for the new" (Berk.).

It is the Lord, the God of Israel, who will give all of these things to His obedient people because He is able and because He wants to do so. It is important to see in this passage an affirmation of God's power as well as His goodwill. We must remember that this word came to a people who were in a world in which all of these benefits were felt to be within the domain of other gods. Thus the passage begins with a denial of the other gods (1-2) and continues with a promise that the God of Israel is *able* and *wills* to give the best to His people. The truth may be peculiarly applicable to our world today, in which modern man has come to feel that all of these blessings lie within his own power to attain. Our problem is not dependence upon images of wood and stone but upon scientific processes, human ingenuity, and chance. Modern man needs reminders that health, plenty, and peace are still within the domain of the Lord.

C. Warning, 26:14-46

1. *If You Will Not Hearken* (26:14-39)

If Israel is not obedient to the **commandments** of the Lord (14), God will respond with chastening, judgment, and destruction. This story is woven into a succession of **if** clauses (14, 15,

18, 21, *et al.*) that describe the disobediences which can lead to increasingly dire results. Here is a chapter that illustrates the reluctance of the Lord to afflict His people, but it also demonstrates the fact that Israel's election did not exempt her from the Lord's demand for obedience. The Scriptures do not say that the laws of moral retribution affect only the non-elect. Rather, the elect will receive the greater condemnation because of their knowledge. Here, however, we see the long-suffering character of God, who chastens in hope of saving His own. Physical sicknesses (16), famine (16, 26), **plagues** (21), **pestilence** (25), war, enemy oppression (17), devastation (30-33), terror, and captivity (33) will result from walking contrary to the law of the Lord.

Verse 16 is clarified by Moffatt thus: "I will subject you to terrible woes, to consumption and fever that waste the eyes and wear life away; you shall sow seed in vain, for your enemies will eat your crops." **Shall avenge the quarrel of my covenant** (25) is better, "I will let loose the sword of war upon you, in punishment for your breach of compact" (Moffatt). Famine conditions are vividly depicted in 26: "When I deprive you of the bread that sustains you, ten of your women will need but one oven for their baking, and your bread shall be doled out in rations, till you never have enough" (Moffatt).

2. *If You Will Confess* (26:40-46)

If Israel can learn from the chastening of the Lord, two conditions can turn the wrath of God: **if they shall confess** (40) and **if** they **be humbled** (41). These will cause the Lord to **remember** the **covenant** (42) which He had made with the fathers and will cause Him to turn His anger and redeem them even as He did their fathers (44-45). How appropriate this chapter is with its philosophy of history for modern nominally Christian nations in the West!

Section XI An Appendix: On Vows and Tithes

Leviticus 27:1-34

The consecration of persons and things to the Lord beyond the demands of the law were known in the OT as vows. Examples are seen in the actions of Hannah (I Sam. 1:11) and of Jephthah (Judg. 11:30-31). **A singular vow** (2) is better "a vowed offering" (Berk.). The provision here is for an **estimation** of the worth of the thing thus promised to God and a commutation of the vow according to value. In most cases cited here there is actually no change in ownership. There is, rather, a payment to the Lord of equivalent value. The evaluation was affected by the standards of the day as to age and sex. The seriousness with which a vow was viewed is seen in Deut. 23:21-23. But the humanitarian character of the Levitical legislation is also reflected in the protection written into the law for the poor (8).

If **a beast** (9) was vowed, the animal vowed had to be offered. No other could be substituted. To make a vow to offer it meant that it had become **holy** (10). It could not return to common life. If it was an **unclean beast** (11), the priest was to place a **value** (12) upon it and sell it. If the offerer wished to **redeem** (13) the unclean animal, he could do so by paying its value plus a **fifth part** (one-fifth). This same treatment was accorded in case a man vowed a **house** to the Lord (14-15).

In the matter of **a field** (16, land) a difference was made between that which was inherited and that which was bought. The meaning of 16 is clarified thus: "When a man sets apart to the Lord a field he owns, then your estimate of it shall be according to the amount of seed required [to sow it], ten bushels of barley means fifty silver dollars" (Berk.). Property was evaluated in terms of **the year of jubile** (16-24). Inherited land could be redeemed for the value plus one-fifth (19). Otherwise it became **holy unto the Lord** (21); i.e., it became the property of the priests. If the property was bought, it was valued in terms of the proximity of the Jubilee (23). The man would give according to its prospective value to him. In **the year of the jubile** (24) it would **return** to the original owner. Verse 25 is clarified thus, "All estimates shall be by sanctuary silver standards; the dollar shall equal ten dimes" (Berk.).

A firstling (26) of the clean animals could not be dedicated to the Lord, since it was His already (Exod. 13:2; 34:19). The firstling of **an unclean beast** (27) was valued and could be redeemed for value plus **a fifth part** (one-fifth). If it was **not redeemed,** it had to be **sold,** since it was unclean and could not be owned by a priest.

The meaning of the term **devoted** (*cherem*) is indicated in vv. 28-29. That which was **devoted** was set apart irrevocably for God. It was **most holy unto the Lord** and as such could not be **sold or redeemed.** It had to be destroyed from among men. The finality of consecration, from God's perspective, is indicated here. Consecration was neither to be done easily nor could it be casually undone. It was an irreversible process.

The tithe (30) likewise could be redeemed if value plus one-fifth (31) was offered. This was true both for the produce **of the land** and of **the herd** or **the flock. Whatever passeth under the rod** (32) is a picture of the shepherd or herdsman setting aside his tithe. Moffatt renders the verse, "The tithe of the herd or of the flock, every tenth animal counted by the herdsman, shall be sacred to the Eternal." This tithe was not to be determined selfishly. A man was not to select either the **good or bad** (33) for God. If a man tried to adjust his tithe by trading animals, he was required to give both the animal offered and the one exchanged for it. Every tenth item was God's without debate.

Bibliography

I. COMMENTARIES

ALLIS, OSWALD T. "Leviticus." *The New Bible Commentary.* Edited by F. DAVIDSON, *et al.* Grand Rapids: Wm. B. Eerdmans Publishing Co., 1953.

BONAR, ANDREW A. *A Commentary on the Book of Leviticus.* New York: Robert Carter and Brothers, 1863.

CHAPMAN, A. T., and STREANE, A. W. *The Book of Leviticus.* "The Cambridge Bible for Schools and Colleges." Cambridge: The University Press, 1914.

ERDMAN, CHARLES R. *The Book of Leviticus.* New York: Fleming H. Revell Company, 1951.

HIRSCH, S. R. *The Pentateuch Translated and Explained,* Vol. III, Parts I and II. Rendered into English by ISAAC LEVY. Second Edition. London: Isaac Levy, 1962.

KEIL, C. F., and DELITZSCH F. *Biblical Commentary on the Old Testament,* Vol. II. Trans. by JAMES MARTIN. Grand Rapids: Wm. B. Eerdmans Publishing Co., 1949.

MICKLEM, NATHANIEL. "The Book of Leviticus" (Exegesis and Exposition). *The Interpreter's Bible.* Edited by GEORGE A. BUTTRICK, *et al.,* Vol. II. New York: Abingdon-Cokesbury Press, 1953.

NOTH, MARTIN. *Leviticus.* "The Old Testament Library." Philadelphia: The Westminster Press, 1965.

RASHI. *Pentateuch with Targum Onkelos, Haphtaroth and Rashi's Commentary.* Translated and annotated by M. ROSENBAUM and A. M. SILBERMANN. New York: Hebrew Publishing Company, n.d.

SNAITH, N. H. *Leviticus and Numbers.* "The Century Bible." Camden, N.J.: Thomas Nelson and Sons, 1967.

II. OTHER BOOKS

ALBRIGHT, W. F. *From Stone Age to Christianity.* Baltimore: Johns Hopkins Press, 1940.

ARCHER, GLEASON. *A Survey of Old Testament Introduction.* Chicago: Moody Press, 1964.

BROWN, FRANCIS; DRIVER, S. R.; and BRIGGS, CHARLES A. *A Hebrew and English Lexicon of the Old Testament.* Oxford: The Clarendon Press, 1907.

DE VAUX, ROLAND. *Ancient Israel: Its Life and Institutions.* New York: McGraw-Hill Book Company, Inc., 1961.

EICHRODT, WALTHER. *Theology of the Old Testament,* Vol. I. "The Old Testament Library." Philadelphia: The Westminster Press, 1961.

KAUFMANN, YEHEZKEL. *The Religion of Israel.* Translated by MOSHE GREENBERG. Chicago: The University of Chicago Press, 1960.

McMILLEN, S. I. *None of These Diseases.* Westwood, N.J.: Fleming H. Revell, 1963.

PAYNE, J. BARTON. *The Theology of the Older Testament.* Grand Rapids: Zondervan Publishing House, 1962.

RINGGREN, HELMER. *Israelite Religion.* Translated by DAVID E. GREEN. Philadelphia: Fortress Press, 1966.

ROWLEY, H. H. *Worship in Ancient Israel.* Philadelphia: Fortress Press, 1967.

III. ARTICLES

BROCKINGTON, L. H. "Presence." *A Theological Dictionary of the Bible.* Edited by ALAN RICHARDSON. New York: The Macmillan Company, 1951.

MICHEL, O. "Mimneskomai." *Theological Dictionary of the New Testament,* Vol. IV. Edited by GERHARD KITTEL. Translated by GEOFFREY W. BROMILEY. Grand Rapids: Wm. B. Eerdmans Publishing Co., 1967.

MOLLER, WILHELM. "Leviticus." *The International Standard Bible Encyclopedia,* Vol. III. Edited by JAMES ORR, *et al.* Grand Rapids: Wm. B. Eerdmans Publishing Co., 1949.

MORRIS, L. L. "Blood." *The New Bible Dictionary.* Edited by J. D. DOUGLAS, *et al.* Grand Rapids: Wm. B. Eerdmans Publishing Co., 1962.

The Book of

NUMBERS

Lauriston J. Du Bois

Introduction

A. Name and Scope

In the English Bible the title of this fourth book of the OT is Numbers, following the title, *Numeri,* of the Latin Vulgate. It is used, no doubt, to highlight the two census reports which are recorded here. The first of these was a part of the program of organizing the people of Israel after their sudden and dramatic exodus from Egypt. The other was a part of the preparation in marshalling them for their trip into the Promised Land. Actually, however, these "numberings" occupy but a small portion of the book, namely, cc. 1—4 and 26. Hence other titles have been suggested from time to time as being more appropriate.

The Hebrews commonly used a distinguishing word from the beginning phrases of a book for its title. Consequently, Numbers was sometimes called "And he spoke" (*Vaidabber*), from its initial word. Most Hebrew Bibles give it the title "In the wilderness" (*Bemidbar*), which is not only the fifth word of the first verse, but speaks also of the setting of the main body of the book.

So far as content is concerned, Numbers might well be designated as the "Book of Moses."[1] Here Moses is portrayed as God's man for the hour in a more profound manner even than in the preceding two books and perhaps even more than in the book which follows. He dominates the scene as lawgiver, as intercessor, as peacemaker, as provider, as wise counsellor, as astute statesman, as clever general, as righteous leader, and as humble servant of God.

The Book of Numbers could also be titled "The Story of God's Faithfulness." The basic story of the book is God working among His people.[2] He is a Pillar of Fire by night, a Pillar of Cloud by day, a Provider of water and manna, a Captain at the front of the armies, a hovering Presence over and around the entire camp. Hence, Numbers contributed greatly, across the centuries, to the Israelites' basic faith in God.

[1]L. Elliott Binns, "The Book of Numbers" (Introduction), *Westminster Commentaries* (London: Methuen and Co., 1927), pp. lvi-lx.

[2]John Marsh, "Numbers" (Introduction), *The Interpreter's Bible,* edited by George A. Buttrick, *et al.,* II (New York: Abingdon Press, 1953), 139.

The object of the book could be pinpointed even more explicitly by such a title as "Pilgrimage," with the key verse, not at the beginning, but deep within the heart of the record: "We are journeying unto the place of which the Lord said, I will give it you: come thou with us, and we will do thee good: for the Lord hath spoken good concerning Israel" (10:29).

Or in looking at the book from the vantage point of Hebrew and Christian history, it might well be called "The Tragedy of a Murmuring People." The book is spotted with records of the murmuring and complaining of the people because of the hardships which were thrust upon them. It also has, as its historical hub, the great sin of unbelief at Kadesh-barnea, in which the people moved from criticism of their leaders to criticism of God himself.[3]

Although this book is thought by some not to be as detailed or as authentic as other of the historical books, yet it is significant to the history of Israel and to the history of God's dealings with His people.[4]

B. The Book's Structure

In several ways Numbers is unique both in its structure and in its treatment of the data it contains. It is not an independent book which carries its own distinctive meaning, but is, with Leviticus, "the middle part of a continuous story which runs from Genesis through Deuteronomy, and indeed into Joshua . . . This means that . . . [they] play a crucial part in understanding the others."[5] Within the book itself, cc. 1:1—10:10 relate back to Leviticus and Exodus and the Egypt-oriented experiences, while the portion following 10:11 points ahead to Canaan-oriented experiences.

Numbers is composed of narrative, instruction, laws, religious rites, and epic literature. The arrangement of these gives the impression that the material could have come from many sources. In certain places, for example, the legislative matter, which is interspersed with the narration, grows out of and shows

[3]Olive M. Winchester, in her classroom teaching of Hebrew history, placed a strong emphasis upon this relationship between murmuring and unbelief.

[4]IB, II, 138.

[5]James L. Mays, "The Book of Leviticus, the Book of Numbers," *The Layman's Bible Commentary,* edited by Balmer H. Kelly, *et al.* (Richmond, Virginia: John Knox Press, 1959), IV, 8.

a natural connection with that narrative. In other instances, however, such a relationship is not evident.[6]

The narrative itself is uneven and broken. It does not unfold as a continuous, fully treated story but is a record of certain incidents, some treated very briefly and others more at length. The book gives detailed attention, for example, to the preparations for leaving Sinai and to the incidents which preceded the spiritual defeat at Kadesh. It gives a bit less attention to the account of the final march to Canaan and to the incidents surrounding it. There is only a short note and very few answers to one's questions regarding the 38 years of the "wilderness wanderings."

The book, then, must be read in the light of this "patchwork" nature. There seems to be no pattern of organization which eases the abrupt transitions, explains the obscurities, or bridges the gaps which abound. It has many beginnings and many endings. However, these empty spots in our full understanding of the structure of Numbers need not weaken its position in the canon of Holy Scripture. It still stands as a trustworthy account of that famous trek of the people of Israel from Sinai to Canaan.

C. The Findings of Archaeology

It is regrettable that there are not more documented helps from the scholarly research of archaeology and related fields which apply to the areas and times covered by the Book of Numbers. The findings to date are limited and few of them are so clearly established as to be uncontested.

As a result, it is necessary to depend heavily upon tradition for such matters as the marking of the route of the journey, the locations of many of the events connected with it, and for other data not made explicit by the biblical record. Such important locations as the mountain called Sinai, the springs of Kadesh-barnea, and many of the stopping places (33:1-37) on the way cannot be pinpointed conclusively on a contemporary map. Thus, any attempt to show the route of the pilgrimage can at best be only an estimate and must contain many probabilities.[7]

[6]Thomas Whitelaw, "Introduction to Numbers," *Pulpit Commentary*, edited by Joseph S. Exell (New York: Funk and Wagnalls, n.d.), p. 11.

[7]Jesse Lyman Hurlbut, *A Bible Atlas* (New York: Rand McNally & Co., 1938), pp. 26 ff. Cf. James L. Mays, *op. cit.*, p. 9.

There are, to be sure, findings upon which the archaeologists place some importance. There are evidences, for example, that these wilderness areas may not always have been as barren and unproductive as they are today. They could, indeed, have given a measure of support to the food needs of as great a host of people as the Scriptures record, even though there was still need for the miracles which God performed in order that they could survive. There are also evidences which indicate that the Sinai area, during these times, boasted a production of metals (iron, copper, and perhaps others). These facts would explain the names found in the record of this period relating to metals, smelting, and the like. They would also support the biblical implication that these areas were not as remote and desolate as modern conditions would suggest.[8]

Certain scholars[9] have felt that the best evidences from archaeology support the "later" date (roughly 1300 B.C.) of the Exodus. There are two of these to which they point as being the most significant. (1) There has been a more exact dating of the origin of the Hyksos dynasty in Egypt, whose beginning is believed to coincide with the days of Joseph and the migration of Jacob and his family to Egypt. (2) There is evidence which supports the idea of a rather sudden appearance of established cities in southern Palestine and in trans-Jordan in the thirteenth century B.C., which condition certainly pertained when the Israelites made contact with these areas in connection with their journey.

There have been speculations concerning the authorship of Numbers, but here again little evidence has been uncovered that changes the traditional position, which holds that Moses was the author of the bulk of the book.[10] This may be maintained in spite of the intimations that interpolations have been made, either by the original compiler or by some later reviser, and in spite of the presence of the rather unrelated pieces of epic literature which could have come from other sources. Firm evi-

[8]J. A. Thompson, *Archaeology and the Old Testament* (Grand Rapids: Wm. B. Eerdmans Publishing Co., 1959), p. 55.

[9]G. Ernest Wright, *Biblical Archaeology* (Abridged Edition; Philadelphia: The Westminster Press, 1960), pp. 34-43. John Elder, *Prophets, Idols and Diggers* (Indianapolis: Bobbs-Merrill, 1960), p. 57. Kathleen M. Kenyon, *Archaeology in the Holy Land* (London: Ernest Benn, Ltd., 1960), p. 206.

[10]See comments as to authorship in the article on "The Pentateuch," pp. 18-19.

dence is lacking which would cause us to assign the basic authorship to any other than Moses.

In the main, the supporting data covering this period is limited, more so even than that covering the later times of the settlement of Israel in Canaan. Hence there is little help from these outside sources in filling the empty spots and little that adds basically to the information which has been preserved in the biblical account.

Outline

I. Preparations at Sinai, 1:1—10:10

- A. The Census, 1:1—2:34
- B. Provisions for the Levites, 3:1—4:49
- C. Social Responsibilities, 5:1-31
- D. The Nazarite Vow, 6:1-21
- E. The Benediction, 6:22-27
- F. Offerings from the Princes, 7:1-89
- G. Cleansing of the Levites, 8:1-26
- H. On the Eve of Departure, 9:1—10:10

II. From Mountain to Wilderness, 10:11—14:45

- A. The Camp Moves Out, 10:11-36
- B. The People Complain, 11:1-9
- C. Moses Feels His Burden, 11:10-17
- D. God Promises the People Meat, 11:18-23
- E. The Giving of the Spirit, 11:24-30
- F. The Quail, 11:31-35
- G. The Sin of Miriam, 12:1-15
- H. Scouting Party Surveys Canaan, 12:16—13:33
- I. Response of the People, 14:1-10
- J. God's Judgment, 14:11-45

III. Wilderness Experiences, 15:1—19:22

- A. The Years of Obscurity
- B. A Review of Certain Laws, 15:1-41
- C. Korah's Insurrection, 16:1—17:13
- D. Levitical and Priestly Duties, 18:1-32
- E. Provisions for Cleansing, 19:1-22

IV. From Kadesh to Moab, 20:1—22:1

A. Happenings at Kadesh, 20:1-21
B. Toward Canaan at Last, 20:22—21:4
C. The Brazen Serpent, 21:4-9
D. Incidents on the March, 21:10—22:1

V. The Drama of Balaam, 22:2—24:25

A. Unique Characteristics of the Section
B. Balak's Invitation and Balaam's Response, 22:2-41
C. The First Prophecy, 23:1-13
D. The Second Prophecy, 23:14-26
E. The Third Prophecy, 23:27—24:13
F. The Fourth Prophecy, 24:14-25

VI. Events in Moab, 25:1—32:42

A. Moral Failures, 25:1-18
B. Another Census, 26:1-65
C. The Law of Universal Inheritance, 27:1-11
D. Joshua Is Selected, 27:12-23
E. The Seasons of Worship, 28:1—29:40
F. The Vows of Women, 30:1-16
G. War Against the Midianites, 31:1-54
H. Settling Outside Canaan, 32:1-42

VII. Miscellaneous Data, 33:1—36:13

A. Camps from Egypt to Canaan, 33:1-56
B. The Boundaries Outlined, 34:1-29
C. Cities of Refuge, 35:1-34
D. Marriage and Inheritance, 36:1-13

Section I Preparations at Sinai

Numbers 1:1—10:10

The opening scene of the Book of Numbers occurs 10½ months after the arrival of the people of Israel at Mount Sinai. It was one month after the completion of the Tabernacle[1] (Exod. 40:1-33) and slightly over a year after the start of the Exodus. The book begins by placing Israel in the midst of the central institutions of her national being, the priesthood and God dwelling in the Tabernacle.[2] It begins abruptly with a command from God to Moses to **take ye the sum** (2; "take a census," RSV) of the congregation.

A. The Census, 1:1—2:34

1. *Purpose of the Census* (1:1-3)

This particular census (numbering) was related closely to one which occurred earlier (Exod. 30:11-16), which centered around the need for income to support the sanctuary and was, in a sense, the basis of a poll tax for this purpose. While this one was military rather than religious in its nature, many scholars feel that, so far as the records were concerned, it was but an extension of the former and that really there were not two numberings, but only one.[3] It is also related to the census taken later in Moab, prior to the Israelites' entering into Canaan (c. 26). That census was related to the assignment of territory to the various tribes.

John Wesley expressed well the purpose of this census. He says it was "partly that the great number of the people might be known to the praise of God's faithfulness in making good his

[1]Or *tent of meeting* (RSV) or *trysting tent,* so called because it was there that God met with Moses (Exod. 25:22). "It is important to distinguish between the *Ohel*—i.e., the *tent*—and the *mishkan*—i.e., the *tabernacle*—which was the building of shittim wood with its curtains which was within the tent" (C. J. Ellicott, "Numbers," *Ellicott's Commentary on the Bible,* edited by Charles J. Ellicott [The Layman's Handy Commentary Series; Grand Rapids: Zondervan Publishing House, 1961], p. 23).

[2]John Marsh, "The Book of Numbers" (Exegesis), *The Interpreter's Bible,* edited by George A. Buttrick, *et al.,* II (New York: Abingdon Press, 1953), 143.

[3]Ellicott, *op. cit.,* pp. 22, 36.

promises of multiplying them; partly for the better ordering of the camp; and partly that this account might be compared with the other at the close of the book, where we read that not one of all this vast number, except Caleb and Joshua were left alive, a fair warning to all future generations to take heed of rebelling against the Lord."[4]

Such exact registrations as these probably formed the core of the genealogical lore which was so important to both the secular and the religious history of the Jews. These served as the "records center" of the nation, preserving for history details which are missing from the cultures of so many other nations. It is quite evident, since the totals were in "round numbers," that the purposes of this census were fulfilled with these general figures.

The command of God was, "Take a census of all the congregation of the people of Israel, by families, by fathers' houses, according to the number of names, every male, head by head; from twenty years old and upward" (2, RSV). **Every male by their polls** (2) is better, "Get a record of every male" (Berk.). This census related to military service, as it involved all **that are able to go forth to war** (3). In this sense it was not unlike the selective service registrations common to many twentieth-century nations. Each male Israelite (except those who were of the tribe of Levi) was a soldier and was to serve in this capacity as Israel pressed toward and into Canaan. It is sometimes assumed that old men were exempt from such military service, but nowhere in the record is an "age of retirement" given. Apparently, physical disability was the only exception to such service.

2. *The Pattern of the Census* (1:4-19)

Moses and Aaron were to accomplish the census with assistance from one **man of every tribe; every one head of the house** (4). It is probable that these were "lay" people, as contrasted to the former census where the Levites were the assistants. The difference might have been occasioned by the fact that this was a political and military census. Even so, the very names of the assistants in most instances embody some reference to God, and seem to indicate that the people felt that God was present with them from the very start of their pilgrimage.[5] "These were the

[4]*Explanatory Notes upon the Old Testament* (Bristol, Wm. Pine, n.d.), I, 449.

[5]IB, II, 144.

ones chosen from the congregation, the leaders of their ancestral tribes, the heads of the clans of Israel" (16, RSV).

It is logical that Moses, Aaron, and these assistants set up stations to which the representatives of the tribes and/or families of the tribes reported. Since the previous census had been taken so recently, it is assumed that the records were already in order and needed only to be presented. The representatives **declared their pedigrees** (18, lit., "announced themselves as having been born"). They were then enrolled under three heads, by (*a*) tribe, (*b*) family, and (*c*) father's house. Such an accurate record made it possible for later generations to trace the genealogy of Jesus.[6]

3. *Results of the Census* (1:20-46)

The results of the census can best be seen and analyzed in tabulation form. For convenience of comparison, the parallel figures for the census in Moab (c. 26) are also given.

Tribe	Sinai Census (*Cc. 1—2*)	Moab Census (*C. 26*)
Reuben	46,500	43,730
Simeon	59,300	22,200
Gad	45,650	40,500
Judah	74,600	76,500
Issachar	54,400	64,300
Zebulun	57,400	60,500
Ephraim	40,500	32,500
Manasseh	32,200	52,700
Benjamin	35,400	45,600
Dan	62,700	64,400
Asher	41,500	53,400
Naphtali	53,400	45,400
Total	603,550	601,730

These figures, of course, included only the "men of war," adults 20 years of age and over. Various rules have been used to seek to determine the number of the total congregation, counting the women, children, the "mixed multitude," and the Levites. The spread suggests 2 million as a minimum and 3 million as a maximum. In any event, it was a sizable group to venture on such a journey.

[6]Ellicott, *op. cit.*, p. 24.

Liberal and conservative scholars have not agreed on the number of people involved. The former have insisted that the figure shown is grossly in error. Their arguments, however, have not been based either on proven flaws in the record or on documented evidence from outside sources. Rather, their reasoning proceeds as follows: Miracles are not possible. The land could not possibly support such a group apart from miracles. Therefore the "modern mind" is forced to discount the scriptural count as inaccurate. Conservative scholars, on the other hand, stand firmly on the confidence that miracles are not only possible but that God performed miracles as the biblical record states. They insist that any suggested errors in calculating these figures have not been authenticated. Moreover, the account concurs with other biblical records such as Deut. 29:5; Ps. 78:26-28; I Cor. 10:4, which support the idea that the Israelites composed a very large number as they moved from Egypt to Canaan. Hence conservative scholars believe that the total of this census as recorded here is basically correct.[7]

The grand total which was tabulated in the census taken in Moab approximates the total given of those who left Sinai, even though there are shifts in the totals of the tribes. Thus there was a "replacement" of the old generation with the new in accord with the statement of judgment which God meted out for the nation's unbelief at Kadesh-barnea (14:27-37).

4. *The Levites Excluded* (1:47-54)

The Levites (47) were excluded from this part of the census and from the regulations which were laid down for the other tribes. There is no reason given why the tribe of Levi was singled out by God for special service. It is most probable that this came about either because Levi was the tribe to which Moses and Aaron belonged or because this tribe was quick to champion the cause of God at the incident of the golden calf (Exod. 32:26). It is apparent that the decree here was but a reaffirming of policy which already had been in operation (cf. Lev. 25:32). In any event God set the Levites apart and gave them specific responsibilities. The command was, **Thou shalt appoint the Levites over the tabernacle . . . and over all things that belong to it** (50).

[7]Details of the pros and cons of this issue can be reviewed in most larger commentaries.

In this connection, the Levites were subject to a separate census (3:1—4:49) and each family within the tribe was given specific responsibilities in this care of the Tent of Meeting. **When the tabernacle setteth forward** (51) is better, "When it is time for the Dwelling to be moved" (Berk.).

5. *The Location of the Tribes* (2:1-34)

One of the important purposes of the census was to organize the camp into a plan of march. It is here, perhaps as at no other point, that the first steps in nationhood are evidenced. In this organization there was an outline of intertribal relationships; the structure of a "city" with addresses where people could be located; a plan of march, so that the movement would be orderly; and a plan of worship, so that the people's religious and political-military activities and interests would not be hopelessly separated.[8] A diagram best explains the outline of the camp.

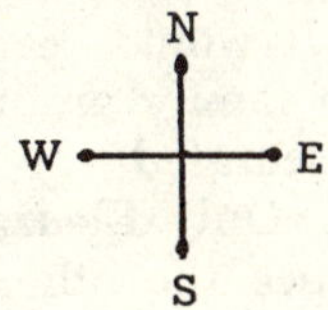

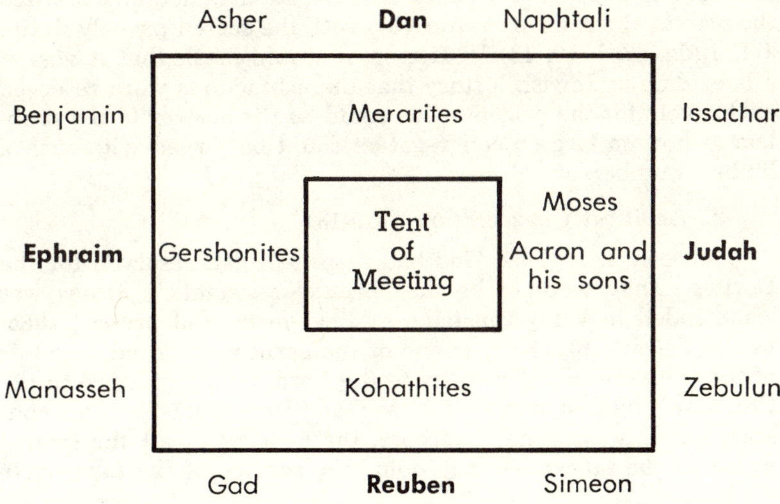

[8]G. Campbell Morgan, *Exposition of the Whole Bible* (Westwood, N.J.: Fleming H. Revell Co., 1959), p. 61.

Significant to the alignment of the tribes was the placing of the Tent of Meeting in the center. The people were never to forget that "God is in the midst of his people." It is also noteworthy that each tribe should **pitch by his own standard, with the ensign of their father's house** (2). We do not have an accurate record of what these ensigns were. Perhaps there were only four, representing the "lead" tribe on each side of the square. Jewish tradition ascribes a *lion* to Judah, a *human head* to Reuben, an *ox* to Ephraim, and an *eagle* to Dan.[9] **Their armies** (9, 18) is better "their companies" (RSV) or "battalions" (Moffatt).

B. Provisions for the Levites, 3:1—4:49

1. *Aaron and Moses* (3:1-4)

Aaron and Moses (1) were of the tribe of Levi and, in one sense, were its leaders. It would seem that Moses' sons found their places in their own family group (Kohathites), while **the sons of Aaron** were **consecrated** (3) or ordained[10] to carry on the duties of the priests. Only **Eleazar and Ithamar** (4) were involved at this time, since the other two sons had met their deaths by offering unholy sacrifices (Lev. 10:1-2). There is some evidence to support the belief that the Levites actually assisted the priests, **the sons of Aaron** (3), with the sacred priestly duties (cf. Judg. 17:5, 10, 13).[11] If true, it would mean that it was at a later date in Jewish history that these functions were reserved exclusively for the priests. This could be the answer to the problem of how so large a congregation could be served with such a limited number of priests.

2. *Levitical Consecration* (3:5-13)

As seen in 1:47-54, God had a special plan reserved for the Levites. They were to be the "priests' assistants." Moses was commanded to **bring the tribe of Levi near, and present them before Aaron** (6). Here is one of the earliest recorded accounts of the consecration of persons to the Lord, an act so basic to the Christian's highest relationship to God (Rom. 12:1-2). This consecration was for a holy purpose, the keeping of **all the instruments of the tabernacle** and doing **the service of the tabernacle**

[9]IB, II, 150.

[10]This word means lit. "to fill the hand."

[11]IB, II, 153.

(8). It was full-time service for the Lord in the fullest meaning of the term. Here also are the seeds of that further truth, that such consecration is exclusively for God's children (John 14:17), for **the stranger that cometh nigh shall be put to death** (10). The word **stranger** is used here (cf. also 1:51; 16:40) as "any unauthorized person"; or in the spiritual setting, "any unclean or unfit person."

The roots of this idea of setting apart certain persons as God's own lay in the Passover (Exod. 13:2, 11-12) when God **hallowed . . . all the firstborn in Israel, both man and beast** (13). But instead of claiming **all the firstborn that openeth the matrix** (12), God took as His own all of the people of the tribe of Levi, including their livestock.

3. *Census of the Levites* (3:14-39)

It was necessary, in harmony with the general plan of the census, to number the tribe of Levi, counting the male children over a month old;[12] but also to number the males between the ages of 30 and 50, who would do the work of caring for the Tabernacle and ministering under the direction of the priests. Chapter 3 reports the results of the general census of the Levites and gives the location of the families in relationship to the Tent of Meeting (see diagram, p. 409). Chapter 4 lists the totals of those who were able to serve in these various tasks. The results of the two tabulations are as follows:

Family	*Males one month old and upward*	*Males between 30 and 50*	*Location*
Gershonites	7,500	2,630	West
Kohathites	8,600	2,750	South
Merarites	6,200	3,200	North
Moses and Aaron			East
Total	22,300	8,580	

The summary total in v. 39 drops 300 from the total of males one month old and upward as listed by families, giving a total of 22,000. Some suggest that there could easily have been an error in the transcription of the total. Others seem to feel that the 300 could have been the "firstborn" of the Levites, who

[12]As contrasted with the other tribes, who were numbered from 20 years.

would already have been the Lord's and hence would not be counted with those who would serve as "substitutes" for the firstborn of other tribes.

For those who seek to analyze these figures meticulously there remain some problems unsolved, but there are no methods of calculation which serve any better than these. In any event, the summary total (39) was used as the base from which was figured the number of those to be redeemed by an offering. For a description of the assignments of the Levitical families, see comments below and on c. 4.

4. *Redemption of Israel's Firstborn* (3:40-51)

In order that the exchange of Levites for all of **the firstborn** (40) of the other tribes might tally out, Moses was instructed to count the firstborn and compare the figure with the totals of the tribe of Levi. There was a differential of 273 (46). To make up this difference there was a "plan of redemption"; i.e., in place of the firstborn sons being given for the service of the Lord, an offering of **five shekels**[13] was presented for each one. This was reckoned by **the shekel of the sanctuary** (47) of **twenty gerahs** (cf. Exod. 30:13; Lev. 27:25). The total of 1,365 shekels probably was not collected from the individual families but was taken from the tribal treasuries and given to Aaron and his sons as a total amount. **The number of the names** (40, 43) is simply "the number" (Berk.).

This plan of redemption is a foregleam of the great plan of redemption in Christ for all men and also underlines God's timeless claim upon man's firstfruits of life and possessions.

5. *Duties of the Levitical Families* (3:25-26, 31, 36; 4:1-49)

Specific duties were assigned to each of the three families of the Levites. This was to make for efficiency in caring for the Tent of Meeting and to expedite the process of dismantling and

[13]Babylonian standards of measure were largely used by the Israelites during this period of their history. The use of terms for weight (**shekels, gerahs,** 47) meant that this was unminted silver. Since the term *shekel* did not uniformly refer to an established weight (varying from slightly over eight ounces to nearly 17 ounces), it is not possible to relate it exactly to a modern equivalent. Some scholars (cf. Berk.) have compared the shekel to the U.S. silver dollar. Probably this is as close as can be determined. On this basis the redemption price would be $5.00 a person, with the total collected amounting to $1,365.

assembling it as need demanded. These duties are specified in cc. 3—4 as follows:

The Kohathites (listed first in c. 4), and in some ways the elite of the Levites, had the care[14] of the sacred utensils of worship—the **table,** the **vessels,** the **altars,** the **hanging,** and all of the **service** pieces (3:31; 4:5-15). They were under the direct supervision of the priest, Eleazer (3:32), and were subject to far more strict regulations than were the others (4:15). Yet there were certain exceptions which had to be made since they were responsible for making these sacred portions of the Tent of Meeting ready for travel (4:17-20). Certainly there should be a reverence for sacred things which ought to permeate all of our lives.

The Gershonites (listed first in c. 3) had the care of the tent, the curtains, and draperies—the "soft goods" of the Tent of Meeting (3:25-26; 4:25-28).

The Merarites were in charge of the heavy, cumbersome pieces—the **boards,** the **bars,** the **pillars,** the **sockets,** and the "solid" part of the fabric (3:36-37; 4:31-32). They were **under the hand** (supervision) **of Ithamar** (4:33), who was also the supervisor during the building of the Tent of Meeting (Exod. 38:21).

C. Social Responsibilities, 5:1-31

The potential social problems involved in such a trek as lay before Israel would stagger the imagination. It was not unexpected, then, that certain laws which had previously been laid down would be reviewed on the eve of departure. Three are mentioned in this chapter that touch those areas in which the most acute problems would arise: *cleanliness, honesty,* and *morality.*

1. One of the serious problems of a large group of people camping in such close proximity with limited (in the modern concept) facilities is that of *health and sanitation.* There were, no doubt, some religious implications in the laws regarding leprosy and perhaps also in the laws regarding contact with the dead. However the fact that diseases with other symptoms were

[14]The intricate and sacred nature of these responsibilities is given in detail in 4:5-15.

also involved seems to underline the hygienic issue. One need only to imagine the sanitation situation which faced Moses, the possibility of epidemics, and the constant threat to the health of the people, to see some of the reasons for the strict rules which were here laid down.

Three specifics are mentioned in v. 2: leprosy (Lev. 13:3); infection (discharge, running sores, etc.; Lev. 15:2); and uncleanness through contact with **the dead** (2; cf. Lev. 21:1). We cannot fully equate all of these regulations to modern-day concepts of the cause and cure of disease, but it is not difficult to see that the health of the people had to be protected. Even with those diseases for which the cause of contamination and/or contagion was uncertain, isolation was still the prescribed procedure. It would appear that areas **without the camp** (3) were designated as places to which infected persons would go and where some care was provided for them.

Beyond this, however, there appears the strong intimation that uncleanness is abhorrent to a holy God. Not only must unclean persons be removed from where they will contaminate others, but also they must not **defile** the camp, **in the midst whereof** (3) the holy God dwells. Integral to this whole issue, so prevalent in the law passages, is the idea that God wants those among whom He dwells to be His people. Uncleanness, moral and spiritual as well as physical, has no place alongside a holy God. In these laws and these commands are found the seeds of two significant concepts with which the Word of God abounds: the "idea of the holy" and the "idea of the family of God" (Lev. 11:44; 26:12). These two come together in the concept of Christian holiness, God's plan for a holy people whom He can call His own.

2. The second serious problem which arises when large groups of people are thrown together in close proximity is the *security of personal property* when dishonesty is not controlled. The property rights of all must be protected (5-10). And so the procedures of dealing with those who have violated this right are outlined.[15] Simply, it is this: restoration of the goods wrongfully taken with a **fifth part** (7) or 20 percent added. Or, in the case where such restitution cannot be carried out, because

[15]A previously given law (Lev. 6:1-7) deals with restoring stolen property. This is a supplement to it (IB, II, 167).

the one wronged has **no kinsman** (8), the amount shall be taken **to the priest,** along with **the ram of the atonement.** An accurate, though not complete, picture regarding the forgiveness of sins, is given. There is the need for *repentance,* the test of *restitution,* and the fact of *reconciliation.*

3. The third problem suggested centers in the marriage relationship (11-31). The issue here was not proved adultery, for laws concerning this were clear and prescribed the death penalty (Lev. 20:10). Rather this regulation related to situations in which infidelity could not be proved (13, 29) or in which a wife's conduct was such as to arouse suspicions (Amp. OT). **Taken with the manner** (13) is better "taken in the act" (RSV).

Under these conditions, the husband could go to the priest with his wife and with an offering. While the procedure suggested is not unlike the "trial by ordeal" of many primitive people, here it had God's blessing. It was no doubt sanctioned by Him in the light of possible similar practices known to the Israelites. There is, however, no instance recorded in the Scriptures where this ordeal was used. According to the Talmud, the provision ceased 40 years before the destruction of Jerusalem, hence during the life of Jesus. These facts give credence to the view that this was an interim provision for the desert and as such was not one of major significance.[16]

However, in the process of preparing the people for their journey, this provision and the principles incident to marital fidelity are given a prominent place. Perhaps the severity of the penalty alone served the purpose intended.

The ordeal centered in the **holy water . . . and dust** from **the floor of the tabernacle** (17). These provisions must have impressed all concerned with God's interest in the issue. The **jealousy offering** (18) was held by the woman. Her head was uncovered; she agreed to the law and the penalty by her **Amen, amen** (22); she drank **the bitter water** (23) which had dissolved the ink on which the law had been written on a parchment. If the woman was guilty, the bitter water would cause serious reactions in the female organs. If she was not guilty, she would be declared clean, and the bitter water would cause her to be fruitful in bearing children.

[16]R. Winterbotham, "Numbers" (Exposition), *Pulpit Commentary* (New York: Funk and Wagnalls, n.d.), p. 41.

Here were provisions both for the man who accused his wife of infidelity and for the wife, that she might not be unjustly condemned. Moral cleanness and marital fidelity must always be the foundations of a society. Honesty and fairness in the marriage relationship must exist if a marriage is to succeed and to have God's blessings.

D. The Nazarite Vow, 6:1-21

1. *Plan for the Vow* (6:1-8)

The vow of a Nazarite (2) was one of the unique provisions of God for His people. It included all who might choose to take the vow, men and women from any tribe and from any station in life. Throughout the OT there are provisions for the priests and the Levites to perform special religious services. This vow, however, sets the stage for the universality of the NT gospel which makes it possible for anyone who chooses to do so to enter the service of God.

The word "Nazarite" is from the Hebrew *nazir,* meaning "to separate." In later Hebrew history this vow was a fairly common practice represented by such well-known persons as Samson, Samuel, and John the Baptist. The vow of the Nazarite was strict, even more so than the vows under which the priests served.

a. The Nazarite vowed to **separate himself from wine and strong drink** (3). The general term would be "intoxicating beverages." **Vinegar** is included in the list of prohibitions because the Hebrews made theirs from intoxicants which had gone sour.[17] Added were the "juice of grapes" and "grapes, fresh or dried" (RSV) (probably in raisin cakes). In fact, the Nazarite was to abstain from everything "produced by the grapevine" (4), even to the "seed or the skins" (RSV) or "unripe grapes or tendrils" (Smith-Goodspeed).

b. The Nazarite was, during the time of the vow, to let his hair grow; **there shall no razor come upon his head** (5). This stood as an outer symbol of his vow to God and indicated, in the language of the rituals, that he was clean.

c. The Nazarite, furthermore, was to **come at no dead body** (6) and thus by such contact make himself ceremonially un-

[17]IB, II, 170.

clean. This was so strict that he was not even to assist with the burial of his own kinfolk (7).

The Nazarite was indeed a "separated" person (Titus 2:14), and during the period of his vow performed specialized services for God. There was also the spiritual implication that **all the days of his separation he** was to be **holy unto the Lord** (8). The vow spoke of personal physical cleanness, of ceremonial purity as related to the law, and of strong moral discipline. The external signs provided an evidence to the world around that the man was a Nazarite.

We see in this relationship a forecast of God's purpose for all of His children, a personal, voluntary choice to be separated persons, holy people, dedicated to God's service. This is clearly related, in spirit and purpose, to the consecration vows of the NT Christian (cf. II Cor. 6:14, 16-18). It points to the heart of God's desire that all of His children be Nazarites in spirit.

2. *Cleansing from Defilement* (6:9-12)

In connection with the ceremonial uncleanness which would result should the Nazarite be thrust inadvertently into contact with death, God made provision for his cleansing. **He shall shave his head** (9) and bring his offering of "two turtledoves or two young pigeons" (10, RSV) to the priest who will make atonement for him. God does not make requirements without providing a means of fulfillment, and an atonement when such is needed (I John 2:1-2). **The head of his consecration** (9) is a figure of speech for "his person" (Moffatt).

3. *Completion of the Vow* (6:13-21)

The Nazarite vow was for a specified period of time as indicated by **the days of his separation** (13). Probably this was for not less than a year, and could be for a lifetime. When the time had elapsed, the Nazarite would appear before the priest with **one he lamb . . . for a burnt offering** (offering of consecration); **one ewe lamb . . . for a sin offering** (for atonement for sins committed during the period of his vows, actually to come in sequence before the burnt offering); **one ram . . . for peace offerings** (14), and **unleavened bread . . . and meat** (cereal) **offering; and drink offerings** (15, for thanksgiving).

This ran the full gamut of the offerings which had been required (Leviticus 1—4). By appropriate ceremonies the priest would absolve the person from his vow and he would then be free to pursue a regular course of life. The shaving of his head was the sign that he had fulfilled his vow and was no longer a Nazarite.

E. The Benediction, 6:22-27

1. *Its Place*

Dropped into the record at this point, without any particular reference to the context, are the delightful words of the benediction known as the "Priestly Blessing." This was the formula which the priests were to use in blessing a consecrated and sanctified people (Deut. 21:5). Attempts to find the origin of this at a much later date have not proved convincing, and there is no good reason to believe that it had not been used earlier (cf. Lev. 9:22) or that it was not formalized at this time in Hebrew history. In any event, it was used extensively in later Jewish worship and, in part at least, has been used in Christian circles.

2. *Its Value*

It would seem that at this stage in Israel's history authority was given to the priests to use the divine name in blessing in a similar manner to which the oriental father blessed his children in God's name. The great value of the text is the manner in which it lifts up the character of God before the people. The blessing consists of three clauses comprising vv. 24-26. Each verse is a couplet with the second portion presenting the application of the grace suggested in the first.

3. *Its Text*

a. **The Lord bless thee,**
and keep thee (24).

"The blessing of God is the goodness of God in action," said John Calvin. This blessing is the assurance of God's *protection* and of His hand stretched out over His own. Such blessing is not alone in the physical affairs of life (Psalms 91) but also in the deeper spiritual issues (John 17:9-15; I Thess. 5:23).

b. **The Lord make his face shine upon thee,**
and be gracious unto thee (25).

The **face** of God is His presence turned toward man or turned away from him. Israel was made conscious ever and again of God's favor as represented by His face turned toward them and His presence and glory in their midst. When God's face is turned toward man in favor, there is *pardon;* the grace of God is thus extended to meet human need (Ps. 21:6; 34:15).

c. **The Lord lift up his countenance upon thee, and give thee peace** (26).

This is God's entire being as it is brought to bear on the salvation of His people. The result is **peace**—that which comes, not by the disciplines of the human mind, but by the presence of the Holy Spirit of peace (John 14:26-27). "It is more than mere absence of discord, expressing rather the positive well-being and security of a man whose mind is stayed on God."[18]

d. **And they shall put my name upon the children of Israel; and I will bless them** (27).

The **name** of the God of Israel means more than the mere letters which form the word. His name is a part of His being and can be disassociated neither from His nature (Exod. 3:13-14) nor from His covenant (Exod. 6:3). Hence, to put the covenant name of God upon the people had real meaning. It could not be done without divine authority. Beyond this is the truth that in accepting the name of God as theirs the people were acknowledging His fatherhood and their sonship. They were taking His nature as well as His family name for their own. This makes possible not only God's blessing upon them but their blessing upon a world. "A like idea is expressed by the New Testament thought of the Church as the body of Christ."[19]

In 22-26 we see "God's Benediction." (1) The consecration of a separated life brings God's blessing of preservation, 24; (2) God's favor is shown in His grace, 25; (3) Fellowship with God is experienced in peace, 26 (G. B. Williamson).

F. Offerings from the Princes, 7:1-89

1. *Equipment for the Levites* (7:1-9)

The readying of the Tent of Meeting and the securing of materials and supplies for worship were a vital part of preparation for the journey from Sinai. Moses set up the Tent of Meeting, **anointed . . . and sanctified it, and all of the instruments**

[18]*Ibid.*, p. 174. [19]*Ibid.*

thereof (1).[20] It was then that the princes of the tribes brought their offerings. The gifts not only served as an act of worship, but also provided the essential equipment and material which the priests and Levites would need as they performed their duties in the future. As should always be the case, these offerings of worship had a practical value in the total work of God.

The six **wagons** and 12 **oxen** went to the clans of **Gershon** (7) and **Merari** (8), so that they could transport the heavy material which made up the Tent of Meeting. Two wagons were for **the sons of Gershon,** who were to handle the "soft goods" (4:25), and four wagons for **the sons of Merari,** who were to transport the heavier boards, bars, pillars, and sockets (4:31-32). There was no need for **the sons of Kohath** (9) to have wagons, because their task was to carry the ark and the sacred utensils of worship on their shoulders.

2. *Offerings from the Tribes* (7:10-88)

Following the initial gift of vehicles, the princes, each on a succeeding day, brought offerings **for the dedicating of the altar** (11). They came in the order to which they were assigned in the camp, beginning with the tribe of Judah. The offering of each prince was identical. It included vessels which would be used in worship and included "one silver plate . . . one silver basin (13) . . . one golden dish" (14, RSV). Each prince also brought the ingredients for a "cereal" (RSV) offering, a **burnt offering** (15), **a sin offering** (16), and **peace offerings** (17). Presumably not all of these provisions were used immediately. Some were kept in reserve for the sacrifices which would be offered later. It is assumed that these offerings were clean and measured up to every specification of the law (Lev. 2:1; 3:1; 4:3).

[20]The act of anointing and sanctifying applied to things as well as sacrifices and persons. This highlights one-half of the meaning of the term "sanctify," i.e., to set apart (cf. dictionary). It is the common usage in the OT, particularly in relationship to things. Several elements are inherent in the meaning: (1) relationship to God, (2) exclusion of the secular, (3) positive dedication to God or sacred uses. This applied not only to the Tent of Meeting but also to the sacrifices, firstfruits, and everything that was hallowed by this setting apart for sacred use. Cf. G. Allen Turner, *The More Excellent Way* (Winona Lake, Ind.: Light and Life Press, 1952), p. 26; and by the same author, *The Vision Which Transforms* (Kansas City: Beacon Hill Press, 1964), pp. 21-22.

After the last of the princes, from the tribe of Naphtali, had brought his offering, **the dedication of the altar** was complete (84). These offerings helped provide a spiritual preparation for the journey. As always is the case, a significant offering cost the people something. With David, at a much later date, they could say in essence, "Neither will we offer offerings unto God of that which doth cost us nothing" (II Sam. 24:24).

3. *God's Answer* (7:89)

This kind of sacrifice pleases God. When the last of the princes had brought his gifts, Moses went into the Tent of Meeting to talk with God. Here he heard **the voice of one speaking unto him from off the mercy seat** (89). It is intimated that from this time on, here in the holy place, Moses received his messages from God.[21] Worship and sacrifice should result in hearing from God (Isa. 6:1-8). It was a good start for the journey toward the Promised Land.

G. Cleansing of the Levites, 8:1-26

1. *The Lights* (8:1-4)

The lighting of **the seven lamps** (2) seemed to mark the completion of the sanctification of the priests (Exod. 40:4). It was in that sense a sign that they were ready to offer sacrifices for the people. In this instance, it was the final step in preparation for the cleansing of the Levites and in making them ready for their sacred duties. The light from the lamps was a constant symbol of the power and presence of God. This symbolism of light also carries a deep spiritual significance today as it illustrates the spiritual truths of the NT. For a drawing of **the candlestick** (4) see Chart *A*.

2. *Instructions for Cleansing* (8:5-15)

Up to this point all that had been said regarding the special, holy service of the Levites was projected into the future. The time had now come when they must begin their duties. But before they could start, they must be spiritually and personally prepared. Only a holy people can perform a holy work. Hence God ordered, **Thus shalt thou do unto them, to cleanse them** (7).

[21]David W. Kerr, "Numbers," *The Bible Expositor*, ed. by Carl F. H. Henry (Philadelphia: A. J. Holman Co., 1960), p. 158.

This was more exactly a rite of purification than merely of consecration.[22]

The steps were thorough; they included a physical cleansing as well as a ceremonial and legal purification. Here is the first recorded use of the **water of purifying** (7), described in 19:9, 17-18. This special agent for cleansing seemingly was made up ahead of time and was available when the priests needed it. How descriptive of the blood of Christ, of which it was indeed a type, instantly available when needed (Heb. 9:13-14; I John 2:1-2).

The steps in the purifying of the Levites suggest God's plan for the cleansing of His children today (cf. Isa. 52:11): (1) Provision for the cleansing (I John 1:7); (2) Preparation for the cleansing (Col. 3:5-8); (3) Fulfillment of the cleansing (Heb. 10:22).

In addition to the ritual, the congregation (by what representatives we are not told) **put their hands upon the Levites** (10). This act signified that they dedicated the Levites to a special service in place of their own firstborn. By thus laying their hands on them they pledged to provide for them as they engaged in this holy service.

3. *God's Plan for the Levites* (8:16-26)

This plan of God for the Levites has appeared several times earlier and here serves as a recapitulation of what has gone before. Perhaps it was a delicate issue or one which was not fully understood. In any event, it was an important part of God's scheme of organization for Israel and Moses repeated it carefully whenever the issue was up for consideration. After the ceremony of cleansing and atonement was completed, the Levites **went . . . in to do their service . . . as the Lord had commanded** (22). Thus was set in motion the pattern which prevailed throughout Israel's history. All able-bodied male Levites between the years of 25[23] and 50 (24-25) performed this service to the Lord. *The Berkeley Version* clarifies v. 26 thus: "Thereafter they shall assist their fellow workers in the meeting tent in keeping with the office, but shall not discharge the regular duties."

[22]*Ibid.*, p. 159.

[23]The difference between the beginning age given here and that stated in 4:3 is best explained by the suggestion that at age 25 an apprenticeship began and that full service did not begin until age 30.

H. ON THE EVE OF DEPARTURE, 9:1—10:10

1. *The Passover Observed* (9:1-14)

The passover (2) was central in the worship pattern for the Israelites (Exod. 12:1-27). However, even though the procedures stipulated were exact, yet in the actual observance there was considerable variance. For example, this was only the second observance, though two years had elapsed since the first. There is no record of another observance short of the arrival in Canaan (Josh. 5:10). Here in connection with preparations for the journey God ordered an observance of the Passover, **in his appointed season: according to all the rites of it** (3).[24] Surely, with all of the tests that lay ahead, Israel needed a time of remembrance of God's great power.

There were exceptions to the rules which were laid down.[25] Those who were **unclean by reason of a dead body, or be in a journey afar off** (10), could observe the Passover one month later—**the fourteenth day of the second month** (11).[26] God's provision here obviously was directed to those who were caught in circumstances beyond their control. In 13, He carefully warned that these circumstances were not to be used as excuses. There was provision also for the **stranger** (14). In this setting the word means a proselyte or a settled alien, one who had cast his lot with the Israelites but who was not a native. Even in this early day of God's dealings with His people, there is a careful blending of the spirit of the law with the letter. The essence of sin is disobedience which is intentional and purposeful, not a failure that is inadvertent.

2. *The Cloud and the Fire* (9:15-23)

The promise of God's abiding presence and of His continual guidance throughout the entire journey of the Israelites from Egypt to Canaan has been a source of help to all generations since. They had enjoyed the pillar of cloud by day and the pillar

[24]There is some indication that modified provisions were allowed in this desert, nomadic setting.

[25]We see in 8 the pattern that Moses sought to follow throughout the journey, i.e., when in doubt, seek the mind of God. This is good procedure in any day and for every man (Jas. 1:5).

[26]The time given for the holding of the Passover preceded by two weeks the command to number the people (1:1). It is probable that the mention of it at this point was related to the exceptions made for those who could not observe it earlier.

of fire by night since their departure from Egypt (Exod. 13:21). But here God assured them that the same hovering presence would be with them as they moved on. From the time the Tent of Meeting was completed it became the resting place of the pillar of cloud and the pillar of fire when the congregation was camped. In addition to these visible symbols of God's presence, the people had the direct **commandment of the Lord** (18) to instruct them as they journeyed. While the text here reflects retrospection, showing that it was edited in the light of a later time, the promise of God on the eve of departure was reassuring. Such promises are indeed timeless (John 16:7, 13; Heb. 13:5).

3. *The Silver Trumpets* (10:1-10)

It was no small task to engineer the movement of so vast a congregation. The camp had been carefully organized to make this easier. In addition, God called for **two trumpets of silver** (2) to be made which were to be blown by the priests for the calling of the assembly and for "breaking camp" (2, RSV). Since these were specified to be of silver, they were probably different from the ram's-horn trumpets called the shofar, which were used in other situations and in later Jewish worship. The silver trumpets used on this occasion were probably made in the shape of a long, slender tube with a flared end. Each probably had a different tone, so that the sounds given out by the two instruments could be easily distinguished.[27]

The sounding of both trumpets signaled for the entire **assembly** to gather (3). The sounding of **one trumpet** called only **the princes** (4). The sounding of **an alarm** (5), a sustained "blast" (Berk.), called the camps to begin their march. The first such signal was for the **camps . . . on the east**; the second was for the **camps . . . on the south** (6). It is inferred that there were third and fourth signals which summoned the camps on the west and north, in harmony with the directions that had previously been given (c. 2).

Following the instructions there is a soliloquy on the place of **trumpets** (8) in the life of Israel. They were to be used to call the armies **to war** (9) and to help celebrate the feast days and **the sacrifices** (10). The use of trumpets was to be **an ordinance for ever throughout** their **generations** (8) and was to be **a memorial before . . . God** (10).

[27]IB, II, 189.

Section II *From Mountain to Wilderness*

Numbers 10:11—14:45

A. The Camp Moves Out, 10:11-36

1. *The Journey Begins* (10:11-13)

Without doubt, in view of all the foregoing preparations, the camp was in a fever of excitement to get moving. The people had been at this one location for the better part of a year (Exod. 19:1). The elapsed time, plus the intensive concentration on departure procedures, must have intensified their anticipation to a white heat. Then the great day dawned! The **cloud was taken up** (11), the trumpets sounded (5), and **the children of Israel took their journeys out of the wilderness of Sinai** (12; see map 3) in the order of march which had been established.

2. *Order of the Tribes and Their Leaders* (10:14-28)

The tribes are listed here, with the names of their leaders given in parentheses. This listing established the order of the march: **Judah** (14; **Nahshon**), **Issachar** (15; **Nethaneel**), **Zebulun** (16; **Eliab**), the Gershonites and Merarites (17) bearing the Tent of Meeting, **Reuben** (18; **Elizur**), **Simeon** (19; **Shelumiel**), **Gad** (20; **Eliasaph**), **the Kohathites** (21) bearing the holy implements of the Tent of Meeting,[1] **Ephraim** (22; **Elishama**), **Manasseh** (23; **Gamaliel**), **Benjamin** (24; **Abidon**), **Dan**[2] (25; **Ahiezer**), **Asher** (26; **Pagiel**), **Naphtali** (27; **Ahira**).

Set forward (28) would be "set out" (RSV). **The rearward** (25) means the rear guard. **Armies** (28) is better "hosts" (RSV).

[1]The Kohathites with the Tabernacle furniture were this far back in the procession in order that the Tent of Meeting, which went on ahead, would be set up (21) and ready to receive the sacred instruments of worship by the time they arrived at the new campsite.

[2]The tribe of **Dan**, and probably those also of **Asher** and **Naphtali**, were assigned the responsibility to be the rear guard. This meant that they would collect stragglers, take charge of those who fainted by the way, and find and restore lost articles (*The Pentateuch and Haftorahs*, ed. by J. H. Hertz [London: Soncino Press, 1952], p. 612).

3. *Moses' Plea to His Brother-in-law*[3] (10:29-32)

Moses' father-in-law, Jethro (Reuel), had joined the Israelite camp soon after it had arrived at Sinai (Exod. 18:1-27), bringing Moses' wife, Zipporah, and her two sons with him. He soon returned to his own land of Midian, but it is evident that one of his sons, **Hobab** (29; not mentioned in the Exodus account), remained with the camp. When plans got under way to move on toward Canaan, Hobab gave indication that he would return to his **own land** (30). Moses pled with him to remain with the Israelites, insisting that they would need his skilled services as a guide. They were moving into **the wilderness** (31), a land with which Hobab was well-acquainted (31). For this service he would be a recipient of all of the blessings God had promised to Israel (32). The record does not so state, but it seems evident that Moses prevailed, for later history shows that Hobab's descendants lived in Canaan (Judg. 1:16; I Sam. 15:6, Amp. OT).

"Not Receiving but Serving" is the theme of 29-32. (1) An invitation to benefit refused, 29-30; (2) An appeal to serve accepted, 31 (G. B. Williamson).

4. *Ceremonial Prayers* (10:33-36)

It would seem from the language used here that **the ark of the covenant** (33) was in advance of the procession, even as it was when the Israelites later crossed the Jordan River (Josh. 3:6). In this position it symbolized the presence of God, and when it stopped, it would determine the next campsite of the company. It is just as probable, however, that the position of the ark referred to here was religious as well as geographical; i.e., it was "foremost" in the camp because it was the most prominent.

The whole procedure of the movement of the camp reflected the fact that God was in the midst. This is indicated by Moses' morning and evening prayers. When the ark set out he prayed:

> *Arise, O Lord,*
> *and let thy enemies be scattered;*
> *and let them that hate thee flee before thee* (35, RSV).

[3]Here Hobab is listed as Moses' brother-in-law. This is probably the true relationship, even though elsewhere (Judg. 4:11) he is listed as Moses' father-in-law and even though Rabbinic tradition holds that Hobab and Jethro are one and the same.

When the ark rested, he prayed:

Return, O Lord,
to the ten thousand thousands
of Israel (36, RSV).

The theme of 10:35-36 is "The Hallowing of Work and Rest." (1) Realization of and aspiration after the Divine Presence—**Rise up, Lord . . . Return, O Lord,** 35-36; (2) The Divine Presence as the Source of all energy—**Rise up, Lord,** 35; (3) The Divine Presence in hours of repose—**Return, O Lord,** 36 (A. Maclaren).

B. The People Complain, 11:1-9

1. *The Fire Burns* (11:1-3)

The murmuring and complaining of **the people** (1) was no new sound to the ears of Moses (cf. Exod. 14:11-12; 15:24-25). Nor would this be the last time he would hear it. In every instance, God dealt severely with such complaints. Here, **the fire of the Lord burnt among them,** consuming some on the outer edges **of the camp.** It **was quenched** (2) only on Moses' supplication.

2. *The Cry for Meat* (11:4-5)

Appetites quickly revolt against plain and simple food. In the extreme situation that faced the Israelites it was inevitable that complaints would soar. They started in this instance with Egypt" (Amp. OT). However, the complaints quickly spread to the main body of the Israelites with the cry, **Who shall give us flesh to eat?** Their taste buds were stimulated by the thoughts of **the fish . . . cucumbers . . . melons . . . leeks . . . onions, and the garlick** (5) which they had in abundance in Egypt.

3. *Manna Was Not Enough* (11:6-9)

The real issue, however, was not the plainness of their desert diet. The complaint focused on the unpalatability of **this manna** (6). But their criticism was a thrust at God, saying, in essence, "What You do for us is not good enough." They complained in spite of the fact that the manna was a miracle food which had actually kept them alive up to this point and would sustain them through the balance of their trek to Canaan (Exod. 16:14-36; Josh. 5:12).

The manna is described here (cf. Exod. 16:14-31) as being like the beedy eye of the **coriander seed,** the **colour of bdellium** (7; "resembling pearls," Moffatt). **The people . . . gathered it, and ground it . . . baked it . . . and made cakes of it. The taste** was that of **fresh oil** (8).[4] The manna was sweet, and it provided a dietary need for the nomadic people, to whom fruits were unobtainable, but its taste no doubt had become tiresome.[5]

C. Moses Feels His Burden, 11:10-17

1. *Weeping People and a Praying Man* (11:10-15)

Even in the light of the punishment by fire (11:1) which had so recently come to them, the people did not cease their complaining. At this point, it took on the proportions of an organized "demonstration" with a unified pattern of weeping throughout the camp. **Every man** wept **in the door of his tent** (10), so he could be heard and so that all could see that he was in favor of the protest.

The sound of weeping among the people, and no doubt the motive which initiated it, caused **the anger of the Lord** to blaze hotly; also "in the eyes of Moses it was evil" (9, Amp. OT). As a result Moses expressed his despair to God. He suggested that perhaps God had **afflicted** him, because he had **not found favour** (11) in God's sight. He felt God had laid the whole burden of these people upon him. The climax to his prayer expressed the complete dependence and helplessness which ultimately characterizes all effective prayer—**I am not able to bear . . . this . . . alone** (14). The prayer continues, "If this is the way it is to be, kill me now, that I may not witness the utter failure of my ef-

[4]Dr. F. S. Boderheimer of the Hebrew University describes manna as a "sweet secretion of various plant lice, cicadas, and scale insects feeding on wilderness tamarisk trees. Insects secrete their excess carbohydrates in the form of the honeydew manna, which evaporates into particles resembling hoar frost" (*Harper's Bible Dictionary,* Madeleine S. Miller and J. Lane Miller, eds [New York: Harper and Brothers, 1954], p. 417).

[5]The true nature of the sin of their complaining lay in the *direction* toward which their appetites pointed. God had not planned that they should eat manna indefinitely. He intended that they should very quickly trade it for the grapes, pomegranates, figs, and other satisfying food of Canaan. However, instead of looking *forward* to the good things God had promised, they looked *backward* to the menu of Egypt. Sin, the carnal mind, in any age can be readily identified by this direction of the appetite.

forts" (15).[6] **Kill me . . . out of hand (15)** would be, "Kill me now" (Berk.).

2. *The Provision for the Elders* (11:16-17)

To ease Moses' load, God instructed him to **gather . . . seventy men of the elders of Israel** (16). Some such council had existed, at least informally, for a year or more, but the purpose of having this group was more spiritual than that of the previous one (Exod. 18:17-26). This group may have been the 70 who went to the mountain with Moses (Exod. 24:9-10). Later Jews traced the pattern of the Sanhedrin to this occasion, but there is no historical tie to support the position.[7]

D. God Promises the People Meat, 11:18-23

1. *The Promise and the Warning* (11:18-20)

The miraculous appearance of quail is usually held both in the Scriptures (Exod. 16:13; Ps. 105:40) and in tradition to have been for the same purpose as the giving of the manna—the survival of the people. However in this instance, at least, the quail came as a plague and were used by God as a punishment for the complaining multitude. The people may have had an earlier experience in mind when they began to clamor for meat, but the answer to their cry on this occasion was one not to be desired. There was tragedy rather than benefit in it (33).

God commanded the people to prepare themselves as if for a religious service: **Sanctify yourselves against tomorrow** (18). Actually, however, this preparation was for chastisement and judgment. It is not difficult to detect a bit of satire in God's instructions to them: You'll have your meat, all right, not just enough for **one day, nor two days, nor five days, neither ten days, nor twenty days** (19), but enough for **a whole month** (20) at one time.

2. *Moses Continues the Dialogue* (11:21-23)

It was difficult even for Moses to comprehend all that God had in mind. He raised questions regarding the extravagant proposition that God had just unfolded—meat for this great a group of **people,** enough for **a whole month** (21). Here again Moses felt the burden of the Israelites, thinking, no doubt, that

[6]Personal Paraphrase.

[7]Winterbotham, *op. cit.*, p. 111.

God expected him somehow to produce all of this meat. True, they had **the flocks and the herds** (22), but these were for sacrifices and were needed to provide milk and other milk products. Certainly these animals would not last long if they were to be slain and used for food. Moses' comment about **all the fish of the sea** must be taken as a statement issuing out of his despair; fish were not available to them at that immediate location.

Verse 23 set a challenge for Moses. It should be remembered every time our faith is weak: "Is the Lord's hand shortened? Now you shall see whether my word will come true for you or not" (RSV).

E. The Giving of the Spirit, 11:24-30

1. *At the Tent of Meeting,* 11:24-25

Moses **gathered the seventy men** as previously instructed **(16-17) and set them round about the tabernacle** (24). There the Lord visited them with an enduement of His Holy Spirit, the same **spirit** that rested on Moses; and **they prophesied, and did not cease** (25). This prophesying meant "sounding forth the praises of God and declaring His will" (Amp. OT). It is the equivalent of the witnessing done by a not dissimilar group on the Day of Pentecost (Acts 1:4-8; 2:4, 6-18). The prophesying of the 70 must have included proclaiming the faithfulness of God thus far on their journey and giving reminders of His deliverance from Pharaoh. **The seventy elders** were thus to build morale for God in the camp.

2. *Eldad and Medad* (11:26-28)

For some reason two of those who had been summoned were not present at the Tent of Meeting. However the Lord poured out His Spirit **upon them** also and they witnessed **in the camp** (26) in the same manner as the others did. **A young man** (27) hurried to report this to Moses. Whereupon **Joshua** (28) recommended that Eldad and Medad be forbidden such prophesying. In response, Moses pointed out a lesson for all times: Not all who effectively serve God receive their commissions in just the same manner, and not all go under the same banner (Luke 9:49-50).

3. *The Promise of the Father Is for All Men* (11:29-30)

Following this interchange between Moses and Joshua, Moses gave a classic proclamation, underlining, even in this ancient day, the universality of the gospel of the Spirit: **Would God that all the Lord's people were prophets** (witnesses), **and that the Lord would put his spirit upon them!** (29) In this proclamation he goes beyond the immediate group who were to be used in a special mission in the work of God; he projects this outpouring as a possibility for all of the children of God (Joel 2:28-29).[8]

F. The Quail, 11:31-35

There went forth a wind from the Lord, and brought quails from the sea (31; the Gulf of Aqaba). Exhausted by their long flight or a possible shift in the wind, they flew only **two cubits** (three to four feet) above the ground. They came in such abundance that they spread **a day's journey** in each direction from **the camp.** The people could easily catch them with their hands, knock them down with sticks, or net them with pieces of cloth. Each person had all the quail he could use; even **he that gathered least gathered ten homers** (roughly 65 bushels).[9] The people then made an effort to preserve the quail which they had caught by spreading **them all abroad** to dry. Some have suggested that the people buried the quail for a short time in the hot sand to prepare them for eating.

There was no benefit from the meat, however. **Ere the flesh was chewed,**[10] **the wrath of the Lord was kindled,** and He **smote the people with a very great plague** (33). It is not certain what was the nature of this plague, other than the suggestion which

[8]It is a profitable study to trace through the Scriptures the concepts of the "people of God" and the "children of God," watching for references to the outpouring of the Holy Spirit. God always challenges His own to be people in whom His Spirit dwells.

[9]Scholars have not been agreed as to the modern equivalent of the homer. The most recent evidence from archaeological sources gives support to the more conservative calculations, with the homer listed in U.S. measures at 60.738 gallons (wet) and 6.524 bushels (dry) (George A. Arrois, "Weights and Measures, Hebrew," *Twentieth Century Encyclopedia of Religious Knowledge* [*An Extension of the New Schaaf-Herzog Encyclopedia of Religious Knowledge*] [Grand Rapids: Baker Book House, 1955], pp. 1165-66. Others (such as Berk.) calculate the homer to be in excess of 10 bushels.

[10]Lit., "ere it was cut off," or "ran short" (LXX). This fits more nearly with what follows: that the punishment came primarily to those who gorged themselves on the meat (L. Elliott Binns, *op. cit.*, p. 74).

God gave in the initial warning to the people (20). In any event, many died and the name **Kibrothhattaava** ("graves of sensuous desire," Amp. OT) was given to the place (34). The record does not state how many died in the plague; perhaps all in the camp who ate of the quail were affected or maybe only those who overate (see fn. 10).

It is important to see that the sin for which the people were punished was deeper than the sin of complaining or the sin of uncontrolled physical appetites. Here, even as it was to be at Kadesh-barnea, the real sin was the sin of unbelief. The people "despised the Lord" (20). They did not believe His promises or heed His warnings. They did not believe that He could take them through to Canaan. They loved the creature comforts of Egypt more than the will of God. They valued their own judgment and their own perspective of the situation more than the pattern which God had outlined for them.

G. The Sin of Miriam, 12:1-15

1. *The Accusation* (12:1-3)

It seems that the murmuring and complaining could not be checked no matter how severely God dealt with it. Now it showed up in the highest echelons of the camp, in **Miriam** (the prophetess, Exod. 15:20) and **Aaron** (the priest). It is quite evident that Miriam was the initiator of the criticism and that Aaron, as usual, was merely a mouthpiece. Their criticism of Moses was twofold: it involved displeasure over his choice of a wife (1), and it raised the question as to why Miriam and Aaron should not be recognized along with Moses as capable of receiving God's messages (2).

The first of these complaints had no foundation in either moral or legal wrong, as would have been the case had Moses married a Canaanite (Deut. 7:1-6). It seems, rather, to have arisen from the heart of a jealous sister over what appears to be a second marriage for Moses; although some hold **the Ethiopian** (Heb., Cushite) refers to Zipporah, to whom Moses had been married for many years (Exod. 2:21), perhaps a long-standing sore point with his sister. There is no indication that God paid any attention to this complaint.

The second complaint had even less foundation, existing only in the minds of Miriam and Aaron. Miriam had been given an unusual place of honor and respect, arising particularly out of her leadership in the victory song following the crossing of the Red Sea (Exod. 15:20-21). Aaron had been designated as Moses' mouthpiece (Exod. 4:10-16) and had more recently become the chief priest of the Israelites (3:1-3). Both Miriam and Aaron, no doubt, still saw Moses as their little brother and resented his place of leadership with the people and his favor with God.

The parenthetical statement, **Now . . . Moses was very meek** (3), more so than any person living, has been interpreted variously by scholars. Some feel it must, of necessity, be an interpolation by later writers, for such a self-commendation was out of character for Moses. However, others[11] point out that the word for **meek** appears frequently in the psalms and, as here, is applied by the writers to themselves (cf. Ps. 10:17, "humbly"; 22:26). "There is about these words, as also about the passages in which Moses no less equivocally records his own faults (20:12; Exod. 4:24-26; Deut. 1:37) that simplicity which is witness at once to their genuineness and inspiration."[12]

2. *The Vindication* (12:4-8)

The sin of undermining the influence of God's leader[13] and of questioning his authority could not go unnoticed or unchallenged. God called the **three** of them **suddenly** to appear before the outer court[14] of the Tent of Meeting. God's presence was evidenced by **the pillar of the cloud,** which moved to this position.

The Lord's vindication of Moses was complete. The focal point of His defense spoke to the manner in which God communicates with His servants. To an ordinary prophet or lesser ones, He speaks through **a vision** or **a dream** (6). But with Moses, God spoke **mouth to mouth** ("directly," Amp. OT; "face to face," Deut. 34:10), clearly and not in riddles (8). The reason for this was that Moses had a unique relationship to God (7). In

[11]Hertz, ed., *op. cit.*, p. 618. (Cf. *Speakers' Bible, ad loc.*)

[12]*Ibid.*

[13]There are intimations that, between vv. 1 and 2, Miriam and Aaron had made their first criticism vocal in the camp, and because some had sought to defend Moses, they offered the second criticism in support of their position. Cf Winterbotham, *op. cit.*, p. 130.

[14]First to the outer court (4) and then to **the door** of the sanctuary (5). Cf. Ellicott, *op. cit.*, p. 90.

the divine economy he was compared to Christ himself (Heb. 3:2, 5-6) as a special envoy **in all mine house.** Therefore God rightfully raised the question with Miriam and Aaron, Why then are you **not afraid to speak against** him? (8)

3. *The Punishment* (12:9-10)

As in other cases, God's displeasure at such questioning of His anointed was immediate. As He finished speaking, **the cloud departed** (10). This action signified a divine withdrawal, as a judge might leave the bench after a sentence. It was different from the *lifting* of the cloud, signifying the time to move camp.[15]

The greatest punishment for sin, whatever its particular manifestation, is this separation from God.

As **Aaron** turned to his sister, he saw that she had been stricken with leprosy. It was a fully developed case, **white as snow** (10), as in the later stages of the disease. Leprosy was a loathsome disease with which the Israelites were familiar in Egypt and for the control of which detailed laws had already been laid down (Leviticus 13—14). Such a penalty is not out of keeping, for leprosy, in the Word of God, is consistently used to typify sin. Miriam, who at one moment had exalted herself in self-pride to the point of thinking she should be coequal in prominence with the leader of all Israel, was the next moment banished from the camp in the most humiliating circumstances. Such is the result of the sin of pride (Prov. 16:18; Isa. 10:33).

4. *The Provision for Restoration* (12:11-15)

Immediately upon seeing Miriam's plight, **Aaron** began his plea, addressing **Moses** as **my lord** (11). This was, indeed, a quick reversal of the attitude reflected earlier in v. 2. Aaron confessed that he and Miriam had **done foolishly** and had **sinned.** This condition of Miriam, he pleaded, was worse than if she had been stillborn (12). Once again **Moses** petitioned God, who had long since proved that He was a God of forgiveness, **Heal her now, O God, I beseech thee** (13). God's answer was that Miriam should be punished at least as much as one whose **father had but spit in her face** (14). The penalty was isolation **from the camp for seven days.** So the entire camp waited until this time was accomplished and **Miriam was brought in again** (15) properly

[15]*Ibid.*, p. 91.

chastened, probably chagrined, and, we must assume, fully cleansed.

H. Scouting Party Surveys Canaan, 12:16—13:33

1. *The Initiation of the Plan* (12:16—13:16)

Soon after the arrival in **the wilderness of Paran** (16; Kadesh-barnea, Deut. 1:19; see map 3), plans were made to send a scouting party (Amp. OT) into Canaan, **that they may search the land** (2). The party was made up of one man from each tribe, with **Ephraim** (8) and **Manasseh** representing **the tribe of Joseph** (11). Since the tribe of Levi was not to participate, the division of **the tribe of Joseph** into Ephraim and Manasseh resulted in the 12-tribe numbering.

It is not certain just how the plan for the spies originated. The account in Deut. 1:22 seems to indicate that the people insisted on such a scouting trip and implies that their request came out of a reluctance to take God's way.

> And when we departed from Horeb, we went through all that great and terrible wilderness . . . and we came to Kadesh-barnea. And I said unto you, You have come to the hill country of the Amorites, which the Lord our God gives you. Behold, the Lord your God has set the land before you; go up and possess it, as the Lord God of your fathers has said to you; fear not, neither be dismayed. Then you came near to me and said, Let us send men before us, that they may search us out the land, and bring us word again by what way we should go up, and the cities into which we shall go up, and the cities into which we shall come. The thing pleased me well, and I took twelve men of you, one for each tribe (Deut. 1:19-23, Amp. OT).

It is clear that a "scouting party," in the military sense, was not needed in this situation. The assurance of success lay, not with accurate intelligence reports, but in the power of God. All the people needed, really, was to trust God and move on in.[16] If it is true that the people were responsible for the plan, the whole project was unnecessary. At best it was permitted by God to appease the people's complaining and to encourage them to follow

[16]There are, however, scholars who feel that the victory of the Israelites over the king of Arad in the extreme south of Canaan (21:1-3) took place at this stage. This would account for the mood with which the people faced Moses and their apparent zeal in asking that a scouting party set out immediately. Cf. J. H. Hertz, ed., *op. cit.*, p. 623.

through on the basic plan to possess Canaan. If this position is correct, the record in vv. 1-2 bypasses the people's involvement and merely records God's instructions to carry out the plan.

2. *The Implementation of the Plan* (13:17-25)

The scouts were to go in by the southern route and follow the "hill country," the ridge which separates the Mediterranean plateau from the Dead Sea and the Jordan Valley. They were to see what **the people** were, whether **strong or weak, few or many** (18); **what the land** was, **whether it be good or bad** (19), **fat or lean** (20); whether or not the people were nomadic—**dwell in . . . tents** (19)—or lived in **cities (strong holds)**; and whether or not the hills were timbered. In addition they were to bring back samples **of the fruit of the land** (20).

These instructions continue to savor of the human. There was no real reason why Moses needed this information. To some of it he could well have had access already, and the rest he did not need. It was God who had promised them this land, and their possession of it did not depend upon a scouting report but only on obeying God.

The scouts went forth, following the instructions, going the length of **the land** to **Rehob,** "at the entrance to Hamath,"[17] the northernmost part of the land. As they returned, at **Eshcol,** near **Hebron**[18] (see map 3), they cut a large **cluster of grapes,** gathered **pomegranates** and **figs** (22-23). To protect the grapes, they carried them on a pole. In all, the scouting trip took **forty days** (25), a period of time which in the Scriptures commonly speaks of a work being completely done.

3. *Pro and Con of the Report* (13:26-33)

On arrival of the scouts back at **Kadesh** (see map 3), representatives of the people gathered together to hear their report. Canaan was a land flowing **with milk and honey** (27), confirm-

[17]Ellicott, *op. cit.*, p. 95.

[18]Moses may have had access to the archives of Zoan, or may have received data from his Egyptian teachers. The reference here (22) to the relationship of Hebron to Zoan appears simply as a "footnote," a "flashback of memory," not as a significant entry in the record. "There is no one but Moses to whom the statement can . . . be traced; a later writer could have had no authority for making the statement, and no possible reason for inventing it" (Winterbotham, *op. cit.*, p. 144).

ing that God was faithful in His promise (Exod. 3:8). But it was also a land occupied by **strong** people living in **walled** cities (28).

The report brought a "buzzing" among the congregation, which was **stilled** temporarily by **Caleb.** He sought to challenge them, **Let us go up at once, and possess it; for we are well able to overcome it** (30). But his fellow scouts (all but Joshua) took exception. **We be not able** (31). **We saw the giants . . . we were . . . as grasshoppers . . . in their sight** (33).

In essence, all of the scouts gave the same factual report: there were good things and bad things. The argument between Caleb and Joshua and the other 10 scouts had to do with whether or not Israel could and should go in and possess the land.

From 13:17-33, Alexander Maclaren preached on "Afraid of Giants." (1) The dispatch and instructions of the explorers, 17-20; (2) The exploration, 21-25; (3) The two reports, 26-33.

I. Response of the People, 14:1-10

1. *An Excuse to Murmur* (14:1-4)

The congregation's response has many of the earmarks of a people who were looking for an excuse to complain. The reference of the majority of the scouts to giants, as well as to the land eating up **the inhabitants**[19] (32), was based on their observation of isolated cases.[20] In this instance the report was false in effect. Certainly not all of the inhabitants were of such a size, nor all of the land barren and desolate. It was purely a case of picking the evidence they wanted to emphasize.

The people were quick to catch the spirit of pessimism which the 10 scouts projected; they began, again, to murmur as ones "peevish and discontented" (Deut. 1:27, Amp. OT). This time the murmuring was not only against Moses and Aaron but against God himself: **Would God that we had died in the land of Egypt! or . . . in this wilderness!** (2) They were afraid that their **wives** and **children** would die by the swords of these giants (3). In fear they proposed to each other, **Let us make a captain, and let us return into Egypt** (4).

[19]This specification may have reference to the barrenness of portions of the land or to the fact that the strife and discord of the tribes over possession of the land made it a precarious place in which to live. Cf. Ellicott, *op. cit.*, p. 98.

[20]Winterbotham, *op cit.*, p. 145.

2. *The Loyal Four* (14:5-10)

Moses,[21] Aaron, Joshua, and Caleb pleaded with the congregation to look at the positive factors which supported their contention that a victorious occupation of Canaan was possible. To lend weight to their judgment, and as an expression of their deep concern, **Caleb** and **Joshua rent their clothes** (6), declaring, **The land . . . is an exceeding good land** (7). They contended that there was no reason why Israel could not enter. **If the Lord delight in us, then he will bring us into this land** (8). Only rebellion and fear could defeat God's people (9), while obedience, courage, and faith were the secrets of victory.

But the people cried out that Caleb and Joshua should be stoned. Such is the world's reward of many who have sought to be true messengers of God across the centuries (Acts 6:8—7:60). The stoning was averted on this occasion, however, by God's intervention. He appeared in His **glory** before the Tent of Meeting, visible to all **the congregation** (10).

The theme of 14:1-10 is "Weighed, and Found Wanting." (1) Faithless cowards, 1-4; (2) The faithful four, 5-9; (3) The all-seeing Lord, 10 (A. Maclaren).

J. God's Judgment, 14:11-45

1. *God Makes Moses a Proposition* (14:11-19)

The first words that God spoke in unfolding the judgment upon the nation for its sin of unbelief were directed to Moses, **How long will this people provoke me?** (11) "How long will it be before they believe Me, for all the signs which I have performed among them?" (Amp. OT) Then followed God's proposition to Moses. He would destroy this people and replace Abraham with Moses as the head of the nation. This was not unlike the situation which faced Moses on Mount Sinai (Exod. 32:1-14) after the incident of the golden calf.

Moses turned the proposition aside, calling attention to God's integrity. **The inhabitants** (14) of Canaan were well aware of God's reputation in His care for the Israelites. To destroy Israel now would be to destroy these nations' respect for God. They would say that "God was not able to bring His people into the land He swore to give them" (16, Amp. OT).

[21]Cf. Deut. 1:29-34.

Moses' appeal was to God's character, which would not allow such a total destruction as had been suggested. "Moses pleads with God to spare His people out of regard for His own self-revealed Thirteen Attributes of Divine Mercy and Forgiveness, enumerated earlier (Exod. 34:6-7) and reproduced here."[22] Amidst the definitions of God, these attributes stand out as describing Him in ethical terms.[23] Such principles must finally prevail, not at the expense of God's law and justice—**and by no means clearing the guilty,** but **visiting the iniquity of the fathers upon the children** (18)—but prevail because of the Cross and God's provision for redemption. Verses 17-18 are translated by Moffatt, "Ah, let the power of my Lord be displayed in carrying out thy promise that the Eternal is slow to be angry, rich in love, forgiving iniquity and transgression."

2. *Condemned to the Wilderness* (14:20-38)

God pardoned this sin of unbelief, **according to** Moses' **word** (20), but there was to be a punishment.[24] "As truly as I live," the Lord said, "and as all the earth shall be filled with the Glory of the Lord (cf. Isa. 6:3; 11:9), because . . . these men have not heeded my voice, surely they shall not see the land" (21-23, Amp. OT). **Ten times** (22) suggests the number of completeness or fullness (Berk.).

This meant that all who were **twenty years** of age and older would die in the **wilderness** (29) and **not come into the land** (30). In 28, God said, **As ye have spoken in mine ears, so will I do to you.** In v. 2 the people had prayed, "Would God we had died in this wilderness!" Now their rebellious prayer would be answered. **Caleb** and **Joshua** were exceptions to this, of course, as two of the scouts who gave a "good report."[25] The time involved in this punishment was 40 years,[26] **after the number of the days in which ye searched the land** (34), one year for each day. This, too, was the minimum time comprising a generation, the time it would take, under normal situations, for the old genera-

[22]Hertz, ed., *op. cit.*, p. 627. [23]*Ibid.*, pp. 364-65.

[24]Cf. Deut. 1:35-40.

[25]It is assumed by some that this also excluded the Levites who were not among those "numbered" in the main census (Ellicott, *op. cit.*, pp. 103-4).

[26]Counting the year and a half which had already passed since they had left Egypt.

tion to pass. While the children did not partake in full measure of the judgment, the wandering aimlessly for 40 years was, in a very real sense, a punishment for them also. **Breach of promise** (34) is better "my displeasure" (RSV). The 10 scouts who **made all the congregation to murmur** (36) **died by the plague** (37) immediately, as a seal upon the judgment which God had outlined.

"Kadesh vs. Consecration'" is the theme of cc. 13—14. (1) Doubt suggested sending the spies, 13:1-2; cf. Deut. 1:21-22; (2) The majority report encouraged unbelief, 13:25-29, 33; (3) Full-grown rebellion instead of total consecration and obedience —the consequences, 14:1-4, 30 (G. B. Williamson).

The great lesson of this passage is missed if it is viewed only as an event in history. The Scriptures plainly teach (Heb. 3: 1-19) that this account has its parallel in personal relationship with God. There is a personal "Canaan," a spiritual "rest" which is the destination, the land of promise, for the Christian. In this personal journey there are often struggle and tears, faith and unbelief at Kadesh-barnea. The tragedy of Christian life is the great number who, starting on the way to Canaan, fail to enter in.

In 14:17-23 we see "Moses the Intercessor." (1) The ground of divine forgiveness, **thy mercy,** 19; (2) The persistency of divine pardon, **thou hast forgiven . . . even until now,** 19; (3) The manner of divine forgiveness—pardon but inevitable consequences, 20-23; (4) The vehicle of divine forgiveness—Moses, the intercessor, a dim shadow of Christ, 19 (A. Maclaren).

3. *Trying Without God* (14:39-45)

When the full force of God's judgment registered with the people, they **mourned greatly** (39). How different from the "weeping" which took place when they first heard the report of the scouts (1)! The first was the weeping of frustration and despair, born of self-centeredness and self-pity. The second was the mourning born out of judgment that had overtaken them, the sorrow of being caught and punished.

When the people felt the pinch of punishment, they sought to push ahead regardless.[27] They would try to redeem their lost opportunities and still enter in. So, **early in the morning,**[28] they

[27]Cf. Deut. 1:41-46.

[28]Contrary to the command of v. 25.

went up to **the top of the mountain, saying, Lo, we be here, and we will go up unto the place which the Lord hath promised: for we have sinned** (40). But it was too late. Keeping a former command, now that God had issued a new one, would not atone for their sin. Moses told them, **Go not up, for the Lord is not among you** (42) . . . **because ye are turned away from the Lord, therefore the Lord will not be with you** (43). The location of the **mountain** of v. 40 is unknown.

But they persisted in their plan and went to battle. **The Amalekites** and **the Canaanites** who lived in the hill country "smote the Israelites and beat them back" (45, Amp. OT). **Hormah** has not been pinpointed as a specific location, but see map 3 for a possible site. The expression could well be an idiom, referring to their total destruction, a state of *hormah,* as it were, much as Anglo-Saxons would speak of one "meeting his Waterloo."

Israel's experience has served as a lesson for the succeeding centuries that to attempt anything without God is never successful. The conflict with the inhabitants of the southern hills also settled the course of Israel's later journey. They must bypass southern Palestine and enter Canaan by another route.

Section III Wilderness Experiences

Numbers 15:1—19:22

A. The Years of Obscurity

1. *A Wandering People*

With the fall of the hammer of judgment, Israel entered into a period of wilderness wanderings which lasted for nearly 38 years.[1] To add to the historical problems, there is a near total blackout of the events that transpired during this period. Neither the Scriptures nor the scholars give an explanation. It is almost as if Moses purposefully drew the curtain, feeling that the story of a people under such severe judgment from God should not be told.[2]

As a result, historians have been forced to speculate regarding the details of this generation. Perhaps the word "wandering" is descriptive enough to tell all that God wanted to reveal of what happened. It may be best that the full, heartbreaking story has not been uncovered.

2. *Some Intimations*

There are, however, certain intimations that should not be overlooked. Moses witnesses that during this period God did not completely abandon His people. They had the divinely given manna to eat and divinely preserved clothes to wear throughout the entire time. Their clothing did not become old nor did their sandals wear off their feet or their feet swell (Deut. 8:2-6; 29: 5-6). Joshua gave a further insight, revealing that the rite of circumcision was not observed during this time (Josh. 5:2-8). It can be assumed that other religious rites were also discontinued. It is clear that the Passover was not celebrated between the time the Israelites left Sinai and their arrival in the land of

[1]In many instances the term "forty years" is used with reference to the time of the wilderness judgment. This must be understood to be an approximate figure, since the 40 years covers the time which elapsed from the exodus from Egypt to the gathering of the tribes at Kadesh preparatory to starting again for Canaan (20:1).

[2]Whitelaw, *op. cit.*, "The Thirty-seven Years Chasm," pp. ii-iv.

Canaan (Josh. 5:10). It is also clear, however, that there was a strict observance of other laws and ordinances, such as that relating to the Sabbath (15:32-36).

Limitations in the religious life of the community should not lead one to suppose that there were no lessons to be learned from these years of wandering. Moses was firm in the belief that God brought purpose to all of this (cf. Rom. 8:28). He wrote:

> You shall remember all the way which the Lord your God has led you these forty years in the wilderness, that he might humble you, testing you to know what was in your heart, whether you would keep his commandments, or not. And he humbled you and let you hunger and fed you with manna . . . that he might make you know that man does not live by bread alone, but that man lives by everything that proceeds out of the mouth of the Lord (Deut. 8:2-3, RSV).

3. *The Course of Events*

The record in Deut. 1:46 indicates that, following the humiliating defeat at the hands of the hill-country armies, the people of Israel remained in Kadesh for "many days."[3] Only later did they follow God's command to "get you into the wilderness . . . [toward] the Red Sea" (14:25). It is presumed that during years that followed there was no organized camp. Families probably scattered according to their individual inclinations. Even so, there must have been a center, probably shifting from time to time, where the ark was located and where Moses and Aaron stayed. It is certain that the camp did not have the full marks of organization that had been laid out for it at Sinai. It can be inferred from the words "even the whole congregation" (20:1) that the return to Kadesh at the end of the 38 years was more exactly a reassembling and that some may have stayed close to, if not at, Kadesh during the entire time.

The transactions recorded in this section (cc. 15—19) are the only record we have of what transpired during the 38 years. They are extremely limited and are not listed in any chronological order or dated in any way. Hence they give little help in piecing together the happenings of these hectic judgment years.[4] They must be viewed as isolated events included by Moses in his record largely because of what they contribute to the lessons God expected Israel to learn. The laws which were given, or repeated,

[3]This means an "indefinite time." [4]Ellicott, *op. cit.*, p. 107.

were prefaced by the words **when ye be come into the land of your habitations** (15:2). They purposefully projected the people's thoughts into the future. These events, then, though they have their origins in the desert setting and happened under judgment circumstances, take on the greatest significance as their timeless spiritual and moral values are revealed.

B. A Review of Certain Laws, 15:1-41

1. *Offerings with a Sweet Savor* (15:1-16)

It would appear that the reason the instructions regarding the offering of sacrifices were repeated (cf. Leviticus 1—3)—besides the minor matter of fixing the quantities for oil, flour, and wine—was to highlight the truth that all of the offerings were to be a **sweet savour unto the Lord** (3, 7, 10, 13-14).

This expresses the idea that God smells a "sweet savour" (Gen. 8:21) whenever a true offering is presented to Him.[5] Christ is pictured in the NT as an Offering of this kind (Eph. 5:2). The NT also points out that the Christian is to dedicate his life to God in a manner that is full and complete (Rom. 6:13) and to present his service to God as a sweet savor (Phil. 4:18). The lesson here is clear: the elements that God requires in an offering to make it acceptable to Him must be foremost in man's thinking too.

There is some indication, furthermore, that with the sacrifice (in contrast to the burnt offering) the worshipper himself partook of a portion of the offering.[6] Hence, the fuller preparation of the sacrifice, with provisions to make it palatable, made the whole act of worship more satisfying and pleasant to the person involved. True worship should bring to man this sense of reality. When this occurs, God is loosed from the bonds of ritual and is enjoyed in fellowship and communion. It would appear that Moses was pointing out a day to come when, free from the limitations which the wilderness imposed on their worship, Israel should indeed experience sweet blessings from the worship of God. This is the kind of worship that Jesus emphasized centuries later (John 4:5-15).

The laws and principles of worship were to be universal. They applied to the **stranger** and sojourner (16) as well as to the native-born Israelite.

[5]IB, II, 215-16. [6]*Ibid.*, p. 215.

2. *Stewardship at Home* (15:17-21)

While this passage is not too clear, it seems that the emphasis is upon stewardship, especially upon the offering which comes from the home. The principle of man's stewardship before God is pinpointed: **Then it shall be, that, when ye eat of the bread of the land, ye shall offer up an**[7] **. . . offering unto the Lord** (19). There must be responsibilities for those who are privileged to enjoy the bounties of life from God's hand.

The law of the offering of the firstfruit of the **threshingfloor** (20) had previously been made clear (Lev. 2:14). It was here extended to include **the first of your dough** (21) from the home. This would expand the idea of stewardship beyond the "industrial" and "agricultural" aspects of life to include the individual and family.

The offering of the "firstfruits" is also identified with the "tithe" or the one-tenth (Lev. 27:30-33; Deut. 26:1-15). It is the God-ordained manner in which God's children express their stewardship as well as the God-ordained plan of supporting His cause.

3. *Moral Responsibility* (15:22-36)

The chief concern of Moses at this point was to compare two types of sin.

The first was described here as sin **committed by ignorance without the knowledge of the congregation** (24). Provisions whereby this "sin of ignorance" may come under God's atonement are described: for **the congregation** (24-26) and again for the individual (27-29).

The second sin is that which is done **presumptuously** (30), "with a high hand" (RSV), or in defiance of God and His law. The one who thus sins knowingly and willfully **shall be cut off from among his people** (30). This penalty is **because he hath despised the word of the Lord** (31). An illustration is given which tells of **a man that gathered sticks upon the sabbath day** (32). Here was a clear case, so they judged, of one who knew the law (Exod. 31:14-15; 35:2-3) and who had no doubt had ample opportunity to see the law in operation. In spite of this, he defied the law and defied God. As a judgment, **all the congregation . . . stoned him with stones, and he died** (36).

[7]Dropping the adjective "heave," as in the RSV, makes for clarity.

Clearly outlined here is a universal principle related to sin—it is *moral*, i.e., it relates to man's choice, to the degree of his knowledge of the law and to the degree of his *willfulness* in disobeying God.

The sins listed here illustrate the two extremes. On one hand, there is that completely inadvertent act, in which there is neither knowledge that it was a sin nor any will to commit sin. The other extreme is that sin which puts to naught the grace of God and completely defies all that God says or wills (cf. Rom. 1:18-31; Heb. 10:26-31; II Pet. 2:20-21). In between, however, there are many hues and tints of sin, involving more or less knowledge and more or less degrees of rebellion. For all of these, there is forgiveness, save for the most extreme apostasy, blasphemy against the Holy Ghost (Matt. 12:31-32; I John 5:16).

4. *The Public Witness* (15:37-41)

God commanded the people to put **fringes in the borders of their garments** (38). The purpose for this was to help them **remember all the commandments of the Lord, and do them; and that** they **seek not after** their **own heart** (39) and that they **be holy unto** their **God** (40).

"The orthodox Jew still wears a *tallith*—an oblong piece of cloth with a hole in the middle for passing over the head and a tassel at each corner."[8]

A visible and audible witness to one's inner spiritual experiences with God is an important part of the NT gospel (Acts 1:8). It had its ceremonial counterpart in this ancient day. The Pharisees of Jesus' day had enlarged their tassels beyond all proportions in order that they might "witness" the more ostentatiously.

C. Korah's Insurrection, 16:1—17:13

1. *A Bid for Leadership* (16:1-2)

In the light of expressions which had come from the people from time to time (cf. 14:4), it was inevitable that there would come a time when the leadership of Moses and Aaron would be actively challenged. Chapters 16—17 tell of such an uprising by

[8]IB, II, 219.

Korah, a Levite of the family of the Kohathites (a "cousin" of Moses and Aaron). He was joined by three men from the tribe of **Reuben**[9]**: Dathan, Abiram,** and **On.**[10]

2. *Challenges of the Mutineers* (16:3-19)

Korah[11] secured the support of 250 representative leaders of the congregation (2), many of whom were from the tribe of Levi (8, 10). This group confronted Moses with the indictment, **Ye take too much upon you, seeing all the congregation are holy** (3). They were, in a very general sense, correct in that all of Israel had been consecrated to the Lord. However, they were wrong when they assumed that the priesthood was an office to which they could assign themselves at will. The priesthood was ordained by God, and Aaron, the high priest, had been anointed under divine direction (3:1-3). These Levites had an important and sacred part in the care of the holy things in the Tent of Meeting (8-9; 4:4-14). They were presumptuous in believing that they had a right to take over, at their own discretion, the office of the priesthood (5).

Moses replied in the exact words of Korah, **Ye take too much upon you** (7; cf. 3). It was assumed by Moses that, in addition to the ambitions of these Levites, Korah himself aspired to the office of high priest in place of Aaron (10). The challenge of Korah and those with him was against the religious leadership of Moses and Aaron.

Dathan and Abiram, in contrast, followed the political line —it was a kind of lay movement.[12] They blamed Moses for blundering. They charged that he had brought the people **out of a land that floweth with milk and honey** (13; Egypt),[13] and

[9]"The tribe that once possessed but now had lost the 'birthright' in Israel, and was, it seems, chafing for the recovery of that primacy" (Hertz, ed., *op. cit.*, p. 638).

[10]**On** drops from the picture immediately, there being no record of his further involvement in the insurrection. Some scholars feel that the name is merely a dittography in the Hebrew text and should be omitted. Cf. Binns, *op. cit.*, p. 109.

[11]It is clear that Korah was the mainspring of this attempted revolution. Cf. 27:3; Jude 11; Winterbotham, *op. cit.*, p. 201.

[12]Probably this was the reason they were not involved in Moses' confrontation with Korah and the 250; cf. 12.

[13]The dissenters used a phrase in connection with Egypt which had consistently applied only to Canaan.

yet had **not brought** them **into a land that floweth with milk and honey, or given** them **inheritance of fields and vineyards** (14; Canaan). They said Moses had blinded the people and had sought to make himself **a prince** (dictator) over them (13). Moses' defense was, **I have not taken one ass from them, neither have I hurt one of them** (15). His leadership was not authoritarian or dictatorial. The accusations were wholly unwarranted and constituted, in essence, a mutiny. The degree of the punishment that God inflicted (31-33) substantiated Moses' claim.

3. *The Punishment* (16:20-50)

Moses was not acting on his own behalf. In contrast to insurrections in a non-theocratic society, Moses had the backing of God. Hence these challenges were met, not alone by argument, but by the manifestations of God's presence and by His punishment.

Those who claimed the priesthood should be open to others than Aaron and his sons were called upon to test their claims (5-7, 16-18) by preparing "censers" (pans) and upon them offering incense before the Lord. **Korah** appeared confident as he **gathered all the congregation . . . unto the door of the tabernacle,** but he did not properly assess God's intervention. **The glory of the Lord appeared** (19) with a proclamation that there would be a judgment by fire. **The congregation** (22) questioned the justice of the destruction of all for the sin of one man, and the **fire . . . consumed** (35) only the 250 who had illegally offered the incense before the Lord (17).

Moses had sent for Dathan and Abiram earlier. They had refused to come, so he went to their camp.[14] Moses requested all to leave who were not involved (26) and announced the test that would be put to these rebels. **Hereby ye shall know that the Lord hath sent me to do all these works,** "for I do not act of my own accord" (28, Amp. OT). The test was, **If these men die the common death** (29), they would be vindicated. **But,** Moses said, **if the Lord make a new thing, and the earth open her mouth, and swallow them up . . . then ye shall understand that these men have provoked the Lord** (30). As he stopped

[14]The phrase **tabernacle of Korah** (24, 27) may indicate that Korah had set up a rival place to the Tent of Meeting; or it may mean only that Korah's tent served as a headquarters for the insurrection.

speaking, the earth **clave asunder** (31) as by an earthquake and **Dathan, and Abiram** and their families (27) perished.

Opinions differ as to the fate of Korah himself,[15] whether he was with Dathan and Abiram or whether he was among the 250 who perished by fire. In any event, God's judgment fell on him for his leadership of the rebellion.[16]

Following the destruction of the 250 by fire, **Eleazar** was commanded to gather **the censers** which had been used. He was told to **scatter** the coals of fire, **for they** were **hallowed** (37), even though the offering had been made by profane hands. **The censers** (38) were to be beaten into covers for **the altar.**

The next day the people accused **Moses** and **Aaron** (41) of being personally responsible for these judgments. As a result a **plague** (46) from God started among the people. The plague was stayed only after Aaron **made an atonement for the people** (47), standing between **the dead and the living** (48). Even so, 14,700 perished (49). All men can take heart that between man's sin and God's judgment are the provisions of divine grace.

4. *A Final Test* (17:1-13)

In an attempt to **make to cease . . . the murmurings of the children of Israel** (5) a test was devised. God sought to ease the strife between the tribe of Levi and the other tribes, as well as to convince the congregation that Aaron's spiritual leadership was indeed of God. **A rod** (6), representing tribal authority, was taken from each of the tribes, with one included for Aaron and the tribe of Levi. The rods were placed in the Tent of Meeting overnight. **And it came to pass, that . . . the rod of Aaron . . . was budded . . . and bloomed blossoms, and yielded almonds** (8).[17] Moses displayed the results to all of the congregation,

[15]There are some indications (cf. 32; 26:10) that he was with Dathan and Abiram in their judgment, though the connection is not clear. A shift of punctuation of 26:10 could just as easily support the position that he was with the 250 who perished by fire. Elsewhere, when Dathan and Abiram are mentioned, Korah is not included (Deut. 11:6; Ps. 106:7). Furthermore, the sons of Korah were not included in their father's judgment, while the families of his two collaborators did not escape.

[16]"The Great Mutiny sank deep into the memory of after-generations in Israel. To the Rabbis, this whole movement, of which Korah was the principal spokesman, became typical of all controversies that had their origin in personal motives" (Hertz, ed., *op. cit.*, p. 638).

[17]The almond tree is a symbol of the bursting forth of spring. Cf. Jer. 1:11.

and then ordered that **Aaron's rod . . . be kept** (10) in the hope that its presence would prevent any such rebellion in the future.

Temporarily, at least, the plan worked. It was a subdued and properly chastened congregation that declared, **Behold, we die . . . Whosoever cometh . . . near unto the tabernacle . . . shall die** (12-13).

D. Levitical and Priestly Duties, 18:1-32

1. *Intermingled Responsibilities* (18:1-7)

The information recorded here, relating to the duties of the priests and the Levites, is not new (cf. 3:1—4:49). It is repeated in this particular setting to underline the principle which had just been dramatically demonstrated, that sacred things should not be profaned. It was repeated also to remind the priests and Levites that, while they had high privileges, they also had serious responsibilities. The priests were responsible for the sanctuary and the Levites were their helpers. The Levites were, however, not to touch the altar or the other sacred furnishings and were to see to it that the people did not come close enough to suffer the penalty of death (17:13).

2. *Priests' Benefits Listed* (18:8-20)

Since the priests were the spiritual servants of the people, they would be unable to work for their living in the same manner as did the others. Hence their support was to come from the main body of the congregation. The promise of God to Aaron was, "I have given you whatever is kept of the offerings made to me, all the consecrated things of the people of Israel; I have given them to you as a portion, and to your sons as a perpetual due" (8, RSV). Then follows a listing of the portions of the sacrifices which the priests could use and detailed instructions as to how they were to do it.

A covenant of salt (19) was "an indissoluble covenant" (Berk., fn.).

3. *The Levites' Dues* (18:21-32)

The Levites were to receive their living from the tithes of the Israelites. In turn they were to **do the service of the tabernacle** (23) and bear responsibility for the spiritual needs of the people. By the same token, they were to give **a tenth part of**

the tithe (26) of what they received to the priests. This would be considered the equivalent of the increase **of the threshing-floor, and as the fulness of the winepress** (27) of the other tribes. God honors the tithe and none is exempt from God's expectation of purposeful, systematic giving as a vital part of his worship. None should be tempted to keep that which should be given (32) and none should rob God (Mal. 3:8-10).

E. Provisions for Cleansing, 19:1-22

1. *The Lord's Command* (19:1-2)

The purpose of this passage is missed if the details of it are given precedence over its theme. Once "God's Provision for Cleansing" is seen as the theme, this must stand as one of the most significant passages of the entire book. The use of the words **the ordinance of the law** (2) is unique and assigns supreme importance to the law about to be given.[18]

The great need of the people was for cleansing. This need was made acute, no doubt, by the particular circumstances of the wilderness wanderings, the death-note imposed by God's judgment, and even the special judgments and plagues which arose from time to time (cf. 16:49). Contact with the dead was the particular cause of the ceremonial defilement underlined here. Actually, however, there were many situations that could cause physical defilement—all of which would bring into sharp focus the problem of uncleanness.

It must be kept in mind that the two[19] issues, hygienic and ceremonial uncleanness, were closely related. The hygienic issue was the more immediate and obvious. It was tied to social contacts and was a part of everyday living. However, the spiritual needs of the people, of which ceremonial uncleanness was representative, were just as real. Religious needs were prevalent, and were, in truth, the target-center of God's basic purpose to have a holy (cleansed) people. In a true sense, the hygienic matters relating to defilement were but illustrations of this deeper spiritual defilement.

[18]Ellicott, *op. cit.*, p. 129.

[19]"There are two distinct views in regard to the laws of purity and impurity; one, that they are hygienic; the other, that they are 'levitical', i.e. purely religious . . . However, while neither . . . can by itself account for all the facts, the two views are not mutually exclusive" (Hertz, ed., *op. cit.*, p. 459).

The law set forth here belongs to the group of commandments dealt with earlier (Leviticus 12—15) which outline the provisions for cleansing of impurity from childbirth, leprosy, and bodily secretions. Here however the law pinpoints the issue of impurity caused by contact with the dead.[20]

The theme of this chapter, then, is the same as that which is central in the entire Bible—God provides moral and spiritual cleansing. Consequently the laws and principles outlined here must be evaluated in the light of the total of scriptural teaching, especially with that which relates to the atonement of Jesus Christ.

2. *The "Water of Purifying"* (19:2-10)

Central to this plan was the preparation of **a water of separation** (9), or "water of purifying" (8:7; cf. 31:23). It was to be used in the **purification for sin** of any who were defiled. It was no doubt prepared ahead of time and was ready when the need arose. It also clearly typifies the atonement of Jesus Christ, prepared ahead of time and instantly available to the cry of the heart that needs cleansing (I John 1:7).

The people of Israel were commanded to bring Moses **a red heifer[21] . . . wherein is no blemish, and upon which never came yoke** (2). The heifer was given to **Eleazar the priest,** and was to be slain **without the camp** (3; Exod. 29:14; Lev. 4:11-12,

[20]"The belief that contact with the dead made a person unclean or brought him into danger is ancient and widespread. It is impossible to fix its origin, though it is unlikely to have arisen in Israel. It is one of the pervasive beliefs of the primitive mind, arising perhaps from the customs of ancester worship, or from the conviction that the spirits of the dead surround a corpse. While the belief in the power of dead bodies to cause defilement is widespread, the remedy prescribed in this chapter is not exactly reproduced elsewhere." There is little doubt but that the principal reason that "contact with the dead" was so universally related to ceremonial defilement in the Mosaic law was because of the relationship of death to sin (IB, II, 234).

[21]This burning of the red heifer has several significant references to the sacrifice of Christ, according to Matthew Henry. The heifer was spotless and without blemish. It was red (Heb. 9:14; I Pet. 1:19), as Christ was a Son of the red earth, red in His apparel, red with His own blood (Isa. 63:1), and red with the blood of His enemies. It was to be wholly burnt, typifying the extreme suffering of Christ (Isa. 53:1-12). The ashes were kept for posterity (nearly 1,000 years, the Jews say) and were sufficient for all the people (Heb. 2:9-10, 14-18) (*An Exposition of the Old and New Testament,* Vol. I [New York: Fleming H. Revell Co., n.d.]).

21).[22] After the ceremonial sprinkling of **her blood** (4), the priest had the heifer totally burned. He then added **cedar wood,** for fragrance and incorruption; **hyssop,** for purification; and **scarlet** stuff (RSV), representing both sin (Lev. 14:4) and the blood which will bring remission of sins. The ashes from this burning became the base, to which water was added. This **water of separation** (9) made possible the "removal of sin" (RSV). Those who took part in the preparation were unclean until evening (7-8).

3. *The Prevalence of Uncleanness* (19:11, 14-16)

These verses point out the problem—there were many who were made unclean because they had come into contact with the dead. They were ceremonially unclean for seven days. This was not an incidental matter, as is indicated by the severity of the penalty for those who did not avail themselves of the provision for cleansing. To add to the problem, uncleanness could come in other ways than personal contact with the dead, as indicated by vv. 14-16.

While this speaks of the prevalence of uncleanness in the camp, it relates, further, to the universal uncleanness which has infected all mankind (Ps. 51:5; Rom. 3:10-23). Just as the uncleanness brought about by sin is universal in its outreach and touches the life of every person, so the atonement of Christ is readily available for all who will receive cleansing (Rom. 5:12-21).

4. *Procedures for Purification* (19:12, 17-19)

The act of purification was to take place **on the third day** and **on the seventh day** (12; cf. RSV). It was to come about by taking **the ashes of the burnt heifer of purification for sin,** to which **running water** "shall be added in a vessel" (17, RSV). **A clean person shall take hyssop,**[23] **and dip it in the water, and sprinkle it upon the tent . . . the vessels . . . the persons . . . and upon him** that is unclean (18). Then **on the seventh day he shall purify himself, and wash his clothes, and bathe himself in water, and shall be clean at even** (19).

[22]Outside the camp because the act had reference to an offering for sin and the uncleanness of death (Ellicott, *op. cit.*, p. 130). Cf. also Heb. 13:12.

[23]Cf. Ps. 51:7.

It is clear here, as elsewhere in the Scriptures, that the cleansing was more than ceremonial. There was a personal physical cleansing brought about by the washing of clothes and the bathing of the person. By the same token, the cleansing of the hearts of God's children is real, cleansing from the root of sin, changing inner affections (Deut. 6:4-5; 30:6), removing the heart of stone and filling the life with the Spirit of God (Ezek. 36:25-38).

5. *The Penalty for Neglect* (19:13, 20-22)

There is clear declaration that a person who did not "cleanse himself" (RSV) **defileth the tabernacle of the Lord** (13). This suggests that uncleanness relates to man's spiritual condition and to his relationship before God. A holy God cannot tolerate lack of holiness in His children. A severe penalty was outlined for the one who refused to allow the water of separation to be sprinkled on him. **He shall be cut off from Israel** (13). This speaks of several universal truths: the atonement is available; the unclean person must willingly receive it; he must obey the requirements to absolve his sin; after the days allotted him are over, he has no recourse; the responsibility for his rejection rests upon the individual; separation from the congregation of God is final. The timeless truth is plain, yet awful—God's grace is full and complete, but the heart that rejects the plan which God has provided for cleansing from sin will be forever lost.

Section IV *From Kadesh to Moab*

Numbers 20:1—22:1

A. Happenings at Kadesh, 20:1-21

1. *The Tribes Gather In* (20:1*a*)

Then came the children of Israel . . . and . . . abode in Kadesh (1). The wilderness wanderings were over. Israel had paid the full price for her sin. The old generation had passed and the new one was ready, after nearly 38 years of interruption, to pick up God's plan. So the tribes and families gathered together again at Kadesh (see map 3), probably in the first month of that forty-first year since the original group had left Egypt. They remained at Kadesh, according to Deut. 1:46, "many days," which may have been as much as three or four months. This was made necessary for at least three reasons: time was needed for reassembling and orienting the new generation to the plans for the movement of the camp (c. 2), a period of mourning over the death of Miriam, and communication with the leaders of Edom.

2. *The Death of Miriam* (20:1*b*)

Miriam died there, and was buried there (1). Miriam has been recognized in history as one of the strong forces under the hand of God in the great event of the Exodus. This is in spite of her one burst of jealousy (c. 12) and the dishonor and humiliation which resulted from it. The principal event in the record which tells specifically of her influence was her leadership in the victory celebration after Israel had crossed the Red Sea (Exod. 15:20-22). We can assume, however, that she gave strong and consistent support to Moses and Aaron and the program which God outlined for Israel. Even so, the record of her death is given in less than a sentence. God's cause is bigger than the most capable and the most celebrated of His workmen. His work moves on even as they are buried.

3. *The People Cry for Water* (20:2-8)

No mention had previously been made of any shortage of water at Kadesh. This lack now could mean that the springs had dried up, or that the flow had decreased so that there was not enough water to supply the full needs of the people. Or perhaps the water was not accessible to all of the people, since the camp was spread over a large area. In any event they complained because **there was no water for the congregation** (2). This followed the pattern which had characterized their murmuring in the past. The most recent instance had followed the rebellion of Korah (c. 16).[1]

The points of issue and the phrasing of their complaint were very much the same as before: **Would God that we had died!** (3) **Why have ye brought** us **up . . . into this wilderness?** (4) **Wherefore have ye made us to come up out of Egypt?** (5) The younger generation, of course, had personally experienced neither the pleasures of Egypt nor the full trials of the journey but no doubt had heard the stories. The complaining at this point could well have been led by the older ones, to whom these events of the past were not as remote.[2] It is apparent that the congregation was ready to pick up any issue that would give them occasion to complain about their plight. Murmuring is not noted for its logic nor is it confined to any one set of circumstances or to any one generation.

In the face of the continued agitation, **Moses and Aaron went . . . unto the door of the tabernacle** and fell prostrate before the Lord. As usual, God was faithful. **The glory of the Lord appeared unto them** (6). **And the Lord spake unto Moses** (7), giving instructions. Moses was to take the rod,[3] assemble the congregation, and "tell the rock before their eyes to give forth its water" (8, Amp. OT). While Moses did not do exactly as God had instructed, nevertheless God was faithful, and "water came out abundantly, and the congregation drank, and their beasts also" (11).

[1]Some authorities place Korah's rebellion toward the close of the years of wandering, which, timewise, would make it near the present uprising.

[2]Cf. Ellicott, *op. cit.*, p. 134.

[3]It is not clear whether this was the rod of Aaron which had budded (17:6-10) or the rod which had been the symbol of God's power in the hand of Moses in the past (Exod. 4:1-5; 7:9-12, 17).

4. *The Sin of Moses and Aaron*[4] (20:9-13)

God was displeased with the conduct of **Moses and Aaron** and told them that they would **not bring this congregation into the land** (12). What the exact nature of the sin was for which these two leaders were punished is not specifically described. However, even when the record is read under the most favorable interpretation, the response of Moses does not coincide with the commands God had given. No doubt it is in this variance that the true nature of the sin comes to light. A comparison is revealing.

a. God commanded Moses to "speak" to "the rock" (8). Instead, Moses **with his rod . . . smote the rock** (11). Here he was guilty of not obeying *explicitly* the command of God. Rather, he followed only the general lines of the command and may have carelessly reverted to a pattern of conduct which he had used on a similar occasion but with God's approval (Exod. 17:1-7). God's indictment was that Moses **believed me not** (12). This unbelief was probably not that Moses lacked faith in God's power to perform the miracle in the manner that God had designated. Rather, because of his personal desires or his mood of the moment Moses lacked the inclination to obey explicitly the will of God without modification. God condemned Moses and Aaron because of their rebellion (24). At the very moment Moses was calling the people **rebels** (10) he himself was refusing to follow the simple and well-defined command of God.

b. God commanded Moses to "gather . . . the assembly together . . . and speak . . . unto the rock before their eyes" (8). Instead, Moses cried out, as he struck the rock, "Shall we bring forth water for you?" (10, RSV) Here **Moses and Aaron** were guilty of projecting themselves and the powers of the human instead of exalting God before the people (12). God judged these leaders because they failed to **sanctify** Him **in the eyes of the children of Israel,** as God had commanded (Lev. 10:3) and as His holy nature demanded (Ps. 99:5, 9). Moses and Aaron were guilty of that very essential and basic of all sins, especially heinous for spiritual leaders—they exalted themselves rather

[4]It is apparent from the fact that Aaron was included in the penalty that he was involved in this sin, as was Moses. However, the record does not state just what his involvement was.

than the Lord. God is most honored when His servants humbly acknowledge that it is not by their hands but by the hand of God that miracles of the Kingdom are accomplished.

c. It is true that God commanded Moses to deal with the water shortage. However, God's spirit and mood was that of patience and love and His instructions were given with calm and poise. There is no reason indicated why Moses should not have followed through with the same pattern. Instead, he lost his grip, both on the situation and on himself. In anger he **smote the rock,** not once, but **twice** (11). In this he was guilty of that great sin in leadership: losing patience with the people whom he was trying to lead and, in this case, losing patience also with God.

In addition, he was guilty of violating his own personality. Moses was a man whose life consistently reflected qualities of meekness and patience even in the face of the most trying circumstances. In a sense these qualities were the hallmark of his character (cf. 12:3). This outburst of heat and bitterness was serious because it thus violated what Moses was because of his faith in God. It is at this point that his sin was properly labeled "unbelief."

d. God's command to Moses, furthermore, reflected love and patience with His children even though they were murmuring and complaining: "So thou shalt give the congregation and their beasts drink" (8). Moses, however, not only struck the rock with his rod but struck out verbally at the people, shouting, **Hear now, ye rebels** (10). Here he was guilty of that greatest of all sins in a society of human beings: deprecating human personality (Matt. 5:22) and failing to recognize that those with whom one is dealing are persons, too.

Whatever was the nature of Moses' and Aaron's acts, God called them sin—unbelief and rebellion. They were essentially sins of the spirit, which are indeed the most basic and the most serious kind. Certainly the penalty which God assessed gives an indication of how serious He considered them. **Therefore ye shall not bring this congregation into the land** (12). Thus these two mighty leaders suffered a similar judgment to that which had come upon the entire older generation. The tragedy of the failure of Moses and Aaron is compounded when the measure of their stature is taken and when it is remembered that, up until this time, they had done so well. But the record stands as a lesson for all generations that faithfulness must be thorough and complete, reaching to the end of life (Matt. 24:13; Heb. 3:6-19).

5. *Appeal to Edom* (20:14-21)

Because of the disastrous defeat suffered previously (14:45), the "way of the spies" was presumably cut off as a route to Canaan. Hence, **Moses** gave consideration to the possibility of searching out a route to the east. The shortest of these would pass through **Edom** (see map 3). These verses tell of Moses' attempt to get a "safe travel permit" from the leaders of the Edomites to go this route.

The message that Moses sent called attention to the fact that Edom was indeed the descendant of Esau, Israel's **brother** (14). Then followed a brief account of the sojourn of the Israelites in **Egypt** (15) and their flight from the Egyptians (16). Moses finally outlined the current situation that made it advantageous for them to go through the territory held by Edom. He assured the Edomites that Israel would not **pass through their fields, or . . . vineyards, neither . . . drink of the water of the wells,** and they would stay on **the king's high way** (17).[5]

Edom refused this request with a threat, **lest I come out against thee with the sword** (18). Moses tried again, insisting that the Israelites would do nothing but march through the land and would **pay** for any **water** which they used (19).[6] On receiving this proposition, **Edom came out** (20) with a show of force, to be sure that Israel did not ignore their refusal and press ahead anyway. **Thus Edom refused to give Israel passage through his border** (21).

B. Toward Canaan at Last, 20:22—21:4

1. *A New Day* (20:22)

It had been a long time. The buildup of expectation was intense, even though this was a new generation. The constant hope through the years of wilderness wanderings must have

[5]**The king's high way** would be simply the main caravan route, not a finished, solid-surfaced highway as the Romans later built, or as moderns would conceive such a road.

[6]These conditions for travel through the land of another were common in that day.

been to finish out the time of judgment and to get on to Canaan. Even the severity of their frustration, heartache, and suffering could not have obscured this hope. Yet the record is put simply, **And the children of Israel . . . journeyed from Kadesh, and came unto mount Hor** (22).

2. *Mount Hor* (20:22)

The exact location and identification of **mount Hor** have never been fully established. The evidences of the most recent scholarship[7] tend to support a site, identified as Jebel Madurah, some 30 miles northeast of Kadesh (see map 3) rather than the traditional site near Petros to the southeast. Such a location would still qualify the site as being on the "border of Edom" (23, RSV) but would place it nearer Canaan. This location makes more intelligible the incident recorded immediately following (21:1-3), which has the southern route into Canaan as its setting and hence more nearly supports the sequence of the text.

3. *The Death of Aaron* (20:23-29)

At Mount Hor, God reminded **Moses and Aaron** (23) that the latter **would not enter into the land** because of his part in the sin **at the water of Meribah** (24). Thus the stage was set for the transfer of the priestly powers from **Aaron** to his son **Eleazar.** God instructed Moses to take the two **up unto mount Hor** (25) and there perform the ceremony of transferring the priestly robes from the older man to the younger. And there on the mount, quietly, humbly, and majestically, **Aaron died.** When **Moses** and **Eleazar** (28) returned from the mount, the people, seeing the signs of the priesthood on Aaron's son, knew that the old priest had died. **They mourned for Aaron thirty days** (29) before continuing their journey.

4. *Defeat and Victory* (21:1-3)

The exact significance of this incident is not clear. Moses may have made plans to try the southern route into Canaan as had been originally planned. This would have been natural in view of Edom's refusal to let the Israelites pass to the east. However, **king Arad**[8] **the Canaanite** (1) learned of this intention. He was fearful of such a large group of people seemingly

[7]Cf. IB, II, 240. Also *Harper's Bible Dictionary*, "Mount Hor," p. 267.

[8]Arad would be only a short distance northwest of Mount Hor.

moving in his direction, and attacked the Israelites with a measure of success.

Whereupon Israel **vowed a vow unto the Lord** (2) that if God would deliver the Canaanites into their hands they would **utterly destroy their cities.** God gave them a notable victory at **Hormah** (3). This may be a given location (see map 3) or it may signify merely that the Canaanites were reduced to a state of utter destruction (*hormah;* cf. 14:45). There is some indication, also, that this account, in addition to depicting a single battle or group of battles, may be incorporating a bit of general prophecy as to the ultimate victory of Israel in her conquest of Canaan (Judg. 1:16-17).

5. *The Route to Moab* (21:4*a*)

It would appear that the Israelites, after they were refused passage across Edom, probed the southern route into Canaan. Then in the face of the resistance they met, or because of reasons not recorded, gave up the idea of entering Canaan by this route. It was then that they circled southward **by the way of the Red sea** (4). To clear the southern border of Edom, they had to travel to the northern tip of the Gulf of Aqaba, nearly half the distance back toward Mount Sinai. They then turned eastward, passing near what is the present port of Eilat (Ezion-geber), in order to get east of the land of Edom (see map 3).

An alternate route has been suggested by some scholars as being more logical. This would have led the Israelites south from Mount Hor to a point midway between the Dead Sea and the Gulf of Aqaba. From there they turned abruptly northeast to Puron, which they locate inside Edom. From thence the route would be to Oboth, which they locate toward the north-central portion of the Arabah. It would then run to the south tip of the Dead Sea, where the Brook Zared empties from the east. Turning to the east they would have followed the Brook Zared, moving between the countries of Edom and Moab, circling Moab to the east and thence to the Arnon River (see place names in 11-13).

C. The Brazen Serpent, 21:4-9

1. *The Plague of Serpents* (21:4-6)

As the congregation moved to the south they encountered tedious travel conditions similar to those that had been such a trial to their fathers in the past. In the face of these desert conditions, the murmuring of the people reached a new height. **There is no bread, neither is there any water** (5), they complained. They were correct, of course, in that there was no natural supply of either bread or water from the land through which they were going. They were wrong in that God had been and was then miraculously supplying their basic needs. Their complaint brought in question the adequacy of what He was providing for them. It was basically this lack of faith that brought God's displeasure upon them.

For this murmuring, the Lord sent a plague of **fiery serpents** (6). They were so designated, probably because of the nature of the poisonous venom which they ejected, and because of their color, which was a bright, copper color.[9]

2. *The Serpent of Brass*[10] (21:7-9)

In the face of the deaths from the plague, the people awakened to the wrong of their complaining and came to Moses. They said, **We have sinned, for we have spoken against the Lord, and against thee** (7). They begged Moses to **pray unto the Lord, that he take away the serpents.** It is noteworthy that the people's petition to Moses in this instance, more than in others, called for intercession to the Lord.

God's instruction was for Moses to make a serpent of brass which was to be placed on **a pole** (8).[11] It was to be lifted high enough above the camp so that it could be seen by all of the people. Those who had been bitten by a serpent could avoid death simply by looking at **the serpent of brass** (9).

While this account is discredited by some, conservative scholars feel that it must stand as one of the great pre-Calvary miracles of the OT. The prime authority for this is Christ himself, who said, "As Moses lifted up the serpent in the wilderness, even

[9]This fact is established through the use of the word *saraph* for "serpent," which seems to mean "burning one." When used in Isa. 6:2, 6; 14:29; Ezek. 1:7, *saraph* carries the idea that the symbolic beings had a metallic luster. This is also supported by the fact that the serpent which God ordered Moses to make was made of shining metal (Winterbotham, *op. cit.*, p. 272).

[10]It is not clear what was the exact composition of this serpent. It could have been brass, or copper, or bronze. Hence the occasional use of the general term, "brazen."

[11]One of the standards or ensigns used to mark the position of the tribes, or a special, longer pole especially set up for the occasion.

so must the Son of man be lifted up: that whosoever believeth in him should not perish, but have eternal life" (John 3:14-15).

The serpent of brass was thus a type of Jesus Christ, who, when lifted upon a Cross, brought salvation and spiritual life to all who but look in faith. There is also implied in this OT account the truth that "like cures like." God gave a miraculous serpent of metal to heal the deadly infection caused by the venom of the fiery serpents. The Scripture says of Jesus, "With his stripes we are healed. . . . and the Lord hath laid on him the iniquity of us all" (Isa. 53:5-6). Also, "[God] hath made him [Christ] to be sin for us, who knew no sin; that we might be made the righteousness of God in him" (II Cor. 5:21; cf. Rom. 8:3).

In 4-9 we see the truth of "The Brazen Serpent." (1) Sin is racial and personal, 4-7; (2) The serpent and the Saviour were lifted up, 8; cf. John 3:14; (3) There is life for a look that is voluntary, contrite, believing, 9; cf. John 3:14-15 (G. B. Williamson).

3. *From Whence the Miracle?*

In all of this there must be a clear understanding that salvation and life came not from the brass serpent, as such. These blessings came from the power of God which was released by faith and by personal acceptance of the plan which He had outlined. Even in that day it was the power of a Cross which was yet to be lifted up that brought healing.

It must be forever established that it is not the symbol which redeems, but the Christ back of that symbol. The Hebrews later fell into the error of worshipping this very brazen serpent which had been preserved (II Kings 18:4). Because of this faulty use, Hezekiah had the serpent taken from the Temple and broken to pieces. Although the brazen serpent had its place in the plan of God in the desert setting and perhaps had a place among the items of reverence in Israel's archives, it was not to become an object of worship, nor was it to be venerated as something which had a supernatural power inherent within itself.

D. Incidents on the March, 21:10—22:1

1. *Some Stations en Route* (21:10-13, 16, 19-20)

The list of the stations at which the Israelites camped on the entire journey from Egypt to Canaan is given in c. 33. At this point only those principal ones, in this leg of the trip from Mount Hor to Moab, are given. It is as if the historian wanted to move the reader with seven-league boots from the desert of Paran to the fertile bowl of the plains of Moab.[12]

The places mentioned cannot be located on modern maps. **Oboth** (10) has been identified merely as "the flinty plateau to the east of Edom"[13] but it cannot be pinpointed more exactly. The name **Ijeabarim** (11) means "the ruins on the other side" but is not identified further.[14] **The valley of Zared** (12) is "on the wady of Zered which flows into the Dead Sea at its southern extremity."[15] **From thence they removed, and pitched** on the north side **of** the river **Arnon . . . the border . . . between Moab and the Amorites** (13). To locate **Beer** ("well town," 16), **Mattanah, Nahaliel,** and **Bamoth** (19) is also all but impossible. **Pisgah** probably speaks of one or more of the high ridges of the Moabite plateau that jut out into the Dead Sea, **which looketh toward Jeshimon** (20). From here the hills of Canaan could be clearly seen.[16] The highest of these was Mount Nebo, on which Moses died (Deut. 34:1).

2. *Bits of Folk Song History* (21:14-18*a*)

These verses present fragmentary snatches of records representative of this period of history. **The book of the wars of the Lord** (14) is not mentioned elsewhere in the Bible. But the fact that data is referred to here, even in a sketchy manner, indicates that such accounts were kept. Here were bits of ballads or folk songs, records of the exploits of great persons or events, which were sung around the campfires or before the courts. These are not unlike other records that have been discovered of the exploits of kings and military leaders of this period of history. The inclusion here of such records, even though they are but snatches, confirms rather than discredits the validity of the account.

The first song speaks of the victories of Israel at **the Red sea, and in the brooks of Arnon** (14). The second tells of the incidents at **Beer,** where a **well** was digged and a song was sung (16). This ancient song has been a source of rich blessing across the centuries to Jews and Christians alike. It speaks of the unique

[12]Cf. alternate locations in comments on 4*a*.

[13]Cf. Deut. 2:1-12.

[14]IB, II, 243.

[15]Hertz, ed., *op. cit.,* p. 660.

[16]IB, II, 244-45.

combination of God's miracles and man's work. God promised, **I will give them water.** But **the princes digged the well, the nobles of the people digged it . . . with their staves** (18). Perhaps the special joy which seems to be inherent in the song came because of this very combination. It marked a transition in the manner in which God dealt with His children. Previously, on occasion, God gave them water miraculously. Now the people themselves had a part to perform. This, indeed, was a transition into their new way of life and responsibility in the conquest of Canaan.

3. *Fate of the Amorites* (21:21-32)

The Amorites (21) were among the principal tribes of the Canaanites (Gen. 10:16). The name is often used in a general way when the broadest reference to the Canaanite nations is intended (cf. Deut. 1:7, 19, 27). Also it is used to denote all of "the inhabitants of Syria before the time of the Exodus."[17] A tribe of the Amorites under the leadership of **Sihon** had only recently moved in from the north of Palestine. They had conquered and taken over the cities of the Moabites, stopping at the river Arnon.

The territory that Sihon occupied was not included in the original promise of God to Abraham (34:2-12). However, the fact that it was now in the possession of a Canaanite people did include it (Gen. 15:18-21; Deut. 2:24).[18] Hence Moses did not hesitate to make contact with Sihon. He **sent messengers** requesting permission to pass through his land to reach the fords of the Jordan opposite Jericho. Sihon refused and came out with his armies, so the Israelites fought them. Even though theirs was not an experienced army, they seemed to have courage, strength, and confidence. God gave them victories and they occupied **all these cities** (25) which they wrested from **the Amorites** (cf. Deut. 2:30-37).

It was about this total victory over the Amorites that **they that speak in proverbs** (27) sang. The song is a combination of gloating over victory and taunting the defeated. It begins with

[17]Hertz, ed., *op. cit.,* p. 662.

[18]This in contrast to the land occupied by the Amorites, the Moabites, the Midianites, and the Edomites, all of whom were Semitic in origin, tracing their descent from Terah (cf. Deut. 2:1-25). Military action against these people (cf. c. 31) was for other reasons.

the victory of **Sihon** (28) over the Moabites and calls to attention the failure of **Chemosh** (29), the Moabite god. It closes with the simple summary of the victory of the Israelites over Sihon (30). The entire song places **Heshbon,**[19] the principal city of the Amorites, in the place of prominence.

4. *The Defeat of Og*[20] (21:33—22:1)

While only a few words are given to the account, the victory over **Og** (33) is significant.[21] While probably, in some ways, Og would be classified as a Canaanite, he was distinctive in that he was one of the last of a tribe of giants. Besides being formidable warriors, the followers of Og had cities which were all but impregnable. Israel would probably not have conquered them had these armies stayed behind their city walls. Instead, **Og the king of Bashan went out against them,** and he was defeated.

In addition to the facts of the victory, it is important to see that the territory which Og controlled reached northward to a point opposite the Sea of Galilee. The fact that this territory was conquered by Israel brought about the request of the tribes of Reuben, Gad, and one-half the tribe of Manasseh to take this area as their inheritance rather than that which would have been given them under the original promise (c. 32; Deut. 3:15-17).

So **Israel set forward, and pitched in the plains of Moab** (22:1), presumedly even while the armies were closing out the campaign against Og to the north. These **plains of Moab** constituted a humid, fertile valley, below sea level across the Jordan from Jericho. This was the first slight taste of the promise that the Israelites would possess a land flowing with milk and honey. Certainly it was a change of atmosphere from the desert setting which had been theirs since they left Egypt.

[19]**Heshbon,** "city of daughters" or "the mother city." Permanent cities were a comparatively new thing in this area. Archaeologists have ascertained that rather suddenly, and that without explanation, the people of these areas gave up the nomadic pattern of living and built permanent, walled cities. This occurred not long before the appearance of Israel in their trek to Canaan. It must be assumed, however, that many of the cities were "in the making," without walls, even as in the case of the cities of Og (Deut. 3:5). These unwalled or partially built cities were dependent upon the "mother city" for protection.

[20]Cf. Deut. 3:10-17.

[21]So much so that the event is referred to many times in the OT (Deut. 1:4; 3:1-13; Josh. 2:10; 9:10; 12:4; 13:12-31; I Kings 4:19; Neh. 9:22; Ps. 135:11; 136:20).

Section V *The Drama of Balaam*

Numbers 22:2—24:25

A. Unique Characteristics of the Section

1. *The "Book of Balaam"*[1]

By whatever measurement used, this section of Numbers is unique. This has caused many to mark it as a completely interpolated passage, with little if any relationship to the body of the book. It has been aptly called the "Book of Balaam." The chief reason, however, that this is seen as a separate bit of literature is the fact that the text of 22:2 can be followed by 25:1 without any break in the flow of the historical account.

Because its setting is completely outside the borders of Israel the question has been asked, "How did Moses get the story?" The most logical answer is that Balaam made a record of the incidents, and at a later date, possibly when Israel overran Moab, the story came to Moses' hand. It could be that at this time the account was edited to give it the definite pro-Israel shadings which it contains.

The mood of the story is lost unless its distinct dramatic accent is kept in mind. It has many of the earmarks of a dramatic production. If it is not the kind that would have been played by actors, at least the dramatic details were clearly in the mind of the author. All in all, the story of Balaam stands as one of the puzzling portions of this otherwise more basically historical book.

2. *The Man Balaam*

Scholars are far from agreed as to just who Balaam was. The account here speaks of him simply as **Balaam the son of Beor to** (of) **Pethor** (22:5). He is identified as one who lived to the east, a resident of the same general area from which came Abraham and the wise men of Jesus' day. This was the area where Laban lived and to which Jacob returned for a wife (Gen. 29:1-35).

[1]As the section was probably known in ancient times. Hertz, ed., *op. cit.*, p. 668.

In seeking to determine the character of Balaam, two extremes of interpretation come into play. There are those who would brand him as a scoundrel, a heathen sorcerer. Though playing the role of a true prophet in blessing Israel, before he departs the scene, he "suggests a peculiarly abhorrent means of bringing about the ruin of Israel."[2] There are others, however, who would exalt him to a high position as a prophet born out of his time, not unlike the place accorded to Melchizedek (Gen. 14: 18-19).

Probably the real answer is found not in the extremes, but in some mid-ground between them. Like Samson, Balaam showed some signs of being pliable to the will of God, when that will was made clear to him. Nevertheless there were things about his character that would not pass a biblical moral standard. Probably it is best not to criticize Balaam too severely, at least for actions in the early stages of the account. He had very limited light and probably only sketchy information as to who Israel was.

An evaluation from a Jewish source brings some light to the perplexing dilemma.[3]

> Because of these fundamental contradictions in character, Bible Critics assume that the Scriptural account of Balaam is a combination of two or three varying traditions belonging to different periods. This is quite unconvincing; it is as if we were to maintain that the current life-story of Francis Bacon, for example, was due to the combination of two or three traditions belonging to different periods of English history, since no one man could at the same time be an illustrious philosopher, a great statesman, and the "meanest of mankind." Such a view betrays a slight knowledge of the fearful complexity of the mind and soul of man. It is only in the realm of the Fable that men and women display, as it were in a single flash of light, some *one* aspect of human nature. It is otherwise in real life. "The heart is deceitful above all things, and desperately wicked; who can know it?" (Jer. 17:9) is, alas, a far truer summary of human psychology.

Able and competent scholars have presented fairly sound evidence on both sides of the issue. It is therefore probably not possible for the average student of the Scripture to come to a wholly satisfactory conclusion in the matter. A brief look at the pros and cons might be of assistance in gaining a workable evaluation of the man Balaam.

[2]*Ibid.* [3]*Ibid.*

3. *The Pros*

The evidences which tend to place Balaam in a favorable light might be listed as follows:

a. He seemed to have an accessibility to God far above the average and to have a basic desire to listen to the voice of God (8, 13, 18), in spite of the relapse which occasioned the experience of the speaking donkey (22:22-31).

b. There is a depth of perception in his transmission of the truths that God gave him which indicates that he was no novice in the deep things of the spirit.

c. It appears that, in the seesaw of good and evil in his experience, the good seemed to be victorious. This was true at least in the initial stages of his contact with Balak and the pressures to either bless or curse Israel.

d. Regardless of other evidence to the contrary, he was used of God to bless Israel and thus thwarted the ingenious plan of Balak to stop them.

4. *The Cons*

The evidences which place Balaam in an unfavorable light might include the following:

a. Jewish history quite generally treats Balaam as an evil man, in spite of the blessing that he gave to Israel at this time.

b. The Scripture record refers to him in a similar light. Jude 11 speaks of Balaam's greed; Rev. 2:14 speaks of his treachery in turning Israel to "eat things sacrificed to idols, and to commit fornication."

c. The most severe indictment, and the one upon which the others rest, is found in the limited reference in 31:8, 16. It would appear from these passages that Balaam, perhaps to square himself with Balak, counseled Balak to encourage the women of his country to beguile the men of Israel (c. 25).

d. Finally, there is reluctance to attribute high spiritual perception to one whose background is so uncertain. It seems inconsistent to attribute to an "occultist and soothsayer" the abilities to speak divine truth as he seemed to speak it.

B. Balak's Invitation and Balaam's Response, 22:2-41

1. *The Setting* (22:2-7)

Balak . . . king of the Moabites (4) was aware of the victories of Israel over the Amorites and over Og. Not knowing that

Moab was not marked for conquest, since it was not a Canaanite nation, he sought to forestall a similar conquest of his own cities. He did not want his country to be "licked up" (4) as were the others. He thought he had a plan to prevent this, which he discussed with **the elders of Midian.** He secured their cooperation and then sent **messengers . . . unto Balaam** (5) to appeal to him for help. **There is a people come out from Egypt,** his message went, **and they abide over against me.** He urged, **Come now . . . curse me this people** (6), in order that they may not overrun Moab and in order that they may be driven **out of the land.** Balak's thinking was like that which prevailed in his day. He felt that if he could get a reputed soothsayer to curse Israel the tides of fortune would go against them.

Hence the messengers, **elders of Moab and the elders of Midian departed with the rewards**—their price for the job of "foretelling" (7)—and brought the message to Balaam.

2. *Balaam's Response* (22:8-14)

Balaam welcomed the messengers, saying, **Lodge here this night** (8). He assured them that he would give them an answer **as the Lord shall speak unto me.** Then follows a conversation between God and Balaam. It began with the question, **What men are these with thee?** (9) The conversation closed, after the mission was explained by Balaam (10-11), with the command, **Thou shalt not go with them; thou shalt not curse the people: for they are blessed** (12). The next morning **Balaam** relayed these instructions to **the princes of Balak** (13) and they returned home.

"Balaam's Blessing" is the theme of cc. 22—24. (1) Man's intended curse may be turned into God's blessing, 22:5-6; 23:7-10; (2) Man's blessing may bring God's curse, 25:3-5; (3) By God's grace and sovereign power all the curse of sin shall be changed to blessedness, II Pet. 3:13 (G. B. Williamson).

3. *Balak Persists* (22:15-21)

Balak was not to be thwarted by a single refusal from Balaam. He sent **more** princes to Balaam, greater in number and **more honourable** (15) than those sent previously. On their arrival, they offered Balaam more than money. They promised **great honour** and a free rein in the project. Balak had sent an offer, **I will do whatsoever thou sayest unto me** (17).

But Balaam was not moved by the offers and expressed his response in a thrilling declaration of dedication and purpose: **If**

Balak would give me his house full of silver and gold, I cannot go beyond the word of the Lord my God, to do less or more (18). Following this, God gave Balaam permission to go with the princes of Balak on condition that **the word which I shall say unto thee, that shalt thou do** (20). And so Balaam "saddled his donkey" (Amp. OT), **and went with the princes** (21).

4. *The Speaking Donkey* (22:22-35)

It is not certain why there is an apparent discrepancy in God's instructions as to whether Balaam was to respond to Balak's request (cf. 20, 22). The reasonable answer lies in a change in Balaam's attitude. So long as Balaam was willing to say what God wanted him to speak, God gave him permission to go. Probably somewhere between the evening and the morning Balaam's decision shifted. Hence **God's anger was kindled** (22) and there was need for the lesson from the angel and from the donkey.

There were three steps in getting Balaam to see and to listen. These are vividly described in 22-31. In the first instance the donkey, seeing the angel[4] **standing in the way . . . with his sword drawn . . . turned aside . . . into a field** (23). The second time the angel blocked the path as Balaam moved through a vineyard where the path was lined on either side by a wall. Seeing **the angel** blocking the way, the donkey moved to one side, **thrust herself unto the wall, and crushed Balaam's foot** (25). Again **the angel** blocked the way **in a narrow place** and, since there was no place to go, the donkey "lay down under Balaam" (27, RSV). In anger, Balaam struck the donkey **with a staff,** more furiously than he had in the two previous instances.

With this, **the Lord opened the mouth of the ass** (28), and she spoke to her master, complaining of the treatment he had given her. The donkey asked, **What have I done unto thee, that thou hast smitten me these three times?** Balaam responded, "Because you have ridiculed and provoked me; I wish there were a sword in my hand, for now I would kill you" (29, Amp. OT). The donkey reminded Balaam that she had never before acted like this, which the man acknowledged. With that Balaam's **eyes** were **opened** and he, too, **saw the angel of the Lord** (31) with

[4]As in the case of the burning bush (Exod. 3:1-6) and Joshua's experience (Josh. 5:13-15), the **angel** was no doubt the Lord himself.

the drawn **sword.** He **bowed . . . his head, and fell flat on his face** before the Lord.

The angel told Balaam that he had appeared in the way because Balaam's behavior was "willfully obstinate and contrary" (32, Amp. OT), and had not the donkey turned aside he would have **slain** Balaam (33). Balaam acknowledged his sin and said, **If it displease thee, I will get me back again** (34). But Balaam was assured of the Lord that if he would certainly "speak what I tell you" (Amp. OT) he could proceed toward Moab. With that understanding, **Balaam went with the princes of Balak** (35).

5. *Balak's Reception* (22:36-41)

Balak went out to meet **Balaam** at the boundary of his country (36). He chided Balaam, presumably for not coming at the first invitation. **Am I not able indeed to promote thee to honour?** (37) Balaam replied that he had indeed **come,** but warned Balak that he had no **power** in himself to **say any thing,** but **the word that God putteth in my mouth, that shall I speak** (38).

The group then returned to **Kirjath-huzoth** (39; location not known), sacrifices were **offered,** and portions were **sent to Balaam, and to the princes** (40). **Balak** then **took Balaam** to the **high places of Baal,** from where they could see the nearest part of the Israelite encampment (41).

C. The First Prophecy,[5] 23:1-13

1. *Preparations* (23:1-6)

In preparation for the work to be done, **Balaam** directed **Balak** to have **seven altars** prepared, upon which were sacrificed **seven oxen and seven rams** (1). Balaam then ordered Balak to **stand by thy burnt offering** (3) as he went away by himself, saying: "Perhaps the Lord will come to meet me" (3, Amp. OT). God did meet Balaam and gave him a message. When **he returned,** he found Balak standing faithfully by the **burnt sacrifice** (6), and he delivered the prophecy that God had given him.

2. *Review of Events* (23:7-9)

The first portion of the prophecy speaks of the events which had brought Balaam to this place: **Balak . . . hath brought me from Aram . . . saying, Come, curse me Jacob** (7). Balaam then

[5]To read these prophecies from the RSV or other versions which line them in poetic form makes for clarity and ease of understanding.

asked, **How shall I curse, whom God hath not cursed? or how shall I defy, whom the Lord hath not defied?** (8) The prophet was reflecting upon his promise to the Lord that he would speak only what God commanded him to speak.

3. *The High Points* (23:9-10)

a. The first insight speaks of the historical loneliness of Israel: **Lo, the people shall dwell alone, and shall not be reckoned among the nations** (9).[6] This prophecy not only spoke of Israel's situation at the moment but saw its loneliness across the centuries.

b. The second section speaks of the fulfillment of the prophecy to Abraham: **Who can count the dust of Jacob, and the number of the fourth part of Israel?** (10) Again, Balaam was speaking not only of what he saw from the high place but what he was seeing through the eye of the spirit in the centuries that were to come.

c. The closing message is a beautiful insight into the character of those whom he was supposed to be cursing: **Let me die the death of the righteous, and let my last end be like his!**[7] Balaam revealed the insight that God had given him: here were good people, not to be cursed but blessed.

4. *Balak's Reaction* (23:11-13)

Balak's reaction was immediate: **What hast thou done unto me? I took thee to curse mine enemies, and . . . thou hast blessed them.** Balaam simply reminded him of the agreement that he would speak only **that which the Lord hath put in my mouth** (12). Whereupon Balak took him to a place from which they could see only a portion of the Israelite camp. He reasoned, perhaps, that Balaam could better curse the camp when not so much of it could be seen.

D. The Second Prophecy, 23:14-26

The Preparation (23:14-17)

As before, **they built seven altars, and offered a bullock and a ram on every altar** (14); then Balaam went aside by himself

[6]Jewish scholars support the reading, "Israel is a people that dwelleth alone, it does not conspire against the nations" (Hertz, ed., *op. cit.*, p. 674).

[7]This wish was not fulfilled (31:8, 15). Better had he said, "Let me live the life of the righteous!"

to **meet the Lord** (15). On his return with his **word** from God (16) he found **the princes of Moab** with Balak standing by the offering (17).

2. *The Character of God* (23:18-20)

The first of this prophecy spoke directly to **Balak** (18) and instructed him as to the character of God. He must understand **God is not a man** (19). God cannot be forced to tell a **lie,** nor can He be persuaded to change His mind about such a matter as was before them. God was seeking to show Balak that He could not be persuaded to change His mind no matter how many times Balaam was asked to prophesy. As Balaam put it: **I have received commandment to bless: and he hath blessed; and I cannot reverse it** (20).

3. *The Source of Jacob's Strength* (23:21-24)

Balaam's blessing, however, went further than telling of God's character. It showed Balak that it would be impossible to predict "misfortune" or "trouble"[8] (RSV) for Israel because the Lord had "forgiven" him (Amp. OT). Balaam continued, **The Lord his God is with him, and the shout** (glory) **of a king** (the Lord) **is among them**[9] (21). God was with Israel and had proved through many evidences that He would not fail His people.

The point was evident. Balaam said, **God brought them out of Egypt** and "they have as it were the horns [strength] of the wild ox" (22, RSV). He further pointed out to Balak that there was "no sorcery in Jacob, neither is witchcraft found in Israel" (23, Berk).[10] "In due season and even now it shall be said of Jacob and Israel, What has God wrought!" (Amp. OT) Israel had a strength which came from Almighty God. There was little use in trying to bring any forces to bear to defeat them.

Then Balaam pointed up a prophecy that was well-known to Israel and no doubt was much repeated around their family circles (Gen. 49:8-9): "Behold, [what] a people!" (24, RSV)

[8]"'Misfortune' and 'Trouble' are preferable to the KJV 'iniquity' and 'perverseness'. They not only accord with the LXX, but more accurately render the Hebrew" (IB, II, 257).

[9]Or, "They shout with praise to a King." This, in acknowledgement of the theocracy which they one day rejected (I Samuel 8) (Berk.).

[10]This, possibly, in contrast in Balak's desire to invoke divination on Israel.

They **shall rise up as a great lion,** and **shall not lie down until he eat of the prey.** The prophecy predicted the ultimate victory of Israel over its enemies, the very truth that Balak did not want to hear.

4. *Balak's Despair* (23:25-26)

At this point, **Balak** was desperate. He just could not get Balaam to speak the words he wanted to hear. So he told the prophet, **Neither curse them . . . nor bless them** (25); in modern parlance, "If you can't say what I want to hear, just don't say anything!" But Balaam stuck by his original proposition: **All that the Lord speaketh, that I must do** (26).

E. THE THIRD PROPHECY, 23:27—24:13

1. *The Prelude* (23:27—24:2)

"So Balak took Balaam to the top of Peor [another high place], that overlooks the desert" (28, RSV). There the same pattern of offering sacrifices was followed (29). However, **when Balaam saw that it pleased the Lord to bless Israel** (1), he did not go apart, as he had done previously, but looked toward the "plain of Moab where Israel was camped" (Berk., fn.). He saw the orderly arrangement of the tents of Israel "tribe by tribe" (RSV), **and the spirit of God**[11] **came upon him** (2).

2. *The Man of the Oracle* (24:3-4)

This poem is less regular than the others and contains perplexities which the scholars have not resolved. It is different from the first two in that it is not directed to Balak but takes on the form of a true prophecy or "oracle" (RSV). Balaam begins by giving his credentials, "The oracle of the man whose eye is opened"[12] (3, RSV; "able now to see the purposes and will of God," Amp. OT). It was "the oracle of him who hears the words of God, who sees a vision of the Almighty" (4, RSV). Balaam claimed divine authority for what he was going to say, taking on the posture of the prophets of a later day.

[11]Here we find an advancement to a more personal, spiritual form of the revelation of God to man. It was the form by which the true servants of God received their messages.

[12]Not clear, but most certainly not simply "closed" as the KJV margin has it. Perhaps "closed" in the sense of being "perfect" (IB, II, 259).

3. *The Picture of Israel* (24:5-9)

Balaam, seeing the orderly rows of the tents of Israel pitched on the plain of Moab, described the scene in poetic language. **How goodly are thy tents, O Jacob, and thy tabernacles, O Israel!** (5) He then likened the orderly alignment of the camp to **valleys** (6), a series of vast fertile plains, **gardens by the river's side.** In Balaam's mind, this picture was like the orchards of his native country which lay along the river Euphrates, where the aloe tree was a symbol of verdant luxury. However, this that lay before him was of the Lord's planting, not man's. There was a perpetual source of life, such as the **cedar trees** which have their roots **beside the waters.**

Then follows a description of the Israel of the future. "Water shall flow from his buckets,"[13] **and his seed shall be in many waters** (7). This is evidently an allusion to prosperity as well as to virility. The strength of the nation is illustrated by its supremacy over its enemies: **His kings shall be higher than Agag, and his kingdom shall be exalted.**

Balaam then continued with a near repetition of his second prophecy, describing the greatness of the nation which God **brought . . . out of Egypt,** whose strength is that of a wild ox (RSV), who **shall eat up the nations his enemies, and shall break their bones, and pierce them through with his arrows** (8).

The picture here shows Israel as a **lion** asleep—a sleep from which no one dare wake him—content with his successful hunting foray. This is in contrast to 23:24, which shows the lion's great might in the time of war. Far from being affected by curses or blessing from others, Israel is rather the standard: **Blessed is he that blesseth thee, and cursed is he that curseth thee** (9). History has, indeed, borne out the fact that God in a very unusual manner has kept His hand upon this people.

4. *Balak's Anger Aroused* (24:10-13)

At the close of the prophecy, **Balak's anger** blazed (10). He clapped **his hands together** as an indication of scorn (Job 27:23), and advised Balaam to **flee** (11) to his home. It is remarkable insight on Balak's part that he credited **the Lord** with keeping

[13]The Jewish version has it, "Water shall flow from his branches." In both cases it speaks of abundant water, which in an arid country is a symbol of the greatest resources.

Balaam from the **honour** which the Moabites had intended to heap upon him. But Balaam was not moved. He held to his initial commitment: **If Balak would give me his house full of silver and gold, I cannot go beyond the commandment of the Lord** (13).

F. The Fourth Prophecy, 24:14-25

1. *A Parting Word* (24:14)

Before Balaam left, **to go unto** his **people,** he added a final prophecy, telling Balak **what this people** (Israel) **shall do to thy people** (Moab) **in the latter days.** This word came without the elaborate preliminary sacrifices or acts of divination which had preceded the earlier prophecies. **I will advertise thee** is simply, "Let me tell you" (Moffatt).

2. *His Credentials* (24:15-16)

In a repetition of the third prophecy, Balaam spoke of himself as one whose eye is "perfect" (RSV, fn.), who "hears the words of God, and knows the knowledge of the Most High, who sees the vision of the Almighty" (16, RSV).

3. *The Star Out of Jacob* (24:17-19)

Balaam caught a vision of **a Star out of Jacob** (17), the King who should rule **Israel** in the future—**not now . . . not nigh.** This has been viewed across the centuries as a vision of the Messiah, whose birth would be marked by the appearance of a star out of the east (Matt. 2:2). Balaam saw that **a Sceptre** would **rise** which would "crush the forehead"[14] (RSV) of **Moab** and **the children of Sheth** (17, "sons of pride")[15] and would **have dominion** (19) over His enemies.

4. *Oracles Against Certain Nations* (24:20-25)

a. The first nation brought into Balaam's sights was "Edom" (18), which was to become "a possession" of Israel. This prophecy was fulfilled in the time of David.

b. Of the Amalekites,[16] he prophesied that they should **perish for ever** (20).

[14]Or "pierce through the temples." [15]IB, II, 261.

[16]Probably **the first of the nations** (20), not in origin or in power, but the **first** to attack Israel (Exod. 17:8-16).

c. **Of the Kenites,** though their **dwellingplace** was **strong** (21), it was said that they would be **wasted, until Asshur**[17] should take them **captive** (22).

d. And then for **Asshur** and **Eber** he prophesied that they, in turn, would **perish for ever** (24) under the hand of a people who would come in **ships** from the coasts of **Chittim.** With the close of this prophecy, Balaam **went . . . to his place** (25). **Balak . . . went his way,** giving up at last on the plan which he had contrived to bring a curse on Israel.

[17]The identity of these nations and events in this and the following verses is not clear, but the best interpretation seems to favor this glossary: **Asshur** (Persia), **Chittim** (Cyprus), **Eber** (rendered "the Hebrews" by LXX, but unknown; it means the people "across," presumedly across the Euphrates) (IB, II, 263).

Section VI *Events in Moab*

Numbers 25:1—32:42

A. Moral Failures, 25:1-18

1. *Israel's Great Problem* (25:1-5)

Israel found it difficult across the generations to keep the command of God not to intermarry with the people into whose lands they went (Exod. 34:12-16; Deut. 7:1-6). Early in their contact with other peoples, "while Israel dwelt in Shittim,"[1] she "began to play the harlot with the daughters of Moab" (1, RSV). This wanton intermingling led Israel to sin in a religious sense as well as in the moral, as it led them to sacrificing to Moab's **gods** and worshiping them.[2] For this **the anger of the Lord was kindled against Israel** (3). He commanded Moses to **hang** "the chiefs of the people" (4, RSV), who were morally responsible. He also instructed **the judges** to **slay** every man who had thus **joined** himself to the god **Baal-peor** (5).

2. *Involvements with Midianites* (25:6-9, 14-15)

A similar pattern developed with regard to the daughters of the Midianites, as represented by the instance noted here. An Israelite man boldly brought **a Midianitish woman** to present as his wife.[3] This was done brazenly, **in the sight of all the congregation,** even while there were supplications and prayers before the Tent of Meeting (6). The prayers related to a **plague**[4] then in progress. Alertly, **Phinehas, the son of Eleazar,** the priest, sizing up the seriousness of the situation, **rose up,** "took

[1]The last camp before the Israelites crossed Jordan, from whence Joshua sent his spies into Canaan.

[2]It appears that many Israelites were invited to join in a sacrificial festival. This worship of Baal-peor was associated with and consisted in the most licentious rites (Hertz, ed., *op. cit.*, p. 68).

[3]Or perhaps he was flaunting his immoral association with the woman in the sight of Moses and all Israel.

[4]**The plague,** no doubt, resulting from this very moral laxity which had overtaken the people (3-6).

a spear in his hand" (7, RSV), and **thrust both of them through** (8). The man's name was **Zimri** and the woman's name was **Cozbi.** He was **a prince** of the tribe of Simeon and she was a princess of Midian (14-15).

3. *Phinehas Is Rewarded* (25:10-13)

Because of his alertness, zeal, spiritual insight, and quick intervention on behalf of Israel, God rewarded **Phinehas** with the **covenant of an everlasting priesthood** (13).

4. *War Against Midian Authorized* (25:16-18)

Because of this seduction of the men of Israel by the women of Midian, God authorized war against the nation. **Vex . . . and smite them** (17), He ordered. This command was carried out and recorded in c. 31. A punishment this severe while Moab was not so punished may be explained by the fact that Midian purposely attempted to destroy Israel morally after they had failed to destroy her through oracles. Balaam seems to have sponsored this seduction (31:16).

B. Another Census, 26:1-65

1. *The Census Ordered* (26:1-4)

After the plague (1), God ordered another numbering of the **children of Israel** (2). This was the third census on record up to this point in the history. The first (Exod. 30:12) was basically for the purpose of organizing the *religious* life of the people. The second (cc. 1—2) was principally a *military* census, to find the number who were "able to go forth to war" (1:28). This third census, while in a measure military, was also *political.* Its purpose was to prepare the tribes for occupation of their respective inheritances in Canaan.

2. *The Census Proper* (26:5-51)

These verses tell in detail of this census and list, tribe by tribe, the numbers which each contained "from twenty years old and upward" (4). The enumeration began with the tribe of **Reuben** (5) and closed with the tribe of **Naphtali** (48). The results totaled 601,730, slightly less than were obtained in the first census.[5] While there were minor internal differences,

[5]See the discussion and tabulation, cc. 1—2.

the total of the new generation was not measurably different from the earlier one.

3. *Plans for Land Division* (26:52-56)

Following the census (and revealing part of the reason for having it) the Lord gave Moses plans for the allotment of the land into which they would soon be entering. Two principles are given: First, the land would be allotted **according to the number of names** (53), i.e., by the sizes of the tribes (54). Second, the land was to **be divided by lot** (55). It would seem best to assume, in the absence of a specific explanation of the relationship of the two, that the Israelites received their locations "by lot." On the other hand, the amount of territory that each tribe received was determined by the needs of that particular tribe[6] (cf. 33:54). From the Hebrew viewpoint, drawing lots was not mere chance, since God "assigned" the locations.

4. *The Levitical Census* (26:57-62)

As was the case with the earlier census, the families of the tribe of Levi were numbered separately, since **there was no inheritance given them among the children of Israel** (62). The principal **families** are listed (57) as they were given in the first census and under which the Levitical duties were assigned (cc. 3—4). The listing here is by **families** (58)[7] one generation removed, probably so given either because of their prominence or because the others, at this point, had died out. Then follows (59-61) a brief genealogy of Moses and Aaron. The total of the Levites enumerated, of **all males from a month old and upward** (62), was 23,000, a gain of roughly 1,000 over the census at Sinai.

5. *A New Nation* (26:63-65)

The closing comments of the chapter turn again to the fact that this was, indeed, a new nation. **There was not a man of them** (64) who was numbered in the Sinai census, **save Caleb** . . . and **Joshua** (65). "The old Israel must be remade before she can enter the Land of Promise, a truth that attains new depth

[6]In at least two cases, that of the two and a half tribes (c. 32) and that of Caleb (Josh. 15:13-19), some consideration was given to personal preferences and tribal needs.

[7]The **Libnites** (58) were from the clan of Gershon (3:21); the **Hebronites** were from the clan of Kohath (3:19, 27); and the **Mahlites** and the **Mushites** were from the clan of Merari (3:20, 33). Cf. Exod. 6:16-25.

when Jesus himself sets up the Israel of God through his own life and death and resurrection."[8]

C. The Law of Universal Inheritance, 27:1-11

1. *The Appeal* (27:1-4)

As a part of the account of the census and the plans for land allotment, and yet reaching far beyond the immediate setting in implication, is the appeal of the **daughters of Zelophehad** (1). **They stood before Moses . . . the priest . . . and . . . the princes** (2) with the request. Since their **father** had **died in the wilderness** of natural causes and since he **had no sons** (3), they should be given his inheritance. **Died in his own sin** means that he was "included in the general punishment prescribed at Kadesh, but not in any rebellious group" (Berk., fn.). It was a request outside of the existing traditions (cf. Deut. 25:5-10), which authorized an inheritance to sons only.

2. *The Answer* (27:5-11)

And the Lord spake unto Moses, saying (6), They **speak right;** "you shall give them possession of an inheritance among their father's brethren" (7, RSV). Here, then, was established the law of inheritance; a man's inheritance might go to his **daughter,** his brothers, his uncles, or **his kinsman** (8-10).

3. *Some Intimations*

This law has more to it than meets the eye. It is, indeed, the forerunner to other great laws and traditions. Certainly the idea that women should have an equal place with men in society, a concept so prominent in the Judeo-Christian tradition, found impetus from such early laws as this. Related to this concept are the emancipation of womanhood and woman suffrage. Beyond the social concepts are those which are more nearly religious—e.g., the universality of the gospel. Such NT truths as Gal. 3:26-29 were certainly in embryo in these early laws: "For ye are all the children of God by faith in Christ Jesus. For as many of you as have been baptized into Christ have put on Christ. There is neither Jew nor Greek, there is neither bond nor free, there is neither male nor female: for ye are all one in Christ Jesus. And if ye be Christ's, then are ye Abraham's seed, and heirs according to the promise."

[8]IB, II, 270-71.

D. Joshua Is Selected, 27:12-23

1. *The Call for a Change* (27:12-14)

The time had come for Moses to step aside as the leader of Israel. The Lord sent him to the **mount Abarim,** to **see the land which** God had **given unto the children of Israel** (12). This was somewhat of a ceremony, wherein God let Moses look at the land but therewith told him he would be **gathered unto** his **people, as Aaron**[9] was (13). This was because Moses had **rebelled against** God's **commandment** at **the water of Meribah** (14; 20:1-13).

2. *The Selection of Joshua* (27:15-23)

Moses spoke to **the God of the spirits of all flesh** (16) regarding the need for a new leader. He insisted that the **congregation** must not be **as sheep which have no shepherd** (17). The new leader must be one who could carry on as Moses had—be the general of their military affairs and able to carry to a completion every activity.

God said that **Joshua** (18) was such a man. Moses was given instructions **to set him before . . . the priest, and before all the congregation; and give him a charge in their sight** (19). During this ordination ceremony **some of the honour** and "spirit of wisdom" (11:25; Deut. 34:9) which had been upon Moses fell upon Joshua (20). The new leader would not have the same authority as had Moses, for with Moses God spoke "face to face." Joshua, on the other hand, needed to go before the priest, who would **ask counsel for him after the judgment of Urim.**[10] But even with this limited access to a knowledge of God's will, Joshua's word would be strong and influential with **the congregation.** At his **word** they would **go out** and **come in** (21).

E. The Seasons of Worship, 28:1—29:40

1. *The Primacy of Worship* (28:1-2)

Worship is an essential part of man's relationship to God. This had been pointed up earlier, but there had been a lapse

[9]"The Rabbis explain this to mean that like Aaron he was to die 'by the mouth of the Lord,' i.e. his also would be 'death by a Divine kiss'" (Hertz, ed., *op. cit.*, p. 692).

[10]**Urim** and Thummim were small objects worn on the priest's garments which were used as sacred lots. They were consulted when the priest wished an oracle from God (Exod. 28:30).

in the pattern of worship in the wilderness. Now there was a need to remind the people of what was expected of them. So **the Lord spake unto Moses** (1) to command Israel to be faithful **to observe to offer** worship to God in **due season** (2). This would be in harmony with the schedule of offerings (Leviticus 23) which covered daily, weekly, monthly, and yearly observances.

These laws may seem to us to be so elaborate and complicated as to be utterly confusing. However, one lesson should stand out—there is an offering to God appropriate in every time and every place. The truth is universal, God's people must be diligent in worshipping Him in every season. To the NT Christian this is the offering of a consecrated life lived every day, every week, every month, throughout all of our years.

2. *The Daily and Sabbath Offerings* (28:3-10)

The daily offerings were the most important in the OT plan. Certainly they underline the necessity for day-by-day faithfulness to God and the need for regular worship. This offering included **two** yearling **lambs** (3) offered, **one . . . in the morning, and the other . . . at even** (4). With these there was to be a "cereal offering" (RSV) composed of **flour** mixed with **beaten oil** (5).[11] There was also a **drink offering** of **wine** poured out **in the holy place** at the base of the altar (or over the altar) **unto the Lord** (7). Both the morning and evening offerings became a **sweet savour** (acceptable) **unto the Lord** (8).

On the sabbath (9) these daily offerings were to be doubled, expressive of the need for additional worship on God's holy day.

3. *The Monthly Offerings* (28:11-15)

On the first of each month **a** large **burnt offering** was required: **two** bulls, **one ram,** and **seven lambs,** all yearlings and **without spot** (11). The cereal offerings and drink offerings were proportionately large (12-14). In addition, there was to be "one male goat" (RSV) **for a sin offering** (15).[12] These monthly offerings were valuable in relating the worship pattern of the

[11]The **ephah** (dry measure) was about 70 pints. The **hin** (liquid measure) was nearly 12 pints.

[12]"Offered on all the Feasts (except the Sabbath) as an expiatory sacrifice to atone for any sin of levitical uncleanness committed unwittingly in connection with the Sanctuary or its sacred vessels" (Hertz, ed., *op. cit.*, p. 695).

Israelites to the passing of time, identified by so many people with the changing of the moon. **A several tenth deal** (13, 21, 29) means simply one-tenth of an ephah, a little over three quarts.

4. *Observances for the Passover Season* (28:16-25)

The passover of the Lord (16) had not been held for the duration of the wilderness wanderings, but the time was near when it would be observed once again. Hence God reminded them of the time on the year's calendar of worship—**the fourteenth day of the first month** (16; Exod. 12:16; Lev. 23:7-8).

Immediately following the Passover, i.e., on **the fifteenth day, the feast** of **unleavened bread** (17; Lev. 23:6-8) was to begin. It was to last **seven days.** This was the offering of the firstfruits of the harvest, the wheat of Pentecost (Exod. 34:22). On the first day there was to be a **convocation** and no **servile work** was to be done (18, 25). On the other days sacrifices were to be offered (19-24).

5. *The Feast of Weeks* (28:26-31)

In this connection, provisions were also made for the Feast of Weeks. The requirements were the same as for the monthly sacrifices and for the Feast of Unleavened Bread.

6. *The Midyear Offerings* (29:1-38)

a. Midway through the year, **on the first day** of the **seventh month** was to be the Feast of Trumpets, so named because it was **a day of blowing the trumpets** (1). The offerings were similar to, but nearly double, those of the other monthly offerings. In one sense this feast was related to the other "new moon" offerings in a similar fashion to which the Sabbath offerings were related to the daily sacrifices. **Servile work** would be "strenuous labor" (Berk.).

b. **The tenth day** (7) was a "day of atonement," so named because at this time the offering was made for the **atonement** for their sins (11; cf. Heb. 9:24-25). The balance of the offering was similar to that which was offered on the first day.

c. On the **fifteenth day of the seventh month** there was to be a feast which was to last for **seven days** (12). The appropriate offerings for each day are listed in 13-38. This time was known as the Feast of Booths and the "offerings were the heaviest of the whole year."[13] This was true probably because at this

[13]IB, II, 278.

time the people not only expressed their gratitude to God for His presence but also thanked Him for the harvests which they had recently gathered.

7. *Formal and Informal Worship* (29:39-40)

The outline of the regulations for worship closes with the admonition that the people should be faithful in their **set feasts** (39) in addition to their individual **vows** and **offerings.** True worship in the formal setting, while rising out of the strength of personal worship, must not be a substitute for it. Both are valid and necessary parts of one's worship of God.

F. The Vows of Women, 30:1-16

1. *The Male Oath* (30:1-2)

Old Testament ethics firmly underlines the fact that a man is unconditionally bound by a verbal vow. This starts with the vows he makes to God but extends to those made to other men. In a day when modern business implements such as notaries, contracts, recorded deeds, and notes were not available, a "man's word must be as good as his bond." Certainly this was true with regard to the vows made to God; **he shall not break his word** but **do according to all that proceedeth out of his mouth** (2).

Such was not the case, however, with certain women, for at this stage of Israel's development the woman's vow was subject to ratification by the man to whom she was responsible.

2. *Two Kinds of Vows* (30:2)

In this verse and throughout the balance of the passage, two kinds of vows are involved, suggested by the terms which are used. The first is the **vow** (*neder*), which is a broad term covering positive vows of every kind. The second is the **bond** (*issar*), which speaks specifically of a negative vow, or one of abstinence, such as that taken by the Nazarites (cf. c. 6). There are also degrees of vows intimated. The one is that **wherewith they have bound their souls** (9), i.e., one which is made seriously and with forethought. The other is that which arises as the "thoughtless utterance of her lips" (8, RSV), spoken quickly and without forethought.

3. *The Vow of the Young Woman* (30:3-5)

The vow of the young woman who was still living **in her father's house** (3) was subject to his approval. If he **shall hold**

his peace . . . her vows shall stand (4). However, if he **disallow her,** then none **of her vows, or other bonds . . . shall stand** (5).

4. *The Married Woman* (30:6-8, 10-16)

The same pattern followed for the woman who was under a vow at the time of her marriage. **Her husband** must take the responsibility of either ratifying or annulling her vow. If the husband knew of the vow and **held his peace . . . then her vows shall stand** (7). But if the **husband disallowed her . . . then he shall make her vow . . . of none effect** (8).

This same rule applied to the woman who took a vow after she was **in her husband's house** (10), i.e., after she was married. The husband was responsible to approve (11) or disapprove (12). In the latter instance the wife was not held to her vow and the **Lord shall forgive her** (12).

5. *The Widow or Divorcée* (30:9)

The exception to the laws of vows regulating women is cited in 9. It speaks to the case of the **widow** and the divorcée, who do not have men to whom they are responsible. These women come under the same rule as do the men. **Every vow . . . shall stand against her.**

G. War Against the Midianites, 31:1-54

1. *The Expedition Called* (31:1-2)

God had instructed Moses previously to "vex the Midianites and smite them: for they vex you with their wiles" and have "beguiled you" (25:17-18). It is apparent that Moses had delayed carrying out that initial command, perhaps so that the attack could catch the Midianites off guard and unprepared, as it did. The Lord's command was given in order to **avenge** (2) what had been a gross evil against Israel by the seducing Midianite women. The righting of this wrong was to be the final act of Moses as leader in Israel. When this was accomplished, he would **be gathered unto** his **people.**

This account of a war of vengeance ordered by a God who is elsewhere in the Scripture pictured as a God of love poses its problems. Some have made these problems unsurmountable and have discounted the record accordingly. Several things must be kept in mind if this account is to be meaningful.

a. Since God commanded the expedition, there must have been moral purpose in it, some of which is not evident to the casual reader.

b. This was a war of judgment upon the Midianites. It was comparable in purpose to the unidentified plague in which 24,000 perished which came upon Israel for their part in the sin (25:9).

c. New Testament standards of morals must not be used as the measuring stick for these OT situations. There are many evidences that God allowed and commanded certain modes of conduct that were compatible with the accepted morality of that day. The highest level of morality was not possible until Christ came.

d. The account is best interpreted for the modern day as it is spiritualized. Certainly all enemies of God and all forces that would corrupt God's people should be dealt with severely. Jesus said, "If thine eye offend thee, pluck it out" (Matt. 18:9).

2. *Preparations* (31:3-6)

Moses directed the people, "Arm men from among you for the war" (3, RSV). **Of every tribe a thousand . . . shall ye send to the war** (4), making an army of 12,000 men. With the army Moses sent **Phinehas**[14] **the son of Eleazar the priest** (6). He also sent along certain unnamed **holy instruments** from the Tent of Meeting [15] and **the trumpets** which were used in sounding the military calls (10:9).

3. *The Results of Battle* (31:7-12)

The results of the battles were swift and sure. The army of Israel no doubt caught **the Midianites** (7) completely by surprise and unprepared. The Midianite **males**[16] who came out to fight were slain, as were five of their **kings** (elders, 22:4; or

[14]Probably as a symbol of God's presence and to give spiritual support rather than as an active leader.

[15]There is some evidence that these might have included the ark of the covenant, as it was later used for just such a purpose (Josh. 6:4).

[16]Probably only certain encampments or crudely built cities were attacked. Since Midian is listed as a strong nation two centuries later (Judges 6), the destruction of **all the males** probably included only those who were encountered.

princes, Josh. 13:21).[17] Along with these **kings** the prophet Balaam was also slain **with the sword** (8) as punishment for his part in counselling the women of Midian to seduce the men of Israel **in the matter of Peor** (16).[18] The Israelites **burnt all their cities** "and all their encampments" (10, RSV). They took their **women** and children as **captives** and **their cattle** and **goods** (9) as spoils of war (11). These they brought **unto Moses, and Eleazar the priest, and unto the congregation . . . unto the camp at the plains of Moab** (12).

4. *Judgment Extended* (31:13-18)

But when the situation was assessed by the leaders (13), **Moses was wroth with the officers** (14) in charge of the expedition because they had saved **the women** and children (15). The command to **kill every male** child and all adult women (17) seems severe in the light of modern Christian morality, yet Moses pointed up the dangers of letting them live. It was the women of Midian who had **caused the children of Israel . . . to commit trespass against the Lord** (16). They could not be allowed to be loose and to victimize the camp a second time. Furthermore, to allow a generation of Midianite male children to grow up under the roofs of Israel would have been to invite national disaster. Only the young girls were kept alive as servants in the households of the Israelite families (18).

5. *Purification of the Men of War* (31:19-24)

In harmony with the laws governing ceremonial impurity through contact with the dead (c. 19), the men of war were commanded to **abide without the camp seven days** (19). They were to **purify** their **raiment,** and all of the possessions they had with them which were **made of skins** and **goats' hair** or **wood** (20). **Eleazar the priest** (21) instructed them that "everything that can stand the fire . . . shall pass through the fire, and it shall be clean" (23, RSV). In addition, it should **be purified with the water of separation** (19:1-10), as would those articles

[17]It would appear, since these kings are listed as "dukes of Sihon" (Josh. 13:21), that they were occupying the upper eastern Jordan country and were also within the scope of God's command to drive out the Canaanites and possess their land. It was this territory which was soon to be given to the two and one-half tribes (c. 32).

[18]Cf. the discussion of the complex problems relating to the character of Balaam in cc. 22—24.

which could not stand **the fire.** Here again we see the underlying relationship between ceremonial uncleanness and spiritual impurity. The cure for both is water (Titus 3:5) and fire (Matt. 3:10-12).

6. *The War Booty Is Divided* (31:25-54)

Moses was then commanded of the Lord to "take a count" (26, Amp. OT) of what had been captured. He was assisted by **Eleazar the priest** and the "heads of the fathers' houses" (RSV). Several general principles were used in dividing the spoil.

a. The first step was to "divide the booty into two (equal) parts" (27, Amp. OT). One part was to be given to the "warriors" (RSV) who actually engaged in the fighting, while the other half was distributed among those who remained "by the stuff" (I Sam. 30:24-25). This principle is not established here as a rule, but no doubt became a recognized practice through the generations. It reveals that, in God's plan, there is an equal responsibility upon those who are "at the front" of His cause and those who remain behind on the "home front" to pray, to give, and to encourage.

b. The second principle related to an **offering of the Lord** (29). It was to be **one soul of five hundred** (28), i.e., 1/5 of 1 percent, of the portion which had gone to **the men of war.** This was given to **Eleazar the priest** (29).

c. The third principle related to an offering for the Levites. This was taken from the portion that belonged to the congregation. It was to be 2 percent—**one portion of fifty** (30). This portion was larger because there were more Levites than priests.

d. The fourth principle involved a special thank offering from the warriors (48-54). The officers said, "There is not a man missing from us" (49, RSV). **We have therefore brought an oblation for the Lord** (50). This offering included all of the **jewels of gold**[19] that the men had taken. These were given to God **to make an atonement for our souls.** The total came to 16,750 shekels (52).[20] The offering was taken by Moses and Eleazar and placed in the Tent of Meeting **as a memorial for the children of Israel before the Lord** (54). It would continue to remind them of the sizable victory that God had given them.

[19]The Midianites were noted for their possession of valuables of this sort (cf. Judg. 8:26).

[20]"About $305,000" (Berk.).

H. Settling Outside Canaan, 32:1-42

1. *The Request of Two Tribes* (32:1-15)

The time was nearing when the Israelites would cross Jordan and enter Canaan. But two of the tribes, **Reuben** and **Gad,** later to be joined by one-half of the tribe of Manasseh (39), had different plans for themselves. It was a simple matter of economics. They **had a very great multitude of cattle: and . . . they saw** that **the land of Jazer, and . . . Gilead . . . was a place for cattle** (1). Basically this was the area in **which the Lord smote** (4) the Amorites and Og. The two tribes requested Moses to let them remain here and to **bring us not over Jordan** (5).

On the surface this appeared to be a logical and innocent request. However, it had several flaws:

a. It was a request based wholly on material factors. The land they sought had rich pastoral potential and these tribes wanted it in order that they might better feed their own cattle and hence build a wealth and security for their future. All of this was without any respect to the will of God, His promises for them in Canaan, or His spiritual purposes for them. Too many, even in the modern day, settle just outside Canaan because they lose sight of God's first requirement to "possess the land."

b. This was a request, also, which apparently disregarded the responsibilities of these tribes to assist in the conquest of Canaan. When they requested, "Do not take us over Jordan" (Amp. OT), Moses interpreted it to mean that they wanted to be free from these military responsibilities. Hence his reply to them: **Shall your brethren go to war, and shall ye sit here?** (6) He felt that in taking such a position these tribes would **discourage** the others (7), even as the 10 spies discouraged the congregation when they returned to **Kadesh-barnea** from their scouting trip into Canaan (8-13). Moses said, **Behold, ye are risen up in your fathers' stead** (14), to bring a like judgment upon **Israel.** There are those in the modern day, also, who stay out of Canaan because of their reluctance to carry the responsibility of conquest. They are a discouragement to countless others, who follow their example.

c. The third flaw in the request related to God's spiritual purpose for all of the tribes of Israel. Canaan was to be their inheritance, and even though the peoples who had been displaced from the east-Jordan country were Canaanites (Amorites; cf. 21:21-35), this was not Canaan proper. These tribes were willing to live "just outside" Canaan. In their thinking it was "not out," but in God's thinking it was "not in." Certainly they represent many Christians who, for material benefit and self-interest, live "this side of Jordan." Because of this exposed position these two and a half tribes were the first to be taken captive by the king of Assyria (I Chron. 5:26).

2. *Their Promises* (32:16-19)

When confronted with Moses' fears, the tribes were quick with their promises that they would, indeed, **go ready armed before the children of Israel** (17). They would **not return unto** their **houses** until all the tribes had received their **inheritance** (18). First, however, they wanted to make provision for their **cattle** and sufficiently rebuild the **cities** that had been captured to give their **little ones** (16) protection and care.

3. *Moses Gives Permission* (32:20-38)

On the basis of these promises from Gad and Reuben, Moses assured them that they could have the land which they had requested. He called in **Eleazar** and **Joshua** (28) and confirmed before them what these tribes were to do. **The children of Gad and . . . Reuben answered, saying, As the Lord hath said unto thy servants, so will we do** (31). So they were given **the kingdom of Sihon . . . the kingdom of Og,** "the land and its cities with their territories" (33, RSV). On this basis these tribes **built** (34), or rebuilt, the **cities** within these boundaries (34-38).

4. *The Inclusion of Manasseh* (32:39-42)

There are problems related to this passage and some missing data as to the exact place that it fills in the total story. It is evident, however, that one-half of the tribe of Manasseh joined in this inheritance east of Jordan (cf. Deut. 3:12-17). They were represented by **the children of Machir the son of Manasseh; Jair,** the great-grandson of Manasseh, on his mother's side;[21] and **Nobah,** probably a subordinate chieftain. They were given this inheritance because of the particular part they had in conquering the land (39, 41-42).

[21]**Jair** was the son of Segub, the son of Hezron, who married the daughter of Machir, the son of Manasseh (I Chron. 2:21-22). Hence he was among those Israelites whom we reckon as belonging to their tribe (Ellicott, *op. cit.*, p. 202).

Section VII *Miscellaneous Data*

Numbers 33:1—36:13

A. Camps from Egypt to Canaan, 33:1-56

1. *Introduction* (33:1-4)

This chapter lists the "stages" (RSV) of the **journeys of the children of Israel** (1) from Egypt to the plains of Moab, from which they moved into Canaan under Joshua. Exclusive of the starting point and the encampment near the Jordan, there are 40 stopping places listed.

These were not names of existing cities or of conspicuous landmarks. They were rather, in many cases, names given to the spots at the time of the encampment with a purpose known only to the congregation itself.[1] Hence the identifications of the locations were in most cases erased soon after the camp moved on. It is not possible, therefore, from the data given here to reconstruct a reliable or detailed itinerary of these journeys. This is distressing to the modern historian who seeks to pinpoint every place and every event. However, the account of Israel's trek from Egypt to Canaan is reliable and the route can be traced sufficiently to give the general directions.

Jewish tradition gives considerable help regarding the purpose of this record of the "stages" of the journey.[2] It was written

> to serve as a memorial not only of historical interest but of deep religious significance. Every journey and every halting place had its suggestions for the instruction, admonition, or encouragement of Israel. The Midrash says, "It may be likened unto a king who had taken his ailing son to a distant place to be cured. On the return journey, the king would lovingly recount to the lad all of the experiences they went through at each of their halting-places. 'At this spot we slept; at that, we had a cool resting-place from the heat; at the other, you were overcome with pains in the head!' Israel is God's child, upon whom He bestows compassion, even as a father bestows compassion on his son."

[1]The naming of Kibrothhattaavah ("the graves of the greedy") (11: 31-35; 33:17) is one of the most dramatic.

[2]Hertz, ed., *op. cit.,* p. 714.

Credit for the record is given to **Moses,** but **the Lord** (2) was the Commander of the journey itself. The starting point was **Rameses** (3; see map 3). The date was the **fifteenth day of the first month,** on the day **after the passover.** Israel's departure was public, made **with an high hand**[3] (cf. Exod. 14:8), while **the Egyptians** were busy burying **all their firstborn** (4). In addition to the blow dealt to the Egyptians, **their gods** were also brought to shame (4).[4]

Their armies (1) is more accurately "their hosts" (RSV).

2. *En Route to Sinai* (33:5-15)

There were 11 encampments on this leg of the trip. This is related in its historical setting to Exod. 12:37—19:2. Two camps listed here, **Dophkah** and **Alush** (13), are not mentioned in the Exodus account. See map 3 for probable locations of some of these sites.

3. *The Wilderness Trip* (33:16-36)

There were 21 encampments during the trip from Sinai to the final appearance at **Kadesh** (36). Many of these names, even more than those on the other two sections of the journey, are not identifiable in terms of modern geography. Thirteen of the places are not mentioned elsewhere in Scripture. This period covers the initial journey from **Sinai** (16) to Kadesh (probably the same as **Rithmah,** 18; cf. 12:16; Deut. 1:19). It also includes the 38 years of wandering until they finally gather in **Kadesh** (36; cf. 20:1). The log of the wilderness wanderings compounds the problem of accurately charting the journey and of relating it to other records (cf. Deut. 10:6-7). See "The Years of Obscurity" introducing the comments on 15:1—18:22.

4. *The Trip to Moab* (33:37-49)

This section begins with a repetition of 20:22-29. It gives the added fact of the age of **Aaron** at his death (39). There are differences between this passage and the record of 21:4-20 which cannot be fully explained. Probably neither was intended to be a complete record. Each was prepared in a particular frame of reference, and both are required to give the full picture.

[3]Confidently and fearlessly, not under cover.

[4]"In smiting the first born of all living things, man and beast, God smote objects of Egyptian worship. Not a single deity of Egypt was unrepresented by some beast" (Exod. 12:12) (*ibid.*, p. 255).

5. *Serious Commands* (33:50-56)

Inserted here, on the eve of Israel's entry into Canaan, is the command to **dispossess the inhabitants of the land, and dwell therein: for I have given you the land** (53)—and the penalty for not doing so was serious. **If ye will not drive** them **out,** then they **shall be pricks in your eyes, and thorns in your sides, and shall vex you** (55). History tells us that the ideal was not reached and this prophecy came true. God did, indeed, **do unto** Israel **as** He **thought to do unto** Canaan (56). This is probably a reference to the captivity in Babylon.

A vital part of this command related to the total destruction of the Canaanite implements of worship: their "figured stones" (RSV), **their molten images** (supposedly made in the likeness of their gods), and **their high places** of worship (52). Success in holding the land and fulfilling God's purpose for them depended on Israel keeping free from the idolatrous worship of the peoples whom they conquered. History again tells us that in many cases Israel failed at this point also.

The basis of these commands was that God had **given** them **the land . . . to possess it** (53). They were reminded at this point that the **families** (tribes, RSV) would be placed in areas of Canaan according to their size and according to lot (cf. 26:52-56). This is repeated here, no doubt, to remind Israel of the individual and tribal responsibilities which lay before them.

B. The Boundaries Outlined, 34:1-29

1. *The Lines Drawn* (34:1-15)

God commanded Moses to draw the lines for the borders of **the land of Canaan** (2). These are given as follows (cf. Gen. 10:19):

a. The line marking the "south side" (3; RSV) began at the south end of the Dead Sea, moving with the western border of **Edom** as far as **Kadesh-barnea** (4). There it turned northwest,[5] following the **river of Egypt** (5, *Wadi el-Arish*), more of a dry wash than a river, which enters the Mediterranean Sea some 45 miles southwest of Gaza.

b. The **western border** is **the great sea** (6) "and its coast" (RSV). Scholars do not agree as to how much of this coast is in-

[5]The locations of the other places mentioned are unknown.

tended. Since the point of departure of the north boundary is not clear, several have been suggested. The one most commonly used puts the northernmost reaches of the western border slightly above the point where the Leontes River enters the Mediterranean Sea, short of the Lebanon Mountains. Jewish authorities, however, insist that the reading here means the *entire* coast, or the *whole* eastern flank of the Great Sea, from its southeastern to its northeastern corners. "If any point on the coast, between these two corners were meant, the text would surely have designated that point."[6] This would take the western boundary to the northeastern border of the Bay of Alexandretta.

c. The **north border** reached on a line from the Mediterranean Sea to **mount Hor** (7).[7] It then reached to **Hamath, Zedad,** and **Hazar-enan** (8-9). While these places cannot be located with certainty, the maps of a later period show a **Hamath** some 100 miles north of Damascus and a **Zedad** halfway between.[8] The location of **Hazar-enan** is also uncertain, but may be the headwaters of the Jordan River, for the name means "enclosure of the spring."[9] This line would be, actually, a northeastern border. If these locations are correct, credence is given to the tradition of the Jews giving the nine and a half tribes a strip the entire length of the eastern coast of the Mediterranean and with widths varying from 30 to 75 miles.

d. **The east border** (10) moves from **Hazar-enan** southward to **the sea of Chinnereth** (11; Galilee or Gennesaret). The intermediate points listed are not identifiable. From **Chinnereth** the border follows the **Jordan** to **the salt sea** (12, Dead Sea).

Verses 13-15 take note of the division of the territories to nine and one-half tribes west of Jordan and to two and one-half tribes east of Jordan.

These boundaries were only ideal, for Israel never fully occupied this territory. They are mentioned in Joshua 15—19 and Ezek. 47:13-20; 48:28. Ezekiel, the prophet, in his day, was

[6]Hertz, ed., *op. cit.*, p. 717.

[7]A satisfactory identification for this northern **mount Hor** has not been made. It was not the Mount Hor of 20:22, where Aaron died.

[8]*Harper's Bible Dictionary*, Maps, edited by G. Ernest Wright and Floyd V. Filson, Plate VI, "The Kingdoms of Israel and Judah in Elijah's Time" (New York: Harper and Brothers, 1954).

[9]IB, II, 300.

still looking forward to the real occupation of all of the territory that God had promised Israel.

2. *Official Assistants* (34:16-29)

God ordered an official committee for the task of dividing the land among the tribes. **Eleazar** and **Joshua** (17) were in charge. **Caleb** (19) represented **the tribe of Judah** for his faithfulness at Kadesh-barnea. The others, **one prince of every tribe** (18), were those whose names indicated that God was with Israel. Thus **Shemuel** (20) means "name of God"; **Elidad** (21) means "God has loved"; **Bukki** (22) means "proved" (of God); **Hanniel** (23), "favor of God"; **Kemuel** (24), "raised by God"; **Elizaphan** (25), "my God protects"; **Paltiel** (26), "God is my deliverance"; **Ahihud** (27), "brother of majesty"; **Pedahel** (28), "God hath delivered."[10] A similar group was chosen to direct the earlier census (1:4-16).

C. Cities of Refuge, 35:1-34

1. *Cities for the Levites* (35:1-5, 7-8)

The Levites did not share in the allotment of the land. God therefore provided that the tribes that received an inheritance should give the Levites **cities to dwell in** (2) and **suburbs** ("pasture lands," RSV) for their **cattle, goods,** and **beasts** (3). There were **forty and eight** (7) of these **cities.** They were to continue as **the possession of the children of Israel** but were to be made available to the Levites as dwelling places and were to be given on the basis of the amount of the tribal inheritances (8).

This law was partially implemented as recorded in Joshua 21. However, it was never fully completed. The general concept, though, was basic throughout Israel's history.

2. *Special Cities* (35:6, 9-15)

Among the cities given to **the Levites,** six were to be set aside as "cities of refuge" (6, RSV).[11] Three were east of Jordan and three in Canaan proper.[12] These were for the protection of **the manslayer,** the one "who kills any person without intent" (11, RSV—i.e., "manslaughter" in modern terminology).

[10] *Ibid.*, p. 302.

[11] Cf. Deut. 19:1-10.

[12] Those established were: Bezer, Ramoth-gilead, and Golan east of the river; Hebron, Shechem, and Kadesh on the west.

The need for such a plan of refuge arose out of practices related to **the avenger** (12). This custom was recognized as a principle of law enforcement in the early stage of Israel's history (Gen. 9:5).[13] This principle allowed the nearest kinsmen of the one who had been wronged to wreak punishment on the person who had been responsible. Hence protection was provided for the one who inadvertently took the life of another, but it applied only until such time as he could be brought **before the congregation** for trial and **judgment.** This refuge was available for all who were included in Israel's society, for the "people of Israel" (RSV), **for the stranger, and for the sojourner** (15).

This principle is basic in the broader idea of "sanctuary," a concept in evidence in many of the laws and regulations by which societies have governed themselves. The idea of the "cities of refuge" also serves as a strong illustration of the "refuge," through divine grace, which exists in the kingdom of God.[14]

3. *Manslaughter and Murder* (35:16-25)

As guidance for all, illustrations are laid down here to show the difference between manslaughter and premeditated murder. Manslaughter came under the provisions for the cities of refuge while murder came under other laws and was punishable by death.

Death caused by specified instruments was *prima facie* evidence that murder was intended. They were **an instrument of iron** (16), **a stone** in the hand (17), or a **weapon of wood** in the hand (18). When murder was evident, the **revenger** could slay the **murderer** at once (19). The same rule applied if the victim was struck **in enmity** (21), i.e., by any instrument used in malice and with purpose to kill.

But it was recognized, even in that day, that there can be an unintentional homicide. **If he thrust** (stabbed) . . . **or cast upon him** (22) . . . **or with any stone . . . seeing him not . . .**

[13]Toned down, however, as Israel increasingly grasped the higher ethical concepts which God was constantly seeking to get through to them and as the principles and laws of procedures governing manslaughter and unintentional homicide were strengthened.

[14]Specifically, in distinguishing the inadvertent crime from that which is intentional. It points up the distinction between these types of sin and the recognition by God that the unintentional act is not sin in the same sense as the other. The unintentional sin is covered by provisions of the atonement.

neither sought his harm (23), the slayer would come under the law of refuge. **The congregation shall judge** (24), and if he was innocent of premeditated murder, he shall be **rescued out of the hand of the revenger.** But he must be kept in **the city of his refuge** to which he had fled, until **the death of the high priest** (25).

Here is underlined the importance of *intent*[15] as the basic ingredient to determine the nature of a crime. This principle is recognized in most civilized countries as the important factor in determining the guilt or innocence of one suspected. It is also a major factor in the biblical concept of sin. It is "willful transgression," not the "inadvertent slip," which God judges as sin.

4. *Applications of the Regulation* (35:26-34)

If the slayer, even after the judgment was passed, came outside **the border of the city,** he could be slain by the avenger, without guilt on the avenger's part (26-27). The slayer, however, was safe if he remained within the city until after **the death of the high priest.** He could then return to his home, free from all penalty (28).

These laws were given as a "statute and ordinance" (29, RSV) for all **generations.** Murder was punishable by **death,** but more than **one witness** was needed to establish this guilt (30). No "ransom" (RSV) could be paid either for one who was a **murderer** (31) or for the one who wished to leave **the city of his refuge** (32) before the death of the high priest. The death penalty must be paid because death polluted the land **wherein** God dwelt (34). This pollution could be cleansed only **by the blood of him that shed it** (33).

D. Marriage and Inheritance, 36:1-13

1. *The Issue* (36:1-4)

This passage supplements 27:1-11, in which the daughters of Zelophehad presented their case for an inheritance in the absence of any brothers. **The chief of the fathers** (1) came to Moses and presented the problem: If their daughters **be married to any sons of the other tribes . . . then shall their inheritance be taken**

[15]The account in Deut. 19:1-10 gives even more emphasis to the intent than to the instrument.

from their tribe (3). Hence, even at the time of **jubile** (4), the inheritance would remain with the tribe of the husband.

2. *The Law Given* (36:5-9)

So Moses spoke **according to the word of the Lord,** saying, "The tribe of the sons of Joseph is right" (5, RSV). And then followed the command: **The daughters of Zelophehad** (6), as well as all other young ladies, were to marry within their father's tribe. This meant that **the inheritance** of a given tribe was not to **remove from tribe to tribe** (7). The provision was established so that **the children of Israel may enjoy every man the inheritance of his fathers** (8). To insure this, the inheritance of one tribe was not to **remove from one tribe to another** (9).

3. *The Law Obeyed* (36:10-13)

"The daughters of Zelophehad did as the Lord commanded Moses" (10, RSV), and they were married to sons of their father's brothers. Thus "their inheritance remained in the tribe of the family of their father" (10-12, RSV).

Bibliography

I. COMMENTARIES

CLARKE, ADAM. *The Holy Bible with a Commentary and Critical Notes,* Vol. I. New York: Abingdon Press, n.d.

CLARKE, W. K. LOWTHER. *Concise Bible Commentary.* New York: The Macmillan Co., 1953.

ELLICOTT, C. J. "Numbers." *Ellicott's Commentary on the Bible* (The Layman's Handy Commentary Series). Charles J. Ellicott, ed. Grand Rapids: Zondervan Publishing House, 1961.

ELLIOTT-BINNS, L. "The Book of Numbers" (Introduction). *Westminster Commentaries.* London: Methuen and Co., 1927.

GORE, CHARLES; GOUDGE, H. L.; GUILLAUME, ALFRED. *A New Commentary on the Holy Scriptures.* New York: The Macmillan Co., 1945.

GRAY, GEORGE BUCHANAN. *A Critical and Exegetical Commentary on the Book of Numbers.* "The International Critical Commentary." Edited by CHARLES A. BRIGGS, *et al.* New York: Charles Scribner's Sons, 1903.

GRAY, JAMES C.; ADAMS, GEORGE M. *The Bible Encyclopedia,* Vol. I. Cleveland: F. M. Barton, 1903.

HENRY, MATTHEW. *Commentary on the Whole Bible,* Vol. I. New York: Fleming H. Revell Co., n.d.

HERTZ, J. H., ed. *The Pentateuch and Haftorahs.* London: Soncino Press, 1952.

KEIL, C. F., and DELITZSCH, F. *Commentary on the Pentateuch,* Vol. III. Edinburgh: T. & T. Clark, n.d.

KERR, DAVID W. "Numbers." *The Bible Expositor.* Edited by CARL F. H. HENRY. Philadelphia: A. J. Holman Co., 1960.

MARSH, JOHN. "Numbers" (Introduction and Exegesis). *The Interpreter's Bible,* Vol. II. Edited by GEORGE A. BUTTRICK, *et al.* New York: Abingdon Press, 1953.

MAYS, JAMES L. "The Book of Leviticus, the Book of Numbers." The *Layman's Bible Commentary.* Edited by BALMER H. KELLY, *et al.,* Vol. IV. Richmond, Va.: John Knox Press, 1959.

MORGAN, G. CAMPBELL. *Exposition of the Whole Bible.* Westwood, N.J.: Fleming H. Revell Co., 1959.

NEIL, WILLIAM. *Harper's Bible Commentary.* New York: Harper and Row, 1962.

WADE, GEORGE W. "Numbers." *A Commentary on the Bible.* Edited by ARTHUR S. PEAKE. New York: Thomas Nelson and Sons, 1962.

WATSON, ROBERT A. "The Book of Numbers." *The Expositor's Bible.* New York: A. C. Armstrong and Son, 1903.

WESLEY, JOHN. *Explanatory Notes upon the Old Testament,* Vol. I. Bristol: Wm. Pine, n.d.

WHITELAW, THOMAS. "Introduction to Numbers." *Pulpit Commentary.* Edited by JOSEPH S. EXELL. New York: Funk and Wagnalls, n.d.

WINTERBOTHAM, R. "Numbers" (Exposition). *Pulpit Commentary.* New York: Funk and Wagnalls, n.d.

II. OTHER BOOKS

ALBRIGHT, WILLIAM F. *Archaeology of Palestine and the Bible.* Westwood, N.J.: Fleming H. Revell Co., 1935.

ARROIS, GEORGES A. "Weights and Measures, Hebrew." *Twentieth Century Encyclopedia of Religious Knowledge.* Grand Rapids: Baker Book House, 1955.

ELDER, JOHN. *Prophets, Idols and Diggers.* Indianapolis: Bobbs-Merrill, 1960.

GEIKIE, CUNNINGHAM. *Hours with the Bible,* Vol. II. New York: James Pott and Co., 1893.

HURLBUT, JESSE LYMAN. *A Bible Atlas.* New York: Rand McNally and Co., 1938.

KENYON, KATHLEEN M. *Archaeology in the Holy Land.* London: Ernest Benn, Ltd., 1960.

MILLER, MADELEINE; MILLER, J. LANE. *Harper's Bible Dictionary.* New York: Harper and Brothers, 1954.

OWEN, G. FREDERICK. *Archaeology and the Bible.* Westwood, N.J.: Fleming H. Revell Co., 1961.

PURKISER, W. T., *et al. Exploring the Old Testament.* Kansas City: Beacon Hill Press, 1955.

THOMPSON, J. A. *Archaeology and the Old Testament.* Grand Rapids: Wm. B. Eerdmans Publishing Co., 1959.

TURNER, GEORGE ALLEN. *The More Excellent Way.* Winona Lake, Ind.: Light and Life Press, 1952.

UNGER, MERRILL F. *Archaeology and the Old Testament.* Grand Rapids: Zondervan Publishing House, 1954.

WRIGHT, G. ERNEST. *Biblical Archaeology* (Abridged Edition). Philadelphia: The Westminster Press, 1960.

WRIGHT, G. ERNEST; FILSON, FLOYD V. "Plate VI, The Kingdoms of Israel and Judah in Elijah's Time." *Harper's Bible Dictionary.* New York: Harper and Brothers, 1954.

The Book of

DEUTERONOMY

Jack Ford

A. R. G. Deasley

Introduction

A. Author and Date

The Book of Deuteronomy is made up almost entirely of speeches attributed to Moses. Besides these there are short historical sections referring to Moses. It is part of the Pentateuch which is referred to frequently in the Old and New Testaments as the law of Moses. For these reasons and others, conservative scholars have attributed its authorship to the great lawgiver of Israel. This does not mean that there are not comments and items of historical information by other hands. But this view takes seriously the statements made in the book and the general testimony of the rest of the Bible regarding Mosaic authorship.

Scholars who adopt what may be called the Wellhausen view, with various modifications, hold that Deuteronomy is a composition, containing some ancient material, part of which may be derived from Moses, but produced by a prophet or a school of prophets sometime before 621 B.C. In that year the book of the law was discovered by Hilkiah in the Temple and read before King Josiah. This initiated a series of reforms which scholars of this persuasion declare were based on Deuteronomy (II Kings 22:8—23:25 and II Chron. 34:14—35:19). Outstanding among these reforms was the removal not only of the idolatrous altars but also of altars erected to the Lord in the high places. The reformers also insisted that sacrifices should be offered only at the central sanctuary in Jerusalem.

The above scholars also claim that the outlook of Deuteronomy is similar to the Book of Jeremiah, the First and Second Books of Kings, and other prophetic literature of the late eighth and early seventh century B.C. They assert that the idea of an exclusive central sanctuary was unknown to such worthies as Samuel and Elijah. These are some of the main reasons put forward for attributing Deuteronomy to a prophetic writer or school about the beginning of the seventh century B.C.

The evidence for this view is not strong enough to bring about a complete consensus among scholars. E. Robertson attributes the editing of Deuteronomy to Samuel. Hölescher, on the other hand, assigns it to the postexilic period.

Moreover, if the book was written to correct the practice of worship in the high places, it is remarkable that such practices are not specifically mentioned. One would have thought that an author writing at the beginning of the seventh century would have been able to work in some allusion to Jerusalem being the central sanctuary, if one of the primary purposes of the author (s) was to centralize all sacrifice there. The similarity in outlook between this book and the prophetic literature could be explained by the influence of Deuteronomy on the prophetic writers.

The fact that the reading of Deuteronomy brought about certain reforms is no more an indication that it was written in the time of the abuses than that the Bible was written just before the Protestant Reformation.

A recent contribution to the subject is *Treaty of the Great King*.[1] Kline asserts that the structure and content of Deuteronomy conform to the pattern of treaties drawn up between a suzerain and his vassal. These began with a preamble identifying the suzerain (cf. 1:1-5), followed by a historical prologue (cf. 1:5—4:49). Then came the stipulations of the treaty (cf. cc. 5—26), followed by a recital of curses in the event of nonobservance and of blessings attendant upon faithful observance (cf. cc. 27—30). The treaty closed with the enlisting of witnesses (cf. 31:16-22; 31:28—32:45), direction for depositing it and its periodic re-proclamation (cf. 31:9-13), also provisions for dynastic succession (cf. cc. 31—34, *passim*). Kline also submits that the structure of Deuteronomy has the closest affinity with the treaties of the second millennium B.C. His whole thesis gives impetus to the view that Deuteronomy is a unity belonging to the Mosaic era.

The subject of authorship is a large and intricate one, and it is not the purpose of this commentary to discuss it in detail. The above brief statement is made to give an indication of some of the main issues and to explain the reason for treating Deuterononomy as substantially Mosaic.

B. Characteristics

It is probable that the title of this book, "Deuteronomy," is taken from *to deuteronomion touto*, the LXX translation of "a copy of this law" (17:18), lit., "this second law." Since most of the book consists of a restatement of the law by Moses on the eve of the crossing of the Jordan into Canaan, it has been accepted as an appropriate title.

[1]M. G. Kline, *Treaty of the Great King* (Grand Rapids: Wm. B. Eerdmans Publishing Co., 1963).

For the most part, Deuteronomy is a series of orations by Moses. They are in the language of the common people and are addressed to all Israel. Their purpose is to remind the old and inform the young concerning the covenant with the Lord and the laws which are a part of it.

Utter loyalty to the Lord is demanded, and also separation from all false gods and their worship (7:5). In this sense the Lord is a jealous God, tolerating no rival and repudiating a divided loyalty (5:7-10). Nothing that is likely to draw His people from Him or debase their character and conduct is to survive (7:5). The licentious Canaanites are to be destroyed, lest they should pollute His people with their evil practices (7:1-4; 20:16-18). The terrible edicts cause a shudder, but the debasing of the race chosen for the advent of Messiah would have had even more terrible effects.

But there are also kindly and generous strains in the book. Here more than in any other book in the Pentateuch, God declares His love for His people (7:13; 10:15; 23:5) and His desire for theirs (6:5; 30:6). God's people are taught to be merciful and generous to the fatherless, the widow, the poor, and the stranger (10:18; 15:7).

There is an uncompromising insistence on justice. Not only must justice be done indiscriminately to rich and poor, great and small (1:16-17), but it extends to correct weights and fair measures (25:13-16).

Deuteronomy is a "neighborly" book. The neighbor's ass must be prevented from escaping and if in difficulty must be given assistance (22:1-4).

Obedience to God is equated with life and blessing; disobedience, with death and cursing (11:26-28; 30:19). This has given rise to the expression the "Deuteronomic view of life": goodness brings prosperity, and wickedness brings adversity and grief. It is asserted that this interpretation of history runs through the historical books of the Bible. It is conceded by its critics that there is a real truth in it, but it has severe limitations. They declare that Isaiah shows greater insight by seeing vicarious suffering as far greater than prosperous righteousness. The Book of Job was probably written in direct contradiction of too wooden an application of the Deuteronomic view. But the value of the discipline of suffering is recognized in 8:2-3. Moses himself is an outstanding example of the righteous man who suffers voluntarily because of his identification with a rebellious people (3:26; 9:18-19).

C. Importance

There can be no question about the abiding value of Deuteronomy. Liberals and conservatives alike are swift to recognize the part it has played in the development of the religion of Israel. The history of Israel is written from its standpoint and her monarchs are weighed in its scales. It was probably read at the reading of the law in the reformation under Ezra and Nehemiah after the return from exile, and it probably figured prominently in the cultural festivals.

Our Lord evidently meditated deeply upon Deuteronomy and met the threefold attack of Satan with a threefold thrust from its armory (8:3; 6:13, 16). He quoted part of the Shema (6:4-5) when asked for the greatest commandment (Mark 12: 28-30). The Apostle Paul applied Moses' description of the law to the gospel when enlarging on its simplicity and accessibility (Rom. 10:6-8; cf. Deut. 30:11-14).

D. Deuteronomy and Holiness

What light does Deuteronomy shed on the doctrine of holiness? Expositors, influenced by Heb. 3-1-11 and other NT scriptures, have seen in the land of Canaan a type of the Spirit-filled, entirely sanctified experience (cf. Acts 26:18). Deuteronomy abounds with promises concerning the land and exhortations to possess the divinely provided inheritance (1:8; 7:1; 11:8-9; *et al.*).

Besides this typological significance, Deuteronomy reminds us that a genuine religious experience is validated by righteous conduct. Religious ecstasy is spurious if it does not find an outlet in fair and neighborly relationships, and in commercial and social justice.

Deuteronomy teaches us that loyalty to God is the essence of true piety. This allows no compromise with anything obnoxious to God and calls for separation from all illegitimate relationships and practices.

The essence of holiness is love. The *Shema* (6:4-9) sums up the supreme duty of man in such terms. God loves His people and seeks their love. He desires them to serve Him with joy. He will make possible this love by removing all that hinders it, so that we may love the Lord with all our hearts (30:6).

Outline

I. Introductory Address: Review, 1:1—4:43

- A. Time and Place, 1:1-5
- B. From Horeb to Kadesh-barnea, 1:6-46
- C. Dealings with Edom, Moab, and Ammon, 2:1-23
- D. Conquest of Sihon and Og, 2:24—3:29
- E. Closing Exhortation, 4:1-40
- F. Appointment of Cities of Refuge, 4:41-43

II. Main Address: The Law, 4:44—26:19

- A. Introduction, 4:44-49
- B. The Ten Commandments, 5:1—11:32
- C. Other Commandments, 12:1—26:19

III. Concluding Addresses: The Covenant, 27:1—30:20

- A. The Ratification Ceremony, 27:1-26
- B. The Covenant Sanctions, 28:1-68
- C. Taking the Covenant Oath, 29:1—30:20

IV. Perpetuation of the Covenant, 31:1—32:47

- A. Preparatory Safeguards, 31:1-30
- B. Impeachment Procedure: The Song of Witness, 32:1-47

V. The Death of Moses, 32:48—34:12

- A. The Blessing of Moses, 32:48—33:29
- B. Death of Moses and Succession of Joshua, 34:1-12

Section I *Introductory Address: Review*

Deuteronomy 1:1—4:43

A. Time and Place, 1:1-5

These be the words, or discourses, **which Moses spake unto all Israel** (1). Deuteronomy was essentially a book for the laity, as Leviticus was a manual for the priests and Levites. It is improbable that all the people would be able to hear Moses at one time, but representatives of the whole nation would be present.

On this side Jordan is literally *eber,* "the crossing," or "valley" of the Jordan. It is used of both the east side (4:41, 49) and the west side (3:20, 25; 11:30). If there is no qualifying expression to indicate which side is intended, surprisingly, it may be taken to refer to the *opposite side* from which the author wrote. If so, the language might indicate that the opening verses were written in the land of Canaan as an editorial explanation of the place where the addresses were given. Adam Clarke suggests that the words might have been added by Joshua or Ezra.[1] But some scholars regard *eber Yorden* as a technical description of the eastern side of the Jordan.

The Hebrew for **wilderness** means any uninhabited tract of land, not necessarily a desert. **The plain** is the Arabah (ERV), the deep valley running north and south of the Dead Sea. The identification of the other places, **Paran, and Tophel, and Laban, and Hazeroth, and Dizahab,** has long been a subject of discussion among scholars. Some take them to indicate the route **from Horeb** (2, another name for Sinai) to the border of the land of Canaan. If so, the reference to them is historical and dramatic as well as geographical. The depression of the Arabah in which the oration was given continued to the gulf of Aqaba (Red Sea; see map 3), and along its western side lay the route to Sinai, where the law was first proclaimed. Another view is that a place called Suph (1; cf. RSV) is intended, not the Red Sea (*yam*

[1]Adam Clarke, *Commentary on the Whole Bible* (London: Wm. Teff and Co., 1854), I, 749.

suph), and that the other names are of places which can no longer be identified in the valley of the Jordan opposite Beth-peor in the land of Moab (cf. 4:46).

The writer adds a pregnant comment: **There are eleven days' journey from Horeb by the way of mount Seir** (the eastern route skirting the borders of Edom) **to Kadesh-barnea** (2). Only **eleven days' journey** but it had taken them almost 40 years! How many condemn themselves for years to wandering in the wilderness of the second best when they could be enjoying the fullness of God's blessing of entire sanctification (cf. Heb. 4:1-11)!

Like Jacob (Genesis 49), Joshua (Joshua 24), Samuel (I Samuel 12), David (I Kings 2), and our Lord (John 14—16), Moses delivered a final exhortation at the close of his life. His leadership finished on a note of victory with the defeat of **Sihon** (4; cf. 2:24-37) and **Og** (cf. 3:1-22).

After the time and place have been carefully indicated, we are informed that **Moses spake . . . according unto all that the Lord had given him in commandment unto them** (3). The basis of his final address was the revelation already given to and through him by God, though some laws are mentioned for the first time and others already given are modified. This was essentially his final exposition of the law—for this is the meaning of **declare** (5).

The Hebrew for "law" is *torah.* "The word *torah* may refer to moral guidance, or to a single specific teaching, as in Prov. 1:8, 'forsake not the teaching (*torah*) of thy mother.' It is also applied to a body of religious precepts or teachings—such as form the central portion of the Book (Deut. xii-xxvi). Often it denotes the entire sum of Israel's religious doctrine and life —the *Torah* of Moses."[2] The law (*Torah*) came to be the Hebrew name for the Pentateuch (Ezra 7:6) and sometimes for the whole OT (Rom. 3:19).

B. From Horeb to Kadesh-barnea, 1:6-46

The first address is mainly a historical review of the Lord's dealings with Israel. Recent investigations have established that the structure of Deuteronomy corresponds closely to the treaties

[2]"Deuteronomy," *The Pentateuch and Haftorahs,* ed. J. H. Hertz (London: Soncino Press, 1938), p. 737.

drawn up by nations of those days between a suzerain and his vassal. These usually began with a historical recital, then a list of conditions setting out the terms of the covenant. They concluded with a pronouncement of blessing on the faithful observance of the conditions and of anathemas in the event of unfaithfulness (see Introduction: Authorship). The form, therefore, of Deuteronomy is a testimony to its unity and antiquity.

1. *Call to Possess the Land* (1:6-8)

Revelation calls for action. Israel was not to encamp indefinitely at Horeb. The Lord called the nation to possess the land of Canaan, of which a clear description is given (7). **The plain** is the northern part of the Arabah, the Jordan valley, ending in the Dead Sea. **The hills** are the central mountain range. **The vale** is the Shephelah, the foothills between the central mountain range and the maritime plain. **The sea side** is the plain extending inward from the coast of the Mediterranean a distance of from four to 15 miles. **The south** is the Negeb, the dry steppe district south of Judah. The mountain range of **Lebanon** in the north and the **Euphrates** in the east are ideal natural boundaries.

Two chief nations are identified with the land. **The Amorites,** or Amurru, were a powerful nation which entered Palestine from the north and settled in the hill country. **The Canaanites,** who occupied the plain, were probably of Phoenician stock.

Verse 8 introduces a theme which recurs throughout the book. **I have set the land before you: go in and possess the land which the Lord sware unto your fathers . . . to give unto them and to their seed.** The land is a divine gift to be possessed by faith in the divine promise which holds good for all generations of believers.

2. *The Appointment of Assistant Rulers* (1:9-18)

Increase has its problems. Would that all our problems were of this kind! God's promise to Abraham that He would make his seed as numerous **as the stars** (10) in the night sky is regarded as having been fulfilled (cf. Gen. 15:5). In v. 12, Moses refers to the difficulty of governing a vast number of people. **Cumbrance** and **burden** probably refer to the general responsibilities of leadership, and **strife** to disputes between groups and individuals. It was not long before Moses realized that he needed assistants. The suggestion came in the first place from Jethro, his father-in-law (cf. Exod. 18:13-27), but it is possible that some such solution had already been in his mind. He adopted it and laid it before the tribes. He first stipulated the qualifications for leadership—"wise, understanding, and experienced men" (13, RSV). Moses then gave the people an opportunity of putting forward candidates acceptable to them, and he appointed them to office. A similar arrangement in the NT is described in the choosing of the first deacons (Acts 6:1-6).

The men thus appointed are described as **heads** (15; *rashim*), **captains** (*sarim*), and **officers** (*shoterim*). The **officers** were either those enforcing the orders of a superior, or else recorders. The word **judges** (16) seems to refer to the **rulers** in their judicial capacity. The equity and compassion which are characteristic of Deuteronomy are shown in **judge righteously. Ye shall not respect persons in judgment**—there was to be impartial dealing for **small** and **great** (17), the **brother** Israelite and **the stranger** (16). The leaders were not to be afraid of men, for they are God's representatives (17). Moses gave general directions (18) and was the ultimate authority (17).

There is guidance here for "Church Leadership": (1) The responsibility of leadership, 12; (2) The sharing and qualification of leadership, 13, 15; (3) The execution of leadership, 16-17.

3. *Exploration of the Land* (1:19-25)

Poignant memories are summed up in v. 19. The modern conflict between Israel and the Arab nations has brought before the world the savage heat and desolation of **that great and terrible wilderness**—the Sinaitic peninsula. But in the days of which Moses speaks the nation was on the march to a land flowing with milk and honey. It is impossible to identify **Kadesh-barnea** with any certainty, but we know it was near the southern border of Canaan (see map 3).

Moses spoke with realism and faith—a good combination. He took account of **the mountain** and **the Amorites** (20), but he saw the land as a gift and a possession. He exhorted the Israelites: **Go up and possess it . . . fear not, neither be discouraged** (21). To **possess** (*yarash*) means "to enter into possession of a land or property by casting out or replacing its previous occupier, whether by conquest or by process of inheritance. It occurs no less than fifty-two times in Deuteronomy."[3]

In v. 22 a new insight is given into the exploration of the land by the spies. In Num. 13:1-2, God tells Moses to send men to spy out the land. The Jewish rabbis emphasize that the Hebrew term is *leka*, "Send for thyself," which they interpret as, "If thou wishest to send spies, do so." In other words, God permits without approving. This may be an indication that the initiative came from the people, as is expressly asserted here. Moses approved (23), confident that the land would bear inspection. Notice the care to see that each tribe was represented in the investigation (23). **The valley of Eshcol** ("cluster," 24) was so named by the spies. It was near Hebron (see map 3). The spies made an excellent beginning when they returned. They showed **the fruit of the land** and bore testimony to its goodness (25). But they failed dismally when they lapsed into the language of unbelief.

4. *The Refusal to Enter* (1:26-33)

The refusal of the people to possess the land is stated forcefully and condemned in the most emphatic terms. First, they **would not go up** (26). Secondly, **they murmured in** their **tents** (27). They stayed at home and refused to take part in the forward march. And, finally, they charged God with hatred. And it all happened because those bringing the report magnified the difficulties and ignored the possibilities (28). For comment on **the Anakims** (28), cf. 2:21. True, **the cities** were **great and walled,** but God could bring the walls down—as, indeed, He did later at Jericho (Josh. 6:20). The Canaanites were stronger and **greater** than Israel; but as Moses rightly reminded Israel, **the Lord** had already delivered them from the Egyptians, a far mightier nation than any in Canaan, and He was going **before** them to **fight for** them (30).

In reply to their absurd accusation that the Lord hated them, Moses speaks tenderly of the Lord's fatherly care **in the wilderness** (31). He envisages God going before them like a shepherd to find the place for them to **pitch** their **tents,** giving His presence **night** and **day** (33).

[3]G. T. Manley, "Deuteronomy," *The New Bible Commentary*, ed. F. Davidson (London: Inter-Varsity Fellowship, 1954), p. 199.

5. *Judgment of the Lord* (1:34-40)

The Lord was as displeased with the Israelites for refusing to enter the Promised Land as He was when they made the golden calf (cf. Num. 14:11-12). Deliberate refusal to receive God's blessings can be as disastrous as positive transgression.

The irrevocable sentence was pronounced: **Surely there shall not one of these men of this evil generation see that good land** (35). We can jeopardize our future usefulness and happiness in a moment of unbelief and rebellion. The people disinherited themselves and held up God's purpose of blessing for an entire generation. But there were exceptions. **Caleb** and **Joshua** stood out against the movement of rebellion at the risk of their lives (Num. 14:10). Because of this God excluded them from the sentence on the rebels and promised them a place in the land. **Caleb** is mentioned first. What finer commendation can a man have than for it to be said that he **wholly followed the Lord** (36)? "Only such men as Joshua and Caleb who take God at his word, and who know that against his might no strength can prevail, are likely to *follow God fully,* and receive the heights, lengths, breadths, and depths of the salvation of God."[4]

Caleb obtained the portion of the land he had surveyed, for his offspring (36; cf. Josh. 14:9, 12). **Joshua** (38) was given the privilege of leading the entire second generation into the Promised Land. What we do and are affects others besides ourselves.

There is a note of personal tragedy in this speech of Moses: **Also the Lord was angry with me for your sakes** (37). "Rather, because of you, on account of you. The Heb. word (*galal*) comes from a root meaning to roll, and signifies primarily a turn in events, a circumstance, an occasion or reason."[5]

The sentence God passed on the rebellious people reminded Moses of the sentence of exclusion which he himself had incurred at Kadesh many years later. Provoked by the complaints of the people, he had behaved in such a way as to displease the Lord. His lapse is described as unbelief resulting in failure to sanctify the Lord (Num. 20:10-12); breaking faith

[4]Clarke, *op. cit.,* I, 678-79.

[5]W. L. Alexander, *Deuteronomy,* "The Pulpit Commentary," ed. Spence and Exell (London: Funk & Wagnalls, 1907), p. 18.

with the Lord and not revering Him as holy (Deut. 32:51, RSV); and a bitter spirit and rash words (Ps. 106:33, RSV). In a very real sense, this was vicarious suffering; for if Moses had not identified himself so completely with the people, he would have consented to their destruction and have become the progenitor of another nation (Exod. 32:10; Num. 14:12). "They angered him also at the waters of strife, so that it went ill with Moses for their sakes: because they provoked his spirit, so that he spake usnadvisedly with his lips" (Ps. 106:32-33).

An indication of the moral stature of Moses is seen when God committed to him the task of encouraging his young assistant, Joshua, to do the job he was forbidden to do himself. Moses' love for his heartbreaking flock was so great that he willingly undertook the task of preparing the man to lead them into the land he was forbidden to enter. No wonder he is a type of the Messiah (cf. 18:18-19; Acts 3:22-23)!

Your little ones, which ye said should be a prey . . . shall go in thither (39). God is always more concerned about the welfare of our children than we are. Going His way may often seem to impose hardship on them, but it is always the best way for them and us. Note the allowance God makes for those not morally accountable. The Hebrew for **little ones** (*tappim*) signifies those who walk with short steps or trip along. The small children would be incapable of arriving at a right decision on such an issue. Even the older ones up to 20 years of age would find it difficult to discern the moral issues involved when all their elders apart from Moses, Aaron, Joshua, and Caleb, were unanimous in refusing to enter the land.

The solidarity of the nation is prominent in this passage. Moses was addressing mainly the children of the chief actors in the drama he was rehearsing, but they were treated as part of the nation which passed through these experiences. Those who were above 12 and even younger children would have some personal reminiscences of the events.

6. *The Price of Presumption* (1:41-46)

It is characteristic of human nature, especially fallen human nature, not to appreciate a good until it is lost. This may be one of the chief pangs of hell. When the Israelites were told that they must not do the very thing they had refused to do, they immediately resolved to do it. Probably there was an awful realization that there was no alternative to 40 years' experience in "that great and terrible wilderness" (19). Anything was better than that.

There is also an element of moral carelessness in the people's attitude. "Often we attempt to make up for our moral failure to do the right thing at the right time by a lighthearted attempt to do now, at the wrong time, what we should have done before."[6]

To insist on doing the right thing at the wrong time is as much rebellion as to do the wrong thing at the right time (43). In spite of the warning that the Lord is **not among you** (42) they presumed to go up. **Presumptuously** (43) is a very strong word in the original. It means "to act insolently, fiercely, wickedly." There could be only one result. **The Amorites** chased them like **bees do** (44). In Num. 14:45 the Amalekites and the Canaanites are mentioned. This is an instance of how the terms Amorite and Canaanite were sometimes used interchangeably. The Amalekites were quick to seize an opportunity for victory (cf. 25:17-18). **Hormah** ("destruction") was in the extreme south, probably a little to the north of Kadesh-barnea (see map 3). They were pursued almost to their camp. Small wonder they wept! But apparently it was remorse rather than repentance, for **the Lord would not hearken** (45).

Verse 46 is an example of Semitic idiom often employed by a writer who is either unable, or has no occasion, to speak explicitly:[7] **So ye abode in Kadesh many days, according unto the days that ye abode there.**

In the story of Israel at Kadesh-barnea we see that "Obedience Means Progress." The key idea is in 2:3. (1) Disobedience brought delay, 38 years of frustration and futility. Obedience would have brought them into the Promised Land in 11 days, 1:2, 26-28; (2) Disobedience always results in restless, wearisome activity with no progress, 2:1, *et al.;* 1:34-35; (3) Obedience results in a sense of right direction toward fulfillment, 2:3-4 (G. B. Williamson).

[6]H. Cunliffe-Jones, *Deuteronomy,* "Torch Bible Commentaries," ed. J. Marsh, *et al.* (London: SCM Press, 1951), p. 34.

[7]S. R. Driver, *Deuteronomy,* "The International Critical Commentary," ed. S. R. Driver, *et al.* (Edinburgh: T. and T. Clark, 1895), p. 31.

C. Dealings with Edom, Moab, and Ammon, 2:1-23

Moses turns from the description of the rebellion at Kadesh-barnea and its tragic outcome to the period preceding the time of his oration. There is only a brief reference to the long years spent in the wilderness in the region of Kadesh-barnea and Mount Seir.

Before referring to the victories over Sihon and Og, Moses refers to the Israelites' dealings with those related to them by blood. "The friendliness shown to Edom, Moab, and Ammon as 'brethren' is characteristic of the patriarchal and Mosaic ages, and a testimony to the contemporary character of the narrative. In the days of the kingdom it gave place to constant wars, and prophecies of bitter wars."[8]

1. *Edom* (2:1-8*a*)

After **many days** (1) in Kadesh-barnea (1:46), the Israelites journeyed in a southeast direction along the border of Edom to the **Red sea** (Gulf of Aqabah). Mainly in this region most of the 40 years were spent with perhaps one or more visits to Kadesh-barnea (cf. 14). According to the account in Num. 20:14-21 it appears that on a journey from Kadesh-barnea Israel requested permission to pass through the territory of Edom. When this was turned down, accompanied by threats of war, they skirted the borders of Edom and journeyed south to the Red Sea (Gulf of Aqabah; Num. 21:4). From here, according to the account before us, God commanded them, **Turn you northward** (3), through the eastern outskirts of the land of Edom (4).

They were to annex no territory, for the Lord had given this area to the descendants of **Esau,** Jacob's brother (5). The Israelites were to possess only the territory assigned to them by the Lord; they were not to be merely a nation of conquerors. They were commanded to **buy** whatever food or drink they required (6). **The Lord** who gave the command had made the fulfillment of it possible by blessing them even in their **wilderness** journeyings (7). Even God's second best has more abiding prosperity in it than the world's best.

We passed by from . . . the children of Esau . . . from Elath, and from Ezion-gaber (8). These are either two names for the

[8]Manley, *op. cit.*, p. 200.

same place or two places in the same vicinity, the northern end of the Gulf of Aqabah (see map 3). The impression is given that Israel kept to the fringes of the Edomite territory. The eastern frontiers were probably not as well defined as the west and not as easily defended.

2. *Moab* (2:8*b*-15)

The Lord gave precisely the same instructions about Moab as He had given concerning Edom.

Most of this paragraph is taken up with a historical note concerning the former inhabitants of **Ar** (9), the chief city. The information may have been added later as an explanatory note after Israel was settled in the land (cf. 12*b*). The Hebrew for **giants** (11) is *Rephaim* (RSV). The *Rephaim* were a giant aboriginal race inhabiting parts of Palestine. They were given different names in different localities. **Emims** (10) may be derived from Emah, "terror." **The Anakims** were notorious for their huge stature. *Anak* may mean "the long-necked [people]."

The account continues with a reference to the destruction by the Edomites of the former inhabitants of Mount **Seir** (12; see map 3). There are two views of **the Horims.** One is that they were cave dwellers, a possible meaning of *horim* (cf. Isa. 42:22, where the term is translated "holes"). A more recent view is that they were the powerful and civilized Hurrians, some of whom settled in Palestine.[9]

Underlying these references is the philosophy of divine sovereignty in human history. Amid the movements and conflicts of nations, overruling human motives and endeavors, God works out His purpose. The battle is not always to the strong. There is another factor in history.

Now rise up, said I, and get you over the brook Zered (13). **The brook Zered** is a mountain torrent, a river in the time of rain, dry at other times. It flowed into the southeast end of the Dead Sea and formed the border between Edom and Moab (see map 2). In Num. 21:12 we are told that the Israelites encamped in this valley. Hence the command to **rise up** (13). This was a definite stage in their journey along the borders of Edom and Moab towards Ammon.

[9]D. J. Wiseman, "Horites, Horim," *The New Bible Dictionary*, ed. J. D. Douglas, *et al.* (London: Inter-Varsity Fellowship, 1962), p. 537.

The period from leaving **Kadesh-barnea** (14) initially to the crossing of **Zered** is given as **thirty and eight years.** God's purpose had to wait until those who stood in the way of it were removed.

3. *Ammon* (2:16-23)

The Ammonites (20) occupied the territory between the rivers Arnon and Jabbok (see map 2) to the west of the territories of the Amorite kings, Sihon and Og. As the Israelites moved along the eastern frontier of Moab, perhaps crossing it near Ar, they would "approach the frontier of the sons of Ammon" (19, RSV). Hence the warning is given again not to annex any of this territory. The Ammonites were to be treated as brethren, even as Edom and Moab.

The original inhabitants of Ammon had also been "Rephaim" (RSV), whom they had called **Zamzummims** (20). This name "has been connected with the Arabic *Zamzamah,* 'a distant and confused noise,' and with **Zizim,** the sound of the *jinn* heard in the desert at night. The word may thus be translated 'Whisperers,' 'Murmurers,' and may denote the spirits of the giants supposed to haunt the hills and ruins of Eastern Palestine."[10]

It was known that the brethren of the Israelites in Edom and Moab had all been able to drive the giants out of the territories given them by God to possess. This fact makes all the more culpable the unbelief of the Israelites concerning His power to give them the land of Canaan in spite of **the Anakims** (21).

Another historical note is added about the **Avims** (23), "Avvim, who lived in villages as far as Gaza" (RSV). These were destroyed **by the Caphtorims** (Philistines), who came from Caphtor (Crete). It may be that they are mentioned because they belonged to the Rephaim, or because they were dispossessed in a similar way by invaders.

These historical notes have their lessons. Verses 10-13, 20-24 suggest: (1) That the present may learn from the past. History, sacred and secular, is a powerful influence in forming the characters of the living race. (2) That the Church may learn from the world. The holy nation is here incited by pointing to what other peoples have done in pursuit of their secular ambi-

[10]W. F. Boyd, "Zamzummim," *Dictionary of the Bible,* ed. James Hastings, *et al.* (Edinburgh: T. and T. Clark, 1929), p. 983.

tions. (3) That the desponding may learn from the successful. It is something to feel that we are not the first who have had to face the giants.[11]

D. Conquest of Sihon and Og, 2:24—3:29

Moses now turns to the recent victories over the two Amorite kings. These were epoch-making. They were not the first victories which God had given to His people (cf. Exod. 17:8-13; Num. 21:1-3). But this was the beginning of the possession of the land.

1. *Sihon of Heshbon* (2:24-37)

The first step in the conquest of Sihon was God's call to action buttressed by His assurance of victory. The victory and the land were Israel's by the gift of God, but they had to be possessed and fought for, mile by mile. There must be a beginning if there is going to be a winning. Morale is a vital factor in warfare. God here promises that He will **begin to put the dread of thee and fear of thee upon the nations that are under the whole heaven** (25). Influence is as vital in service as morale is in warfare. We must depend on God if we are rightly to affect the hearts of those whom we seek to win for Him.

Although aware of what the response was likely to be, Moses approached **Sihon king of Heshbon** (26) with a peaceful and reasonable proposal. We must act rightly even though we know our neighbor will do the opposite. It appears from Moses' proposition that some at least of the Edomites and Moabites had dealings with the Israelites as they travelled along the eastern frontiers (28-29). Were there merchants among them who could not miss business, or kindhearted folk who were moved by Israel's need?

As in the case of Pharaoh, so here God is said to have **hardened** Sihon's **spirit, and made his heart obstinate, that he might deliver him** (30) into the **hand** of Israel. In a very real sense, all the processes of life, material and moral, are attributable to the sovereignty of God. The more a man resists God and good, the more prone he will be to do so, because of the very character he is forming, and the less easy it will be to choose the right. In the case of Sihon and Pharaoh there may well have

[11]*Pulpit Commentary, loc. cit.*

been a judicial hardening as a climax to a course of deliberate rebellion and self-will. "Whom the gods destroy they first make mad." Thus Sihon willfully and deliberately set himself and his people on a course which brought deserved judgment upon them. The iniquity of their nation was now full (cf. Gen. 15:16) and they must give place to a people who would remove evil out of the land.

The battle was fought **at Jahaz** (32), which was probably on the route to **Heshbon** (26), the capital city. Moses attributes Israel's decisive victory to **the Lord our God** (33). All the cities with all the inhabitants were put to the ban (*cherem*), i.e., totally **destroyed** (34; cf. 20:16-18). It was not done in blood lust nor wanton destruction, but lest the inhabitants should teach the Israelites "to do after all their abominations, which they have done unto their gods" (20:18). These abominations included child sacrifices, ritual prostitution, and sodomy. Nevertheless our hearts turn sick at the thought of the total destruction of men, women, and especially the little children. And they should. But sin is a sickening thing with sickening results, and sometimes death alone can arrest its course. On the Cross the Son of God himself died to put it away.

The whole of Sihon's kingdom **from Aroer, which is by the brink of the river of Arnon . . . even unto Gilead** (36) was subdued. This gave Israel a possession on the frontier of **Ammon,** which they left inviolate, and up to **the river Jabbok** (37), the frontier of Og, to whom the story now turns.

2. *Og of Bashan* (3:1-29)

Chapter 3 deals first with the defeat of Og, then with the distribution of his territory. It closes with Moses' request of God to enter the land west of the Jordan, now that the possession of it on the eastern side had begun.

a. The conquest (3:1-11). **Og** was **the king of Bashan,** the kingdom to the north of Sihon's territory. It lay above the river Jabbok, with **Edrei** (1) and Astaroth (1:4) as its capitals. The king was a formidable contestant in himself, being of the giant Rephaim race. But Israel, stimulated by the victory over **Sihon** (2) and encouraged by God, invaded his territory and completely defeated him at Edrei. These two victories made a deep impression on the national consciousness of Israel and were celebrated in speech (Neh. 9:22) and song (Ps. 135:11; 136:19-20). To live in the past is a sign of decadence, but to learn lessons from the past and take heart is the secret of future success.

This account is part of Moses' oration. There is a point in his rehearsing the number of cities and their strong defenses: **fenced with high walls, gates, and bars** (5). The spies had dwelt on the impossibility of possessing Canaan because of its "cities . . . great and walled up to heaven" and the giant Anakim (1:28). But trusting in God, Israel had been able to capture the strongly fortified cities of Bashan and overthrow its giant king.

Again the **cities** (5-6) were put to the ban (*cherem*). It seems terrible to us to slay the people and save **the cattle** (7). But man, so much higher than the beasts, can sink so much lower that his presence constitutes a threat in a way that the presence of beasts cannot.

Verse 8 gives the extent of the territorial accessions: **from the river of Arnon,** the border of Moab (see map 2), right up to **mount Hermon** in the north, a distance of about 120 miles. On the eastern border was the territory of Ammon. So Moses was permitted to see Israel in possession of a considerable territory before his death. Note the names for **mount Hermon** (9), visible from most parts of the Promised Land. They are all descriptive: **Hermon,** "the lofty peak"; **Sirion** and Senir (RSV), the glittering "breastplate" of ice. Verse 10 enumerates the gains in terms of **cities:** "cities of the tableland" (RSV), **and Edrei,** the royal city, and "Salecah" (RSV) in the extreme west. **Gilead** and **Bashan** were excellent pasturelands.

Scholars are divided as to whether v. 11 refers to Og's iron **bedstead** or stone coffin (sarcophagus). There are many such stone coffins in the area made of black basalt which contains a percentage of iron. The measurements are thirteen and a half feet by six feet.[12] Apparently the Ammonites took possession of it and preserved it in their capital city, Rabbah or **Rabbath.**

b. The distribution of the territory (3:12-22). Apparently the best portion of the territory, though not the largest, was that between the rivers **Arnon** and **Jabbok.** This was given to the two tribes, Reuben and Gad (12, 16). The rest of the terri-

[12]Cf. Driver, *op. cit.*, p. 53.

tory northward was given to **the half tribe of Manasseh** (13). **Jair** (14), a descendent **of Manasseh,** took possession of the northern part of Og's territory, called **Argob,** up to the frontiers of the **Geshuri and Maachathi,** two Syrian tribes located east of Hermon. He called the villages after his name, "Havoth-jair" (RSV), i.e., "tent villages" of Jair. **Machir** (15) was either the name of the leader of the Manassites who possessed Gilead or another name for the tribe of Manasseh. The eastern border of the two and a half tribes was the east side of the Jordan valley **from Chinnereth** (17, a city after which the Sea of Chinnereth, the Sea of Galilee, was called) to **the salt sea** (Dead Sea).

Moses reminded the two and a half tribes of their obligation. They were to help the other tribes possess their inheritance west of Jordan even as the others had enabled them to possess the territory on the east. Their **wives** and children and **cattle** might remain in their recently acquired territory but the men would not be discharged from their obligation until their **brethren** had entered into their inheritance (18-20).

With this glance across the Jordan, Moses encouraged **Joshua** to take courage for the future from the triumphs of the past (21-22).

These verses reveal "Qualities of a Leader": (1) Recognition of past divine triumphs, 21*a*; (2) Realization of future assistance, 21*b*; (3) Refusal to fear, 22.

c. *The request of Moses* (3:23-29). Moses makes no disguise of his deep longing to enter the Promised Land. The places where he refers to this unfulfilled desire are among the saddest portions of Deuteronomy. The tragedy is that the one who desired most to enter the land found it bolted against him by an uncharacteristic attitude of unbelief and an act of folly on his part. We may not understand this fully, but it clearly illustrates the principle that much light implies great responsibility.

I pray thee, let me go over, and see (25). **But the Lord was wroth with me for your sakes** (26). Some scholars interpret this as purely vicarious suffering by Moses on behalf of the people. Admittedly, **for your sakes** is a different Hebrew expression from that in 1:37. It seems, however, that a similar thought is present here as there, and in both places the translation in the RSV is "on your account."

The Lord . . . would not hear me: and the Lord said unto

me, Let it suffice thee; speak no more unto me of this matter. Some take **Let it suffice thee** to mean simply, "That's enough"; others, that Moses had had privileges enough without asking for more.

Yet half of his prayer was answered. He was permitted to see the land from Pisgah's height, nearby, even though he was not allowed to enter. And he was assured that the enterprise he had begun would be carried through to a successful conclusion by **Joshua** (28).

This was not the last that Moses was to see of the land. "For on some 'goodly mountain' (Hermon or Lebanon) Moses and Elias stood with the Saviour of the world, and spake of a far more glorious conquest than Joshua's, even 'His exodus, which he should fulfil at Jerusalem' (Luke 9:31)."[13]

This paragraph gives us an insight into the "Principles of Prayer": (1) Prayer should begin with praise, 24; (2) Prayer should include aspiration, 25; (3) Prayer calls for believing and obedient conduct, 26; (4) Prayer is answered in God's way, 27-28.

E. Closing Exhortation, 4:1-40

Having brought the historical review to an end, Moses launched into his final exhortation. This is also interwoven with appeals to the past experiences of the nation to give point to the substance of his appeal.

1. *The Privilege of Israel's Revelation* (4:1-8)

Moses commences his peroration by enlarging upon the great privilege of being recipients of divine revelation. This revelation calls for a practical response. It must be heeded and translated into active obedience: **hearken . . . do** (1). Some scholars make no distinction between **statutes** (*chuqqim*) and **judgments** (*mishpatim*). Others regard **statutes** as revelations of abiding validity (*choq* is "engraved or inscribed") and sanctioned by God and conscience. By contrast, **judgments** are rules of law "laid down by authority or settled by ancient custom, by which a judge (*mishpat*) must be guided in certain specific cases."[14] Ac-

[13]C. H. Waller, "Deuteronomy," *A Bible Commentary*, ed. Charles J. Ellicott (London: Marshall Brothers, n.d.), II, 18.

[14]Manley, *op. cit.*, p. 201.

cording to the Jewish tradition **statutes** are the precepts, the reason for the observance of which is withheld in order to inculcate discipline and obedience—e.g., the dietary laws (cf. 14: 3-20).[15] **Commandments** (2, *mitswoth*) is a more general term for anything which is commanded by God, including such temporary regulations as the gathering of the manna (Exod. 16:28).

To the law of God nothing must be added or taken away (2). The main idea is that there must be no attempt to pervert the plain meaning of the divinely given law. Jesus charged the Pharisees with "making the word of God of none effect through . . . [their] tradition" (Mark 7:13). The law must be reverently preserved as well as observed. To keep God's word means life; to disobey means death, as witness the fate of those who died as a result of succumbing to the seductions of the Moabitesses in worshipping **Baal-peor** (3; cf. Num. 25:1-9). Baal means "Lord." Among the nations in and around Canaan each place had its local god or baal. Immorality was a regular part of Baal worship and child sacrifices were also offered. **Baal-peor** was the name of the local deity of Peor. Beth-peor (3:29; "house of Peor") may well have been the site of his temple. **Cleave** (4) is a word of strong allegiance (cf. Acts 11:23).

Note **teach** (1) and **taught** (5). Deuteronomy is an exposition of laws already given, with the new conditions in the Promised Land especially in mind. The keeping of these laws would impress the surrounding **nations** with the **wisdom** and **understanding** of Israel (6). In like manner, when the Christian Church takes God's Word to heart, the world respects her. The paragraph closes with an exclamation concerning the greatness of Israel. There was no other contemporary **nation,** not even the greatest, whose god was as near **as the Lord** was to Israel, near enough to hear her every **call** (7). There was no other **nation** which was exalted by such a **righteous . . . law** (8).

2. *The Peril of Idolatry* (4:9-31)

The great privilege of God's revelation to Israel carried with it a special responsibility.

a. The original revelation must be remembered (4:9-14). Time and again in Deuteronomy, Moses takes the nation back to the historic revelation of God at **Horeb** (10). The main facts must

[15]Hertz, ed., *op. cit.*, p. 756.

be kept firmly in mind and taught to successive generations. Moses especially emphasized the absence of any form that could give ground for idolatry. **A voice** (12) was **heard** giving commandments and making a covenant, appealing to conscience and faith, but there was **no similitude** ("form," RSV). Moses was delegated **to teach** them **statutes and judgments** (14), thereby validating divine revelation through a chosen man. But nothing that could be seen or touched was in evidence at Horeb, lest worship should be materialized and sensualized, and matter exalted over spirit. As with Israel, so with Christians; we must constantly refer to the original revelation given in the NT and keep our faith and service pure.

b. The revelation must not be corrupted with idolatry (4:15-24). The various forms of idolatry are given in this paragraph. Israel was warned against **graven** (*pesel,* "carved") images (16). No figure or form was to be copied. **The likeness of male or female** may well refer to the adulation of sex in heathen worship in which the sex organs were worshipped with obscene rites. Beasts, birds, insects, reptiles, and **fish** (17-18) were all worshipped by the Egyptians and other nations.

Verse 19 prohibited Israel from worshipping **sun, moon,** or **stars,** which were the dominant influence in Babylonian religion. What is the meaning of **which the Lord thy God hath divided unto all nations under the whole heaven** (19)? Some take it to mean that this form of worship was permitted by God to nations without the special revelation of Israel as a stage toward the true worship (cf. Acts 14:16-17; 17:30). But for Israel to stoop to this was apostasy and repudiation of **the covenant of the Lord** (23), who had delivered them. **Out of the iron furnace** (20) is a metaphor for severe affliction (cf. I Kings 8:51; Isa. 48:10; Jer. 11:4). **A consuming fire . . . a jealous God** (24) indicates the burning love which will tolerate no rival and destroys everything contrary to His nature. Moses' reference to the Lord's anger towards him, excluding him from the Promised Land, is repeated here (21-22). The purpose was probably to warn the people that the Lord is not to be trifled with and also to urge them not to forget the covenant when Moses would no longer be with them to enforce its claims.

c. God will deal with Israel on the basis of the revelation (4:25-31). If the Israelites despise the unique revelation given by God, He will chastise them; but if they repent and turn to Him again on the terms of the covenant, He will restore them.

Moses foresaw the peril of forgetfulness in the coming generations. The further we are in years from the days of the original covenant, the greater the danger of spiritual decay unless the covenant is renewed in fresh accessions of the Spirit. The word translated **remained long** (25) contains the idea of growing old and stale. This can happen even to those who have entered into the Canaan of heart holiness. Because the covenant is not renewed, their experience becomes stale and they lose their inheritance.

Moses called **heaven and earth to witness** (26). This was either an appeal to celestial and human witnesses or a poetic appeal to the fixed phenomena of nature outlasting the passing generations of men. He affirms that judgment will inevitably attend any form of idolatry transgressing the covenant. A complete reversal of the blessings of faithful observance will take place: they will be dispossessed of the promised **land,** and their **number** will be reduced (27). Again they will be in bondage to idolatrous nations and in serving them will eventually be in bondage to their gods, man-made, blind, dumb, and inanimate.

But the God who is a consuming fire is also a **merciful God** who does not **forget the covenant** (31). In exile He will hear the cry of His people if they **seek him with all** their **heart and with all** their **soul** (29) and **turn to** Him and obey **his voice** (30).

Moses, as "the first and greatest of the long succession of prophets,"[16] was given such insight into the character of God and the frailty of His people that he was able to lay down the pattern of future events. Beside this, like others of the prophets, he was no doubt given ecstatic visions of the future.

3. *The Privilege of Being God's Elect* (4:32-40)

The speech of Moses moves to a magnificent climax in this paragraph.

a. A unique privilege (4:32-34). These verses are in the form of rhetorical questions. Moses invites time (32*a*) and space (32*b*), history and geography, to furnish any other instance of a nation having the experience of God which Israel had. No other

[16]F. F. Bruce, *Israel and the Nations* (Exeter, England: Paternoster Press, 1963), p. 14.

nation had heard God **speaking out of the midst of the fire** and survived (33). No other god had taken for himself **a nation** from the grip of a greater **nation** (34). **Temptations** are trials. Some refer these to Pharaoh, others to God's testings of Israel. Probably both are right. **Signs** are significant acts; **wonders,** supernatural deeds; **war,** the overthrow of the Egyptian army in the Red Sea. **A mighty hand, and . . . a stretched out arm** represent divine omnipotence in action. **Great terrors** are terrifying demonstrations of divine power. The redemption of Israel was grounded in history, and ours is too, in the Cross and the Resurrection. Of three Greek words used for NT miracles, two are found here in the LXX: *semeion,* "sign," and *teras,* "wonder." The third is *dynamis,* "work of power" (cf. Heb. 2:4).

b. The purpose of the privilege (4:35-38). God chose the Israelites **because he loved** their **fathers** (37). It was an election based on divine love and grace; but the response of faith and obedience on the part of the patriarchs, notably Abraham, must not be overlooked. Because of His love, God gave Israel not only His power but His presence (cf. Exod. 33:14-15). And His purpose in it all was, first, that they might **know that the Lord he is God; there is none else beside him** (35). Davies declares that 35 and 39 "teach absolute monotheism."[17] Second, that they might be taught ("disciplined," RSV) in His ways (36); and, third, that He might settle them in the Promised Land (37-38).

c. The obligation of the privilege (4:39-40). The Israelites were not the pampered favorites of an indulgent God. Such a conception is an insult to the divine character. To be His elect people carried with it the obligation to honor Him **in** the **heart** as supreme (39) and to **keep . . . his statutes** (40). Only thus could it **go well** with them. There is a vital truth in the Deuteronomic emphasis. Ultimately we are preserved by keeping God's Word or broken by breaking it.

F. Appointment of Cities of Refuge, 4:41-43

It appears that this action was taken between the first and second discourses. The account could be by the hand of Moses or in the nature of an editorial note. For the purpose of a city of refuge see comments on 19:13, also on Num. 35:6, 11-34.

[17]"Deuteronomy," *A Commentary on the Bible,* ed. A. S. Peake (London: T. Nelson and Sons, 1948), p. 234.

It is impossible to locate these three cities with certainty. **Bezer** (43) is thought to have been due east from the place of the oration in the territory of Reuben. **Ramoth** is identified with Ramoth-gilead. This, however, was in the territory of Manasseh rather than of Gad. **Golan** is thought to have been in the north of Manasseh's territory. All the cities would be chosen so as to be readily accessible to the majority of the population in order that the unintentional killer would have an opportunity of declaring his innocence. **On this side Jordan** (41) here clearly refers to the eastern bank (cf. comments on 1:1).

Section II *Main Address: The Law*

Deuteronomy 4:44—26:19

The main section of the book is devoted to an exposition of the law of God. This begins with the Ten Commandments, then proceeds to deal with other religious, civil, and social laws.

A. Introduction, 4:44-49

The law is here described in terms of **testimonies** (45), **statutes,** and **judgments** (ordinances). For **statutes** and **judgments,** see comments on 4:1. **Testimonies** is a literal translation of *edoth.* Here it stands for "solemn declarations of God's will on matters of moral and religious duty."[1]

The place **on this side Jordan** (46) is the same as indicated in 1:1, 5 and 3:29. In the former references it is defined as being in the land of Moab, whereas here it is stated to be in the freshly conquered territory of **Sihon king of the Amorites.** But this part of Sihon's kingdom had formerly belonged to the Moabites (cf. Num. 21:26).

For the conquest of Sihon and Og (46-49), cf. 2:26—3:17. The name for Mount Hermon, **Sion** (48; "lifted up"), should not be confused with Mount Zion, "sunny mountain."

B. The Ten Commandments, 5:1—11:32

1. *Their Content and Communication* (5:1-33)

a. Setting (5:1-5). This chapter commences with a recital of the Ten Commandments. They are treated as the basis of the **covenant** (2) between God and Israel. The covenant is declared to be not only with men of the past generation, who dismally failed to discharge their obligations, but also with those now addressed, many of whom, as children and adolescents, were present at Horeb (2-3).

The form of the Decalogue has affinities with the form in

[1]Hertz, *op. cit.*, p. 764.

which international treaties were cast in those days, especially treaties between a superior power and vassal states.[2]

b. Content (5:6-21). This recital of the Ten Commandments should be compared with that in Exod. 20:1-17. There are slight differences, but the two accounts are substantially the same. Some think that the original words written on the tables of stone contained just the brief commands and that Moses added inspired interpretations.[3] The interpretations in Deuteronomy are particularly suited to life in Canaan.

The first commandment begins with the mention of the divine name (6; cf. Exod. 3:13-14). No other god is to intrude between the Lord and His redeemed people.

The second commandment forbidding idolatry (8-9) follows naturally upon the first. But it includes not only the making of images of other gods but also the representing of the Lord in the form of celestial, terrestrial, or marine creatures, as was probably the motive in making the golden calf. Verses 8-9 should be taken together. This is not a prohibition against carving statues or painting pictures as such, but only against making them for worship.

That **the children** suffer for the sins of their parents is a fact of life. They also benefit from the piety of their parents. This is life as God has made it, part of its social bond. How grave therefore is the responsibility of parents to give the children whom they love a good legacy! Ezekiel makes it clear that God readily receives the penitent children of evil parents (Ezek. 18: 14-17). And whereas **the iniquity of the fathers** is visited upon **the third and fourth generation** (9), the **mercy** ("steadfast love," RSV) of the Lord extends to **thousands** of generations of those who **love** Him and **keep** His **commandments** (10).

The third commandment (11) is especially related to oaths: taking up **the name of the Lord** upon the lips lightly or in falsehood. One of the marks of allegiance to a deity was to use his name in oaths (cf. 6:13). To use the sacred name to buttress a false statement is the height of cynical unbelief. **The Lord will not hold him guiltless.** The third commandment is thus designed to inculcate reverence and truth.

The fourth commandment (12-15) relates to keeping (Exod. 20:8, "Remember") **the sabbath day.** The two main ideas are

[2]Bruce, *op. cit.*, p. 16

[3]Manley, NBC, p. 204.

rest (*shabbath,* "to sit down," "to cease") and sanctity (12). God's ordinance is six days' work and one day's rest. We should need fewer tranquillizers and have fewer nervous breakdowns if we observed this law of spiritual and physical hygiene. In Exod. 20:11 the example of the Lord is quoted and the commandment is related to His creative work. Here the emphasis is upon rest for the entire household (14). It is enforced by a reminder of the grim servitude **in the land of Egypt** (15) and the Lord's gracious deliverance from it. One can almost hear Jesus saying, "Freely ye have received, freely give" (Matt. 10:8).

The fifth commandment (16) is quoted by Paul as "the first commandment with promise." He applies the promise of long life and well-being to Christians who observe it (Eph. 6:2-3). This commandment lies at the foundation of true religion and national well-being. It is often associated with the first four commandments, which deal with piety towards God, because parents stand in the place of God so far as their children are concerned.

The next five commandments all relate to social righteousness; they are linked together by the Hebrew conjunction "and." The Lord is a righteous God and demands righteous dealings in human relationships. The first five commandments have explanatory clauses, warnings or promises. The last five are brief and self-explanatory. Conscience and our own experience supply the rationale.

Thou shalt not kill (17) is better translated, "Thou shalt not murder." The Hebrew word *ratsach* is always used in this way in the OT.

Thou shalt not **commit adultery** (18). This is a sin against both partners in the marriage, and if there are children, against them too. It is both callous and cruel.

Thou shalt not **steal** (19). The three commandments above are connected. Murder is taking a man's life; adultery is taking his wife (or *vice versa*), and stealing is taking his property. In each case the transgressor exalts his own desires and requirements above his neighbor's, judging himself of more worth than his brother. In so doing he sins against God.

The ninth commandment deals with the sin of the lips, **false witness against thy neighbour** (20). This covers not only perjury but all lying detrimental to our fellowmen. God's ideal is a society in which every man speaks the truth with his neighbor (Eph. 4:25).

The tenth commandment deals with the sin of the heart (21). It was this commandment that brought home to Paul his need of a salvation which could change the heart (Rom. 7:7). In Exod. 20:17 the **house** is mentioned before the **wife,** whereas here the order is reversed. Perhaps in the former account "house" is used in the sense of "household," and here the dwelling place is more in mind, so the wife is mentioned first in order of importance.

The Ten Commandments stand in a category of their own: "He added no more" (22). They are fundamental to right living and right thinking. No nation can be great which ignores them. No Christian would want to break them. Yet all of us have transgressed them in motive and spirit. We need a Saviour who can redeem us from the curse of the law and give us the promise of the Spirit by faith (Gal. 3:13-14). Thus we can have the law written in our hearts (Heb. 10:16) and rejoice in that love which is the fulfilling of the law (Rom. 13:9-10).

c. *Communication* (5:22-33). This section dwells on the historic occasion of the giving of the law to Israel with all the impressive accompaniments of its communication. It stresses again **the fire, the cloud, the thick darkness,** the **great voice,** and the **two tables of stone** inscribed by the divine hand (22).

The awe-inspiring majesty of it all was overpowering. The leaders of Israel, fully convinced of the authenticity of the revelation, besought Moses to act as an intermediary between them and God, lest they should die (23-27). In this Moses is a type of the "one mediator between God and men, the man Christ Jesus" (I Tim. 2:5). There are a number of references in Scripture to the overpowering effect of the supernatural on the natural (e.g., Dan. 10:5-19; Matt. 28:2-4; Acts 9:3-9; Rev. 1:17). This is probably one of the reasons why God communicates with the spirit of man rather than through the five senses. In the case of Moses there was such a deep spiritual relationship between him and God that he was able to approach God's glory in a way impossible to others. Even so, there were limits to this approach (cf. Exod. 33:20).

The leaders' request was granted by the Lord, especially in view of their promise to **hear** and **do . . . all that the Lord our God shall** speak unto Moses (27). The divine exclamation (29) is characteristic of the tenor of the book: reverence from the heart, resulting in keeping **all** the **commandments always,** issuing in well-being to **them** and **their children.**

The people were allowed to return to their **tents** (30), but the man of God was detained to wait upon God to receive the full revelation (31). Every Christian in this dispensation has direct access to God. But in a very real sense those ordained to the ministry have a special obligation to wait on God for His word for the flock. No amount of activity is any substitute for this.

The paragraph closes with a reminder by Moses (32-33) of the people's obligation to keep the promise made by the nation on the occasion of the historic communication of the divine law.

In this "second giving of the law" none of the former supernatural phenomena were present. The essence of this occasion was the communication of God's will for His people. The divine truth remained and was set before them again by Moses. It needed no further authentication. It simply required obedience, and God's blessing would automatically follow. Likewise, we make a mistake if we crave external phenomena. The inward gift of the Spirit is available to all who ask, believe, and obey (Luke 11:13; Acts 5:32; 15:8-9). His indwelling fullness is the essence of NT Christianity.

2. *The Dedication God's Commandments Deserve* (6:1-25)

The Ten Commandments are still the main theme, since they are the basis of the covenant with God and the nucleus of the Torah (law).

a. Inward and outward dedication (6:1-9). Verse 2 sums up the content of the entire chapter. Reverence for the Lord expresses itself in keeping **all . . . his commandments . . . all the days** of our lives and teaching our children to do the same.

Verses 4-5 are part of what is called the *Shema* (Heb. for "hear"). This is the creed of Judaism. Either "The Lord our God is one Lord" or "The Lord is our God, the Lord is one" is a valid translation. **The Lord** in the KJV stands for the Hebrew word *Yahweh,* which the Jews regarded as too sacred to be pronounced and so substituted the word *Adonai,* "my Lord." *Yahweh* means literally "He is" or "He becomes." It is translated by Moffatt as "the Eternal." The words of v. 4 declare that the

Lord is the God of **Israel,** that He is the only God, and that He is the same everywhere. This was probably in opposition to the gods of the surrounding nations, particularly the Baals, who were worshipped in different forms and with different rites in various localities. The word **one** is not inconsistent with the Christian doctrine of the Trinity, i.e., three Persons of the same substance in the one Godhead. Indeed, **God** is regularly in the plural form in the Hebrew Scriptures and is so here.

The confession of faith is followed by an exhortation to love. This occurs in Deuteronomy 10 times, and not elsewhere in the Pentateuch.[4] This love must include the total personality: **heart . . . soul . . . might** (5). These three terms include the whole man, his inner and outer life, his mind, will, desire, psychic emotions, mental and physical energy, and even his possessions. When asked for the first commandment in the law, Jesus quoted the *Shema,* adding "mind," probably to bring out the LXX *dianoia,* "understanding." He also added Lev. 19:18, "Thou shalt love thy neighbour as thyself." Those who have a low estimation of the OT should remember that from its pages the Son of God was able to define vital religion in terms of love. "Jesus' answer was in keeping with the best Jewish thought on the subject, with the result that this law for both Jews and Christians is considered to be God's primary requirement, the sum of all other requirements."[5]

The Scriptures declare, **These words . . . shall be in thine heart** (6). The heart of religion is in the heart. But it must not be confined to it. It must issue into the activities of life. The word of God must be taught to the **children,** talked of in the **house** and in **the way,** the last thing at night, and the first thing in the morning (7). How far this is to be taken literally, each individual must decide. There is a saying that "what possesses the heart wags the tongue." We may all ask ourselves whether what should be first in our lives is sufficiently prominent in our conversation.

There is a difference of opinion as to whether vv. 8-9 were intended to be taken literally. Driver states, "It seems on the

[4]J. Battersby-Harford, "Deuteronomy," *A New Commentary on Holy Scripture* (London: Society for Promoting Christian Knowledge, 1928), p. 156.

[5]G. Ernest Wright, "Deuteronomy," *The Interpreter's Bible,* ed. G. A. Buttrick, *et al.* (New York: Abingdon-Cokesbury Press, 1951), p. 372.

whole to be more probable that the injunction is intended to be carried out literally."[6] On the other hand there is little biblical or extra-biblical evidence of its being put into practice until the time of the Maccabees (c. 167 B.C.). The custom among the Jews, from the second century A.D., has been to use four sections from the law, Exod. 13:1-10; 13:11-16; Deut. 6:4-9; and 11:13-21. They put these passages in leather cubes on straps and bind them to their left hands and on their foreheads before morning prayers. They are called *tephillin,* "prayers," or *phylacteries,* probably "a means of protection." Also the Jews put Deut. 6:4-5; 11:13-20 in a metal or glass case and fixed it to the right-hand doorpost of the outer entrance of every dwelling room in the house. This was called a *mezuzah,* "doorpost." Jesus' censure of the Pharisees was probably not because they wore phylacteries but because they ostentatiously displayed them. This ostentation was part of their tragic mistake of exalting the trappings of religion above the attitude of the heart.

The theme of 4-11 is "God Is One Lord." (1) Lord in personal experience, 5-6; (2) Lord in family life, 7-9; (3) Lord of abundant provision for heaven on earth, 10-11; cf. 11:21 (G. B. Williamson).

b. Constant dedication (6:10-19). The commandments and covenant of the Lord call for a constant dedication. This will be tested especially by prosperity. The very goodness of God, if not accepted in a humble and thankful spirit, can be a source of temptation. Think of what **great and goodly cities** (10), **houses full of all good things . . . wells . . . vineyards and olive trees** (11) would mean to a nation which had spent 40 years in the wilderness. And all were gifts. Man in plenty soon forgets his adversity, and, alas, too often the One who has brought about the change. There would also be a temptation to adopt some of the **other gods** (14) of the surrounding agricultural nations, now that Israel had become an agricultural people themselves. But **the Lord** will tolerate no rivals (15). Jesus quoted 13 when tempted to worship Satan (Matt. 4:10; Luke 4:8). Did He see it as a temptation to conform to worldly methods? He interpreted **fear** of v. 13 as worship.

Christ also quoted 16 when tempted to force God's hand to work a miracle (Matt. 4:7; Luke 4:12). He must have meditated

[6]*Op. cit.,* p. 93.

much on this chapter. It is a privilege to follow His example. **For Massah** see Exod. 17:1-7. God's deliverances and provisions come to those who **diligently keep** His **commandments** (17) **and do that which is right and good in** His **sight** (18).

c. Communicated dedication (6:20-25). The covenant was not intended for one generation only. A part of the dedication demanded of those to whom the law and the covenant were given was to communicate them to their children.

God expected that the faithful observance of His laws by His people would attract the attention of their children (20). No precept is worth much unless it is enforced by example. On the other hand, the parents were expected to be familiar with the history of God's deliverance and be able to instruct their children in the fundamentals of their faith. In Deuteronomy there is a recurring emphasis on the fact that the divine commandments are for human benefit (24). His will and our highest good are one.

Regarding the statement **it shall be our righteousness** (25) Clarke writes: "[Observance of the law shall be] the *evidence* that we are under the influence of the fear and love of God. Moses does not say that this righteousness could be wrought without the influence of God's mercy, nor does he say that they should purchase heaven by it; but, God required them to be conformed to his will in all things, that they might be holy in heart, and righteous in every part of their moral conduct."[7]

3. *Separation Demanded by the Law* (7:1-26)

There is a negative as well as a positive side to keeping the commandments and covenant of God. In the marriage covenant a man separates himself from marriage with all other women to be the loyal husband of one wife. This chapter indicates the division which must come between Israel and the Canaanites because of the covenant with God.

a. Separation from nations which defile (7:1-5). The defeat and dispossession of the nations in Canaan is all attributed to God. His is the victory. **The Hittites** (1), or sons of Heth, were a powerful, civilized nation which held sway in Syria and Asia Minor from 1800 to 900 B.C. **The Jebusites** were a Canaanite peo-

[7]*Op. cit.*, p. 769.

ple inhabiting the hills about Jebus (Jerusalem). **The Girgashites** (in Heb. always in the sing.) are little known, except that they appear to have inhabited a part of Canaan west of the Jordan (Josh. 24:11). **The Hivites** were located in the north at Lebanon and Hermon (Judg. 3:3; Josh. 11:3) and towards the south in Kirjath-jearim and Beeroth (Josh. 9:17). Those in Gibeon made peace by guile with the Israelites (Josh. 9:17). For **the Amorites, and the Canaanites** cf. comment on 1:7. All of the six mentioned above are listed in the line of Canaan, the grandson of Noah (Gen. 10:15-18). **The Perizzites** seem to have dwelt mainly in the hill country. In Josh. 17:15 they are associated with the *Rephaim* or giants.

All persons belonging to these nations were to be destroyed—"put to the ban" (*cherem*)—lest they should corrupt the Israelites (2, 4). No **marriages** were to be contracted with them (3; cf. Num. 25:1-9). All relics of their worship were to be eliminated (5). The **groves** were trees or wooden poles set up as sacred symbols, perhaps images of Asherah, a Canaanitish goddess of the sea, the consort of El or Baal.[8]

There are several things which should be borne in mind when reading such passages as this. First, this command of God was given to a particular nation which had been chosen to receive His revelation and was to be trained to produce the Messiah and prepare the minds of men for His ministry (cf. Rom. 9:4-5). This nation needed an object lesson in the dire results of idolatry and licentiousness. Secondly, the command to destroy was given concerning nations that had become a festering cancer in the human corpus, practicing child sacrifices, sodomy, bestiality, idolatry, and witchcraft (cf. 7:5; 18:9-12; Lev. 18:21-25). Thirdly, the command was given at a stage in the education of the chosen people when the distinction between mercy to the defeated and compromise with their evil ways was imperfectly understood.

The writer of the Epistle to the Hebrews makes clear that the OT is the record of a progressive revelation which finds its full expression only with the incarnation of the Son of God (Heb. 1:1-3). To apply these commands to warfare today would be a gross misapplication of scripture. There can be no doubt that, armed with the Christian gospel and endued with the Holy

[8]For a full discussion see Driver, *op. cit.*, pp. 201 ff.

Spirit, Paul would have entered Canaan as he entered Corinth to show God's triumph over evil in transformed lives (cf. I Cor. 6: 9-11). Nevertheless, there is a permanent principle in the Deuteronomic judgments. God as Lord of history ever judges nations which grossly break His laws. He used Assyria as His rod (Isa. 10:5), Nebuchadnezzar as His servant (Jer. 25:9), and the legions of Rome as the harbingers of His judgment (Luke 21:22; cf. Matt. 22:7).

b. Separation to God, who blesses and gives victory (7: 6-26). God calls Israel **holy,** separated and sanctified; a **special people,** "a people for his own possession" (RSV; cf. Titus 2:14). **Special** is the same adjective David uses to describe his personal wealth as distinct from the state treasury, over which he had control as king (I Chron. 29:3).

Verses 6-8 suggest "Chosen by God": (1) To be holy, 6*a*; (2) To be His, 6*b*; (3) To be humble, 7; (4) To be heirs, 8.

God was not attracted to the people of Israel by their numbers. He called Abraham as a childless man, and took his descendants to himself when they were a minority as slaves in Egypt. The cause of His choice is to be found in His love (8; cf. Rom. 5:6, 8; I John 4:10). The result of His choice was the deliverance from **Egypt,** which demonstrated His faithfulness and love. God is **the faithful God** (9), stable, dependable, and consistent. He is the One on whom the obedient and believing can utterly rely to keep His covenant, and One whom His enemies must inevitably encounter in judgment (9-11). "Behold therefore the goodness and severity of God" (Rom. 11:22).

In 12-15 the promises of blessing flow like a river over a faithful and obedient people. They relate to the multiplication of the nation: fruitfulness in children, the products of the **land,** and of the **cattle** (13-14). Also included is a promise of freedom from **all sickness** (15). Egypt was notorious for its unhealthful conditions. Pliny describes it as "the mother of worst diseases."[9] Canaan, if they were obedient, should be noted for its health.

The fact that God blesses His obedient and believing people is on every page of Scripture. It is natural that this should be manifest in nations in a visible and material way. In the case of the individual, material blessing is often withheld that greater and more abiding blessing may be given. This was true of Him

[9]Hertz, *op. cit.*, p. 780.

who is the best and most beloved of all, the Christ himself. Providing this is borne in mind, Deuteronomy's message is authentic and eternal.

Verses 16-26 deal with the power of God to make His people victorious. The God who wrested His people from the clutch of **Pharaoh** will wrest Canaan from the hand of those who have defiled it. The appeal is made to God's past deliverances to strengthen faith for the forthcoming task (17-19). Moses exhorts, **Thou shalt . . . well remember** (18). The **temptations** (19) is better "tests" (Berk.). God's victory will be strategic as well as mighty. **The hornet** (20) will assist it, but the wild **beasts** will be restrained (22). Some think that **the hornet,** which was the badge of Thothmes III and his successors, is a reference to Egyptian invasions weakening the resistance of the Canaanites.

The purpose of this speech was to build up the morale of a fearful people (18, 21). There must be no debacle as at Kadesh-barnea. God is able to take confidence from the hearts of His enemies and put it into the hearts of His servants.

Once the victory is gained, there must be no compromise with the evil overthrown (16, 24-26). The Canaanites will perish because of their **abomination** (25). The same fate will overtake Israel if there is any compromise with devastating evil (25-26). God is not removing one nation to make room for His favorites. He has a consistent purpose throughout of purging the land from unspeakable evil.

4. *Danger of Forgetting the Commandments* (8:1-20)

The basis of all the blessings which God has in store for Israel is His commandments. In order to keep this firmly in mind it is necessary to remember the lessons of the past.

a. Remember the lessons of divine discipline (8:1-6). God prepares us for His blessings. No man can stand success without the necessary divine discipline. Many of us would be more successful if we would submit to the necessary apprenticeship. On the other hand, with some of us the training is unnecessarily drawn out because we "fail our exams." This was the case with Israel. It was 40 times as long as it need have been.

But the discipline was good. It **humbled** (3) and it tested. It showed the real motives of the **heart** (2). It took the form of an unusual diet for which they were literally dependent on God every day. Some scholars think the **manna** (3) was the excretion of two types of scaly insects which feed on the tamarisk tree.[10] If this was so, and we do not really know, then the reference to humbling is appropriate indeed! This diet was a food that neither the Israelites nor their **fathers** had previously known. But chiefly God humbled His people by making them dependent on His commands and His promises. The important thing in life is to be rightly related to the Giver of food for soul and body (cf. Matt. 4:4; Luke 4:4).

Some take the the statement, **Thy raiment waxed not old upon thee** (4), to mean that the clothes of the Israelites did not wear out during the 40 years. It probably means that by God's provision they were able to renew their clothing, even though they were nomads in the wilderness. By the same divine care their feet did not suffer. In v. 5 the emphasis is not on **chasteneth** but on **his son** (cf. Heb. 12:7-8). The point of the discipline is applied: **Therefore thou shalt keep the commandments of the Lord** (6).

Verses 1-6 suggest the theme "Lest We Forget": (1) Past trials, 2; (2) Past lessons, 3; (3) Paternal care, 4-5.

b. Remember the Giver of the land (8:7-20). A faithful description of Canaan as it was in the time of Moses is given (7-9). Charles Wesley describes the experience of perfect love in terms of the land of Canaan:

A land of corn and wine and oil
Favoured with God's peculiar smile
And every blessing blessed . . .

The **iron** (9) probably refers to the black basalt stone with about 20 percent content of iron. For **brass** read "copper" (RSV). In recent days the mineral wealth of Canaan has been exploited as never before.

The theme of 6-10, "Live by the Word of God," is suggested in 3*b*. (1) Live by obedience to God's commandments, 6; (2) Live by acceptance of God's disciplines, 5; cf. Heb. 12:5-11; (3) Live by faith in God's promises, 7-10 (G. B. Williamson).

It is human nature to move from scarcity to plenty with an initial gratitude which after a time gives place to a spirit of self-congratulation, complacency, and sometimes haughty rebellion.

[10]G. E. Wright, *op. cit.*, p. 386.

This tendency is exposed in these verses and safeguards are indicated. **Beware . . . lest when thou hast eaten and art full . . . thine heart be lifted up, and thou forget the Lord** (11-14), **and thou say in thine heart, My power . . . hath gotten me this wealth** (17). Happy the man who can balance a full stomach with a thankful and lowly heart. Too often the tendency is the other way. The haughty heart inhibits the memory of the Lord's goodness and explains the prosperity in terms of human ability and good fortune. The sad outcome often is the turning away from our Benefactor and the transfer of allegiance to a less demanding form of religion which gives greater scope to the lower desires. This tendency is only too abundantly illustrated by Israel's history. In the graphic words of Moses' song: "Jeshurun waxed fat, and kicked" (32:15).

Moses gives a sure prescription for the prevention of such an eventuality. Israel is to remember the Lord in the keeping of His **commandments,** and to keep ever in mind His deliverance from **Egypt** (11, 14). They are to recall His guidance, protection, and provision in the wilderness. They must never forget that behind all ability **to get wealth** lies His power (18). Finally, apostasy to the false gods will bring on Israel the fate of **the nations** they dispossessed (19-20).

5. *Divine Grace Behind the Law* (9:1—10:11)

Law and grace are often contrasted. Here we see the covenant of God with Israel, based on the Ten Commandments, rooted in divine grace.

a. A warning against self-righteousness (9:1-6). In 7:17-24, Moses encouraged a fearful people. Here he follows the assurance of the Lord's victory over the Canaanites with a warning against pride when once the apparently impossible task has been accomplished. Moses does not anticipate that the Israelites will immediately attribute the victory to their own prowess. Rather they will be tempted to say that the Lord has used them as the executors of His purpose because of their own **righteousness** (4). Pride can creep in through devious means, but Moses had the foresight to forestall its entry. **Not for thy righteousness** (*tsedeqah,* "rectitude of conduct"), **or for the uprightness of thine heart** (*yosher,* "rectitude of motive and purpose"): **but for the wickedness of these nations the Lord** will **drive them out** (5).

Therefore the conquest of Canaan should be a constant warning to Israel of the peril of wickedness, a peril to which she had succumbed more than once.

b. A rehearsal of Israel's rebellion (9:7-29). Most attention is given to the disgraceful apostasy of the golden calf at the very time of the establishing of the covenant (8-21; cf. Exodus 32—33). **Also in Horeb** (8) is better translated "even in Horeb" (RSV). The account is substantially the same as in Exodus, bearing in mind that it was given nearly 40 years after and in a condensed form. It is not clear whether Moses twice fasted **forty days and forty nights** or whether 9 and 25 refer to the same event.

Kline is of the opinion that **the two tables of stone** (11) were two separate tables, each containing all the Ten Commandments, written on the front and back (Exod. 32:15). He states that it was customary for treaties between suzerains and vassals to be drawn up in duplicate in this fashion. One was to be kept by the suzerain and the other by his vassal, each in the sanctuary of his god. In the case of Israel, both copies were deposited in the ark in the sanctuary of the Tabernacle because the Lord was both Israel's Suzerain and God. On this interpretation, Moses' act in breaking the tables when he saw the golden calf was not merely an act of exasperation—though he was understandably angry (Exod. 32:19)—but was symbolic of the breaking of the covenant (cf. 15, RSV). Some commentators who are not committed to Kline's view nevertheless interpret the breaking of the tables in this way (Hertz, Alexander, Waller, *et al.*).[11]

Moses reminded the people of his intercession on their behalf. **The Lord** (12) knew all that was taking place at the foot of the mountain. His threat, **Let me alone, that I may destroy them** (14), was actually an invitation to intercession. Exodus states that Moses immediately interceded for the people and was heard by God. Nevertheless he made haste to descend **from the mount** (15) to take steps to put the people's sin away. If we lived close enough to God to tremble at His **hot displeasure** (19) against sin, how much more effective our intercession would be! The substance of Moses' intercession was that Israel was the Lord's people and heritage—an appeal to His love; that He had promised the land to the patriarchs—an appeal to His faithful-

[11]Kline, *op. cit.*, p. 74.

ness (27); and that the Egyptians would misunderstand His action—an appeal to the honor of His name (28).

Moses' intercession suggests "Persuasive Petitions": (1) Destroy not Thy people, 26; (2) Remember Thy servants, 27; (3) Safeguard Thy name, 28.

The other incidents to which Moses referred were at **Taberah** (22; Burning), where the people murmured (cf. Num. 11:1-3); **Massah** (Temptation, Trial; cf. comments on 6:16); **Kibroth-hattaavah** (the Graves of Lust), where the people lusted for flesh (Num. 11:4-35); and **Kadesh-barnea** (23; cf. comments on 1:19-46).

c. *God's renewal of the commandments* (10:1-11). It appears that the Lord supplied the first tables of stone for the commandments (Exod. 24:12). After the Israelites had broken the covenant, they, through Moses, were called upon to supply the **two tables of stone** for the renewal (1). In both instances, the Lord wrote the commandments on them. The **ark of wood** refers either to the ark later made by Bezaleel (Exod. 37:1) or to a temporary one made until the permanent ark was ready. **There they be** (5) fits in very appropriately with a speech made by Moses. The covenant had been renewed.

The next four verses are in the form of a historical insertion though they bear directly on the context. Apparently the journey from **Beeroth of the children of Jaakan** (6; Heb. *Bene*) is mentioned to lead up to **Mosera** (Chastisement), where Aaron died. Moseroth (pl.) is mentioned in Num. 33:30, but this account in Numbers seems to refer to a visit some time previous to Aaron's death. However, in the wilderness journeyings it seems that places were sometimes visited more than once. **Mosera** was probably at the foot of Mount Hor (see map 3). Aaron's death is mentioned to show the priestly succession. For **Gudgodah** (7) cf. Hor-hagidgad, Num. 33:32-33; and for **Jotbath,** cf. Jotbathah, Num. 33:33-34; these were in the same vicinity as **Beeroth** and **Mosera.**

At that time (8) refers, not to the death of Aaron, but to the rebellion at Horeb, when the Levites responded to the call of Moses (Exod. 32:26). The duties of the Levites are given in Num. 3:25-26, 30-31, 36-37. Besides their care of the Tabernacle they were expected generally to assist the priests and, probably at a later date, assist as choirs in worship. The duty of the Levites was to serve the Lord, for which they were freed from the cultivation of the land and provided with the tithes of the other tribes. This is the meaning of **the Lord is his inheritance** (9).

Though they were rebellious, God pardoned the people because of the intercession of Moses. **The Lord hearkened unto me . . . the Lord would not destroy thee** (10). In spite of the shocking episode of the golden calf, God renewed His promise of **the land** (11). The history of the covenant was a history of the failure of the people, and the continuing grace of God.

6. *Closing Exhortation* (10:12—11:32)

The section 5:1—11:32 reaches its climax in this magnificent exhortation.

a. God's requirements (10:12-22). Both Moses and Micah asked the question, **What doth the Lord thy God require of thee?** Micah answered it in terms of justice, mercy, and humble piety (Mic. 6:8). Moses puts supreme emphasis on the relationship to God. A total response is demanded and five things are required: (1) **fear,** awe at His deity; (2) **walk,** activity in His ways; (3) **love,** personal affection; (4) **serve,** dedication to His service; (5) **keep,** observance of His commandments (12-13). This would result in good for themselves and others. God's commandments lead to personal and social well-being for us as well as for Israel.

Immensity and condescension are wedded in 14-15. **Heaven,** remote and mysterious, and **earth,** very much with us and demanding, are both under God's sovereignty. Yet He is interested enough to "set his heart in love upon" (RSV) individuals and nations and to choose them to fulfill His purpose. Israel should therefore respond by ceasing to be obstinate, circumcising **the foreskin of the heart** (16). Here God clearly indicates that man can meet His requirements by yielding his heart fully to God and trusting Him to remove the hindrance (cf. 30:6).

What a revelation of God is given in vv. 17-18! Here we have sovereignty, immensity, power, awesomeness, and equity. How terrible if power and equity were divorced! "This demand to *love* the alien is without parallel in the legislation of any ancient people."[12] The life of Christ is a commentary on v. 18. The unfortunate and outcast always drew His compassion. Note the

[12]Hertz, *op. cit.*, p. 790.

relationship between God and His people. Because *He* loves **the stranger** (18), so must *His people,* helped by the memory of their own experience (19). For v. 20, cf. comments on 5:11; 6:13.

He is thy praise (21) may mean either "the object of your praise" or "your honour and glory." "It is an eternal honour to any soul to be in the friendship of God."[13] The exhortation closes with an appeal to history and experience (22). On **threescore and ten persons,** cf. Gen. 46:27.

b. Manifestations of God's power (11:1-7). Genuine **love** and obedience to **his commandments** (1) go together. Israel had good cause to both love and obey the One who had demonstrated His love in **miracles** and **acts** (3). Moses made a distinction between those who were old enough to remember the events of which he was about to speak and their **children** (2) who were born in the wilderness. **Chastisement** has the meaning of both education and correction.

Two miraculous acts of God are mentioned: the defeat of **the army of Egypt** (4), and the overthrow of **Dathan and Abiram** (6). They would represent both external and internal foes. **Unto this day** (4) probably means that Egypt had made no further attempt against the Israelites but had been decisively defeated. Korah is not mentioned, although he was one of the leaders of the rebellion (cf. Num. 16:1-35). This omission may be because his sons did not perish with him (Num. 26:11) as in the case of Dathan and Abiram and therefore the same total destruction did not overtake his family. It may also be because his descendants were present at the oration and Moses may have spared them the mention of their father's name.

c. Blessing or cursing (11:8-32). The theme that runs throughout the book is prominent at the close of this section: obedience brings blessing, and disobedience brings a curse (cf. c. 28). Here this theme is especially related to **the land.** If **the commandments** are kept, Israel will **possess the land** (8) and **prolong** his **days** there (9). **Egypt** is a notoriously dry land where irrigation is a major problem. **Wateredst it with thy foot** (10) may refer to the channeling of water with the foot, or the use of the foot in working irrigation machinery. Canaan, with its **hills** (11) in contrast to Egypt's plains, has an abundant rainfall. The **first rain** descends in October and November, just after the

[13]Clarke, *op. cit.*, p. 778.

sowing of the seed, and **the latter rain** comes in March and April to swell the grain (11-12, 14-15).

There is an outline here on "The Land of Canaan": (1) A land of plenty, 9; (2) A land with a difference, 10; (3) A land under heaven's smile, 11-12.

The statement that the rains are conditional on obedience (13-17) causes some difficulty. In the first place, Jesus declared that God sends the sunshine and the rain on both the just and the unjust (Matt. 5:45). Also, good Christian farmers have suffered through drought. It may well be that God used special methods in educating the elect race. However, most scholars would admit that obedience and well-being are connected, and that even nature serves moral ends. Faith affirms that blessing follows obedience, and if material prosperity is withheld, it is only that the blessing may be given in a deeper and more lasting form (cf. comments on 7:12-15).

Because the laws of God are the laws of survival, every means must be used to insure that they are not forgotten (18-20; cf. comments on 6:7-9). If they were obeyed, wherever the Israelites placed their **feet** would be their possession, and the frontiers were large enough to challenge faith (24; cf. comments on 1:7).

In 22-25 we see the theme "Possess the Land." (1) The condition for successful conquest is obedience to God, 22-23; (2) Continued obedience means permanent possession, 24; (3) Those who identify with God are the dread of their enemies. Resistance melts away in His presence, 25 (G. B. Williamson).

In order to enforce the alternative of blessing and cursing, a national drama was to be enacted, with **mount Gerizim** representing **blessing** and **mount Ebal** the **curse** (29; cf. comments on 27:11-26). They would be clearly visible from where Moses spoke, occupying a central position in the land **over against Gilgal** (30; probably not the Gilgal near Jericho, but Gilgal in the vicinity of Shechem), "beside the oaks of Moreh" (ERV). Here God had said to Abraham, "Unto thy seed will I give this land" (Gen. 12:7). **Champaign** would be flat, open country.

C. Other Commandments, 12:1—26:19

The second division of the main section of the book deals with the other commandments which, with the Decalogue, made up the corpus of laws for the land. The opening words of c. 12 make it clear that another phase of the subject is being introduced.

1. *Laws Concerning Religion* (12:1—16:17)

At the head of these laws are the regulations concerning the central sanctuary on which the main scholarly controversy concerning Deuteronomy has centered.

a. The central sanctuary (12:1-32). **The high mountains** and **the hills** (2) were the favorite places of worship among the Canaanites. They were probably chosen because of their supposed accessibility to the heavenly gods. The **green tree** would offer shade, besides being regarded as sacred. These sites proved a snare to the Israelites and became places of irregular and, more serious, idolatrous worship. Such practices were strongly condemned by the prophets (cf. Jer. 2:20; Ezek. 18:6; Hos. 4:13). All trace of Canaanitish worship was to be obliterated, including the **groves** (3; cf. comments on 7:5) and the **pillars** (*mazzebah,* lit., something "set up"). The latter were heathen symbols of the Canaanites (7:5; Exod. 23:24), alluded to as erected in or near temples of Baal (II Kings 3:2; 10:26-27) and in proximity to the Asherim, symbols of the Canaanite goddess Asherah (I Kings 14:23; II Kings 17:10).[14] It is possible that the pillar represented the male deity and the grove (Heb. *asherah*) the female deity. However, the word *mazzebah* can refer to a perfectly legitimate monument (e.g., Gen. 28:18; Exod. 24:4; Isa. 19:19).

Ye shall not do so unto the Lord your God (4). This refers to the multiplication of shrines by the Canaanites, as the following verse makes clear. Some rabbis, however, took it to refer to destroying the names of the false **gods** (3) and understood it to mean that the name of the Lord was not to be destroyed like that of heathen deities. This is why Hebrew books in which the sacred name occurs are reverently buried rather than destroyed when they can no longer be used.

The Israelites were to come **unto the place which the Lord your God shall choose out of all your tribes to put his name there** (5). To this place they were to bring **burnt offerings** and **sacrifices** (Leviticus, cc. 1—7), **tithes** (cf. comments on 14:22-29),

[14]Cf. Driver, *op. cit.,* pp. 203-4.

heave offerings (*terumah,* the priest's portion of sacrifices, Exod. 29:27-28; Lev. 7:14, 32; *et al.*), **vows** ("votive offerings," RSV), **freewill offerings** (a voluntary offering, as the name implies), **and the firstlings of your herds** and **flocks** (6; Exod. 13:12-13). This passage presupposes the teaching of the other books of the Pentateuch concerning the items mentioned in v. 6.

Nothing could be more natural than the teaching of this chapter concerning the central sanctuary. This had been no problem before. Ever since the deliverance from Egypt the nation had been a unit under the leadership of Moses. Now the leader was to be taken away, the land was to be entered and conquered, leaving women and children of three tribes on the eastern side of the Jordan. Already the campaigns against Sihon and Og and the settling of the women and children of Reuben, Gad, and half the tribe of Manasseh had disrupted the normal life of the nation and the closely knit pattern of government and worship. This is probably the meaning of v. 8. Moses envisaged that it would probably be some time before the regulations of the central sanctuary would be capable of regular fulfillment. **But when ye go over Jordan . . . and when he** (God) **giveth you rest from all your enemies round about** (10), **then there shall be a place** (11) to be the center of the worship and also a court of appeal and a place of guidance. This had been in mind from the beginning in the earliest days of the covenant. In its primary forms it had envisaged the appearing of every male before the Lord three times a year, at the Passover, Pentecost, and the Feast of Tabernacles (Exod. 23:14-17; 34:18-23). Now on the eve of entering the land the provision was made explicit.

The occasions of the visits were to be festivals of social intercourse and joy. Gladness is one of the characteristics of Deuteronomy (14:26; 16:11; 26:11). These times of holy fellowship would strengthen the faith of the individual and the unity of the nation. They would also safeguard against apostasy to false gods. The chief peril of the Israelites was that they might lapse into the practices of the Canaanites, use their shrines, build altars in their localities, and worship the Lord or even the local Baal with the rites of the Canaanites (cf. 29-31). Therefore regular sacrificial worship was confined to the central sanctuary (13-14).

Previously, all slaughter of beasts for food had been done at the Tabernacle. Meat was not part of the daily diet of the Israelite; it was something of an occasion when it was eaten. With the

Tabernacle so accessible, this presented no problem. Now the regulation was relaxed and the slaughter of beasts purely for food, not as an act of sacrifice (17-18, 26-28), was permitted—**Thou mayest kill and eat flesh in all thy gates** (15). The term **lusteth** here means "to desire." The only restriction, and it was an important one, was that **the blood** must not be eaten (16). **The blood is the life** (23). It was not to be eaten, for it belonged to God and normally was offered to Him on the altar. But lest it should be offered on a heathen altar, the command was given for it to be poured out **upon the earth as water** (24). This had been the practice in the case of wild animals such as the **roebuck** (22; "gazelle," ERV) **and the hart.** Also both **the clean** and **the unclean** were permitted to eat of domestic animals so killed, since they were not offered in sacrifice (15, 22).

How far did this law of the central sanctuary prohibit sacrifice elsewhere? It certainly prohibited the ordinary individual from erecting an altar according to his inclination (13). But provision was made in the early form of the covenant for "an altar of earth" to be made for the sacrifice of "burnt offerings" and "peace offerings." And God gave the assurance that, in every place where He recorded His name, He would come and bless (Exod. 20:24). In the case of "an altar of stone," it had to be unhewn stone (Exod. 20:25). In 27:5-7, Moses commanded that an altar of this description should be built on Mount Ebal and "burnt offerings" and "peace offerings" be offered upon it. The Tabernacle was still in existence with the brasen altar and these would undoubtedly be part of the central sanctuary.

It seems that, while altars could not be erected according to the individual's inclination, an inspired prophet or authorized leader could erect one and use it in special circumstances. This was also obviously true in the case of a theophany (a special appearance of God; cf. Judg. 6:25-26; 13:15-20; II Sam. 24:17-18). There was the time, in the absence of the central sanctuary at Shiloh, when Samuel sacrificed at different altars (I Sam. 7:9; 9:12; 16:5). Also in the time of the divided kingdom, Elijah rebuilt an altar on Mount Carmel (I Kings 18:30-31).

It was recognized in the regulations for the central sanctuary that certain conditions were required for their proper fulfillment: **rest from all your enemies round about, so that ye dwell in safety** (10). This was said to be the condition of Israel on three occasions: at the close of the conquests under Joshua

(Josh. 23:1); in the time of David (II Sam. 7:1); and in the time of Solomon (I Kings 5:4), in whose reign the Temple was built. Unhappily, the kingdom was divided in his son's reign.

As stated in the introduction, those who adhere to a modified form of the Wellhausen hypothesis insist that the explicit regulations for a central sanctuary are a distinct advance on Exod. 20:22—23:33, and at variance with it. They claim that the explanation is that Deuteronomy is several centuries later than the Exodus passage, which is assigned to what they call the Elohistic source. There is a tendency today among scholars of this persuasion to see a far greater similarity between Exod. 20: 22—23:33 and Deuteronomy 12 than previously they would admit. They also concede that the idea and existence of a central sanctuary was present in Israel from the first. This seems a trend in the right direction.

The interpretation given above is in keeping with conservative scholarship, with the general tenor of Scripture and a high view of its inspiration.[15]

b. Apostasy (13:1-18). This chapter deals with three cases of possible apostasy.

(1) The first is through **a prophet, or a dreamer of dreams** (1-5). Both of these were classes of persons through whom the Lord communicated His will to His people (cf. Num. 12:6). They existed also in the heathen religions. In Israel, as in the case envisaged, there were false prophets who for various reasons spoke contrary to the will of the Lord (cf. I Kings 22:6, 8, 20-23; Jer. 6:13; 28:1-17). It is conceded in the text that it was possible for a false prophet to give **a sign or a wonder** which would be fulfilled; in other words, to do something which appeared to be supernatural or miraculous.

The Lord would permit this to test His people's **love** and loyalty (3). The test that they were to apply to the prophet was not whether he could perform the spectacular but whether he adhered to the law of God (2). We may well take to heart this evidence of a true prophet (cf. Isa. 8:19-20). The danger is fore-

[15]For a good, concise statement of the conservative position cf. G. Ch. Aalders, *A Short Introduction to the Pentateuch* (London: Tyndale Press, 1949), c. xi, and Hertz, *op. cit.*, pp. 939-41. For the modified Wellhausen position cf. Driver, *op. cit.*, pp. 136-50 and Gerhard von Rad, *Deuteronomy* (London: SCM Press, 1966), pp. 89-94.

stalled with a negative warning (3) reinforced by a positive command: **Ye shall walk after the Lord your God, and fear him, and keep his commandments, and obey his voice, and ye shall serve him, and cleave unto him** (4). The real safeguard against backsliding is total commitment to God. **The Lord** comes first in the original and the pronoun **him** is first in each clause. The emphasis of the life should be on *Him.* A fully consecrated, cleansed, and Spirit-filled life is the best defense against sin, as an active, healthy body is the best defense against disease.

There is a warning here also against a too credulous attitude toward those holding official positions. Officers within the church are entitled to respect and support insofar as they are loyal to God and His Word. But Deuteronomy, the layman's guide, makes it clear that even one whose office calls for respect may fail in his responsibility (cf. Aaron, 9:20-21). If he departs from the revealed will of God, his authority is to be rejected.

The false **prophet** or **dreamer of dreams** must be **put to death** because he is guilty of attempting to entice the people from loyalty to their God and their Redeemer. The false leaders try to **thrust** the people **out of** God's **way** of life (5). In the RSV, the rendering is "because he has taught rebellion against the Lord your God." Kline states that in the ancient suzerainty treaties (cf. Intro. and comments on 9:7-17) it was required of the vassal that he must not connive at evil words spoken against the suzerain. In the case of active rebellion the suzerain must undertake military measures against the offenders. Moreover the vassal must manifest fidelity to his lord in such cases, no matter who the offender might be, whether prince or nearest relative.[16]

(2) This brings us to the second case of possible apostasy: through a relative or friend (6-11). The first temptations was envisaged as coming through one with religious authority. These verses deal with instances of seduction through natural affection. This seems to have been the cause of Adam's fall. He was not deceived by the serpent's lie (cf. I Tim. 2:14) but seems to have yielded to the persuasion of the wife he loved; cf. **the wife of thy bosom** (6). Note the intimacy of the relationships: **the son of thy mother,** a much closer relationship than the son of the same father but different mothers in the case of plural

[16]*Op. cit.,* p. 84.

wives; **thy friend, which is as thine own soul.** The prophet *says* (2); the beloved associate *entices.*

It matters not what the degree of the temptation is, it must be rejected. Throughout Deuteronomy the false religions in the land are regarded as the greatest threat (cf. 6:14; 7:1-5; 12:2-3; 20:15-18). False gods, wherever they may be, divide the dedication which belongs to the Lord alone and must be utterly rejected. Not only must the outward act be refused, but also inward **consent** (8) or the slightest sign of a sympathetic hearing. If it is a choice between repudiating God or the most beloved associate, there must be no hesitation. God must be cleaved to (4) and the relative or friend exposed. This assumes that the associate persists in his apostasy, for undoubtedly the one who is the object of the seduction would be expected to try to win him back to the God of Israel before delivering him up. Even though it is known that exposure will mean death, the death of a loved one must be accepted rather than conniving at treachery against God. **Thou shalt stone him with stones** (10) was the usual Hebrew form of execution.

Christ makes the same supreme demand on the allegiance of His disciples as God does in these verses (cf. Matt. 10:34-39). This is one of the evidences of His deity, for only God has such a supreme right. As Creator, His claims take precedence over all His gifts in creation: material, mental, or personal.

(3) The third source of apostasy was through **children of Belial** (13), i.e., "sons of worthlessness." "The term [is] repeatedly used in scripture for abandoned criminals, *base* in word, thought and action."[17] There is no pretext in this case. It is a high-handed flinging off of restraint and embracing of a religion that panders to the lower nature. This is much in evidence today when evil practices which belong to the dark ages of the human race are being shamelessly advocated by those with "progressive" views. In the case in point, it is assumed that the whole **city** readily consents to this defiant rebellion against the God of Israel.

(4) The execution of justice (14-18). What is of particular interest in this case is the scrupulous care which must be exercised to establish beyond doubt that such an apostasy has taken place before the judgment is executed. They must **enquire,**

[17]Hertz, *op. cit.*, p. 807. Cf. also p. 808 on v. 17.

and make search, and ask diligently (14). Only if it is established that the charge is true and certain must radical action be taken. If we would be as scrupulously fair to our brethren when gossip is circulated about them and refuse to believe anything detrimental to their characters unless it is established beyond doubt, backbiters would have a lean time.

The fate prescribed for the apostate **city** (15) is a terrible one. It is to be "put to the ban" (*cherem*), destroyed **utterly** with **all that is therein.**

Two points are worthy of notice. First, no advantage is to accrue to the executors of the sentence. Heresy hunting is not to be made a profitable occupation, as alas too often it was in the middle ages. **And there shall cleave nought of the cursed thing to thine hand** (17). Cf. Achan (Joshua 7). Secondly, the Israelites must administer the same severe treatment to those of their own number as they are called upon to mete out to the Canaanites if their own communities identify themselves with the practices of the Canaanites. Cf. the fate of Gibeah and its surrounding cities (Judg. 20:37, 48).

Three reasons are given for taking drastic action with inveterate apostates. First, **so shalt thou put the evil away from the midst of thee** (5). Secondly, as a deterrent to others: **And all Israel shall hear, and fear, and shall do no more any such wickedness as this is among you** (11). Firm and fearless action at the right time can nip evil in the bud. It is said that Kerensky, the liberal Russian leader, could have scattered the Bolsheviks with a whiff of grapeshot if he had fired it at the psychological moment. Thirdly, **That the Lord may turn from the fierceness of his anger, and shew thee mercy . . . and multiply thee** (17). If we want God's blessing, we must eliminate from our midst the things that cause Him grief.

The whole setting of this chapter fits the time of Moses and the pre-monarchic period. It is another evidence of the authenticity of the book.

c. *Clean and unclean food* (14:1-21). The purpose of this section is indicated in the two opening verses. Because **ye are the children of the Lord** (1), practices inconsistent with such a privileged relationship must be shunned. The cutting of the flesh and the hair of the forehead in connection with the dead "had heathen associations, and may have been designed to help in concluding a covenant with the departed, at whose grave the shed blood or cut hair might be offered."[18]

In like manner Israel is described as "a people holy to the Lord . . . chosen . . . to be a people for his own possession" (2, RSV). Therefore the Israelites must **not eat any abominable thing** (3).

In some cases the animals listed were unfit for human consumption and in these instances the rules may be regarded as dietary laws to safeguard the health of the Lord's people. In other cases the reason for the prohibition is not readily apparent. The Jews regarded keeping the dietary laws as having two values over and above health reasons. First, the laws separated them from the other nations and made manifest their elect character. Second, they gave an opportunity for the exercising of faith in and obedience to the divine statutes, which transcended human reasoning. In the NT dispensation they no longer apply (Mark 7:19; Rom. 14:14; I Tim. 4:4), though common sense in the care of the body, the temple of the Holy Spirit (I Cor. 6:19), will dictate avoidance of harmful food.

The clean beasts were classified as those that part **the hoof** and chew **the cud** (6). Permission was given to eat fish with **fins and scales** (9). The list commences with the domestic animals, followed by game permissible for diet. Prohibited animals are listed in vv. 7-8. Prohibited **birds** are mentioned in 12-18, and **every creeping thing** is forbidden in v. 19. The RSV is more reliable in identifying the creatures listed than the KJV, but not all those referred to can be identified with certainty.

For obvious health reasons any animal dying **of itself** (21) should be avoided, though apparently there were foreigners both within and outside of the borders of Israel who were not so particular.

The prohibition to **seethe a kid in his mother's milk** (21) is regarded by some scholars to be based on humanitarian principles. Others incline to the opinion that it refers to a Canaanitish ritual, probably a fertility charm.

d. Tithes (14:22-29). The regulations for tithing in these verses are plain and straightforward. Each year **the increase of**

[18]W. J. Moulton, "The Social Institutions of Israel," *Commentary on the Whole Bible*, ed. A. S. Peake (London: T. Nelson and Sons, 1948), p. 110.

the seed sown in their fields had to be tithed by the Israelites; i.e., a tenth of it set aside for a special purpose. This with **the firstlings** of the **herds** and the **flocks** had to be taken to the central sanctuary and eaten in a religious feast **before the Lord** (23). If the central sanctuary was **too far** (24) from the home of the tither, he was permitted to sell the tenth of his produce and the firstlings of his herds and flocks and with **the money** purchase whatever he desired for the feast at the sanctuary (25-26). In this feast **the Levite** (27) had a share.

Every third year, **the tithe** (28) and firstlings were laid up **within** the **gates** of the tither to provide a feast for **the Levite . . . and the stranger, and the fatherless, and the widow** (29).

Since every seventh year the ground was allowed to lie fallow (Lev. 25:1-7), there would be no tithing during that year.

In Num. 18:21, 24, it is clearly stated that the Levites should receive the tithe from their brother Israelites. The question arises, How can the regulations of Deuteronomy be reconciled with this statement? Broadly speaking, there are two views. Some think that the regulations in Deuteronomy refer to the official presentation of the tithe which takes place in a ceremonial feast which the tither and his family share with the Levite. This takes place in the tither's locality every third year, and **the stranger, the fatherless,** and **the widow** share in the feast too. On each occasion, the Levite retains the bulk of the tithe which remains after the religious feast.

The Jewish view is that the provisions in these verses refer to a second tithe over and above the first tithe, which was given in full to the Levite according to Num. 18:21, 24. This means that almost a fifth of the income is given in tithes, but most of the second tithe, apart from every third year, is consumed by the tither and his family. This is not only a theoretical opinion on the passage, but has been a practice among the Jews.

If Jews living under the law could so acknowledge the sovereignty of God in the disposal of their income, how readily should a Christian give regularly, proportionately, and gladly in the light of God's unspeakable Gift!

e. Release for debtors (15:1-11). The word **release** (2) means to remit a debt, as here, or to let ground lie fallow, as in Exod. 23:11, both of which were commanded for the seventh year.

The remission of debts on this occasion was limited to the fellow Israelite, **neighbour** and **brother.** This privilege was not to be extended to the **foreigner** (3; *nokri,* a member of another nation who in this case has commercial relations with Israel). The **foreigner** is distinct from the stranger in 14:29 ("sojourner," RSV, Heb. *ger*). This "stranger" belongs to another race but has made his home in Israel.

The context of these verses is the conditions of an agricultural community in which debt is incurred because of poverty. It does not apply to a commercial nation where credit is an essential part of the economy. When conditions changed, Hillel in the first century A.D. modified the regulations here to apply to a commercial community.

Some scholars hold the view that no more is intended in these provisions than that the creditor should not press his claim for the payment of the debt during the seventh year, when the land of his debtor would be lying fallow.[19] But Jewish interpreters understand it as a literal discharge of debt; in this they are supported by the majority of scholars. It is assumed that, should circumstances change, the debtor would be free to repay the amount loaned to him, but the creditor would not be able to enforce collection of it.

There is no inconsistency between v. 4, **Save when there shall be no poor among you,** and v. 11, **For the poor shall never cease out of the land.** Moffatt renders vv. 4-5, "Though indeed there should be no poor among you (for the Eternal your God will prosper you in the land which the Eternal your God assigns to you as your own possession), provided that you are attentive to the voice of the Eternal your God, and mindful to obey all these commands laid down by me today." Ideally there should be no poor in the land if Israel is fully obedient. But Moses' past experience caused him to doubt whether the condition would be fulfilled, and therefore to legislate for the poor. If Israel indeed would give wholehearted obedience to the Lord's commands, not only would there be no poor in the land, but she would be a creditor—**Thou shalt lend unto many nations** (6). There have been fulfillments of this promise in such eras as the reigns of David and Solomon. When the Israelites were driven from agriculture into finance, they exercised great power as

[19]Cf. Alexander, *op. cit.,* p. 253.

financiers, though how far this was because of their obedience to the law is open to question.

Two characteristics of Deuteronomy are present in these verses: a concern for the poor and an emphasis upon the attitude of the heart. **Thou shalt not harden thine heart, nor shut thine hand from thy poor brother** (7). As Matthew Henry puts it, "If the hand be shut, it is a sign the heart is hardened."[20]

Moses is quick to anticipate an attempt on the part of the selfish to forestall the benefits of this humane legislation. Some will consider not their brother's need, but the possibility of repayment. A refusal to lend because **the year of release, is at hand** (9) is attributed to "a base thought in your heart" (9, RSV). A base thought entertained in the heart can issue in a base act, bringing guilt before God and sowing the seed of a base character. Ungrudging giving will bring divine blessing on **all our works** (10).

Perhaps Jesus had this chapter in mind when He uttered the words recorded in Luke 6:30-36.

In these verses we see "Heart and Attitude." (1) The hardened heart and the shut hand, 7; (2) The wicked heart and the evil eye, 9; (3) The ungrudging heart (RSV) and the wide-open, God-blessed hand, 10-11.

f. Release for slaves (15:12-18). Slavery was a part of the contemporary environment, but the Mosaic legislation modified its rigors and provided for its termination on generous terms. These verses are an amplification of Exod. 21:1-6. The woman slave is included as well as the man (Exod. 21:7-11 refers to the special case of a father selling his daughter for betrothal).

After serving **six years** (12), the slave shall be given his discharge **in the seventh.** This does not appear to refer to the sabbatical year as in the case of debts, but to any period of seven years from the time of the commencement of service. According to v. 14, with gifts from his master's **flock, floor,** and **winepress,** the discharged slave would be able to commence life anew with sufficient to make him independent. The master is given a threefold motive for so treating him: first, because he himself has been generously treated by **the Lord** (14); second, he, or rather his

[20]*An Exposition of the Old and New Testament* (London: James Nisbet and Co., 1857), I, 787.

forefathers, were slaves in **Egypt, and the Lord . . . redeemed** them (15); and third, in having his former slave as a permanent member of his household, he has received twice the benefit of a **hired servant** (18), who worked only specified hours.

Provision was made for the slave to stay if he wished to do so (16-17). In such a case, on confession of love for his master and his household, he received the mark of lifelong love-slavery at the threshold of his master's house. This custom included the female slave as well as the male—**Unto thy maidservant thou shalt do likewise** (17). Perhaps Paul was referring to this custom when he said, "I bear in my body the marks of the Lord Jesus" (Gal. 6:17). There are scars which may be received in the Master's service.

There are three characteristics of "God's Love Slave." (1) His determination: **I will not go away from thee;** (2) His motive: **because he loveth thee and thine house;** (3) His reason: **because he is well with thee,** 16.

g. The firstlings (15:19-23). It is here emphasized that the firstborn **males** of the **herd** and **flock** (19) must be dedicated to **the Lord** to be used according to His commandment. There must be no tampering with the dedication by using the firstborn **bullock** in the **work** of the farm nor by taking the wool of the firstborn **sheep** for the use of the household. If there was **any blemish** (21) in the firstborn animal, it must be treated as ordinary livestock. It could be eaten as common meat, the only condition attaching to it being the pouring out of its **blood** on the **ground** (23; cf. 12:23). Thus the Lord's people were taught to consecrate only the best to God and to consecrate it entirely.

Thou shalt eat it before the Lord (20). In Num. 18:17-18, the firstlings are given to the priests, and it is the opinion of some that the words **thou and thy household** refer to them.[21] Other scholars take these words to refer to the second tithe (cf. comments on 14:22-29).

Thou shalt eat it . . . year by year. "I.e. the offering must not be delayed beyond a year. This is not at variance with what was stated in Exodus xxii 29-30 'on the eighth day thou shalt give it Me', for the Mechilta explains that to mean from the eighth day onwards; cf. Lev. xxii 27."[22]

[21]Hertz, *op. cit.*, p. 814.

[22]*Ibid.*

h. The national gatherings (16:1-17). The feasts described in this chapter are the three feasts that were to be celebrated at the central sanctuary when Israel was settled in the land. They are referred to in terms similar to v. 16 in Exod. 23:14-17; 34: 18-23. For the full list of feasts see Lev. 23:1-44 and Num. 28:16—29:40.

(1) *The passover and feast of unleavened bread* (1-8). The word **Abib** (1) means "the green ears of corn." After the Babylonian exile the name of the month was changed to Nisan. It is equivalent to March—April in our calendar. The purpose of **the passover** was to remind the Israelites of the fateful night in Egypt when the Lord smote the firstborn of the Egyptians and saved the firstborn of Israel through the blood of a lamb. The reference to **the flock and the herd** (2) is probably to the lamb or the kid for the Passover sacrifice and to the bullocks for the festival sacrifice (cf. Num. 28:16-19). However, some scholars think that, while a lamb or a kid was specified at the first Passover, the rule was relaxed in Deuteronomy. **Roast** (7; *bishshel*) is translated "boil" in RSV. It can have this meaning, though it is also used in the general sense of "cook." In Exod. 12:8 emphasis is laid upon the lamb being roasted. In the celebration of the Passover recorded in II Chron. 35:1-19, it is stated "and they roasted [the same verb as in Deut. 16:7] the passover lamb with fire according to the ordinance; and they boiled [same word] the holy offerings [the bullocks] in pots, in caldrons, and in pans" (II Chron. 35:13, RSV).

The Passover was to be eaten with **unleavened bread** (3), reminiscent of the **affliction** of the Egyptian slavery and the **haste** with which they left the land. **Six days shalt thou eat unleavened bread: and on the seventh day shall be a solemn assembly** (8) means six days plus the seventh were days on which unleavened bread was eaten, seven in all (cf. 3-4).

At the first Passover, the lamb was killed and its blood applied to the lintel and doorposts of the dwellings. However, when settled in the land of Canaan the Israelites were to assemble at the central sanctuary (2, 5-6).

For the significance of the Passover for a Christian, cf. I Cor. 5:6-8.

(2) *The feast of weeks* (9-12). This feast was to be held **seven weeks** (50 days, hence the Gk. word "Pentecost," "fifty")

after the beginning of the barley harvest. This was calculated from the presentation of the sheaf of the firstfruits on the sixteenth of Abib (cf. Lev. 23:4-11). It was to be a time of grateful, joyous, and compassionate giving, with an eye on the past to promote gratitude and obedience (12). The feast was to be observed at the central sanctuary—**the place which the Lord thy God hath chosen** (11).

(3) *The feast of tabernacles* (13-15). This festival celebrated the final ingathering, not only of the harvest of barley and wheat, but of the vineyards and the fruit trees (13). For **seven days** (13) a feast of rejoicing and thanksgiving was held, the most joyous of all Israel's festivals. All were to partake in this feast: the family and the household, **the Levite, the stranger, and the fatherless, and the widow** (14).

Verses 16-17 recapitulate the teaching of the previous verses.

In this section note the "Pattern of Religious Conventions": (1) They should recall fundamental truths, 1, 3, 6, 12; (2) They should be times of grateful joy, 11, 14; (3) They should be opportunities for grateful giving, 10, 17.

2. *Laws Concerning Government* (16:18—21:23)

From religious laws the theme of the book passes on to laws concerning government. It begins with those who are to administer the law.

a. Officials (16:18—18:22). We have already been informed of the duty of judges (1:16-18). Now additional information is given.

(1) *Judges* (16:18—17:7). Provision is made for **judges and officers** (18; cf. comments on 1:15) to be appointed in the various localities of the land. The gate was the place where the elders of a city sat and important matters were dealt with. But here **in all thy gates** probably means no more than a city or town (cf. 5, 11, 14). The method of appointment is not stated but it would probably be on the principle observed in 1:13-15. In 1:16-17 similar instructions were given to the judges as here. At this point special emphasis is laid on refusing bribes, the greatest evil in corrupting the administration of justice. Bribes can blind and pervert even **the wise** (19) and **the righteous** (or subvert "the cause of the righteous," RSV). Moffatt translates the first part

of 20, "Justice, justice you must aim at."[23] This sums up the tenor of the OT messages regarding civil and social relationships.

The command to appoint judges is followed by three cases of religious offenses. The first is a prohibition to "plant any tree as an Asherah [cf. comments on 7:5] beside the altar of the Lord your God which you shall make" (21, RSV; cf. comments on 12:3). Verse 21 is fatal to the theory that Deuteronomy was written in the century before Josiah's revival, with a view to centralizing all worship in Jerusalem. Here, obviously, some altars were permitted besides the central sanctuary.

The second religious offense mentioned is the sacrificing to the Lord of any **bullock, or sheep** (17:1) with any defect (cf. comments on 15:19-23).

The third offense is the case of apostasy (17:2-7). Normally, religious issues are not dealt with by civil judges, but in a theocracy where God is King, religious offenses are an affront to the Sovereign, and offenders may be liable to capital punishment. Hence they would come under the jurisdiction of the judge. In the case of apostasy care was to be taken in making certain that the charge was proved beyond doubt (4; cf. comments on 13:14). There must be **two . . . or three witnesses** (6; cf. I Tim. 5:19), and grave responsibility was laid upon them (7).

(2) *The supreme court* (17:8-13). If the local judges could not come to a decision, they must go to the central sanctuary—**the place which the Lord thy God shall choose** (8). These cases might be **blood and blood** (homicide), **plea and plea** (civil actions), or **stroke and stroke** (assault). At the central sanctuary the Levitical **priests** (cf. comments on 18:1) and **the judge** (9; the chief judge, e.g., Joshua, Gideon, Samuel) would try the case and give a verdict in keeping with the law (cf. II Chron. 19:5-11). This verdict was to be final and anyone **presumptuously** refusing to abide by it was guilty of a capital offense (12; cf. comments on 1:43).

(3) *The king* (17:14-20). This passage fits the time of Moses on the eve of entering **the land** (14) as it fits no other time. The monarchy is treated as a permitted institution but not commanded; it was a concession to the people's desire to be **like** the **nations** round **about.** For by far the greater part of her history,

[23]Cf. an extended note on the Hebrew conception of justice. *Ibid.*, pp. 820-21.

Israel existed as a nation without a king. The **king** (15) must avoid the vices of the oriental monarchs: love of power (16), women and wealth (17). It was the second of these which caused Solomon's downfall (I Kings 11:1-13), and by multiplying **horses** he entered into commercial relations with Egypt (16; cf. I Kings 10:28-29). The king had to write for himself a copy of the law, probably Deuteronomy but possibly the entire Pentateuch. He was to read it constantly and observe it, in order that he might have a long reign and be succeeded by his children. He was to be chosen from his **brethren** (15) and remain a brother, though a king (20). He must be God's choice (15), probably expressed through His servants the prophets and endorsed by the people (cf. I Sam. 10:24; 16:11-13; II Sam. 5:1-3; II Kings 9:1-13).

(4) *Priests and Levites* (18:1-8). The consideration of various officials responsible for administering the divine will throughout the nation continues with **the priests** and **the Levites** (1). **The priests** are properly included in such a context. The modern distinction between sacred and secular was foreign to the ancient Israelite, who regarded the whole of life as being grounded in God and therefore amenable to divine control. This explains the otherwise bewildering ease with which the book moves from religious to civil regulations and back again. Here this general characteristic is illustrated—the priest is associated with the judge in the administration of justice (17:9).

The priests are described here and in various other places in Deuteronomy (e.g., 17:9, 18; 21:5; 24:8; 27:9) as **the priests the Levites** (1) or "the priests the sons of Levi." It is a standard point with Wellhausen[24] and his followers that this implies that all Levites were priests. This position is a material contradiction of the rest of the Pentateuch (e.g., Lev. 1:5-9), according to which the priests were drawn solely from the sons of Aaron. All priests were Levites but not all Levites were priests. This so-called "discrepancy" is then used by Wellhausen to support the conclusion that the Levites were demoted from the position they held in Deuteronomy, and consequently the Levitical law must be later rather than contemporary with Deuteronomy, as it claims to be.

Admittedly, there are obscurities in the relationship between priests and Levites. Here as elsewhere the law was not

[24]*Prolegomena to the History of Ancient Israel* (New York: Meridian Books, 1957), c. iv.

always observed to the letter, either through rank disobedience or because of the political exigencies of the time. Consequently it is perilous to seek to deduce the law from Israelite practice.[25]

Nothing in the immediate context requires the conclusion that all Levites were priests. The phrase itself does not, and the fact that the passage proceeds to legislate separately for the needs of the **Levite** (6) demonstrates that in the mind of the author the two roles were distinct. The usage of other OT writers who recognized the distinction confirms this (e.g., II Chron. 30:27, cf. 25; Mal. 3:3). Consequently in v. 1 the second phrase, **all the tribe of Levi,** is to be interpreted, not as an equivalent, but as an expansion of **the priests the Levites** (KJV and ERV marg. are to be preferred to ERV and RSV).[26] From the side of archaeology, after an examination of the relevant data, Albright concludes: "We are not justified . . . in throwing overboard the standard Israelite tradition regarding priests and Levites."[27]

The purpose of this passage (18:1-8) is to provide for the material support of the priests and the entire tribe of Levi. Since this tribe was dedicated to the service of God, Levi was apportioned no territorial area of Palestine as were the other tribes, but was given **the Lord** (2) for its **inheritance.** What this meant in practice was that the Levites should share in the offerings made to the Lord.

Having laid down the general principle (1-2), the author defines in turn the respective shares of the priests and the Levites. The parts of the sacrifices allotted to the priests differ from those named in Lev. 7:30-34. There is nothing inherently surprising in this. As is now widely recognized, the basic pattern of Deuteronomy is that of an ancient suzerainty treaty.[28] Its life

[25]For an examination of alleged violations of the law see W. H. Green, *The Higher Criticism of the Pentateuch* (London: Richard D. Dickinson, 1895), pp. 150-54.

[26]This rendering is perfectly in accordance with the Hebrew. See G. E. Wright, IB, II, 444.

[27]*Archaeology and the Religion of Israel* (Baltimore: The Johns Hopkins Press, 3rd ed., 1953), p. 110. For fuller treatments of the relation of the priests and the Levites, see J. Orr, *The Problem of the Old Testament* (London: James Nisbet and Co., 1906), pp. 184-90; and D. A. Hubbard, "Priests and Levites," NBD, pp. 1028-34.

[28]E.g., M. G. Kline, *op. cit.*, c. 2; E. W. Nicholson, *Deuteronomy and Tradition* (Oxford: Basil Blackwell, 1967), pp. 78-79.

setting is the renewal of the covenant between God and Israel in view of the impending death of the mediator, Moses. At such renewals "new documents were prepared in which the stipulations were brought up to date. Deuteronomy is such a covenant renewal document; hence its repetition with modernizing modifications of the earlier legislation."[29] As to why this particular alteration was made, it has been plausibly suggested that it was to avoid confusion with Canaanite heathen practice according to which the right shoulder was the priest's portion.[30]

Despite the subordinate character of their duties (see 10:8) similar provision was made for **a Levite** (6) who came to serve at the Lord's altar.[31] The provision was made quite apart from any revenue accruing from the sale of personal (as opposed to tribal) inheritance (8; cf. Jer. 32:6-15).

It is significant that thus early in the history of God's people provision should be made for the support of His ministers. Paul appealed to the law to sustain his rights in this connection even though he declined to exercise them (I Cor. 9:8-18). The passage under review establishes (1) The principle, 1-2; (2) The method, 3-4; and (3) The measure, 8, of such support.

(5) *The prophet* (18:9-22). A crucial question throughout the history of religion has been: How may the will of God be known? It was particularly important that it be answered for the Israelites before they entered Canaan, because after they arrived they would find many other answers which accorded ill with the faith they now held. Against this background three points were made:

(*a*) They were not to be guided on this point by current Canaanite practice (9-14). The abysmal depths to which **those nations** (9) had sunk[32] are aptly indicated by the examples listed. There were child sacrifice—making one's **son** or **daughter to pass through the fire** (10; cf. 12:29-31)—sorcery, and necromancy. Where reason gave no guidance, man has sought light in

[29]Kline, *op. cit.*, p. 20.

[30]*Ibid.*, p. 100. For other possible explanations see Driver, *op. cit.*, pp. 215-16.

[31]On the meaning of **the place which the Lord shall choose** (6), cf. comments on 12:5.

[32]"The sedentary culture which they encountered in the thirteenth century seems to have reflected the lowest religious level in all Canaanite history" (Albright, *op. cit.*, p. 94).

the nonrational. But Israel's God is the God of rationality, who will make His will plain in a moral, not a magical, way.

(*b*) The way in which **the Lord** (15) will guide His people is through His servants the prophets (15-19). Just as Moses was the divine intermediary at **Horeb** (16), so he will be succeeded by others who will fulfill the same role. That it is a succession of prophets rather than a single individual that is in mind is made plain by the test of the true **prophet** (20-22). More than one is plainly implied. The task of the prophet is to be the mouthpiece of God—**He shall speak . . . all that I shall command him** (18; cf. Exod. 7:1-2). The mediator of the covenant is also and in the same act the revealer of the divine will. The prophets are repeatedly presented in this role, summoning Israel back to her allegiance to God (see I Sam. 11:14—12:25; I Kings 18:19-39).[33]

However, it is more than simply a succession of prophets that is promised. This is made equally plain by 34:10, which evidently glances back to this passage.[34] Other prophets have arisen since Moses' death but none who knew the Lord as directly as he. From then on Israel repeatedly looked for "that prophet" (e.g., John 1:21; 7:40). They did not find him till they found Him whose glory was "as of the only begotten of the Father" (John 1:14), who was himself "the brightness of his glory, and the express image of his person" (Heb. 1:3; cf. Acts 3:22-23).

(*c*) If there were true and false ways of seeking knowledge of the divine will, there were also true and false prophets. How could one tell the difference? A test is supplied: nonfulfillment of prediction is the mark of a false prophet: **If the thing follow not, nor come to pass . . . the Lord hath not spoken** (22). This indeed is not the only mark. The question had already arisen and the fundamental principle had been laid down that no prophet who tried to lead Israel after other gods was true (see 13:1-5). For Moses, the chief part of revealing the divine will consisted in guiding the life of the community. But another and yet related part of the prophetic ministry lay in the unfolding of things to come, as it also did for Moses. Here this further test would find its place.

[33]For documentation of the covenant role of the prophets see Nicholson, *op. cit.*, pp. 78-79.

[34]See F. F. Bruce, art. "Messiah," NBD, pp. 812-14, on the Messiah as the Antitype of Moses.

The word of God to His ancient people speaks powerfully to our condition still. The real theme of these verses is the age-old question, How can man find God? In reply two points are made: (1) The frustration of man's search for God, 9-14. "The secret things belong unto the Lord our God" (29:29) and man cannot by searching find them out. (2) God's self-revelation of himself to man, 15-19: partially and progressively through the prophets, fully and finally through His Son (Acts 3:22-23; Heb. 1:1-2). Particularly striking is the disclosure of the standard which God expects of man: **Thou shalt be perfect with the Lord thy God** (13). It is impossible to improve upon Manley's comment: "The command to be perfect is given (Gen. 17:1; Matt. 5:48) because God can ask for nothing less. Absolute perfection is unattainable by sinful man, but it is possible to have a perfect heart (I Kings 11:4; Col. 2:10)."[35]

b. *Laws for nation and family* (19:1—21:23). Having dealt with various administrators of justice, Moses turned to the task of making detailed applications. These laws are a mixture of statutes and judgments (4:1). Statutes are in the form of "thou shalt" and "thou shalt not." Judgments, or case laws, are phrased, "If a man . . ." These types are common in the treaty-covenants and laws of the Ancient Near East.[36]

(1) *Justice for the defenseless* (19:1-21). The three examples are of unequal length but equally important. They reflect the needs and standards of an early society.

(*a*) *Justice for the unintentional killer* (1-13). In ancient Israel, as in other societies in which state organization was at a simple stage, the right of blood revenge lay with the kin of the deceased. Far from being vengeance, this was a safeguard of the sanctity of life. As such, the present law was not concerned with abolishing it—the willful murderer was still to **die** at the hands **of the avenger of blood** (12). This legislation was concerned with curbing unjust applications of blood revenge. Chief among these was the possibility that an outraged relative might exact retribution from an unintentional killer (4-6). The **helve** (5) would be the "handle" (RSV).

To guard against such miscarriage of justice, places of refuge

[35]*Op. cit.*, p. 213.

[36]K. A. Kitchen, *Ancient Orient and the Old Testament* (London: Tyndale Press, 1966), p. 147.

were provided where the killer might find sanctuary until the case could be investigated. In the earliest times the altar was such a place (Exod. 21:14). But in the changed circumstances of Canaan, in which one could be many miles from the central altar (see v. 6), further provision was needed. This God had promised (Exod. 21:13;[37] Num. 35:9-29) and partly provided (Deut. 4:41-43). Orders are now given for **three cities** of refuge (2-3, 7) with the possibility to **add three . . . more** (9). To the willful murderer, however, they afford no protection (11-13). In such cases justice must be done by **the elders of his** own **city** handing the criminal over for execution (12).

(*b*) *Justice for the landowner* (14). In a society in which wealth was based on land ownership, it was important, especially for the poor, that possession should be guaranteed. This was done by the use of marking-stones on which the boundaries of the property were inscribed. To remove these was to undermine an owner's claim and livelihood. Hence God gave the command, **Thou shalt not remove thy neighbour's landmark.**

(*c*) *Justice for the accused* (15:21). The rule that the evidence of at least two witnesses was required to sustain a capital charge had already been laid down (17:6). Here it is extended to cover **any iniquity, or . . . any sin** (15). Moreover a deterrent is introduced against perjury prompted by malice towards the accused. When such is suspected, the evidence is to be sifted carefully. If convicted, the perjurer is to suffer the penalty he sought to bring upon **his brother** (18). **Diligent inquisition** means "diligent inquiry" (RSV).

These three laws are a most interesting window on the spirit and temper of ancient Israelite society. Three things are especially noteworthy.

(i) The mental context of the laws and the ultimate ground of justice is God. This emerges most clearly in the Law of Witness where a disputed case is tried **before the Lord, before the priests and the judges** (17). But it is not absent from the Law of Refuge. Kline points out that the cities of refuge were Levitical cities (Josh. 20:7-8 with 21:11, 21, 32) and the period of refuge was continuous with the life of the high priest (Num. 35:25).

[37]"Mine altar" (Exod. 21:14) is not the "place" "I will appoint" (Exod. 21:13). See Adam Welch, *The Code of Deuteronomy* (London: James Clarke, 1924), pp. 138-39.

"The cities of refuge were then extensions of the altar as a place of asylum. All this contributes further to the emphasis of this section of laws on the judicial importance of the priesthood and the central altar."[38] This but illustrates the continuous theme of Deuteronomy: that all of life is God's and injustice offends God as much as the injured.

(ii) In comparison with similar laws in other nations these show a high degree of ethical insight. Thus, while in other nations the willful murderer could buy his life, in Israel he must die. Unlike the Babylonians, the Hebrews valued life more than property.[39]

(iii) The repudiation of pity (13, 21) and the enjoining of retaliation (19, 21) do not contradict this. It is true that both are contrary to the Christian standard (Matt. 5:38-48). But in this OT setting they represent an advance on the primitive standard of unlimited vengeance. They are thus an example of God taking man where he is and introducing a higher element for which alone He is responsible.[40]

(2) *Justice and war* (20:1-20). The justice of God which was to characterize the internal affairs of Israel was also to guide her relations with other nations, even when these were her enemies. Not only her worship but her war was also to be holy. The presentation of war as a sacred institution falls oddly on Christian ears, yet it pervades the entire history of Israel.[41] Her God was a God of war (Exod. 15:3), and when she went **out to battle** (1) not only did He lead her (II Chron. 13:12) but Moses promised, He will **fight for you against your enemies** (4). Hence she is to place her trust in neither weapons nor manpower but in God (Hos. 1:7). When she went out, she did so with His blessing (I Sam. 30:7), and all that she gained in battle belonged to Him (Josh. 6:17-19). This is a prominent theme in Deuteronomy (6:18-19; 7:1-2, 16-26; 9:1-6; 11:22-25; 12:29; 19:1;

[38]*Op. cit.*, p. 102.

[39]M. Greenberg, "Some Postulates of Biblical Criminal Law," in "Yehezkel Kaufmann Jubilee Volume" (Jerusalem: Magnes Press, The Hebrew University, 1960), pp. 5-28.

[40]On the theme of the progressiveness of revelation see the penetrating comments of Orr, *op. cit.*, pp. 465-77.

[41]For an account of the Holy War in Israel see Roland de Vaux, *Ancient Israel, Its Life and Institutions* (London: Darton, Longman and Todd, 2nd ed., 1965), pp. 258-67.

31:3-8).[42] In the present chapter the idea is expounded and rules laid down for its execution.

(*a*) *The presence of God in battle and its implications* (1-9). Particularly in their earliest years in Canaan the Israelites lacked the military organization and weapons characteristic of the more developed nations. A volunteer army led by a charismatic leader employing surprise tactics (see I Sam. 11:1-11) was more to her taste than facing **horses, and chariots** (1) in pitched battles. However, even in these circumstances she was not to fear, for the God who delivered her **out of the land of Egypt** was with her. **The priest** would remind the troops of this as they stood poised for **battle** (2-4).

As proof of God's help, and also out of justice, certain classes of people were to be exempted from military service. In principle those exempted were persons who had undertaken certain responsibilities and had not yet enjoyed the privileges accruing from them: the man who had **built a new house** (5), just **planted a vineyard** (6), or **betrothed a wife** (7). Also all who were **fearful or fainthearted** (8) were to be sent home (cf. Judg. 7:3). When the **officers** (*shoterim*) had raised the army from among the tribes, they would then appoint **captains** (*sarim*) over them (9). All of this plainly presupposes an early date.[43]

(*b*) *Rules for the conduct of war* (10-20). A distinction is made between the treatment meted out to **the cities which are very far off** (15) and **the cities of these people** (16). The former were to be offered the option of **peace** on condition that they became **tributaries** (11; gave "forced labor," RSV) to Israel. If they spurned peace, they were to be overthrown, although the ban (**thou shalt smite every male,** 13) was to be executed against men only (14). But **the cities of these people** (16, the Canaanites) were to receive no such consideration. They were to be totally destroyed, as a menace to the preservation of Israel's faith (16-18; cf. 7:1-6).

A final law forbade the destruction of fruit-bearing **trees** (19), a common policy among invaders, on the ground that everything that supports human life should be preserved. This

[42]See the treatment in G. von Rad, *Studies in Deuteronomy* (London: SCM Press, 1963), c. 4.

[43]G. T. Manley. *The Book of the Law* (London: Tyndale Press), pp. 112-13.

is the most probable meaning of the parenthesis, **For the tree of the field is man's life** (cf. 24:6).

To the modern mind this chapter may well appear a curious mixture of enlightened humanitarianism and primitive savagery. The Christian mind particularly will query the notion of the sanctity of war. The teaching of Deuteronomy here, as elsewhere, must be seen in the total context of the progressiveness of divine revelation.

That war is here an instrument of divine policy means no more than that, as society then was, Israel could not have survived without it. But this does not imply permanent approval. Even in the OT, David is denied the privilege of building the Temple because his hands are stained with blood (I Kings 5:3), and the Messianic kingdom is seen as involving the abolition of war (Isa. 2:4; Mic. 4:3). That society today still resorts to war proves nothing except that men are terribly resistant to the grace of God. However, the recognition of neutrality and the contemporary revulsion against war contrasted with the glorification of it in earlier days indicate that some steps have been taken towards the biblical ideal.

On the moral problem inherent in the command to exterminate the Canaanites see comments on 7:1-6. Hertz writes: "The Canaanites were put under the ban not for false belief but for vile action; because of the human sacrifices and foul immorality of their gruesome cults. The judicial extirpation of the Canaanites is but another instance of the fact that the interests of man's moral progress occasionally demand the employment of stern and relentless methods."[44]

It is legitimate to interpret this chapter typologically of the advance of God's righteousness. He is active in the world through His people in the interests of His kingdom (1-4); to those who will submit to Him comes the offer of peace (10-11); to those who resist comes judgment (12-18), a judgment that is total and final where sin is stubbornly persisted in (17-18).

(3) *Justice in nation and family* (21:1-23).

(*a*) *Unknown murderers* (1-9). Since the shedding of innocent blood must be requited (Gen. 4:10; Num. 35:33), victims of unknown murderers presented a peculiar problem. In the absence of the criminal it became the corporate responsibility of

[44]*Op. cit.*, p. 833.

the nearest **city** to provide a substitute in the form of **an heifer** (3) which would bear the murderer's penalty. It was not a sin offering, for the ritual prescribed for such an offering was not observed (Lev. 4:1-21; cf. Exod. 13:13). However, sanctity attached to it. The ceremony must take place in **a rough valley** (4; an area untouched by man) and with a heifer which had "never been worked" (3, RSV). By washing **their hands over the heifer** (6) and declaring their innocence (7), the elders secured forgiveness for the **people** (8).

Of particular interest is the role played by the various officials. The **elders** (2; *zeqenim*) of the adjacent cities were a sort of city council (19:12).[45] They would be accompanied by the **judges** (see comments on 16:18-20); these would be the successors of those appointed by Moses (Exod. 18:13-26; Deut. 1:9-17). The judge would ensure that there was no trickery in determining which city was nearest to the scene of the crime.[46] Thereafter the initiative rested with **the elders of that city** (4) and **the priests the sons of Levi** (5). They were recognized as the major judicial functionaries: "By their word every dispute and every assault shall be settled" (5, RSV). Again, the ultimate unity of justice and faith, law and religion, is implied (see comments on 19:15-21); the seriousness of sin and the provision of forgiveness are underlined.

(*b*) *Marriage with captive women* (10-14). Since marriage with Canaanite women was specifically prohibited (7:3), the **beautiful** women (11) in question must have been from more distant nations (20:14-15). Even though these women were part of the booty, they were to be treated with respect. They might not be married forthwith. First they must formally break with heathenism—**shave her head, and pare her nails** (12), and put off captives' clothes (13; cf. Lev. 14:8; Num. 8:7). Second—and humanely—they must be allowed a **month** to mourn for their parents and adjust to their new surroundings (13; cf. Num. 20:29).

If later their husbands ceased to like them, they might not be returned to the slave status from which marriage to the conqueror had released them (14). **Have no delight** is better "do not care for her" (Moffatt). Kline comments that "the case of a captive woman is used as a case in point for establishing the

[45]de Vaux, *op. cit.*, p. 138. [46]Welch, *op. cit.*, pp. 147-48.

rights of the wife, perhaps because the principle would obviously apply *a fortiori* in the case of an Israelite wife."[47]

(*c*) *Unwanted heirs* (15-17). Just as 10-14 legislates against the arbitrary treatment of women, so 15-17 prohibits the arbitrary treatment of heirs. Polygamy, which was tolerated here as was divorce in the previous verses (cf. Matt. 19:8), is fruitful of strife. Dislike of the mother of his **firstborn** might prompt a father to seek to transfer the right of primogeniture which carried with it a double portion of the inheritance (17; Gen. 48: 22; II Kings 2:9). In ancient Israel there were no such things as written wills;[48] the division of property was indicated prior to death (cf. Gen. 24:36). When it was made, the strict right of primogeniture was to be observed (16-17). **The beginning of his strength** (17) is better "the first flush of his father's manhood" (Moffatt).

(*d*) *Depraved sons* (18-21). Even in the cases of depraved sons, paternal rights of punishment were limited. If family discipline proved ineffective, then resort must be had to the duly constituted legal authority, **the elders** meeting in **the gate** of the city (19). These alone could impose the death penalty, which would be carried out by **the men of his city** (21).

It may seem that the death penalty, exacted here and for other non-capital offenses (e.g., 22:20-27), is severe. However here, as elsewhere (see closing comments on c. 19), comparison with the rest of the ancient Near East shows the superiority of the Israelite code. Israelite law, unlike that of other nations, restricted capital punishment to offenses against purity of worship, the sanctity of life and sexual relationships. This, as de Vaux points out,[49] is the outcome of the connection between law and religion. Indeed, beyond these areas Israel's law was distinguished by the humaneness of its sentences.

(*e*) *Hanging executed criminals* (22-23). The penalty of **death** (22) would be increased by exposure of the bodies. Hanging was not a means of execution but a sign of disgrace, a public declaration that the criminal had broken the covenant law, and was therefore **accursed of God** (23; cf. Num. 25:4; II Sam. 4:12). Just as the land in a figurative sense could be forgiven by the shedding of the blood of the heifer (9), so it could be **defiled** by

[47] *Op. cit.*, p. 107.

[48] de Vaux, *op. cit.*, p. 53.

[49] *Ibid.*, p. 149.

the display of the corpse of an accursed criminal. Hence such bodies **shall not remain all night upon the tree.** For the Christian application of these ideas see John 19:31; Gal. 3:13.

3. *Laws Concerning the Covenant Community* (22:1—25:19)

This section of Deuteronomy is concerned with practicing righteousness within the bounds of the covenant community and between its members.

a. The covenant and divine institutions (22:1-30). From the implementation of God's righteousness in society, the author now turns to the divine institutions upon which society, indeed life itself, is founded. Here also the divine order must be recognized and respected. But first come a series of laws illustrating that the bond and cement of the covenant community is neighborly love.

(1) *The basis of obedience—love* (1-4). In the center of the legal section of the book this series of injunctions exemplifies the fact that laws themselves are largely useless where the law-abiding spirit is absent. Thus in the examples given no one can tell whether or not the lost property in question has been deliberately overlooked. A basic attitude of goodwill towards one's neighbor alone will insure law observance. This bespeaks the presupposition of the entire book: that religion and law are one and "true community is dependent upon proper worship."[50] In the parallel laws in Exod. 23:4-5 the lost property is that of one's enemy. George Adam Smith points out that the "substitution of the term brother renders this law not narrower but wider."[51] "Enemy" referred to a private rather than foreign enemy. These laws are thus remarkable anticipations of Matt. 5:44, and demonstrate that the old covenant was concerned with inward attitudes as much as with outward actions, however little it could do to cure the former (Jer. 31:31-34). To **hide thyself** (1, 3, 4) means to "withhold your help" (RSV).

(2) *The covenant and the order of nature* (5-12). The Covenant-Lord declares not only that righteousness shall prevail within His community; but as Creator, He decrees that it shall characterize the attitude towards those institutions without which

[50]G. E. Wright, IB, II, 329.

[51]*The Book of Deuteronomy,* "The Cambridge Bible" (Cambridge: University Press, 1918), p. 259.

community and even life would be impossible. Thus the natural world, as His, must be used in accordance with the laws of its Maker.

It is this principle that is illustrated by the examples in vv. 5-11. These seem to be pointed at heathen abuses of nature; as Welch says, "It is a legitimate inference that in the few cases where it is not possible to make sure of the origin, the same principle is at work."[52] The wearing by one sex of a **garment** (5) peculiar to the other is forbidden as a blurring of the distinction between the sexes which, in pagan practice, led to gross moral improprieties.[53] No ritual reason is known as to why the mother bird should be spared (6-7). George Adam Smith observes that, were it kindness, the taking of the whole brood would be forbidden.[54] It may be that endangering the balance of nature was in mind. Birds are important in Palestine for keeping down pests.

Of greatest value in the created order is the **blood** of **man** (8). The flat **roof,** widely used for enjoying the air, was to have **a battlement** (railing) to prevent the spilling of blood by accident.

Verses 9-11 forbid the mixing of **seeds, an ox and an ass** in plowing, and kinds of cloth in **a garment.** Hos. 2:5, 9 suggest that the Canaanites attributed different products to different Baals, in which case garments of mixed cloth could have a pagan significance.[55] The mixing of seeds was prohibited for a religious reason, because the consequence would be the defilement of the harvest. The RSV interprets v. 9, "Lest the whole yield be forfeited to the sanctuary," i.e., be placed under the ban. The precise explanation is unknown, but is probably related ultimately to the distinctness of species as created by God (Gen. 1:11). A similar explanation may be inferred for v. 10. The wearing of **fringes** (12) or tassels on the **four** borders of the outer garment was a sign of submission to the rule of God (see Num. 15:37-41).

(3) *The covenant and the institution of marriage* (13-30). As well as the divinely ordained boundaries in nature the cove-

[52]*Op. cit.*, p. 202.

[53]See Driver's note, *op. cit.*, p. 250.

[54]*Op. cit.*, p. 250.

[55]Wheeler Robinson says, "Perhaps the union of male and female deities was tacitly recognized by this (Egyptian?) cloth" (*Deuteronomy and Joshua*, "Century Bible" [Edinburgh, T. and T. Clark, n.d.], p. 168).

nant people must observe the divinely ordained boundaries in marriage. Various transgressions of these laws, together with the appropriate penalties, are treated here.

The first law relates to charges against **a wife** (13, bride). If a man marries for purely sensual reasons and, quickly hating his wife (cf. II Sam. 13:15), seeks to divorce her by alleging premarital relations on her part, the case shall be brought to trial. In the Near East **the tokens of the damsel's virginity** (15) were the blood-stained bed linens of the wedding night, retained thereafter as evidence by the bride's father. If these were produced, the husband was chastised (flogged), amerced (fined), and deprived of his right of divorce (18-19). If, however, the charge was **true** (20), the woman was stoned at **the door of her father's house** (21), because she had disgraced him. The second law relates to adultery, the penalty for which was death for both parties (22).

The next three laws relate to the seduction of unmarried girls. The first two relate to betrothed virgins, these being treated separately because betrothal was tantamount to marriage, since the bride-price was already paid (see v. 24, where the damsel is referred to as **his neighbour's wife,** and Matt. 1:20). If the woman has offered no resistance, symbolized by her failure to call for help which, in **the city** (23), was available, **both** were to **die** (24). If on the other hand she was attacked **in the field** (25), where there was no help, only her attacker was to **die** (25-27). The seducer of a **virgin . . . not betrothed** (28), if discovered, must pay the bride-price, **fifty shekels of silver** (29), marry her, and forfeit his right of divorce.

The final law forbids the taking of a stepmother as wife (30). To spread the **skirt** over a woman meant to take her as wife (cf. Ruth 3:9). Moffatt translates the verse clearly: "No man shall marry a wife of his father or have intercourse with her." Lev. 18:6-17 lists this and other relationships within which marriage is prohibited. This one may be singled out here either as representative or as indicating the prevalence of such unions, which were known as late as the time of Ezekiel (Ezek. 22:10). Such intercourse seems to have been regarded as proof of the right to inherit the father's property (II Sam. 3:7; 16:22; I Kings 2:22). This may explain the frequency of its occurrence.

This chapter speaks with chastening soberness to a lawless

age such as ours. (*a*) To a generation which is exploiting natural resources with terrifying thoroughness, and flouting long-set distinctions, it speaks of the divine order in nature (5-12), which can be ignored only at our peril. This may not, indeed, be used to justify hidebound prejudice; on the other hand the final consequences of every scientific breakthrough are not always seen in advance, and many a breakthrough leads ultimately to a breakdown. (*b*) To an age which condones increasingly the exploitation of human beings as pawns in the game of sex, it speaks of the divine order among men (13-30), requiring recognition of the sanctity of marriage. People are not simply bodies to be played with. (*c*) To an age that is intent on throwing off all restraints it speaks of the basis of an orderly world (1-4). This basis is not law itself but rather respect for law, manifested in an attitude of brotherly care for one's neighbor and his property. To defy this order is to court not only liberty but anarchy. "We cannot break God's laws; we can only break ourselves against them."

In 22:8, there is a suggested theme, "Safeguard Your Home." (1) Build a battlement of home influences (good books and magazines, pictures, music, radio, and television); (2) Build a battlement of parental example; (3) Build a battlement of family altars; (4) Build a battlement of love with discipline and patience (G. B. Williamson).

b. Righteousness and the covenant congregation (23:1-18). The righteousness which God requires is now shown as it regulates entry into and conduct in the covenant community.

(1) *Membership in the congregation* (1-8). Various categories of people are excluded permanently from **the congregation of the Lord** (Israel). Permanently is the meaning of **even to** the **tenth generation** (2-3). First, those who have been emasculated by any method (1), because such mutilations were part of pagan worship. Second, the **bastard** (2, *mamzer*), which probably means the child of an incestuous marriage (cf. 22:30). Third, the **Ammonite** and **Moabite,** because of their unfriendly treatment of the Israelites when they fled from **Egypt** (3-6). This does not contradict 2:29, as may appear on the surface. Driver comments: "The expression used suggests that the Moabites were not forward in offering them food in a friendly spirit (cf. Isa. 21:14), and is not necessarily inconsistent with their having sold

it to them, perhaps under compulsion, in return for money payment."[56]

These specific regulations are but applications of the underlying principle that God requires perfection of His people (cf. Deut. 18:13). Such physical impediments do not permanently disqualify their bearers from the spiritual fellowship of the people of God where "it is the spirit that quickeneth; the flesh profiteth nothing" (John 6:63; cf. Isa. 56:4-5; Acts 8:27, 38). The **Edomite** and the **Egyptian** (7) were not to be excluded beyond the second **generation** (8). To **abhor** (7) was to "detest" or to "reject." The Edomites, despite displays of enmity (e.g., Num. 20:18-21), were Israel's kin (Gen. 36:1). The Egyptians, despite the enslavement of the children of Israel, saved the family of Jacob in a time of famine (Gen. 42:1 ff.). Of course, any of these foreigners who entered the congregation must profess Israel's faith.

(2) *The purity of the camp* (9-14). When the nation was prosecuting holy war (see comments on 20), she must be sure that the camp was holy. Provision must be made outside the camp for the necessities of nature listed in 10-13 (cf. Lev. 15:16-17). Although these laws also had sanitary value, their main purpose was to demonstrate a reverence for God, who led His people in battle. God wanted **no unclean thing in thee** (14; lit., the nakedness of anything). He wanted nothing indecent in the camp.

(3) *Two examples* (15-18). The righteousness of the congregation is illustrated in the treatment of runaway slaves (15-16) and the banning of prostitution (17-18). **The servant which is escaped** (15), in contrast to the harsh treatment accorded him in surrounding nations, might remain in Israel, free.[57] Prostitution, male and female, was a leading feature of pagan worship. It was to find no place in **Israel**; nor were its returns, **the hire of a whore, or the price of a dog** (18), to find any place in **the house** of Israel's **God. A dog** here denotes a male prostitute.

So is summarized the character of the people of God. (1) They are to be a holy people, 1-8. (2) They are to be such because they are the beneficiaries of a Holy Presence, 14. (3) Their holiness is to be demonstrated not merely in their own personal state but in holy practice, 15-18. The righteousness re-

[56]*Op. cit.*, p. 43.

[57]de Vaux, *op. cit.*, p. 87.

quired of God's ancient people foreshadows that required of the Church, for the same reason and with similar consequences (II Cor. 6:14—7:1; Eph. 5:25-27; Titus 2:14).

c. *Righteousness and the covenant members* (23:19—25:19). The righteousness which conditions entry into the congregation is to characterize the treatment of fellow members, various groups of which are now considered.

(1) *Neighbors* (23:19-25). Dealings with neighbors were to be governed by neighborly love (cf. 22:1-4). Exod. 22:25 forbade the taking of interest (**usury**) on loans made to distressed Israelites, a law which Lev. 25:35-37 extends to resident aliens. Verse 19 repeats the law of Exodus, forbidding interest on any loan, whether in cash or in kind. Verse 20 does not contradict the law of Leviticus, for here commercial rather than personal loans are in mind. Rates of interest in neighboring countries were high, sometimes as much as half; to the poor these would be ruinous, and no Israelite must encompass the ruin of his brother.

Verses 24-25 enjoin similar neighborliness on those passing through the **vineyard** or the field of another. Hunger may be satisfied but not greed; the property rights of the owner must be respected. The Pharisees violated both the spirit and the letter of this law when they accused the disciples of reaping on the Sabbath (Mark 2:24).

Sandwiched between these laws is the law of vows (21-23). If the Israelite must keep covenant-loyalty with his neighbor, even more must he keep it with his **God** (21). No one was obliged **to vow** (22), but if he did he must keep his word (23).

In 21-23 we find the theme "Perform Your Vows." (1) Consider your ability to pay before you promise, 22; (2) Pay your vows to God, 21; (3) Keep even rash promises or obtain honorable release. Learn, then, to make vows with due consideration, 23 (G. B. Williamson).

(2) *Wives* (24:1-5). This is not a law instituting divorce. No OT law encourages divorce. Rather its attitude is that of Mal. 2:14-16. This is a law restricting the practice of divorce, here taken as a fact, in the particular case of a twice-divorced woman or widowed divorcée. Certain formalities were required in all divorces. They were designed to prevent a husband, who alone had the right of divorce, from exercising it hastily. Thus

(*a*) There must be a serious cause. **Some uncleanness** (1) is a vague expression which, says Driver, "is most natural to understand of immodest or indecent behaviour."[58] It does not mean adultery, which was punishable by death (cf. 22:20-21). (*b*) The due legal procedure must be observed: **a bill of divorcement** must be handed over and the woman formally dismissed from her husband's home. But if a woman had been duly divorced twice, or divorced once and bereaved, she must not remarry her first husband **after that she is defiled** (3-4). Her second union placed her in an adulterous relation to her first husband (cf. Lev. 18:20; Num. 5:13-14, 20, where "defile" is used to express the same result). C. F. Keil comments: "The marriage of a divorced woman is thus treated implicitly as tantamount to adultery, and the way is prepared for the teaching of Christ on the subject of marriage."[59] The whole concession of divorce presupposed here, Jesus sweeps away in Matt. 19:7-9. Verse 5 shows further the esteem in which marriage was held by exempting men from military and other public service during their first year of marriage (cf. 20:5-9).

(3) *The needy* (24:6-22). Special care must be taken of those unable to care for themselves. The laws in this section are concerned with three main themes:

(*a*) *Goods given in pledge* (6, 10-13, 17-18). While it was forbidden to exact interest on loans (23:19-20), it was permissible to take a **pledge** (6, security) for them. The very poor, however, would possess only the necessities of life, so that the security for a loan might endanger their continued existence. Hence two guidelines are given. First, nothing must be taken as security that would endanger **life.** Thus the **upper** of the two round millstones used to grind corn was not to be taken, for this removed the source of food. **The nether** is better "a mill" (RSV) or "handmill" (Moffatt). If the outer garment was taken, it was not to be kept overnight (12-13, 17), since the peasant, who used it as a blanket, would perish in the cold without it (Exod. 22:26-27; Amos 2:8). Second, the choice of **pledge** was to be made by the borrower, not the lender, who was therefore forbidden to enter the borrower's **house** (10-11). The "means test" could too easily become the mean test.

[58]*Op. cit.*, pp. 270-71.

[59]Quoted in Driver, *op. cit.*, p. 272.

(*b*) *Security of the person* (7-9, 16). A man's life was sacred in Israel. Hence the kidnapping of a fellow Israelite to sell him into slavery was banned on pain of death (7). Similarly, during epidemics of **leprosy** (8) care was to be taken to **observe** the laws to contain it (Leviticus 13—14; cf. Mark 1:44). These laws were exemplified in the exclusion of **Miriam** (9) from the camp on express divine orders when she was afflicted (Num. 12:10-15). **Leprosy** is a term used in Scripture for various skin diseases besides leprosy proper.[60]

Finally, the principle of individual responsibility is laid down—**Every man shall be put to death for his own sin** (16). In many countries of the ancient Near East the family rather than the individual was the unit of society, so that if one member committed a crime the whole family was punished (Esther 9:13-14; Dan. 6:24). The repeated emphasis upon personal responsibility in the OT (e.g., II Kings 14:6; Jer. 31:29-30; Ezek. 18:19-20) suggests that Israel was in danger of falling a prey to this view; hence this law against it.[61] The legal repudiation of the idea of such corporate guilt in no way nullifies the reality of corporate suffering which the sin of an individual can bring. It is this corporate suffering that is expressed in the third commandment (5:9). But the inevitable processes of life are not to be made the principles of law.

(*c*) *Care of the poor* (14-15, 19-22). Advantage was not to be taken of a needy **servant** (14). He was to be given **his hire** (15) when he had earned it. At **harvest** time no **field** (19) or **olive tree** (20) or **vineyard** (21) was to be stripped. Anything missed was to be left **for the stranger, for the fatherless, and for the widow.**

These laws concerning the needy are notable, not only for their humanitarian concern, but also for the humane way in

[60]A. P. Waterson, art., "Disease and Healing," NBD, p. 314.

[61]It is widely held, chiefly on the basis of Josh. 7:24-25 and II Sam. 21:1-9, that this view also prevailed in Israel. Driver points out that the instances quoted are exceptional and cannot support a general inference (*op. cit.*, p. 277). For a discussion contending that social and individual elements were always present in Israelite thought, see Th. C. Vriezen, *An Outline of O.T. Theology* (Oxford: Basil Blackwell, 1958), pp. 324-25. Vriezen holds interestingly that the alternation of the singular and plural forms of address, which is such a marked feature of Deuteronomy, is proof of his contention.

which that concern was to be expressed. It is not enough to be prepared to help the needy; one must be ready to help them in a way that makes it easy for them to accept help. Manley says, "These rules are illustrations of that 'gentleness' which is the fruit of the Spirit, for they inculcate respect for the feelings as well as for the needs of the borrower."[62] The lender is not to enter the borrower's house (10-11); the needy servant is not to have to ask for his wages (14-15), nor the poor for the leftovers of the harvest (19-22). They are individuals in their own right and are to be treated as such despite their poverty. The same spirit carries over into Christianity, where Paul was beseeching men to come to Christ although he had the dignity of an ambassador (II Cor. 5:20). To use Denney's phrase, we must "preach the Gospel in the spirit of the Gospel."[63]

(4) *The helpless* (25:1-19). Attention now turns to situations in which individuals are largely or wholly at the mercy of others. It has been said that the treatment of the helpless is the touchstone of civilization. This is true chiefly because the converse is also true: that the exercise of power is one of the most searching tests of character. As Lord Acton said, "Power tends to corrupt, and absolute power corrupts absolutely." The lofty moral tone of Deuteronomy shines through again in these verses.

(*a*) *Fair punishment for the guilty* (1-4). Condemned prisoners are particularly vulnerable, where, as in ancient Israel, there were no prisons and corporal punishment was more frequent. Hence strict conditions were laid down for its administration. First, it must take place only after trial by authorized **judges** (1; contrast Acts 16:22-24, 37-39). Second, it must be administered in the presence of **the judge . . . before his face** (2). Third, it must be **according to his fault** (proportionate to the crime) and the strokes must be only a certain number, a safeguard against administration in anger. And fourth, the number must not exceed **forty** (3). To avoid error on this last point it became traditional in Judaism for the maximum to be restricted to 39 (II Cor. 11:24).

The purpose of these restrictions was to avoid the humilia-

[62]NBC, p. 216.

[63]*The Second Epistle to the Corinthians* ("The Expositor's Bible," London: Hodder and Stoughton, 1894), p. 216.

tion of the prisoner. Cunliffe-Jones says pertinently: "The personality of the offender must be respected even in punishment. The criminal law must not harm either judge, by causing him to indulge in contempt of his brother, or criminal, by causing him to lose that self-respect which is the foundation of his humanity."[64] It is interesting to note that although the offender is among **the wicked** (1) he is still **thy brother** (3). **Seem vile** is better "be degraded" (RSV).

To this law is appended one about not muzzling **the ox** (4), thereby extending the principle of consideration to dumb animals. To **muzzle** an ox while its very hooves were separating the grain from the ears would be a refinement of cruelty. Paul's comment on this law in I Cor. 9:9-10 probably owes more than is commonly allowed to the Hebrew idiom whereby a comparison is expressed in terms of absolute contrast.[65]

(*b*) *Fair treatment for the dead* (5-10). The custom of levirate marriage (from the Latin, *levir,* husband's brother) was widely practiced in the ancient world. Its background varied from nation to nation. In ancient Israel it centered in the fear of the extinction of a family line (Ruth 4:5, 10; I Sam. 24:21; II Sam. 14:7). Perhaps this fear existed because of the incomplete revelation of the character of the life to come, and childlessness was regarded as a disaster for the dead. The associated idea of perpetuating the inheritance of the dead by not marrying outside of the family (5; Ruth 4:5, 10) may confirm this. The alienation of a man's property through the marriage of his widow to a stranger would mean the loss of his allotted share in the Promised Land. Hence if a man died childless, it was his brother's duty to fulfill the role of husband to his widow. Any child of the union was regarded as the offspring of the deceased (Gen. 38:6-9).

The law as expressed here has several distinctive features. First, it was to apply only **if brethren dwell together** (5), i.e., had a common establishment; and if the first marriage was childless, as opposed to sonless (this seems to be implied by the right

[64]*Deuteronomy*, "Torch Bible Commentaries," ed. J. Marsh, *et al.* (London: Student Christian Movement Press, 1951), p. 140.

[65]See the comments of E. E. Ellis, *Paul's Use of the Old Testament* (Grand Rapids: Wm. B. Eerdmans Publishing Co., 1957), pp. 46-47.

of inheritance of daughters provided for in Num. 27:4-11).[66] Second, only **the firstborn** (6) was to take the name of the dead; subsequent children would take the name of their physical father. Third, contrary to earlier practice (Gen. 38:8-10), a brother could repudiate the responsibility, though this was regarded as a grave dereliction of fraternal duty. In such cases after **the elders** had been informed (7) and had endeavored unsuccessfully to dissuade him (8), he would formally renounce his obligation in their **presence.** This was symbolized by the removal of his sandal by the woman. As one occupied land by walking on it, the **shoe** became the symbol of taking possession; its removal symbolized loss or rejection. Such repudiation of duty involved lasting disgrace (10).

(c) *Fair treatment for the attacked* (11-12). Intervention of a **wife** (11) on her husband's behalf by a grossly immodest attack on his assailant is to be penalized by cutting **off her hand** (12). "That the act forbidden includes contempt for the covenant sign and not just indecency is suggested by the apparent similarity in the nature of the punishment and the sign, both involving a mutilation."[67] This view is supported by de Vaux, who sees it as the only physical application in Israelite law—and that in symbolic form—of the *lex talionis* (19:21).[68]

(d) *Fair weights and measures* (13-16). The customer was at the mercy of the vendor, who could easily use heavy **weights** (13) for buying and **small** for selling. This was not unknown (Amos 8:5), though royal standards for these **weights** were fixed in the time of David (II Sam. 14:26). Such practice was an **abomination** not only to men but to **God,** as is shown by the blessing attached to **just weight** (15) and the curse to **all that do unrighteously** (16).

In 13-16 we see "Strict Honesty." (1) Shaded honesty is dishonesty, 13-14; (2) Perfect honesty is rewarded, 15; (3) Dishonesty is condemned, 16 (G. B. Williamson).

(e) *Fair treatment for the Amalekites* (17-19). After the above illustrations by way of example, the section concludes with an illustration by way of warning. Etched indelibly into the Israelite memory was the shameful treatment they suffered at

[66] J. S. Wright and J. A. Thompson, art., "Marriage," NBD, p. 789.

[67] Kline, *op. cit.*, p. 118.

[68] *Op. cit.*, p. 159.

the hands of the Amalekites when they came **forth out of Egypt** (17). Exod. 17:8-16 records the battle. Here sniping at the **feeble,** the **faint and weary** (18), beleaguered Israelite rear-guard, is recalled with especial bitterness (cf. I Sam. 15:2). No one who **feared . . . God** would have done it, but the Amalekites did; and the same justice that enjoins fair treatment of the needy involves condemnation of those who withhold it (19; see comments on 20:17-18).

We may gather together the thought of this entire section (23:19—25:19) by seeking its message for us today. The faith of Deuteronomy was obviously no individualistic pietism with its force exhausted when it achieved personal acceptance. On the contrary, the whole thrust of this section is that holy faith must issue in holy action; the effect of the sanctification of souls is the sanctification of society. The Israelites were to be not merely holy individuals; they were to be a holy nation (7:6). Hence the intensely concrete social applications of holiness contained in this section. Christianity stands in the same tradition. In Wesley's celebrated words: "Christianity is essentially a social religion, and to make it into a solitary one is to destroy it . . . The gospel of Christ knows of no religion but social religion; no holiness but social holiness . . . Faith working by love is the length and breadth and depth and height of Christian perfection."

The section before us may be said to suggest "Four Ways of Showing Christian Righteousness." (1) By the practice of Christian neighborliness, 23:19-25. Whereas Deuteronomy distinguishes various categories of neighbor (e.g., "brother" and "stranger," 23:19-20), the Christian definition of neighbor was given once and for all in the parable of the Good Samaritan (Luke 10:25-37). Our neighbor is anyone whom we are in position to help. (2) By respect for Christian marriage, 24:1-5. Again Christ goes beyond the position of Deuteronomy, with even its limited acceptance of divorce, returning to the original institution of the creation when marriage was ordained to be lifelong (Gen. 2:23-24; Matt. 19:3-9). (3) By Christian care for the needy, 24:6-22. According to Jas. 1:27 this enters into the very heart of pure religion. (4) By Christian charity for the helpless, 25:1-19. The concern for those found guilty at law is a particular rebuke to this age, which has witnessed the return of torture and the invention of brainwashing. In Cunliffe-Jones's words: "The principle that punishment should be limited to the least possible compatible with the vindication of the claim of just law to obedience is of great importance and permanent application."[69]

The extent to which contemporary society reflects these features is the extent of the influence of the faith of Deuteronomy and its Christian successor. The extent to which it fails to do so, or is departing from doing so, is the measure of our challenge.

4. *Liturgies Acknowledging God as Lord* (26:1-15)

The legal section of this document, containing the terms of the covenant between God and Israel, closes with two **rituals.** These are liturgies for services in which the people acknowledge God as their Benefactor and declare that they have observed the terms of the covenant.

a. A liturgy for the offering of firstfruits (26:1-11). After the Israelites had entered the land they were, in season, to **take of the first of all the fruit of the earth** (2) and carry it **in a basket** into the sanctuary. They were to stand before **the priest** (3) and declare that God's covenant promise (1:8) had been fulfilled. Thereupon the priest would place the basket **before the altar** (4) and the worshipper would recount the mighty deliverances that had brought him thither. Jacob's deliverance from Laban and Israel's deliverance from Egypt are cited as examples. Jacob is described as **a Syrian** (5; Aramaean) both because his mother was from Aram-naharaim (Gen. 24:10) and because he spent many years there serving Laban (Genesis 29—31). The worshippers were to tell of their **hard bondage** (6) in **Egypt,** from whence they were freed by **the Lord** (7-8). Now, in acknowledgment that the new land was God's gift, the worshippers presented the basket of **firstfruits,** placing it before the altar, from which they had picked it up (cf. 4) while reciting the liturgy (5-10).[70] The ritual would be followed by a sacred feast in which **the Levite** (11) and foreigners would join with the household.

According to Num. 18:12-13 and Deut. 18:4 the firstfruits belonged to the priests, though no ritual for their presentation is prescribed. This lack is made up here—fittingly enough since, in Welch's phrase, Deuteronomy "is not a handbook for the guidance of the priests . . . it is a law-book for the laity."[71] It is uncertain whether the basket contained all of the firstfruits or only

[69]*Op. cit.*, p. 140.

[70]Hertz, *op. cit.*, p. 860.

[71]*Op. cit.*, p. 93.

a token,[72] the main part being used at the feast (11). What the liturgy was designed to underline was that credit for the fertility of the land belonged to **the Lord thy God** (repeated nine times),[73] not to some Canaanite Baal.

All the main emphases of Deuteronomy are embodied in this passage: the divine providence in the nation's history, and the consequent thanksgiving symbolized by the payment of God's dues and gifts for the poor. It is the characteristically biblical pattern of grace and gratitude (see, e.g., Rom. 12:1).

b. A liturgy after the distribution of tithes (26:12-15). Whereas in the first and second years **the tithes** (12) were used for sacred feasts (14:22-27), in **the third** they were given to the Levites and the poor (14:28-29). When this was duly done, the worshipper would appear before the Lord at the sanctuary (14: 23; 15:20) and avow that he had obeyed the divine **commandments** (13). He would affirm in particular that he had avoided polluting his tithe from three specific sources: by eating of it when **mourning** (14), which would render it ceremonially unclean (Hos. 9:4); by distributing any of it when he was ritually **unclean**; or by offering any of it to **the dead**—a possible allusion to the Canaanite funeral custom of consecrating part of the offering to the deity of vegetation.[74] On the basis of this declared obedience he prayed for the continuance of the divine blessing.

Just as in Numbers the firstfruits are allotted to the priests, so **the tithes** are allotted entirely to the Levites (Num. 18:21-32). The traditional Jewish explanation of this discrepancy with Deuteronomy is to say that Deuteronomy speaks of a second tithe.[75] More probably it is to be explained as an amendment in

[72]The first **of** (Heb. *min*) in v. 2 may be emphatic (see RSV). Again, the sacred meal (11) may be that accompanying the Feast of Weeks (16: 11), at which the firstfruits may have been offered. See Driver, *op. cit.*, p. 290.

[73]**The Lord thy God** is used in Deuteronomy 299 times, frequently with associations of the Exodus and Sinai. " 'Yahweh thy God' expresses a personal and exclusive relationship between Yahweh and Israel, and suggests the consciousness that there is a fundamental difference between Israel's God and those of the nations" (G. T. Manley, *The Book of the Law*, p. 41).

[74]*Ibid.*, pp. 108-9.

[75]See Driver, *op. cit.*, pp. 170-71, for an account of this view and objections to it.

view of the changed conditions in Canaan. In the wilderness, only cattle tithes would be available, as Num. 18:27, 30 implies, and in the confined circumstances of the desert the Levites would require them all. In the land of plenty, however, where field produce would be available in abundance, there would be more than enough, and in this overflow the worshipper and the poor might share.

The following points may be added: (1) The fundamental law of the tithe in Lev. 27:30-33 specifies nothing regarding its distribution. It lays down the basic principle that it is "holy unto the Lord" (Lev. 27:30), a principle that is honored in all the laws of tithing. (2) The fact that in Deuteronomy the Levites receive a share rather than the whole of the tithe may be hinted at in the distinction between the tithe and the heave offering (*terumah,* "contribution of the hand," 12:6, 11, 17), the offering being the Levite's share of the tithe. In this case the heave offering may bear the same relation to the tithe as the basket to the whole of the firstfruits (26:2, 11). (3) The differing emphases upon the destination of the tithes in Numbers and Deuteronomy may be explained by the differing historical backgrounds and audiences of the two books. Numbers gives directions for the religious officials against the straitened background of the wilderness. Deuteronomy gives guidance to the lay worshippers against the more ample background of the Promised Land.[76] (See also comments on 14:22-29.)

Without doubt the details of the procedure were clearer to the Israelites than they are to us. What is perfectly clear is the main purpose of the liturgy. It was to avow that the tithes had been used for the ends for which they were sanctified by God, not for the practice of Canaanite fertility rites.

5. *Conclusion: Declarations of Loyalty* (26:16-19).

Although the word *covenant* is not used in these verses, the thought is plainly of the conclusion of a contract between God and Israel. Since there was only one such covenant—that concluded at Sinai (Exod. 24:7)—the setting must be that of a covenant renewal. **This day** (16) the terms of the covenant had been read in their fullness. The terms included **statutes** (*huqqim*) or

[76]For a fuller exposition of this view (though with some variations) see A. H. Finn, *The Unity of the Pentateuch* (London: Marshall Brothers, n.d.), pp. 196-99.

laws enforced by conscience; **commandments** (*mizwoth*), orders capable of once-for-all fulfillment; and **judgments** (*mishpatim*), case laws—in short, everything contained in the book (16-17; cf. 12:1).[77]

Israel had committed herself to observing them and in so doing had bound God to be her God. This is the force of **avouched** (17-18), which means to "cause to acknowledge." It is probably a technical, legal term used by the contracting parties in a covenant. God, on the other hand, had caused Israel to acknowledge that she was **his peculiar** (particular) **people** (18). Yet this acknowledgment was not a shackle but a privilege, the fulfillment of His promise to her to make her His **holy people** (19). Holiness of heart is more than an obligation; it is an honor.

This chapter pictures Israel as being in the Promised Land (1), enjoying its benefits (9, 15). Lest prosperity should make her forget the God who had brought her thither, there are enjoined upon her "Three Acts of Worship for a Prosperous People": (1) The worship of testimony, 1-11; (2) The worship of tithing, 12-15; (3) The worship of rededication, 16-19.

Now that the end of the main legal section of Deuteronomy (12:1—26:19) has been reached, it may be useful to make some general observations on the arrangement of the laws. At many points it is difficult to see why a particular law comes where it does, and easy to suggest a better place for it. Thus 19:14 has no obvious connection with its surroundings; while 21:10-14 and 23:9-14 might be more aptly placed in c. 20. Examples could be multiplied, as could the despairing confessions of scholars and commentators that the problem of the order of Deuteronomy is insoluble.[78]

However, while no complete solution is known as yet, there are several factors that offer guidance. Thus the widespread recognition of the covenantal form of Deuteronomy, as indicated by Mendenhall,[79] means that the basic plan and development of

[77]See Manley, *The Book of the Law*, pp. 71-73.

[78]For one of the latest see E. W. Nicholson, *op. cit.*, pp. 32-33.

[79]*Law and Covenant in Israel and the Ancient Near East* (Pittsburgh, Pa.: The Biblical Colloquium, 1955), pp. 31-35. The recognition that the *whole* of Deuteronomy answers to this pattern encompasses all shades of the theological spectrum from von Rad (e.g., *Studies in Deuteronomy*, pp. 14-15) to Kline on the conservative side (*Treaty of the Great King*, pp. 27-44), who applies the idea with great thoroughness.

the book are clear. This, in turn, yields a further clue. If, at covenant-renewal ceremonies, the covenant was subject to modernization and addition,[80] then the process whereby this was done may explain the order of the laws in their present form. Daube has shown how, when additions were made, they were frequently made at the end, whether or not they treated the theme of the final law of the existing code.[81]

Comparative evidence from the ancient Near East shows further that, if a law was displaced by another with a different or opposite effect, the original was not necessarily excised.[82] Allowance must therefore be made for "the law of change in the Bible,"[83] whereby a basically Mosaic code was modified and augmented to meet the needs of an ever-changing situation.

In the words of F. F. Bruce: "No matter in how many parallel or successive recensions his laws might be preserved and from time to time repromulgated, no matter how they might be expanded and applied to changing conditions of life, in written form or in oral tradition, Israel's law would never cease to be known as the law of Moses. Rightly so: for the principles laid down in his time, before the settlement in Canaan, remained the principles of Israel's law for all centuries to come."[84] Accordingly, it is right both to seek to interpret Deuteronomy as a coherent whole and also to refrain from forcing connections where they obviously do not exist.

[80]So Kline, *op. cit.*, p. 20.

[81]*Studies in Biblical Law* (Cambridge: University Press, 1947), C. II, "Codes and Codas."

[82]Cf. K. A. Kitchen, *op. cit.*, p. 128, fn. 63; pp. 134-35, 148-49; Greenberg, *op. cit.*, pp. 5-7.

[83]The phrase is the title of Chapter II of H. M. Wiener's *Early Hebrew History* (London: Robert Scott, 1924). In it he demonstrates that Moses did not regard his laws as immutable for all time. He modified them himself (cf. Num. 27:1-11, which modifies the rule that sons alone have the right of inheritance). He also provided for others to do so by envisaging the monarchy (Deut. 17:14-20) with the changes inseparable from it, and the succession of prophets who would occupy his place (Deut. 18:9-22). The touchstone of such alterations is that they should not minister to apostasy (cf. Deut. 13:1-5; 18:20).

[84]*Israel and the Nations* (Exeter: Paternoster Press, 1963), p. 16.

Section III Concluding Addresses: The Covenant

Deuteronomy 27:1—30:20

The recital of the terms of the covenant was now complete. It remained for the people formally to commit themselves to it. In covenants characteristic of the ancient Near East in the time of Moses such a ceremony, comprising various elements, was the customary climax of the concluding of a covenant.[1] Chapters 27—30 embody this ratification procedure. The leading features are the repetition of the blessings and curses that will attend respectively the observance and infraction of the covenant (28); and the actual ceremony of oath taking (29—30).

A. The Ratification Ceremony, 27:1-26

A covenant imposed by a conqueror upon his vassal was usually renewed in two stages. The first occurred before the suzerain's death, and the second after the accession of his successor. Such a pattern seems to be in view here, where Moses is about to die and to be succeeded by Joshua. The ritual for the second stage seems to be embodied in this chapter (its fulfillment is recorded in Josh. 8:30-35). Insofar as it interrupts the sequence between 26:19 and 28:1, it may be because it anticipates this later stage. The order of parts in such treaties was by no means constant.[2] This may explain why Moses felt free to depart from a more logical order, especially when such a departure enabled him to enjoin obedience to God in future days when he would no longer be leading God's people.

1. *Ceremonial Writing of the Law* (27:1-8)

On arrival in the Promised Land the Israelites were to set up **great stones, and plaister them with plaister: and . . . write upon them all the words of this law** (2-3). The inscribing of

[1]See Kitchen, *op. cit.*, pp. 90-99, for a summary and comparison.

[2]Mendenhall, *op. cit.*, p. 32. See also J. A. Thompson, *The Ancient Near Eastern Treaties and the Old Testament* (London: Tyndale Press, 1964), p. 15.

laws upon stones was commonplace in the ancient world. The code of Hammurabi, the famous Babylonian king of the eighteenth century B.C. is about 8,000 words long, engraved on a block of diorite. The Persian code carved into the Behistun rock is twice as long as Deuteronomy 12—26. The method of writing enjoined here is Egyptian. It involved applying a layer of stucco to the surface of the stone and writing with some black pigment rather than carving.

More important than the method of writing the law was its significance. The publication of law implies the proclamation of it as the law of the land where it is published. This public inscription of God's covenant with Israel at the moment of her arrival in Canaan would signify the nation's acceptance of it as the rule of her life in the new land. The inscribed stones would bear permanent testimony to this act and to the content of the law.

That this is the meaning of the writing of the law is confirmed by the command to offer sacrifice, a customary part of covenant-ratification procedure (cf. Gen. 15:9-18; Jer. 34:18).[3] An altar was to be erected in **mount Ebal** (4) made **of whole stones** (6), i.e., unhewn stones, untouched by **any iron tool** (5). The Hebrew word for **whole** (*shelemoth*) comes from the same root as *shalom* (peace). The physical character of the stones is indicative of their spiritual function and effect. Thus, as at Sinai (Exod. 24:5, 11), the conclusion of the covenant would be attended by a sacrificial feast as the people rejoiced **before the Lord thy God** (7).

It is significant that Moses found no incongruity between the erection of an altar on Mount Ebal and the law of the central sanctuary in 12:1-14. On the contrary, as Manley says, he "uses the very words of Exod. 20:24 which Deuteronomy is supposed to revoke."[4] This suggests strongly that, while 12:1-14 looks forward to a central sanctuary, it permits worship of the true God at any authorized place (see comments on 12:1-14).

2. *A Solemn Reminder* (27:9-10)

In the midst of directions for the future there is interjected this reminder that **Israel** is always to be **the people of the Lord**

[3]J. A. Thompson, *op. cit.*, pp. 25-26. [4]*The Book of the Law*, p. 134.

thy God (9). The covenant would need to be ratified later, but it was also in process of ratification as Israel listens to its terms from the lips of Moses in the plains of Moab (see map 3). Obedience to **the voice of the Lord thy God** (10) was therefore a present as well as a future obligation (10). Von Rad observes that these verses show strikingly that the covenant is the free gift of God. It was not the reward of Israel's obedience, for as yet she had not had the opportunity to obey its provisions for life in Canaan. Obedience indeed is required, but it is the consequence rather than the cause of the covenant.[5]

This section shows an affinity, in language and content, with 26:16-19 and c. 28. Far from interrupting the sequence, it serves to bind these chapters together.

3. *Blessings and Curses* (27:11-13)

The thought here returns to the ratification ceremony in the future after the land had been entered. The blessings and curses are the sanctions of the covenant (11:26-28). Their content is indicated in c. 28. The precise form of the ritual of blessing and cursing may be inferred at least in part from 11:29 and Josh. 8:30-35.

Six of the tribes were to stand on **mount Gerizim to bless** (12) and six on **mount Ebal to curse** the people (13). Whether the tribes recited the blessings and curses or simply had them recited to them is not clear. In the midst of this natural amphitheater stood the priests with the ark of the covenant. The substance of the blessings and curses is omitted here, presumably because of its inclusion in c. 28.

The principle on which the tribes were allotted to the mount of blessing or cursing appears to be genealogical. The sons of Jacob's legitimate wives were appointed to bless, and the sons of his concubines to curse. However Reuben, who forfeited his birthright (Gen. 49:4), and Zebulun, Leah's youngest son (Gen. 30:19-20), were transferred to the second group to make up even numbers. At the same time a geographical basis is not impossible. The first group, with the doubtful exception of Issachar, are tribes that settled south of Esdraelon. The second group, including Reuben and Gad from Transjordan, settled in the north (see map 4).

[5]*Deuteronomy,* p. 166.

4. *The Covenant Oath* (27:14-26)

These verses represent a ritual distinct from that of blessing and cursing. This is evident from the fact that here **the Levites** (14) pronounce the curses and **all the people** (15), rather than merely half of them, respond. Also this ceremony is constituted entirely of curses. A formal oath of obedience was as much a part of the conclusion of a treaty in the ancient Near East as the reading of its terms or the pronouncement of its sanctions.[6]

It is likely that this feature, in which the vassal called down maledictions upon himself if he broke the provisions of the treaty, is embodied in these verses.[7] Exod. 24:7 and Josh. 24:16, 21, 24 probably refer to the same kind of ceremony. As the curses were read out, the people indicated their assent by responding with the **Amen** (15).[8] For other biblical instances see Num. 5:22; I Kings 1:36; Neh. 5:13.

All of the misdemeanors cursed here are outlawed elsewhere in the Pentateuch, though not in any single place. Thus making a **graven or molten image** (15) is banned in Exod. 20:4; dishonor of **father** or **mother** (16) in Exod. 20:12; Deut. 21:18-21; removal of the **landmark** (17) in 19:14; misleading **the blind** (18) in Lev. 19:14; perversion of justice (19) in 24:17; various forms of incest (20, 22-23) in Lev. 18:8-9, 17; bestiality (21)—a pagan rite to procure fertility—in Lev. 18:23; murder (24) in Lev. 24:17; the receiving of bribes for murder (25) in Exod. 23:8; Deut. 16:19.

The striking thing about this collection of evils, and that which gives it cohesion, is the note of the secrecy of these sins. This note is explicit in vv. 15, 24, and implicit in 16, 17, 18, 25 as well as in the wide area of sexual sins (20-23). Such offenses might escape human eyes and evade human justice, but they would not evade the sight and justice of God. "There is something splendid," says von Rad, "about the way in which Israel . . . acknowledges Yahweh's will . . . as binding on those occasions when a man believes he is alone by himself."[9] As the Psalmist

[6]Cf. Kitchen, *op. cit.*, pp. 92-94; Thompson, *op. cit.*, p. 14.

[7]So Kline, *op. cit.*, p. 124; Kitchen, *op. cit.*, p. 98.

[8]Cf. J. B. Pritchard, *Ancient Near Eastern Texts* (Princeton, N.J.: Princeton University Press, 1950), pp. 353 ff.

[9]*Deuteronomy*, pp. 168-69.

discovered (Psalm 139) there was no part of his interior life that was unknown to God.

As this chapter and the ceremony it describes spoke to Israel of the acknowledgment of the divine lordship, so it speaks to us of "The Coming of the Reign of God." There is (1) The acknowledgment of God's reign, 1-8, which is the secret of blessing, 3. There is (2) The grace of God's reign, 9-10. His will to bless requires obedience, but as a consequence, not a precondition. Finally there is (3) The sphere of God's reign, 11-26—everything down to the secret springs. If He is Lord of the heart, He will be Lord of everything else.

B. The Covenant Sanctions, 28:1-68

Now that the second stage in the covenant renewal has been dealt with, Moses returns to the first. He is concerned with the submission of the people to God **this day** (1) as he speaks to them in the plains of Moab. In thought, therefore, 28:1 is the sequel to 26:19 and 27:9-10. A leading feature of this ceremony of submission was the recital of the blessings and curses which would follow obedience or disobedience to the terms of the covenant.[10] These blessings and curses, embodied in c. 28, constituted the sole sanctions of the covenant, a further indication that the people were answerable directly to God.

In comparison with the parallel sections of other ancient covenants, c. 28 has several notable features. First, whereas the usual order is curses, then blessings, here that order is reversed. "This," says Kitchen, "would appear to be a specifically O.T. feature, not unconnected with the difference in kind of witnesses involved."[11] Israel's God comes first to bless. Second, and apparently contradictory of the first point, the blessings (1-14) are heavily outweighted by the curses (15-68). While this has analogies in other ancient treaties,[12] the explanation probably lies in Israel's tendency to go astray. This tendency was already well attested during her journey through the wilderness.

[10]See F. C. Fensham, "Malediction and Benediction in Ancient Near Eastern Vassal-Treaties and the O.T.," in *Zeitschrift Für Die Alttestamentliche Wissenschaft* (Berlin: Töpelmann, 74 Band, 1962), Heft 1, pp. 1-8.

[11]*Op. cit.*, p. 97, fn. 39.

[12]Kitchen, *op. cit.*, p. 97, fn. 41.

1. *Blessings* (28:1-14)

Obedience to **the voice of the Lord thy God** (1) and His **commandments** expressed in the covenant will bring **these blessings** (2). They are spelled out in the succeeding verses. First, there is a series of six beatitudes—**Blessed shalt thou be** (3-6). They promise blessing in every area of life. The last three especially indicate their comprehensiveness. Prosperity is promised in **basket and store** (5; kneading trough). The **basket** was used to garner, and the kneading trough to prepare the produce of the soil for eating. Verse 6 means that their work would be blessed from start to finish.

After this comprehensive blessing three areas are specified in which further blessing is promised, and these become the motif of the rest of the chapter. If obedient, the nation will enjoy victory over her **enemies** (7). Though they advance against her bravely in a single body, they will be routed in every direction. Further, she will enjoy blessing in her **storehouses** (8), i.e., material prosperity. Israel shall also know moral and spiritual well-being in that God **shall establish** her as His **holy people** (9). These blessings are repeated in reverse order in vv. 10-14. In 10 the expression **shall see that thou art called by the name of the Lord** is more properly rendered "shall see that the Lord's name is called over thee." This expresses divine ownership, as does v. 9.[13] Verses 11-12 promise material prosperity. **His good treasure** (12) refers to **the rain . . . in his season.** Verse 13 corresponds to 7, holding out the expectation of rising power and influence. Throughout, the dependence of this blessing upon obedience is emphasized (1, 9, 13-14).

2. *Curses* (28:15-68)

After the blessings come six groups of curses. The first (15-19) consists of the reversal of the blessings in 3-6. Then follow three cycles of curses (20-26, 27-37, 38-48) on the pattern of the blessings of 7-14. The nation may be blessed militarily, materially, and spiritually, but she will be cursed in these same areas if she breaks the covenant. The most dire of these curses—military defeat—is taken up and expounded as a single curse (49-57). The chapter ends with a warning curse summarizing all the others

[13]See Driver's note, *op. cit.*, p. 306.

(58-68). The whole sequence is one of the most solemn and eloquent in Scripture. It produces much of its effect through repetition.

a. The reversal of covenant blessings (28:15-19). Obedience will bring blessing (8); disobedience will bring **all these curses** (15). This is expressed strikingly in that these verses are an exact reversal of the boons promised earlier. Verse 15 corresponds to v. 1; vv. 16-19, with a slight change, follow the order of 3-6.

b. Curses of man and nature: cycle one (28:20-26). Verses 20-24 describe the cursing of the physical and material realms. Man and nature are both afflicted—man with disease,[14] and nature with plague and drought. **Blasting** (22) refers to the withering effect of the scorching east wind from the desert. Verse 23 refers to withholding the rain. There shall be no clouds—the **heaven** will be as bright as **brass.** The **earth** will be dry and crusted—as hard as **iron.** The withholding of rain leads the author to combine the thoughts of **blasting** (22) and drought in 24. The only **rain** would be the **dust** with which the east wind filled the air as it blew in from the sands of the desert. Verses 25-26 describe military disaster. Verse 25 is the reversal of v. 7. The last clause of 25, **And shalt be removed into all the kingdoms of the earth,** is better rendered, "And you shall be a horror to all the kingdoms of the earth" (RSV). The thought is that of Jer. 18: 15-17. The defeat in battle would be such that it would lead to the dissolution of the nation. The final indignity would be that man, who was made to have dominion over the creatures of the earth (Gen. 1:26), would become their hapless prey. There would not even be anyone to **fray** (drive) **them away** (26).

The fact that these disasters come from the hand of **the Lord** (20-22, 24-25) is indicative of His repudiation of Israel as His people (9-10).

c. Curses of man and nature: cycle two (28:27-37). The same theme continues in this section although the cursing of man takes predominance (27-35). The rejection of the people by God is more explicit than in the preceding cycle (36-37). Kline notes[15] that of the four forms of curse mentioned in 27-35, dis-

[14]For attempted medical identifications of the diseases listed in 21-22 see George Adam Smith, *op. cit.*, p. 311.

[15]*Op. cit.*, p. 127.

ease, madness, oppression, frustration, the first three lead up to the fourth and then are repeated after it in reverse order: i.e., the arrangement is inverted.

The curse will affect man physically. "The boils of Egypt . . . the ulcers and the scurvy and the itch, of which you cannot be healed" (27, RSV), may be forms of plague. The curse will also affect man mentally, resulting in **madness** (28, confusion) worse than physical blindness (29*a*). At 29*b* it becomes clear that one of the agents of divine judgment is the foreign invader—**Thou shalt be . . . oppressed.** Hence man's social life will also be thrown into chaos. The frustrations that men were exempted from military service to avoid (20:5-7) will come upon them inexorably (30). Property will be expropriated **before** their very **eyes** (31). Their children will be sold into slavery while they **look** on in palsied helplessness (cf. 32-34). Verses 33-35 repeat these same judgments in reverse order.

The climax of this cycle is the rejection of the people by **the Lord** (36), symbolized by national exile and the worshipping of **other gods, wood and stone.**

d. Curses of man and nature: cycle three (28:38-48). The material curse occupies 38-44, though the note of military defeat is present in 41. The basic theme is that judgment in the form of pests and blight will reduce the Israelites to poverty. In reversal of the promise of vv. 12-13, they will have to borrow from **the stranger** (43-44). The cause of **these** material **curses** is spiritual defection (45-46). Israel's rejection of **God** (47) will be sealed by His rejection of them in handing them over to their **enemies** (48).

e. The curse of national overthrow (28:49-57). In this section the most fearful of all the curses—military defeat—is expanded as a single curse. This constitutes the climax, since there could be no greater mark of divine disapproval than the overthrow of the nation.

The horrors that attend it will be as bad as the curse itself. These will come from without and within. From without will come the invading foe of such a character as to strike terror. It will be **a nation . . . as swift as the eagle** (vulture, 49), speaking an unknown **tongue** and utterly pitiless (50). Besides spoiling the **land** (51) he will **besiege** and overthrow the cities (52). As a result of **the siege** (53), privation will be such that the beleaguered Israelites will resort to cannibalism. **The man that is tender** (54, the most refined) will be reduced to such straits that he will not share, even with his **wife** and surviving **children, the flesh of his children** (55) he is now consuming. Not even maternal instincts or feminine propriety will be able to withstand the intense privation. The lady of rank, who **would not adventure to set the sole of her foot upon the ground** (56), accustomed as she is to being borne in a litter, would devour her afterbirth (cf. RSV) and **her children** born during the siege. But she would do so **secretly** to avoid having to share even this grisly meal with her **husband** and other children (56-57).

f. A warning summary curse (28:58-68). To this point the vast majority of the curses have been in the indicative. Now as the final series commences, the conditional—**if thou wilt not observe** (58)—with which they began (15) is resumed. This is to remind Israel that these drastic results are not inevitable but will occur only through disobedience. The theme of this final series is roughly like the first (15-19), namely, the reversal of covenant blessings. Here, however, the blessings with which the curses are contrasted are those of the original covenant promise to Abraham (Gen. 12:2), subsequently confirmed in the miraculous deliverance from Egypt.

Obedience brought exemption from the plagues of Egypt (Exod. 8:22-23; 9:4, 6-7, 26; 10:23; 11:7). In contrast disobedience would bring not only these **plagues** (59) but other judgments **not written** (61) in the covenant. **Wonderful** (59) is better "extraordinary" (RSV). If obedience enabled the Israelites to multiply even under oppression (Exod. 1:12), the divine judgments would decimate them (62). If obedience brought them to the Promised Land (Gen. 12:1), disobedience would drive them **from off the land** (63). They would become a scattered remnant, reduced to pagan servitude (64). Even in exile they would **find no ease** (65). Seeing their lives hanging **in doubt** (66), they would be a perpetual prey to anxiety (67). They are pictured as being transported in slave traders' **ships** again to **Egypt** to a bondage worse than that of their forefathers. They would suffer the ultimate indignity of being undesired even as **bondmen and bondwomen** (68).

Prophecy and curse mingle as the penalty of disobedience assumes the form of banishment from **the land** (63-64). There is no inconsistency between this and the threat of return to Egypt, which became a symbol of divine rejection (Hos. 8:13).

This chapter is the most sustained exposition in the book of one of the central doctrines of Deuteronomy, that obedience brings prosperity and disobedience disaster. According to many scholars this view is peculiar to what is identified as the Deuteronomic theology. It is a pragmatic theology which "teaches that the fortunes of Israel will inevitably reflect its religious loyalty, and that when it is faithful and pure in its worship and life, prosperity will mark its way, while religious declension will be followed by disaster and curse."[16] In the light of NT teaching such a view is at best a half-truth, since in many cases faithfulness to God brings the reverse of prosperity.

The author of Deuteronomy would not have denied this. Indeed George Adam Smith points out that there is at least one passage in the book which explains suffering in didactic rather than corrective or retributive terms (8:2-3).[17] That, however, is not the point which the book needed or intended to emphasize. The emphasis required as the Israelites were about to enter Canaan with all its temptations was that disobedience would bring disaster.

Even if all suffering cannot be explained on such terms, an important part of it can be. If the universe was created and ordered by God it will—although fallen—reflect His character. Hence the truly "natural" life is the life lived according to His will. To live otherwise is to live against the grain of life, to rub life the wrong way. This cannot be the way to peace or prosperity. Baines Atkinson summarizes the matter judiciously when he says: "The issue is that there is a measure of material prosperity promised by God to His people,"[18] a conclusion that is surely justified by our Lord's words in Matt. 6:33.

Within this area the chapter teaches of "Blessing and Judgment in Human Life." (1) God's primary intent is to bless. The precedence of the blessings over the curses, in contrast to the

[16]H. H. Rowley, *The Growth of the Old Testament* (London: Hutchinson's University Library, 1956), p. 27.

[17]*Op. cit.*, p. xxxviii.

[18]*The Beauty of Holiness* (London: Epworth Press, 1953), p. 131. His whole treatment of prosperity as one of "The Fruits of Perfect Love" (pp. 128-31) is finely balanced.

reverse order in secular covenants, is striking. Vriezen rightly protests against the misrepresentation of the God of the OT as a God of judgment in contrast with the God of mercy in the NT.[19] Hos. 11:8-9 and Lam. 3:32-33 are typical of OT passages which speak with the same voice as John 3:17 and 12:47. (2) The way to blessing is obedience. (3) The penalty of disobedience is judgment. This principle, whose operation Deuteronomy shows in the temporal realm, obtains also in the eternal. Those who will not receive Christ as Saviour will face Him as Judge (John 3:18, 36).

C. Taking the Covenant Oath, 29:1—30:20

The contents of the covenant, including the benefits of obeying and the penalties for breaking it, have been set forth. There remains only the sealing of the covenant by the taking of the oath. It is this act and its accompaniments that are the subject of cc. 29—30. To underscore the solemnity of the oath the leading elements of the covenant are repeated in brief, so that these chapters are to a degree a recapitulation of the entire covenant. Thus 29:1-9 answers to the historical prologue in 1:6—4:49; also 29:16-29 answers to the sanctions of 28:1-68; and 30:8, 10-14 alludes to the stipulations of the covenant embodied in 5:1—26:19; while 30:15-20 contains the summons to the oath and the invocation of witnesses, as yet unmentioned but integral parts of the standard treaty pattern.[20] Here, as throughout Deuteronomy, there is a strong note of exhortation. The book is not merely a legal covenant but a collection of material for the public proclamation of a covenant. It might be called a "preached covenant"—hence the strong hortatory element.

1. *Exhortation on the Basis of History* (29:1-9)

Verse 1 is regarded as 28:69 in the Hebrew text. Grammatically, it may be either the subscription of c. 28 or the superscription of c. 29. **The words of the covenant** (1, 9) may refer back to the terms of cc. 5—26, or more probably forward to the words Moses is about to speak (cf. 4:45; 5:1).[21]

The **covenant . . . made . . . in Horeb** (1) is about to be renewed in **Moab.** As Israel enters into this renewal, **Moses** re-

[19]*Op. cit.*, pp. 274-76. [20]Mendenhall, *op. cit.*, pp. 32 ff

[21]Manley, *The Book of the Law*, pp. 151-52.

minds her of the blessings received from her **Lord** in the past (2). Three are recalled. First was the deliverance from **Egypt** (2-3). **Temptations** (3) is better "great trials" (RSV). Second was the miraculous provision **in the wilderness** (5-6); and third, the victories over **Sihon** and **Og** (7-8; 2:30—3:11), whose lands they now occupied. Yet despite these displays of supernatural power, given to evoke faith in **God** (6; cf. 8:2-4), Israel was still untrusting (4). "In attributing their dullness of heart to Jehovah, Moses only adopts the mode of thought, which runs throughout the Old Testament, of attributing all things to Jehovah as their ultimate source."[22] Regarding this renewed **covenant** things must be different (9).

2. *Parties to the Covenant* (29:10-15)

The people were assembled for the taking of the covenant oath: leaders (10), children, **wives,** foreigners, servants—all were included (11). Nor was it merely the living who were incorporated. The covenant extends to those as yet unborn—to **him that is not here with us this day** (15). The purpose is twofold, as are the parties: that Israel should be Jehovah's **people** and that He should be their God (13; cf. 26:17-18). Indeed, Israel's taking the oath of loyalty to God is but the fulfillment of God's oath to her founding fathers (Gen. 17:7).

3. *Exhortation Based on Covenant Sanctions* (29:16-29)

The covenant was to be observed not only because of God's past blessings, but also because of the dire consequences of disobedience. The chief threat to Israel would be idolatry, and this section begins with a double warning, although this is obscured in the KJV. At the beginning of vv. 16 and 18 some such words as "Take heed" have to be supplied. However alluring idol worship might appear, its results would be disastrous. The poisonous **root** (18) would yield bitter fruit. Such defection might well take place on the part of one who imagined that the **curse** (19, "sworn covenant," RSV) guaranteed unconditional security. So far from doing so, infringement of it would bring the destruction of the entire nation. For the expression **to add drunkenness to thirst** (19) read, "This would lead to the sweeping away of moist and dry alike" (RSV), a proverb indicating general ruin.

[22]Manley, NBC, p. 218.

In 21-29, the perspective both widens and lengthens. In 18-21, the emphasis has been on some treacherous individual. The effect of his action on the nation has been mentioned incidentally (19). Now, however, he is seen to have been a source of infection to the whole nation, and the tone changes from warning to prediction. The fearful consequences are portrayed in a dramatic dialogue between **your children that shall rise up after you** (22; Israelites of the future) and **the stranger,** foreign visitors for whom Israel has become a grisly tourist attraction, a second **Sodom** (23; cf. Gen. 14:2; 19:29). And even the astonished heathen will understand the cause of the dereliction—**Because they have forsaken the covenant of the Lord God** (25). They themselves felt bound to their own gods, false as they were. Faithless Israel had shown a perfidiousness which not even the pagans could match (26); hence her overthrow and exile (27-28). The warning is therefore repeated. **The secret things** (29) of the future are in the mind of **God** alone. Israel's business is to live by what she knows now—**this law,** the covenant, the will of God.

4. *Obedience a Cure for National Overthrow* (30:1-10)

The tone is now unmistakably predictive. Exile is not a threat but a certainty—**when all these things are come upon thee** (1). This passage looks beyond **the blessing and the curse** to the period of restoration. As such it is an apt sequel to 29:16-29. While imperfect connections of thought *may* be explained by dislocation of the text, the character of Deuteronomy as a "preaching of the law" may also be a contributory factor. As Manley says: "The stream of words flows on, as befits a discourse, with various turnings, and not as in a formal document. . . . The arrangement is therefore governed by the lawgiver's dominant religious motive and the various matters which required his attention. Caution should therefore be exercised before passages are put down to later insertions, when they may be merely digressions."[23]

The future overthrow of the nation need not be final. If idolatry brought disaster, obedience will bring restoration. The purposes of God are merciful and He "will restore your fortunes, and have compassion upon you" (3, RSV). From "the ends of heavens" (4, Berk.) He will bring them back to the promised

[23]*The Book of the Law*, p. 68.

land (5), blessing them with prosperity (9) and cursing their erstwhile **enemies** (7). This, however, is conditional upon whole-hearted obedience (2, 8, 10), an obedience which God himself will enable them to render. The sign of Israel's covenant was circumcision of the flesh. In His own time God will visit them with a spiritual circumcision whereby, from renewed and willing hearts, they will yield the voluntary obedience that He requires (Jer. 31:31-34; Ezek. 36:26-28; Rom. 2:28-29; Col. 2:10-11).

5. *Summons to Decision* (30:11-20).

The secret of that future obedience will be its ease. But with that thought the mind of the lawgiver leaps back to the present and to all those who "stand this day . . . before the Lord your God" (29:10). For them also obedience is possible. The divine requirements are easy both to ascertain and to understand. Its availability is the chief feature of the divine law: it is **in thy mouth, and in thy heart, that thou mayest do it** (14).

Consequently the time for exposition is past. This is the moment for decision. The alternatives are set forth starkly: **life and good** (15) are dependent upon obedience; **death and evil** are consequent upon disobedience (15-18). **Denounce** (18) means to "declare." These alternatives are the essence of the theology of the book. As if to add solemnity, **heaven and earth** (19) are summoned to witness that the opportunity for free choice has been offered. The speech closes with an exhortation to **choose life** and its accompanying benefits (19-20).

From these chapters it is easy to derive "Modern Lessons from the Old Faith." For while the new covenant supersedes the old, it is in the sense of fulfilling rather than nullifying it. Christ is the Fulfillment of the promise to Abraham (Gen. 12:3; Gal. 3:29), and the principles of the divine dealings with men are unchanging. Three lessons are particularly stressed here: (1) The conditionality of security, 29:16-29, esp. 19-20. The covenant guarantees blessing only on condition of obedience (cf. Amos 9:10). (2) The possibility of inward obedience, 30:1-14, esp. 6. For us, through Christ, the devotion of the whole heart to God without division has become a practical possibility. This is the essence of the new covenant. (3) The demand for decision, 30:15-20.

In 15-20 we see "Make Your Choice." (1) God makes clear the alternatives, 15-18; (2) Man makes the decision, 19; (3) Final consequences are certain, 17-18, 20 (G. B. Williamson).

Section IV *Perpetuation of the Covenant*

Deuteronomy 31:1—32:47

Significant elements in many covenant documents were provisions for the succession, for the depositing of a copy of the covenant in the Temple, and orders for the regular public reading of it. There was also a list of witnesses guaranteeing the covenant, and an outline of the procedure which would be followed if the vassal rebelled. It cannot be accidental that precisely these elements are present in this final section of Deuteronomy. It is true that their order differs from that of many secular treaties, but as Mendenhall pointed out,[1] these themselves show variation in order, omission, etc., so that the pattern was not rigid.

Again these chapters maintain the hortatory note observed elsewhere in Deuteronomy, so that the book is not a bare legal document but rather a simultaneous presentation of the covenant and exhortation to obey it. It seems fair therefore to regard these chapters as pointing to a renewal of God's covenant with Israel in view of the impending death of Moses, who combined in his person the roles of divine mediator and national representative and head.

A. Preparatory Safeguards, 31:1-30

1. *Naming a Successor* (31:1-8)

The death of Moses was approaching. On two counts he could not lead the Israelites into Canaan. First, age had exhausted his powers of leadership. He could **no more go out and come in** (1), though cf. 34:7. Second, he had been divinely banned from crossing **Jordan** on account of an earlier sin (cf. 4:21-22; Num. 20:12). God had, therefore, named his successor. **Joshua** (3), already ordained as the nation's leader (Num. 27:18-23; Deut. 1:38), was the divine appointee. But God himself would be their real Leader and they could expect victories in the future like those over **Sihon and . . . Og** (4-5; cf. 2:32—3:

[1]*Op. cit.*, p. 32.

10). Joshua was not to **be afraid** (6), and for the same reason: **The Lord, he it is that doth go before thee** (6-8).

2. *Orders for Reading the Covenant* (31:9-13)

Israel's covenant was to be read **every seven years**[2] in **the year of release** (10; cf. 15:1-15) at **the feast of tabernacles** (cf. 16:13-15). The responsibility for reading was entrusted jointly to the **priests** and **elders** (9), i.e., religious and civil authorities. Whereas males alone were under orders to attend the feast (16: 16), in the seventh year **all Israel** was to gather: **men . . . women . . . children,** and **stranger** (11-12). All who enjoy the benefits of the covenant must also be made aware of its obligations. Although this was not the only occasion on which the facts and meaning of the covenant were to be taught (cf. 6:6-7, 20-25), it would be a dramatic and memorable reminder to the entire nation.

3. *The Charge to Joshua, and a Prediction* (31:14-23)

Two themes are fused in these verses, the commissioning of Joshua and the writing of the Song of Moses. Some scholars hold that these verses are badly arranged. For this, as well as for other reasons,[3] they assign them to an independent and inconsistent source. But the way in which Moses and Joshua are associated in both the commissioning ceremony (14) and the writing of the song (19; cf. 32:44) may indicate that Joshua is being especially commissioned in the full knowledge of Israel's future rebellion.

The tabernacle of the congregation (14) or tent of meeting was the place of personal encounter with God (Exod. 25:22; 29: 42; 30:36). Here **Joshua,** who had already been commissioned through Moses (7-8; Num. 27:18-23), was confirmed in his commission by the immediate presence of **the Lord** (15, 23). Moreover, it was made plain to him, as Israel's future leader, that the nation would **forsake me, and break my covenant** (16). Together with Moses he was charged to **write** a **song** of witness and **teach it** to **the children of Israel** (19). This **song** would fulfill the function of witnesses to the covenant (see comments on 32:1).

[2]Among the Hittites, to whose treaties Deuteronomy bears closest resemblance, covenants were read publicly every one to three years (Mendenhall, *op. cit.*, p. 40).

[3]See Driver's summary, *op. cit.*, pp. 337-38.

When Israel played false, the song, by its existence as well as its contents, would testify that she was knowingly breaking her word (20-21).

4. *Placing the Document with the Ark* (31:24-27)

The ark was already known as **the ark of the covenant** (25) because it contained the tables of the Sinai covenant. In this case, however, the covenant was to be placed "by the side of" (26, RSV) rather than inside the ark. Here it would fulfill the role of being a covenant **witness** in addition to the song.

The reference to the **writing** (24) activity of Moses is interesting (cf. 9, 22; Exod. 17:14; Num. 33:2). While such phrases need not mean that he was in every case the actual scribe of every part, there is no reason to doubt that in a fundamental sense he was the architect and author of the Book of Deuteronomy.

5. *Public Reading of the Song* (31:28-30)

Two witnesses have already been named, the song (19-21) and the covenant document placed by the side of the ark (26). However, the song must be read publicly (28), so that when in the future God punished the Israelites for their disobedience (29), none would be able to plead ignorance as an excuse. The song itself was a witness, but Moses also called **heaven and earth to record against them** (28). He summoned the entire created universe to testify that the covenant had been concluded between Israel and God.[4]

The central commands in this chapter—that the covenant be read regularly, that the Song of Witness be written and taught to Israel, and that the covenant document be placed by the side of the ark—embody a single fear, that Israel will forget her promise and break it. It was an ever-present danger then and is so still. John Wesley believed that an important "means of increasing serious religion, which has been frequently practiced by our forefathers, and attended with eminent blessings"[5] was to

[4]A typical Hittite suzerain-vassal treaty lists "the mountains, the rivers, the springs, the great Sea, heaven and earth, the winds and clouds—let these be witnesses to this treaty and to the oath" (J. B. Pritchard, *op. cit.*, pp. 203-5).

[5]*Journal*, Aug. 6, 1755 (Standard Edition, ed. Nehemiah Curnock; London: Epworth Press, 1938), IV, 126.

renew "in every point our covenant that the Lord should be our God."[6] He conducted his first Covenant Service on August 11, 1755, and since the first Sunday of 1782 it has marked the opening of each new year for Methodists around the world. The recalling of our promises to God is a necessary complement to recalling His promises to us. Done corporately it will instruct our children (13); done individually it will quicken us.

High heaven that heard that solemn vow
That vow renewed shall daily hear
Till in life's latest hour I bow,
And bless in death a bond so dear.

(P. Doddridge)

B. Impeachment Procedure: The Song of Witness, 32:1-47

The typical ancient Near Eastern treaty contained a list of witnesses to the terms of the covenant. A further feature was a procedure for taking action against a rebellious vassal.[7] This contained many of the elements of the covenant itself, but recast in the form of a lawsuit.[8] The Song of Moses fuses these two elements of witness and lawsuit.

It has been pointed out that Deuteronomy 32 goes beyond the normal lawsuit form by contemplating restoration after judgment (26-43). On this ground it has been described as a later reformulation of the lawsuit pattern for the purposes of confession and instruction.[9] However Deuteronomy is not simply a legal document. When it uses legal forms it does so for its own purposes, and there is no reason why it should not have adapted the secular lawsuit pattern to convey its own message. The lan-

[6]*Journal,* Dec. 25, 1747 (ed. *cit.*), III, 328.

[7]Mendenhall, *op. cit.,* pp. 35 ff.

[8]See Julien Harvey, "Le 'Rib-Pattern' Réquisitoire Prophétique Sur La Rupture de L'Alliance," *Biblica,* XLIII (1962), 172-96, to which the pattern of the exegesis of c. 32 offered below is greatly indebted.

[9]G. Ernest Wright, "The Lawsuit of God: A Form-Critical Study of Deuteronomy 32," in *Israel's Prophetic Heritage, Essays in Honour of James Muilenburg,* ed. Bernhard W. Anderson and Walter Harrelson (London: SCM Press, 1962), pp. 26-27, 40-41, 54-58.

guage as well as the poetic structure tends to confirm this.[10] This lawsuit or controversy pattern later became a standard weapon in the hands of the prophets for charging Israel with breach of faith (cf. Isa. 1:2; Hos. 4:1; 12:2; Mic. 6:2).[11]

1. *The Summons of Witnesses* (32:1-3)

The procedure for bringing the rebellious people to trial begins with the summoning of the covenant witnesses, **heavens** and **earth** (1), to give evidence that the compact was legally made. But the summons also includes an affirmation of the rightness of the covenant. The **doctrine** (2) or teaching of the covenant has the effect of **rain** on vegetation because it is the word of God. It should be received in this spirit (3). **Doctrine** (2, *leqah*) is used only in the wisdom literature, as Prov. 1:5; 4:2; Job 11:4; and Isa. 29:24.

2. *Preliminary Statement of the Charge* (32:4-6)

Israel's God is **the Rock** (4; cf. 15, 18, 30-31, 37), the essence of stability and reliability. His government of the world is **perfect: for all his ways are** just. This perfection of performance is but the expression of His perfection of character, which is faithful, **without iniquity, just and right.** His people present a sad contrast, and with v. 5 the charge begins. "They have dealt corruptly with him, they are no longer his children because of their blemish" (5, RSV). In v. 6 the charge is pressed interrogatively. Where is the wisdom in repudiating **thy father,** who rescued the nation from bondage in Egypt? (Cf. 8:1-5.) **Hath he not made thee, and established thee?**

3. *The Indictment in Detail* (32:7-18)

The charge against Israel is that she has repaid God badly for His multiplied blessings. This idea, outlined in 4-6, is now developed at length, recounting God's goodness in 7-14. Israel's ingratitude is described in 15-18. The benevolence of God dates from **the days of old** (7), indeed from the very founding of **the nations** (8), when each was allotted its **inheritance.** At that early time the nations were so disposed as to leave adequate

[10]For the former see W. F. Albright, "Some Remarks on the Song of Moses in Dt. 32," *Vetus Testamentum,* IX (1959), 339-46. For the latter see Patrick W. Skehan, "The Structure of the Song of Moses in Deuteronomy," *Catholic Biblical Quarterly,* XIII, No. 4 (Oct., 1951), pp. 153-63.

[11]Mendenhall, *op. cit.,* pp. 44 ff.

space for **Israel** (cf. Gen. 10:32). The people of Israel then became **the Lord's portion** (9).[12]

In v. 10 the thought advances to the wilderness wanderings—overlooking the deliverance from Egypt in order to emphasize the divine care. Israel was **found . . . in a desert,** like an abandoned child (10; Ezek. 16:3-6). God cared for her **as the apple** (pupil) **of his eye.** Since God is constantly watching Israel, her image is reflected in the pupil of His eye. The metaphor of the **eagle** (11, vulture) which stirs the fledglings out of the nest to teach them to fly, but hovers nearby to bear them up if they fall, further emphasizes God's care. The coming accusation is anticipated by the assertion that God **alone led them** without the aid of any **strange god** (12).

The third mark of favor to Israel is the occupancy of the Promised Land, "flowing with milk and honey." Possession of **the high places** (13) implies undisputed ownership. After the restricted if adequate diet of the desert, the lush produce of field and flock was blessing indeed (13-14). It is sometimes claimed, in proof that the song cannot be Mosaic, that 7-14 look back on the Exodus and occupation of the land as events of the remote past. This is either to overlook or deny the predictive element in them, as in the earlier passages on which they are based; e.g., 28:15-68; 9:16—30:10.

In 8-14 we see God's care of His people pictured "As Eagles." (1) God feathers the nest, 8-10, 12-14; (2) God stirs up the nest, 11*a*; (3) God teaches the young to fly as nature intended, 11*b*; (4) God upholds the falling one, 11c (G. B. Williamson).

The splendor of the divine beneficence serves but to highlight the baseness of Israel's response. **Jeshurun** (15, "upright") comes from the same root as the word "Israel," for which it is an alternative. It may be a pet name. There is thus great irony in its use here. Israel responded to God's goodness like an overfed beast, becoming refractory and even contemptuous of the

[12]An alternative explanation of 8-9 has been suggested on the basis of the text of the last clause of 8 preserved in the Gk. OT and the text of Deuteronomy from Cave 4 at Qumran. It reads, "According to the number of the sons of God." The "sons of God" are held to be God's heavenly council of supernatural but inferior beings, through whom He administers the universe (cf. I Kings 22:19-22; Job 1:6). The meaning would then be that, whereas other nations are ruled by God's subordinates, Israel is the direct responsibility of God.

God who **made him.** Not content with ignoring Him (18), Israel turned to **strange gods** (16) and the **abominations** that went with them (cf. 18:9-12). These gods are called **devils** (17). In Ps. 106: 37, the only other OT occurrence of the word, they are the recipients of human sacrifice. These were **gods they** never **knew . . . new gods** whom their **fathers** had never heard of. Any god was good enough and none too bad for Israel to serve (16-17), while the God who "begot you, and . . . gave you birth" (RSV, 18) was ignored.

4. *The Sentence* (32:19-25)

The sentence now follows in two parts. In 19-21 the principle is emphasized; in 22-25 the particulars are added. The principle is that of strict justice. Since His children had ignored Him (18), He would **hide** His **face from them** (20). Since they want to go their own way, He will let them and **will see what their end shall be.** Note the recurrent formula in Rom. 1:24, 26, 28, "God gave them up." Dodd writes, "Paul . . . sees that the really awful thing is to fall out of His hands, and to be left to oneself in a world where the choice of evil brings its own moral retribution."[13] Since Israel had **provoked** God with a no-god and foolish idols, He will provoke them with a no-**people** and a **foolish nation** (21). They prefer foolishness; they shall have it. The perfect match for a god who is the denial of everything divine is a people who are a denial of everything civilized—a horde of savage barbarians. Having all of what you want, as Midas discovered, is a good definition of hell. This judicial abandonment by God, far from being a shrugging off of responsibility on His part, is **a fire . . . kindled** (22) against sin which encompasses the universe, reaching to the depths of the nether world.[14] **The lowest hell** is here "Sheol" (RSV), the grave; not the eternal abode of the wicked, as in the NT.

The second part of the sentence expounds the ways in which the penalty will be imposed by the infliction of the covenant curses (cf. 28:15-68). Like a hunter in hot pursuit, God **will spend** His **arrows upon them** (23). **Hunger** (24), pestilence, and

[13] *The Epistle of Paul to the Romans*, "The Moffatt New Testament Commentary" (London: Hodder and Stoughton, 1932), p. 29.

[14] Contrast Dodd's version of the wrath of God, not as "the attitude of God to man," but as "an inevitable process of cause and effect in a moral universe" (*op. cit.*, p. 23).

plague will culminate in invasion in which street warfare will spare neither **young man** nor **virgin** nor **the man of gray hairs** (25).

5. *The Promise of Mercy* (32:26-43)

The sentence, which is obviously about to pass over into one of death and annihilation for Israel, is suddenly brought up short. It is stopped by the divine fear of the effect that such an ending would have upon the invader. **Scatter them into corners** (26) is better "scatter them afar" (RSV). In the stupefaction of their triumph over Israel, **the enemy** (27) would infer that their own might had brought them victory. **The wrath of the enemy** means "provocation" (RSV). **Behave themselves strangely** means to "judge amiss" (RSV), i.e., fail to see the truth. Far from revealing the glory of God, such a reaction would call it in question.

This mistaken interpretation of their victory by Israel's conquerors is developed in 28-35. If they had insight they would see that ultimate judgment was to be **their latter end** (29; cf. 34-35). The defeat of Israel's hosts by their puny adversaries could have but one explanation, that God had deserted Israel (30). It certainly could not be explained by any moral superiority of the enemy, whose **vine is of the vine of Sodom** (32). If anything, they are worse than the Israelites. Consequently, judgment is inevitable. The deadly harvest is **laid up** in the storehouses of God (34). Soon the moment of divine **vengeance** (vindication) will come as **calamity** descends (35).

The thought now turns directly to Israel (36-43). On the brink of total ruin, she sees the tide turn at the eleventh hour. In the moment of her helplessness, when **there is none . . . left,** "bond or free" (36, RSV), God will step in to **judge his people, and repent himself for his servants.** He will vindicate His people and show them compassion. The depth of Israel's extremity will compel her to acknowledge His power. The gods in whom she fondly trusted—her **rock** (37), as they are called ironically—have let her down. There is but one God who alone holds the power of life and death (39). And He now swears that He will **whet** His **sword** (41) and **render** to His **enemies** their due. He lifts up His **hand,** taking an oath that, as **I live for ever,** so justice will be done (40-41). In 42, the sword swings into action. "I will make my arrows drunk with blood, and My sword shall devour flesh with the blood of the slain and the captives, from the long-haired heads of the foe" (42, Berk.). Their long hair marked either their fierce, unkempt appearance or their religious dedication to warfare (Ps. 68:21).

The song concludes with a summons to all **nations** to **rejoice** (43) in God's righteous intervention. The saving of Israel is cause for rejoicing, for through her all nations of the earth shall be blessed (Gen. 12:3). The occasion of rejoicing is, first, the exhibition of justice, and second, the exercise of mercy. **Be merciful** means "make atonement." The same God who requites sin forgives and cleanses it; He is both "a just God and a Saviour" (Isa. 45:21), both "just, and the justifier of him which believeth in Jesus" (Rom. 3:26).

6. *Moses' Exhortation* (32:44-47)

As indicated by 31:14, 19, Joshua was associated with Moses in both writing the song and teaching it to Israel. **Hoshea** (44, Salvation) was his original name, which Moses changed to Joshua (Jehovah is salvation, Num. 13:8, 16). The occurrence of **Hoshea** here is probably a spelling mistake, created by the omission of one jot (cf. Matt. 5:18). Moses exhorts **all Israel** (45) to give heed to **all the words** (46) of the song, so that they may teach them to the rising generation. This **is not a vain thing** (47, trifle), for their **life** is at stake.

The Song of Moses is a powerful exposition of the doctrine of God's judgment in history, as the story of Israel is a striking example of it. The biblical doctrine of the divine lordship of history—of which judgment is but one aspect—is here dramatically affirmed. If God has an agreement with Israel to bless her, He also has an agreed procedure for bringing her to book in the event of sin and rebellion. God does not, as Carlyle thought, sit in heaven and do nothing. There are times and places where right appears to be flouted and wrong unrequited, so that it is difficult to "justify the ways of God to men." In such times, with Forsyth, we may "trust in Christ" for what we cannot "trace in affairs."[15] Moses first and Israel later found the justification of God in that act whereby in forgiving sin He also condemned it (32:43). In vaster measure we may find it in that similar act whereby He accomplished the same for the whole world. It was the sublime demonstration of His justice and love in the cross of His Son (Rom. 3:21-26).

[15]*The Justification of God* (London: Independent Press, 1948), p. 192.

Section V The Death of Moses

Deuteronomy 32:48—34:12

With the Song of Witness the treaty pattern in Deuteronomy comes to an end. The two remaining chapters are concerned with the death of Moses. Chapter 33 records his blessing of the tribes of Israel, and c. 34 his mysterious death. The section ends with a reflection, by some other writer, on Moses' unparalleled greatness (34:10-12). However, these chapters are more than "simply a supplement to record the end of Moses,"[1] a tailpiece to round off the story and satisfy curiosity about what became of the great leader. It is difficult to resist the conclusion that, besides recounting the death of Moses, these chapters see it as holding significance for the covenant as a whole. It has been maintained that Deuteronomy embodies the covenant between God and Israel renewed in the plains of Moab in view of the impending death of Moses. If this be true, it follows that the death of Moses is tantamount to the activation of the covenant.

The decease of one leader and the succession of his appointed heir, Joshua, is the proof of the nation's fidelity to its word. The inclusion of the ritual for the ratification of the covenant (c. 27), the charging of Joshua (31:1-8, 14-23), and many features of cc. 33—34 seem to support this view. Hence the Blessing of Moses and the account of his death, while completing the biography of a great man of God, also have direct covenantal significance.

A. The Blessing of Moses, 32:48—33:29

1. *The Impending Death of Moses* (32:48-52)

The departure of Moses was more imminent than had yet been realized. **That selfsame day** (48) he was summoned to Mount Nebo to die. **This mountain Abarim, unto Mount Nebo** (49) is better translated "this mountain of the Abarim, Mount Nebo" (RSV). **Abarim** probably means "the mountain of the borderlands" and denotes a range of which Nebo is the highest

[1]Kitchen, *op. cit.*, p. 128, fn. 63.

peak.[2] Moses will not die, however, before he views the Promised Land. If "view" has the legal sense suggested in the comments on 34:1-4, then in a legal sense Moses was receiving possession of Canaan on behalf of Israel. Nevertheless, that legal possession would not be made actual for him in a personal sense. Like his brother **Aaron** before him, he must die without entering Canaan (Num. 33:37-39)—and for the same reason, sin—in his case at **Meribah-Kadesh** (50-51; cf. 1:37). **Ye sanctified me not** (51) is better, "You did not revere me as holy in the midst of the people of Israel" (RSV).

2. *The Blessing of Moses: Introduction* (33:1-5)

The blessing of their offspring by those about to die was commonplace in many ancient societies. It was moreover important, because in nomadic societies which used writing little a spoken blessing was binding,[3] having the validity of a last will and testament (cf. Gen. 27:34-38). Like Jacob before him (Gen. 49:1-27), Moses **blessed the children of Israel before his death** (1). The actual blessings (6-25) are placed in a framework (1-5, 26-29) which refers to Moses in the third person. Verses 1 and 4, like the narrative of his death, were evidently supplied by another hand. The blessings themselves however show every sign of being Mosaic. They allude to contemporary events (8, 9, 21), and the form of words, poetic diction, and structure require an early date.[4]

The claim that many of the individual blessings imply events or circumstances later than the time of Moses, e.g., 6-7, ignores the prophetic element in such blessings (cf. Luke 2:28-35). In content the blessings have a theocratic reference in contrast to the predominantly secular tone of the blessings of Jacob. They also contrast strikingly with the tone of the Song of Witness. If threat and warning are part of the covenant, blessing shall be the last word.

[2]Manley, *The Book of the Law*, p. 60.

[3]C. H. Gordon, "Biblical Customs and the Nuzu Tablets" (*Biblical Archaeologist*, III, No. 1, Feb., 1940, 8) cites an example from Nuzu or Nuzi in N.E. Iraq in the fifteenth century B.C. in which an oral blessing was upheld in court.

[4]F. M. Cross and D. N. Freedman, "The Blessing of Moses," *Journal of Biblical Literature*, LXVII (1948), 191-92.

The verses introducing the blessings constitute a poem in praise of the greatness and goodness of **the Lord** (2), Israel's God, particularly for His gift of the law. He is pictured as a fiery dawn over **Sinai,** a common figure in the OT (Judg. 5:4; Hab. 3:3). He is attended by **ten thousands of saints** (holy ones), described in the last clause of 2 and v. 3. These verses are best rendered, "At his right hand proceeded the mighty ones, yea, the guardians of the peoples. All the holy ones are at thy hand, they prostrate themselves at thy feet, they carry out thy decisions."[5] The giving of the **law** (covenant) through **Moses** (4) and its ratification by the assembly **of Israel** (5) was the recognition of God as Israel's King.

3. *Individual Blessings* (33:6-25)

Blessings are now invoked on each of the tribes except Simeon, soon to be absorbed by Judah (Josh. 19:2-9). The number 12 is made up by counting Joseph as two (17). The tribes of the sons of Jacob's wives are blessed first, followed by the tribes of the sons of the handmaids.

Reuben is blessed first (6), as he was by Jacob also. The qualified "not" (Gen. 49:4) is repeated here in the prayer that the tribe will **not** be extinguished. **The blessing of Judah** (7) is difficult to interpret; it may be a prophetic prayer that God will heal the breach between **Judah** and the northern tribes (I Kings 12:16-20). The blessing **of Levi** (8-11) is a confirmation of the tribe in the role with which it had already been invested. Scattered throughout Israel at the word of Jacob (Gen. 49:5-7), Levi had been raised to the rank of priestly tribe. They were keepers of the **Thummim** and **Urim** (8), the sacred breastplate through which the will of God was revealed (see comments on Exod. 28:30). **At Massah** and **Meribah,** Levi, in the persons of Moses and Aaron, was tested and failed (Exod. 17:1-7; Deut. 6:16). *Their* testing of God was the exposure of their own unbelief and so also God's testing of *them.* Nevertheless, at the episode of the golden calf they had remained loyal to God even at the expense of disowning their **brethren** (9; cf. Exod. 32:26-29). Accordingly **they shall teach Jacob** (10), exercising the functions of the priesthood, instruction in the law and sacrifice. A prayer is of-

[5]*Ibid.,* p. 193. RSV, *contra,* seems to envision the persons of 2 and 3 as different groups.

fered for **the work of his hands** (11) and the destruction of his enemies.

Having blessed the tribe of Jacob's firstborn and the royal and priestly tribes, Moses now turns to the tribes of the sons of Rachel. **Benjamin** (12), the child of Jacob's old age, is blessed in terms befitting his place in his father's affections. Not only will he be secured and protected, but God himself **shall dwell between his shoulders.** The term **dwell** comes from the Hebrew word for God's dwelling among His people, while **shoulders** is used of the hill in Jerusalem on which the Temple was to stand (Josh. 15:8; 18:16, RSV). The meaning is that the Temple would be built within the boundaries of Benjamin.

The longest of the blessings is reserved for **Joseph** (13-17; cf. Gen. 49:22-26). In 13-16 material prosperity is invoked upon him. Throughout these verses read "with" instead of **for.** In 14, **the moon** is conceived as contributing to plant growth. **Him that dwelt in the bush** (16) is a reference to God's manifestation of himself to Moses (Exod. 3:2). Military power is the subject of 17, **horns** being a symbol of strength. **Ephraim** and **Manasseh,** the sons of Joseph, became the recipients of the double portion taken from Reuben, whose it was as firstborn, and given by Jacob to Joseph (Gen. 48:22).

Zebulun and **Issachar** share the next blessing (18-19). In Gen. 49:13, Zebulun is depicted as a seafaring tribe, while in the two following verses Issachar is pictured as following agriculture. These interests are confirmed in Zebulun's **going out** and in Issachar's **tents** (18). Both tribes are further represented as calling other **people** (19) to their religious festivals, at which trade would also be discussed. **Treasures hid in the sand** (19) probably refers to the manufacture of glass known to have taken place in the sands of Accho.

The remaining blessings are upon the sons of Zilpah and Bilhah, the handmaids of Leah and Rachel respectively. **Gad** is blessed (20-21) because of his military prowess. First of all the tribes to choose an inheritance, he settled in Transjordan (Num. 32:1-5). "He chose the best of the land for himself, for there a commander's portion was reserved" (21, RSV). Although the tribe had received its own inheritance, Moses was certain that, in accordance with its word (Num. 32:6-33), it would fight alongside the other tribes until they received theirs (21*b*). **Dan** (22) is credited with the capacity for sudden attack, demonstrated in their overthrow of Laish in **Bashan,** in which afterwards they settled (cf. Josh. 19:47; Judg. 18:27). **Naphtali** (23), whose lot was Upper Galilee, will be as favored by nature as by the blessing of the Lord. **West** (23) is an error. The word means "lake." Naphtali is to "possess the lake [of Galilee] and the South" (Berk.). The final blessing is upon **Asher** (24), situated upon the northwest border of Israel. Prosperity is invoked upon him, in population, popularity, and wealth. To use **oil** upon the feet was a sign of affluence. The territory of Asher was noted for its natural wealth (cf. Gen. 49:20). In view of the exposed geographical position, **strength** was also promised (25). This **strength** would be in armaments and manpower.

These individual blessings repay study. First, they should be compared with those of Gen. 49:1-27. This comparison shows that, while some tribes remained in the grip of their weaknesses or vices (e.g., Reuben), others underwent a transformation (e.g., Levi). The blessings, however, are significant in themselves, showing, as they do, the qualities God desires in and for His people: worship (Levi), honest work (Zebulun and Issachar), selflessness (Gad), security (Benjamin), and strength (Asher). Each tribe did not have the same need, but whatever its need, God could meet it. Finally, the blessings are significant as a group in that the note of harshness and cursing, present in the blessing of Jacob, is wholly absent. It would appear that, for all the fact and propriety of the warnings and threatenings of earlier chapters, Deuteronomy is to find its final note in the blessing of God. "A bruised reed shall he not break, and smoking flax shall he not quench, till he send forth judgment unto victory" (Matt. 12:20; Isa. 42:3).

4. *The Blessing of Moses: Conclusion* (33:26-29)

The introductory verses of the blessing recall the creation of the nation at Sinai (1-5). These concluding verses look forward to the successful occupation of the land with such confidence that in the Hebrew past tenses are employed in 27-28 (rather than futures as in KJV). The ground of this confidence is Israel's unique, incomparable **God,** who rides to Israel's **help** through **the sky** (26). He is their "dwelling place" (Ps. 90:1), and His support of His people (27) is as **eternal** as His being—His **arms** are never exhausted. He will deal with Israel's **enemy** so that she will be safe and prosperous. **The fountain of Jacob**

(28) refers to her people. Because her God is a unique God, **Israel** (29) is a unique people. They are **saved** (victorious) through His **shield** and **sword.** Her **enemies** will fawn upon her, i.e., yield lying obedience. She will occupy their **high places** (commanding heights of their territory).[6]

In 26-29 we see "God Incomparable." (1) God is an eternal Refuge, 27; (2) God is a dependable Support, 26; (3) God is the Source of abundant supply for every need, 28; cf. Phil. 4:19 (G. B. Williamson).

B. Death of Moses and Succession of Joshua, 34:1-12

Chapter 34 records the fulfillment by Moses of the command received in 32:48-52, of which narrative it is the continuation. The events recounted here are designed at least in part to show that, on the decease of Moses, Israel remained faithful to her covenanted word, and the divinely appointed successor was duly acknowledged. How long after the death of Moses this account was written it is impossible to say. Verses 10-12 imply that enough prophets had arisen since then to make a comparison possible.

1. *The Death of Moses* (34:1-8)

The time for Moses' death had come, but he ascended the mount not merely to die. First of all, he was shown the Promised Land. From Mount **Nebo** (1), the top of the serrated ridge or *pisgah*[7] of the mountains east of Jericho, "the bulk of W. Palestine is in sight."[8] The entire land was shown to Moses, rather than **all the land of Gilead.** The RSV reads: "And the Lord showed him all the land, Gilead as far as Dan, all Naphtali," etc. To the west he saw "Judah as far as the Western Sea" (2, RSV, i.e., the Mediterranean). To **the south** was **Jericho,** famed for its **palm trees** as far as **Zoar** (3). This was the land promised to the patriarchs, and Moses was seeing it fully. Daube, on the basis of legal analogy, suggests that in Hebrew thought the look was a symbol of acquisition by which property became legally if not

[6]Kitchen interprets the meaning as "tread upon their backs" (*op. cit.,* p. 164).

[7]**Pisgah** is a common noun with probable meaning as indicated. Cf. Num. 21:20; 23:13-14 for two other examples, and Manley, *The Book of the Law,* pp. 61-62.

[8]George Adam Smith, *op. cit.,* p. 378.

actually that of the viewer (cf. Gen. 13:14-15).[9] Moses was thus accepting from God ownership of the Promised Land on behalf of the entire people of Israel. But this merely adds poignancy to the inescapable tragedy of the situation. He sees but will never actually possess it. For a sin that was his own, though occasioned by the sin of others (3:24-29), he was permanently excluded.[10] **So Moses . . . died,** the **servant of the Lord** even to death, and was **buried** in an unknown grave (5-6). No one will worship at the tomb of either the mediator of the old covenant or the Mediator of the new. It is emphasized that, despite his great age, **his eye was not dim** (7), thus stressing that he saw the land full well and so entered into full legal possession.[11] The phrase **nor his natural force abated** suggests that his death was not natural but **according to the word of the Lord** (5). Verse 8 records the period of **thirty days** of official **mourning.**

2. *The Succession of Joshua* (34:9-12)

The nation's leader, who had represented God to the people and the people to God, had gone, but there was no crisis of obedience. The leaders may change but God's work goes on (Josh. 1:1). The nation, in obedience to Moses' command (31:1-8), acknowledged the succession of **Joshua** (9).

Although Joshua was Moses' successor, he was not his equal. Indeed of all the prophets who have appeared since, none has been **like unto Moses** (10; cf. 18:15-19; Num. 12:6-8). Thus Deuteronomy ends with a forward look. In glancing back to 18:15-19, and affirming that no prophet like Moses had yet appeared, it also points forward to Him who, centuries later, offered to His assembled followers the cup of the new covenant sealed in His own blood (Mark 14:23-24).

[9]*Op. cit.*, pp. 24-35.

[10]For a piercing exploration of the tragedy of Moses and of its spiritual lessons see H. H. Farmer, "Life's Frustrations," in *The Healing Cross* (London: Nisbet, 1949), pp. 65-75.

[11]Daube, *op. cit.*, p. 39.

Bibliography

I. COMMENTARIES

ALEXANDER, W. L. "Deuteronomy." *The Pulpit Commentary.* Edited by H. D. M. SPENCE and JOSEPH S. EXELL. London: Funk and Wagnalls, 1907.

BATTERSBY-HARFORD, J. "Deuteronomy." *A New Commentary on Holy Scripture.* Edited by CHARLES GORE, *et al.* London: Society for Promoting Christian Knowledge, 1928.

CLARKE, ADAM. *The Holy Bible with a Commentary and Critical Notes,* Vol. I. London: Wm. Tegg and Co., 1854.

CUNLIFFE-JONES, H. *Deuteronomy.* "Torch Bible Commentaries." Edited by J. MARSH, *et al.* London: Student Christian Movement, 1951.

DAVIES, T. W. "Deuteronomy." *A Commentary on the Bible.* Edited by ARTHUR S. PEAKE. London: T. Nelson and Sons, 1948.

DRIVER, S. R. *Deuteronomy.* "The International Critical Commentary." Edited by S. R. DRIVER, *et al.* Edinburgh: T. and T. Clark, 1895.

HENRY, MATTHEW. "Deuteronomy." *An Exposition of the Old and New Testament,* Vol. I. London: James Nisbet and Co., 1857.

HERTZ, J. H. (ed.). *The Pentateuch and Haftorahs.* London: Soncino Press, 1938.

MANLEY, G. T. "Deuteronomy." *The New Bible Commentary.* Edited by F. DAVIDSON. London: Inter-Varsity Fellowship, 1954.

MOULTON, W. J. "The Social Institutions of Israel." *A Commentary on the Bible.* Edited by ARTHUR S. PEAKE. London: T. Nelson and Sons, 1948.

ROBINSON, H. WHEELER. *Deuteronomy and Joshua.* "The Century Bible." Edinburgh: T. C. and E. C. Jack, n.d.

SMITH, GEORGE ADAM. *The Book of Deuteronomy.* "The Cambridge Bible." Cambridge: University Press, 1918.

VON RAD, GERHARD. *Deuteronomy.* "The Old Testament Library." London: SCM Press, 1966.

WALLER, C. H. "Deuteronomy." *A Bible Commentary.* Edited by CHARLES JOHN ELLICOTT, Vol. II. London: Marshall Brothers, n.d.

WRIGHT, G. ERNEST. "Deuteronomy." *The Interpreter's Bible.* Edited by GEORGE A. BUTTRICK, *et al.,* Vol. II. New York: Abingdon-Cokesbury Press, 1951.

II. OTHER BOOKS

AALDERS, G. CH. *A Short Introduction to the Pentateuch.* London: Tyndale Press, 1949.

ALBRIGHT, W. F. *Archaeology and the Religion of Israel.* Baltimore: The Johns Hopkins Press, Third Edition, 1953.

Anderson, G. W. *A Critical Introduction to the Old Testament.* London: Gerald Duckworth and Co., 1959.

Atkinson, J. Baines. *The Beauty of Holiness.* London: The Epworth Press, 1953.

Bruce, F. F. *Israel and the Nations.* Exeter: Paternoster Press, 1963.

Daube, D. *Studies in Biblical Law.* Cambridge: University Press, 1947.

Denney, J. *The Second Epistle to the Corinthians.* "The Expositor's Bible." London: Hodder and Stoughton, 1894.

de Vaux, Roland. *Ancient Israel, Its Life and Institutions.* London: Darton, Longman and Todd, Second Edition, 1965.

Dodd, C. H. *The Epistle of Paul to the Romans.* "The Moffatt New Testament Commentary." London: Hodder and Stoughton, 1932.

Ellis, E. E. *Paul's Use of the Old Testament.* Grand Rapids: Wm. B. Eerdmans Publishing Co., 1957.

Farmer, H. H. *The Healing Cross.* London: Nisbet, 1949.

Finn, A. H. *The Unity of the Pentateuch.* London: Marshall Brothers, n.d.

Forsyth, P. T. *The Justification of God.* London: Independent Press, 1948.

Green, W. H. *The Higher Criticism of the Pentateuch.* London: Richard D. Dickinson, 1895.

Kitchen, K. A. *Ancient Orient and the Old Testament.* London: Tyndale Press, 1966.

Kline, M. G. *Treaty of the Great King.* Michigan: Wm. B. Eerdmans Publishing Co., 1963.

Manley, G. T. *The Book of the Law.* London: Tyndale Press, 1957.

Mendenhall, G. E. *Law and Covenant in Israel and the Ancient Near East.* Pittsburgh, Pa.: The Biblical Colloquium, 1955.

Nicholson, E. W. *Deuteronomy and Tradition.* Oxford: Basil Blackwell, 1967.

Orr, James. *The Problem of the Old Testament.* London: James Nisbet and Co., 1907.

Pritchard, J. B. *Ancient Near Eastern Texts.* Princeton, N.J.: Princeton University Press, 1950.

Rowley, H. H. *The Growth of the Old Testament.* London: Hutchinson's University Library, 1956.

Thompson, J. A. *The Ancient Near Eastern Treaties and the Old Testament.* London: Tyndale Press, 1964.

Von Rad, G. *Studies in Deuteronomy.* London: SCM Press, 1963.

Vriezen, Th. C. *An Outline of Old Testament Theology.* Oxford: Basil Blackwell, 1958.

Welch, A. C. *The Code of Deuteronomy.* London: James Clarke, 1924.

Wellhausen, J. *Prolegomena to the History of Ancient Israel.* New York: Meridian Books, 1957.

Wesley, J. *Journal.* Standard Edition. Edited by Nehemiah Curnock. London: The Epworth Press, 1938.

Wiener, H. M. *Early Hebrew History.* London: Robert Scott, 1924.

Young, E. J. *An Introduction to the Old Testament.* London: Tyndale Press, 1960.

III. ARTICLES

ALBRIGHT, W. F. "Some Remarks on the Song of Moses in Deuteronomy 32." *Vetus Testamentum,* IX (1959), 339-46.

BOYD, W. F. "Zamzummim." *Dictionary of the Bible.* Edited by JAMES HASTINGS, *et al.* Edinburgh: T. and T. Clark, 1929, p. 983.

BRUCE, F. F. "Messiah," NBD, pp. 812-14.

CROSS, F. M., and FREEDMAN, D. N.: "The Blessing of Moses." *Journal of Biblical Literature,* LXVII (1948), 191-92.

FENSHAM, F. C. "Malediction and Benediction in Ancient Near Eastern Vassal-Treaties and the Old Testament." *Zeitschrift Für Die Alttestamentliche Wissenschaft,* 74 Band (1962), Heft 1, pp. 1-8.

GORDON, C. H. "Biblical Customs and the Nuzu Tablets." *Biblical Archaeologist,* III, No. 1 (Feb., 1940), 8.

GREENBERG, M. "Some Postulates of Biblical Criminal Law." *The Yehezkel Kaufmann Jubilee Volume.* Jerusalem: Magnes Press, The Hebrew University, 1960, pp. 5-28.

HARVEY, J. "Le 'Rib-Pattern,' Réquisitoire Prophétique Sur La Rupture de L'Alliance." *Biblica,* XLIII (1962), 172-96.

HUBBARD, D. A. "Priest and Levites." NBD, pp. 1028-34.

KLINE, M. G. "Ten Commandments." NBD, p. 1251-52.

MANLEY, G. T. "Book of Deuteronomy." NBD, pp. 307-10.

MOTYER, J. A. "Prophecy, Prophets." NBD, pp. 1036-46.

SKEHAN, P. W. "The Structure of the Song of Moses in Deuteronomy." *Catholic Biblical Quarterly,* XIII, No. 4 (Oct., 1951), 153-63.

STEWART, R. A. "Passover." NBD, pp. 936-38.

THOMPSON, R. J. "Sacrifice and Offering. 1. In the Old Testament." NBD, pp. 1113-22.

THOMSON, J. G. S. S. "Tithes." NBD, p. 1284.

WATERSON, A. P. "Disease and Healing." NBD, p. 314.

WISEMAN, D. J. "Horites, Horim." NBD, p. 537.

WRIGHT, G. E. "The Lawsuit of God: A Form-Critical Study of Deuteronomy 32." *Israel's Prophetic Heritage. Essays in Honour of James Muilenburg.* Edited by B. W. ANDERSON and W. HARRELSON. London: SCM Press (1962), pp. 26-67.

WRIGHT, J. S., and THOMPSON, J. A. "Marriage," NBD, p. 789.

Map 1

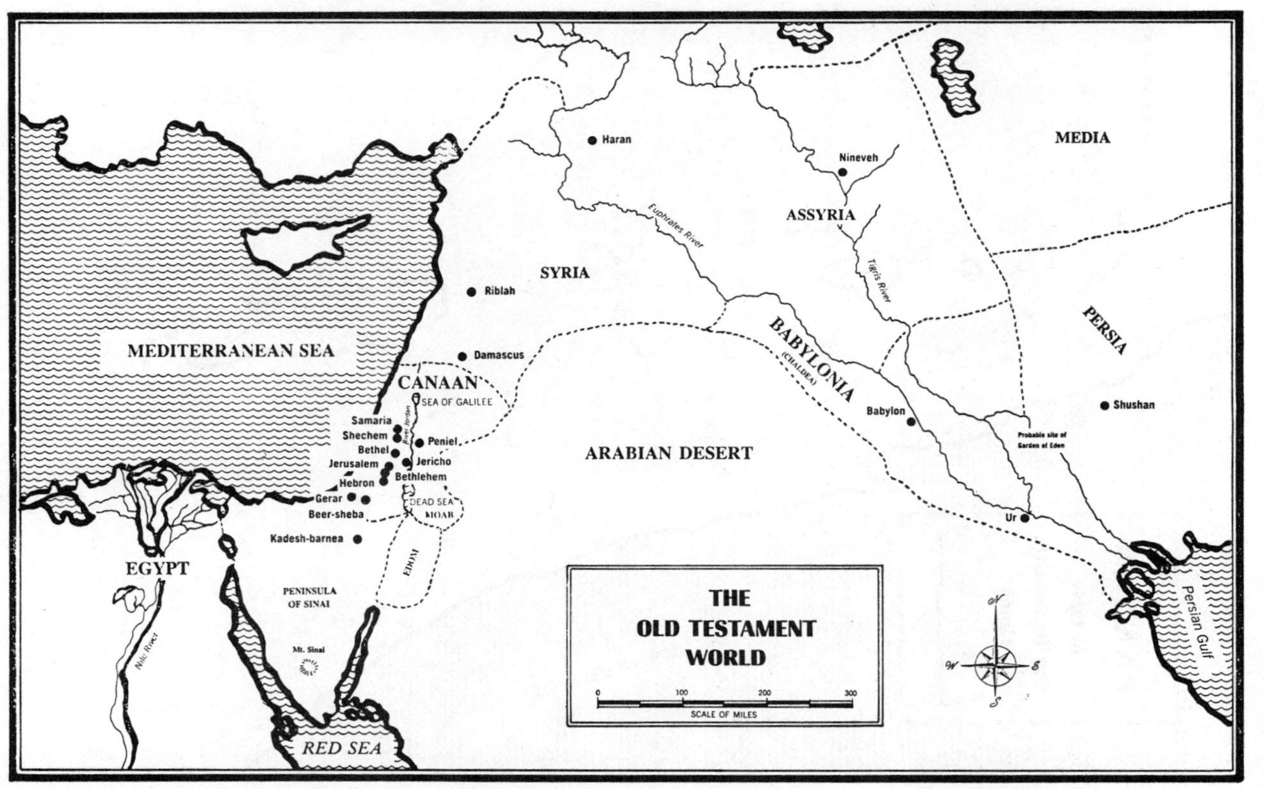
MEDIA
Haran
Nineveh
ASSYRIA
Euphrates River
Tigris River
SYRIA
Riblah
PERSIA
BABYLONIA
(CHALDEA)
MEDITERRANEAN SEA
Damascus
CANAAN
SEA OF GALILEE
River Jordan
Samaria
Shechem
Bethel
Jerusalem
Hebron
Gerar
Beer-sheba
Peniel
Jericho
Bethlehem
DEAD SEA
MOAB
EDOM
Kadesh-barnea
ARABIAN DESERT
Babylon
Shushan
Probable site of Garden of Eden
Ur
Persian Gulf
EGYPT
Nile River
PENINSULA
OF SINAI
Mt. Sinai
RED SEA
THE
OLD TESTAMENT
WORLD
0
100
200
300
SCALE OF MILES

Map 2

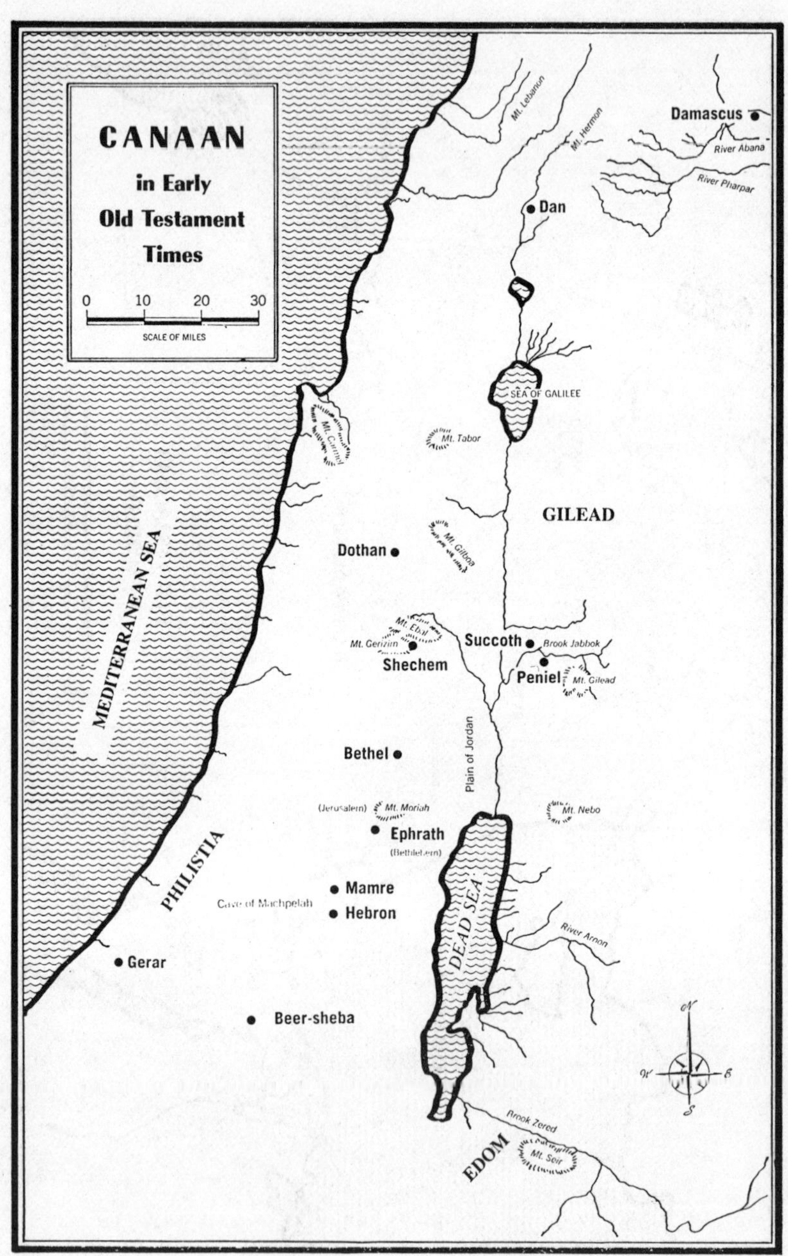

CANAAN
in Early
Old Testament
Times
0 10 20 30
SCALE OF MILES
MEDITERRANEAN SEA
Mt. Lebanon
Mt. Hermon
Damascus
River Abana
River Pharpar
Dan
SEA OF GALILEE
Mt. Carmel
Mt. Tabor
GILEAD
Mt. Gilboa
Dothan
Mt. Ebal
Mt. Gerizim
Shechem
Succoth
Brook Jabbok
Peniel
Mt. Gilead
Plain of Jordan
Bethel
(Jerusalem)
Mt. Moriah
Mt. Nebo
Ephrath
(Bethlehem)
PHILISTIA
Mamre
Cave of Machpelah
Hebron
DEAD SEA
River Arnon
Gerar
Beer-sheba
N
W
E
S
Brook Zered
Mt. Seir
EDOM

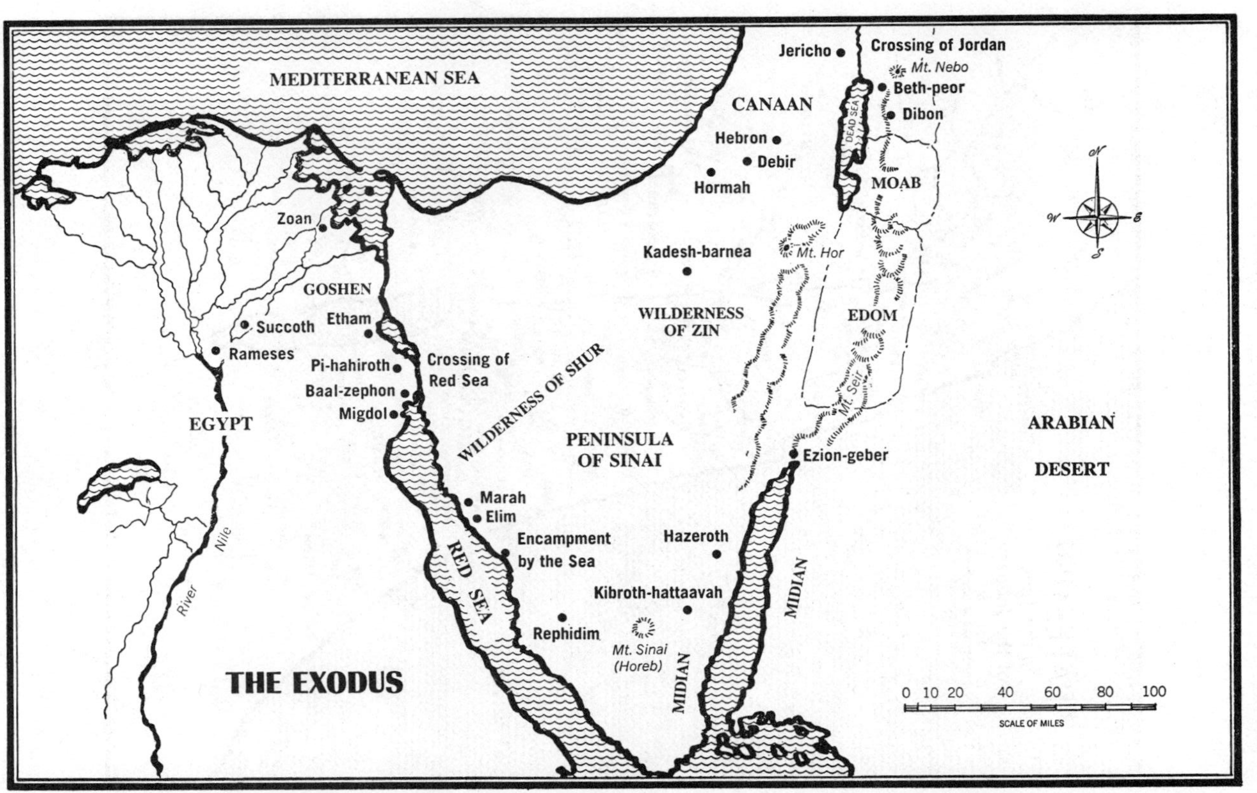

MEDITERRANEAN SEA
Jericho
Crossing of Jordan
Mt. Nebo
Beth-peor
Dibon
DEAD SEA
CANAAN
Hebron
Debir
Hormah
MOAB
Zoan
Kadesh-barnea
Mt. Hor
GOSHEN
WILDERNESS OF ZIN
EDOM
Succoth
Etham
Rameses
Pi-hahiroth
Crossing of Red Sea
Baal-zephon
Migdol
Mt. Seir
WILDERNESS OF SHUR
EGYPT
PENINSULA OF SINAI
Ezion-geber
ARABIAN DESERT
Marah
Elim
Encampment by the Sea
Hazeroth
RED SEA
Nile River
Kibroth-hattaavah
MIDIAN
Rephidim
Mt. Sinai (Horeb)
MIDIAN
0 10 20 40 60 80 100
SCALE OF MILES

THE EXODUS

Map 4

PALESTINE
in the Time
of the Judges
0 10 20 30
SCALE OF MILES
SYRIA
Hobah
Damascus
River Abana
River Pharpar
Mt. Lebanon
Mt. Hermon
PHOENICIA
Sidon
Zarephath
Tyre
Dan
Beth-rehob
Heleph
Kedesh
Hazor
Zebulun
Waters of Merom
Golan
MANASSEH
Achzib
ASHER
Accho
NAPHTALI
ZEBULUN
Sea of Galilee
Aphek
MEDITERRANEAN SEA
Mt. Carmel
Plain of Esdraelon
River Kishon
Kitron
Mt. Tabor
Endor
River Yarmuk
Dor
Megiddo
Shunem
Jezreel
Beth-barah
Edrei
Ramoth-gilead
ISSACHAR
Beth-shean
Dion
Kerioth
Dothan
Jordan River
GILEAD
Jabesh-gilead
MANASSEH
Samaria
Manahaim
Salcah
Mt. Ebal
GAD
Pirathon
Shechem
Brook Kerioth
Succoth
Mt. Gerizim
Zaretan
River Jabbok
Mt. Gilead
EPHRAIM
Joppa
Adam
Penuel
DAN
Gilgal
Shiloh
Ephraim
Rabbath-ammon
Bethel
Beth-horon
Mizpeh
Ai
Michmash
Makkedah
Ekron
Ajalon
BENJAMIN
Jericho
Shittim
Elealah
Beth-shemesh
Gibeon
Ramah
Gilgal
Heshbon
Kirjath-jearim
Jerusalem
Ashdod
Timnath
Bethlehem
Brook Kidron
Mt. Nebo
AMMON
Askelon
Gath
Azekah
Beth-peor
Baal-meon
PHILISTIA
Adullam
Hareth
Tekoa
REUBEN
Eglon
JUDAH
Hebron
Bezer
Gaza
Lachish
Engedi
Dead Sea
Dibon
Debir
Carmel
River Arnon
Gerar
Zanoah
Maon
Sharuhen
Hazor
Arad
Beer-sheba
Moladah
Kir
Ziklag
MOAB
Bered
Rehoboth
SIMEON

Chart A

PLAN OF THE TABERNACLE IN THE WILDERNESS

30 Cubits Long, 10 Cubits Wide, 10 Cubits High (45′ x 15′ x 15′)

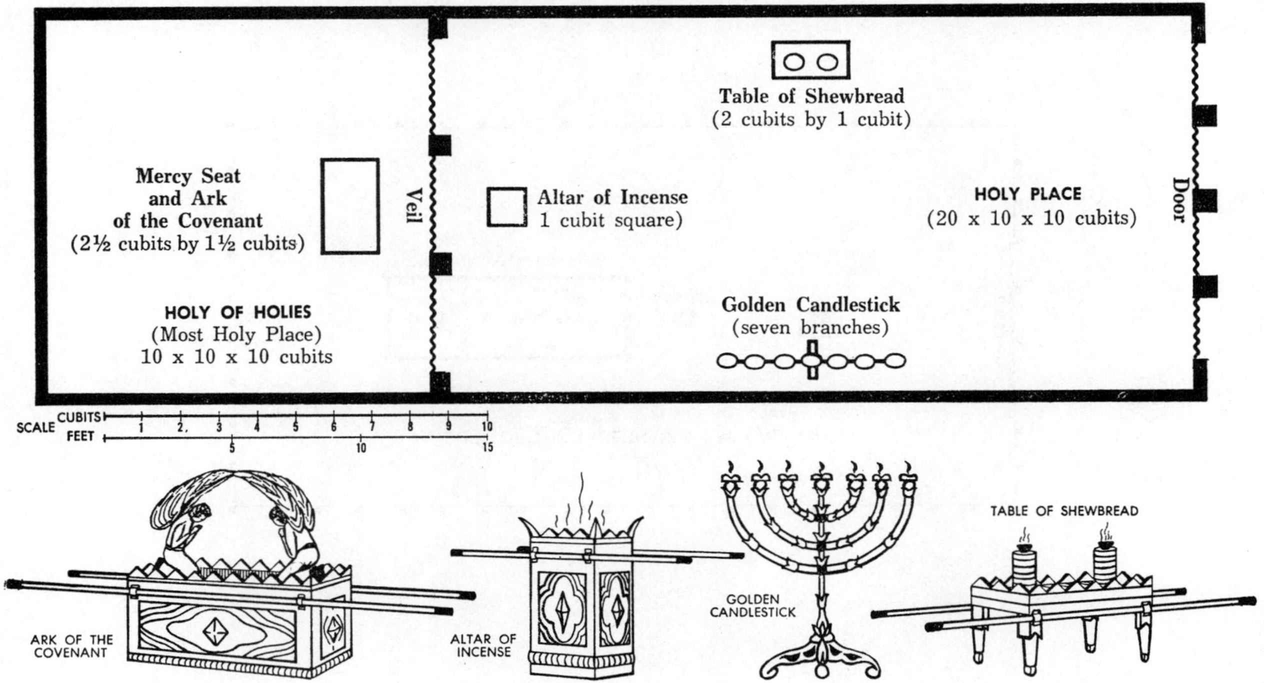

Mercy Seat
and Ark
of the Covenant
(2½ cubits by 1½ cubits)

HOLY OF HOLIES
(Most Holy Place)
10 x 10 x 10 cubits

Veil

Altar of Incense
1 cubit square)

Table of Shewbread
(2 cubits by 1 cubit)

Golden Candlestick
(seven branches)

HOLY PLACE
(20 x 10 x 10 cubits)

Door

SCALE
CUBITS 1 2 3 4 5 6 7 8 9 10
FEET 5 10 15

ARK OF THE COVENANT

ALTAR OF INCENSE

GOLDEN CANDLESTICK

TABLE OF SHEWBREAD

Chart B

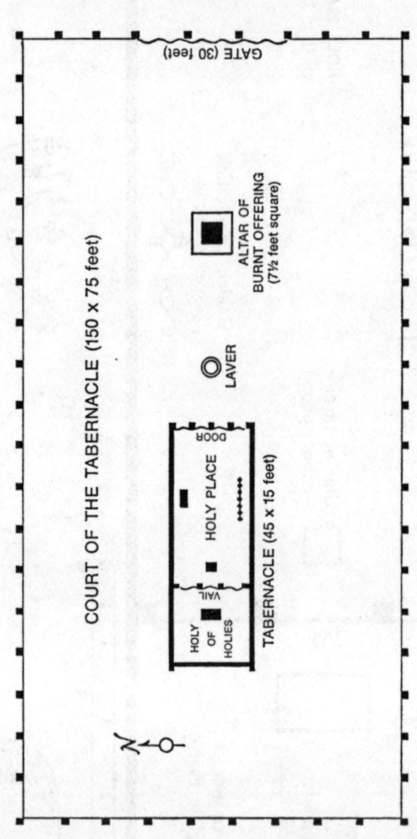
COURT OF THE TABERNACLE (150 x 75 feet)
GATE (30 feet)
ALTAR OF BURNT OFFERING (7½ feet square)
LAVER
DOOR
HOLY PLACE
VAIL
HOLY OF HOLIES
TABERNACLE (45 x 15 feet)
N